SOFTWARE PRODUCT ASSURANCE

Techniques for Reducing Software Risk

SOFTWARE PRODUCT ASSURANCE

Techniques for Reducing Software Risk

William L. Bryan and Stanley G. Siegel

P T R Prentice Hall
Englewood Cliffs, New Jersey 07632

Library of Congress Cataloging-in-Publication Data

Bryan, William L. (William Littell), 1928–
   Software product assurance.

   Includes bibliographies and index.
   1. Computer software—Quality control.   I. Siegel, Stanley G.   II. Title.
QA76.76.Q35B79 1987   005.1   87–5360

© 1988 by P T R Prentice-Hall, Inc.
A Simon & Schuster Company
Englewood Cliffs, New Jersey 07632

Printed in the United States of America
10 9 8 7 6 5 4 3 2 1

ISBN   0-13-500505-1   02I

Prentice-Hall International (UK) Limited, *London*
Prentice-Hall of Australia Pty. Limited, *Sydney*
Prentice-Hall Canada Inc., *Toronto*
Prentice-Hall Hispanoamericana, S. A., *Mexico*
Prentice-Hall of India Private Limited, *New Delhi*
Prentice-Hall of Japan, Inc., *Tokyo*
Simon & Schuster Asia Pte. Ltd., *Singapore*
Editora Prentice-Hall do Brasil, Ltda., *Rio de Janeiro*

To

Ann

Bena
Gary
Deborah
Rachel

CONTENTS

LIST OF FIGURES

LIST OF TABLES

PREFACE

We wrote this book to convince senior managers and software project managers that software product assurance can significantly help them. We also wrote this book to help software product assurance managers and software product assurance practitioners better perform their jobs. *Software product assurance* is a management support discipline that offers a measure of *assurance* that a *software product*

1. does what the customer really wants it to do
2. is delivered on or before the date the customer specified and
3. costs no more than the customer said he wanted to spend.

We wrote this book because our experience in the software industry convinced us that attitudes such as the following are the rule rather than the exception on many software projects:

"Our schedule simply does not permit us to document before we code!"

"Mr. Customer, you tell me what you need and the next time you see me is when I deliver your working computer system to you."

"I have the best programming staff in the industry. When they tell me the code is ready for delivery, I know I can call the customer to tell him to pick up his system."

"Sure, I know what is happening on the software project that I manage. I talk to my development staff every day."

"Yes, we have software standards on this project. But our customer knows that if he wants his computer code on time, we will have to ignore them."

"Of course we have design reviews! They are never more than forty-five minutes long, no questions are asked, and the customer goes away believing that everything is okay."

As a result of such attitudes, software projects often result in software products that

1. do not do what the customer really wants them to do
2. are not delivered on or before the date the customer specified and/or
3. cost more than the customer said he wanted to spend.

It is clear that software projects do attain success. However, as one well-known software veteran has written, the following psychology has emerged in the software industry:

> So many [software] projects fail in some major way that we have had to redefine "success" to keep everyone from becoming despondent. Software projects are sometimes considered successful when the overruns are held to thirty percent or when the user only junks a quarter of the result. Software people are often willing to call such efforts successes, but members of our user community are less forgiving. They know failure when they see it.[1]

We make no claims that the product assurance techniques we discuss guarantee project success—even as redefined above. But our experience unequivocally shows that applying these techniques can reduce the ever-present risks of unsatisfied customer requirements, schedule slippages, and cost overruns—hence the subtitle of this book.

This book is intended for the following three audiences:

1. senior managers
2. software project managers and product assurance managers
3. current and potential product assurance practitioners.

These three audiences generally have widely disparate information needs. Consequently, each of the book's seven chapters is partitioned into three parts—text; followed by exercises; followed by references and additional readings. These three categories of information and their intended audiences are depicted in Figure P1.1. The purpose of each of these information categories is the following:

---

[1] T. DeMarco, *Controlling Software Projects*. New York: Yourdon Press, 1982, p. 4.

Information Category	Purpose
Chapter text	Defines terms
	Introduces principles
	Explains application of principles through analogies, examples, and sample problems
Exercises	Explores nuances of concepts and principles introduced in the chapter text
	Extends ideas introduced in the chapter text
	Provokes you to think through, down to the "how-to-do-it" level, how to do product assurance
References and additional readings	Points to supporting and contrasting views regarding material introduced in the chapter text
	Introduces (primarily via short extracts from the references cited) concepts related to those explained in the chapter text
	Points to more detailed discussions of topics not treated in depth in the chapter text

Senior managers will probably satisfy their information needs by reading the chapter text, and skipping over exercises and references. The text deals with how product assurance can benefit senior managers and their organizations by reducing project risks. It presents concepts, principles, and trade-offs necessary for applying product assurance constructively. To supplement and substantiate these ideas, the chapter text also includes real-world examples and sample problems concretely illustrating the benefits of product assurance. For senior managers who are looking for an added challenge, the text sometimes suggests end-of-chapter exercises especially pertinent to this reader group. (The approach to working these exercises is the same as that used to work the sample problems appearing in the chapter text. Also, many of these exercises include hints to get you started.) Some software applications and associated project management issues have mathematical overtones, and for this reason some of the examples and sample problems included in the chapter text are mathematical in nature. Recognizing that some of our intended readership may not want to wrestle with mathematical discussions, we issue an alert whenever the chapter text is about to deal with mathematics. Readers wishing to skip over this material can do so without significant loss of continuity.

Software project managers and product assurance managers, in addition to reading the chapter text, should read the third category of material (references and additional readings). Augmenting the chapter text, this material offers these technical managers insight into what others have written on product assurance. Armed with such alternative viewpoints, tech-

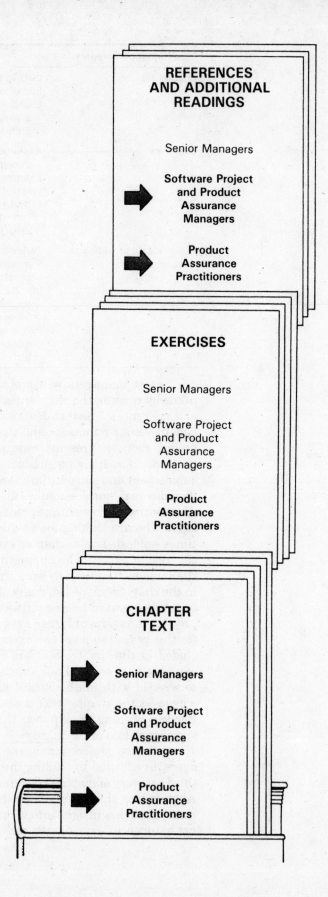

FIGURE P1.1. The three
parts of each chapter
in this book and their
intended audiences.

nical managers should be better able to direct the practitioners reporting to them. This third information category also points to some important specific product assurance techniques, particularly valuable for product assurance managers. By understanding these techniques, product assurance managers should find it easier to direct their practitioners to use the same techniques. Software project managers should furthermore gain a greater appreciation of these techniques, and will profitably inculcate their product development specialists with these same techniques elaborated in this third information category. Some project managers and product assurance managers may wish to work the exercises—especially those dealing with the advantages (and disadvantages) for management of using product assurance. For these managers—and for senior managers—we provide pointers to specific exercises particularly pertinent for these audiences. These pointers are listed at the end of the text in each chapter.

Product assurance practitioners should not only read the chapter text and the third category of material, but they should seek out and read some of the references listed in this third category. To be well rounded, a product assurance practitioner needs exposure to alternative and contrasting points of views, such as those described in these references. Furthermore, product assurance practitioners should attempt to work most of the exercises (particularly those focusing on product assurance practices). Assimilating the ideas in the first and third information categories is not sufficient for readers who aspire to be product assurance practitioners. These readers, and readers who are product assurance practitioners seeking to improve their skills, need to know how to formulate and implement product assurance procedures. Many of the chapter exercises are thus designed to make these readers probe and extend the ideas in the other two information categories. These exercises thereby help the product assurance practitioner understand how to perform product assurance *effectively*, i.e., in a manner that appeals to product developers while simultaneously accommodating management's need for cost and schedule control. Most of these exercises will challenge even those individuals who have been in the software industry for many years. Readers with backgrounds in mathematics will find some of these exercises particularly challenging to their analytical skills.

The exercises, which total over 100, are taken mainly from our on-the-job software experience. They include extensive introductions defining the context for answering the exercise questions. Consequently, this exercise material makes up a substantial portion of the book. Furthermore, the Chapter 1 text presents three sample problems (one aimed at each of the three audiences shown in Figure P1.1). These sample problems, and the ones included in each of the remaining chapters, not only elucidate principles and practices discussed in the remainder of the chapter text, but they also serve as models indicating how the exercises at the end of each chapter can be approached. For these reasons, and for the additional reason that many of the exercises at the end of each chapter are intended to provoke extensive discussion, we believe that this book can be used as an advanced undergraduate or graduate textbook in courses on software engineering and software management. To facilitate student use, an ample margin has been left on each page for notes.

A comment is in order here about the book's approach. To a great extent, the material is organized in graduated layers. That is, we treat topics in progressively greater levels of detail as the book is traversed from Chapter 1 to its seventh and final chapter. For example, in Chapter 1, intuitive arguments demonstrate that four comparison processes are useful to apply throughout the software life cycle to produce software with the characteristics listed at the outset of this Preface (these four processes are classically referred to as quality assurance [QA], verification and validation [V&V], test and evaluation [T&E], and configuration management [CM]). In Chapter 2, this train of thought continues as we explore some specific aspects of these four processes, frequently by using simplified examples of software products. In Chapter 3, we bring to light the common features of these processes; identification of these features then allows the introduction of three fundamental product assurance functions—control, auditing, and bookkeeping. Introducing these functions allows us to describe product assurance in terms of three related but essentially disjoint entities. A chapter is then devoted to each of these entities—Chapter 4 to control, Chapter 5 to auditing, and Chapter 6 to bookkeeping. Chapter 7 then explores the integrated application of these tasks in the real world where resources are limited, development schedules are tightly constrained, and software customers change their minds regarding what they want. Thus, at the risk of being slightly redundant, we make return visits to concepts and ideas as the reader is led in a relatively painless manner into the details of how to do software product assurance. The reader not interested in such detail can bypass this material with no loss in continuity. We believe that this cyclic approach is appropriate on pedagogical grounds because it reinforces key points in a natural manner (e.g., after understanding the intuitive basis for product assurance, the reader is likely to be receptive to understanding *what* product assurance entails, which then naturally makes him receptive to understanding *how* product assurance is to be performed).

A word is also in order about the figures in the book and their relationship to the general approach described in the preceding paragraph. A brief glance at these figures shows that they are not typical of the illustrations found in computer science and software engineering texts. For the most part, they contain friendly, nonthreatening symbology to convey ideas and concepts (such as a sponge to symbolize software). We use few block diagrams—our classroom experience convinces us that such diagrams are deadly as teaching aids. Because this book is intended for the three diverse audiences identified in Figure P1.1, and because this book deals with complex software management issues, our figures are designed to put all three audiences at ease while at the same time illuminating ways of dealing with these issues. Our experience in our seminars and published articles has confirmed that such figures are effective teaching aids. However, do not be misled by the light touch characterizing our figures. This book deals with some very complicated issues that, in our opinion, are still not being addressed in the software industry and that must be addressed in any book on software product assurance seeking to deal seriously with the subject. Some of these issues have deep technical roots (e.g., how does one properly test mathematical formulas embedded in computer code?). In order not to lose the senior management readers who may wish to omit these discussions, we have for the most part placed such highly technical issues in the exercises at the end of each chapter. Senior managers can easily skip this material without loss of continuity. Nevertheless, despite the book's nonthreatening appearance, it addresses topics that should challenge even the most sophisticated software technologists.

The captain who went down with the *Titanic* was informed—so history tells—that his ship was in iceberg-populated waters. Although he (and his crew and passengers) may have indeed felt that the *Titanic* was unsinkable, would he (and his crew and passengers) not have been better off knowing where the icebergs were and how big they were, so that he had an option of navigating around them? It is time that the software industry seriously approaches each software project with the candid realization that it is indeed a voyage through iceberg-infested waters (or worse!). If this attitude is honestly adopted, then common sense and the natural instinct for self-preservation can only lead to one conclusion—that some way must be found to steer clear of the icebergs to the extent prudently possible. With this idea in mind, let us begin our study of techniques for reducing software risk.

ACKNOWLEDGMENTS

We wrote this book while employed full-time with Grumman-CTEC, Inc. Without the support and cooperation of the Grumman-CTEC organization (now part of Grumman Data Systems) and many of our colleagues, this book would never have been written.

To Harold Crane, the founder and president of CTEC before it became part of the Grumman family and our long-time friend and associate, goes our appreciation for giving us encouragement and company time and resources, without which this book would have remained only an idea. To Robert Fellows, our manager, go our thanks for supplying us with further resources and giving us the encouragement to see this project through to completion. We consider ourselves fortunate indeed to have had such uncompromising management support and commitment. To our colleagues and friends go our special thanks for their constructive comments and criticisms of drafts of the words and pictures that have finally made it into print. These people gave us much to think about. Without their reviews, we would have missed the mark in many instances. To Earl Meiers goes our appreciation for helping steer us in the right direction, particularly while the manuscript was in its early stages. We thank Frances Lawson for her meticulous review of the entire manuscript and galleys. To Elizabeth C. Below, we are indebted for her continuing support throughout the entire production period of the book, including review of the manuscript, galleys, and page proofs, and for her assistance in preparing the indices. Of course, where we may still have missed the mark, the responsibility is ours. To Jo Elder, the Grumman-CTEC librarian, we are particularly grateful for her help in fulfilling our numerous requests for books and articles. We also thank her for handling the permissions correspondence. To the Grumman-CTEC publications department goes our deep appreciation for the monumental task of helping us transform our words and pictures into something that others could read. Carol Winthers Barbour was our always dependable editor, and Carol Ann Quarto was responsible for the considerable body of computer graphics-derived artwork. Mary Crider and Sonia Hale did the bulk of the typing.

To the many organizations which contracted to obtain product assurance services from Grumman-CTEC, we owe a debt of gratitude. This work and the product assurance services supplied internally within Grumman-CTEC gave us opportunities to use the techniques described in this book. Through these experiences, we were able to understand what can, cannot, should, and should not be done in the real world of software projects. Obviously, without this exposure, we would have had little more to draw on than the ideas of two zealots on how product assurance should theoretically be applied to software projects.

To Ken Metzner, we wish to express our appreciation for his encouragement during the very early days of this undertaking.

To the staff of Elsevier go our thanks for patience, understanding, and suggestions. We thank Betsy Brown for her patience while we labored to finish the manuscript and her understanding of our special concerns while the book was wending its way through production. We thank Christine Hastings, the book's desk editor, who helped us smooth our prose and who patiently answered our many questions regarding matters of style, consistency, and grammar. And we thank Regina Dahir, the book's designer, who went out of her way to produce artwork that met our many zany demands. Producing a textbook is not easy. These individuals, with their agreeable manner, at least made it pleasant.

Any book project, even one done in a company environment, cannot be accomplished without some impact on home life. To our wives and families, we express our gratitude for their patience while we took time away from them on evenings and weekends to write this book. Because this time can never be recovered, we are grateful for their understanding. Special thanks go to Deborah Siegel; her ideas and suggestions regarding many of the illustrations appearing in this book were invaluable.

We gratefully acknowledge permission to reprint selections from the following:

"Software Engineering Under Deadline Pressure" by S. H. Costello in *ACM SIGSOFT Software Engineering Notes*, vol. 9, no. 5 (October 1984). Used by permission of the author.

"Two Observations on Large Software Projects" by Dick Dunn in *ACM SIGSOFT Software Engineering Notes*, vol. 9, no. 5 (October 1984). Used by permission of the author.

"The Impact of Rapid Prototyping on Specifying User Requirements" by H. Gomaa in *ACM SIGSOFT Software Engineering Notes*, vol. 8, no. 2 (April 1983). Used by permission of the author.

"Software Maintenance: Penny Wise, Program Foolish" by G. Parikh in *ACM SIGSOFT Software Engineering Notes*, vol. 10, no. 5 (October 1985). Used by permission of the author.

ANSI/IEEE Std 729-1983, Copyright 1983, The Institute of Electrical and Electronics Engineers, Inc.

ANSI/IEEE Std. 730-1984, IEEE Standard for Software Quality Assurance Plans © 1984 The Institute of Electrical and Electronics Engineers, Inc.

Per Brinch Hansen, THE ARCHITECTURE OF CONCURRENT PROGRAMS, © 1977, pp. 226–227. Reprinted by permission of Prentice-Hall, Englewood Cliffs, New Jersey.

Donald C. Gause and Gerald M. Weinberg, *Are Your Lights On? How to Figure Out What the Problem Really Is*. Copyright © 1982 by Little, Brown and Company (Inc.). Reprinted by permission.

D. H. Hansen, *A Case Study of Successful Systems Development—Up and Running*. Copyright © 1984. Used by permission of Yourdon Press.

W. E. Perry, *Cleaning Up a Computer Mess*. Copyright © 1986 Van Nostrand Reinhold Company.

"Case Study: The Space Shuttle Primary Computer System" by A. Spector and D. Gifford in *Communications of the ACM*, vol. 27, no. 9 (September 1984). Copyright © 1984 The Association for Computing Machinery.

Complete Guide to Software Testing by W. Hetzel. Copyright © 1984. Reprinted with permission of QED Information Sciences, Inc. 170 Linden Street, Wellesley, MA 02181.

"A Practical Experience with Independent Verification and Validation" by G. Page, F. E. McGarry, and D. N. Card in *Proceedings of COMPSAC 84*. Copyright © 1984 The Institute of Electrical and Electronics Engineers, Inc.

"Need for Software Testing Moves into Spotlight" by William Suydam. Reprinted with permission from the Volume 24 #25 issue of *Computer Design*. Copyright 1985, PennWell Publishing Company, Advanced Technology Group.

"One Day in the Programming Department" by D. A. Feinberg in *Computer*, Vol. 17, No. 11 (Nov. 1984). Copyright © 1984 The Institute of Electrical and Electronics Engineers, Inc.

Reprinted from *Controlling Software Projects* by DeMarco, copyright 1982, by permission of Yourdon Press.

"Panosta Laotuun Ohjelmistotyossa" by W. L. Bryan and S. G. Siegel in *Elektroniikka & Automaatio*, nos. 14 (Au-

7, 8. Reprinted by permission of Prentice-Hall, Inc., Englewood Cliffs, N.J.

Software Reflected by R. L. Baber. Copyright © 1982 Elsevier Science Publishers B.V.

B. Beizer, *Software System Testing and Quality Assurance.* Copyright © 1984 Van Nostrand Reinhold Company.

A Structured Approach to Systems Testing by W. E. Perry. Copyright © 1983. Reprinted with permission of QED Information Sciences, Inc. 170 Linden Street, Wellesley, MA 02181.

"Data Collection: A Perspective" by W. J. Ellis in *Third Software Engineering Standards Application Workshop.* Copyright © 1984 The Institute of Electrical and Electronics Engineers, Inc.

"Data Collection Standards" by F. E. McGarry in *Third Software Engineering Standards Application Workshop.* Copyright © 1984 The Institute of Electrical and Electronics Engineers, Inc.

"Position Paper on Data Collection Standards for Software Engineering" by J. Vosburgh in *Third Software Engineering Standards Application Workshop.* Copyright © 1984 The Institute of Electrical and Electronics Engineers, Inc.

From WHO OWNS INNOVATION? by Richard A. Spanner. Copyright © 1984 Dow Jones-Irwin. All rights reserved.

SOFTWARE PRODUCT ASSURANCE

Techniques for Reducing Software Risk

chapter 1

MOTIVATION

1.1 Introduction

The primary purpose of this chapter is to convince you that the rest of this book is worth reading. We indicate in our Preface that we are writing this book for three groups of people—senior managers, software project managers, and product assurance practitioners. Therefore, "convincing" will require arguments relevant to the special interests of each of these groups.

If you are a senior manager, we need to convince you that in some important ways software projects require special care if they are not to become a threat to the stability and growth of the company or organization that you help to manage. If you are a software project manager (or want to become one), we need to convince you that the day-to-day management of your project depends upon certain activities that may at first appear unnecessary because they do not contribute directly to software product development. If you are a software product assurance practitioner (or want to become one), we need to convince you that, to ply your trade successfully, you need to be aware not only of "how-to-do-it" product assurance techniques but also of how the application of these techniques may have an impact on other personnel on the software project you are supporting.

A good way to get people to think about what product assurance has to offer is to use examples of specific product assurance issues. These issues will stimulate you to consider things that you may not have thought about previously. An effective way to present these issues is in the form of problem statements or exercises. Consequently, in each of the following three sections we present a sample problem and explain how it may be addressed (at least from our point of view). Section 1.2 presents and explains a problem suited to the interests of senior managers; Section 1.3 presents and explains a problem suited to the interests of software project managers; and Section 1.4 presents and explains a problem suited to the interests of software product assurance practitioners. These sections should also give you insight into the methodology needed to attack the exercises at the end of this chapter and the remaining chapters. In Section 1.5, we preview the remainder of the book.

Before proceeding to the sample problems, we need to give you initial definitions of three concepts—*product assurance, requirement,* and *software development* (the qualifier "initial" is used because we elaborate on them in subsequent chapters). These concepts provide a frame of reference for the sample problems. More important, they are central to the ideas put forth in the remainder of the book.

A software product is developed to satisfy the need of the product's intended recipient. It therefore seems reasonable that during product development some assurance should be provided that these needs are being satisfied. Proceeding from this idea, we define product assurance[1] as follows:

Product assurance is a set of checks and balances interwoven into the software development process whose primary purpose is to assure (i.e., give confidence) that a software product satisfies the needs of the intended recipient. More specifically, these checks and balances are activities performed by the product developers, project management, and/or some other organization (which we refer to as a product assurance group) aimed at making a software product visible so that explicit determination can be made of product conformance to the intended recipient's needs.

A key point deriving from the above definition is that product assurance as presented in this book extends far beyond a "kick-the-tires" philosophy of product testing. It is the institutionalizing of a product examination philosophy spanning the entire software development cycle—from the time the product needs are formulated to the time software code is fielded for operational use and upkeep. By "institutionalizing" we mean that product assurance is part and parcel of the development process itself, and even though specific product assurance activities may at times be accomplished by individuals identified as "product assurance practitioners," these activities, as well as the product examination activities performed by the product developers and project management, are generally indistinguishable as to whether they are product development or product assurance activities. You should therefore not be surprised, even at this early stage, by the intimate relationship involving product assurance, product development, and project management. This relationship is examined at length in subsequent chapters.

Our definition of requirement is the following:

A *requirement* is a need as perceived by the intended recipient (or, as we subsequently refer to this recipient, *customer* or *user*) for a software product. This need is to be satisfied by one or more capabilities embodied in the software product.

A key phrase in the above definition is "as perceived by the intended recipient." As we emphasize many times in this book,

---

[1] Throughout this book, we use the terms "product assurance" and "software product assurance" synonymously, since the focus of the book is on software.

the basic software management challenge is to achieve convergence between a customer's perception of his need and the software developer's perception of that need. Examples of requirements implied by the above definition include the following (when we define *software* in Chapter 2 we elaborate on this definition):

Drawing a map on a display device

Drawing a map of the East Coast of the United States on a display device

Drawing a map of the East Coast of the United States between latitudes 30°N and 40°N on a display device

Drawing a map of the East Coast of the United States between latitudes 30°N and 40°N in three colors on a display device

Drawing a map of the East Coast of the United States between latitudes 30°N and 40°N in three colors on a display device within three seconds

Note how each item in the above list is more specific than its predecessor. Such a sequence of stating a requirement with increasing precision is not unusual. Often, the initial statement of a need by a customer lacks precision. During the course of the software development process—particularly when product assurance has been included in the process—the customer's needs are elicited with increasing specificity. The fact that a requirement when it is first articulated may embody more than meets the eye is a notion that we explore in subsequent chapters. This notion is closely tied to the basic software project management challenge cited earlier—that of achieving convergence between a customer's perception of his need and the software developer's perception of that need.

Our definition of software development is the following:

Software development is the process of transforming a customer's requirements into computer code that operates in the customer's environment in accordance with these requirements. This transformation is typically accomplished through stages of increasing specificity—from "what" to "how" to "implementation." These stages may be revisited one or more times until the desired convergence between "what" and "implementation" is achieved.

For the present, you should note the following about the above definition:

Software development is viewed as an evolutionary process over which are superimposed "revolutions" (i.e., revisits to stages) resulting from a basic fact of life—that a customer generally does not know what he really wants (at least until the development process has been going on for some time).

Our definition does not specify the number of stages from

"what" to "implementation." Depending on their size, complexity, and other factors, different software projects may require different numbers of stages.

Classically, software maintenance is distinguished from software development. Martin and McClure and others define software project maintenance as "changes that have to be made to computer programs after they have been delivered to the customer or user."[2] By contrast, our definition of software development includes the concept of maintenance. As we explain in Chapter 2, revisiting stages is tantamount to performing the classically defined maintenance function. For this reason, we often do not refer to maintenance in this book (except when the pull of tradition compels us to use the term); strictly speaking, the term "software development and maintenance" is a redundancy.

To orient your thinking toward the sample problems in the next three sections, we offer the following observation regarding the three concepts just defined:

Software development is aimed at satisfying customer requirements. Product assurance integrates a system of checks and balances into software development to raise the likelihood that this aim is achieved in each product resulting from this development. These checks and balances help make the software development process more visible (thus facilitating its management) by spotlighting discrepancies between a software product and customer requirements. These checks and balances also provide a means for tracing software development. Its evolution thus manifest, a software product's further evolution becomes easier to manage.

This observation is so important that we have put its first two sentences in Figure 1.1 to remind you that software product assurance is inseparable from software development. If you keep Figure 1.1 in mind as you read the following sample problems, you should be convinced of the value of reading this book.

1.2 Product Assurance and the Senior Manager—A Sample Problem
Background and Questions

Suppose you are president of a company that, among other things, develops software for systems. Suppose further that these systems are such that if the software fails to operate properly people might get killed (e.g., software that drives air traffic control display devices). Finally, suppose you have been approached by a large insurance company offering to insure your company against lawsuits resulting from the failure of your software to operate properly. Although the protection that the policy offers appears attractive, the premiums are expensive.

A. Why should you consider buying insurance in the first place?

B. What approaches to software development do you have

---

[2] See Reference 7 at the end of this chapter, p. 3.

FIGURE 1.1. The inseparability of software product assurance from software development—why software product assurance deserves the attention of a senior manager, a software project manager, and a software product assurance practitioner.

Software development is aimed at satisfying customer requirements. Product assurance integrates a system of checks and balances into software development to raise the likelihood that this aim is achieved in each product resulting from this development.

that might induce the insurance company to reduce its premiums?

C. From your responses to parts A and B, what can you deduce about one possible role for product assurance on a software project?

Solution Approach[3]

A. As president of the company, you are naturally concerned about your company's fiscal well-being. Insurance is

---

[3] Notice that we are providing not solutions to these problems, but rather *solution approaches*. There are no absolute or unique solutions to these sample problems or to the exercises at the end of the chapters. There are many valid ways to respond to the exercises;

worth purchasing only if it offers protection against some identifiable risk. You are of course worried about people getting killed. But what is the nature of the risk in software development? Consider, for example, the statistics quoted in Figure 1.2. Being a prudent businessman, your interest may be aroused by these statistics. After all, the failure on your part to deliver software as contracted may leave you liable beyond contract matters. For example, an outmoded, overburdened system may have to continue to be used rather than be replaced by your system. But still you may be skeptical. After all, you can legitimately ask about the other 85 percent of software projects that at least deliver something. Even if your management largesse extended to an occasional 100 or 200 percent overrun, you might want to do a little more reading on the track record in the software industry (assuming that your company's other business interests occupy most of your attention so that you are not well read on this subject). Most of the references at the end of this chapter would at least get you started; see also the references in Exercise 7.16 at the end of Chapter 7 regarding legal liability and software malfunction.

At this point, we know that the most skeptical among you are thinking "These guys are stacking the deck with *their* references! The software industry really cannot be so shaky that I need to buy an expensive insurance policy on the outside chance that I'll wind up in court some day defending my company against the relative of someone killed by my company's malfunctioning software." Okay. Even if you think we may be stacking the deck with our references, and even if your company develops software whose malfunction may not kill people (but may ultimately kill your customer base if the malfunctions happen with sufficient frequency), why not talk to your software development staff to get software project data that you might find more credible? Do not bother asking them about their experiences on software project failures (naturally you pride yourself on hiring only good software people, so the chances that these people will recall such failures would probably not be worth your time pursuing). Simply ask them about their experiences with what they would consider software project successes where they had to redefine customer requirements in some major way (let them define "major") two or more times before the software could be delivered. Ask them how many times customer requirements had to be cut back so that a customer's delivery date (and/or customer's budget) could be satisfied. You may find that at least some of these software project successes turned out that way by definition.[4]

in fact, the purpose of many of these exercises is to stimulate you to think about various *alternative* ways of dealing with software management issues. We return to this point in Section 1.5.

[4] We have participated in several such projects. As will become apparent in subsequent chapters of this book, we could also be accused of defining success so that failure is unlikely. We would not argue with this accusation, other than to note that the purpose of this book is to show how, through the application of product assurance, potential failure (i.e., nonsatisfaction of customer requirements) can be spotted early enough that there is time to do something—if there is a desire to do so. Sometimes the desire to heed these

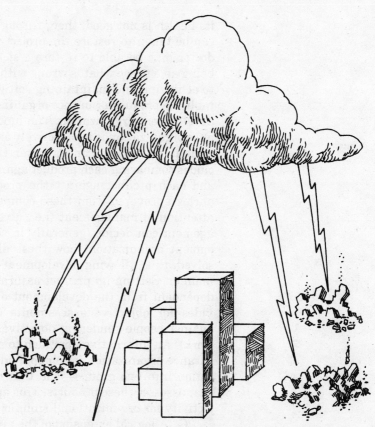

FIGURE 1.2. Some statistics on software projects. Quotations from T. DeMarco, *Controlling Software Projects* (New York: Yourdon Press, 1982), p. 3.

"Fifteen percent of all software projects never deliver anything; that is, they fail utterly to achieve their established goals."

"Overruns of one-hundred to two-hundred percent are common in software projects."

B. In this part of the problem, you are asked to think about approaches to software development that might induce the insurance company to reduce its premiums. (Presumably, having thought about arguments like those presented in A above, you are at least still considering buying insurance to protect your company's future. If you are one of those who remains unconvinced by such arguments, you may at this point consider returning the book to the publisher and asking for a refund. We will be the first to admit that many people still view the software industry through rose-colored glasses, even if we don't.) Just as some life insurance companies reduce premiums for a person who has no chronic ailments, so the insurance company here might be expected to reduce its premiums if the software development process in your company is in good health. Logic would seem to dictate that if this process is visible (i.e., people participating in the project—managers and the technical staff—can see what is going on) its health can be assessed. If

warnings is not there, and project success becomes an exercise in cutting back customer requirements in a mad rush to meet fast-approaching delivery dates. We explore this subject in Chapter 7.

its health is not good, then, through this visibility, measures can be taken to restore the project to health (the same way a doctor may be able to restore a sick person to health by first being able to see what is wrong with the person). One approach to achieving and maintaining software project health is to establish a product assurance organization independent from the development organization. The function of this product assurance organization is to objectively assess each software product as it is developed. Among other things, this assessment includes comparing each product against customer requirements and each product against the predecessor product. Discrepancies uncovered from these comparisons are brought to the attention of management (i.e., given visibility) so that management can decide (generally in conjunction with the development organization) how these discrepancies should be resolved, thus allowing development to proceed in a controlled manner. Setting up product assurance as an organization independent from the development organization generally provides for objective assessments (human nature militates against people rendering objective assessments of their own work). An alternative approach to an independent product assurance organization is to subdivide the development organization into two groups—one that develops products and one that assesses these products. This approach sacrifices some objectivity for organizational simplicity.

C. A logical extension of the arguments in A and B is that product assurance itself can be viewed as a form of insurance against being unaware of unsatisfied customer requirements (and hence project trouble). By raising the visibility of the software development process, product assurance offers management alternative insight into the activities of the development organization. Product assurance thus acts as a stabilizing influence on software development. Management determines how to react to these alternative views of the development activity. While you as the president of a company that produces potentially lethal software may want some insurance against legal proceedings, you may find your chances of a courtroom appearance significantly diminished if you staff your software projects with (independent) product assurance organizations. Of course, if your company produces software whose failure may only cause you to lose customers (to one of your competitors) with little or no threat of legal action, then you may find the insurance offered by product assurance sufficient for your software project needs and the continued success of your company.

We want to stress that we are not advocating the practice of product assurance as a form of disaster insurance. We argue many times throughout this book that, as illustrated in Figure 1.3, investing in product assurance pays dividends in avoiding wasted project resources resulting from false starts and ex-

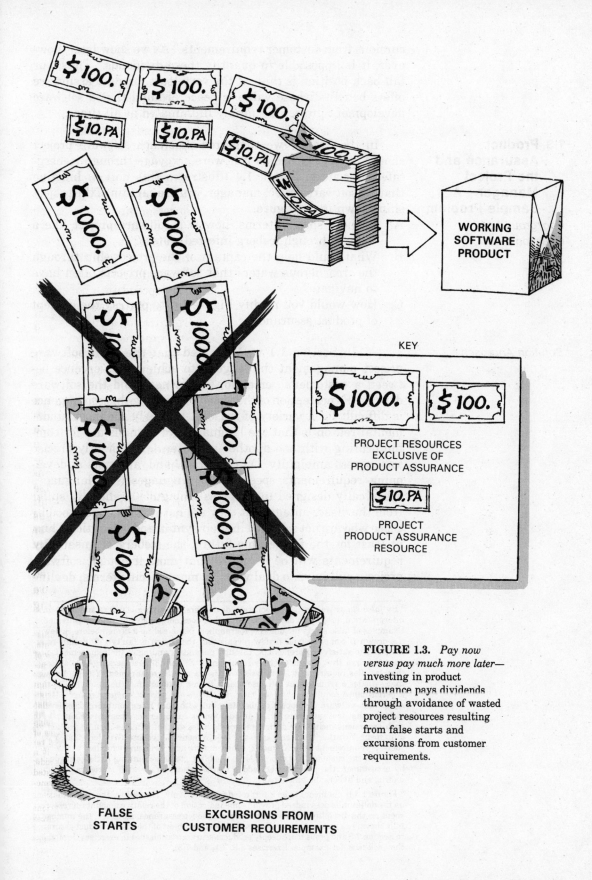

KEY

$1000. $100.

PROJECT RESOURCES
EXCLUSIVE OF
PRODUCT ASSURANCE

$10.PA

PROJECT
PRODUCT ASSURANCE
RESOURCE

WORKING
SOFTWARE
PRODUCT

FALSE
STARTS

EXCURSIONS FROM
CUSTOMER REQUIREMENTS

FIGURE 1.3. *Pay now versus pay much more later—* investing in product assurance pays dividends through avoidance of wasted project resources resulting from false starts and excursions from customer requirements.

cursions from customer requirements.[5] As we show later, however, it is impossible to quantify these dividends.[6] Thus, our fall-back position is that, at the very least, product assurance offers benefits whose value is peace of mind that a software development project is suitably illuminated at all times.

1.3 Product Assurance and the Project Manager—A Sample Problem

Background and Questions

In the Preface we suggested that each software project should be approached as if it were a voyage through iceberg-infested waters. Figure 1.4 illustrates this notion. Imagine that, as software project manager, you are captain of the project ship shown in the figure.

A. In more specific terms, how is a software project like a voyage through iceberg-infested waters?

B. What could help the captain of the project ship through the treacherous waters that software projects often have to navigate?

C. How would you modify Figure 1.4 to portray the concept of product assurance?

Solution Approach

A. In Section 1.1 we indicated that the basic software project management challenge is to achieve convergence between a customer's perception of his need and the software developer's perception of that need. Achieving this convergence is difficult for a variety of reasons. Probably the most fundamental reason is that the languages we humans use for communicating with one another are often insufficiently precise to suppress ambiguity. On the other hand, attempts at developing requirements specification languages (i.e., languages specifically designed to suppress ambiguity) generally suffer from the disadvantage that they are not readily understood by those who are not schooled in their syntax and semantics. Thus, at least for the foreseeable future, the iceberg of unsatisfied requirements will be a hazard that most if not all software projects will have to deal with. In more specific terms, dealing

---

[5] By *false starts* we mean that software developers, through misunderstanding or misinterpretation, proceed to develop software that does not satisfy customer requirements. Examples of false starts include (1) programmers begin coding a design before review of the design is complete (and review reveals that the design is faulty); (2) designers attempting to satisfy requirement X, through misunderstanding of the requirement, produce a design that does not satisfy requirement X; and (3) designers produce a design that satisfies requirement X but fails to satisfy a related requirement Y (e.g., a design that satisfies a requirement to retrieve data from a database may be so inefficient that a performance requirement is not met). By *excursions from customer requirements* we mean that software developers deliberately but with good intention proceed to develop software that is a substitute for, or an addition to, customer requirements. Examples of such excursions include (1) designers provide a design that satisfies an unexpressed requirement Y rather than an expressed requirement X, because they feel that Y is a "better" requirement than X; and (2) programmers add "bells and whistles" to the code, for which the customer has expressed no need (e.g., to an accounting package requested by a customer, the programmers add a mathematics library with statistical, trigonometric, and hyberbolic functions).

[6] Figure 1.3 is not meant to be interpreted quantitatively. The ratio of the denominations on the dollar bills does indeed provide some indication of the relative amounts of resources spent on the disciplines of development and product assurance. However, the number of bills shown has no significance. We touch upon the subject of the cost of product assurance in Section 7.3 and probe more deeply product assurance cost issues in exercises throughout the book (see, for example, Exercises 3.8, 7.1, and 7.5).

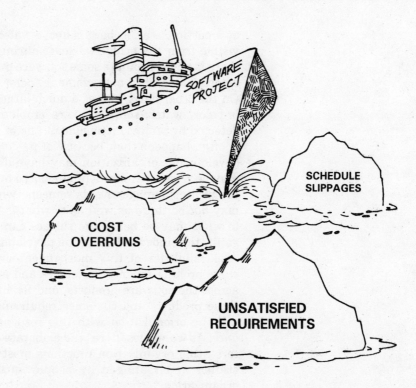

FIGURE 1.4. Typical hazards faced by a software project.

with this hazard means that a software project manager must have the ability to recognize unsatisfied requirements so that he can take appropriate corrective action. It follows that the longer these requirements remain unsatisfied, the greater the likelihood that the other icebergs shown in the figure—cost overruns and schedule slippages—will threaten the project ship. If, for example, it is not until software coding is well under way that requirement ambiguities are discovered, then to address these ambiguities the project manager may have to redirect considerable resources to resolve the ambiguities in requirements and design documentation and to modify what has already been coded. But such redirection of resources is just another way of saying that costs may overrun and schedules may slip because such redocumenting and recoding may not have been planned at project outset. Thus, the iceberg of unsatisfied requirements often fragments into the additional icebergs of cost overruns and schedule slippages. Without a way to detect this process of iceberg proliferation, a software project can easily and quickly be stopped dead in the water (or worse).

B. To avoid the icebergs, the captain of the project ship will need some way to know where they are. More specifically, the project manager will need to have some insight into the software products (and the customer requirements) so that he can determine to what extent these products may have to be changed to make them conform to customer requirements (or, as is sometimes the case, to what extent customer requirements may have to be changed to make the project doable). Now, just as a portion of an iceberg is above water and therefore clearly visible from the bridge (at least during daylight hours when there is no fog around), some software problems may be readily detected by project management and/or the development staff. On the other hand, just as a much larger portion of an iceberg is below water, some software problems may not be readily detected by project management and/or the development staff. It often happens that, because of its closeness to its work, the development organization may have difficulty noticing what may be missing from its products. To overcome this tendency, the project manager needs someone who is sensitive to what may *not* be there as well as to what *is* there. This sensitivity to what may be below the surface can be achieved by an organization independent of the development organization. The responsibilities of this independent organization should include probing for inconsistencies and ambiguities within and across the software products, and for inconsistencies between these products and customer requirements. In this book, we call the organization with this responsibility *product assurance*. As we suggest here (and elaborate on in subsequent chapters), this organization functions most effectively when it is staffed and managed by people outside the development organization.

C. Based on the discussion in A and B, Figure 1.4 could be modified in one or more of the following ways to portray the concept of product assurance (some of the strengths and weaknesses of each portrayal are indicated):

1. There could be a lighthouse on the shore that enables the ship to navigate clear of the icebergs. This portrayal carries with it the possible interpretation that product assurance is applied only near the end of the project journey (or near the beginning of the journey), when the ship is close enough to land to benefit from the visibility afforded by a lighthouse. The notion of independence is suggested by the location of the lighthouse—outside the confines of the ship and not under its control (the trade-offs associated with placing the product assurance organization outside the control of the project manager as well as the development organization are explored in subsequent chapters—see, for example, Exercise 3.10). Of course, a lighthouse affords limited visibility, its illumination being dimmed or blotted out by fog and heavy rain, and so it is on some software projects. For a variety of reasons (e.g., tightly constrained budgets), product assurance may be limited to cursory reviews of software products; such reviews may also be widely spaced (much like the alternating periods of light and darkness associated with the sweep of a lighthouse beam).

2. There could be a radio tower on the shore that beams iceberg and fog alerts to ships. This portrayal carries with it a more global interpretation than that of the lighthouse.

As in 1, the notion of independence is suggested by the shore-basing of the radio tower. However, unlike the lighthouse, if the power output of the tower is sufficiently large, the beams can afford the ship's captain visibility throughout the voyage. Of course, such sustained and high-powered visibility does not usually come cheaply. Good software auditors (as some product assurance people are called) command high salaries. However, such salaries can be justified, as we argue in subsequent chapters, because, for example, a thorough audit done early in the software project can give visibility to problems that may be much cheaper to resolve at that time than later in the project.

3. There could be an airplane flying in the vicinity of the ship and equipped with devices to detect potential hazards on the water surface (even through fog) and to detect potential subsurface hazards. With a communication link to the ship, this independent source of information would offer the ship's captain comprehensive visibility as long as the captain believed he could afford to keep the plane in the air. Compared to the product assurance portrayals in 1 and 2 above, the airplane portrayal carries a connotation of "deluxe" or possibly even "overkill." We simply observe here that such "deluxe" product assurance coverage is often warranted in circumstances where software failures would result in loss of life (e.g., a software-controlled missile run awry) and/or large financial loss (e.g., a software logic error that corrupts thousands of personal and business accounts at a major bank). In subsequent chapters, we return to this issue of risks associated with software failure and the need for visibility into software development that (independent) product assurance can provide.

As an overall comment on C, we observe that the portrayals of product assurance have been in terms of entities not attached to the project ship and thus presumably not under the direct control of the ship's captain. These portrayals are intended to stress the desirability of organizational independence for product assurance. Each portrayal has its onboard counterpart (e.g., the lighthouse could be replaced by searchlights affixed to various parts of the ship). Such sources of visibility would be under direct control of the ship's captain. Our experience shows that while such control offers the project manager the potential for firmer overall control of his project, it carries with it the risk that the lights may not be turned on when they are most needed or that they may be beamed in the wrong directions. For example, there is a tendency on many software projects not to turn the product assurance lights on early in the project (and thus be blind to such things as requirements conflicts), but to wait until coding is far along (with the result that such requirements conflicts come to light through testing, thus precipitating an expensive recoding-retesting cycle that might have been avoided or at least sharply reduced in scope and cost). The issue of organizational independence for product assurance is explored in subsequent chapters.

As an overall comment on this sample problem: It could be surmised from Figure 1.4 that the three questions posed at the outset of this sample problem are pertinent only for luxury-liner-class software projects (i.e., projects with large budgets that take years to complete). But such an inference would be incorrect. In Exercise 1.6, at the end of this chapter, we ask you to reconsider the preceding discussion from the point of view of smaller projects.

1.4 Product Assurance and the Product Assurance Practitioner—A Sample Problem

Background and Questions

At the end of Section 1.1, we commented that, through a system of checks and balances interwoven into the software development process, product assurance raises the likelihood that software products will satisfy customer requirements. These checks and balances help make the software development process more visible by spotlighting discrepancies between a software product and customer requirements; they also provide a means for tracing software development. What are some specific product assurance activities, and how do they help raise the visibility of the software development process and thread it with traceability?

Solution Approach

The software development process is inherently less visible than other development processes (such as the designing and manufacturing of an automobile). To understand why software development is inherently less visible, it is sufficient here to state that a software product is a packaging of information embodying functions that are ultimately intended for machine processing. In Chapter 2 we formally define what we mean by software. We thus see that, unlike a piece of hardware (such as a nut or bolt), software does not have readily perceived physical characteristics (such as length, width, height, weight, or color). A nut or bolt can be straightforwardly compared with a specification drawing showing its physical characteristics to determine whether the object matches its specification; in addition, a nut or bolt can be joined with another hardware piece in accordance, say, with an exploded-parts diagram in a readily perceptible manner to test whether the nut or bolt is the proper size and shape. The software analogues of such activities (and other such product assurance activities) are generally not easy to visualize, let alone carry out. However, common sense suggests that such activities need to be performed in the software world for the same reasons they need to be performed on other products—the primary reason being that product assurance serves to raise the visibility of the development process. Just as comparing a bolt against an engineering drawing of that bolt gives insight into the degree to which the manufactured object conforms to what was asked for (as defined in the drawing), so comparing software code against a requirements or design specification (i.e., the software analogues of engineering drawings) gives insight into the degree to which the software code conforms to what was asked for (as defined in specification documentation). Also, through such comparisons, a cycle is set in motion whereby discrepancies become apparent, changes (to the code and/or specifications) are formulated to resolve these discrepancies, these changes are incorporated, the comparisons are repeated, and so forth, until convergence between what was produced and what was asked for is achieved. This cycle amounts to a trace of product development.

From the arguments in the preceding paragraph, it follows that the activities listed below can help assure that a software product satisfies customer requirements. Also indicated below are ways that these activities help raise the visibility of the software development process and thread it with traceability.

A. Frequently, one or more standards may be imposed on the software development process. Such standards may specify the format and content of requirements or design specifications; they may specify the language constructs permitted or disallowed in computer code; they may indicate the type and number of documents that should be produced during software development. An important product assurance activity is the application of procedures, techniques, and tools throughout software development to help assure that a software product meets such established standards. A standard can be viewed as a form of checklist that reduces the likelihood that something is left out of a software product. Checking conformance with this checklist may uncover discrepancies between a product under development and a standard. These discrepancies shed light on missing or incompletely thought through parts of the product. Brought to the attention of management, such omissions and lack of definition have a greater likelihood of being systematically dealt with, particularly if they are discussed early in the product's development, than if they spontaneously come to light subsequent to customer delivery. Also, as such discrepancies and proposed solutions become part of the record of this development, a trace of this development is maintained that generally facilitates subsequent development activities (and the resolution of subsequently appearing discrepancies). Because software is malleable (more so, at least, than, say, a piece of steel), software projects often turn out to be highly dynamic, with backtracking a frequent occurrence. The traceability thread resulting from product assurance activities (such as standards checking) helps prevent such backtracking exercises from degenerating into a series of resource-consuming hit-or-miss trials.

B. A logical extension of the standards comparison activity described in A is the comparison of a software product against the predecessor product (e.g., computer code against the design specification for that code) and the comparison of a software product against a requirements specification for that product (the predecessor product and the requirements specification can be thought of as standards governing the content of the product being examined). Such comparisons serve to raise the visibility of the software development process by shedding light on product inconsistencies with customer requirements and by shedding light on mismatches between a product and its predecessor. Brought to light, such discrepancies, together with the product, themselves provide a trace of the software development process. This trace serves to reduce the likelihood that previously encountered problems will reoccur in other areas of a project, so that subsequent development can proceed more efficiently. (This argument is based on the assumption that requirements and design specifications are produced on a development project. See Exercise 1.10 for considerations regarding whether such specifications should be produced.)

C. There is a special case of the comparison discussed in B above that deserves separate mention. This special case is the software analogue of taking an automobile out for a test drive before deciding whether to buy it. In the software industry, this activity is often referred to as *acceptance testing*. Typically, a software system is "test driven" by installing the system on the customer's hardware and exercising the software in an environment that at least approximates the environment in which the customer intends to use the system. As distinguished from so-called unit and integration testing (presumably performed by the developer on individual parts of the software and on collections of these parts), test driving the software focuses on determining the extent to which this software performs the functions that the customer asked for in accordance with customer-specified performance criteria. The test drive is conducted by following written test plans and procedures that embody customer requirements.[7] Thus, test-drive anomalies amount to departures from customer requirements. Such departures give visibility to the software development process by bringing to light specific incompatibilities between customer-stipulated functions that the software code is to perform and the actual operation of this code. Again, just as was explained

---

[7] By *test plan* we mean a document that specifies the test organization, test schedule, allocation of resources, and the assignment of responsibilities for the conduct of an acceptance test. The plan prescribes a set of tests whose execution will demonstrate the fulfillment of customer needs. By a *test procedure*, we mean the document resulting from the translation of a test specified in a test plan to a sequence of instructions to a tester to enable him to demonstrate the fulfillment of the objective of the test. A test procedure, which is derived from a requirements specification and a design specification, specifies tester actions to be taken and the results expected from those actions. The names, types, and hierarchy of test documentation are not yet standardized within the software industry. We use the simple schema of test plans, procedures, and reports in this book for exemplification purposes (see Chapter 5).

in B above, such incompatibilities, together with the code and the requirements specification, provide a trace of the software development process. This trace provides the means of achieving convergence between customer requirements and software code operation through the (visible) cycle of test-recode-test-recode . . . until the difference between what the customer asked for and what the developer can produce falls below a mutually acceptable threshold.

D. The application of the product assurance activities described in A, B, and C above generally results, as indicated, in changes to software products. Providing a forum for evaluating these changes, and providing a means for tracking this evaluation process, are necessary adjuncts to the product assurance activities previously described. Thus, it seems logical that these adjuncts should also fall into the product assurance domain. They serve to raise the visibility of the software development process by shedding light on the trade-offs associated with proposed software changes. The tracking of these trade-offs serves to trace this process.

Note that in this sample problem we have focused on four major product assurance activities and touched on some of their interrelationships. We have pursued this course with malice aforethought. In subsequent chapters, we delve into these activities in considerable detail. In this sample problem, our aim has been to demonstrate that software product assurance is nothing more than a set of coupled comparison activities stemming from common-sense considerations of what, in specific terms, is meant by attempting to answer the following question:

How can a determination be made that a software product embodies what the customer asked to be contained in the product?

In Figure 1.5, we show these activities as gears whose meshing action is concentrated on resolving the foregoing question. We highlight the basic function for each activity to show that they are all comparison activities (note that the function of evaluation contains the notion of comparison). We hope that we have provided some insight into the definition of product assurance presented at the outset of this chapter. To reiterate, it is a set of checks and balances (effected through a series of comparison activities) interwoven into the software development process (because it serves as a catalyst in the product change cycle by bringing to light the source of change—discrepancies between the product and other items governing that product's development) whose primary purpose is to assure that a software product satisfies the needs of the intended recipient (the basic software management challenge to achieve convergence between those needs and the software developer's perception of those needs).

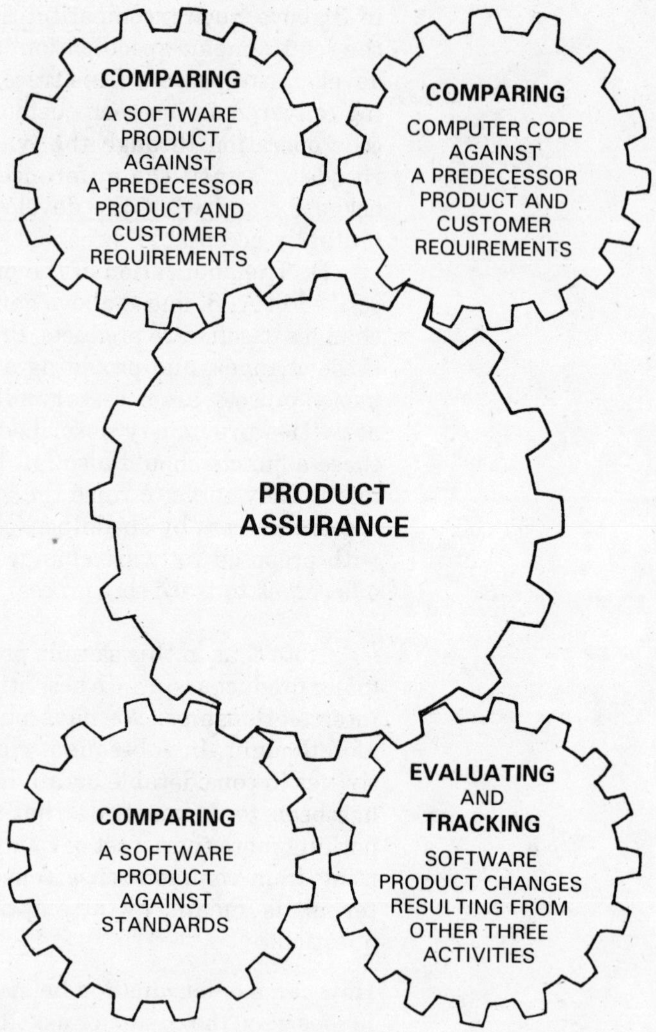

FIGURE 1.5. Product assurance is a set of four coupled activities for determining that a software product does what it is supposed to do.

The gears in the figure are labeled:

- **COMPARING** A SOFTWARE PRODUCT AGAINST A PREDECESSOR PRODUCT AND CUSTOMER REQUIREMENTS
- **COMPARING** COMPUTER CODE AGAINST A PREDECESSOR PRODUCT AND CUSTOMER REQUIREMENTS
- **PRODUCT ASSURANCE**
- **COMPARING** A SOFTWARE PRODUCT AGAINST STANDARDS
- **EVALUATING** AND **TRACKING** SOFTWARE PRODUCT CHANGES RESULTING FROM OTHER THREE ACTIVITIES

1.5 Preview

We conclude this chapter by previewing the remainder of the book. In Chapter 2, we formally define and illustrate the key concepts that make up a working vocabulary needed to describe software product assurance. In Chapter 3, we analyze the discipline of product assurance. The discussion in Chapters 2 and 3 will build upon the notions introduced in Sections 1.2, 1.3, and 1.4. The remaining four chapters of the book dwell on the detailed mechanics of product assurance and on software project management issues from a product assurance perspective.

Chapter 4 describes the basic elements needed to control software changes visibly and traceably. It introduces the concepts of evolutionary and revolutionary changes and focuses on the organizational body that lies at the center of change control—the configuration control board (CCB)—along with the procedures and forms used for change control.

Chapter 5 describes the basic techniques involved with comparing software products against one another and themselves to determine whether these products are being developed logically and are congruent with what the customer asked for. It covers the general classes of discrepancies found in software, and specific techniques for assessing a software product's content, both when the product is a document and when it is computer code.

Chapter 6 describes the bookkeeping required to support the activities discussed in Chapters 4 and 5. This description includes how to keep a record of CCB activity and how to establish and maintain a project archive; it also includes a discussion of bookkeeping automated aids.

Chapter 7 discusses some of the authors' real-world experiences to demonstrate that product assurance can help safely navigate a software project through iceberg-infested waters. It shows that application of the concepts and techniques described in the preceding six chapters can make a difference under certain circumstances.

In closing this chapter, we want to make an important point regarding the exercises in this book. An extensive set of exercises immediately follows the text of each chapter. These exercises are designed to let you demonstrate to yourself that you understand and can apply the material that we present in the chapter text. Product assurance is a complex and multi-faceted discipline. These exercises reflect this situation in that they call upon you to think about some of these complexities and facets from the perspective of your own environment.

We do not believe that product assurance can be reduced to a cookbook formulation with only one prescribed way for accomplishing its functions. We already alluded to this state of affairs in our presentation of the three sample problems in this chapter. When we discussed these sample problems, we emphasized that we were presenting solution *approaches* to the questions posed. In these solution approaches, you have seen how several possible answers can be given to a particular question (recall, for example, the discussion in Section 1.3 of three ways to portray the concept of product assurance—a lighthouse, a radio tower, or an airplane). Thus, the exercises at the end of each chapter are different from those found in mathematics and scientific texts, which typically have one right answer. Our exercises generally have more than one possible answer. For this reason, we do not provide solutions to these exercises. Rather, you must consider various possible solutions in terms of the factors and principles involved (often we assist you here by offering hints suggesting some of these factors and principles) and in terms of your experience and environment.

We indicated in the Preface that we did not expect managers reading this book to plunge into these exercises. For those managers who choose to bypass this material, we want to emphasize that you will not be shortchanged—the chapter text does provide what we believe is the essence of product assurance. However, those managers who do work some of these exercises will find that the thinking that these exercises demand will serve to deepen their understanding of the material in the chapter text. Even if you choose not to take pencil in hand and actually work through an exercise, simply reading it may bring to mind issues that may not have occurred to you as you read the chapter text.

Senior managers in particular may wish, after reading an exercise, to pass the issues raised in the exercise to their subordinates for their consideration. These senior managers may then subsequently want to discuss with their subordinates how they would deal with these issues. Based on our teaching experience, this mode of working the exercises benefits all the participants, because through the interchange of ideas each individual gains a greater understanding of the issues being examined. Furthermore, this approach aids the participants in arriving at the "right" answers. That is, the participants will know that the possible answers are right after they discuss the pros and cons of the issues raised in the exercise and come to a common understanding of these pros and cons (which is *not* the same thing as coming to an agreement as to how a particular issue should be resolved).

Let us begin our exploration of product assurance.[8]

EXERCISES

1.1   In the comments on the state of the software industry that we quoted from DeMarco's book (see Figure 1.2), it was noted that cost overruns of 100 to 200 percent are common on software projects. Elsewhere in his book, DeMarco contrasts these figures with the situation in another industry: "A construction job is considered a debacle if it overruns by six percent" (p. 4). In your opinion, what factors could explain this large difference between typical cost overruns on software projects and cost overruns on construction projects? For example, are the products developed on a software project different in some fundamental ways from the product developed on a construction project? If so, in what ways are these products different, and how can these differences help explain the larger overruns typically experienced on software projects? If in your opinion these products are basically similar from the point of view of the management techniques needed to control their development, what other reasons can you offer to explain the cost overrun differences between software and construction projects?

---

[8] Senior managers may want to consider the following exercises before proceeding to the next chapter: Exercise 1.1, on factors influencing cost overruns; Exercise 1.4, on insurance for nonlethal software systems. Project managers and product assurance managers may want to consider the following exercises: Exercise 1.2, on product assurance providing peace of mind; Exercise 1.3, on planning for a software development effort with product assurance; Exercise 1.5, on considerations in software development management; Exercise 1.6, on problems of small projects and the possibility of product assurance assistance; Exercise 1.7, on product assurance assistance in averting possible project failure.

1.2 In what specific ways do you think that product assurance can provide a software project manager with peace of mind during project evolution? For example, is product assurance like a tranquilizer that dulls the senses and thus elevates a project manager's threshold of pain? Or, for example, is product assurance like a magnifying glass through which a project manager can see what is happening on a project? (If you choose to think along the lines of the second example, consider the relationship between "peace of mind" and the availability of a "magnifying glass" that may allow you to see some adverse project happenings.)

1.3 Suppose you have just been appointed manager of a two-year $1 million software development effort that the company you work for has just won. What the customer wants is specified in a one-page statement of requirements. This statement essentially consists of a list of twelve one-sentence descriptions of functions that the customer wants his software system to perform. Recalling the notions of visibility and traceability that were mentioned in the text, what is the first product that you think your engineering staff should develop for you? Why? What are subsequent products that this staff and your programming staff should develop? Why? When should product testing be performed and why? Besides testing, what other product assurance functions do you think should be performed (i.e., what functions would you like those on your staff who are not doing product development to perform to help to see what the developers are doing)? When should these other product assurance functions be performed, and on what products? Why? (Assume that before you initiate product development you prepare a project management plan that specifies for the customer (1) how you intend to organize and manage the project, (2) what products are to be developed, (3) what functions are to be performed to ensure that these products satisfy customer requirements, and (4) a product delivery schedule.)

1.4 Rework the sample problem in Section 1.2 without the supposition that people might get killed if the software in the systems your company develops fails to operate properly.

1.5 Some people (including veterans of many software projects) contend that the nature of the software beast makes control (i.e., management) of its development nearly impossible. The best you can do, they claim, is try to keep the beast at bay so that it does not consume the project participants (the main course being the project manager) and the user. What do you think are some reasons for this attitude? Is the development of software fundamentally different from, say, the designing and building of a house or the designing and production of an automobile? Is the development of software more akin to the painting of a picture by an artist where the idea of telling the artist what color to select or how to apply the paint to canvas would be tantamount to suppressing artistic expression? If you believe that software development is akin to an exercise in artistic expression, do you think that applying product assurance to software development is akin to suppressing this artistic expression? (*Hint:* In responding to these questions, consider why it is beneficial to *any* project manager to be able to see what is going on and to trace the course of project events. Consider also why these two capabilities may be particularly beneficial to a *software* project manager.)

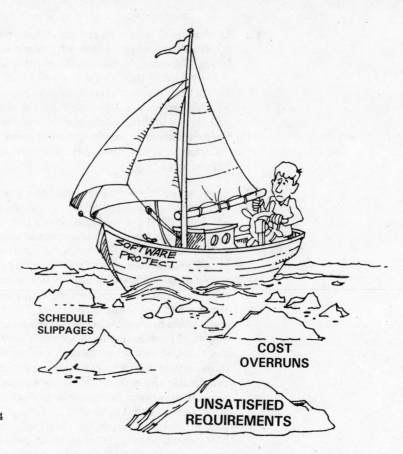

FIGURE E1.1. A small-project analogue to Figure 1.4 (Exercise 1.6).

SCHEDULE SLIPPAGES

COST OVERRUNS

UNSATISFIED REQUIREMENTS

SOFTWARE PROJECT

1.6   At the end of the discussion in Section 1.3, we indicated that the ideas treated there may not be restricted to luxury-liner-class software projects (see Figure 1.4). Consider now the small-project analogue to Figure 1.4 depicted in Figure E1.1. Respond to the following questions by modifying and/or augmenting the discussion in Section 1.3 to account for the differences in software projects implied by Figures 1.4 and E1.1.

    (a) What is the nature of the difference of the icebergs depicted in Figure E1.1 versus those depicted in Figure 1.4 in terms of threat to the software projects shown in the figures?

    (b) What would help the captain of the vessel shown in Figure E1.1 sail through the treacherous waters?

    (c) How would you modify Figure E1.1 to portray the concept of product assurance?

    (d) What do your responses to the preceding parts of this exercise and the discussion in Section 1.3 suggest about the applicability of product assurance to any software project?

1.7   Some people (including veterans of many software projects) contend that the key element for ensuring project success is a well-conceived project plan. Specifically, they claim that if this plan contains the information listed below, then all project management needs to do is have periodic staff meetings to check on project progress and give direction for continuing project activities.

Milestones with clearly defined products (including a test report reflecting the results of testing the computer code prior to customer delivery)

Product delivery schedules consistent with the experience of project personnel and the perceived complexity of the development effort (and of course consistent with the customer's delivery expectations)

A budget (preferably broken down by specific tasks related to project milestones) with a contingency fund to accommodate unforeseen circumstances, consistent with the experience of project personnel and the perceived complexity of the development effort (and of course consistent with the contents of the customer's pocketbook)

What are some reasons that a project with a well-conceived plan, an experienced project manager, an experienced staff of product developers, a reasonable schedule, and a sufficient budget still might not succeed (here "succeed" means "products delivered on time, delivered within budget, and congruent with customer needs")? Based upon the notion of product assurance that we discussed in this chapter, in what ways might product assurance help to avert possible project failure stemming from these reasons? *Hint:* Consider the following questions:

(a) In what ways is a project manager able to determine project progress?

(b) What is the tendency of most people when they are reporting progress to project management on their assigned tasks—to be optimistic or pessimistic?

(c) How can a project manager determine whether a product scheduled for customer delivery is consistent with customer needs?

(d) What potential difficulties does personnel turnover present to the project manager—particularly sudden, unexpected loss of key technical personnel?

(e) In what ways is a project manager able to determine the impact of revised customer needs on project schedules and deliverable products?

(f) What are some risks the project manager might be taking if detailed examination of a product's contents is left solely to the product developers as opposed to a technically qualified group of individuals who did not develop the product?

(g) What are some potential impacts on the project budget and schedule if the project manager chooses to conduct detailed examination of a product's content using a group of technically qualified individuals who did not develop the product?

(h) Do the impacts in (g) serve to increase or decrease the likelihood of project success? Why (not)?

1.8 Recall the definition of *requirement* given in Section 1.1. Consider each statement listed below and indicate whether you think the statement represents *what* a customer needs a developer to do (i.e., a requirement) or whether it represents *how* something is to be done (or both). Give at least one reason to justify each of your answers.

(a) Build me a black box that manages my stock portfolio.

(b) The system you build for me should respond to all keyboard inputs within five seconds.

(c) The system you build for me should be coded in FORTRAN.

(d) The software you code for me should use only mnemonic variable names and should not use GOTO statements.

(e) The system needs to process a maximum of 500 messages per hour.

(f) The software must be up and running no later than six months after you start work.

(g) The software you build for me is to be delivered to me untested.

(h) I need all the capabilities in this list for no more than $10,000.

(i) The design specification that you will use as the basis for software coding is to be written in English supplemented by pseudo-code.

(j) The number of lines of software code you produce is not to exceed 100,000.

(k) No subroutine you code is to contain more than 100 source language statements.

(l) Each subroutine you code will contain comments explaining its purpose and the mathematical equations it contains.

(m) What I really need is a checkbook-balancing capability coded in COBOL.

1.9 The operations of governments and military organizations are frequently supported by intelligence activities. A primary role of these activities is to gather information and make assessments regarding things that may be of some interest to the governments and military organizations that the intelligence activities support. Of course, governments and military organizations have the option of ignoring the information (which often takes the form of warnings regarding the course of future events) these activities provide. With the preceding as background, consider the following:

(a) Based on the discussion in this chapter, list at least three ways that the role of product assurance on a software project could be viewed as being similar to the role of an intelligence activity. Give at least one reason to justify each item on your list.

(b) Suppose that an intelligence activity frequently reports that nothing untoward has occurred or is about to occur. Does such a situation call the utility of the activity into question? Why (not)?

(c) Suppose that an intelligence activity frequently reports things that the customer perceives as being of little consequence (and sometimes prove to be incorrect or off the mark). Does such a situation call into question the utility of the activity? Why (not)?

(d) Based on your responses to (a), (b), and (c), give at least two reasons why it may be difficult to assess the value of product assurance on a software project.

1.10 On many software projects the documentation task (i.e., writing requirements and design specifications and writing descriptions of what computer code is supposed to do) is addressed as an afterthought—something that gets done after the code is produced, if time permits. The cartoon in Figure E1.2 illustrates this state of affairs. A view diametrically opposed to this figure was expressed in 1977 by the author of a computer programming book:

> I . . . would like to make the following suggestion to professional programmers: *One way to improve the quality of programs drastically is to take the view that the main purpose of*

FIGURE E1.2. Does software development in the real world have to be done this way? (Exercise 1.10). Clem Scalzitti, *Software News,* vol. 5, no. 11 (November 1985), p. 23. Reprinted by permission of Clem Scalzitti.

"Writing the program is a breeze... it's writing the documentation that gets me."

a programming project is to write a highly readable manual describing a program. The program itself is merely a useful by-product of the effort. (P. B. Hansen, *The Architecture of Concurrent Programs* [Englewood Cliffs, N.J.: Prentice-Hall, 1977], pp. 226–227.)

The attitude adopted in our book runs counter to that depicted in Figure E1.2 and is more in sympathy with the attitude expressed in the above quotation. That is, we adopt the attitude that computer code is something that should result *only* after requirements that the code is to satisfy are formalized and *only* after a design based on these requirements has been formulated and agreed to by software project participants. With the preceding as background, and based on your own experience in the software industry (or if you have little or no such experience, based on what others may have told you about the software industry), consider the following:

(a) What may be some reasons why software code is often produced in the manner depicted in Figure E1.2?

(b) Given these reasons and your perception of human nature, is it reasonable to assume that imposing discipline on a software project (so that, contrary to Figure E1.2, computer code is produced from requirements and design documentation and not in spite of it) cannot meaningfully be accomplished because it is a constraint that is artificial (i.e., runs counter to human nature because, for example, everybody knows that it is computer code and not documentation that makes computer systems operate)?

(c) What are at least three kinds of problems that may arise if computer code is developed in the manner suggested by Figure E1.2? For each problem you cite, give at least one reason why the problem may arise. (*Hint:* Consider what may be going through the mind of the onlooker in Figure E1.2, assuming that he is the user or the buyer of the program.)

(d) For each problem you identify in (c), indicate at least one way that product assurance as we describe it in this chapter may be able to reduce the likelihood of the problem arising, and give at least one reason why.

(e) For each problem you identify in (c), indicate at least one way that some means other than product assurance may be able to reduce the likelihood of the problem arising, and give at least one reason why.

(f) Suppose you are a manager of a software project where the attitude depicted in Figure E1.2 does *not* exist, and suppose your software development staff (including specification writers) really believed in the documentation philosophy expressed in the above quotation from the Hansen book. Under such circumstances, do you think that the four product assurance activities depicted in Figure 1.5 need to be performed on your project? Give at least three reasons to justify your answer.

(g) If your response to (f) is that the four product assurance activities depicted in Figure 1.5 need to be performed, list at least three advantages and at least three disadvantages of having your development staff (as opposed to a separate product assurance staff) perform these activities.

(h) Based on your responses to the preceding parts of this exercise, is product assurance indeed inseparable from software development as Figure 1.1 suggests? Why (not)?

(i) If your response to (h) is that product assurance is inseparable from software development, should there be an organization separate from the development organization whose primary responsibility is to perform the four activities shown in Figure 1.5 on a software project? Why (not)? (*Hint:* You may want to temper your response by considering such factors as project size [e.g., number of people working on the project at a given time], project duration, complexity of the customer requirements [e.g., is the software to be produced something that has never been done by software before?], and project budget size [e.g., is the project amply funded?].)

1.11 In this book our thesis is that the application of product assurance can make it more likely that a software project will succeed (i.e., yield software products that do what the customer asked for, on time, and within budget). We do not claim that product assurance alone will solve all or even most of the ills from which the software industry suffers. To stimulate your thinking about a factor other than product assurance and the relationship of this factor to product assurance in contributing to software project success, consider the discussion below, which is an excerpt from C. A. R. Hoare, "Programming: Sorcery or Science?" *IEEE Software,* vol. 1, no. 2 (April 1984), pp. 5–16.

> In earlier times and in less-advanced societies, the welfare of a community depended heavily on the skill and dedication of its craftsmen—the millers and blacksmiths, spinners and weavers, joiners and thatchers, cobblers and tailors. A craftsman possessed special skills, not shared by his clients, which he acquired by long and ill-paid apprenticeship to a master of his craft. He learned by imitation, by practice, by experience, and by trial and error. He knew little of the scientific basis of his techniques, or geometry or even of drawing, of mathematics or even of arithmetic. He could not explain how or why he did what he did, yet he worked effectively, by himself or in a small team, and could usually complete the tasks he undertook within a predictable timescale, at a fixed cost and with results that were satisfactory to his clients.

The programmer of today shares many attributes with the craftsman of yesterday. He learns his craft by a short but highly paid apprenticeship in an existing programming team engaged in some ongoing project, and he develops his skills by experience rather than by reading books or journals. He knows little of the logical and mathematical foundations of his profession. He does not like to explain or document his activities. Yet he works effectively, by himself or in small teams, and he sometimes manages to complete the tasks he undertakes at the predicted time, within the predicted costs, and to the satisfaction of his client.

In primitive societies of long ago, the welfare of the community depended on another class of specialist. Like the craftsman, he was dedicated to his task and regarded with respect—perhaps tinged with awe—by his many satisfied clients. Several names were given to such a man—seer, soothsayer, sorcerer, wizard, witch doctor, or high priest. I shall just call him a high priest.

There were many differences between the craftsman and the high priest. One of the most striking was that the high priest was the custodian of a weighty set of sacred books, or magician's manuals, which he alone was capable of reading. When he was consulted by his client with some new problem, he referred to his sacred books to find some spell or incantation that had proved efficacious in the past; and having found it, he told his client to copy it carefully and use it in accordance with a set of elaborate instructions. If the slightest mistake was made in copying or in following the instructions, the spell might turn into a curse and bring misfortune to the client. The client had no hope of understanding the nature of the error or why it evoked the wrath of his deity— the high priest himself had no inner understanding of the ways of his god. The best the client could hope for was to go right back to the beginning and start the spell again. If this did not work, he went back to the high priest to get a new spell.

And that brings up another feature of the priesthood. When something went wrong, as it quite often did, somehow it was always caused by the client's ignorance or stupidity or impurity or wickedness. It was never the fault of the high priest or his god. When the harvest failed, it was the high priest who sacrificed the king, never the other way around.

Present-day programmers share many attributes with the high priest. We have many names—coder, systems analyst, computer scientist, informatician, chief programmer. (I will just use the word "programmer" to stand for them all.) Our altars are hidden from the profane, each in its own superbly air-conditioned holy of holies, ministered to night and day by a devoted team of acolytes, and regarded by the general public with mixed feelings of fear and awe appropriate for their condition of powerless dependence.

An even more striking analogy is the increasing dominance of our sacred books, the basic software manuals for our languages and operating systems which have become essential to our every approach to the computer. Only 30 years ago, our computers' valves and tanks and wires filled the walls and shelves of a large room, which the programmer would enter, carrying in his pocket his programming manual—a piece of folded cardboard known as the FACT CARD. Now the situation is reversed: the programmer enters a large room whose walls and shelves are lined with software manuals, but in case he wants to carry out some urgent calculations, he carries in his pocket—a computer.

With the preceding as background, and recalling the discussion of product assurance in this chapter, consider the following:

(a) Suppose that a software project were staffed by software developers who were engineers in the professional sense of the word (and thus were not craftsmen or high priests in the sense described by Hoare). Would it be sufficient to leave the job of product assurance entirely to the software developers, or would it still be at least desirable (if not necessary) to have a group independent from the developers perform at least some product assurance functions? Why (not)? Give at least three reasons to support your answer. (*Hint:* In your response, consider factors such as project size and complexity, the experience of the development staff with the application to be automated, the value of an independent opinion, and the cost of an independent opinion.)

(b) In referring to software developers as high priests, Hoare states that they are "regarded by the general public with mixed feelings of fear and awe, appropriate for their condition of powerless dependence." Assuming that some senior managers and software project managers may share with members of the general public their attitudes toward software developers, what are some ways that the application of product assurance (by either the developers themselves, an independent group, or both) may help management overcome the condition of powerless dependence referred to by Hoare? (*Hint:* Consider how the application of product assurance may help management be better able to see what is happening on a software project.)

(c) As long as software developers turn out working products on time and within budget, does it really matter that they perform like craftsmen or high priests? Why (not)?

1.12 Refer to Figure 1.3. Observe that there are no product assurance resources shown falling into the trash cans, and answer the following questions:

(a) Do you think we should show some product assurance resources falling into the trash cans, in the sense that product assurance resources spent uncovering false starts and excursions from customer requirements are also wasted project resources? Why (not)?

(b) Suppose the developers on a project made no false starts or excursions from customer requirements. Would all resources spent for product assurance be wasted? Why (not)? (*Hint:* Consider the situation of a person who gets an annual physical examination, hoping to have medical problems detected early and possibly to avoid major medical [and expense] problems later. If the doctor informs the patient that he is completely healthy [i.e., that he has no medical problems], has the patient wasted his money on the examination? Or has the patient purchased peace of mind? Who on a software project might obtain peace of mind if the product assurance organization uncovers no false starts or excursions from customer requirements?)

(c) The authors are familiar with one multiyear, multimillion-dollar software project where product assurance was installed and functioning even before the software developer was selected (see discussion of Project Saturn in Section 7.1). This project was canceled in the coding stage (which began several years after the project started), partially due to the false starts and excursions from customer requirements uncovered in this stage by product assurance efforts. Because the entire project was canceled and no working software code was produced, do you think that the product assurance efforts were wasted resources? Why (not)?

(d) If the development effort described in (c) had resulted in producing some working code (say, an initial operating capability) before being canceled, would you change your answer to (c)? Why (not)?

REFERENCES AND ADDITIONAL READINGS

1. Baber, R. L. *Software Reflected*. New York: North-Holland, 1982.

   Baber's book explains in layman's terms what is wrong with the way software is currently developed. It is atypical in that it focuses on the history of the software industry and describes three paths that the industry might take in the future. The book's thesis, with which we are in sympathy, is the following (pp. 11–12):

   > This book proposes that the activity of programming—specifying in detail, designing, and developing computer software—is by nature an engineering discipline but that it is not generally regarded as such in our society today. Some of the most serious consequences of our current non-engineering approach to computer programming are:
   >
   > Disappointing and shoddy products, often containing simple errors of a fundamental nature
   >
   > Unnecessarily low productivity
   >
   > Frequent failures of such size that major projects must be aborted at a late stage of development
   >
   > Diversion of considerable effort to fundamentally unproductive tasks
   >
   > Generation of confusion, fear, frustration and misunderstanding among direct and indirect users of computer based systems

   The book is short, qualitative, and easy to read. It closes by leaving the reader to consider the following regarding the activity of programming as defined in the book (p. 190):

   > In your view, the detailed specification, design, and development of computer software is
   > a. a science or an engineering discipline
   > b. an art
   > c. a craft
   > d. a trade
   > e. a racket

2. Biggs, C. L., E. G. Birks, and W. Atkins. *Managing the Systems Development Process*. Englewood Cliffs, N.J.: Prentice-Hall, 1980.

   Biggs et al. present a highly structured approach to managing the development of systems with software content. In describing the special management challenge that such system development efforts present, they state:

> One of the primary reasons underlying the often unfulfilled promise of computers and data processing is the lack of attention to basic management techniques by systems and data processing personnel. Even the rudimentary fundamentals of management (planning, organizing, executing, measuring, and correcting) are often disregarded by systems and data processing organizations. These basic management techniques must be introduced, practiced, ingrained, and enhanced if the promise of the computer is to be fulfilled. These management techniques are integral to successfully managing the systems development process (p. 3).

Emphasing visibility and traceability in the system development process, they summarize their methodology:

> This methodology is appropriate for developing the specific plans and programs called for by the systems projects that support an organization's objectives and goals. It specifically defines the phases of the systems development process— planning, requirements, development, implementation, and maintenance. The definition includes the standard activities that should be produced. These standards provide for a controlled approach to the definition and development of information systems required to meet objectives and goals. The end items specify a structured method for establishing how the organization will utilize the system and what costs and benefits should result from various alternatives. In many cases, the planning process will identify a number of versions or releases of a new system over a time period that meets existing needs, allows for evolutionary change, and permits a realistic scope of development effort (pp. 5–6).

One aim of our book is to support the planning process as defined in the last sentence above. The overall perspective of our book complements the perspective in the Biggs et al. book—theirs is the full scope of activities that a manager needs to be aware of to handle his project, while ours focuses on the specific activities of the product assurance organization that supports the project manager by providing him an alternative view of the activities of the product development organization.

3. Boehm, B. W. *Software Engineering Economics.* Englewood Cliffs, N.J.: Prentice-Hall, 1981.

Boehm's book applies economics to the software development and maintenance process. Its thesis is that software can and should be engineered (as opposed to being artistically created). Chapter 3 ("The Goals of Software Engineering") is particularly pertinent to the discussion in our Chapter 1. Boehm begins by defining the magnitude of the software industry and its growing impact on our daily lives. For example, the author notes on page 17 that in 1980 the annual cost of software in the United States was approximately $40 billion (27 percent of the gross national product). Commenting on the large and increasing impact software is having on human welfare, Boehm states:

> By 1985, roughly 40% of the American labor force will be

relying on computers and software to do their daily work, without being required to have some knowledge of how computers and software work. Thus, this 40% of the labor force will be trusting implicitly on the results produced by computer software (pp. 18–19).

In discussing the importance of software cost estimation, Boehm presents an example drawn from a U.S. Air Force software project. The winning bidder's estimate was $400,000. At its conclusion, the project's cost multiplied almost tenfold to $3,700,000! (For this project, the cost overrun iceberg shown in our Figure 1.4 would seem especially fitting.) A cost overrun of this magnitude is by no means unique. The discussion in our Chapter 1 hints at how the visibility and traceability afforded by the application of product assurance can reduce the likelihood of such overruns. Subsequent chapters reinforce this point a number of times.

4. Canan, J. W. "The Software Crisis." *Air Force,* vol. 69, no. 5 (May 1986); pp. 46–52.

Canan discusses semi-quantitatively the extent to which software has been, and will continue to be, a major problem for the U.S. Air Force in particular and the U.S. Department of Defense in general. He defines the software crisis as a demand for software that far exceeds the available supply of software professionals. A growing headache for the Air Force (and the Department of Defense) is the rising cost of fixing error-ridden software. Canan notes that the Air Force has had difficulty in catching software errors early in the life cycle where, as we subsequently indicate (see, for example, the first sample problem in Section 5.1), such errors are generally easier and less costly to correct. He also mentions that late delivery of software is precipitating delays in installing badly needed changes to operational weapons systems such as fighter aircraft. The article stresses that the software crisis is not confined to the American military establishment but also extends to the civilian sector which in turn exacerbates the crisis for the military due to the generally more attractive salaries and benefits of civilian software jobs. To illustrate this point, the article indicates that the General Motors Corporation spent almost as much money on software in 1985 as did the entire U.S. defense establishment in that year (the Department of Defense spent about $10 billion in 1985 for software, a figure that, Canan notes, is expected to triple by 1990; he also notes that by 1990, software will account for ten percent of the Air Force budget). Echoing a theme that we reiterate in this book, the article states that software development is often undisciplined with the result that software productivity can be vastly improved (recall Figure 1.3). In its closing paragraph, the article soberly notes that, unless this productivity improves (with concomitant declines in software costs), the U.S. software industry could suffer the same fate in the world marketplace that befell the U.S. steel industry—with grave consequences for the U.S. military.

5. DeMarco, T. *Controlling Software Projects*. New York: Yourdon Press, 1982.

DeMarco describes how measurement is essential to achieving control of software projects. Chapter 1 supplements the ideas in our Chapter 1 (as suggested by our quotes from DeMarco's book in our Preface and in Figure 1.2).

6. Keider, S. P. "Why Projects Fail." *Datamation,* vol. 20, no. 12 (December 1974), pp. 53–55.

    By describing the indicators of an unsuccessful project, this article discusses why software projects fail. Keider defines a successful project as one that satisfies the user's needs and is completed within time and cost estimates. He begins his analysis of project failure by indicating that any project can be time-divided into five distinct phases. For each of these phases, he then points out some of the errors that have major impact on project success. Particularly noteworthy for our purposes are such errors as:

    Lack of depth in project reviews

    Failure to adhere to standards and specifications

    Failure to provide adequate test time

    Lack of analysis or consideration in design reviews

    Failure to appoint a project manager

    We discuss these errors in subsequent chapters.

7. Martin, J., and C. McClure. *Software Maintenance: The Problem and Its Solutions.* Englewood Cliffs, N.J.: Prentice-Hall, 1983.

    As the title indicates, Martin and McClure discuss software maintenance, which they define as "changes that have to be made to computer programs after they have been delivered to the customer and user" (p. 3). The concept of software maintenance that we put forth in our book is broader in scope than Martin and McClure's. Their ideas complement many of ours. The opening chapter of this book ("The Maintenance Mess") builds a case for why software maintenance is a problem that demands attention now. (The book's front cover depicts an iceberg representing software costs; the iceberg's exposed portion is labeled "Development," the submerged portion is labeled "Maintenance." Note that this iceberg differs in meaning from our icebergs in Figure 1.4.) In particular, Martin and McClure note the following about the software industry:

    > Programming projects take longer to complete and cost more than planned. . . . Instances of actual costs running 300% over budget and actual schedules running 200% over estimates are the rule rather than the exception. . . . Managers are bewildered by their inability to apply normal management practices to the data-processing function. Users are frustrated and antagonized by applications that are difficult to change and do not work as expected. Software professionals are at a loss to understand why one project succeeds and the next one fails (pp. 5–6).

    The authors further explain that designing systems with maintenance in mind goes a long way toward alleviating the software cost iceberg phenomenon.

8. Peters, T. J., and R. H. Waterman, Jr. *In Search of Excellence: Lessons from America's Best-Run Companies.* New York: Harper & Row, 1982.

    In Search of Excellence has nothing to do with software (except for a few stories about computer companies), but it has much to say to all industry. Its message is best summarized in the following extract from the introduction:

[This book] will define what we mean by excellence. It is an attempt to generalize about what the excellent companies seem to be doing that the rest are not, and to buttress our observations on the excellent companies with sound social and economic theory. And, finally, it will employ field data too often overlooked in books on management—namely, specific, concrete examples from the companies themselves (pp. xxv–xxvi).

Perhaps the material in chapter 6 ("Close to the Customer") is the most pertinent to the ideas that we discuss in our book. It opens this way:

That a business ought to be close to its customers seems a benign enough message. So the question arises, why does a chapter like this need to be written at all? The answer is that, despite all the lip service given to the market orientation these days, . . . [business experts] are right: the customer is either ignored or considered a bloody nuisance (p. 156).

Recalling our Figure 1.4, we see that a problem plaguing the software industry is that software does not do what the customer wants. Peters and Waterman offer the following message:

All business rests on something labeled a sale, which at least momentarily weds company and customer. A simple summary of what our research uncovered on the customer attribute is this: the excellent companies *really are* close to their customers. That's it. Other companies talk about it; the excellent companies do it (p. 156).

We return to this point a number of times in our book.

9. Shooman, M. L. *Software Engineering: Reliability, Development, and Management.* New York: McGraw-Hill, 1983.

As stated in its preface, the objectives of this textbook are the following:

This book presents software engineering methodologies for the development of quality, cost-effective, schedule-meeting software. This approach serves a diverse audience: (a) upper-level undergraduates or graduates studying computer science, electrical engineering, mathematics, operations research, or industrial management, and (b) programmers, system analysts, software engineers, digital system engineers, engineering managers, or quality and reliability engineers in industry and government (p. xvii).

Shooman's chapter 6 ("Management Techniques") complements and supplements concepts presented in our book. Written as a textbook, it contains problems at the end of each chapter (which is not common in software engineering publications). To aid study, answers to selected problems are included. A good portion of the book utilizes mathematics (particularly probability theory and statistics).

10. Spanner, R. A. *Who Owns Innovation? The Rights and Obligations of Employers and Employees.* Homewood, Ill.: Dow-Jones-Irwin, 1984.

Spanner, a lawyer, focuses on how to preserve the secrecy of proprietary information. Chapter 3 ("What Information Is Protectable?") contains a four-page section on software. In our Chapter 1 discussion, we suggested that software development is a process in constant need of increased visibility. That software is indeed something difficult to perceive is reflected in the following excerpt from Spanner's book:

> Software has given courts trouble. Computer programs are so complicated and unintelligible on their face that it seems that they must be valuable secrets, but for the same reasons it is difficult to identify *what* is secret and unique about them (p. 21).

If in the courtroom, where probing and cross-examination are a matter of course, software poses visibility problems, is it any wonder that software should pose visibility problems during its development? The references listed in Exercise 7.16 probe in considerable detail legal issues pertaining to software.

11. U.S. Government Accounting Office. "Contracting for Computer Software Development—Serious Problems Require Management Attention to Avoid Wasting Additional Millions." Report to the Congress by the Comptroller General of the United States, FGMSD-80-4, November 9, 1979.

This report should be read in its entirety. It documents in project-specific terms our assertions that software is typically delivered late, delivered over budget, and does not do what it is supposed to do. Figure 5 in the report is a graphic illustration of these assertions.

12. Weiss, D. M. "The MUDD Report: A Case Study of Navy Software Development Practices." Naval Research Laboratory Report 7909, May 21, 1975.

If an industry as young as the software industry can claim to have classic publications, this report should be included in this category. The following quotation from the document's preface succinctly summarizes its purpose:

> This report is one result of a year-long investigation into Navy software problems. During this investigation, the author talked to many people associated with Navy software development. All of these people, from contracting personnel to program managers to programmers, were keenly interested in finding ways to improve software quality. Although it is not yet possible to give an algorithm for producing reliable software [and we believe that we still have a long way to go], many mistakes can be avoided by staying aware of problems encountered in the past. The purpose here is to describe some of these problems in a context familiar to Navy software developers in the hope that they can recognize and avoid similar errors in the future.
>
> This report chronicles the development of a mythical software system and describes where and how the developers went awry. The report is based on more than 30 interviews with people responsible for development of various kinds of Navy software in more than ten Navy activities. The pitfalls described typify problems which actually occurred in software development efforts, but all persons and situations described in this report are fictional.

Despite its serious subject, the report is written with a humorous touch that makes for easy reading.

chapter 2

LEARNING THE VOCABULARY

The job of a software manager is to *plan* the software development cycle, *direct* others to produce software products according to this plan, and *control* activities during plan execution. To accomplish each of these functions, the manager needs insight into what is happening. With this insight, the manager can then make intelligent, informed decisions on how to proceed. To understand more specifically how product assurance can facilitate this decision-making (and thus facilitate the manager's job), we need a working vocabulary of concepts bearing on the interplay between planning/directing/controlling and product assurance. From these concepts, we can then construct principles whose application can help the software project manager and his boss(es) avoid the project-threatening icebergs described in Chapter 1. The purpose of this chapter is to define and illustrate these concepts.

Before the product assurance practitioner decides to skip this chapter as being pertinent only to managers, we hasten to assure the practitioner that study of this chapter is necessary to obtain the full benefit from the remainder of this book. First of all, the concepts presented here are the base on which we construct the principles of product assurance presented in subsequent chapters. Without this base, which includes specific definitions and illustrations of concepts central to product assurance, the practitioner will have difficulty comprehending the full impact of the principles we present. Further, the practitioner needs the material provided in this chapter to understand why he is practicing his trade. It allows the practitioner to see the purpose behind what he does, and thus enables him to practice his trade more professionally.

Because the focus of this book is on software, we begin in Section 2.1 by formally defining and illustrating this concept. In Sections 2.2 and 2.3 respectively, we define the fundamental software project management concepts of visibility and traceability that were informally introduced in Chapter 1. Next, in Section 2.4, we introduce the notion of life cycle and relate it to the concepts of visibility and traceability. In Section 2.5, we expand upon our view of software and introduce the closely related concepts of software change, software baseline, software baseline update, software parts, and software configuration. With this solid foundation, we finally introduce, in Section 2.6, a notion that ties all these other concepts together—product integrity. That section provides a fitting transition to Chapter 3, which deals with the role of product assurance in achieving product integrity. In Section 2.7, we summarize the main ideas of the chapter. We illustrate the concepts introduced in each section through examples. Following the approach used in Chapter 1, we also probe nuances of some of these concepts using sample problems. These problems also serve to prepare you to tackle the exercises at the end of the chapter, which further probe and extend the concepts introduced.

2.1 Software

What do we mean when we use the term "software products"? Classically, software has been looked upon as computer code (or programs) that, once installed on computer hardware, makes the hardware do its intended job. We find this viewpoint too restrictive in presenting our ideas on product assurance. To unify many extant software management concepts that are scattered around under different names, we prefer to think of software in more panoramic terms. Specifically, in this book, *software* is formally defined as shown in Figure 2.1.[1] Note from

FIGURE 2.1. A concept of software. E. H. Bersoff, V. D. Henderson, and S. G. Siegel, *Software Configuration Management: An Investment in Product Integrity* (Englewood Cliffs, N.J.: Prentice-Hall, 1980), p. 10. Reprinted by permission of the publisher.

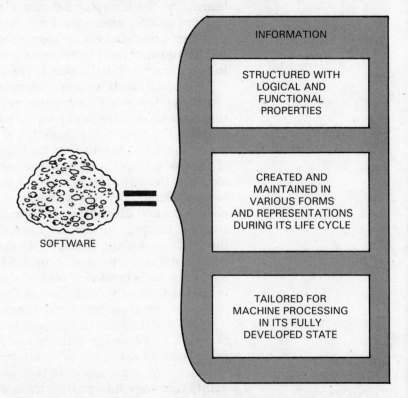

SOFTWARE

INFORMATION

STRUCTURED WITH LOGICAL AND FUNCTIONAL PROPERTIES

CREATED AND MAINTAINED IN VARIOUS FORMS AND REPRESENTATIONS DURING ITS LIFE CYCLE

TAILORED FOR MACHINE PROCESSING IN ITS FULLY DEVELOPED STATE

[1] E. H. Bersoff, V. D. Henderson, and S. G. Siegel, *Software Configuration Management: An Investment in Product Integrity* (Englewood Cliffs, N.J.: Prentice-Hall, 1980), p. 10.

this definition that software includes not only computer programs but also all associated specification and requirements documentation. Thus, for example, a design specification that gives birth to software code is itself software (as is the requirements documentation that gives birth to the design specification). It is crucial to your understanding of this book that you be constantly aware of our definition of software—after all, this is a book about software. If you consider software only as code, you will often be confused in the pages that follow. To help you retain this key concept, we reiterate it graphically in Figure 2.2. Note that in Figures 2.1 and 2.2 we associate our definition of software with a graphic that is suggestive of a sponge. We use this graphic throughout the book to portray software's susceptibility to change and to highlight the need for periodic checks to contain its evolving shape. However, in those instances where we refer to a specific software product which usually exists only in the form of documentation (e.g., a requirements specification), we symbolize this specific software product as a book.

Let us now probe some of the nuances of the software concept shown in Figure 2.1 by considering the sample problem below. We use the format introduced in Chapter 1—"Background and Questions" followed by "Solution Approach." After the problem, we present and describe some examples of software based on the definition given in Figure 2.1.

FIGURE 2.2. Our definition of software encompasses both specification documentation and code.

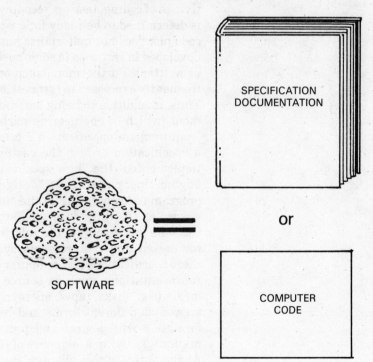

SPECIFICATION
DOCUMENTATION

SOFTWARE

or

COMPUTER
CODE

A PANORAMIC
CONCEPT OF
SOFTWARE—A
SAMPLE PROBLEM
*Background and
Questions*

Our definition of software includes not only computer programs but also all associated specification and requirements documentation.

A. What fundamental engineering notion underlies the definition given in Figure 2.1?

B. In terms of what a project manager is called upon to do on a software development effort, how can our panoramic definition of software (with the underlying engineering notion alluded to above) be helpful?

Solution Approach

A. The development of a system (whether or not it contains software) typically proceeds from broadly defined statements of customer needs, to a specification of how these needs are to be designed into the system, to construction of the physical entity that is the system. In engineering parlance, this evolutionary process is described in terms of a life cycle (by analogy, we suppose, with the evolution of living organisms from a less mature to a more mature state). In Section 2.4, we formally introduce the notion of *software life cycle*. For the present, it is important to observe that our definition of software anticipates this notion.

B. Suppose we had defined software to be simply "computer programs." Then, strictly speaking, software project management would be management of computer program development which presumably would involve overseeing the activities of coding, testing, recoding, retesting . . . until the code is determined to be ready for customer delivery. But computer code just does not materialize out of thin air. It presumably is developed in response to some customer need (either verbalized or written). Furthermore, such customer need statements are frequently expressed in terms of *what* the customer wants done. Thus, in addition to being derived from a customer need statement (which in engineering parlance is often referred to as a "requirements specification"), computer code is also based upon a specification of *how* the customer need statement is to be implemented (the "how specification" is often referred to in engineering parlance as "design"). Consequently, computer program code operating in the customer's environment can be viewed as the fully developed state (having been tailored for machine processing) of the information embodied in predecessor design and requirements specifications. In other words, these specifications and computer code—with its many possible representations, such as source and object code on various media (e.g., disks, tapes, microprocessor chips, paper)—can be viewed as different forms and representations of a set of information with logical and functional properties (i.e., information specifying a sequence of functions to be accomplished). At the outset of this chapter, it was asserted that the job of a software manager is to plan the software development cycle, direct others to produce software products, and control activities during plan execution. Thus, by defining software to include computer code and predecessor specification documents, we in effect reduce software project management to a set of replications of planning/directing/controlling activities applied (and reapplied if necessary) to a body of evolving information. Because, for example, the information in a software design is, from this point of view, nothing more than a less mature form of computer code (and a more mature form of a requirements specification), management of the development of this design should be no different from management of the development of computer code. Thus, by embedding the notion of life cycle in the definition of software, what a software project manager is called upon to do takes on a systematic, less imposing air than might be the case if, for example, software design were viewed as something other than software.

As an overall comment on the sample problem above, we want to stress that we have not simply defined away the complexity of the job confronting a software project manager. Managing a software project is definitely not for someone with a weak will or faint heart. We know few software project managers (or ex-managers) who bear no physical or mental scars from their experiences. Our purpose in the preceding sample problem was to present arguments for saying that the transition from customer requirements specification to operational computer code can be viewed as a series of repeating processes (i.e., product development, product audit/test, product redevelopment, product reaudit/retest, . . . , product delivery) each calling for the same kind of management activity. In subsequent chapters we elaborate on this point from the perspective of product assurance as a catalyst for this activity.

In closing this section on our definition of software, we show in Figure 2.3 and briefly discuss below some examples of software that follow from this definition. Chapter 1 of the Bersoff et al. book (Reference 2 at the end of this chapter) discusses this definition at length. (Note in Figure 2.3 that, to highlight the greater detail of the software as it matures toward an operational product, the backgrounds of the software examples become increasingly more filled in.)

EXAMPLES OF SOFTWARE

1. Requirements specification. As indicated in the sample problem discussed above, *what* the customer wants done is often embodied in something called a *requirements specification*. Sometimes also referred to as a *functional specification*, this document specifies what functions a system is to perform. In general, some of these functions will be performed by hardware, others will be performed by people, and the remainder will be performed by computer code operating on some of this hardware. Thus, a requirements specification usually

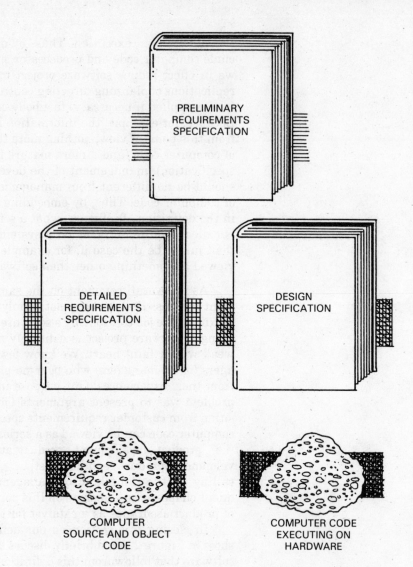

FIGURE 2.3. Examples of software.

PRELIMINARY REQUIREMENTS SPECIFICATION

DETAILED REQUIREMENTS SPECIFICATION

DESIGN SPECIFICATION

COMPUTER SOURCE AND OBJECT CODE

COMPUTER CODE EXECUTING ON HARDWARE

consists of information only some of which is software. Furthermore, as a system proceeds through development, what started out as a hardware or human function may subsequently become a software function, and vice versa. As a result, the software content of a requirements specification often varies throughout the system life cycle. On some large and/or lengthy software projects, a hierarchy of requirements specifications may be produced. For example, a frequent occurrence on such projects is a two-tiered hierarchy—a *functional* or *preliminary requirements specification* and a *detailed requirements specification*. The former document typically sets forth in broad, qualitative terms (and in the customer's vernacular) what the software is to do; by contrast, the latter document typically sets forth in detailed, quantitative terms (and possibly using some computer terminology) what the software is to do. A preliminary requirements specification may, for instance, contain a statement such as the following:

The software shall maintain monthly counts of the number of days during the month when rain fell and the number of days when snow fell.

In elaborating on the above statement, a detailed requirements specification may, for instance, read as follows:

In maintaining monthly counts of rain days and snow days, the software shall conform to the following rules:

A. **A day begins at midnight local time and terminates 24 hours later.**

B. **If rain totaling at least 0.02 inch fell during the 24-hour period defined in A, the number of rain days shall be incremented by 1. (Note: If during one continuous period of rain that overlaps two days at least 0.02 inch fell, but at least 0.02 inch did not fall in either day, then the number of rain days shall be incremented by 1.)**

C. **If snow totaling at least 0.5 inch fell during the 24-hour period defined in A, the number of snow days shall be incremented by 1. (Note: If during one continuous period of snow that overlaps two days at least 0.5 inch fell, but at least 0.5 inch did not fall in either day, then the number of snow days shall be incremented by 1.)**

2. Design specification. In the sample problem discussed above, we indicated that a design specification describes *how* a requirements specification is to be implemented. In contrast to the customer-oriented language of a requirements specification, the language of a design specification is couched in computer terminology. For instance, recalling the rain/snow counting example described earlier in connection with the discussion of a detailed requirements specification, item B in that specification might be carried through to a design specification in a manner such as the following:

To compute the number of rain days in a month, proceed as follows:

A. **Retrieve a record for day X from file RAINM containing the following elements: (1) hourly rainfall amounts; and (2) overlap flag.**

B. **Sum the hourly rainfall amounts.**

C. **If the sum is greater than 0.02, add 1 to the value of RAINDAYS in file PRECIPCOUNT.**

D. **If the sum is less than 0.02 but the overlap flag is set to 1, retrieve a record for day X − 1 from file RAINM; sum backward from midnight the hourly rainfall amounts until a 0 hourly rainfall amount is encountered; if this sum plus the sum from day X is greater than 0.02, add 1 to the value of RAINDAYS in file PRECIPCOUNT.**

As we indicated above in the discussion of the requirements specification, large and/or lengthy software projects often produce a hierarchy of requirements specifications. Such projects also often produce a hierarchy of design specifications, such as a *preliminary design specification* and a *detailed design specification*. The former document typically sets forth the first several levels of detail regarding how the requirements specification is to be implemented; the latter specification (in the ideal limit) sets forth all the detail needed to produce computer code unambiguously. A preliminary design is analogous to an architect's first sketches of a house to be built, showing the exterior and the layout of the rooms; a detailed design is analogous to a detailed engineering drawing of the house, showing information such as room dimensions and quantities of building materials.

3. Computer source and object code.   Source code is the first step in a two-step process by which software physically interacts with computer hardware. Source code is (or at least should be) produced from a design specification and is written in one of the many source code languages. These languages are based on logic constructs and syntax rules that bridge the gap between the way people think in solving problems and the way computer hardware functions in solving problems. To effect communication with this hardware, these languages must be processed by other software called compilers and assemblers, which produce something called *object code*. This latter code directly communicates with the hosting computer hardware in the binary language of zeros and ones that this hardware can understand. In general, source and object code can each be represented in a number of different ways. For example, the information in a FORTRAN program can manifest itself as printed lines on a program listing and as magnetic recordings on a disk or cassette.

4. Computer code executing on hardware.   Computer code executing on hardware is perhaps the most difficult to visualize. It is the information embodied in object code that streams through the logic circuits of computer hardware making the hardware do its intended job.   □

As you proceed through this book, keep in mind that, unless otherwise indicated, when we use the term *software* we are in general referring not just to computer code. We are referring to that set of information that starts out as a statement of customer needs, goes through various stages of detailing, and ultimately flows through computer hardware logic circuits.

2.2 Visibility

How can a ship's captain direct the ship's course if he cannot see where he is? Similarly, how can a manager of a software project direct its course if he cannot see where he is? In Section 1.3 we argued that it is prudent to view any software project as a voyage through iceberg-infested waters (the icebergs being unsatisfied requirements, cost overruns, and schedule slippages). This situation and the question just raised prompt us to introduce a management concept fundamental to system development in general and software development in particular. This concept is *visibility*, and it is formally defined in Figure 2.4 in terms of three aspects. Note that the first aspect ("permitting software to be seen") is an adaptation to the software world of a conventional usage of the word visibility. The remaining two aspects go beyond this conventional usage. In the first row of Figure 2.4, on the left side, the woman is asking the man where the software product is so that she can see what it looks like. The man pictures the software in his head, but the woman cannot see the man's mental image of it. On the right side of this figure, the man has made the software manifest and it is now visible to both the man and the woman.

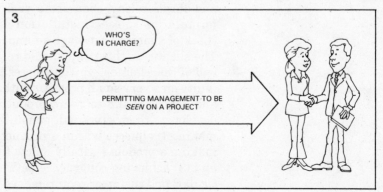

FIGURE 2.4. The three aspects of visibility. E. H. Bersoff, V. D. Henderson, and S. G. Siegel, *Software Configuration Management: An Investment in Product Integrity* (Englewood Cliffs, N.J.: Prentice-Hall, 1980), p. 348. Text reprinted by permission of the publisher.

From this aspect, visibility means permitting software to be seen. (If you are wondering who the two people in this row are, refer to Exercise 2.15.)

The second aspect of visibility is permitting management to see what is happening on a project. In the second row of Figure 2.4, the man on the left, a manager, is wondering how a project is progressing. When he has visibility into the project, as on the right, he can see the software as it evolves from stage to stage; that is, he can see what is happening on the project.

The bottom row of Figure 2.4 illustrates how visibility permits management to be seen on a project. On the left, the woman is wondering who is in charge on a certain project. When the proper visibility is provided (as on the right), the woman can see her manager. Our rationale for introducing a threefold concept of visibility is probed in the sample problem below. (It is recommended that senior managers and project managers read through this sample problem because it is as equally pertinent to them as to product assurance practitioners.)

THE THREE ASPECTS OF VISIBILITY—A SAMPLE PROBLEM
Background and Question

Recalling the discussion of product assurance in Chapter 1 and the software concept introduced in Section 2.1, how does the application of product assurance on a software project help achieve each of the three aspects of visibility listed in Figure 2.4?

Solution Approach

In the discussion below, each aspect of visibility is examined. This discussion also touches upon some relationships among the three aspects.

Visibility Aspect 1: Making Software More Visible to People

In Section 1.4, we indicated that, unlike a piece of hardware (such as a nut or bolt), software does not have readily perceived physical characteristics (such as length, width, height, weight, or color). In Section 2.1, we formally defined software to be information with the characteristics shown in Figure 2.1. Thus, because of software's abstract nature (i.e., its lack of physical characteristics), it is easy to literally lose sight of what is embodied in software as it evolves from a requirements specification, to a design specification, to computer code. This lack of visibility has a debilitating effect on software projects of even modest size (say, involving about ten people) and duration (say, spanning a year or less from requirements formulation to code installation and customer acceptance). (Lack of visibility can have an impact on even a small project. The skeptic on this point should consider Exercise 2.13 at the end of this chapter, which explores the impact of a lack of visibility on a very small project.) Without insight into the nature and details of the software products under development, the developers themselves will generally experience difficulty (1) making the pieces within a product fit together smoothly, (2) making a product logically follow from a predecessor product, and (3) achieving congruence between computer code (in particular) and customer requirements. The application of product

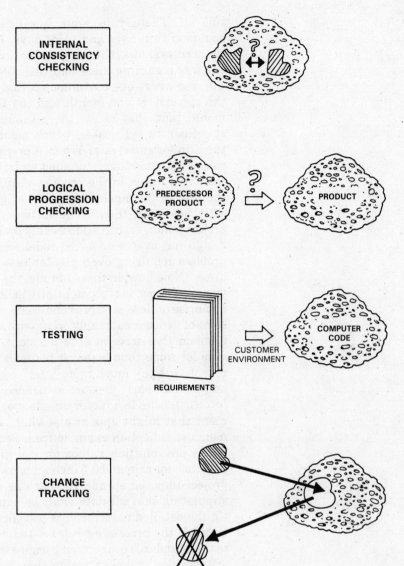

INTERNAL
CONSISTENCY
CHECKING

LOGICAL
PROGRESSION
CHECKING

PREDECESSOR
PRODUCT

?

PRODUCT

TESTING

REQUIREMENTS

CUSTOMER
ENVIRONMENT

COMPUTER
CODE

CHANGE
TRACKING

FIGURE 2.5. Four ways of permitting software to be seen.

assurance can help head off such difficulties by making software more visible in ways such as those shown in Figure 2.5 and discussed below (cf. the discussion in Section 1.4):

A. *Way 1: Internal Consistency and Standards Checking.* By examining a requirements specification for completeness and internal consistency, and by comparing the specification against project-imposed standards, product assurance raises the visibility of the software products and of the software development process by shedding light on incomplete statements and internal inconsistencies within the specification (see the first row of Figure 2.5) and by uncovering items called for in standards that are either incompletely addressed or not addressed at all in the specification. To appreciate more specifically what such findings may mean, recall the discussion of the detailed requirements specification example given in Section 2.1. There, rules were specified for computing monthly counts of rain days and snow days. A careful examination of these rules shows that the specification is incomplete in at least one way regarding these counting rules. The rules do not cover the case where one continuous period of precipitation overlaps the last day of one month and the first day of the following month (and that meets the minimum precipitation criteria specified). In such cases, which month is to be credited with the rain (or snow) day? When it prepares a written account of this apparent software product omission, product assurance is making a defect in the product visible for the developers and the project manager. If this defect is detected before design activities begin, then the developers (under direction from the project manager) can address this problem before it affects the design (or, even worse, the code) and thus becomes a bigger problem requiring even greater resource expenditures to address. (Note how, in this example, the problem, like many software problems, is of a potentially insidious type because it will not arise unless several conditions are simultaneously met, some of which presumably occur with relative infrequency. The problem therefore may lie dormant in operational software code for some time before it becomes apparent.) Similar "pay now versus pay much more later" benefits (recall Figure 1.3) accrue from early product assurance detection of (1) internal inconsistencies in a requirements specification (such as a statement that might appear elsewhere in the detailed requirements specification example from Section 2.1 specifying minimum precipitation values for counting purposes other than 0.02 inch for rain and 0.5 inch for snow) and (2) deviations from project-imposed standards (such as a standards convention stipulating that all data shall be expressed in metric units). (In the detailed requirements specification example from Section 2.1, the processing rules listed do not appear to conform to this standards convention because the precipitation amounts are specified in inches, rather than centimeters, as implied by the standard.)

B. *Way 2: Logical Progression Checking.* By comparing a software product against a predecessor product to see if the latter logically follows from the former (see the second row of Figure 2.5), product assurance raises the visibility of the products and of the software development process by shedding light on areas where a product may not be carrying through the intent of the predecessor product. To illustrate this point, recall the discussion of the detailed requirements specification and the design specification given in the example in Section 2.1. Close examination of the design specification shows that it does not appear to completely carry through the intent of item B in the requirements specification. In particular, note that item C in the design specification reads:

If the sum is greater than 0.02, add 1 to the value of RAINDAYS in file PRECIPCOUNT whereas the intent of item B in the requirements specification appears to require the following wording in item C in the design specification (the changed wording is shown in boldface):

If the sum is greater than **or equal to** 0.02, add 1 to the value of RAINDAYS in file PRECIPCOUNT.

When it prepares a written account of this apparent logical disconnect between the requirements and design specification, product assurance is making visible for the developers (and the project manager) this disconnect. What is the value of this visibility? Repeating our arguments from A above if the disconnect is reported before coding begins, then the developers (under direction from the project manager) can address this problem before it becomes embedded in code and thus becomes an even bigger problem (first trying to locate the problem and second trying to fix it without vitiating other code). Note how this problem, like the requirements specification problem discussed in A (Way 1), is of a potentially insidious type because it will arise only on those presumably infrequent occasions when the rainfall on a particular day is exactly 0.02 inch. If no provision for such an occasion is made in the software code derived from this design, there is in general no way of predicting how the code will function on such an occasion. By the way, when you read the software examples in Section 2.1 your first (or even second or third) time through that section, did you spot the logical disconnect between the design and requirements specification just discussed? Did you spot other potential disconnects between these two software products? Consider these questions carefully, because they are intended to drive home the point that the issue of visibility is real and ever-present on software projects.

One additional comment regarding the requirements specification problem discussed in A above and the logical disconnect problem just discussed is in order here. Note how the former problem bears an interesting relationship to the latter problem. Because the requirements specification is silent on how to perform counting at the end of a month, is the design specification logically inconsistent with the requirements specification if the design explicitly addresses end-of-the-month counting? Yes and no. Yes in the sense that the design in this case would appear to include something not called for in the requirements; no in the sense that end-of-the-month counting is a contingency that needs to be taken into account and is therefore implicit in the requirements specification. Product assurance can offer assistance in such "yes-and-no" situations by once again raising the visibility of the software development process in a manner such as this:

Suppose that when product assurance examined the detailed requirements specification discussed in A it did not uncover the end-of-the-month counting omission (nobody is perfect!). Design begins, and the designer, say, because of his experience, automatically incorporates the end-of-the-month counting situation into the design. When product assurance subsequently compares this design to the detailed requirements specification, it would presumably notice this potential logical disconnect. By giving visibility to this disconnect in the manner previously described, product assurance offers the project the opportunity to clarify the requirements specification through incorporation of statements that explicitly address end-of-the-month counting. Although we elaborate on this point in subsequent parts of this book, bringing a requirements specification into conformance with a design specification is much more than a matter of making the project documentation "look good" (after all, it could be argued that if the design is okay there is no need to update the requirements specification, since code is to be produced from the design and not the requirements). In general, it is the requirements specification that provides the context for enhancements and new requirements. If the requirements specification is not kept up to date, it will be difficult (and possibly not feasible) to incorporate these enhancements and new requirements into future software upgrades. □

C. *Way 3: Testing.* By preparing and executing written test plans and procedures, product assurance raises the visibility of the software products and of the software development process by shedding light on incongruities between the coded form of software and customer requirements (see the third row of Figure 2.5). As we pointed out in Section 1.4, this product assurance activity (typically performed prior to software delivery to the customer) is the software analogue of taking an automobile out for a test drive to determine whether it does what it is supposed to do (product assurance is viewed as a surrogate customer—a view that increases in tenability as the degree of independence of the product assurance organization from the software development organization increases). In Chapter 5, we talk at length about this testing activity. Anticipating some of that discussion, we make the following observations here:

In this book, product assurance testing is (unless otherwise indicated) the preparation of written tests embodying customer requirements (and possibly design) and the execution of these tests using software code installed on the customer's hardware and operated in an environment that at least approximates the customer's environment. Because the tests are specifically created to exercise customer requirements, the cycle of testing/ recoding/testing . . . (described in Chapter 5) generally leads to convergence between customer requirements and the functions performed by software code. During each testing activity in this cycle, product assurance documents discrepancies between computer code operation and the expected results of this operation as stipulated in the test documentation. These discrepancy reports give visibility to incongruities between the code and requirements. These discrepancy reports are presented at a forum attended by management, the developers, and the product assurance organization (this forum and its mode of operation are discussed at length in Chapter 4). These parties decide how to resolve the discrepancies (which in some cases may result in changes to customer requirements). Implementation of these decisions (which may require one or more testing/recoding loops) serves to align computer code and customer requirements—in a visible, and hence manageable, way. □

As a foretaste of the treatment of testing in subsequent chapters, it is useful to illustrate some aspects of the preceding discussion. For this purpose, we return to the detailed requirements specification example from Section 2.1. This example contained rules for counting the number of rain and snow days during a month. Recall that item B in the detailed requirements specification contained the following counting rule for rain days:

> If rain totaling at least 0.02 inch fell during the 24-hour period defined in A above, the number of rain days shall be incremented by 1.

Suppose that the product assurance organization prepared a test procedure designed to exercise the above requirement that consisted of, among other things, feeding a broad range of precipitation values into the software code and then checking the resulting number of rain days to see whether the code generated the number expected on the basis of the above statement. Suppose further that for a certain set of rain values input to the code during testing the software code counted five rain days, but the result expected in the test procedures was only four days because only four of the input rain values were at least 0.02 inch each. As a result of this testing, the product assurance organization would document this discrepancy between software code operation and customer requirements in a manner such as the following:

Execution of test procedure 31, which was designed to exercise the customer's rain-day-counting requirement, produced the following discrepancy:

	Rain Days	
Input Rain Values (inches)	Expected	Observed
0.02, 0.19, 0.01, 0.33, 1.75, negative 0.10	4	5

As a result of this discrepancy report, management would presumably direct the developers to change the rain-day-counting code (unless it was determined during the forum where the report was presented that the product assurance organization did not run the test properly). After this change (and possibly other changes resulting from other discrepancy reports) is incorporated into the code, the product assurance organization would test the recoded software. If as a result of this test the expected and observed counts agreed, the requirement would be considered successfully tested; if these counts did not agree, management would presumably direct the developers to change the code again, after which the product assurance organization would test the recoded software, and so forth, until the expected and observed counts agreed. This code/test/recode/ test . . . cycle would be invoked and continued for all the test cases in the product assurance test documents. The cycle would continue until either (1) no unresolved discrepancies remain (which implies that the computer code and the customer requirements are congruent, assuming that the test documentation spans the entire set of the requirements) or (2) the remaining unresolved discrepancies are not of sufficient significance (as determined by management, presumably in consultation with the customer) to warrant additional recoding and testing. (Note that in this latter instance the unresolved discrepancy reports give visible testimony to the extent of the incongruities between customer requirements and the soon-to-be-operational computer code; presumably, these remaining discrepancies will be resolved some time after delivery of the software code to the customer.)

D. *Way 4: Change Tracking*. By keeping track of the software changes resulting from the activities described in A, B, and C (see fourth row of Figure 2.5), product assurance raises the visibility of the software products and of the software development process by shedding light on changes needed, changes being evaluated, and changes implemented. For example, by maintaining an archive of the discrepancy reports and their resolutions generated during testing, as discussed in C, product assurance gives visibility to the specific changes needed to align computer code and customer requirements. Therefore, the archive is useful in avoiding wasteful excursions away from customer requirements (recall Figure 1.3). It also provides an experience bank that can be exploited to facilitate incorporation of new requirements and enhancements to existing requirements. This experience bank can also be exploited on other projects, since it contains a record of mistakes made and a record of accomplishments and their costs.

Visibility Aspect 2: Permitting Management to See What Is Happening on a Project

In Sections 1.1 and 1.3, we indicated that the basic software project management challenge is to achieve convergence between a customer's perception of his need and the software developer's perception of that need. In Section 2.1 and the just concluded look at Visibility Aspect 1, we discussed at length why software is inherently difficult to see and how the application of product assurance can help raise its visibility. From this discussion, it should also be apparent that the *process* of software development and maintenance is inherently difficult to see. Not only does the project manager need some visibility into the software products themselves, but he and his managers also need visibility into this process (as indicated in Figure 2.4). Without being able to see what is happening on a project, management will be hard-pressed to avoid the icebergs of unsatisfied requirements, cost overruns, and schedule slippages pictured in Figure 1.4. Giving management increased insight (i.e., visibility) into what is happening on a project permits management to make decisions—for planning, directing, and controlling software development—based on information rather than on guesses. To understand in more specific terms how the application of product assurance can help give management increased visibility into project happenings, we reconsider the test discrepancy reporting discussion from C under Visibility Aspect 1. In that discussion, we indicated that the discrepancy reports generated during testing gave visibility into the extent of the mismatches between customer requirements and computer code. From a management perspective, this visibility provides the project manager and those to whom he reports with information needed to help them make decisions regarding the following:

Can the remaining discrepancies be resolved within existing budget and schedule constraints?

How many more testing/recoding loops are likely to be needed before the remaining discrepancies are resolved?

If all remaining discrepancies cannot be resolved within existing budget and schedule constraints, which ones can be?

If all remaining discrepancies cannot be resolved within existing budget and schedule constraints, how much of a cost overrun and/or a schedule overrun is likely to result if all these discrepancies are resolved?

The last item above is particularly noteworthy. It implies that product assurance helps to warn management of impending cost and/or schedule overruns. However, the question "If product assurance can only warn of, but not prevent, disaster, what good is it?" is often asked. Naturally we all strive for guarantees, but our experience teaches us that there are few sure things in life. The "good" that derives from product assurance providing visibility into the software development process is the ability to steer clear of the unexpected. A warning of impending trouble (or worse) at least offers management the opportunity to replan and redirect so that the blow can be softened and control can be maintained. Being blindsided can (and on software projects often does) result in an irrecoverable situation. It is, for example, not good to find out at the beginning of testing that the software code, through a latent design flaw, cannot support one or more customer requirements, but it might be disastrous to discover this situation after the software has been delivered to the customer (who might be, say, a bank that uses the software to keep track of securities transactions [see the end of Section 7.1 for a real-world example], or who might be a military organization that uses the software to guide missiles to their targets). As a final comment on this second aspect of visibility, it should be evident from the preceding discussion of testing that each of the three other ways that product assurance makes software more visible described under Visibility Aspect 1 also increases the visibility of the software development process. That is, each of these ways permits management to see what is happening on a project, thus facilitating management's job—that of planning, directing, and controlling project resources for the ultimate purpose of delivering software meeting customer requirements on time and within budget.

Visibility Aspect 3: Permitting Management to Be Seen on a Project

In the discussion of Visibility Aspect 2, we explored the relationship between that aspect (permitting management to see what is happening on a project) and the basic software project management challenge (achieving convergence between a customer's perception of his need and the software developer's perception of that need). Experience shows that, to meet this challenge, it is generally not sufficient for management to see what is happening on a project. A complementary relationship between management and the other project participants must also exist. That is, in addition to seeing, management must also *be seen* on a project (as shown in Figure 2.4). The absence of visibility of management on a project fosters a "nobody cares" attitude and serves as a deterrent to successful software product development and maintenance. Like a ship without a captain (or whose captain is not manifestly in charge), a software project without a visible manager will flounder and eventually run head-on into cost overruns, schedule slippages, and unsatisfied customer requirements. Making management visible provides a focus for project activities and thus serves to reduce the likelihood that these project calamities will occur.

How does the application of product assurance help achieve this aspect of visibility on a software project? In responding to this question, it is important to recognize that just because management sees what is happening on a project, it does not necessarily mean that management will be seen on a project. Management can, and indeed sometimes does, observe the project from afar, choosing not to inject itself into, or strongly influence, the day-to-day affairs of the project. However, what can and often does happen in such situations is that management abdicates its decision-making responsibility and becomes a slave to project events and/or to the organizations that it is supposed to be directing. Once management finds itself in this situation, software's inherent lack of visibility tends to exacerbate this situation.

To begin to understand how the application of product assurance acts to keep management involved in a project, thus avoiding such situations, it is helpful to recall here the following words used in Chapter 1 to define our concept of product assurance:

Product assurance is a set of checks and balances interwoven into the software development process whose primary purpose is to assure that a software product satisfies the needs of the intended recipient.

Here we focus on the word "interwoven." Product assurance aims at fostering constructive interaction between management and other project participants where all project participants adopt attitudes such as the following, because they really believe that software development success cannot be achieved without such attitudes:

A customer seldom really knows precisely what he wants or needs.

Even if a customer knows precisely what he wants or needs, at least some of these wants or needs are likely to be misinterpreted by project participants sometime during the project.

To reduce wasteful project excursions, it is necessary to document discrepancies between what is being produced and what was asked for, so that such discrepancies can be systematically resolved.

Software product developers often become so close to their work that they may frequently be unaware of discrepancies between what they are producing and what was asked for. An organization independent from the development organization may be more sensitive to such discrepancies.

A direct result of such attitudes is the realization that all software products need to be subjected to constructive peer review before customer delivery. Furthermore, such review, if it is to influence subsequent project activity properly, must be orchestrated by management. This orchestration includes ensuring that product discrepancies are documented and presented at a forum involving management, the development organization, the product assurance organization, and sometimes the customer. This orchestration also includes *management decision regarding how discrepancies are to be resolved* which is just another way of saying that product assurance, through an interwoven set of checks and balances, permits (or, more accurately, compels) management to be seen on a project. (In Chapters 4 through 6, we describe the mechanics of conducting these forums, including management's decision-making role.)

In the preceding discussion, we probed some of the nuances of each of the three aspects of visibility listed in Figure 2.4 and some of their interrelationships. We presented arguments and examples to demonstrate how the application of product assurance can raise the visibility of the software development process in the threefold sense shown in Figure 2.4. We now turn our attention to a concept closely allied with the visibility concept—traceability—and begin to explore the relationship between traceability and product assurance. A good portion of the remainder of this book is aimed at elaborating on the relationships among visibility, traceability, and product assurance.

2.3 Traceability

The captain must know where his ship is so he can direct its future course; he must also know where he has been. (He can determine future progress because he knows how much progress he has achieved to that point.) The importance of knowing where you have been as an aid to determining how to proceed prompts us to introduce another fundamental management concept, traceability, as follows:

Traceability is the thread that links one event to another.

Our concept of traceability is shown in Figure 2.6, which portrays several events linked together. The "events" in the definition of traceability refer, in broad terms, to those happenings associated with a software product's development (and maintenance). More specifically, included in the notion of "event" are happenings such as the following:

A. The appearance or reappearance of a software product for purposes of determining what it embodies (e.g., publication of a draft or revised requirements or design specification, such as Event m in Figure 2.6)

B. Determining what a software product embodies (e.g., testing computer code in the customer's environment to determine whether it embodies his requirements, such as Event n in Figure 2.6)

C. Holding a meeting to present and resolve discrepancies recorded against software products (e.g., meeting to decide how to resolve discrepancies between computer code and a requirements specification which were generated during testing of the code, such as Event o in Figure 2.6)

D. Customer submittal of new or revised requirements (e.g., presentation by the customer, in the midst of design specification development, of a capability not addressed in the design, such as Event p in Figure 2.6)

E. Modifying a software product in response to a previously authorized change (e.g., adding new computer code to existing operational code to incorporate a new capability, such as Event q in Figure 2.6)

Establishing traceability on a software project means creating a record of happenings like those listed above so that linkages among these happenings become manifest. The result is a cause-and-effect chain that makes the evolution of a software product manifest so that its subsequent evolution can be more effectively managed.

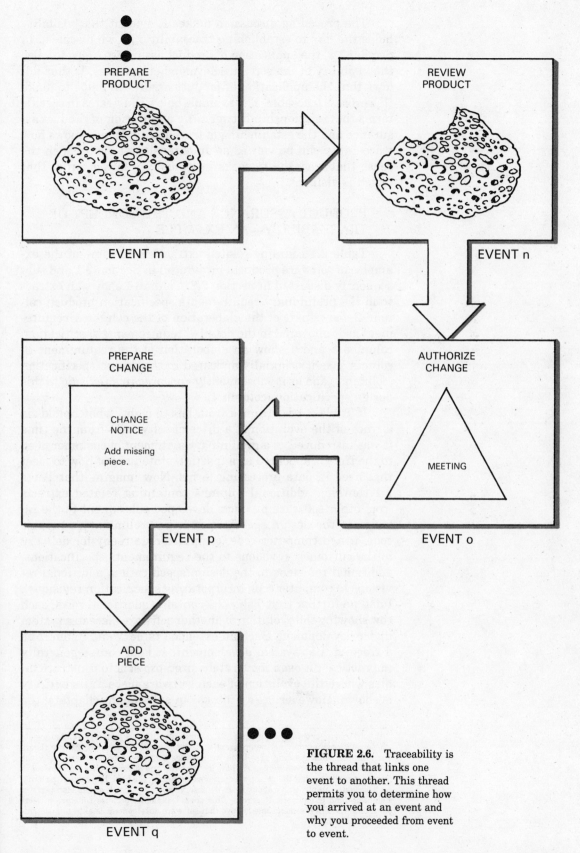

EVENT m

EVENT n

PREPARE PRODUCT

REVIEW PRODUCT

PREPARE CHANGE

CHANGE NOTICE

Add missing piece.

AUTHORIZE CHANGE

MEETING

EVENT p

EVENT o

ADD PIECE

EVENT q

FIGURE 2.6. Traceability is the thread that links one event to another. This thread permits you to determine how you arrived at an event and why you proceeded from event to event.

55

The preceding discussion makes it evident that visibility holds the key to establishing traceability. As we discussed in Section 2.2, the application of product assurance helps to raise the visibility of the software development process. It thus follows that the application of product assurance helps to make this process traceable. The example below illustrates in specific terms this relationship between the application of product assurance and the establishing of traceability. It also shows how traceability can be viewed as an extension of visibility in the sense that traceability seeks to logically relate or order that which is visible.[2]

PRODUCT ASSURANCE AND THE CONCEPT OF TRACEABILITY—AN EXAMPLE

Table 2.1 contains related extracts from some of the examples of software products introduced in Section 2.1 and subsequently discussed in Section 2.2. Column 1 shows an extract from the preliminary requirements specification product; column 2 shows part of the elaboration of the column 1 requirement as it appeared in the detailed requirements specification; columns 3 and 4 show an elaboration of the requirement in column 2 as it originally appeared in the design specification (column 3) and as it subsequently appeared in a revision to this design specification (column 4).

If Table 2.1 is scanned from left to right, what unfolds is a trace of the evolution of a piece of software—from the time it was introduced as a preliminary statement of customer need to the time it appeared as a (partial) statement of how to meet that need in data processing terms. Now imagine that Table 2.1 contains additional columns containing related extracts from other software products developed subsequent to the revision to the design specification (e.g., preliminary computer code, tested computer code, computer code ready for delivery to the customer, revisions to the requirements specifications, additional revisions to the design specification, additional revisions to computer code incorporating specification revisions). Imagine further that Table 2.1 contains additional rows, each row showing the evolution of another software piece in a system under development. Such an extended table would in effect be a trace of that system development. It is of course generally impractical on even moderately sized projects to construct tables where the evolution of each software piece in its entirety is shown. However, as we discuss in subsequent chapters, the

---

[2] As part of our everyday experience, we observe or otherwise perceive related events whose relationships may not be apparent to us (at least at the time we observe them). For example, while passing by a bank we may see someone (among others) enter the bank; some time later we may again pass by the bank and observe police cars parked in front, not realizing that the person we earlier saw entering the bank had robbed the bank. As a second example, think about what we observe when we watch a magician perform sleight-of-hand maneuvers. Regarding this second example, because software projects often lack visibility, some people believe that software development is akin to a sleight-of-hand maneuver.

TABLE 2.1. RELATED EXTRACTS FROM SOFTWARE PRODUCTS: AN ILLUSTRATION OF TRACEABILITY

Preliminary Requirements Specification	Detailed Requirements Specification	Design Specification (original)	Design Specification (revised)
The software shall maintain monthly counts of the number of days during the month when rain fell. . . .	B. If rain totaling at least 0.02 inch fell during the 24-hour period defined in A above, the number of rain days shall be incremented by 1. . . .	(B) Sum the hourly rainfall amounts [for day X]. (C) If the sum is greater than 0.02, add 1 to the value of RAINDAYS in file PRECIPCOUNT.	(B) Sum the hourly rainfall amounts [for day X]. (C) If the sum is greater than **or equal to** 0.02, add 1 to the value of RAINDAYS in file PRECIPCOUNT.

application of product assurance, through ways like those described in the sample problem in Section 2.2, yields synthesized versions of Table 2.1 on actual software projects.

In particular, as a result of the product assurance auditing activity, an entity called a *traceability matrix* is frequently developed. When an auditor compares software products with one another, he looks for corresponding pieces of software. The result of this search is often summarized in a table laid out like Table 2.1 that contains paragraph numbers or some other labels identifying software pieces. These labels are a shorthand for the information such as that shown in Table 2.1. When displayed in a table formatted like Table 2.1, they provide visibility into software evolution (sometimes, to enhance this visibility, each label is augmented with a phrase or sentence that gives some insight into the nature of the software piece that the label represents). For example, if a column contains a blank entry, then management is alerted to a potential problem because a customer requirement (or requirements) may be unsupported in a software product under development. In addition to generating traceability matrices, product assurance helps build and organize a record of project events. For example, the proceedings of project meetings held to decide what to do with proposed changes to software products are compiled and archived by product assurance (specific examples of such meetings can be found in the discussion of testing in the sample problem in Section 2.2; see also Chapter 4).   □

Some general comments are now in order regarding the traceability and visibility concepts formally introduced in this section and the preceding one. We argued in Section 1.3 that it is prudent to view each software project as a voyage through iceberg-infested waters (recall Figure 1.4). We cannot overemphasize this analogy. It derives from our experience and the experience of others in the software industry. A corollary of this experience is that management, if for no reason other than self-preservation, should take more than perfunctory steps to ensure that software development proceeds in a visible and traceable manner. The philosophy advocated in this book is that much of this visibility and traceability can be achieved through product assurance. We have offered some examples to illustrate and justify this. Much of the remainder of this book amplifies this philosophy. In particular, we repeatedly demonstrate how sustained and sincere interaction among management, the development organization, and the product assurance organization perforce leads to visible and traceable software development, which in turn makes it unlikely that the project ship will run afoul of the icebergs pictured in Figure 1.4.

In Chapter 1, we defined *software development* in terms of a series of information transformations—beginning with a statement of customer requirements and culminating with computer code operating in the customer's environment in accordance with these requirements. Now that we have introduced the concepts of visibility and traceability, we can formalize this notion of information transformation by introducing a concept borrowed from the system engineering world—*life cycle*. As we will explain, this concept is a useful tool for infusing visibility and traceability into the software development process.

2.4 Life Cycle

When we are hungry, we enjoy consuming a big meal. But no matter how hungry we may be, we cannot generally swallow the meal whole without choking. In managing a software development and/or maintenance effort, we should not emulate a glutton's approach to eating. To avoid indigestion on a software project, it is prudent and healthful to divide the project into courses or pieces, each course or piece representing a readily digestible portion of the effort (which is thus easier to manage than the uncut whole). This idea of dividing a software project into smaller, more manageable pieces gives rise to the allied notion of attributing a life cycle to software development and maintenance. We remarked in Section 2.1 that the concept of software introduced there anticipates the notion of life cycle. Our definition of *software development* in Chapter 1 implicitly introduced this notion by referring to the *stages* (i.e., the analogy of courses during a meal) that software passes through during its transformation from a statement of customer requirements to computer code. We now formally examine the notion of life cycle stages and its relationship to product assurance, visibility, and traceability.

In what sense does software have a *life* cycle? At the beginning of a project, the software is in a state of infancy—its features are outlines and sketchy definitions. Later in the project, these outlines and sketches are filled in with detail on structure, processing, and data; the software acquires a distinctive "personality." Ultimately (barring sickness, such as faulty design), it achieves its fully developed state when it becomes operational and ages gracefully through a metamorphosis resulting from the incorporation of enhancements, new capabilities, and fixes to latent defects.

The concept of life cycle can be viewed as a tool that helps management acquire insight into the software development and maintenance process. Implicit in the discussion in the preceding sections of this chapter and in Chapter 1 is a synergism between the application of this management tool and the application of product assurance. For example, in the sample problem on visibility in Section 2.2, we indicated in the discussion of Visibility Aspect 2 (i.e., permitting management to see what is happening on a project) how the application of product assurance provides management with insight into the process that yields software products (as well as insight into the products themselves). Conversely, partitioning a software project into a sequence of stages through which the software passes as it matures is fundamental to effective application of product assurance. Each stage yields one or more software products. For example, in the discussion of the software concept in Section 2.1, we indicated that in the early stages of the software life cycle, requirements specifications are typically produced; in subsequent stages, design specifications and computer code are typically produced. As we indicated in Section 1.4 and in the discussion of Visibility Aspect 1 in the sample problem in Section 2.2, products such as these are the focus of product assurance activities. We saw, for example, how product assurance seeks to compare these products with one another to determine the extent to which they logically follow from one another and the extent to which they conform to the customer's stated needs. In Section 2.3, we illustrated how this comparison helps to build a thread that explicitly traces a product to products from predecessor stages (or products from the same stage—such as an earlier draft of a specification document [see Table 2.1])—which, in turn, raises the visibility of the software development and maintenance process (i.e., the life cycle).

Throughout this book, we rely on the life cycle concept to explain and amplify product assurance and allied software management techniques. It is therefore important for you to realize at the outset that a life cycle "stage" is *not* something that is passed through once, never to be revisited. As we mentioned in Section 1.1, from the point of view of software development, any life cycle stage may be revisited a number of times before the software falls into disuse (i.e., dies). In fact, this notion of revisiting a life cycle stage is the primary reason that this book does not look upon "maintenance" as a separate stage in the software life cycle (an attitude that is at variance with a substantial portion of software life cycle management literature). We prefer to think of a revisit to a life cycle stage as the enhancing, correcting, and/or adapting of what was done during the previous visit to that stage. But this process is nothing more than "maintenance" in the dictionary sense of the word (namely, "the act of keeping in existence or continuance; the act of keeping in a specified state"[3]). In this book, we therefore adopt the attitude that "maintenance" is an integral part of the activities associated with *any* life cycle stage. As an example illustrating this attitude, recall the software product extracts depicted in Table 2.1. In that table, we illustrated how a revisit to a design stage resulted in a design specification revision whose ultimate purpose was to maintain the design in conformance with what was done in the requirements specification stages.

The preceding discussion leads to the following observation:

A software life cycle is in reality a series of recycles through part or all of a sequence of stages that begins with a statement of customer need and ends with customer acceptance of software code operating in the customer's environment in accordance with this need.

The point of view embodied in this observation is the basis of much of the discussion in the remainder of this book.

The number of life cycle stages utilized on a particular project is basically a function of how much visibility is desired (and affordable). This number may also be a function of organizational policies. For example, your company may have a blanket policy stipulating that all projects should be partitioned into a specified number of stages. Furthermore, once a project is under way, it may be desirable to change the number of stages agreed to at the outset of the project because, for example, the project budget has changed, the customer may want more visibility, or customer delivery dates have changed. As mentioned at the outset of this section, the idea of partitioning a software effort into stages is useful for avoiding management indigestion. Just as a number of factors govern how someone chooses to slice up the elements of a meal before consuming it, so too there are a number of factors governing how a life cycle should be partitioned. The fundamental point is that there is no single "preferred" partition of the life cycle that should be applied to all projects.

In this book, we use the life cycle stages shown in Figure 2.7. In this figure, we also depict symbolically typical products resulting from activity in these stages. There is nothing magical or preferred about the partition given in this figure. We need a basis for illustrating in specific terms product assurance techniques, and the life cycle depicted in Figure 2.7 is intended to serve this purpose. Through examples and sample problems, we suggest how product assurance techniques can be applied to the life cycle partition(s) you may choose for your projects. (In fact, you have already been exposed to this approach in the sample problem and software examples in Section 2.1, in the

---

[3] *Random House College Dictionary* (New York: Random House, 1982).

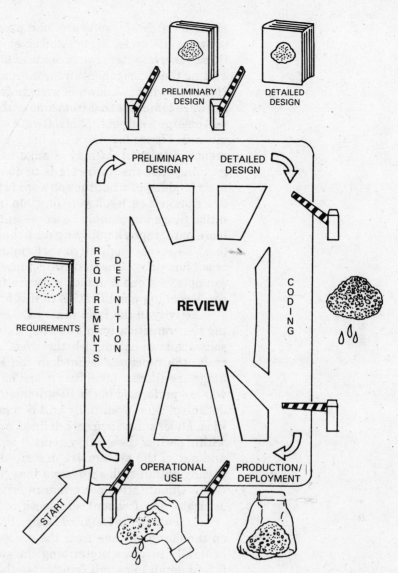

PRELIMINARY
DESIGN

DETAILED
DESIGN

PRELIMINARY
DESIGN

DETAILED
DESIGN

REQUIREMENTS

DEFINITION

REVIEW

CODING

REQUIREMENTS

OPERATIONAL
USE

PRODUCTION/
DEPLOYMENT

START

FIGURE 2.7. A software life cycle and the allied concepts of review and revisits to preceding life cycle stages.

sample problem on visibility in Section 2.2, and in the traceability example in Section 2.3. See also Exercise 2.14 at the end of this chapter.)

At this point, we describe in a simplified way the software development activity associated with each stage in our illustrative life cycle. The purpose here is merely to introduce these stages. In subsequent sections and chapters, we elaborate on these stages. You may find it helpful to relate the discussion of Figure 2.7 to the definition of software development given in Chapter 1 and to the implicit discussion of life cycle given in the preceding sections of this chapter.

Activity in the Requirements Definition Stage focuses on *what* the software is to do. In many cases, it is probably more appropriate at this stage to refer to what the *system* is to do— that is, the functions to be performed by the integrated operation of hardware, software, and people. At this stage of the software life cycle, it may not be evident what each of these three generic system components is to do. The boundaries separating these components from one another may be amorphous. However, what is known of system development projects with software content is that from among the system functions there will emerge a subset that is software according to the definition given in Figure 2.1. Over the life cycle of the system, the elements of this subset may change as decisions are made regarding what the hardware is to do and what the people are to do (and hence what the software is to do).[4] In any event, the description of each software function in the Requirements Definition Stage may simply be a one-sentence definition or one or more paragraphs amplifying particular aspects of the function (e.g., its scope, qualitative performance, characteristics, and/or subfunctions). The first two columns in Table 2.1 provide an example of a one-sentence software function definition and a corresponding amplification of this function's scope.

Activity in the Preliminary Design Stage focuses on making the transition from *what* the software is to do to *how* the software is to accomplish the *what*. At this stage of the life cycle, the functions defined in the Requirements Definition Stage are allocated to software and hardware (if this allocation was not performed in the Requirements Definition Stage). The outline of what eventually will become computer code is specified. Major subsystems are defined, and the top-level structure within each of these subsystems is broken out. Data flows into and out of the system are described together with the processing within each subsystem that transforms inflows to outflows. Quantitative performance criteria (e.g., how fast, how accurate, how frequent) are specified.[5]

Activity in the Detailed Design Stage focuses on expanding on the design outline from the preceding stage. This activity generally involves prescribing the software structure in sufficient detail to permit coding (see the fourth column of Table 2.1 for an example of this detail and how it contrasts with the detail in the first two columns of the table). Ideally, the level of detail should be such that the activity in the Coding Stage is little more than a secretarial transcription into some com-

---

[4] In Section 4.3 of this book, we touch upon the intertwining of the software, hardware, and system life cycles characteristic of system development efforts with software content. In particular, we point out the kinds of coordination needed to ensure that hardware and software development proceed in harmony with each other and in harmony with the development of the system of which they are a part.

[5] Such quantitative performance criteria may sometimes be specified in the Requirements Definition Stage. For example, a customer may want a message processing system that, because of known message volumes, must be capable of processing a specified number of messages per hour. Frequently, however, quantitative performance criteria derive from qualitative statements of customer requirements. These quantitative criteria thus represent *how* to accomplish *what* the customer asked for—and thus represent design. For example, a customer may have a qualitative requirement for display of realistic animation of human motion. From this (qualitative) requirement for realistic (as opposed to, say, freeze-frame or jerky) animation may be derived a (quantitative) software design performance criterion of a specified number of display images that the software must produce each second on a video device (such as a CRT).

puter language (such as FORTRAN, Ada,[6] COBOL, PASCAL, ALGOL, or an assembly language) of the words in the design documentation. The detailed design for software is like an engineering drawing of a hardware component showing all the parts, their dimensions, their interconnections, and the material from which they are to be constructed (this material may embody performance characteristics). Also during the Detailed Design Stage, the databases needed for system operation are designed.[7] In addition, user documentation (i.e., manuals prescribing the commands and other procedures for operating the software) is developed. Concomitant with this development activity, product assurance is preparing plans and procedures for testing the software code in subsequent stages.

Activity in the Coding Stage focuses on turning the detailed design into language that computer hardware can understand. This coding activity ultimately yields a product that is intended for end use by the user in his own environment. This product must be tested at multiple levels as it is being put together and on completion of this integration, to assure that the detailed design has been correctly fulfilled and the user's needs have been fully satisfied. In the sample problem on visibility in Section 2.2, we provided some initial insight into the mechanics of this latter testing activity. In Chapter 5, we talk at length about the role of independent testing as a necessary part of the transition from coding to delivery of code to the customer.

Activity in the Production/Deployment Stage focuses on mass-producing the software code after satisfactory completion of all testing in the Coding Stage, and on packaging the tested software code (with user documentation) and shipping it to the customer for operational use. If the product is intended for a range of customers with specialized needs, activity in the Production/Deployment Stage also includes the tailoring of the product from the preceding stage to these needs. In conjunction with this tailoring, testing similar to that performed in the Coding Stage is conducted to provide a degree of assurance that the tailored product conforms to customer needs.

Activity in the Operational Use Stage focuses on use of the software by the customer in his environment. A by-product of this activity is customer detection of latent software defects and customer definition of enhancements or new capabilities that precipitate revisits to one or more of the preceding stages.

Regarding revisits to life cycle stages, it is worthwhile at this point to consider this notion in terms of Figure 2.7. In this figure this notion is illustrated by the side paths branching off from the life cycle path. These side paths feed into an area labeled "Review." At the end of each stage in our life cycle,

---

[6] Ada is a registered trademark of the U.S. government (AJPO).

[7] According to the definition of software given in Figure 2.1, is a database design software? Should this design be subjected to product assurance? If so, is this activity *software* product assurance?

there is a gate (one might even say a tollgate, since following a disciplined software development path requires payment of some toll—we have more to say about this matter in subsequent chapters). The gate, when closed (for example, at the end of the Coding Stage as shown in Figure 2.7), forces the software products developed during a stage to undergo review before the project team proceeds to the next life cycle stage. If the products pass their review satisfactorily, the project team returns to the diverting gate via the side path, the gate is opened (for example, at the end of the Detailed Design Stage as shown in Figure 2.7), and the project team proceeds into the next stage. If the review uncovers some need for change to the reviewed or a preceding product, some members of the project team will take one of the side paths leading to the beginning of one of the preceding stages. In the sample problem in Section 2.2 on the three aspects of visibility, we gave a specific example of such revisits. In the discussion of Visibility Aspect 1 in that sample problem, we described an omission in a requirements specification (regarding end-of-the-month counting of rain and snow days). We indicated circumstances whereby that omission did not come to light until after design activity began (i.e., until a stage subsequent to the Requirements Definition Stage was entered). We then indicated how this design activity precipitated a change to the requirements specification (i.e., a revisit to the Requirements Definition Stage). Specifically, we indicated how a product assurance review of a design specification and comparison with a requirements specification brought to light a logical disconnect between the two specifications; resolution of this disconnect resulted in an update to the requirements specification to bring it into conformance with the design specification.

In subsequent chapters, we describe in considerable detail the review process alluded to in Figure 2.7. In particular, we examine its central role in ensuring visible and traceable transitions between, and revisits to, life cycle stages.[8] We now turn to some concepts needed to describe the mechanics of this review process in particular and the mechanics of software life cycle management in general.

2.5 Changes, Baselines, Baseline Updates, Software Parts, and Software Configuration

Many system development efforts (whether or not they involve software) embody attempts to improve how things work without being precisely sure of what is wanted. Often, these efforts begin with such customer thoughts as:

Wouldn't it be nice if I could do such and such?

What I really need is a system that will do. . . .

Today I do processes X, Y, Z, . . . separately. It would be more efficient if I could integrate X, Y, Z, . . . into a single system.

---

[8] In the discussion of testing in the Section 2.2 sample problem, we already touched upon this review process.

FIGURE 2.8. The wizardry of software development: Figuring out what the customer wants. B. Parker and J. Hart, *The Wizard of ID* (Irvine, Calif.: News America Syndicate, September 30, 1983). Reprinted by permission of Johnny Hart and News America Syndicate.

From the system developer's perspective, development, once initiated (by such customer thoughts as those listed above), may be pushed along by developer thoughts like:

I think the customer would be happier if I could make his system do such and such instead of what it does now.

Although the design I have developed meets customer needs, now I realize that there are other designs that will meet these needs more efficiently.

I now have a better understanding of what the customer wants, so I think that I will implement his new capability as follows. . . .

The point is that system development is a challenge to the inventive nature of both the customer and the developer. They get ideas and try to flesh them out during subsequent development stages. At any particular point in this development process, they generally do not have all the answers regarding how well the system will satisfy customer needs. Thus, to a certain extent, system development is a process of trial and error where each error makes the customer and the developer a little smarter regarding how they should proceed (if they are willing to learn from their mistakes). But this trial and error process is simply another way of saying that *change* is indigenous to system development. The developer develops, the customer and the developer analyze the results of this development, they change their minds in response to this analysis, the developer develops some more, and the cycle continues until they achieve what they want.

A microcosm of at least one iteration of this cycle is depicted in the cartoon in Figure 2.8. While it is not meant to suggest that software developers are wizards (who are often asked to perform magical feats), this figure serves to reinforce the fundamental point made at the beginning of Chapter 1— that the basic software project management challenge is to achieve convergence between a customer's perception of his need (i.e., what he wants) and the software developer's perception of that need. As Figure 2.8 suggests, this convergence is achieved by iteratively determining what the customer wants and then developing products to satisfy these wants. Management of this interplay between customer and developer is central to much of the discussion in the remainder of this book. For this reason, it is appropriate at this juncture to illustrate in specific terms how this interplay typically takes place. To emphasize that the search for convergence between customer and developer underlies *any* system development effort, and to make readily apparent the universal character of this search, the example below is set in a nonsoftware context and portrays a situation many homeowners have probably encountered.

WHAT IS IT YOU REALLY WANT?—AN EXAMPLE

Suppose you hire a contractor to finish your basement, which consists of a cement floor and walls with exposed two-by-four studs. You tell the contractor what you want—which might be, for example, paneling on the walls, a drop ceiling with fluorescent lighting, and bookshelves along part of one wall. After the contractor draws up plans based upon your stated desires (i.e., your "requirements," in system development parlance), you review and approve them and agree upon a cost and work schedule. Work begins. Each day you go down to the basement and look over the work (i.e., you "gain visibility into the project"). As a result of these daily visits to your evolving basement, you begin to see things you did not think of at the outset of the project. Thus, you want the contractor to do something that differs from the original agreement. Once again, you tell the contractor what you want (i.e., you give him your "new or revised requirements"). You tell him, for example, that you want a closet in one corner of the room, you want the bookshelves to be extended so that they fill one wall, and you want five fluorescent lights instead of six. After the contractor draws up revised plans based upon your updated requirements, you review and approve them and agree upon a revised cost and work schedule. Work continues. This cycle continues (with possibly several additional revisits to the requirements and design stages) until your basement is finished (hopefully to your satisfaction). □

Fundamental to the success of the development effort to finish the basement are well-defined reference points against which to specify requirements, formulate a design, and specify changes to these requirements and the resultant designs. Following conventional system development practice, we use the term *baseline* to denote such a reference point. We formally define this term as follows:

A baseline is an approved snapshot of the system at a given point in its evolution.

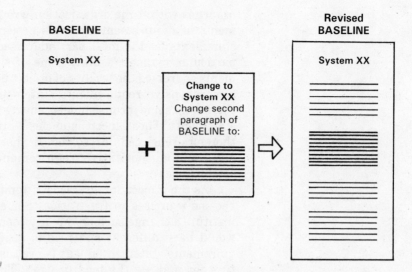

BASELINE

System XX

Change to System XX
Change second paragraph of BASELINE to:

Revised BASELINE

System XX

FIGURE 2.9. The concepts of baseline and change.

For the present, it is sufficient to note that "approved" in this definition is the result of successfully completing the review process alluded to in Figure 2.7. What constitutes "approved" is examined at length beginning in Chapter 4.

As the word literally implies, "baseline" is a line that establishes a formal base for defining subsequent change. Without this line (i.e., reference point), the notion of change (which we stated earlier is indigenous to system development) is meaningless. Figure 2.9 illustrates the concepts of baseline and change and highlights their intimate relationship. In this figure, we show on the left a baseline of a system called XX (e.g., a design specification). We also show a change to be made to the baseline of System XX (e.g., the second paragraph of the design specification must be expanded to clarify an ambiguity). The figure indicates that the revised baseline shown on the right incorporates the change into the original baseline (i.e., the second paragraph of the design specification has been replaced as defined in the change). It should be particularly noted that, without the establishment of the baseline, the formulation of the change to System XX is meaningless.

The example below gives an idea of the importance of establishing software baselines. It is based on an actual project that the authors observed.

WHY ESTABLISH SOFTWARE BASELINES?—A REAL-WORLD EXAMPLE

Project A was a multimillion-dollar effort to establish a large network of computer centers for a national organization. This organization's top management decided to develop the software for the computer center network using only in-house resources. Accordingly, because of the assumed intimacy of the software development team, top management saw no need to write a comprehensive statement of requirements. Over a period of four years, managers of various user departments and branches within the organization wrote seven different statements of requirements for this project. These requirements statements for the most part addressed only the needs of the particular manager's unit. None of the requirements statements addressed the totality of project needs—that is, no single comprehensive requirements statement existed. In addition, there were some inconsistencies among the seven requirements statements. These inconsistencies were never addressed and therefore remained unresolved. In short, no clear, comprehensive, and authoritative requirements baseline was ever established.

As the project "progressed," attempts to institute changes became exercises in frustration. For example, attempting to institute a change such as "Modify capability Y as follows . . ." would have different end results depending upon which requirements statement(s) was (were) used as a point of departure for making the modification. The originator of such a change might be told that his suggested change had been successfully implemented and yet find that the need underlying the change had not been satisfied.   □

Under the circumstances, who could fault the software designers for having no clear idea of what they were to design? Or the product assurance practitioners, for what they were to audit and test? Or the users, for what they were delivered? In sum, the absence of a *requirements baseline* on this project was a primary cause of its ending in failure. In terms of the scenario portrayed in Figure 2.8, this project failed primarily because the wizard and the king had no unambiguous basis for resolving their differences.

We can now relate the concept of baseline to the concept of life cycle previously introduced. A baseline formally marks the completion of a particular journey through a life cycle stage; the act of completion is embodied in an approved product that is a snapshot of the system at that stage in its evolution. In other words, a baseline is the product that emerges from a life cycle stage after successfully completing the review process alluded to in Figure 2.7. We illustrate this important point in more specific terms by considering the two design stages shown in Figure 2.7. The preliminary design document shown in the figure, after successfully emerging from the review process alluded to in the figure, formally marks the completion of a particular journey through the Preliminary Design Stage. Several drafts of the document may be produced before success is achieved. This document constitutes a baseline from which activity in the Detailed Design Stage proceeds. In a manner similar to that discussed in the basement-finishing example presented earlier, this detailed-design activity may precipitate some rethinking of the preliminary design (e.g., what was originally a single subsystem in the preliminary design may be split into three subsystems in the detailed design)—that is, a revisit to the Preliminary Design Stage. This revisit, in turn, may precipitate a revised preliminary design specification.

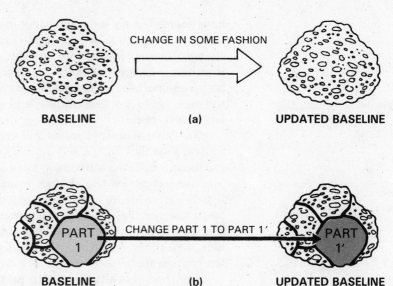

FIGURE 2.10. Why distinguish software parts? In (a), software is viewed as a monolithic entity. Viewed in this way, software change is difficult to visualize and trace because it is difficult to pin down just what is changing. In (b), by contrast, the software baseline is viewed as having identifiable parts, one of which has been changed. Dividing a baseline into such parts makes change to the baseline visible and traceable, thereby facilitating management of the software life cycle.

Such revised baselines we refer to as *baseline updates*.[9] Thus, for each of the life cycle stages shown in Figure 2.7, except the Operational Use Stage, we have a corresponding baseline—namely, Requirements Definition Baseline, Preliminary Design Baseline, Detailed Design Baseline, Coding Baseline, and Operational Baseline. The Operational Use Stage has no termination point until the software system is no longer used, and thus has no associated baseline. During this stage, the Operational Baseline is used. Note that on many software projects the Coding Baseline (the product of the Coding Stage) and the Operational Baseline (the product of the Production/Deployment Stage) are the same because no formal distinction is made between the coding activity and the production and subsequent deployment of the code. For each of these baselines we have zero or more baseline updates (e.g., Requirements Definition Baseline Update 1, or Detailed Design Baseline Update 3).

Are these baselines (and their updates) monolithic in structure? Possibly, but such a monolithic structure provides little visibility into a baseline or traceability between baselines. A preferred approach would be to divide each baseline into parts—we call these subdivisions *software parts*. The rationale for this subdivision is basically the same as that for dividing the software life cycle into stages—better visibility and traceability, yielding improved management (i.e., better planning, directing, and controlling).

To visualize these advantages, consider Figure 2.10. In part (a) of the figure, we show a software product—a baseline, to be more specific—which is viewed only as a whole, i.e., we

---

[9] While a baseline is being established, it may, as noted earlier, be revised one or more times. These drafts are *not* baseline updates. As used in this book, *baseline update* refers to each *approved* reissue of a baseline after the baseline is first established. For a complementary discussion of the baseline update concept, see Bersoff et al., *Software Configuration Management*, pp. 103–105.

have identified no software parts in this baseline. When the baseline is updated, we can state only that the baseline has changed in some fashion; we have no way to point to the part(s) that have changed so that by comparison we can determine how these parts are changed. We have little visibility into the software product or the change, and without this visibility we have no traceability.

We have actually applied a change in some fashion to the software symbol on the left side of part (a) of Figure 2.10 to produce an updated software symbol on the right side. Perhaps you did not notice the change when you first looked at the figure—after all, it is not very apparent. When you have located the change, try this experiment: write down what the change was in specific terms. Without dividing the symbol into identified parts, we think you will find it difficult to describe the change specifically.

Contrast this situation with part (b) of Figure 2.10. Here we have divided the baseline into identifiable parts. We labeled one part for this illustration; we advocate labeling every part of a software product, but omit the additional labeling here to reduce cluttering in the figure. The change to the baseline—substituting part 1' for part 1—is certainly visible and traceable. We have also changed the software symbol in Figure 2.10(b). If you repeat the experiment described above on part (b) of the figure, you will find it much easier to describe the change than you did in part (a). In summary, Figure 2.10 graphically shows how improved visibility and traceability result from dividing software products into parts.

What is a "software part"? Quite simply, it is a subdivision of a software baseline. Since a baseline is a software product, a software part is any piece of information that satisfies the definition of software given in Section 2.1. Recalling the discussion of software examples in that section, it is seen that the following are examples of software parts:

A paragraph (or a sentence, or a chapter) in a design document

A single line (or a group of lines) of computer source code (recorded on magnetic media, or printed on paper)

The information recorded in a piece of computer firmware (such as a read only memory module) or on a tape cassette containing a library of applications programs that connects to a personal computer

A collection of software parts[10]

---

[10] That a software part can itself be made up of software parts should not seem surprising. This recursive property of software parts is simply an adaptation of the familiar recursive property of hardware parts. For example, when viewing an automobile in a showroom to decide whether to buy it, that system is generally thought of as consisting of parts such as an engine, a trunk, an air conditioner, dashboard components, a steering wheel, seats, and headlights. After the automobile is bought and its maintenance becomes important, at least some of these parts are generally looked at differently. For instance, the engine is no longer simply an engine; rather, it is viewed as being made up of parts that may need repair or replacement, such as a carburetor, spark plugs, an air filter, a fan belt, a

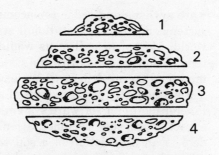

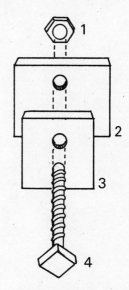

FIGURE 2.11. The concept of software configuration and a hardware analogue.

PARTS LIST

1. Introductory chapter in a three-chapter preliminary design specification itemizing the types of computations to be performed within a mathematical software package.

2. Chapter 2 in the above preliminary design specification describing the algorithms to be used in performing the computations itemized in Chapter 1.

3. Chapter 3 in the above preliminary design specification indicating the range of validity and accuracy of each algorithm described in Chapter 2.

4. Appendix in the above preliminary design specification listing error messages indicating how each algorithm described in Chapter 2 responds when it receives improper input.

PARTS LIST

1. 1/4″ hex nut
2. 4″ x 3″ steel plate 1/2″ thick
3. 3″ x 3″ steel plate 1/2″ thick
4. 2″ x 1/4″ bolt

Software parts are the basic entities over which the software manager needs to exercise control. In subsequent chapters, we explain how product assurance provides the software manager with the means for dealing with software parts, thereby helping him control software evolution.

In addition to the concepts of *change, baseline*, and *software part*, we wish to introduce a related concept because of its importance in subsequent discussions. That concept is *software configuration*, which is defined as follows:

A software configuration is a relative arrangement of software parts.[11]

This definition derives from incorporation of the word *software* into one of the dictionary definitions of *configuration*.[12] Figure 2.11 depicts our concept of software configuration together with a hardware analogue. The right side of the figure depicts an exploded parts diagram of a simple four-part hardware system; it also shows a parts list corresponding to this diagram. The utility of such diagrams and parts lists is familiar to all of us. Among other things, they are used to help us assemble hard-

---

radiator, and so forth. As the automobile ages, there may be a tendency to view it as a jumble of mostly worn-out nuts and bolts.

[11] Bersoff et al., *Software Configuration Management*, p. 108.

[12] *Webster's New Collegiate Dictionary* (New York: G. & C. Merriam Company, 1979). See Reference 6 at the end of this chapter for examples of definitions of *configuration* appearing in the software engineering literature.

ware systems and order replacement parts to maintain these systems. Such documentation is standard fare in the hardware world. Most if not all of us would not pay hundreds or even tens of dollars for hardware systems (e.g., a bicycle, a lawn mower, a power drill) without expecting this documentation. Yet we typically pay hundreds of thousands or millions of dollars (or more) for software systems and typically do not get (or expect to get) such documentation. The left side of Figure 2.11 depicts an abstraction of a software exploded parts diagram using the symbology introduced in Figures 2.1 and 2.2; it also shows a corresponding parts list assuming that the software exploded parts diagram symbolizes a three-chapter preliminary design specification (with one appendix) for a mathematical software package. In this parts list, software parts are individual chapters and the appendix in the specification. Thus, in this example, these chapters and this appendix, from a configuration management perspective, are like pieces of hardware such as a nut, a bolt, or a steel plate. Note that although the nut and bolt in Figure 2.11 are labeled as separate parts, they could have been labeled as a single part to emphasize that together they perform the function of fastening. In a similar vein, chapter 2 in the preliminary design specification could itself have been divided into a number of parts, one for each algorithm described in the chapter. This finer subdivision may be accomplished in the detailed design specification derived from this preliminary design specification to give greater visibility into the subsequent software coding of each algorithm. (Recall our comment earlier that a software part may itself be comprised of software parts.) It should be noted regarding Figure 2.11 that, as with any analogy, the analogue in the figure should not be carried to extremes. It is not the intent of the figure to convey the impression that chapter 1 in the preliminary design specification bears the same relationship to a hex nut that the appendix in the preliminary design specification does to a bolt.

From our earlier discussion of the concept of software part, it should now be evident that a software part can be almost anything—from something small such as a single line of computer source code, to something large such as a thousand-page detailed design specification. It therefore follows that a software configuration can be almost anything. But the concept of software configuration is not so arbitrary as this argument might suggest. The important point regarding this concept is the following:

At a given point in time, software project participants should agree on a set of software parts making up a software configuration, and they should subsequently change this configuration only by using formal procedures.

In this book, we focus on product assurance techniques that provide the software manager (and other project participants) with means for agreeing on what constitutes a software configuration at a given point in time; we also focus on product assurance techniques that serve to formalize the procedures for changing a software configuration. More specifically, we describe in subsequent chapters how the application of product assurance provides software project participants with the following:

Visibility into a software configuration in a to-be-established baseline so that it can be determined whether to establish this baseline as the point of departure for subsequent software development

Visibility into proposed changes to one or more parts in a software configuration making up an established baseline so that it can be determined whether the baseline should be updated

As we close this section, it is instructive to return to the king and the wizard portrayed in Figure 2.8. At the beginning of Chapter 1, we asserted that product assurance imposes a system of checks and balances on software development. These checks and balances raise the likelihood that customer requirements will be satisfied—that is, that the king can answer the wizard's question posed in Figure 2.8. Through the visibility and traceability afforded by product assurance, the arrangement of software parts in a baseline provides the king with something he can relate to his needs at a given point in time. With this information, the king can better understand what he really wants, thereby making him better able to respond to the wizard's question. The king's response will generally precipitate changes and updates to existing baselines as well as the creation of new baselines as life cycle stages are entered for the first time. The visibility and traceability afforded by product assurance illuminates these changes, updates, and new baselines, thereby increasing the likelihood that the wizard will develop what the king really wants.

2.6 Product Integrity

We have emphasized (1) that the aim of software development is to satisfy customer requirements and (2) that product assurance helps achieve this aim by making the development process and its products visible and traceable. From the perspective of software development management, achieving this aim includes other important considerations that should be constantly kept in mind. To give these considerations the attention they deserve, it is useful to define a concept called *product integrity* that links these considerations to the aim of customer requirements satisfaction. This concept is defined as follows:

A software product that has integrity is one that—
1. **Fulfills customer needs**
2. **Can be easily and completely traced through its life cycle**

3. Meets specified performance criteria
4. Meets cost expectations
5. Meets delivery expectations[13]

Regarding the last four attributes in the above definition, several general observations are worth making. The absence of the second attribute (that a product's evolution is easily and completely traceable) in many "operational" systems lies at the heart of the classical software maintenance problem that we alluded to early in Chapter 1. In their book on software maintenance, Martin and McClure offer the following comments that we believe graphically illustrate some of the implications of the absence of this product integrity attribute:

> Users are dissatisfied not only because of system bugs and failures [i.e., non-satisfaction of user needs—the first product integrity attribute listed in the definition above] but also because of poor documentation . . . and the inability of programs to be responsive to their changing requirements [which we contend derives at least in part from the lack or absence of the second product integrity attribute listed above]. . . . Maintenance of existing software systems is diverting valuable and scarce resources away from new development efforts. It is a major contributor to the growing backlog of applications waiting to be programmed. Maintenance dominates the software life cycle in terms of effort and cost. [To illustrate this point, Martin and McClure at this point refer to a figure that also appears on the cover of their book: an iceberg representing software costs, the exposed portion being labeled "Development" and the submerged portion being labeled "Maintenance."][14]

Martin and McClure also bring up another significant consequence of developing software without concern for the second product integrity attribute:

> The cost of failing to design systems for maintenance is very high. Often this is calculated to be the overt cost of doing the maintenance. There is, however, a hidden cost which is often higher. The system becomes fragile so that data-processing managers are reluctant to change it. Any change has unforeseen consequences which often cause problems elsewhere, annoy users, and waste precious personnel resources.
> So business executives are told that programs cannot be changed. . . . Even trivial changes are resisted. Executives cannot obtain the information they need for decision-making. Improvements in proce-

---

[13] Bersoff et al., *Software Configuration Management*, p. 58.

[14] J. Martin and C. McClure, *Software Maintenance: The Problem and Its Solutions* (Englewood Cliffs, N.J.: Prentice-Hall, 1983), pp. 6–7.

dures do not occur. Better forms of customer service are avoided. The business *should* be changing rapidly but the data-processing department is digging in its heels. Dynamic executives become frustrated. They constantly perceive changes they want to make but have increasing difficulty doing so. It is like swimming in slowly solidifying gelatin.[15]

Thus, if the software life cycle is difficult or impossible to trace, either the software must be forever frozen or its subsequent evolution becomes a high-risk venture with a small likelihood of a good return on the development investment.

The third product integrity attribute (that a product meets specified performance criteria) can be viewed as a special case of the first attribute (fulfilling customer needs). What are performance criteria? They generally address issues such as:

How many?

How often?

How long?

For example, a customer may have a requirement for his software to operate eighteen hours a day (how long?), to suffer no more than two failures during this period (how often?), and to process 10,000 incoming messages during this period (how many?). Such stipulations tend to focus more on the performance of the software (how well the software is to do something), whereas a stipulation such as that the software shall process incoming messages tends to focus on what the software is to do. On some software projects, significance is attached to the difference between a functional requirement (what the software is to do) and a performance criterion (how well the software is to perform). For example, a developer may be paid a certain amount for producing software that meets all functional requirements and be paid a bonus for producing software whose operation exceeds specified performance criteria. On other software projects, there may be no reason to distinguish between "customer needs" and "performance criteria," in which case our first and third product integrity attributes merge into a single attribute.

The final two product integrity attributes (that a product meets cost and delivery expectations) call attention to the effectiveness of the software development process that yields the software products. Accordingly, they reflect management effectiveness in getting the job done. At the outset of this chapter, we asserted that the job of a software manager is to plan the software development cycle, direct others to produce software products, and control activities during plan execution. More compactly stated, this job is one of managing project budget and schedule. There is also another way to look at the fourth

---

[15] Ibid., pp. 7–8.

and fifth product integrity attributes. Like the third attribute, these two can also be viewed as special cases of the first attribute. Generally, when a customer stipulates what he wants done (and how well), he will also stipulate how much he is willing to pay and how long he is willing to wait for his software. From the perspective of software project management, however, it is generally more useful to separate the customer's money and schedule requirements from his functional and performance requirements.

To summarize the preceding general discussion of the concept of product integrity, we note that it is a measure of the customer's need; it also encompasses technical, cost, and schedule dimensions. Consistent with our panoramic definition of software, our concept of product integrity spans the entire software life cycle—not just those life cycle stages wherein computer code is produced, tested, and turned over to the customer. Our motivation for introducing a panoramic product integrity concept stems from our experience and the experience of others on software projects—the likelihood of producing computer code that has integrity is small if predecessor requirements and design products lack integrity. We illustrate this concept in Figure 2.12. Notice that the requirements specification is incomplete—we can surmise from the grade given on the product integrity report card that some important user need was overlooked. The design resulting from the requirements is also

FIGURE 2.12. The aim of software development is to turn out software products that have integrity. The likelihood of producing computer code that has integrity is small if predecessor requirements and design products lack integrity.

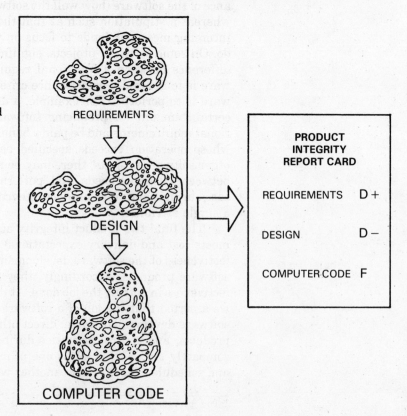

REQUIREMENTS

DESIGN

COMPUTER CODE

PRODUCT
INTEGRITY
REPORT CARD

REQUIREMENTS   D +

DESIGN   D −

COMPUTER CODE   F

given a low grade in product integrity in the figure. The design in one sense reflects the requirements in that the piece missing from the requirements is correspondingly missing from the design. However, the design is distorted with respect to the requirements, possibly because one or more of the other product integrity attributes was not achieved; for example, the allowed time for the design stage may have been substantially exceeded. The result of this lack of integrity in the requirements and design specifications is that the computer code generally has even less integrity and is quite likely to get a failing grade on the report card. In the illustration, the computer code is missing the code to satisfy the omitted requirement. Further, it is also distorted, symbolically indicating a failure to achieve one or more product integrity attributes. For example, as a result of the schedule overrun in the design stage suggested above, a horde of additional coders may be put on the project to make up for lost time. The result of this measure might well be a considerable cost overrun. Thus, the lack of software product integrity in requirements and design is continued or expanded in the code.

In this book, product integrity is a fundamental concept. It would take us too far afield to probe various nuances of this concept through protracted discussion in this chapter. Consequently, to assure proper understanding of this concept, it is strongly suggested that managers as well as product assurance practitioners attempt to work Exercise 2.6 at the end of this chapter. Parts (a) and (b) of that exercise explore some nuances of the product integrity concept from the senior management viewpoint; parts (c) and (d) ask you to think about product integrity as a quantitative measure of a product's interim value and as a means for assessing management performance. Below we present examples to ensure that the concept is broadly understood, followed by the introduction and discussion of the requisite disciplines for attaining and maintaining product integrity on a software project. This discussion establishes the framework for the treatment of software control in Chapter 4.

PRODUCT INTEGRITY—EXAMPLE 1

A deluxe, custom-built house that craftsmen build from the finest materials on a rocky islet probably does not have product integrity for a man confined to a wheelchair. On the other hand, to a rugged outdoorsman, the same house could truly possess all the attributes that fulfill that customer's expectations and thus get the highest marks for product integrity. □

PRODUCT INTEGRITY—EXAMPLE 2

In the same vein as Example 1, a vacation home that takes five times as long to build as expected and is ten times as expensive to construct as anticipated lacks integrity, even if all the customer's needs are satisfied. By the time the home is built, the owner may even be too old to enjoy it and have long since gone bankrupt. Even if he is not, the failure to meet cost and schedule expectations constitutes a product lacking in integrity (because, for example, of the psychological impact on him and the physical impact on his bank account).[16] □

As we reiterated at the outset of this section, the aim of software development is to satisfy customer requirements. On the basis of the preceding discussion, we now broaden this statement as follows:

The aim of software development is to turn out software products with integrity.

This book concentrates on the role of product assurance in achieving this aim. However, proper understanding of this role must begin with a top-level understanding of the roles of those who should be involved with a software project if it is to turn out products with integrity. For this purpose, consider Figure 2.13.[17] This figure depicts a triangle. At each vertex is a group of disciplines—a management group at the top (the project manager and his staff, the manager to whom the project manager reports, and the manager above these managers), a de-

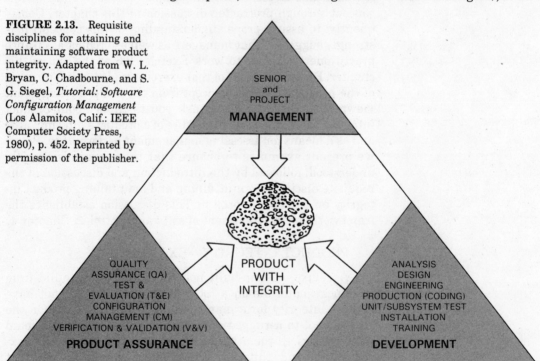

FIGURE 2.13. Requisite disciplines for attaining and maintaining software product integrity. Adapted from W. L. Bryan, C. Chadbourne, and S. G. Siegel, *Tutorial: Software Configuration Management* (Los Alamitos, Calif.: IEEE Computer Society Press, 1980), p. 452. Reprinted by permission of the publisher.

SENIOR and PROJECT
MANAGEMENT

QUALITY ASSURANCE (QA)
TEST & EVALUATION (T&E)
CONFIGURATION MANAGEMENT (CM)
VERIFICATION & VALIDATION (V&V)
PRODUCT ASSURANCE

PRODUCT WITH INTEGRITY

ANALYSIS
DESIGN
ENGINEERING
PRODUCTION (CODING)
UNIT/SUBSYSTEM TEST
INSTALLATION
TRAINING
DEVELOPMENT

---

[16] W. L. Bryan and S. G. Siegel, "Panosta laotuun ohjelmistotyossa" (Finnish translation of an article written in English entitled "Attaining and Maintaining Software Product Integrity Through Product Assurance"), Part I, *Elektroniikka & Automaatio* (Finnish trade journal), no. 14 (August 31, 1982), p. 54.

[17] W. L. Bryan, C. Chadbourne, and S. G. Siegel, *Tutorial: Software Configuration Management*, IEEE Catalog No. EHO169-3 (Los Alamitos, Calif.: IEEE Computer Society Press, 1980), p. 452.

velopment group at one base vertex, and a product assurance group at the other base vertex. Our experience in the software industry is that attaining and maintaining software product integrity on a software project require judicious application of these three groups of disciplines. Before we turn the spotlight on the product assurance group, we briefly discuss the role of all three groups in achieving product integrity. In this way, we hope to make clear at the outset that product integrity cannot be achieved without the interplay of all three groups. Once this is established, we can delve into the details of product assurance mechanics and at the same time maintain perspective on how these mechanics fit into the overall scheme of things on a software project.

An overall comment about Figure 2.13 is in order before we examine its parts. We use a triangle in the figure not just because we are depicting *three* groups of disciplines but to convey the notion of total interconnectivity. Unlike higher order polygons (e.g., quadrilaterals, pentagons), a triangle has the property that every vertex is directly connected to every other vertex in the triangle (by contrast, for example, opposite vertices of a quadrilateral are not connected). This notion of total interconnectivity carries with it the derivative notion of inherent checking and balancing (i.e., stability)—movement at one vertex (e.g., management call for action) precipitates movement at another vertex (e.g., the issuing of a new draft product), which in turn precipitates movement at the third vertex (e.g., product assurance review of the draft product), which in turn precipitates movement at the management vertex (e.g., determining what to do with the results of the product assurance review), and so forth. Take one of the vertices out of Figure 2.13 and the triangle collapses, and this natural project rhythm disappears. For example, take management out of the picture, and the development group will in all likelihood proceed like a ship without a captain, unsure of what the course is for meeting customer needs on time and within budget;[18] take product assurance out of the picture, and management loses visibility into development because of the absence of a source inherently more objective than the development group (recall, for example, the sample problem discussed in Section 1.3); and, take the development group out of the picture, and of course no products are developed (nor is there any work for the other two groups).

In many ways, the organizational structure embodied in Figure 2.13 parallels that of the U.S. federal government. The top of the triangle in this figure—management—can be viewed as the analogue of the legislative branch; the lower right of the triangle—developers—can be viewed as the analogue of the executive branch (i.e., in response to the requirements laid

---

[18] The authors know of a number of software projects where no one was in charge (for example, see Project Neptune in Section 7.1). Not surprisingly, numerous problems of the type depicted in Figure 1.4 were encountered.

down by management, the developers carry out the directives of management regarding product development); and the lower left of the triangle—product assurance practitioners—can be viewed as the analogue of the judicial branch (i.e., in response to the requirements laid down by management, the product assurance practitioners check the activities of the developers and advise management regarding these activities). Let us now see in more specific terms how this project "government" acts to serve the will of the customer (so that the customer receives a product with integrity).

The disciplines in the development group are assigned the responsibility for creating (and re-creating, if necessary) the software during its various life cycle stages, transforming it into an operational product installed at the customer's site, and preparing changes to the operational product (enhancements, new capabilities, and fixes for latent errors); they are also responsible for examining and testing their work before handing it over for independent product assurance review.[19] These disciplines are typified by the activities shown in the lower right of Figure 2.13—analysis (such as that performed by operations research analysts in formulating requirements), design, engineering (such as that performed to integrate hardware and software portions of a system), coding, unit/subsystem test,[20] installation,[21] and training (such as that provided to the customer at the time of installation). To carry out their role in achieving product integrity, the developers need to be technically and managerially disciplined to cope with a project at all stages of product development—from requirements definition through operational use (recall Figure 2.7). Part of this coping means knowing what technical and dollar resources are needed to get the job done, when they are needed, and then applying these resources vigorously in the right mix at the right time.[22] The developers need to ensure that adequate documentation is not only produced, but produced systematically. Software in the form of documentation produced out of sequence—for example, computer code developed before a design specification (see Exercise 1.10)—can disrupt traceability back to customer needs and thus detract from the product's integrity (recall the second product integrity attribute discussed earlier in this section). Systematically produced software, particularly in the form of documentation, serves to maintain visibility of the evolving software product for management and the cus-

---

[19] The discussion in the remainder of this section is an adaptation of the original English that was subsequently translated into Finnish in Bryan and Siegel, "Panosta laatuun ohjelmistotyossa," pp. 54–55.

[20] This testing is a form of product assurance that the developers perform before handing their work over to the product assurance group for independent testing.

[21] That is, installing the product intended for operational use at the customer site(s).

[22] These resource allocation tasks are typically the responsibility of management within the development group (e.g., a design specification task manager, a coding task manager), as opposed to the project and senior management shown at the triangle apex in Figure 2.13.

tomer. The development group needs to accept and support the product assurance efforts as constructive, allied, and indispensable to the health of the project. It is counterproductive for the developers to withhold their work from product assurance review. A developer should not adopt the attitude of someone who is the prey in a hunt. Instead, a developer should assume the attitude of a craftsman who is more than willing to submit his product to review so that the degree of product conformance with customer requirements can be determined (see Exercise 1.11). Finally, the development organization must be ever cognizant of the customer and the need to accurately and completely communicate project progress—and problems—to the customer.

The disciplines that comprise the product assurance group provide management with a set of checks and balances with respect to the activities of the developers. As we discuss later, these checks and balances offer a measure of *assurance* that *product* integrity is attained and maintained (hence, our use of the term *product assurance* to label these checks and balances). The product assurance group includes four disciplines—quality assurance (QA), verification and validation (V&V), test and evaluation (T&E), and configuration management (CM). We already informally introduced and discussed these disciplines in Section 1.4 and in the sample problem on visibility in Section 2.2; we formally define and describe these disciplines in Chapter 3.

Product assurance plays the role of the devil's advocate—but in a constructive, not destructive, sense. There is a natural inclination to view anyone who reviews someone else's work as an adversary (the "bad guy" or the "guy in the black hat"), but when performed properly, product assurance truly aids the development process. By "performed properly" we mean, for example, benevolent (but probing) questioning of a software product's contents. The object of this benevolent questioning should always be determination of the extent to which the product conforms to customer requirements, thereby helping to achieve convergence between the wizard and the king depicted in Figure 2.8. By establishing procedures for conducting product reviews (the forum for constructive interchange among the three groups of disciplines regarding these questions) and obtaining management and developer concurrence regarding these procedures, product assurance institutionalizes a set of checks and balances serving both management and the developer throughout the software life cycle. Typically, the development disciplines and the product assurance disciplines perceive project progress from different viewpoints—the former perhaps more optimistically and the latter perhaps more pessimistically. Product assurance needs to provide management with a potentially contrasting view so that management has the opportunity to make more intelligent decisions. As an adjunct to establishing product review procedures, product assurance needs to confirm that product development is disciplined by providing the procedures for creating and controlling baselines and baseline updates. In confirming that product development is disciplined, product assurance needs to ensure that a balanced blend of product assurance activities commensurate with project complexity and importance is invoked (we have more to say about this point in Chapter 7). This balanced blend is realized by applying technical skills needed to effect the product assurance disciplines. Finally, product assurance must proceed with consummate finesse to ensure that all other project participants understand and support the product assurance effort. In this regard, it is particularly important for product assurance to indicate clearly to these participants the following fundamental point that is often overlooked and then to perform accordingly:

Product assurance does not normally address the "goodness" of a product through subjective judgments. Product assurance primarily addresses the degree to which a product satisfies customer requirements. Requirements satisfaction is determined through objective comparisons as embodied in the disciplines of product assurance.

In performing product assurance, the authors are frequently asked such questions as "How good is the latest software product created by the developers?" or "How good are the developer's programmers?" Our answer to the first question is shown in Figure 2.14. Similarly, we define a "good" programmer as one who produces "good" software products. Thus, product assurance in the strictest sense of the concept does not, for example, offer insight into whether a software design is elegant in the way it exploits computer hardware memory (unless, of course, "elegant hardware memory management" is a customer requirement); the design is "good" from the product assurance perspective if it satisfies customer requirements.[23]

The disciplines in the management group provide direction to development and product assurance activities to effect synergism among these activities. This group consists of the disciplines of project management and senior management. Project management provides direction to the development and product assurance groups at the level of day-to-day activity associated with product development. Senior management provides this direction generally at the level above a particular project organization and promulgates corporate guidelines and policies. Typically, this direction concentrates on sorting things out with respect to two or more projects that may be competing for corporate resources. In this book, when we refer to "senior management," we mean (unless otherwise indicated) the person or organization to which the project manager reports.

---

[23] However, management can, if it chooses, call upon product assurance to render such subjective judgments. The pros and cons of using product assurance in this way are explored in Exercise 7.9.

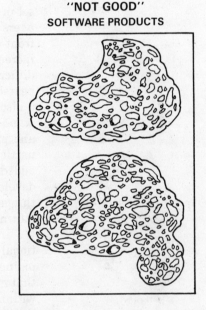

CUSTOMER REQUIREMENTS

FIRST REQUIREMENT

SECOND REQUIREMENT

⋮

LAST REQUIREMENT

"GOOD" SOFTWARE PRODUCT

"NOT GOOD" SOFTWARE PRODUCTS

FIGURE 2.14. What is a "good" software product? A software product is "good," by our definition, if it embodies all customer requirements and does not embody anything the customer did not ask for.

Senior management has a key role to play at the outset of a project. It must see to it that a project is given stature within the corporate structure commensurate with the project's importance as perceived by senior management, its complexity, and its projected cost. Lacking this stature, the project may be pushed to the bottom of the corporate stack and thereby be stifled in the competition for limited corporate resources (and thus lose visibility within the overall corporate context). Senior management must also ensure that a qualified project manager is assigned to lead the project. Senior management must delineate the project manager's responsibilities, particularly with respect to the product assurance disciplines.[24] It must give the project manager sufficient authority to marshal adequate corporate resources to support product development. Senior and project management must establish a well-defined ac-

---

[24] The trade-offs associated with product assurance autonomy versus project management authority and responsibility are discussed in subsequent chapters. Exercise 3.10, for example, presents some different organizational approaches to product assurance and asks you to consider advantages and disadvantages of each approach.

countability chain so that who is supposed to do what for whom is clearly understood at project outset and throughout product development. Project management must adequately distribute project resources between development and product assurance organizational entities (see Exercise 7.1). Unfortunately, the practice in the software industry has too often been to dump resources into the development disciplines in an attempt to meet fast-approaching product delivery dates. The all-too-typical mad scramble to meet delivery dates often comes about because management did not ensure a front-end investment, particularly in the product assurance disciplines. The principle of "pay now versus pay much more later" is an issue that both senior and project management must face squarely at the outset of a project (recall Figure 1.3). Philosophically, most managers probably do not find it difficult to accept the need for front-end endeavors and concomitant expenditures in order to increase the probability of project success. What is generally difficult for managers to appreciate (and what this book repeatedly stresses) is the extent to which they must act to effect a disciplined approach to product development and to effect a *balanced* application of available resources to the development and product assurance disciplines.[25] The project manager, in particular, must see himself as a catalyst to be continually added to project activity to stimulate interaction between the development and product assurance disciplines and to make things happen effectively. This book offers some techniques (but no formulas!) for performing this catalysis.[26]

In closing this section, we need to touch upon one additional topic in connection with Figure 2.13. As we have explained, Figure 2.13 portrays the three groups of disciplines that must interact on any software project if software products with integrity are to result. However, to appreciate more fully the implications of the figure in terms of an actual project environment, we need to say something about the three archetypical parties that interact on most software projects. These parties are:

The user of the software system. This party generally is the one with the requirements that the software is being developed to satisfy.

The buyer of the software system. This party generally is the agent for the user; the buyer can thus be thought of as a surrogate user. The buyer typically interacts with the third party, listed below, in seeing to it that the software

---

[25] By "balanced" we do not mean "50–50." In Exercise 7.5, we address the issue of how much product assurance is necessary to achieve product integrity. Just as token application of product assurance is usually of little or no benefit, too much product assurance can actually be counterproductive. Finding somewhere in between these two extremes is what we mean by "balanced."

[26] It is worthwhile to recall here a comment made in the MUDD Report (Reference 12, Chapter 1): "It is not yet possible to give an algorithm for producing reliable software."

system is being developed in accordance with user requirements. Sometimes the buyer and the user are the same. The buyer and the user are the "customer" to whom we have been referring in preceding discussions. In subsequent discussions, we generally use the terms *customer* and *buyer/user* interchangeably.

The seller of the software system. This party is hired by the buyer to develop the software system for the user. As we subsequently explain, the seller is not the same as the development group of disciplines shown in Figure 2.13 (but they are related). Sometimes, when no confusion will result, we will use the terms *seller* and *developer* interchangeably.

Based upon the discussion of Figure 2.13 earlier in this section, it follows that the likelihood of achieving software product integrity on a project is heightened if the user, buyer, and seller are organized in the manner depicted in Figure 2.15. Thus, for example, the seller should have a project manager, and of course developers who will turn out the software products requested by the customer; also, the seller should have a product assurance group that reviews the products before they are shown to the customer. Correspondingly, the buyer/user should have a project manager (who should interface with the seller project manager in a manner such as that described in Chapter 4); also, the buyer/user should have a staff skilled in the development disciplines to support the buyer/user project manager (in a manner such as that described in Chapter 4); finally, the buyer/user should have a staff skilled in the product assurance disciplines to review the products received from the seller. Note that seller management, development, and product assurance personnel may be organized into independent

FIGURE 2.15. The likelihood of achieving a software product with integrity increases if the user, buyer, and seller are each organized with management, development, and product assurance personnel.

MANAGEMENT

SOFTWARE PRODUCT WITH INTEGRITY

User, Buyer, and Seller Organizations

PRODUCT ASSURANCE

DEVELOPMENT

☐ = organizational unit

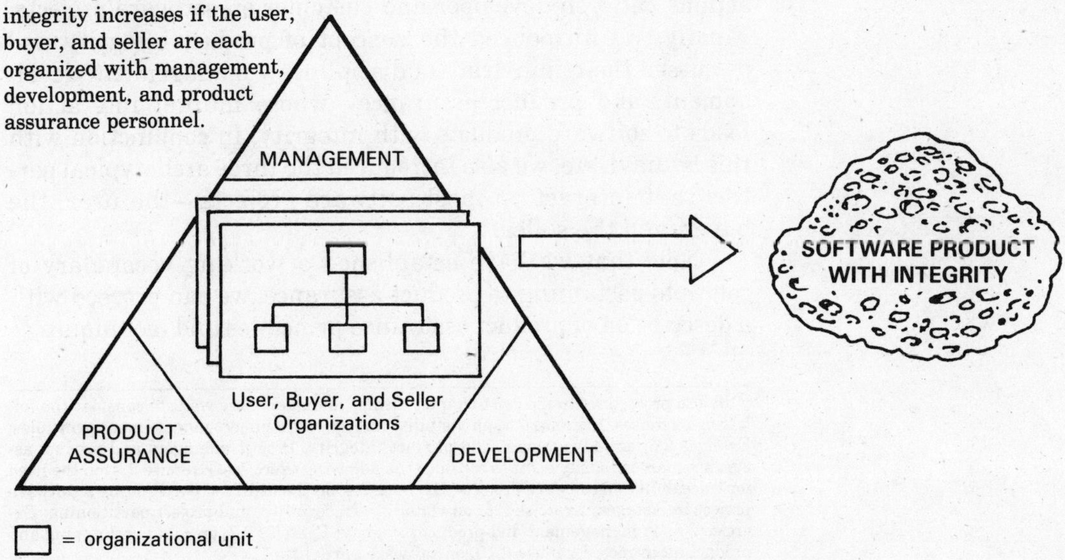

groups, into a single group, or into combinations of groups. The same organizational structure applies to the buyer and the user.

In subsequent chapters, we discuss at length how the march around the life cycle in Figure 2.7 is effectively accomplished within the organizational framework of Figure 2.13. In particular, we describe how the wizard and the king depicted in Figure 2.8 are likely to agree upon what needs to be done if each is backed by this organizational framework.

2.7 Summary

In this chapter, we formally defined a number of concepts needed to elucidate the product assurance principles and techniques presented in subsequent chapters. We began by giving a panoramic definition of software which encompasses not only computer code but also predecessor requirements and design specifications. To clarify the role of product assurance, we next introduced the concepts of visibility and traceability. We indicated how the application of product assurance serves to raise the visibility of software development and infuse it with traceability. As a result, management is better able to make intelligent, informed decisions about how a software project should proceed. To provide the context for illustrating in specific terms how product assurance is to be accomplished, we then introduced a specific software life cycle. Probing further into the concept of software introduced earlier, we next defined the allied notions of software change, software baseline, software baseline update, software part, and software configuration. In conjunction with these notions, we reinforced the fundamental point made in Chapter 1—that the basic software project management challenge is to achieve convergence between a customer's perception of his need and the software developer's perception of that need. For this purpose, we used a comic strip (Figure 2.8) that we asserted was a microcosm of the interactions between developer and customer on software projects. Finally, we introduced the concept of product integrity and discussed the triumvirate of disciplines—management, development, and product assurance—whose mutual interaction leads to software products with integrity. In conjunction with this triumvirate, we also introduced the three archetypical parties that interact on most software projects—the user, the buyer, and the seller.

Now that we have established a working vocabulary of concepts pertaining to product assurance, we can proceed with a description of product assurance principles and techniques.[27]

---

[27] Before proceeding to the next chapter, senior managers may want to consider the following exercises: Exercise 2.2, on visibility and software project management principles; Exercise 2.6, on management and product integrity. Project managers and product assurance managers may want to consider the following exercises: Exercise 2.3, on the need for traceability on software projects; Exercise 2.4, on the utility of partitioning a software project into stages; Exercise 2.5, on visibility, traceability, and project partitioning; Exercise 2.6, on management and product integrity; Exercise 2.7, on rapid prototyping and product assurance; Exercise 2.10, on software parts lists.

2.1 Recall the sample problem on the concept of software in Section 2.1. Rework part B of that problem from the product assurance viewpoint instead of from the perspective of the project manager. That is, address the following question:

In terms of what product assurance is called upon to do on a software project, how can the panoramic definition of software given in Figure 2.1 be helpful?

2.2 Recall the three aspects of the concept of visibility listed in Figure 2.4. From the point of view of software project management principles, how does each of these aspects complement the other two aspects? (For example, what does the aspect "permitting management to be seen on a project" suggest to you about management's ability to focus project resources that the aspect "permitting software to be seen" may not?) In responding to this question, review the discussion of the three aspects of visibility given in the sample problem in Section 2.2.

2.3 When we introduced the concept of traceability in this chapter, we intimated that a project manager is better able to plan how to proceed if he knows where he has been. Do you think that this potential payoff to management is about the same for all or most types of software projects? That is, do you think that the need for traceability on, say, a research and development (R&D) project (where part of the project's objective is to experiment and explore different alternatives) is more or less critical than or about the same as it is on, say, a project whose principal objective is to produce an operational system on a fixed date with a budget that cannot be changed? (*Hint:* Recall Table 2.1 and the accompanying discussion in Section 2.3. Then consider which types of software projects really require traceability aids such as that illustrated in Table 2.1 and which types can proceed without such aids.) What does your response to this question suggest about the trade-offs associated with determining how much traceability you need on a software project? (*Hint:* In addressing this latter question, consider such factors as the cost associated with acquiring a degree of traceability, the criticality of the software to the operation of the system in which it is embedded, and the experience of the software development staff.)

2.4 In introducing the concept of life cycle in this chapter, we intimated that this concept simplifies the approach to a project by breaking it into pieces and thus facilitating its management. Do you think that this concept is useful to invoke on any software development or main-tenance project? Or do you think that some software projects would be made more complex by partitioning them into life cycle stages? What kinds of projects do you think would fall in the latter group? (*Hint:* Consider the relationship between project size [in terms of, say, its budget and planned duration] and the number of life cycle stages that might facilitate management of the project. You may also want to consider the relationship between the number of life cycle stages and the amount of visibility into project happenings that can be realized.)

2.5 Recall the concepts of visibility, traceability, and life cycle defined in this chapter and consider the following questions:

(a) Is it possible to have traceability on a project without visibility? Why (not)? (*Hint:* Review Section 2.3.)

(b) Is it possible to have visibility on a project without traceability? Why (not)?

(c) In what ways does partitioning a software development effort into stages increase visibility for the project manager (and the other project participants)? (*Hint:* To start your thinking, consider the functions of milestones and signs placed along roads and highways.)

(d) In what ways does partitioning a software development effort into stages serve to instill traceability into the project? (*Hint:* To start your thinking, imagine the traceability thread as a chain. You could also recall Table 2.1.)

(e) In your opinion, which analogy listed below best describes the notion of developing a software system by partitioning it into life cycle stages? Give at least two reasons to justify the analogy you select.

1. Putting together a jigsaw puzzle
2. Painting a still-life picture
3. Constructing a house
4. Designing and constructing an addition to a house
5. Getting dressed
6. Writing and producing a play
7. Some combination of (parts of) 1–6 (If you make this selection, you should specify which [parts of] items 1–6 make up your analogy.)
8. None of the above (If you make this selection, you should construct your own analogy.)

2.6 Review the discussion of product integrity given in Section 2.6 and consider the following questions:

(a) Suppose you are a senior manager in a software development company. Suppose further that reporting directly to you are a number of project managers, each responsible for day-to-day management of a software project. One of your responsibilities is to evaluate the performance of these project managers to determine (among other things) their advancement potential. How might you use the attributes in the definition of product integrity to assist you in this determination?

(b) Suppose you are president of a company that develops and sells software systems. Naturally you are interested in making a profit. You are also interested in expanding your business. With these two motives in mind, which attributes in the definition of product integrity would you direct your project managers to be most concerned about, and why? Which would you direct them to be least concerned about, and why? ("Concern" here carries with it the implication that the magnitude of the salary increases given these project managers will greatly depend on how well the software products they develop manifest the product integrity attributes of greatest concern.)

(c) From the point of view of attempting to assess the worth of a software product, is it useful to claim that the product has no integrity unless it manifests all five of the product integrity attributes? Does it make sense to say that a product has a little bit of integrity because, for example, it possesses the first four attributes but was delivered two months (or two years) late? More generally, does it make sense to ascribe different degrees of integrity to a product in accord with the extent to which the product possesses the five integrity attributes? For example, does a product that does what it is supposed to do and is delivered three months early have more integrity than a product that does what it is supposed to do and is delivered two months early or delivered exactly on time? Why (not)?

(d) (*Note:* This part of this exercise is intended for readers with a background in mathematics. It is adapted from an unpublished manuscript by E. H. Bersoff, V. D. Henderson, and S. G. Siegel.) Reconsider some of your answers to part (c) above in quantitative terms. More specifically, how would you define a product integrity index that would indicate quantitatively how much integrity a product has? (*Hint:* Consider, for example, product integrity as a vector with five components—the five product integrity attributes. For each of these attributes, define a scale of values representing in quantitative terms how much of that attribute is present in a product. To assess the integrity of a product, assign a value to each of these attributes based on your [perhaps subjective] judgment of "how much" of that attribute is in the product. Now compute the dot product of the vector with itself to obtain a "product integrity index" for that product. How useful might such an index be, say, for dealing with such issues as those raised in parts (a) and (b) of this exercise?)

2.7 In Figure 2.8, the wizard asks the king, "What is it that you really want?" Many veterans of software projects contend that often the user or buyer of a software system really does not know what he wants. For this reason, these veterans argue, it is not really productive on a software project to spend much time trying to define (on paper) what the user wants (or thinks he needs). It is more productive, they argue, to forgo much of this so-called requirements analysis and quickly build a prototype of the system that the user thinks he needs. The proponents of this so-called rapid prototyping approach to software system development claim that, once in the user's hands, this prototype helps the user quickly determine what he needs, primarily because he has the opportunity to manipulate with his own hands something that works, thereby experiencing firsthand what he may not want or need. (See, e.g., H. Gomaa, "The Impact of Rapid Prototyping on Specifying User Requirements," *ACM SIGSOFT Software Engineering Notes*, vol. 8, no. 2 [April 1983], pp. 17–28. This paper describes the successful use of rapid prototyping to assist in the specification of requirements for a system to manage and control an integrated circuit fabrication facility. Following use of the prototype, "a more formal software engineering approach was used in developing the production system than was used in the prototype" [p. 26]. The development of the production system was completed on time and turned out to be extremely easy to use. See also Exercise 4.3.) With the preceding as background, and in light of the software management concepts introduced in this chapter, consider the following:

(a) In what ways is visibility into the development process achieved with rapid prototyping?

(b) Using rapid prototyping, how does a developer know what to build for the user? (*Hint:* What constitutes the requirements that the prototype is to satisfy? Is the answer to the wizard's question in Figure 2.8 a modification to the prototype itself and/or to some document?)

(c) What role, if any, would product assurance play in rapid prototyping? (*Hint:* Consider how a determination is made of whether the wizard in Figure 2.8 responds correctly to what the king tells him after the wizard asks the question shown in the figure.)

(d) Is rapid prototyping feasible in the automobile or housing industry? What does your answer to this question suggest to you about the types of software systems amenable to rapid prototyping?

(e) Is traceability a useful concept for managing rapid prototyping software efforts? Why (not)?

(f) After the prototype is built to the satisfaction of the user, how are latent defects subsequently removed, enhancements incorporated, and new capabilities added? How is it determined that these three classes of change are correctly made?

2.8 When we discussed Figure 2.8, we said that it served to reinforce the fundamental point made in Chapter 1—that the basic software project management challenge is to achieve convergence between a customer's perception of his need (what he wants) and the software developer's perception of that need. In system development parlance, the determination of these wants or needs is often referred to as "requirements analysis." Requirements analysis is probably more of an art than an engineering discipline because of the difficulty associated with translating customer stipulations into language that developers can use to fabricate systems satisfying these stipulations. The questions below probe some of the nuances of this translation process.

(a) In the first frame of the comic strip in Figure 2.8, the king asks the wizard a question. In your opinion, does the second frame indicate that the wizard answered the king's question? Does the third frame indicate that the wizard answered the king's question? What is the king doing in the third frame—amending the original question? Why does the wizard have to ask the question shown in the fourth frame?

(b) In your opinion, which of the following items does the king in Figure 2.8 really want?
1. Shelter from the rain
2. Something other than rain or snow
3. To see what the wizard can do
4. None of the above (If you select this item, indicate in specific terms what you think the king really wants.)

(c) Suppose the wizard in Figure 2.8 is a software developer who is approached by the king (i.e., customer) who asks the wizard to build him a software system that does the following:

Predicts the weather based on data fed into the computer system from visual observations made by the king's subjects

Tells the king what to wear based on the forecast

Given this list of system requirements, and recalling the scenario in Figure 2.8, what would you as the wizard do as your first step in developing the system that the king has stipulated?

(d) Suppose the process that you, the wizard, go through with the king in (c) corresponds to the Requirements Definition Stage shown in Figure 2.7. Suppose further that you agree with the king that you will develop his system according to the life cycle shown in Figure 2.7. Finally, suppose the king considers work in each stage complete when you have produced a specification (or computer code in the case of the Coding and Production/Deployment

Stages). With these suppositions, what is the relationship between the product produced in one stage and the product produced in a successor stage? (*Hint:* Recall Table 2.1.)

(e) Suppose you are a software developer and a customer presents you with a one-page statement of requirements for a new system he wants you to build for him. Suppose further that you have been in the software business a long time and are therefore quite familiar with the scenario depicted in Figure 2.8. Finally, suppose you use the life cycle shown in Figure 2.7 to develop your software systems. With these suppositions, at what point in this life cycle are you when the customer hands you his one-page statement of requirements? Express your answer in terms of a particular life cycle stage shown in Figure 2.7 and indicate whether you are at the beginning of the stage, at the end, or somewhere in-between. Give at least one reason to substantiate your answer.

2.9 Suppose that the comic strip in Figure 2.8 represents a (highly compressed) version of (a portion of) a system life cycle. With this supposition, refer to the life cycle stages shown in Figure 2.7 and consider the following questions:

(a) Which stage(s) does (do) the first frame in Figure 2.8 correspond to most closely? Why?

(b) Which stage(s) does (do) the second frame in Figure 2.8 correspond to most closely? Why?

(c) Which stage(s) does (do) the fourth frame in Figure 2.8 correspond to most closely? Why?

(d) Refer to Figure 2.13. The application of which of the three groups of disciplines shown in this figure most closely corresponds to the king's activity in the third frame in Figure 2.8? Why?

2.10 Refer to Figure 2.11 and consider the following questions:

(a) Suppose you purchase unassembled the four-part hardware system depicted in the figure. What are at least two ways that you might use the hardware parts list shown in the figure?

(b) Suppose the four software parts shown in the figure are a portion of a software design from which software code is yet to be produced. Recalling your answers to (a), what are at least two ways that you might use a software parts list like that shown in the figure?

(c) Suppose computer code is produced from the design referred to in (b). Suppose further that some time later this code is changed but that the design is not correspondingly changed. What are at least two problems that may arise from subsequent changes to this code?

(d) Refer to Figure 2.13. How might you as a software project manager uncover the discrepancy between the code and design mentioned in (c)? (*Hint:* Recall the discussion of Table 2.1.)

(e) Given that the action you might take in (d) to uncover the discrepancy costs time and money, would you, as project manager, spend this time and money? Why (not)?

2.11 Refer to Figure 2.7 and consider the following questions:

(a) The gates and the side paths linking the life cycle stages to the review area seem to suggest that product assurance activities continually present time-consuming and money-consuming obstacles to the software development process. Would not the trip around the life cycle board be more expeditious without these "obstacles"? Why (not)?

(b) What are some advantages associated with proceeding from the Requirements Definition Stage, through the review area, and then into the Coding Stage? What are some disadvantages associated with this "shortcut"?

(c) The word "testing" is not shown in the figure. Why?

(d) In Reference 7 of Chapter 1, we quoted a definition of maintenance from the book *Software Maintenance* by Martin and McClure. How would you interpret this definition in terms of Figure 2.7? In responding to this question, consider each of the following types of changes:

1. Correction of a latent code-logic error
2. Enhancement of an existing capability
3. Incorporation of a new capability

2.12 Refer to the comic strip in Figure E2.1. Imagine that it represents an interaction between a system developer (the wizard) and a buyer/user (the man who wants a potion). Recalling the life cycle concept discussed in connection with Figure 2.7, consider the following questions:

(a) Which of the life cycle stages shown in Figure 2.7 corresponds most closely to the first frame of the comic strip?

(b) Which of the life cycle stages shown in Figure 2.7 corresponds most closely to the second frame of the comic strip (where presumably the buyer/user is drinking the potion)?

(c) Which of the life cycle stages shown in Figure 2.7 corresponds most closely to the third frame of the comic strip?

(d) From the system developer's perspective, does his product have integrity in the sense defined in this chapter?

(e) From the buyer/user's perspective, does the developer's product have integrity in the sense defined in this chapter?

(f) From your answers to (d) and (e), what can you conclude about the concept of product integrity?

(g) What does the scenario in Figure E2.1 suggest about the need for visibility on a software project?

(h) How might the situation shown in the third frame of the comic strip have been avoided? (*Hint:* Recall the triangle diagram in Figure 2.13 and reconsider (g). Recall also Table 2.1.)

(i) What does your response to (h) suggest to you about the need for product assurance on a software project?

FIGURE E2.1. A typical clash between the buyer/user and system developer? (Exercise 2.12). B. Parker and J. Hart, *The Wizard of ID* (Irvine, Calif.: News America Syndicate, October 11, 1984). Reprinted by permission of Johnny Hart and News America Syndicate.

WIZARD OF ID   BY BRANT PARKER & JOHNNY HART

2.13 If you own or have access to a programmable calculator or personal computer, perform the following experiment:

Enter into the calculator or computer a simple program that you have constructed (e.g., a program that takes the average of a set of input numbers, or a program that stores and allows you to retrieve information on the caloric and nutritional content of different foods). After you have entered the program, convince yourself that it works properly by testing with various input values. When you have convinced yourself that this program works to your satisfaction (making any corrections or changes you feel are needed), do not document the program in any way; simply store it in the calculator or computer memory. Do not use the program for two weeks. Then, recall the program from the calculator or computer memory and attempt to use it.

  (a) What happened when you tried to use the program?

  (b) What does your response to (a) suggest about the concept of visibility introduced in this chapter?

  (c) Given that you were asked to construct only a simple program, what does your response to (a) and (b) suggest about the types of problems that may be encountered on software projects involving more than one person and/or the development of software code of even a modest degree of size or complexity (e.g., several thousand lines of source language statements)?

  (d) Keeping in mind your response to (b), list at least two things you might have done as part of the development of the calculator/ computer program to alleviate some of the difficulty you may have experienced in your attempt to reuse your program after a two-week hiatus. Give at least one reason to justify each item that you list.

  (e) What does your response to (d) suggest to you about the need for visibility on *any* software project? Why?

  (f) Classically, software maintenance is the repair and enhancement of operational software code (cf. Perry's definition quoted in Reference 9 of this chapter and Martin and McClure's definition quoted in Reference 7 of Chapter 1). Martin and McClure (and many others) contend that, like an iceberg, the majority of software costs lies under the water (i.e., beyond the sight of the customer who purchases the software code without realizing that this cost is but one of many that are yet to follow). What does your response to (e) suggest about how the software cost iceberg might be replaced by something whose dimensions are more manifest?

  (g) Given that the software industry is profit-driven (like most competitive industries), and given that most software customers are as likely to be as unsure of their needs as the king in Figure 2.8, is the software cost iceberg referred to in (f) an immutable law governing software project economics? Why (not)? (*Hint:* Think of visibility as being like a sonar, and ask how a sonar might be used to estimate the size of the submerged portion of an iceberg.)

2.14 In discussing the life cycle depicted in Figure 2.7, we stressed that there was nothing magical about the partition shown. Experience indicates that on any software project it is useful to partition it into stages. The exact number of these stages and their character depend on many factors, including the size and complexity of the software to be developed, the experience of the project team, the length of the

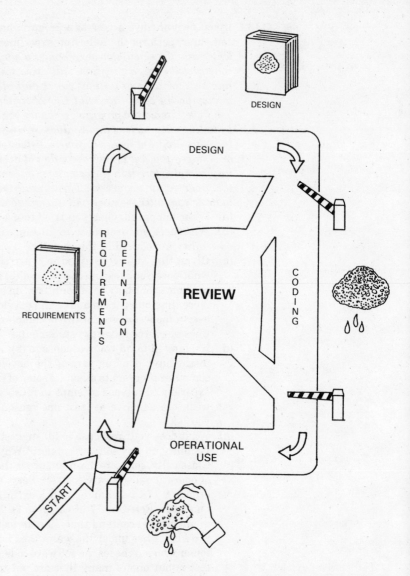

FIGURE E2.2. The life cycle referred to in Exercise 2.14.

projected schedule of the development effort, and the projected number of software products to be developed. To gain appreciation of some of the trade-offs involved with deciding on a life cycle partition for a project, consider the life cycle partition shown in Figure E2.2. The four stages in this figure are defined as follows:

Requirements definition, which focuses on defining *what* the software is to do

Design, which focuses on defining *how* the *what* defined in the Requirements Definition Stage is to be accomplished

Coding, which focuses on translating the design into language that computer hardware can understand

Operational use, which focuses on use of the software by the customer in his environment, the detection of latent defects, and the formulation of new requirements and/or modifications to existing requirements

With Figures 2.7 and E2.2 and the above definitions in mind, consider the following:

(a) In Figure 2.7, design activity is divided into two stages (Preliminary Design and Detailed Design), while in Figure E2.2 these stages have been merged. Write down at least two circumstances where the design approach in Figure 2.7 may be preferable to that shown in Figure E2.2, and give at least one reason for the judgment you made in selecting each circumstance. (*Hint:* Recall the concepts of visibility and traceability introduced in this chapter, and relate these concepts to such factors as those mentioned above.)

(b) Write down at least two circumstances where the design approach in Figure E2.2 may be preferable to that shown in Figure 2.7, and give at least one reason for the judgment used to select each circumstance.

(c) The life cycle in Figure 2.7 includes a stage between the Coding and Operational Use Stages. In Section 2.4, we defined this intermediate stage, which we called Production/Deployment, as that which focuses on mass-producing the software code after it has been thoroughly checked out, packaging the tested software code (with user documentation), and then shipping it to the customer for operational use. In Figure E2.2, the Coding Stage is followed by the Operational Use Stage. Exploiting the hint given in (a), write down at least two circumstances where having a distinct Production/Deployment Stage as defined above may actually be counterproductive, and give at least one reason for selecting each circumstance.

(d) Write down at least two circumstances (and the rationale for their selection) where having a distinct Production/Deployment Stage as defined above may save time and/or money over the life cycle approach shown in Figure E2.2.

(e) The life cycle shown in Figure E2.2 has fewer gates than the life cycle shown in Figure 2.7. Does this reduction in product assurance "obstacles" necessarily imply that if we took the same application and developed it twice—once according to the life cycle in Figure 2.7 and once according to Figure E2.2 using equally experienced project personnel—the time and money expended in going from the Requirements Definition Stage to the Operational Use Stage would be less if we go the Figure E2.2 route? (Indicate yes, no, maybe, or some combination of these three, and give at least three reasons to support your answer.)

(f) Why do you think we enclosed the word "obstacles" in quotes in (e)?

(g) Imagine that the life cycle shown in Figure E2.2 is modified to eliminate the Design Stage so that the Requirements Definition Stage is followed by the Coding Stage. Suppose also that, in this three-stage life cycle, design activity is made part of the Requirements Definition Stage (i.e., suppose the product of this stage is a document that specifies both what the software is to do and how this what is to be accomplished). Using arguments similar to those you employed in responding to (b) and (c), write down at least two circumstances where this three-stage life cycle may be preferable to that shown in Figure E2.2, and give at least one reason for selecting each circumstance. In what sense may this three-stage approach be riskier than the approach shown in Figure E2.2? Why? (*Hint:* Recall the concepts of visibility and traceability.)

(h) Redo (g) by replacing the second sentence in that part by the following sentence:

Suppose also that, in this three-stage life cycle, design activity is made part of the Coding Stage (i.e., suppose that the product of this stage is computer code which includes comment statements defining the design upon which the code is presumably based).

(i) Imagine that the life cycle shown in Figure 2.7 is modified to split the Requirements Definition Stage into the following two stages (recall Table 2.1):

Preliminary requirements definition, which focuses on defining in general, high-level terms what the software is to do

Detailed requirements definition, which focuses on defining in detail the general statements specified in the Preliminary Requirements Definition Stage

Using arguments similar to those you employed in responding to (a) and (d), write down at least two circumstances where the requirements definition approach defined above may be preferable to the requirements definition approach shown in Figure 2.7 or Figure E2.2, and give at least one reason for selecting each circumstance.

(j) Write down at least two circumstances where breaking the Requirements Definition Stage into two (or more) stages as described in (i) may actually be counterproductive, and give at least one reason for selecting each circumstance. (*Hint:* Recall your response to (c).)

(k) Based on your responses to preceding parts of this exercise, deduce at least three guidelines that can be used to define a life cycle tailored to specific project characteristics. (*Hint:* An example of a guideline might be: "If the software to be developed is state-of-the-art and thus is a high-risk endeavor, then increased visibility through a greater number of life cycle stages is required.")

2.15 Figure 2.4 illustrates the three aspects of our concept of visibility. The first aspect (permitting software to be seen) is depicted in terms of an encounter between two people wherein the question "Where's the software?" is raised. Presumably, when this question is first raised, the software exists only in somebody's head. Subsequently, the software exists so that it can be seen by the person who initially asked the question "Where's the software?" Figure 2.4 does not indicate the relationship of the two people depicted in the encounter. For each situation listed below, give at least two reasons why the question should be raised and answered. In giving your reasons, indicate when the question should be answered (i.e., at the beginning of a software project, at the end of a project just before delivery of the computer code to the customer, at some point or points in between the beginning and code delivery to the customer). (*Hint:* Recall Figure 2.2, which indicates what our definition of "software" encompasses.)

(a) The questioner is the software project manager and the other person is the software development manager.

(b) The questioner is a software developer and the other person is the questioner's boss.

(c) The questioner is a software developer and the other person is another software developer working with the questioner on the same project.

(d) The questioner is the customer and the other person is the software project manager.

(e) The questioner is the product assurance manager and the other person is the software project manager.

(f) The questioner is the customer and the other person is the software product assurance manager.

(g) The questioner is a member of a software product assurance organization and the other person is the questioner's boss.

(h) The questioner is a member of a software product assurance organization and the other person is the software project manager.

2.16 In Figure 2.6, which illustrates the concept of traceability, the sequence of events shown indicates that a software product is changed (Event q) because of a meeting wherein the change was authorized (Event o). The need for this change presumably arose from the review conducted in Event n, which presumably uncovered a missing piece in the software product prepared in Event m. Now, Figure 2.6 is generic in the sense that the software product depicted in Event m (and subsequently in Events n and q) could be either a specification document or computer code. Discuss how the missing piece depicted symbolically in Events m and n can be detected in practice for each of the following software products (this exercise anticipates some of the concepts that we examine in detail in Chapter 5):

1. Computer source code
2. Computer code operating on computer hardware
3. Design specification (a document that specifies *how* customer requirements are to be incorporated into computer code)
4. Requirements specification (a document that specifies *what* the customer ultimately wants computer code to do)

(*Hint:* Consider what event or events might immediately precede each of the products listed above. It may be useful to refer to the life cycle shown in Figure 2.7.)

REFERENCES AND ADDITIONAL READINGS

1. Abbott, R. J. *An Integrated Approach to Software Development.* New York: John Wiley & Sons, 1986.

   The twofold purpose of Abbott's textbook is stated in its preface:

   This book is intended as a text in software engineering courses and as a day-to-day working reference for practicing software engineers.

   1. It could be used as a software engineering text in computer science departments and in systems analysis courses in business and engineering. In the latter capacity, chapters 2 and 3 would be most relevant.
   2. For practicing systems analysts, software engineers, and programmers this book can serve as a useful reference for the development of requirements and software design documents, system specifications, and testing documentation (p. v).

   The chapters 2 and 3 referred to in the above citation comprise about one-third of Abbott's 300-page book and deal with the subject of requirements definition. This material probes at length the nuances that we associate with the dialogue between the wizard and the king portrayed in our Figure 2.8. It thus provides additional insight into the issue that we address at length in our book of getting an answer to the wizard's question. As indicated in item 2, quoted above, Abbott's book also addresses test documentation throughout the book and reflects the author's attitude toward the need to integrate product assurance into the software life cycle from its outset. Because the book is intended in part to be a textbook for classroom use, it includes exercises to reinforce and extend concepts discussed in the text.

2. Bersoff, E. H., V. D. Henderson, and S. G. Siegel. *Software Configuration Management: An Investment in Product Integrity*. Englewood Cliffs, N.J.: Prentice-Hall, 1980.

The definitions of most of the concepts in our Chapter 2 are based upon material in Bersoff et al. The discussion in chapter 3, on attaining and maintaining product integrity, complements and expands some of the points we make in Section 2.6. The user/buyer/seller relationship that we touch upon in Section 2.6 is addressed at length in chapters 2 and 3.

3. Driscoll, A. J. "Software Visibility and the Program Manager." *Defense Systems Management Review*, vol. 1, no. 2 (Spring 1977). Reprinted in D. J. Reifer, *Tutorial: Software Management*, 2nd ed. (Silver Spring, Md.: IEEE Computer Society Press, 1981 [IEEE Catalog No. EHO189-1]), pp. 45–58.

This article talks about the problems of making the software component of weapon systems produced by the Department of Defense (DoD) more visible so that its development can be managed. For example, the author notes in the introduction to his article that "the key for any Program Manager in obtaining suitable software is to elevate software—remove it from the category of 'data' and plan for its development on a level of importance with hardware." Here he is in effect saying that the visibility of software needs to be raised so that it can be properly managed. Pursuing this point, the author subsequently states the following, which calls to mind some of the things we mentioned in Chapter 1 and in our definition of product integrity in Section 2.6:

> What does the Program Manager need to know and be concerned about regarding the software in his weapon system? Essentially, he needs to know the same basic things that he is required to know about his hardware. The basics are:
>
> Does the software meet performance requirements?
>
> Is the software within cost?
>
> Is the software on schedule?
>
> In tne "DoD Weapon Systems Software Management" study report prepared by Johns Hopkins University [Technical Report AD-A022 160, June 1975], it is stated that a lack of software visibility, when compared with that of hardware, contributed to the fact that software was not well managed. The report also says that visibility could be increased by putting software on a par with hardware (p. 44).

The article also touches upon the topic of independent verification and validation (IV&V) and its role in raising software visibility (recall Figure 2.5). Regarding this role, the author notes the following, which should be compared with our discussion of Figure 2.13 and the user/buyer/seller relationship at the end of Section 2.6:

> The discussion of software verification to this point has been restricted to that done by the development contractor. An adjunct to verification by the development contractor is the use of an independent verification contractor—an excellent means of providing software visibility for the Program Office and the Program Manager. . . . This practice originated with a requirement for the independent check of software to insure nuclear safety and is becoming widespread. The practice, known as Independent Validation and Verification (IV&V), has been expanded to include software performance as well as nuclear safety criteria. When used properly, the IV&V contractor can provide the Program Manager comprehensive knowledge of all phases of software development. Because of having to verify that requirements have been met, the IV&V contractor is in an excellent position to provide feedback as to the testability of the requirements and the design at early design reviews (pp. 49–50).

In subsequent chapters, we return to the above points regarding IV&V in particular and product assurance in general.

4. Evans, M. W., P. H. Piazza, and J. B. Dolkas. *Principles of Productive Software Management*. New York: John Wiley & Sons, 1983.

This compact, 228-page book focuses on the project management discipline shown in Figure 2.13. It also pays considerable attention to the product assurance disciplines indicated in that figure, including a chapter on configuration management and one on testing. The book's first chapter, "The Trouble with Software," builds a case for the need to discipline software development and in the process argues strongly for product assurance. The book's approach is to "describe what is involved in making the software development process an orderly set of tasks leading to the production of a quality system that meets customer requirements" (p. 4). Thus this book offers some insights that complement and supplement some of the ideas presented in our book.

5. Gause, Donald C., and Gerald M. Weinberg. *Are Your Lights On? How to Figure Out What the Problem Really Is*. Boston: Little, Brown, and Company, 1982.

This humorous but serious 157-page book is a thought-provoking look at the implications of the wizard's question in Figure 2.8 (the book's unusual title is explained in a story therein, pp. 96–101). The book defines a *problem* as follows:

> A problem is a difference between things as *desired* and things as *perceived* (p. 15).

(Based on the above definition, does the king in Figure 2.8 have a problem?) Probing the nuances of problem formulation (which the authors point out can itself be a problem) and solution approaches, the book contains a series of maxims whose truth is amply illustrated through funny yet pointed stories. Examples of such maxims particularly pertinent to our book (especially with respect to the issue of closure between the wizard and the king in Figure 2.8) are the following:

> You can never be sure you have a correct definition [of a problem], even after the problem is solved (p. 41).

> You can never be sure you have a correct definition [of a problem], but don't ever stop trying to get one (p. 44).

> In spite of appearances, people seldom know what they want until you give them what they ask for (p. 143).

Among the topics the book addresses is problem displacement—making "problems less troublesome by putting them in someone else's back yard" (p. 53). The notion of problem displacement has particular relevance for software development and maintenance, as indicated by the following statements from the book:

> The problem of displacement is compounded by the existence of *designers*—special people whose job it is to solve problems, in advance, for other people. Designers, like landlords, seldom if ever experience the consequences of their actions. In consequence, designers continually produce *misfits. A misfit is a solution that produces a mismatch with the human beings who have to live with the solution.* Some mismatches are downright dangerous (p. 56).

(It should be noted that the above excerpt is *not* limited to a software context.) As we indicated in the sample problem on visibility in Section 2.2, and as we discuss in subsequent chapters, a primary function of software product assurance is to bring misfits to the attention of management sufficiently early in the life cycle so that, if management chooses, it can attempt to resolve the misfits.

One of the authors of the book (G. M. Weinberg) has written a number of books and articles on software-related subjects. As a result, some of the examples in *Are Your Lights On?* are set in a software context. One that has particular relevance for some of our subsequent discussion on the value to management of product assurance is the following, which Gause and Weinberg use to illustrate the importance of clearly wording a problem:

> In school, of course, we've learned that giving problems with tricky wording is "unfair"—just another way in which the school fails to prepare us for the unfair world outside its ivy-covered walls. Any computer programmer can supply a dozen examples of a misunderstood word, a misplaced comma, or an ambiguous syntax that cost someone $10,000, $100,000, $1,000,000, or just about any price you care to name.
>
> In one case, the program's specification reads, in part, "The exception information will be in the XYZ file, too."
>
> The programmer took this to mean "*Another* place the exception information appears is the XYZ file."
>
> He assumed, therefore, that the exception information was duplicated somewhere else, so he saw no need for his program to preserve it.
>
> Actually, the writer had meant "Another type of infor-

mation that appears in the XYZ file is the exception information."

Nothing was implied about this information being duplicated elsewhere, and, indeed, it wasn't duplicated. As a result, valuable and unrecoverable information was lost. Before the differing interpretations were discovered, the cost of the lost information had mounted to about $500,000—rather a large bill for one carelessly placed "too" (pp. 73–74).

This example indicates in quantitative terms how product assurance—whose application costs time and money—may save time and money (recall Figure 1.3). As we point out in subsequent chapters, one function of product assurance is to make visible ambiguities in software products such as the one illustrated above *when they first appear*—thus reducing the likelihood that they will be propagated into later life cycle stages as costly misfits. (Recall the discussion associated with Table 2.1 in Section 2.3.)

6. "IEEE Standard Glossary of Software Engineering Terminology." ANSI/IEEE Standard 729-1983, Institute of Electrical and Electronics Engineers, February 18, 1983.

The foreword of this thirty-eight-page document explains its purpose and reads in part as follows:

Software engineering is an emerging field. New terms are continually being generated, and new meanings are being adopted for existing terms. The Glossary of Software Engineering Terminology was undertaken to document this vocabulary. Its purpose is to identify terms currently used in software engineering and to present the current meanings of these terms. It is intended to serve as a useful reference for software engineers and for those in related fields and to promote clarity and consistency in the vocabulary of software engineering. It is recognized that software engineering is a dynamic area; thus the standard will be subject to appropriate change as becomes necessary.

The definitions given in this standard for software, life cycle, baseline, and (software) configuration should be compared with the definitions given in this chapter. For example, the standard gives the following three definitions for the term *configuration*:

1. The arrangement of a computer system or network as defined by the nature, number, and the chief characteristics of its functional units. More specifically, the term configuration may refer to a hardware configuration or a software configuration.
2. The requirements, design, and implementation that define a particular version of a system or system component.
3. The functional and/or physical characteristics of hardware/software as set forth in technical documentation and achieved in a product.

7. Lehman, M. M. "Programming Productivity: A Life Cycle Concept." *Proceedings of the IEEE Computer Society's 23rd International Com-*

puter Conference (COMPCON Fall 81), Washington, D.C., September 14–18, 1981. Silver Spring, Md.: IEEE Computer Society Press, 1981 (IEEE Catalog No. BG341), pp. 232–241.

The life cycle that we use in this book for exemplification is not unique in the number or names of its stages or even in its approach. This article presents several alternative approaches to our exemplification of the life cycle concept. Based on a top-down analysis of the programming process, the author develops a life cycle consisting of a series of transformations of representational models of the application concept. He then suggests that each of these transformation steps uses the same step structure.

Despite the considerable difference in his approach to the definition of a life cycle, the author espouses many of the same principles that we set forth in this book. Among them are:

The software life cycle must be partitioned in some fashion, so that it can be properly managed.

"The individual manager [of a stage or stages] seeking to meet time targets or to reduce expenditure attributable to him may cause a significant decrease of the quality or productivity associated with subsequent work on the system or increased cost of that work, for example, by permitting the introduction of unnecessary complexity or through careless fault eradication" (p. 233).

"Maintenance of all the [representational] models is of course essential if the system is to be effectively and cost-effectively maintained in a changing environment over a long period" (p. 235).

Each iteration of the common step structure requires the performance of vertical verification, horizontal verification, and validation. Vertical verification entails assessing whether the transformation from one model to the next has been made precisely, retrievably, and understandably, i.e., whether there is precise correspondence between representation models. Horizontal verification is defined by the author as the demonstration "that the set of decisions that have been taken [in the creation or modification of a model] are consistent and, in some sense, complete, covering at the very least all the requirements implied by the source [i.e., preceding] model" (p. 238). Validation is defined as the determination of "whether, in terms of one's knowledge and expectation of the remainder of the total process and of the implementation technology, the successive design activities at each step can reasonably be expected to ultimately lead to a satisfactory operational system. Moreover, for operational characteristics that have been left unspecified, validation should provide an estimate of what they are likely to be, or at least that they are in an acceptable range" (p. 238).

"The maximum degree of verification and validation at each step, leading to early discovery of faults, should make a major contribution to productivity growth both in their own right and because their application must simplify the subsequent development of a system as a consequence of the reduced error content" (p. 239).

We will elaborate on these principles in subsequent chapters. It is important to note here that they are independent of the particular life cycle chosen to represent the software development and maintenance process.

8. Metzger, P. W. *Managing a Programming Project.* 2nd ed. Englewood Cliffs, N.J.: Prentice-Hall, 1981. First edition published in 1973.

In 240 pages the author covers a lot of territory. The emphasis is on the practical, which probably explains why the book's first edition went through numerous printings. The author's approach is aptly summarized in the following extract from the preface to the first edition:

> Students in art classes often try to ape everything the instructor says and does in the vain hope that they might find his "secret." The famous watercolor instructor, John Pike, holds aloft a certain brush and with a mischievous wink proclaims that "this is the magic brush!" Needless to say, no student ever painted a masterpiece simply by using the same brush as the teacher. What's really needed is a mastering of principles, a little inspiration, and plenty of hard work. The same applies to running a programming project. You can get a lot from a book—tools, guidelines, advice, warnings, maybe even some inspiration—but no magic brush! (p. xiii)

The following states the aim of the book and gives an indication of the author's style:

> The aim of this book is to get you, the manager, to *plan*, and then *control* your project according to that plan. Almost any plan is better than none at all. You really have a clear choice: plan now and enjoy a successful project, or order yourself space in the management graveyard (p. 4).

Thus, this book offers insight into the mechanics of the project management discipline depicted at the top of the triangle in Figure 2.13.

9. Perry, W. E. *Managing Systems Maintenance.* Wellesley, Mass.: QED® Information Sciences, 1981.

This book contains many product assurance notions that complement some of the ideas presented in this and subsequent chapters. For example, the author's description of systems maintenance, which should be compared with our discussion of revisits to life cycle stages in connection with Figure 2.7, is as follows:

> System maintenance includes any activity needed to ensure that applications programs remain in satisfactory working condition. This encompasses a broad range of activities involving error correction, need specification, system and program design, coding, testing, training, and monitoring the implementation of change. The management of maintenance is the management of change (p. 1).

The author notes that "maintenance" has been given a broad range of definitions through various modifiers that actually represent different aspects of the activity defined above. In particular, the author lists (p. 1) the following types of maintenance generally performed in the software industry:

> *Corrective maintenance*—Maintenance that is conducted for the purpose of eliminating an existing error or problem.
>
> *Deferred maintenance*—Maintenance that is needed but is postponed until appropriate resources are available.

Preventive maintenance—Maintenance that occurs in anticipation of problems. For example, an application may install a fix to prevent a problem that has already occurred in another application.

Emergency maintenance—Unscheduled maintenance that is designed to eliminate a current problem situation which has stopped or otherwise affected successful operation of the application.

File maintenance—The addition, modification, or deletion of systems specifications.

Program maintenance—The addition, modification, or deletion of program instructions.

Scheduled maintenance—Maintenance that occurs at a predetermined time.

In explaining the purpose of his book in the preface, the author echoes a point that we in our book stress about spending time and money (through performing product assurance) to save time and money:

> The practices in this book may appear to be time consuming, but they work. It takes time to read a map and plot a course, but using a map gets you to your destination. The maintenance destination is more effective maintenance at a reduced cost. This book provides you the map and the direction.

10. *Proceedings of the IEEE Computer Society's Seventh International Computer Software and Applications Conference (COMPSAC 83),* Chicago, November 7–11, 1983. Silver Spring, Md.: IEEE Computer Society Press, 1983 (IEEE Catalog No. 83CH1940-6), pp. 636–639.

The articles listed below from these *Proceedings* offer some complementary and contrasting views on the concept of software visibility introduced in this chapter.

G. A. Heidenrich, "Improving Software Management Visibility Through a Detailed Quality Measurements and Objectives Program," pp. 636–637. This two-page paper reports progress on a program to improve software productivity in a 400-person organization. Echoing the theme from our Chapter 1, the paper begins:

> Since most organizations have discovered by now that software development has failed as an art form, their attention has turned to giving it some dignity as an engineering discipline. Practically every large organization has purchased or constructed a methodology, even tight budgets can be stretched a bit to obtain a promising software tool, training materials and courses in advanced techniques are becoming common, but the pressure is still on to produce more and better systems.
>
> A study of 25 large U.S. and Japanese information systems organizations conducted by the author several years ago revealed a rather dismal state of affairs in the area of software productivity. At the root of the problem was a widespread tendency to subordinate long-term improvements to short-term heroic efforts and/or quick fixes that have cumulatively resulted in enormous legacies of treacherous, unstable, costly deteriorating software (p. 636).

The purpose of the paper is subsequently explained as follows:

This paper is a progress report on the strategic improvement program adopted by one of the clients of the earlier study, and highlights the success factors that have made that program work. Those factors are:

Management visibility and commitment

A supportive corporate environment

A coordinated, multidimensional approach

A prioritized, success factor oriented decision algorithm

A total commitment to quality

Although the paper does not explicitly define what is meant by "management visibility," it appears that this term is used in the sense of "management making its presence felt," which is akin to the third aspect of our concept of visibility listed in Figure 2.4.

G. E. Murine, "Improving Management Visibility Through the Use of Software Quality Metrics," pp. 638–639. This paper talks about visibility in terms akin to the first two aspects of our concept of visibility listed in Figure 2.4. It attempts to quantify the degree to which software products can be seen by management (and others) during their development by employing a methodology called Software Quality Metrics (SQM).

11. Rosenau, M. D., Jr., and M. D. Lewin. *Software Project Management: Step by Step*. Belmont, Calif.: Lifetime Learning Publications/Wadsworth, 1984.

This book focuses on the *management* of software projects (as opposed to the other two elements of the triangle in Figure 2.13, development and product assurance). It is divided into six parts, entitled as follows:
1. Defining Software Project Goals (3 chapters)
2. Planning a Software Project (5 chapters)
3. Leading the People (4 chapters)
4. Monitoring Project Progress (5 chapters)
5. Completing the Software Project (2 chapters)
6. Other Issues (2 chapters)

Chapter 13, "The Role of the Computer Software Project Manager," deals with the infrequently addressed topic of the importance of the project manager's ability to influence other project team members ("influence rather than authority," as the authors put it). Chapter 15, "Software Project Reviews," touches on product assurance related activities that we deal with in our Chapters 4 and 5.

12. Shlaer, S., D. Grand, and S. J. Mellor. "The Project Matrix: A Model for Software Engineering." *Third Software Engineering Standards Application Workshop*, San Francisco, October 2–4, 1984. Silver Spring, Md.: IEEE Computer Society Press, 1984 (IEEE Catalog No. 84CH2071-9), pp. 77–82.

This paper reports on a (nonautomated) project management tool that, among other things, helps raise the visibility of the software development process and injects traceability into it. It complements the ideas introduced in this chapter (and discussed throughout the remainder of this book) because it indicates how visibility and traceability may be achieved on a software project without product assurance as we deal with it in this book.

chapter 3

THE ELEMENTS OF SOFTWARE PRODUCT ASSURANCE

In Chapter 2, we introduced definitions of many of the concepts upon which software product assurance is based. We are now in a position to analyze the discipline of software product assurance. We begin by recalling the definition of software product assurance given in Chapter 1:

Product assurance is a set of checks and balances interwoven into the software development process whose primary purpose is to assure (i.e., give confidence) that a software product satisfies the needs of the intended recipient. More specifically, these checks and balances are activities performed by the product developers, project management, and/or some other organization (which we refer to as a product assurance group) aimed at making a software product visible so that explicit determination can be made of product conformance to the intended recipient's needs.

From the discussion of the product integrity concept in Chapter 2, we can restate the purpose of software product assurance as follows:

The purpose of software product assurance is to give confidence that a software product with integrity is achieved.

In this chapter, we show how this purpose is achieved by describing the processes and their constituent functions underlying the above definition.

In Section 3.1, we present an overview of four processes that have historically been associated with the pursuit of product integrity (quality assurance, test and evaluation, configuration management, and verification and validation) and that we have therefore chosen to associate with our concept of software product assurance. We illustrate each process in terms of the precipitation-day counting example introduced in Section

107

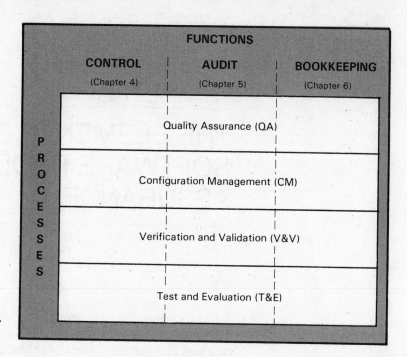

FUNCTIONS		
CONTROL (Chapter 4)	**AUDIT** (Chapter 5)	**BOOKKEEPING** (Chapter 6)
Quality Assurance (QA)		
Configuration Management (CM)		
Verification and Validation (V&V)		
Test and Evaluation (T&E)		

(P R O C E S S E S)

FIGURE 3.1. Product assurance processes and their common functions.

2.1. Our intent in Section 3.1 is to define each of these processes (subsequent chapters describe the mechanics of these processes) and to explain in terms of the above definition why we include them in the software product assurance discipline. In Section 3.2, we dissect these four processes and point out that each of them performs the same basic functions, the processes being distinguished from each other by the software products and other entities on which they operate. These basic functions—control, audit, and bookkeeping—and their relationship to the four processes are illustrated in Figure 3.1. This figure also highlights the organization of the following three chapters of this book—we devote a chapter to each function and describe how the function applies to the four processes. In this way, we are able to focus on the most basic entities underlying the product assurance discipline, while at the same time maintaining connectivity with extant literature that for the most part addresses the four processes. We conclude Section 3.2 with a sample problem illustrating the fundamental point that the three basic product assurance functions are applied not only to software products undergoing review, but also to proposed changes to reviewed products that have been approved. The purpose of the sample problem is to highlight the broad applicability of the three basic product assurance functions, thereby laying the foundation for discussions in subsequent chapters. To synthesize the concepts presented in this chapter and to emphasize that product assurance entails the integrated performance of the three basic functions, we present in Section 3.3 a simple product assurance analogue based on the notion of a balance (an instrument for determining weight). We refer to this analogue in subsequent chapters to maintain an integrated view while concentrating on the individual functions. In Section 3.4, we summarize the ideas in this chapter.

3.1 Processes Included in Product Assurance

Among the processes involved in software development and maintenance are four that are included in our definition of software product assurance. As shown in Figure 3.2, these processes are the following:

Assessing the degree to which a software product conforms to specified standards

Visibly and traceably controlling software changes

Assessing a software product's congruence with a predecessor product and with requirements

Exercising software code and assessing its operation

We subsequently discuss these processes in detail. The extent of the application of these four processes and the organizational element applying them vary widely from project to project and

FIGURE 3.2. Processes included in software product assurance.

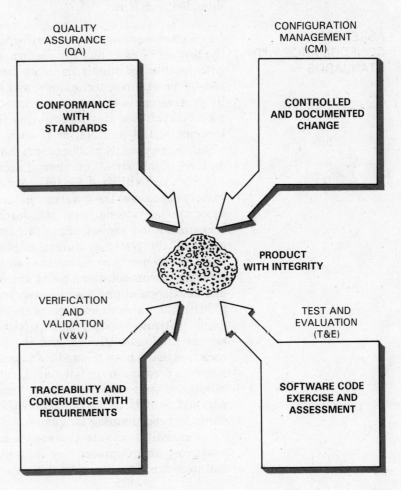

from company to company. What the processes are named also varies; there is no uniform terminology for these processes in the software industry. For example, the labels assigned by various organizations to the last process in the above list include *test and evaluation, quality assurance, acceptance testing, system testing,* and *functional configuration audit.* The labels assigned to these processes are not important in themselves. (For exposition purposes, we assign one of the commonly used labels to each of these processes when we describe them.) What is important is that each of these processes (whatever it is called), when integrated into a software development or maintenance project, provides a measure of assurance that product integrity is attained and maintained.

To substantiate our assertion that these four processes are included in our definition of software product assurance, we first describe the processes and indicate their function as a check and balance contributing to the achievement of product integrity. In terms of an example introduced in Chapter 2, we then illustrate how these processes make more visible the extent to which software products conform to the needs of the intended recipient.

ASSESSING CONFORMANCE WITH STANDARDS

Software quality assurance (SQA) is the label we assign to the process of assessing the conformance of software products with established standards. More formally defined, SQA consists of procedures, techniques, and tools applied impartially by professionals to determine whether a software product meets established standards during the development or maintenance of the product, or if such standards do not exist, whether the product reaches some minimum generally agreed-on level of industrial/commercial acceptability.

Standards utilized for this comparison may come from a variety of sources: the government, professional and industrial associations, international standards organizations, private companies, and project organizations within companies. For example, the National Bureau of Standards and the Department of Defense have established standards and guidelines on software documentation, codes for information interchange, and development and specification practices. Professional and industrial organizations such as the American National Standards Institute (ANSI), the Institute of Electrical and Electronics Engineers (IEEE), and the Electronic Industries Association (EIA) have created standards and guidelines for such items as programming languages, information-processing vocabularies, and software quality assurance plans. The International Standards Organization (ISO) has developed standards on programming languages.

Generally, private companies have their own policies, practices, and/or procedures for software development and maintenance. Often project organizations within a company establish supplemental practices and procedures for use on their particular projects. (Reference 8 at the end of this chapter contains an annotated bibliography of 128 software development standards applicable to scientific software. Reference 9 contains the names and addresses of organizations publishing catalogs and indices of standards, some of which are applicable to the field of software development and maintenance. These catalogs and indices can serve as a starting point for the selection and specification, adoption, or adaptation of standards for SQA use.)

One point of possible confusion must be clarified here. The standards referred to in our definition of SQA do not specify when software is "of high quality" or "of poor quality"—that is, they do not define what quality is. Without a specific definition of quality, the assessment of quality is a matter of judgment or speculation. These standards do specify what should or must be (or not be) in software products. Quality, in this case, refers to the degree that a software product conforms to the specified standards. It can be objectively determined by a process of comparison.

Quality assurance compares all software products to these established standards, regardless of their source, to assess the conformance between product and standard. This conformance is generally measured in terms of structure, format, and information content. SQA is applied throughout the software life cycle. During the early stages of a development effort, it is applied primarily to the documentation form of software. In the latter stages of a development effort, SQA is applied both to the program code and to the documentation defining the code as built.

This process of assessing the conformance of software products to established standards (which we call quality assurance) is one of the desired checks on, and balances to, the development activities. Development project management or buyers prescribe the standards that are to be adhered to in the development of software. The development organization attempts to conform to these prescribed standards in the step-by-step development of the software products. The SQA organization checks each software product to assess its conformance to the applicable standards. This independent check provides greater visibility to management with regard to the state of a software product (by identifying any discrepancies between the product and the standards governing its development). This increased visibility, in turn, enhances the traceability of the product's development. This visibility and traceability provide insight into the degree to which user needs are satisfied, and costs and schedules are met, thus providing a measure of assurance that product integrity is attained and maintained. For these reasons we have chosen to associate SQA with our concept of software product assurance.

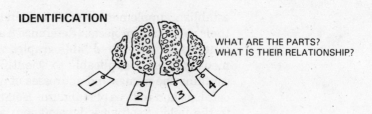

IDENTIFICATION

WHAT ARE THE PARTS?
WHAT IS THEIR RELATIONSHIP?

CONTROL

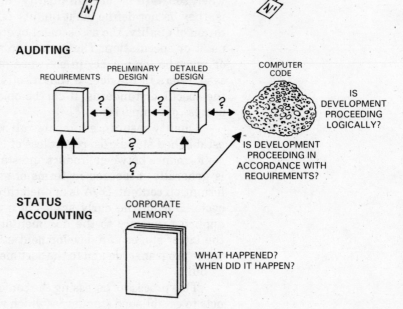

WHAT IS THE IMPACT IF
WE MAKE THIS CHANGE?

SHOULD WE MAKE
THIS CHANGE?

FIGURE 3.3. The four component elements of software configuration management. Adapted from W. Bryan and S. Siegel, "Product Assurance: Insurance Against a Software Disaster," *Computer,* vol. 17, no. 4 (April 1984), p. 79. Reprinted by permission of the publisher.

AUDITING

REQUIREMENTS   PRELIMINARY DESIGN   DETAILED DESIGN   COMPUTER CODE

IS DEVELOPMENT PROCEEDING LOGICALLY?

IS DEVELOPMENT PROCEEDING IN ACCORDANCE WITH REQUIREMENTS?

STATUS ACCOUNTING   CORPORATE MEMORY

WHAT HAPPENED?
WHEN DID IT HAPPEN?

CONTROLLING SOFTWARE CHANGES

For the process of controlling software changes, we use the label *software configuration management* (SCM). SCM has the primary objective of cost-effective management of a system's life cycle products. Compactly stated, SCM is a management discipline for visibly, traceably, and formally controlling software evolution.

Fundamental to SCM is the management of software baselines (recall Figure 2.9). Management of these baselines and the products contained therein entails the exercise of the four component elements of SCM shown in Figure 3.3.[1]

One element of SCM is configuration identification. Identification entails determining the constituent parts of a software product and the relationship among those parts, and labeling the parts thus determined (recall Figure 2.11). In Figure

---

[1] For a detailed discussion of these four SCM elements, see Reference 2 at the end of this chapter.

3.3 we suggest this identification by illustrating the labeled parts of a software product and the relationship among these parts. If the configuration is to be properly managed, the components of any software configuration (such as a requirements or a design specification) must be identified, for the following reasons:

Configuration identification provides greater visibility of the software. We have uniquely labeled each part and shown how the parts relate to each other.

Identification facilitates communication about the software. It is usually more effective to state, for example, that "part 2" is to be replaced than "the function that validates operator entries of action due dates according to the priority of the action item" is to be replaced.

Consequently, identification promotes the exercise of management control. With greater visibility and improved communications, management decisions can be made and executed more knowledgeably.

The second element of SCM is software configuration control. Software configuration control provides the administrative mechanism for precipitating, preparing, evaluating, approving/disapproving, and implementing all changes to software throughout the system life cycle. In Figure 3.3, we have indicated a change to a software configuration in progress, with the part labeled N being replaced with the part labeled N'. This change processing is applied to changes in requirements, correction of software design deficiencies, enhancements of system capabilities, and all other suggested modifications to the software. To evaluate, and approve or disapprove, these changes formally, a *configuration control board* (CCB) is established. The CCB exercises the desired control in a formal and recorded manner. (The CCB is the forum referred to in Chapters 1 and 2. It is discussed at length in Chapter 4.)

The third element of SCM is configuration auditing. The primary functions of software configuration auditing are configuration verification and configuration validation. Configuration verification checks that whatever is intended for each component of a software configuration as specified in one baseline is actually achieved in the succeeding baseline. Verification thus facilitates the achievement of traceability, one of the attributes of product integrity. Configuration validation ascertains that the software configuration is congruent[2] with software requirements, i.e., that the software requirements are

---

[2] See Figure 3.4 for a definition of the concept of *congruence*. In the figure, requirement A is associated with the left-hand piece of the software product (a one-to-one relationship), requirements P and X are associated with the top piece of the software product (a many-to-one relationship), and requirement Z is associated with the two right-hand pieces of the software product (a one-to-many relationship). Notice that we are not using congruence in the mathematical or geometric sense. We elaborate on this concept of congruence in Chapter 5.

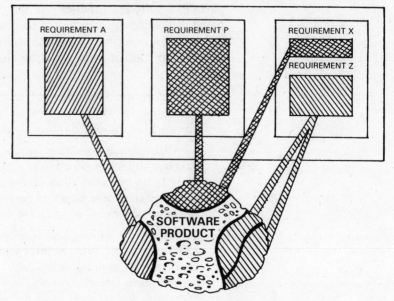

FIGURE 3.4. A software product is congruent with the requirements specification when each software requirement can be associated with piece(s) of the product. A software piece may be associated with more than one requirement, and one requirement may be associated with more than one piece.

fulfilled. Thus, validation is directly involved with two of the attributes of product integrity—satisfaction of user needs and fulfillment of performance criteria. Verification in Figure 3.3 has been represented by the lines between successive software products. Validation in this figure is represented by the lines from the various software products leading back to the requirements for software.

The fourth element of SCM is configuration status accounting. This element records the activity associated with the other three SCM elements. As indicated in Figure 3.3, configuration status accounting provides answers to the questions "What happened?" and "When did it happen?" It therefore provides the means for tracing the development of the software system. As indicated in Chapter 2, this traceability is one of the attributes included in our definition of product integrity.

Change occurs continually to software throughout its life cycle. Changes are made to software documentation and to software code by the development organization. By ensuring that the process of changing the software is disciplined and documented, SCM balances the incorporation of change by the development organization. SCM involves the formal identification of each change and the tracking of the status of each change from inception to incorporation. SCM assures that each change is approved by proper authority, is authorized for the current version of the software, and is correctly made. Consequently, SCM provides visibility into the precise configuration of the developing software at all points in its life cycle and provides traceability of the software throughout its life cycle. For these reasons, we have chosen to associate SCM with our concept of software product assurance.

ASSESSING CONGRUENCE WITH A PREDECESSOR PRODUCT AND REQUIREMENTS

We assign the label *verification and validation* (V&V) to the process of assessing traceability and congruence of software products with predecessor documents and requirements. V&V is quite close to software configuration auditing, which we discussed in the preceding subsection. In contrast to software configuration auditing, V&V deals with issues that do not pertain solely to the software configuration (e.g., validating that a user's manual contains information on how to use the system to satisfy every system requirement, or verifying that a software specification addresses performance criteria set forth in a system specification). Verification and validation are defined as follows:

Verification is the assessment of whether a software life cycle product logically follows from a predecessor product.

Validation is the assessment of whether a software life cycle product is congruent with requirements.

The process of assessing traceability among the software products and the congruence of these products with user requirements is directed toward the attainment of several attributes in our definition of product integrity. These attributes are the satisfaction of user needs and performance criteria, and the establishment of traceability throughout the software life cycle. By helping keep the software development effort on track, this process indirectly assists in achieving the product integrity attributes of meeting cost and schedule expectations. Starting from the software requirements, the developers create a sequence of software products, each product based upon a predecessor software product. The V&V process verifies that the requirements can be traced through the entire sequence of software products and validates that each software product in the sequence is congruent with the requirements. These checks determine whether the development of the software product has remained on track and ensure that any oversights or deviations from requirements are made visible. For these reasons, we have chosen to associate V&V with our concept of software product assurance.

EXERCISING SOFTWARE CODE AND ASSESSING ITS OPERATION

Test and evaluation (T&E) is the label we assign to the exercising of software code and the assessment of its operation. T&E assesses whether software code meets its objectives by executing the code in a live or nearly live environment[3] using written test plans and procedures. Generally, a functional testing approach is stressed to demonstrate explicitly the presence (or absence) of functional capabilities called for in requirements and design specifications. This testing of individual software functions is usually combined with performance testing

---

[3] By a *live or nearly live environment,* we mean an environment that is identical to or closely approximates the environment in which the user operates. We discuss this subject in Chapter 5.

to demonstrate the satisfaction (or lack thereof) of performance requirements stipulated in requirements and design specifications. The execution phase of T&E follows the completion of unit and integration testing[4] of the software functions, which are typically performed by the development group. Planning for T&E must occur earlier in the life cycle. In particular, during the design stages of the software life cycle, T&E activities focus on reviewing the capabilities documented in the requirements and design documents to plan appropriate strategies for testing the software capabilities. These strategies are expanded into detailed, step-by-step test procedures that, when executed, demonstrate the extent to which the software requirements and the specifications contained in the design document have been fulfilled.

The objective of T&E is to provide a high degree of confidence in the validity of the following assertions:

> The software system under test will satisfy the user's specified requirements and performance criteria.

> The system will operate in accordance with its user's manual and its operator's manual. (By *user's manual* we mean instructions provided to the user of a system that enable him to apply it to his problem. An *operator's manual* instructs the computer system operator how to start and run the computer system.)

> The system will operate for some specified period of time without failure.

> When the software system fails, it can be returned to operation after only a brief delay.

> The system will not be missing any of its software parts.

To achieve this objective, T&E is performed on the software system. As a result of T&E, shortfalls in the validity of these assertions are made visible. The developer responds to eliminate these shortfalls, and T&E will again be performed. This iterative process continues until there is a high degree of confidence that the above assertions are valid (i.e., that the software code has integrity).

The process of exercising software code and assessing its functionality (which we call test and evaluation) has objectives similar to the process of assessing traceability and congruence to requirements (V&V). By exercising and assessing the functionality of a (coded) software product, the T&E process provides visibility into how well the software product meets user needs and performance criteria and whether the software product logically follows from predecessor software design documents. In essence, T&E inspects the coded form of software and

---

[4] By *unit testing,* we mean the exercising of a unit (a separately compilable sequence of code statements) to ascertain whether it meets its design specifications. By *integration testing,* we mean the exercising of progressively larger collections of units to check out the integrated operation of each collection of units. The final step in integration testing is the exercising, as a single entity, of all the units in the system under development.

compares its operation against reference standards calibrated with information from requirements and design documentation. For these reasons, we have chosen to associate T&E with our concept of software product assurance. In Chapter 5, we explore the mechanics of the T&E process.

EXEMPLIFICATION OF THE FOUR PRODUCT ASSURANCE PROCESSES

We now exemplify the four product assurance processes just discussed in general terms to illustrate in specific terms how they make more visible the degree to which software products conform to the intended recipient's needs. As a vehicle for this illustrative process, we use the precipitation-day counting example introduced in Section 2.1 and subsequently elaborated on in Sections 2.2 and 2.3. Recall that Section 2.1 introduced a portion of a requirements specification and a portion of a design specification for a system to maintain monthly counts of days with measurable precipitation. For convenience, these partial specifications are reproduced in Figures 3.5 and 3.6, respectively. (Figure 3.5 contains more of the detailed require-

FIGURE 3.5. Portion of detailed requirements specification for precipitation-day counting system.

---

3. In maintaining monthly counts of rain days and snow days, the software shall conform to the following rules:

   a. A day begins at midnight local time and terminates 24 hours later.

   b. If rain totaling at least 0.02 inch fell during the 24-hour period defined in a above, the number of rain days shall be incremented by 1. (Note: If during one continuous period of rain that overlaps two days at least 0.02 inch fell, but at least 0.02 inch did not fall in either day, then the number of rain days shall be incremented by 1.)

   c. If snow totaling at least 0.5 inch fell during the 24-hour period defined in a above, the number of snow days shall be incremented by 1. (Note: If during one continuous period of snow that overlaps two days at least 0.5 inch fell, but at least 0.5 inch did not fall in either day, then the number of snow days shall be incremented by 1.)

   •
   •
   •

7. Upon user request, the software shall produce a precipitation-day report for all months for which data are available in the calendar year specified by the user. This report shall contain the following information:

   • Month.

   • Number of rain days (i.e., days in which more than 0.02 inch of rain fell) in month.

   • Number of snow days (i.e., days in which more than 0.5 inch of snow fell) in month.

   • Number of precipitation-days (i.e., number of rain days plus number of snow days) in month.

4.2 To compute the number of rain days in a month, proceed as follows:

(1) Retrieve a record for day X from file **RAINM** containing the following elements:

    (a) Hourly rainfall amounts.

    (b) Overlap flag.

(2) Sum the hourly rainfall amounts.

(3) If the sum is greater than 0.02, add **1** to the value of **RAINDAYS** in file **PRECIPCOUNT**.

(4) If the sum is less than 0.02 but the overlap flag is set to **1**, retrieve a record for day X-1 from file **RAINM**; sum backward from midnight the hourly rainfall amounts until a **0** hourly rainfall amount is encountered; if this sum plus the sum from day X is greater than 0.02, add **1** to the value of **RAINDAYS** in file **PRECIPCOUNT**.

FIGURE 3.6. Portion of design specification for precipitation-day counting system.

ments specification than Section 2.1 showed.) Section 2.2 touched on the example again in discussing four ways to make software more visible. We now reexamine these ways in light of the four product assurance processes we have been discussing.

Way 1: Standards Checking. In the detailed requirements specification shown in Figure 3.5, rules are specified for computing monthly counts of rain days and snow days. These rules are examined with respect to their conformance with two standards whose use was specified for the project. Portions of these standards are reproduced in Figures 3.7 and 3.8. The first standard (Figure 3.7) imposes documentation content and format conventions for the company, including provisions that all documents must be complete, internally consistent, unambiguous, and testable. The other standard (Figure 3.8) was established for the particular project developing this system and contains provisions unique to the project. One of these provisions stipulates that all data shall be expressed in metric units.

Comparison of the detailed requirements specification with these standards reveals the following three discrepancies:
1. The detailed requirements specification does not conform to paragraph 4b of the XYZ Company Software Documentation Standard (Figure 3.7) because the rules in the detailed requirements specification are incomplete. The rules do not cover the case where one continuous period of precipitation overlaps the last day of one month and the first day of the following month (and that meets the minimum precipitation criteria specified on both days). It is not clear which month is to be credited with the rain (or snow) day.

```
┌─────────────────────────────────────────────────────────────────────────┐
│                            XYZ Company                                    │
│                  Software Documentation Standard                          │
│                                                                           │
│     . . .                                                                 │
│                                                                           │
│  2.   Scope.  This standard applies to all software developed and maintained by this │
│       company . . . .                                                      │
│                                                                           │
│                                                                           │
│     . . .                                                                 │
│                                                                           │
│  4.   General Standards.  The following standards apply to all software documents produced │
│       on a project:                                                        │
│                                                                           │
│                                                                           │
│     . . .                                                                 │
│                                                                           │
│  b.   All documents produced in accordance with this standard shall be complete, │
│       internally consistent, unambiguous, and testable.                   │
│                                                                           │
│                                                                           │
│     . . . .                                                               │
│                                                                           │
└─────────────────────────────────────────────────────────────────────────┘
```

FIGURE 3.7. Portion of XYZ Company Software Documentation Standard.

2. The detailed requirements specification does not conform to paragraph 4b of the XYZ Company Software Documentation Standard (Figure 3.7) because the specification is internally inconsistent. Section 3 of the detailed requirements specification in Figure 3.5 states that the minimum precipitation values for counting purposes are at least 0.02 inch for rain and at least 0.5 inch for snow, while section 7 specifies the minimum values as more than 0.02 inch for rain and more than 0.5 inch for snow.

3. The detailed requirements specification does not conform to paragraph 6a of the Project PRECIP Software Standard (Figure 3.8). The requirements rules do not conform to the project standard in that minimum precipitation values in the specification are stated in inches rather than in millimeters or centimeters, as called for by the standard.

FIGURE 3.8. Portion of Project PRECIP Software Standard.

```
┌─────────────────────────────────────────────────────────────────────────┐
│                           Project PRECIP                                  │
│                        Software Standard                                  │
│              . . .                                                        │
│                                                                           │
│                                                                           │
│     2.   Scope.  This standard applies to Project PRECIP . . . .          │
│                                                                           │
│                                                                           │
│              . . .                                                        │
│                                                                           │
│     6.   Data.                                                            │
│                                                                           │
│          a.   All data will be expressed in metric units.                 │
│                                                                           │
│                                                                           │
│              . . . .                                                      │
│                                                                           │
└─────────────────────────────────────────────────────────────────────────┘
```

This way is clearly the process we labeled *quality assurance* (QA)—assessing conformance with standards. Performing QA in this example has made visible three defects in the detailed requirements specification, presumably before any design has been undertaken. How has this effort contributed to the achievement of product integrity for this development effort? Certainly the process contributes to making the detailed requirements specification more complete and consistent. This contribution, in turn, increases the likelihood of satisfying the user's needs. In addition, resolving these discrepancies at this point in the life cycle (before the design stage has begun) prevents wasteful expenditures of time and money designing and implementing features that are incorrect or undesired (recall Figure 1.3). This prevention contributes to achieving the desired software end product within budget and on schedule.

Way 2: Logical Progression Checking. When the design specification (Figure 3.6) for the precipitation-day counting system is produced, the product assurance organization of the company developing the software compares the document to the detailed requirements specification to check whether the former document logically follows from the latter document and whether the former document is congruent with the latter document. We labeled this comparison process *verification and validation* (V&V). (Since the predecessor product is the detailed requirements specification in this case, this comparison could be considered either verification or validation.) The process proceeds by finding corresponding (in terms of functional capabilities) parts (sentences, paragraphs, or pages) of the two documents. The product assurance practitioner then compares these parts to assess whether the design specification is congruent with the detailed requirements specification.

This V&V activity uncovers two discrepancies in the partial documents given in Figures 3.5 and 3.6. Both these discrepancies (shown in Figure 3.9) have an impact on the achievement of product integrity. For certain data sets, rules 3 and 4 of the design specification will produce an incorrect count of the number of rain days in the month being calculated. The algorithm contained in the design specification is therefore unreliable. Thus, the user's need to count rain days in a month is only partially satisfied, and his need for reliable performance has not been obtained. Correction of this problem will require replacement of the algorithm in the design document with another algorithm that satisfies the requirements specification. It is clearly less expensive to replace the algorithm at this point in the software life cycle (before any code has been written) than to correct it later on, say, during acceptance testing.

This V&V activity continues throughout the life cycle, with each software product being compared to its predecessor, to assess whether the product logically follows from the predecessor, and to its requirements, to assess whether the product is congruent with these requirements.

V&V Discrepancies Observed in Precipitation-Day Counting System

1. Rule 3 of the design specification specifies an action to be taken if the sum of hourly rainfall amounts for a day is <u>greater than</u> 0.02 inch, while paragraph 3b of the detailed requirements specification requires the same action if the sum of hourly rainfall amounts for a day is <u>at least</u> 0.02 inch. The two documents thus require different actions by the system when the rainfall sum is exactly 0.02 inch.

2. Rule 4 of the design specification is inconsistent with the note in paragraph 3.b of the detailed requirements specification for the following data sets:

Data Set	Rationale
a. X = 1, i.e., day X is the first day of the month; the overlap flag is set; the only rainfall on day X = 1 is 0.015 inch from 12 m. to 1 a.m.; and the only rainfall on the last day of the previous month is 0.015 inch from 11 p.m. to 12 m.	If X = 1, then X-1 = 0, i.e., day X-1 is the zeroth day of the month. Presumably file RAINM will not contain a record for day 0 of a month. The design is silent on what will happen if a nonexistent record is referenced, but probably an error message is given. It is unlikely that the number of rain days will be incremented if the design is followed in this case. On the other hand, during one continuous period of rain that overlapped two days, at least 0.02 inch of rain fell, but at least 0.02 inch of rain did not fall in either day. This set of data satisfies the note in paragraph 3.b of the requirements specification, and thus the number of rain days should be incremented by one.

b. The overlap flag is set for day X, and the only rainfall amounts on days X-1 and X are as follows:

Day	Time	Rainfall (inches)
X-1	11 p.m. - 12 m.	0.005
X	12 m. - 1 a.m.	0.006
X	6 p.m. - 7 p.m.	0.01

The sum of rainfall for day X is 0.016 inch and the overlap flag is set. In accordance with paragraph 4.2 (4) of the design specification, the rainfall at the end of day X-1 (0.005 inch) is added to the sum of rainfall for day X (0.016 inch) which is greater than 0.02 inch. Thus, the design indicates that the number of rain days is incremented by one. Note, however, that the rainfall during the continuous period overlapping days X-1 and X is 0.011 inch. Since this amount is less than 0.02 inch, the note in paragraph 3.b of the requirements specification does not apply. Since the rainfall on both day X and day X-1 is less than 0.02 inch, the number of rain days is not incremented for this data set according to the requirements specification.

c. The overlap flag is set for day X, and the only rainfall amounts on days X-1 and X are as follows:

Day	Time	Rainfall (inches)
X-1	11 p.m. - 12 m.	0.03
X	12 m. - 1 a.m.	0.005

The rainfall on day X (0.005 inch) is less than 0.02 inch and the overlap flag is set. In accordance with paragraph 4.2 (4) of the design specification, the rainfall at the end of day X-1 (0.03 inch) is added to the sum of rainfall (0.005 inch) for day X, yielding a sum (0.035 inch) greater than 0.02 inch. Thus, the design would cause the number of rain days to be incremented by one. However, per the note in paragraph 3.b of the requirements specification, the number of rain days will be incremented by one only if at least 0.02 inch did not fall in either day X or X-1. Since that amount of rain was exceeded on day X-1, the number of rain days is not incremented in accordance with the requirements specification.

FIGURE 3.9. Discrepancies observed as a result of verification and validation in Section 3.1.

Way 3: Testing. The activity described as Way 3 in Section 2.2 was clearly the process we have labeled *test and evaluation* (T&E). We discuss the testing activity at length in Chapter 5. Here we confine our discussion to how T&E might be employed on our precipitation-day counting system. This activity begins in the form of test planning right after the requirements specification has been approved as a baseline. One of the central aspects of this planning is specification of a set of tests documented in written step-by-step test procedures to be executed to demonstrate that the final software product satisfies the detailed requirements specification. Such a set might be the following:

Test	Purpose
. . .	
30	Calculate monthly accumulated precipitation
31	Count monthly rain days
32	Count monthly snow days
. . .	

After the tests have been specified, a step-by-step test procedure is developed to fulfill the purpose of each test. Development of the test procedures follows the baselining of the design specification and reflects the design specification in the details of the actions to be taken and of the results to be expected. Thus, these step-by-step test procedures are an amalgamation of the detailed requirements specification and of the design specification.

Finally, prior to delivery to the customer, these test procedures are executed using the software system that has been developed. During this execution, the observed results of exercising a test procedure step may differ from the expected results derived from the requirements and design specifications. This difference is reported in each such instance. For example, the following report (previously shown in Section 2.2) might be made:

Execution of test procedure 31, which was designed to exercise the customer's rain-day-counting requirement, produced the following discrepancy:

	Rain Days	
Input Rain Values (inches)	Expected	Observed
0.02, 0.19, 0.01, 0.33, 1.75, negative 0.10	4	5

The rain days expected are those whose rainfall values were at least 0.02 inch—namely, 0.02, 0.19, 0.33, and 1.75. The test observation of the number of rain days in the input data set (5) could be the result of the following or some other software problems:

The software code does not recognize negative numbers, and thus counted negative 0.10 inch as a rain day.

The software code uses 0.01 inch as a threshold value, and thus counted 0.01 inch as a rain day.

The software code counts threshold values twice and thus counted 0.02 inch twice.

The net effect of this process is to compare the software system with the requirements and design specifications through the use of the test procedures and to report any observed discrepancies.

Way 4: Change Tracking. Recall from the discussion in Section 2.2 that Way 4 to achieve software visibility was to keep track of the software changes resulting from the activities of the other three ways. We have now seen in the discussion immediately preceding that these other three ways are the processes of QA, V&V, and T&E. Each of these processes as exemplified above involved comparing a software product with something else (sometimes another software product) and reporting the results of the comparisons as discrepancies (unless there were no discrepancies, in which case the report would indicate such). These discrepancies, when resolved, would lead to changes in the software. The activity we are discussing here—the tracking, controlling, and accounting for software changes—is the process we have labeled *software configuration management* (SCM).

How would SCM be applied to our precipitation-day counting system? It would be applied continually throughout the life cycle in a variety of ways. One way is to keep track of the discrepancies revealed by the processes of QA, V&V, and T&E, as exemplified in the preceding paragraphs. These discrepancies are identified (configuration identification) and then investigated. The results of these investigations are considered at a meeting convened to resolve discrepancies, and decisions on their disposition are made (configuration control). An archive that records each step in this process is maintained (configuration status accounting).

We have provided portions of the detailed requirements specification and the design specification in Figures 3.5 and 3.6, respectively. These documents (and other software products produced during the development of this system) will be identified (configuration identification) and audited (configuration auditing), and decisions will be made as to whether to establish them as baselines (configuration control).

Other changes in the precipitation-day counting system may be introduced during its development. Suppose, for example, that it is desired to extend the system to include counting days on which a specified amount of sleet fell. The SCM process would identify, audit, control, and account for this change as well as for all others. ☐

This discussion completes our exemplification of the four product assurance processes. We have shown how each of these processes provides a check and balance to the efforts of the software developers. This discussion also completes our gradual delineation of these four processes. In Chapter 1 we introduced four (unnamed) product assurance activities which helped raise the visibility of the software development process and threaded it with traceability. Then in Chapter 2 we sketched four ways that product assurance can make software more visible and added detail to the processes and illustrated them in simple situations. Now we have completed their introduction by providing a definition, a full description, and an example of their function as a check and balance.

The four product assurance processes provide confidence that software products with integrity have been achieved. Performance of all these processes involves management personnel, development personnel, and other personnel independent of the developers. This latter group of people may be known by different job titles—quality assurance practitioners, configuration managers, auditors, or testers—but note that they are all independent from the developers. Organizational independence is a relative matter. Here independence does not mean that these personnel must be from outside the company or agency or department or any other group. The sole constraint is that these personnel should be independent from the development personnel. This organizational independence is necessary to maintain an adequate check and balance on development activities, i.e., an unbiased alternative viewpoint to present to management.[5]

At the beginning of this section, we asserted that the four processes—QA, SCM, V&V, and T&E—were part of the product assurance discipline. The foregoing descriptions indicate how each of these processes is a check and balance on other software development and maintenance activities for the purpose of giving confidence that software products with integrity are achieved. Quality assurance checks whether a software product conforms to established standards making visible any items of nonconformance. SCM balances the incorporation of change by developers and provides a discipline for visibly, traceably, and formally controlling software evolution. The process of V&V is applied to every software product created or modified by the developer during the life cycle. It makes visible any oversights or deviations from requirements and from predecessor products. Finally, T&E applied to the coded form of software makes shortfalls from requirements and design documents visible. Each of these processes falls within the purview of software product assurance as defined at the beginning of this chapter because, as we have explained, each gives confidence that a software product with integrity is achieved.

3.2 Basic Functions of Software Product Assurance

Thus far in this chapter we have taken a look at four processes—QA, SCM, V&V, and T&E—that are included in the software product assurance discipline. In this section, we dissect these four processes into their basic functions and observe that the same basic functions are common to all the processes (recall Figure 3.1). Exploiting this observation, we can then construct a simple functional model that applies to all four product assurance processes.

In the descriptions presented in Section 3.1, the reader may have noticed that the four processes all incorporate the fundamental function of comparison. In QA, a software product is compared with a standard; in SCM, with its preceding configuration; in V&V, with its predecessor software product and with its requirements; and in T&E, with its design document and its requirements specification. As a result of this common comparison function, the processes can be shown to be partially equivalent; that is, QA, SCM, V&V, and T&E are in some measure equivalent processes operating on different entities.

Consider, for example, the performance of test and evaluation on software code in a live or nearly live environment. T&E is performed according to a set of test plans and procedures developed from predecessor software documentation—

---

[5] Readers interested in additional consideration of the subject of organizational independence should do Exercise 3.10 at the end of this chapter.

namely, the software requirements and the preliminary and detailed design specifications (recall Figure 2.7). These test procedures state that specific actions be taken with respect to the software under test and indicate the corresponding results expected from those actions. From a different viewpoint, however, this T&E process could also be considered the performance of QA. From the QA viewpoint, the predecessor documentation can be considered the standard against which the software product is compared. (Here, we use the connotation of standard as "something established for use as a rule or basis of comparison" as opposed to the connotation "criterion set for usages or practices."[6]) This standard, the predecessor documentation, specifies that certain results should be obtained if certain actions are performed. The execution of a test using the test procedures assesses whether the software product conforms to the standard. However, this activity is, by our definition, a description of a QA process. Therefore, the process of executing software in a live or nearly live environment according to written test procedures embodying requirements and design can be viewed functionally as both a T&E and a QA process.

Similarly, the performance of T&E can also be viewed as a V&V process. As stated in the preceding paragraph, the test procedures are based on the software requirements and design documentation. Execution of the test procedures, a T&E process, involves verification that the software code being tested meets the specifications of the design documents, and validation that the tested software code is congruent with the software requirements. That is, execution of the test procedures is functionally also a V&V process.

The V&V process (comparison of a software product with a predecessor product and a requirements document) can be viewed as equivalent to a QA process (comparison of a software product against a standard). A predecessor product can be viewed as a standard for the product of the next subsequent stage, and the requirements document can be viewed as a standard for validating all subsequent products. That is, V&V can be viewed as a form of QA.

It was previously mentioned that the configuration auditing element of SCM is an activity quite similar to V&V. From the preceding paragraphs, we saw that V&V is in some sense equivalent to QA and to T&E. Similar arguments can be applied to indicate that there is functional equivalency between configuration auditing and QA and between configuration auditing and T&E. In truth, the four processes labeled QA, T&E, V&V, and SCM are not distinct in nature but have considerable functional equivalency.

Does this equivalency indicate that the performance of all four processes results in considerable overkill in striving for

---

[6] *Webster's New World Dictionary,* Second College Edition (Cleveland: William Collins Publishers, 1980).

our objective of assuring that software products satisfy the needs of their intended recipients? Could three of the four processes be eliminated to avoid this "duplication" of effort? The answer to these questions is a resounding "No." These processes are not duplicates; each looks at a software product from a different point of view and operates on different entities. The results provided by each process are in general different. The processes simply include the fundamental function of comparison. Each process is a separate check and balance interwoven into the software development process. All are needed if we are to obtain our objective of developing software products with integrity.

This function of comparison—which we term the *audit function*—that is common to all four of the product assurance processes leads to other common functions among the processes. Consider that the act of comparing two entities will at some point generally lead to the uncovering of discrepancies between a software product and the software product or other entity with which it is being compared. All these discrepancies must be recorded, resolved, and accounted for, if the audit function is to serve any useful purpose. For example, the outcome of T&E effort may be a test report, listing actual results of executing test procedures that differed from expected results. A QA report may list instances where a software product does not conform to prescribed standards. A V&V report may list verification discrepancies where a software product did not logically follow from its predecessor software product, or validation discrepancies where a software product was incongruent with its requirements specification.

Resolution of the discrepancies resulting from the audit function will, in general, lead to changes in the audited software product and/or to changes in other software products. (In the latter case, for example, a discrepancy observed when auditing a design document—such as a capability being included in the design that was not required by the requirements specification—might lead to a change to the requirements specification.) These changes to software products must be carefully controlled. Control is necessary if product integrity is to be achieved. If control is not exercised over the resolution of these discrepancies, some discrepancies may be overlooked, and some changes may be overlooked, or incorrectly formulated, or incorrectly made, or inappropriately applied (possibly counteracting or corrupting another change). Lack of change control will cause the loss of the visibility and traceability obtained through the audit function.

In addition to audit and change control, a third function common to all four product assurance processes can be observed—bookkeeping. Many events occurring when the four product assurance processes are executed need to be recorded, stored, and reported. These events include audits of software products, the discrepancies arising from the audits, the change control decisions, and the changes themselves. Bookkeeping of these events maintains and enhances the visibility and traceability on a project. Bookkeeping enables us to know what happened when. It keeps events from being overlooked, forgotten, ignored, or misperceived.

From the preceding discussion, we have seen that each of the four product assurance processes has at its heart a comparison or audit function. From this audit function, each of the four processes produces discrepancies which are reported. Change control must be exercised by each process over these discrepancies and the audited software products. Finally, each process must maintain a record of project events to enhance visibility and traceability. These three functions—audit, change control, and bookkeeping—are the basic functions of each of the four product assurance processes (recall Figure 3.1).

Having analyzed the product assurance processes to obtain their three basic functions, we now synthesize these functions into a simple model of the product assurance discipline. This model is shown in Figure 3.10. Let us now observe how the basic functions interact and how the model relates to the product assurance processes.

In the context shown in Figure 3.10, a software product has been produced as a result of activities undertaken during the current life cycle stage. The circle labeled "Current Life Cycle Stage" represents the development of this software product; it does not represent all the current life cycle stage activities, since the ensuing product assurance activities also occur within the current life cycle stage. The software product may be a requirements specification, a design specification, computer source or object code, computer code executing on hardware, or any other product meeting our definition of software given in Section 2.1. We now explain each of the three product assurance functions just discussed and their interaction in terms of Figure 3.10. This explanation establishes the framework for the remainder of the book.

THE AUDIT FUNCTION

The audit function of software product assurance (discussed in detail in Chapter 5) compares the software product to several other entities to determine whether any discrepancies exist between the two compared items. The entities with which the software product is compared may include a predecessor product, the requirements specification, a test specification, or standards. We have defined the comparison of a software product to a predecessor product as *verification*. If the developed software product is the requirements specification, no predecessor product exists, and verification is not performed.

The comparison of a software product to the requirements specification—*validation*—is a key element in determining whether product integrity has been achieved in the software

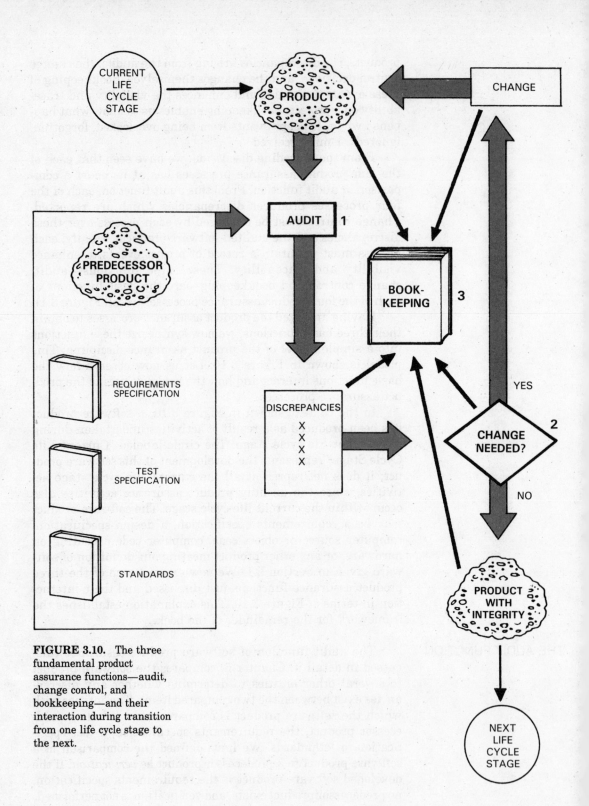

FIGURE 3.10. The three fundamental product assurance functions—audit, change control, and bookkeeping—and their interaction during transition from one life cycle stage to the next.

product. As in the case of verification, validation is not performed if the software product is the requirements specification (but the product is checked for internal consistency and potential language ambiguities).

The comparison of a software product in the form of code to the requirements and design specifications using written test procedures executed in a live or nearly live environment is the process we have labeled *test and evaluation*.[7] A test procedure, as we use the term, is a step-by-step procedure to carry out the purpose of a specific test. As we have previously discussed, each test procedure is derived from the requirements specification and the design specification.

We have labeled comparison of a software product with standards *quality assurance*. This comparison applies to any software product, provided that appropriate standards have been established prior to development of the software product.

Whenever a comparison reveals discrepancies between the two compared items, the discrepancies are recorded and reported. These discrepancies may be reported on an individual basis or incorporated into an audit report. The resolution and disposition of these discrepancies is handled by the change control function.

THE CHANGE CONTROL FUNCTION

The second function of software product assurance is to control software changes visibly and traceably (this function is discussed in detail in Chapter 4). As discussed in Section 2.5, these changes are indigenous to software development. The discrepancies revealed during a software product assurance audit are a prime source of change. They must be investigated and their cause determined. A way to remove the cause of the discrepancy must be determined, and the impact of this removal must be assessed. With this information, a forum is convened to consider each discrepancy and decide its disposition. The details of this function are explained in Chapter 4; suffice it to say here that this forum basically decides whether to change a software product.

A decision not to change the software product might result for several reasons. For example, it might be determined that the discrepancy had resulted from a misunderstanding on the auditor's part, that the software product was already being changed as a result of a previous discrepancy, or that it was not feasible to change the software and that the user could accept the situation without having his needs fulfilled.

When a decision to change is made, the software product is changed accordingly, and then, as shown in Figure 3.10, it is reintroduced to the software product assurance process. That is, the changed software product is again audited and any dis-

---

[7] Note that visual comparison of computer source code on a computer listing (i.e., in the form of a document) with test procedures or with the underlying requirements and design specifications is a form of verification and validation.

crepancies in the comparisons are made manifest. As a result of this iteration, the software product converges to a point either where it has no discrepancies or where the forum mentioned above decides no further changes to the product are needed. At this point, we have achieved a software product with integrity.

This iteration is a key point in the process of producing software products with integrity, and one which is frequently omitted and overlooked. In our experience, we have frequently heard comments such as:

> "The contract only calls for a one-time delivery of this specification. It was never planned to modify it or maintain it or to make cosmetic changes to it. We don't have the time or the money to do so, and besides it will be a throwaway document as soon as we get the code produced!"

> "Certainly we're going to correct the specification, but we definitely are not going to reaudit it. We don't have the time or the money for that. Besides, you'll just uncover more problems, which will delay us even more! We'll never get to coding if we keep reauditing until the specification has no problems."

If the entire project team is committed to the objective of developing products with integrity, it is difficult to believe that statements such as the above can be made. Yet they are made frequently, often by managers who sincerely wish to develop successful products. The problem lies in their focus on short-range goals—meeting an (often unreasonable) delivery date regardless of product state, commencement of coding (a highly visible activity that shows "something is getting done"), or "resolving" problems by putting extra programmers on the job rather than determining what it is that the programmers should be doing. In the process, longer-range goals—maintainability, user satisfaction, minimization of total project lifetime resource expenditures—are overlooked or ignored. Decisions that optimize one activity's success at the expense of other activities are often made. For example, decisions that facilitate completion of coding may create considerable problems in system integration, in acceptance testing, or in maintenance. The forum used to control change must keep these longer-range goals in mind, if product integrity is to be achieved. (We return to this subject of long-range and short-range goals in Section 7.2.)

THE BOOKKEEPING FUNCTION

The third function of software product assurance is that of bookkeeping—the recording of project events, and the storing and reporting of this recorded information. This function is discussed in detail in Chapter 6. As Figure 3.10 shows, events are recorded during the software product assurance process as well as at other points during a life cycle stage. Since this event recording occurs during each stage of the life cycle, it is pervasive throughout the entire development process.

Significant events recorded as shown or implied in Figure 3.10 include:

Completion of development of a software product and its introduction to the software product assurance process

Completion of an audit

Discrepancies made visible as a result of an audit, either as individual items or consolidated into an audit report

Analyses of individual discrepancies

Results of meetings of the change control forum, e.g., minutes including decisions made regarding discrepancies

Establishment of a software product as a baseline

Completion of approved changes to a software product and its reintroduction to the software product assurance process

To be available for reports, the event information recorded must be stored in an archive. This archive can subsequently be accessed to inform the project participants and senior management of such things as the status of changes, the status of baselines, and the results of meetings on change control.

The combination of project event recording and the storing and reporting of this recorded information tells where the project is at any time and where it has been. It provides visibility and traceability to the process of software development and thereby contributes to achievement of software products with integrity.

We explained Figure 3.10 in the context of reviewing a software product developed during the current life cycle stage. Software product assurance can be applied in other contexts— for example, upon the submission of a change request. Such a request applies to a software product that has previously been reviewed and approved as a baseline. As a foundation for discussions of the three basic functions of product assurance in the next three chapters, we now present a sample problem showing that our product assurance model in Figure 3.10 is valid for contexts other than that of initially developed software products.

THE SOFTWARE PRODUCT ASSURANCE MODEL APPLIED TO A CHANGE REQUEST—A SAMPLE PROBLEM
Background and Questions

A change request (see Chapter 4 for a definition and description of a change request) is a document recommending that a software system be changed by the addition of a new capability, the modification of an existing capability, or occasionally the deletion of a current capability. (Recall Figure 2.8 and our assertion that software development is a continuing endeavor to answer the wizard's question: "What is it that you [the user] really want?") For example, consider the following change request submitted on the precipitation-day counting system introduced in Section 2.1 and further discussed in Sections 2.2, 2.3, and 3.1:

In addition to counting the number of days during the month

when rain fell and the number of days when snow fell, also count the number of days during the month when sleet fell.

Would you modify the model shown in Figure 3.10 if the initiator of the software product assurance process was a change request? If so, how?

Solution Approach

The question basically asks how Figure 3.10 should be modified if the representation of a software product in the figure is replaced by a representation of a change request. Recall the definition of software product assurance given at the beginning of this chapter. The focus of that definition is on software products. The question naturally arises as to whether a change request is a software product. Recalling the definition of software given in Section 2.1 and the example of a change request given above, we would answer that a change request is indeed a software product. It is not a software product in the sense of the expected and planned sequence of products generated as the software evolves in its life cycle from its requirements specification to its operational baseline. Rather, this software product is unplanned and unexpected. It might be originated by any member of the project team or by the user, and it might be introduced during any stage of the life cycle. (We expand on this concept of planned versus unplanned changes in Section 4.1.)

Since a change request is a form of software product, our model of the software product assurance process given in Figure 3.10 is not changed at all when the initiator of the process is a change request.

Let us look at how the sample change request given above would be processed. This change request is an enhancement of the preliminary requirements specification given in Section 2.1. Thus, it would be audited by comparing it to the standards established for the project. Because one of those standards (as stated in Section 3.1) required consistency within any project document, the change request would be reviewed with respect to the preliminary requirements document to ensure that no inconsistencies had been introduced.

Any discrepancies found through the audit would be handled under the change control function. The forum performing that function would decide what actions to take on the individual discrepancies. An assessment of the impact of the change request would be made by the development organization. Based upon this impact assessment and upon the audit discrepancies and their resolutions, the change control forum would decide what action to take on the request.

If the change request is not approved, the bookkeeping function would record that action, as it records other events during the software development life cycle, and place the change request in its archives. If the change is approved, the new capability to count monthly days of sleet will be successively added to all the existing baselines—namely, the requirements specification, the design specification, and the source code. Each of these revised baselines would again pass through the software product assurance process to assure that product integrity is achieved.

Note that test procedures would also have to be modified to reflect this sleet-day counting capability, so that the revised source code for the system can be audited.

From the foregoing discussion and sample problem, you can see that our model represents the performance of product assurance (and of the four processes included in product assurance) in two different applications. We have specifically shown the applicability of the model in handling the planned sequence of changes arising as a development project proceeds through its life cycle. We have also specifically shown its applicability in handling unplanned and unexpected changes that may (and typically do) arise at any time during the software life cycle. The operation of our model is explained in more detail for each of these two applications in subsequent chapters.

3.3 An Analogue to Software Product Assurance

To conclude our discussion of the elements of software product assurance, we present in this section a simple analogue of software product assurance that embodies our definition of software product assurance given at the beginning of the chapter and the model of software product assurance presented in Section 3.2. This analogue embodies the prime elements of software product assurance—the four processes (QA, CM, V&V, T&E) and the three basic functions (audit, change control, bookkeeping) that we introduced in Figure 3.1—and emphasizes that product assurance involves the integrated performance of these basic functions. Each of the next three chapters concentrates on one of these basic functions. However, there is considerable interaction among these functions, and it is necessary to maintain an integrated view of them to understand fully how to perform product assurance. Our analogue is designed to assist the reader in maintaining this integrated view.

The analogue we have chosen is the balance shown in Figure 3.11. Using this balance, a software product is compared with various weighted entities to determine whether product integrity has been achieved in the software product. If product integrity has been achieved, that event is duly recorded. If software product integrity is not achieved, the discrepancy is noted, and a decision is made as to how to change the software product in order to achieve product integrity. The product is changed and the set of weights is used again to determine whether product integrity has been achieved. Notice that these actions control software evolution visibly, traceably, and formally—and thus encompass the process we have labeled software configuration management.

What is the set of weights for our product assurance bal-

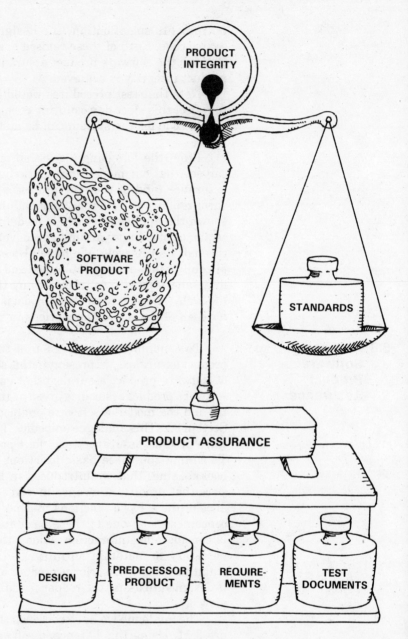

FIGURE 3.11. An analogue to software product assurance.

ance, and when are they used? We have shown five weights in Figure 3.11—predecessor product, requirements, test documents, standards, and design. The predecessor product weight is used for verification—the assessment as to whether the software product follows logically from a predecessor product. The requirements weight is used for validation—the assessment as to whether the software product is congruent with requirements and user needs. With these two weights, we are able to assess traceability and congruence of software products with requirements (the process we have labeled V&V).

With the test documents weight, we can perform the process of T&E—the conduct and evaluation of functional demonstrations of software products. This weight is used only with the coded form of software products. This weight also implies that the tests defined in the test documents are executed in a live or nearly live environment. Since, as we discussed in Section 3.2, the test documents are derived from the requirements specification and the design specification, we could substitute the requirements weight and the design weight for the test documents weight to conduct this functional demonstration.

The standards weight is used to assess the conformance of the software product to specified established standards—quality assurance. This weight is used with every software product assessed, regardless of its form.

Strictly speaking, some redundancy exists in this set of weights. Both the requirements weight and the design weight are instances of the predecessor product weight. This redundancy is deliberate to emphasize the specific role that the requirements specification and the design specification play in the software product assurance process.

3.4 Summary

In this chapter, we introduced four processes that individually contribute to the achievement of product integrity. We assigned to these processes the classical labels of quality assurance, software configuration management, verification and validation, and test and evaluation. We next discussed our rationale for including these processes in the software product assurance discipline. We analyzed the four processes and pointed out that they each contained the same three basic functions—audit, change control, and bookkeeping. Then we presented a model for performing software product assurance, emphasizing the three basic functions of software product assurance. Finally, we suggested an analogue for software product assurance: a balance whose balance point is marked "product integrity" and a set of weights for effecting comparisons with software products.

Now that we have formally introduced the elements of software product assurance, we are ready to describe the mechanics of how to do each of the three fundamental software product assurance functions, beginning in the next chapter with change control.[8]

---

[8] Senior managers may want to consider the following exercises before proceeding to the next chapter: Exercise 3.4, on establishment of a single product assurance department versus separate QA, SCM, V&V, and T&E departments; Exercise 3.5, on qualifications of a product assurance manager; Exercise 3.10, on organizational independence of a product assurance group. Project managers and product assurance managers may want to consider the following exercises before proceeding to the next chapter: Exercise 3.2, on a product assurance approach by a manager who replaces a recently fired manager; Exercise 3.4, on establishment of a single product assurance department versus separate QA, SCM, V&V, and T&E departments; Exercise 3.6, on how standards should be selected and instituted on a software project; Exercise 3.8, on minimum product assurance activities; Exercise 3.9, on organization of a product assurance department; Exercise 3.10, on organizational independence of a product assurance group.

EXERCISES   Many of the following exercises emphasize the four product assurance processes, and only a few relate to the three functions that comprise product assurance. This emphasis is deliberate. A number of exercises on each of the three product assurance functions can be found at the end of the next three chapters, each of which is devoted to one of the functions.

3.1   In a sample problem in Section 2.2 and an example in Section 3.1, we discussed how the application of the four processes of QA, SCM, V&V, and T&E provides a software project manager with increased *visibility* and as a result increases the likelihood that products with integrity are attained. Based upon our definitions of these processes given in this chapter and in terms of the precipitation-day counting system first introduced in Section 2.1, list in specific terms how the application of these four processes provides increased *traceability* so that intelligent decisions on how the project should proceed can be rendered.

3.2   Assume that you have just been appointed manager of a software project to replace the manager who was just fired because the project budget has already overrun and the scheduled product delivery date was six months ago. In your attempt to determine where and why things went wrong, you learn after a few days of searching and talking with project participants that no product assurance of any kind has been used on the project. Being a realist and an experienced software project manager, you know that it would be impractical to institute a full-blown product assurance effort (at least overnight) to help get the project out of trouble. Given that the project is already over budget and at least six months behind schedule, what software product assurance activities would you institute? Assume the following about the current state of the project:
1.   The project began two years ago.
2.   No documentation has been produced.
3.   Working computer code was to be delivered to the customer six months ago.
4.   You have no written record of any project meetings.
5.   Remarkably, you have had no personnel turnover.
6.   You will lose money on this project. Your objective is to minimize your losses and hope to satisfy your customer so that you can obtain follow-on business.

3.3   In analyzing why software projects fail, DeMarco (see Reference 5, Chapter 1) writes:

> A lot of software projects fail, but we software developers are not such dummies that our sheer incompetence can account for them all. Software managers are no less adept at managing their people and their subject areas than are managers in other disciplines. In my years of auditing software projects, I have seen many total failures where lack of competence and drive could never have been considered the cause. I have known project managers who excelled in those characteristics that I associate with good management:
>
> Strong motivation of project staff members
>
> Clear understanding of the issues
>
> Adequate grasp of relevant technologies
>
> Evident capability in the political sphere

Yet their projects failed. Why? They didn't design poorly or code slowly or introduce too many bugs. In most cases, they simply failed to fulfill original expectations. I am convinced that most project failures are of this very nature, and, in most cases, it is not the fault of the project team at all. It is rather the fault of *inflated and unreasonable expectations*. The sad consequence of unreasonable expectations is that projects are dubbed failures without regard for the quality and quantity of work actually done. (T. DeMarco, *Controlling Software Projects* [New York: Yourdon Press, 1982], p. 4.)

Recalling Figure 2.8, consider how applying software product assurance may help software project managers reduce the likelihood of project failures because of inflated and unreasonable expectations. (*Hint:* In what ways is the wizard's question in Figure 2.8 related to DeMarco's contention about project failure and inflated and unreasonable expectations? In what ways can each of the four software product assurance processes help provide answers to the wizard's question and thus help to keep a software project within reasonable bounds?)

3.4 Discuss the trade-offs associated with establishing one product assurance department on a software project versus establishing separate QA, SCM, V&V, and T&E departments on the project. Each approach has its advantages and disadvantages. For each approach, list some of these advantages and disadvantages and give reasons to support your answers. (For other considerations in organizing to perform product assurance, see Exercise 3.10 which focuses on the trade-offs associated with making the product assurance group organizationally independent from the development group.)

3.5 You are a senior manager of a company interviewing candidates for the job of manager of your company's newly formed seventy-five person software product assurance division. Given that you have already interviewed twenty candidates for the job (after you and your company's personnel manager sifted through hundreds of resumes), and given that the three candidates whose backgrounds are listed in Figure E3.1 are the best of the twenty, which candidate would you select and why? What additional qualifications would you want the candidate you selected to have (so that you can help that candidate acquire those qualifications after being hired) and why?

FIGURE E3.1. The backgrounds of the three job candidates referred to in Exercise 3.5.

CANDIDATE #1	CANDIDATE #2	CANDIDATE #3
Twenty years' experience in the software industry on projects ranging in size from 50 to 100 persons.	Fifteen years' experience in the software industry on projects ranging in size from 10 persons up to 500 persons.	Twenty years' experience in the software industry on projects involving at most 30 persons.
Gets along well with people.	Twelve years' experience with QA, SCM, V&V, and T&E.	Six years' experience with QA, SCM, V&V, and T&E.
Sharp analytical mind.	No management experience other than informally overseeing the activities of groups of testers consisting of up to 20 persons.	No management experience (and now wants some).
Weak in writing skills.		Communicates very well in writing (except for a tendency to misspell words).
Five years' experience testing computer programs.	Communicates very well in writing.	Gets along well with people.
No formal V&V experience (other than the above-cited testing experience).	Tends to be headstrong and abrasive toward people who do not believe in product assurance.	
Has effectively managed groups of up to 50 programmers.		

3.6 We defined *software quality assurance* as the comparison of a software product against established standards (such as a documentation or coding standard) to determine the degree to which the product conforms to these standards. A fundamental standards issue that frequently must be addressed on software projects is the following:

How should standards be selected and instituted on a software project?

The purpose of this exercise is to probe some of the nuances of the above issue.

(a) List at least three functions of a software standard. For each, indicate the relationship between that function and raising the likelihood that a software product will have integrity, as defined in Section 2.6. To start your thinking on this matter, the following is a possible example of a standards function and its relationship to the realization of a product with integrity:

Function   A documentation standard prescribes the format for a specification (e.g., a preliminary design specification) and describes the content of each section specified in the format.

Product integrity   By requiring a specification document to follow a prescribed format, the standard raises the likelihood that no important topic is omitted from the specification, i.e., that the specification will be complete. Even a "Not Applicable" statement for a given section indicates that a topic has been considered in developing the specification. By raising the likelihood that the specification will be complete, the standard contributes to making the specification congruent with the requirements, that is, to the satisfaction of user needs, one of the elements of product integrity.

(b) Based on your answers to (a), list at least two advantages and two disadvantages of giving each of the following organizations responsibility for selecting and/or developing the standards to be used on a software project:
  1. Customer
  2. Seller development organization
  3. Buyer product assurance organization
  4. Seller product assurance organization

(c) Given that a set of standards has been selected and instituted on a project, consider the following scenario for effecting conformance to some of the standards in the set:
Suppose that the development organization and the product assurance organization work together to produce an annotated outline of each specification document to be produced by the development organization. Each annotated outline represents a joint developer/product assurance agreed-upon interpretation of the standard for the specification document. As a result of this joint agreement, the product assurance organization prepares a quality assurance checklist for each specification that itemizes the things that the product assurance organization will be examining to de-

termine the degree to which the specification conforms to the standard. A copy of each checklist is given to the development organization.

List at least two advantages and two disadvantages of the above approach to achieving conformance with software project standards. Relate these advantages and disadvantages to the likelihood of achieving, and not achieving, product integrity. Referring to (b), do these advantages and disadvantages depend on which of the organizations listed in (b) selected and/or developed the product specifications? If so, how? If not, why not?

3.7   Suppose you are working on a software development effort that has thus far produced and baselined the following two documents (recall Figure 2.7):
1.   Requirements Specification (RS)
2.   Preliminary Design Specification (PDS)

Suppose further that a draft of a Detailed Design Specification (DDS) has just been produced and that you have been assigned the task of performing V&V on the DDS. You first verify the DDS against the PDS and find no discrepancies. You are about to begin to validate the DDS against the RS when you recall that three months ago the PDS was compared against the RS and was found to be consistent with it. Under these circumstances, is it superfluous (and, perhaps more important, is it wasteful of project resources) for you to now compare the DDS against the RS? (Indicate yes, no, maybe, or some combination of these three and give at least two reasons to support your answer.)

3.8   Suppose you work for a company that develops, sells, and maintains software systems (presumably for a profit). Suppose further that you have just been appointed manager of a software development effort that is just getting started. In addition, suppose your past experience with software projects has convinced you of the need for, and importance of, product assurance. Finally, suppose your boss is (1) primarily interested in keeping project costs to an absolute minimum (to maximize company profit) and (2) unfavorably disposed toward "overhead functions" such as product assurance. You are therefore placed in a position of reducing product assurance to a bare minimum. After presenting various product assurance proposals to your boss, the guidance you receive is that you are permitted to fund *only one* of the product assurance activities shown in Table E3.1.

(a)   Which one of the four activities listed in Table E3.1 would you select? Give at least one reason to support your choice. (*Hint:* Recall the concepts of visibility and traceability introduced in Chapter 2.)

(b)   For each of the three activities you did *not* select, write down at least one reason why you judged it to be less desirable than the one selected.

(c)   Suppose you were able to induce your boss to let you fund any *two* of the activities listed in Table E3.1. Which two would you select? Give at least one reason to support your choice.

(d)   Suppose you estimate that it would cost $25,000 to do each of the four activities listed in Table E3.1. Suppose further that your boss gives you $50,000 and allows you to fund *any* combination of the four activities. With this budget constraint, indicate how you would reallocate funds to these activities and how you would change their scope to reflect this reallocation.

TABLE E3.1. CANDIDATE PRODUCT ASSURANCE ACTIVITIES FOR EXERCISE 3.8

1. Weekly configuration management meetings attended by yourself, your development staff, and customer representatives to review project progress and consider proposed software changes. (Assume that minutes of these meetings and the status accounting of these software changes will be accomplished by a group independent from the development staff.)

2. V&V of selected software products which will consist of the following items (developed in the order listed below—recall Figure 2.7):

   Requirements Specification (and updates)

   Preliminary Design Specification (and updates)

   Detailed Design Specification (and updates)

   Computer code (and updates)

   (Assume that you have sufficient resources to do an in-depth, comprehensive V&V job on either of the last two products listed above and at most two updates to either of these products.)

3. Development and execution (in the customer's environment) of test procedures to determine customer acceptance of the computer code that your development staff produces. (Assume that your development staff will test this code before it undergoes testing at the customer's site. Assume also that a group independent from this staff will develop and execute the tests at the customer's site.)

4. QA (in the sense defined in Section 3.1) of each of the products listed in 2 above (including their updates). (Assume that this QA activity includes the development of project standards as well as the comparison function of software products to standards. Assume also that a group independent from the development staff will perform this QA activity.)

3.9 This exercise is intended to probe some of the nuances underlying the product assurance concepts discussed in Section 3.1.

   (a) Table E3.2 lists examples of activities pertaining to software products. Using Section 3.1 as a guide, and recalling the definition of software from Chapter 2, indicate for each of the activities in the table whether it is an example of one (or more) of the following:

   QA

   Verification

   Validation

   T&E

   Configuration identification

   Configuration control

   Configuration auditing

   Configuration status accounting

   None of the above

   (b) Assume that the objective of software product assurance is to discover *all* types of discrepancies pertaining to software products. Based upon this assumption and your responses in (a), indicate what types of activities—in addition to QA, SCM, V&V, and

TABLE E3.2. ARE THESE PRODUCT ASSURANCE ACTIVITIES? IF SO, WHAT KIND(S) ARE THEY? (EXERCISE 3.9)

Examples of Activities Pertaining to Software Products

1. Comparing a listing of computer code against a predecessor detailed design document to see whether the code logically follows from the design

2. Numbering or otherwise labeling paragraphs, sections, and/or chapters in a design specification from which computer code is to be written

3. Comparing a listing of computer code against a contractual statement of work to see whether the code satisfies contractual requirements

4. Preparing a proposal for changing computer code that is currently operational

5. Archiving the proposal in 4, together with its disposition

6. Comparing a software design document against a documentation standard to check for conformance to the standard

7. Recording the minutes of a meeting held for the purpose of considering and approving (or disapproving) a software design document or proposed changes to this document

8. Examining the derivation of a mathematical formula appearing in a design document to check that the formula (which is to be turned into computer code) is correct

9. Checking a software specification for internal consistency (e.g., to see if one chapter or section does not contradict another chapter or section)

10. Examining a listing of computer code (comments and computer language statements) for spelling errors

11. Checking a software specification document for grammatical and punctuation errors

12. Writing a(n internal) label on a magnetic tape (using tape labeling software code) containing computer code

13. Pasting a label on a magnetic tape cassette containing keystroke sequences for a programmable calculator

14. Executing software code on hardware according to a test procedure and comparing the results of executing this test procedure with the results predicted by the test procedure

15. Executing a simulation of a software system (that has yet to be built) and comparing these simulation results with a document specifying the functions that the actual software code will perform when it is built, to see if these functions are being performed

16. Distributing the minutes of a software change control board meeting to the meeting attendees

17. Comparing a software part embedded in computer code with a presumed oountorpart item in the predecessor design document to determine whether the former item logically follows from the latter item

18. Comparing a specification of software functions against a contract from which the specification was directly developed to determine whether the specification and contract are mutually consistent

19. Modifying a contract to incorporate a software enhancement included in a specification document approved at a software change control board meeting

20. Checking the internal consistency of a contractual statement of work specifying requirements for a software system

21. Checking the activities of a T&E group to ensure that their test procedures are complete and that all the procedures are properly executed during a testing session

T&E—might be useful for a product assurance organization to perform.

(c) Suppose you have just been given the responsibility for setting up and managing a software product assurance department to provide centralized product assurance support in the company or organization you work for. Assume also that your company or organization has heretofore not had a single organizational entity that has had the responsibility for software product assurance (i.e., product assurance has been handled in different ways by each project manager in your company or organization, the handling depending on the experience and personality of each project manager). How might you use the information in (a) and (b) to help you set up your department? Considering that we indicated at the outset of this chapter that the definitions of QA, SCM, V&V, and T&E are not standardized in the software industry, what potential value (if any) is there in the assignments you made in (a) and (b) as far as structuring the organization of your department is concerned?

(d) From the point of view of actually performing product assurance on a project, does it really matter what a specific product assurance activity is called? What really matters regarding these activities? (*Hint:* In responding to these two questions, consider the intrinsic significance of the name of something versus the intrinsic significance of the relationship between that name and a definition spelling out what that name means.)

3.10 Our definition of product assurance states that product assurance activities are performed by product developers, project management, and a product assurance group. In our discussion of the triangle diagram in Figure 2.13 and of product assurance in this chapter, we intimated that the product assurance function is best performed if the product assurance group is organizationally independent from the development group. In actuality, industry practice regarding product assurance spans a broad spectrum—from none at all to a product assurance group that reports to an authority higher than, and totally independent from, the software project manager. Our experience indicates that a particular product assurance philosophy that works well on one type of project may not work so well on another type of project. To stimulate your thinking regarding the trade-offs associated with different approaches to product assurance, we list below and illustrate in Figure E3.2 some of these approaches and ask that, for each one, you write down at least two advantages and two disadvantages of that approach. (If the description of an approach does not mention a product assurance activity, assume that it is not performed as part of that approach.) To focus your thinking, recall that the ultimate objective of product assurance is to give confidence that a software product with integrity is achieved. (The terms QA, SCM, V&V, and T&E are used below in the sense defined in this chapter. As we emphasized, these terms are not uniformly defined in the literature.)

(a) The development group performs T&E and a group independent from the development group performs V&V of this testing activity in the sense that this latter group checks to determine the degree to which (1) test documentation is complete (is congruent with design and/or requirements specifications) and (2) test execution

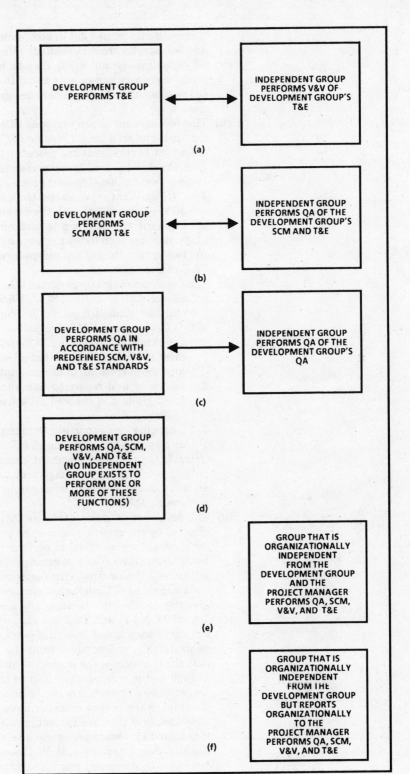

FIGURE E3.2. How do we organize to perform product assurance? (Exercise 3.10).

Within the figure:

(a)
DEVELOPMENT GROUP PERFORMS T&E ⟷ INDEPENDENT GROUP PERFORMS V&V OF DEVELOPMENT GROUP'S T&E

(b)
DEVELOPMENT GROUP PERFORMS SCM AND T&E ⟷ INDEPENDENT GROUP PERFORMS QA OF THE DEVELOPMENT GROUP'S SCM AND T&E

(c)
DEVELOPMENT GROUP PERFORMS QA IN ACCORDANCE WITH PREDEFINED SCM, V&V, AND T&E STANDARDS ⟷ INDEPENDENT GROUP PERFORMS QA OF THE DEVELOPMENT GROUP'S QA

(d)
DEVELOPMENT GROUP PERFORMS QA, SCM, V&V, AND T&E (NO INDEPENDENT GROUP EXISTS TO PERFORM ONE OR MORE OF THESE FUNCTIONS)

(e)
GROUP THAT IS ORGANIZATIONALLY INDEPENDENT FROM THE DEVELOPMENT GROUP AND THE PROJECT MANAGER PERFORMS QA, SCM, V&V, AND T&E

(f)
GROUP THAT IS ORGANIZATIONALLY INDEPENDENT FROM THE DEVELOPMENT GROUP BUT REPORTS ORGANIZATIONALLY TO THE PROJECT MANAGER PERFORMS QA, SCM, V&V, AND T&E

is complete (is carried out in accordance with test documentation and test results are documented). (*Hint:* What are some reasons why the development group may be better able than any other group to prepare and execute tests? In what ways may this group be less able than an independent test group to prepare and execute tests?)

(b) The development group performs SCM on all software products (i.e., code and predecessor documentation) in accordance with predefined SCM standards and procedures, and a group independent from the development group performs QA of this SCM activity; assume that the development group's SCM activity also includes T&E. (*Hint:* What are some cost trade-offs associated with placing the SCM responsibility with the development group versus some other group? Which group is performing V&V? Is this product assurance approach likely to create more or less friction between the two groups than if the independent group had the SCM and T&E responsibilities?)

(c) The development group performs QA on all software products in accordance with predefined SCM, V&V, and T&E standards, and a group independent from the development group performs QA of this QA by doing the following:

1. Checking and reporting to management that the development group has checked that all software products have been produced according to documentation standards

2. Checking and reporting to management that the development group has checked all software products in the V&V sense

3. Checking and reporting to management that the development group has performed T&E

(*Hint:* Is QA of the development group's QA activity necessarily redundant? Why may management find it useful to know from an independent source to what extent the development group is performing QA?)

(d) The development group performs QA, SCM, V&V, and T&E as directed by the project manager; no group independent from the development group exists to perform one or more of these functions. (*Hint:* How does this arrangement simplify project accomplishment? Under what circumstances may this approach save time and money? Under what circumstances may this approach give rise to schedule slippages and cost overruns?)

(e) QA, SCM, V&V, and T&E are all performed by a group that is not only independent from the development group but also organizationally independent from the project manager; assume that the manager of the product assurance group stands at least as high on the organization chart as the project manager. (*Hint:* Under these circumstances, is the project manager the captain of his ship? Is the project manager more likely to receive objective assessments of the development group's activities than he would if the product assurance group also reported to him organizationally? See, for example, M. W. Evans and J. J. Marciniak, *Software Quality Assurance and Management* [New York: John Wiley & Sons, 1987], pp. 60–66, 240–242, 251–253.) To further stimulate your thinking on the pros and cons of this product assurance approach, we mention here the Space Shuttle Challenger disaster. The Presidential Commission on the Space Shuttle Challenger

Accident issued its report on June 6, 1986. The objective of the commission was to prevent recurrence of the failure related to the January 28, 1986, accident which killed seven astronauts and to reduce risks in future flights. The Commission's report contained six major recommendations, including one having to do with safety and quality assurance. This recommendation read as follows (p. 199):

> *Safety Organization.* NASA should establish an Office of Safety, Reliability and Quality Assurance to be headed by an Associate Administrator, reporting directly to the NASA Administrator. It would have direct authority for safety, reliability, and quality assurance throughout the agency. The office should be assigned the work force to ensure adequate oversight of its functions and should be independent of other NASA functional and program responsibilities.
>
> The responsibilities of this office should include:
>
> The safety, reliability, and quality assurance functions as they relate to all NASA activities and programs.
>
> Direction of reporting and documentation of problems, problem resolution and trends associated with flight safety.

(f) QA, SCM, V&V, and T&E are all performed by a group that is independent from the development group and that also reports organizationally to the project manager (in contrast to the situation postulated in (e)). (*Hint:* Under these circumstances, is the project manager captain of his ship? Is the project manager more likely to receive objective assessments of the development group's activities than he would if the product assurance group did not report to him organizationally?)

(See Exercise 3.4 for a related exercise on organizing to perform product assurance.)

TABLE E3.3.   ACTIVITIES THAT MIGHT BE PERFORMED ON A SOFTWARE PROJECT (EXERCISE 3.11)

1. Comparing a design document against a requirements document from which the design document is presumably derived

2. Preparing and executing tests of individually compilable software modules

3. Reviewing the test results generated in 2

4. Recording the minutes of a software change control meeting where changes are reviewed and then rejected or approved

5. Reporting the competence of the development organization

6. Reporting the status of the project

7. Documenting the derivation of a mathematical formula used in software code

8. Evaluating the "goodness" of a software design document

9. Comparing computer code against a coding standard

Continued

10. Looking for spelling and grammatical errors in a software specification document

11. Recommending that certain members of the development organization be replaced

12. Preventing the release of software code to a customer because of code failure during testing

13. Rewriting a portion of a software specification

14. Analyzing software code in search of coding errors or discrepancies with design

15. Preparing reports documenting inconsistencies among software products

3.11   Table E3.3 lists activities that might be performed on a software project. Refer to the triangle diagram in Figure 2.13 and indicate for each activity whether you think it should be performed by the product assurance group. Give at least one reason to justify each product assurance activity you select. For each of the other activities, indicate whether it should be performed by management and/or the development organization (and possibly in conjunction with the product assurance group). Give at least one reason to justify your selection. For those activities that you feel should be performed by more than one element of the triangle, indicate why joint responsibility may be called for.

REFERENCES AND ADDITIONAL READINGS

1.   Beizer, B. *Software System Testing and Quality Assurance*. New York: Van Nostrand Reinhold Company, 1984.

This humorously written book deals with both software product assurance philosophy and practice. Chapters 1, 2, and 10 address philosophy and should be of interest to senior and project managers. Some topics covered in these chapters are:

Testing Versus Debugging

Designer Versus Tester

Builder Versus Buyer

Do Bugs Exist?

Equal Rights for Bugs?

Tasks for a Quality Assurance Department

Who Wants QA?

The QA Manager's Role

Who Deserves the Credit, Who Deserves the Blame?

Many of the ideas in those chapters complement the ideas presented in our Chapters 1, 2, and 3. The middle chapters of the book address the mechanics of testing. As such, they complement and extend the material that we present in Chapter 5. To give an idea of the author's humorous style, the extract below is from a section that discusses nine qualities that Beizer believes are beneficial in a good QA worker. The passage quoted here is his discussion of the quality of tenacity.

> *Tenacity.* The picture of an English bulldog fastened on the burglar's ass comes to mind. A QA worker has to go after an objective and hold on either until she's satisfied or until the objective has been redefined. The programmer must know, from the QA worker's personality, that the problem will not be allowed to go away. QA workers are inherently organized. They use files, indexes, records, and all the other tangible accoutrements of an organized mind as second nature. There's too many things for QA to look after to trust to memory. If QA is committed to seeing to it that the little things are noticed, then there's no room for scatterbrained individuals (p. 381).

2. Bersoff, E. H., V. D. Henderson, and S. G. Siegel. *Software Configuration Management: An Investment in Product Integrity.* Englewood Cliffs, N.J.: Prentice-Hall, 1980.

   Chapters 4–7 of Bersoff et al. examine in detail the four component elements of software configuration management shown in Figure 3.3.

3. Bryan, W. L., and S. G. Siegel. "Making Software Visible, Operational, and Maintainable in a Small-Project Environment." *IEEE Transactions on Software Engineering,* vol. SE-10, no. 1 (January 1984), pp. 59–67.

   This article, based on our experience working on actual projects, presents practical suggestions for effectively managing software development in small-project environments (i.e., no more than several million dollars per year). The suggestions are based on an approach to product development using a product assurance group that is independent from the development group.

4. Bryan, W. L., S. G. Siegel, and G. L. Whiteleather. "Auditing Throughout the Software Life Cycle: A Primer." *Computer,* vol. 15, no. 3 (March 1982), pp. 57–67.

   This article describes in elementary terms how the product assurance function of auditing can help achieve a software product that has integrity. It represents some of our earlier thinking on the concepts included in this chapter and Chapter 5.

5. Freedman, Daniel P., and Gerald M. Weinberg. *Handbook of Walkthroughs, Inspections, and Technical Reviews: Evaluating Programs, Projects, and Products.* 3rd ed. Boston: Little, Brown, and Company, 1982.

   This publication is a how-to-do-it (and why) book on software product assurance primarily as it applies to computer code. Its format is unconventional in that it consists of a series of questions and answers. The following excerpt complements some of the things we say about the checks-and-balances role of product assurance, particularly with regard to raising the visibility of the software development process:

Is There Any Difference Between These Formal Technical Reviews and the Progress Reports We Now Use?

The analogy between formal technical reviews and progress reports is a good one. Formal technical reviews can be thought of as a kind of progress reporting system—one that contains checks and balances that ensure the reliability of the progress information.

Many systems exist for reporting "progress" in programming projects. Some report on how many hours have been spent on a particular project segment. Others report on the number of lines of code produced or pages of documentation written. These components of "progress" are then charted against master schedules and resource allocations to inform management of potential trouble areas. Such systems can be very effective *if the progress they report is true progress.*

Without checks and balances, however, there is no way of ensuring that 1,000 lines of code represent any useful work at all. The programming business is all too familiar with "progress" reports of 99 percent completion when the project in question isn't even 10 percent finished. Why? Because the 1,000 lines of code may be completely wrong, or partly wrong, or wrong in just one or two tiny places—places that may take 2,000 man-hours of work to correct.

A system of formal technical reviews is needed to give *meaning* to the marks on the progress reporting charts. Without *quality* measures—as provided by the formal technical reviews—quantity measures are likely to be *more dangerous than no measures at all* (pp. 9–10).

6. "IEEE Standard for Software Quality Assurance Plans." IEEE Standard 730-1984, Institute of Electrical and Electronics Engineers, June 14, 1984.

This publication defines minimum requirements for SQA plans pertaining to the development and maintenance of critical software (where "critical software" is defined in the standard [at least implicitly] as software whose "failure could impact safety or cause large financial or social losses" [p. 9]). The standard defines "quality assurance" as follows:

A planned and systematic pattern of all actions necessary to provide adequate confidence that the item or project conforms to established technical requirements (p. 9).

Our definition of QA (see Figure 3.2) is contained within the above definition (in a proper subset sense), as can be seen by making the following word substitutions:

Replace "the item or project" by "a software product."

Replace "technical requirements" by "standards."

7. Perry, W. E. *A Structured Approach to Systems Testing.* Wellesley, Mass.: QED® Information Sciences, 1983.

This book presents a panoramic approach to testing—a process integral to *each* life cycle stage and not just a check of computer code before delivery to the customer. Specifically, Perry (p. 1) defines testing as encompassing the following three concepts:

> The demonstration of the validity of the software at each stage in the system development life cycle
>
> Determination of the validity of the final system with respect to the user needs and requirements
>
> Examination of the behavior of a system by executing the system on sample test data

This how-to-do-it book contains, among other things, a compendium of forty-two testing tools (which includes, for each tool, a qualitative estimate of the cost to use it and the advantages and disadvantages of using it).

8. Wilburn, N. P., "Standards and Guidelines Applicable to Scientific Software Life Cycle." Hanford Engineering Development Laboratory, Westinghouse Hanford Company (a subsidiary of Westinghouse Electric Corporation), HEDL-TC-2314, Richland, Wash., January 1983.

This report contains an annotated bibliography of 128 software development standards surveyed by the report's author to determine their applicability to the development of scientific software (which the author defines as "software written to model physical processes such as the thermal-hydraulic processes occurring in a nuclear reactor, . . . chemical processes occurring in the various chemical industries" [p. 1]). The author gives the following as a reason for preparing the report:

> The attributes of good quality software can be obtained by applying good engineering practice across the software life cycle; good engineering practice will be strongly enhanced by adherence to established guidelines and standards (p. 3).

This report thus provides some specific insight into the relationship between the QA function (as we define it) and overall software life cycle management. Also of interest in the report (p. 2) is the following list of software factors:

> *Correctness* (Does it do what I want?)
>
> *Reliability* (Does it do it right all the time?)
>
> *Efficiency* (Does it run as well as it could?)
>
> *Integrity* (Is it secure from intrusion?)
>
> *Usability* (Is it easy to use?)
>
> *Maintainability* (Can I fix it?)
>
> *Testability* (Can I test it?)
>
> *Flexibility* (Can I modify it?)
>
> *Portability* (Can I move it to another computer?)
>
> *Reusability* (Does it consist of general modules?)
>
> *Interoperability* (Does it interface well with other systems?)

Note that "integrity" as defined above is different from our definition of "product integrity" given in Chapter 2. Note also the relationship between the factors "correctness," "maintainability," and "flexibility," defined above, and our definition of product integrity.

9. The following organizations publish catalogs or indices of standards, some of which are applicable in the field of software development and maintenance:

Organization	Catalog/Index
American National Standards Institute 1430 Broadway New York, NY 10018	Catalog
Electronic Industries Association 2001 Eye St., N.W. Washington, DC 20006	Catalog
IEEE Computer Society 345 East 47th St. New York, NY 10017	Catalog
Instrument Society of America P.O. Box 12277 Research Triangle Park, NC 27709	Catalog
National Technical Information Service 5285 Port Royal Road Springfield, VA 22161	National Bureau of Standards Federal Information Processing Standards (FIPS) index
Superintendent of Documents U.S. Government Printing Office Washington, DC 20402	Department of Defense (DoD) Index of Specifications and Standards
Naval Publications and Forms Center 5801 Tabor Avenue Philadelphia, PA 19120	Individual DoD standards and specifications
International Standards Organization Case Postale 56, CH-1211 Geneva 20, Switzerland	Catalog

chapter 4

ESTABLISHING AND MAINTAINING CONTROL

The king in Figure 2.8 is the archetypical software customer. He has some idea of what he wants—but he does not know exactly. We pointed out in Chapter 2 that probably the most fundamental aspect of software development is iteratively determining what the customer wants and then developing products to satisfy these wants. In the current chapter, we turn our attention to describing controls that can be instituted on a software project to achieve convergence between what the king thinks he wants and what the wizard thinks the king wants—with the ultimate result that the wizard produces what the king wants (and can use).

4.1 Evolutionary and Revolutionary Change

Achieving convergence between the king and the wizard is tantamount to saying the following:

A customer's wants migrate through a sequence of changes and ultimately become a product embodying the wizard's (and hopefully the king's) perception of these wants.

In terms of the life cycle depicted in Figure 2.7, this migratory process can be further described as follows:

A planned sequence of transitions from a life cycle stage to a subsequent one overlaid by unplanned transitions within stages or back to preceding stages or forward to succeeding stages.

We refer to a planned transition from one life cycle stage to a subsequent stage as *evolutionary change* because such a change embodies the orderly (i.e., planned) growth of the software from one level of detail to a greater level of detail. We refer to the overlay of unplanned transitions within stages or back to preceding stages or forward to succeeding stages as *revolutionary changes* because each such change embodies an unanticipated alteration to the planned growth of the software. Figure 4.1 illustrates our concept of these two categories of change. Keeping this concept in mind, consider the following

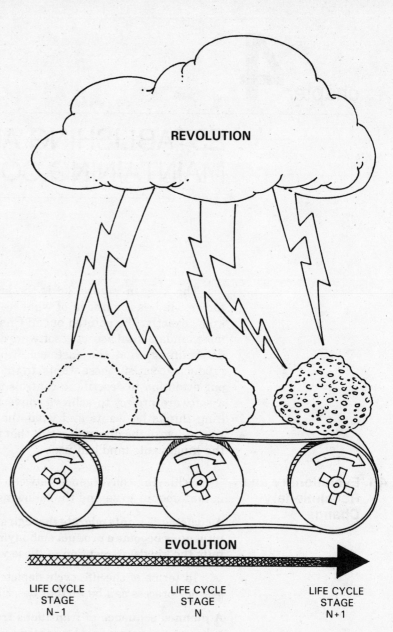

FIGURE 4.1. The concepts of evolutionary and revolutionary change. Evolutionary change is orderly growth of software from one level of detail developed in one life cycle stage to a greater level of detail developed in the next stage. Revolutionary change is unanticipated change within a stage or an unplanned transition from one stage to a succeeding one (or ones) or to a preceding one (or ones).

REVOLUTION

EVOLUTION

LIFE CYCLE STAGE N−1

LIFE CYCLE STAGE N

LIFE CYCLE STAGE N+1

examples of these two classes of change based on Figure 2.7:

1. Suppose that a preliminary design specification for a software system, derived from a requirements specification for that system, listed the functions each of three software subsystems is to perform. Suppose that a detailed design specification describes how each of these functions is to be performed by computer code. This description of "how" is just an embodiment of the orderly growth of the software system and is thus an example of an evolutionary change.

2. Suppose that during the development of the detailed design specification in the preceding example it was discov-

ered that a fourth subsystem (in addition to the three identified in the preliminary design specification) was incorporated into the detailed design because the developers thought this additional subsystem was needed to satisfy the intent of the requirements specification. (Presumably this fourth subsystem was not noticed during the development of the preliminary design specification because, for instance, the absence of design detail did not make manifest this requirements satisfaction issue.) The modification of the preliminary design specification to incorporate this fourth subsystem (presumably after the detailed design specification is approved) is an alteration to the orderly growth of the software that was not anticipated at the time the software was evolving from the Requirements Definition Stage to the Preliminary Design Stage. This modification is thus a revolutionary change.

3. Suppose that computer code was developed from the detailed design specification in the preceding example, tested, and then deployed for operational use. Suppose further that some time subsequent to this deployment a malfunction was discovered in the computer code (which presumably was not noticed during predeployment testing) that resulted from a misinterpretation of the detailed design specification. Modification of the computer code to correct this malfunction is an alteration to the orderly growth of the software that was not anticipated at the time the software was evolving from the Coding and Production/Deployment Stages to the Operational Use Stage. This correction is thus a revolutionary change.

4. Suppose that in the preceding example a review of the detailed design specification was scheduled to determine the feasibility of refining some of the functions in one or more of the software's subsystems (e.g., to make them operate more efficiently). As a result of this feasibility study, suppose that the detailed design specification was modified to incorporate these enhancements to the existing functions and that the computer code was also modified to incorporate these enhancements. These modifications to the detailed design specification and the computer code represent the orderly growth of the (already operational) software system and are thus examples of evolutionary changes.

5. Suppose that the feasibility study referred to in the preceding example, in addition to specifying refinements to existing functions, revealed a logic flaw in the detailed design that had heretofore gone undetected during operational use of the computer code (because, for example, the logic flaw becomes apparent only under a rarely occurring combination of circumstances—recall Figure 3.9). As a result of this feasibility study, suppose that the detailed de-

sign specification was modified to correct this logic flaw (as well as incorporating the enhancements to the existing functions) and that the computer code was also modified to correct this logic flaw. These modifications to the detailed design specification and computer code to correct this latent logic flaw constitute alterations to the orderly growth of the software that were not anticipated at the time the software was evolving from the Detailed Design Stage to subsequent stages. These design and code modifications are thus examples of revolutionary changes.

6. Suppose that, as a result of operational use of the computer code referred to in the three preceding examples, a need arose to add new functions to one or more of the existing subsystems. Suppose further that, as a result of this identified need, the requirements specification was augmented to incorporate these new functions and the preliminary design specification, detailed design specification, and computer code were correspondingly modified to incorporate these new functions. These modifications to these four software products represent the orderly growth of the (already operational) software system and are thus examples of evolutionary changes. Alternatively, it could be argued that these modifications were not anticipated at the time the software was evolving prior to first operational use and thus are examples of revolutionary changes. (From this latter perspective, it thus follows that any new capabilities added to an operational system are revolutionary.) ☐

In earlier chapters we stressed the relationship between software's malleability and the ease with which software projects can get into trouble. In this chapter we focus on techniques for establishing and maintaining control over this high susceptibility to change, thereby reducing the likelihood of encountering trouble during the life cycle. In describing these techniques, we frequently find it convenient to distinguish between evolutionary and revolutionary changes. However, the distinction between evolutionary and revolutionary change is sometimes blurred, as example 6, above, indicates. Other examples of the difficulty of thus categorizing changes are (1) when a change control organization, while reviewing a design specification, finds a feature that the change control organization feels is a needed addition to the system and should be incorporated into the requirements specification or (2) when a change control organization, in response to an audit finding that as-built software code documentation (for example, in a programmer's manual) contains a software code module description that reads "To be determined (TBD)," directs that the missing description be incorporated into the document.

If it is sometimes difficult to distinguish between revolutionary and evolutionary change, what difference does it make what kind of change it is? The prime reason that this distinction is important is to assure that all changes are given the requisite visibility and are handled in a unified way. Let us hasten to explain this somewhat paradoxical statement. Many people in the software development world do not recognize that the planned transitions of software from stage to stage are a form of change, i.e., that they are evolutionary changes as defined here. Lacking this perception, these people exercise little or no control over this evolving software. To illustrate this point, consider the following story based on the authors' actual experiences (names in this and other stories have been changed):

WHY CONTROL EVOLUTIONARY CHANGE?—
A STORY

Tom Smith was the seller's project manager for the development of a large management information system called ATLANTIS. He believed that product assurance had some usefulness, and he established a product assurance organization and procedures early in the life cycle of System ATLANTIS. He decreed that a succession of baselines was to be established, one at the end of each life cycle stage to serve as a point of departure for efforts in the next stage.

However, Tom did not view this succession of baselines as evolutionary changes to be controlled. He wanted his software engineers to be able to introduce different ideas easily "if they found a better way to do things." Because his engineers thus did not regard the preceding baseline as a rigid specification, the next baseline did not logically follow from its predecessor—with plenty of surprises for everyone who read it. In Tom's view, each baseline superseded its predecessor. His concept was strengthened by his contractual list of deliverables—the contract called only for a single delivery of each software product and did not suggest maintaining any software product. Not having to maintain the baselines saved him time and money and, from his viewpoint, increased the likelihood that his project would be completed on schedule and within budget.

Of course, Tom's product assurance organization kept pointing out that he had no visibility into what was going to be in a baseline until it was produced, that by discarding each baseline as its successor was produced he had destroyed all traceability in his project, and that he had effectively lost all control over his project. Their reports were an embarrassment to Tom, particularly when his senior management began asking questions about them. So Tom took the obvious step to solve what he perceived his problem to be—he disbanded his product assurance organization!

By this time, however, the user/buyer was observing the fledgling system undergoing integration testing. His observations told him that the project was going to be late and over budget (because the numerous problems introduced by the software engineers needed correcting) and that System ATLANTIS did not come close to solving his needs. Without hesitation, the buyer terminated the contract to avoid further loss, and System ATLANTIS was never heard of again. □

The moral of the story is that *all* change—both evolutionary and revolutionary—must be controlled in order to attain visibility and traceability in a project. We distinguish between the two categories primarily to assure that the former category is not omitted or overlooked.

A secondary reason for distinguishing between revolutionary and evolutionary changes is that they do have some different attributes. One such attribute is direction. Evolutionary change always moves forward from baseline to a succeeding baseline, much the same way that human development evolves. Revolutionary changes, on the other hand, may cause transitions either within a stage, back to a preceding stage, or forward to a succeeding one (recall Figure 4.1). Particularly important are the revisits to baselines resulting from revolutionary changes, with the result that all project baselines are maintained, and visibility and traceability are retained.

Another attribute distinguishing these two types of change is that revolutionary change processing is often more tightly time-constrained than evolutionary change processing. This time constraint generally has an impact on some of the details of the change evaluation and approval steps as we explain in subsequent sections.

Using this twofold categorization of change, we describe in the remainder of this chapter how software change can be handled on a software project in a visible, traceable, and hence manageable manner. Our approach is as follows:

In Section 4.2, we describe change processing from the perspective of the organizational body—the configuration control board (CCB)—that ideally should be the focal point of this processing. We step through the generic event sequence underlying both the evolutionary and revolutionary change process. Using the life cycle in Figure 2.7, we then illustrate this sequence in more specific terms—first for evolutionary change, then for revolutionary change.

In Section 4.3, we turn our attention to the topics of CCB composition and modus operandi. Starting from the triangle diagram introduced in Figure 2.13, we discuss the project disciplines that should staff the CCB. We then discuss how the CCB provides a forum for the user, buyer, and seller to interact continually and effectively on a software project for the purpose of managing change. This discussion is extended to the notion of CCB hierarchy. In this discussion, we explain some of the relationships between project size and complexity, and CCB tiers. We tie this discussion back to concepts treated earlier in the section—

namely, CCB composition—and look at the interactions among various kinds of CCBs—those homogeneous in their composition (i.e., CCBs composed only of users, buyers, or sellers) and those not homogeneous in their composition (i.e., CCBs composed of mixtures of users, buyers, and sellers). In treating the topic of CCB modus operandi, we examine the types of decisions a CCB must typically make. We illustrate this decision-making activity by returning to the evolutionary and revolutionary change process described in Section 4.2. We also discuss the trade-offs associated with establishing a CCB voting mechanism. In conjunction with this discussion, we address the issue of who should chair the CCB; the context for examining this issue is once again the discipline triumvirate depicted in Figure 2.13.

In Section 4.4, we focus on the paperwork needed to support the CCB as it acts to establish and maintain control over software development. We introduce three questions that encompass all the situations that could precipitate a software change. We then associate with these questions a set of forms that gives visibility to, and establishes a trace of, events pertaining to software changes (both evolutionary and revolutionary). We provide guidelines on forms design and step through the design of one form—an incident report—in a sample problem. We provide examples of all the forms in our set and illustrate their use in three scenarios matching the three questions referred to earlier to give you ideas on how to design forms pertinent to your own software project environment.

In Section 4.5, we summarize the main ideas presented in the chapter. This summary also serves as a transition to Chapter 5 by raising the issue of how the CCB knows when a software change may be needed.

4.2 The Processing of Changes

In the preceding section, we divided software changes into evolutionary change and revolutionary change. We intimated in Section 2.5 that changes are inevitable on any software project. Evolutionary changes, of course, will occur by definition on any project having more than a single stage. (As we discussed in Chapter 2, the division of a software project into a number of stages is essential to managing the project.) As we proceed through the project life cycle (for example, the one we illustrated in Figure 2.7), a baseline will be created at the end of each stage, as we discussed in Chapter 2. Each baseline embodies what was done during a given stage. This planned sequence of baselines represents the orderly growth of the software during the project life cycle; by our definition, each of these baselines is an evolutionary change.

Revolutionary changes are also inevitable on any software

project of any complexity. These changes arise from our fallibilities as human beings, from our general lack of complete experience, and from our inability to communicate perfectly among ourselves. Because of these limitations, it becomes necessary to continually make unplanned changes to correct misperceptions or misunderstandings. From stage to stage, we gain more insight and knowledge on a project and recognize the need to change the results of the current stage and of other stages. The larger and more complex the project, the larger and more convoluted the communications paths and the more likely the need for revolutionary change. Figure 2.8 encapsulates some of these concepts. The wizard apparently misperceived the king's question stated in the first frame ("Can you stop the rain?"). In the third frame, the king may be reformulating his requirement, based on the insight and experience he gained since he asked his question in the first frame.

In the preceding section, we noted the importance of revisits to baselines resulting from revolutionary changes. These revisits precipitate baseline updates, as discussed in Section 2.5. Note that the update of a revisited baseline is a revolutionary change. As a result of this change, baselines intermediate between the revisited baseline and the current baseline must also be updated (as scheduled activities) to maintain visibility and traceability. Thus, the intermediate baseline updates are evolutionary changes, according to our definition. We can observe, then, that revolutionary changes often precipitate evolutionary changes. If the former are inevitable, the latter are also inevitable.

It is important to acknowledge this inevitability of change on a software project. Our objective in establishing and maintaining control of changes is not to prevent change but to control it. To understand why we adopt this objective, consider the story below (modeled after experiences of the authors).

THE INEVITABILITY OF CHANGE—A STORY

As project manager on a new software development project, Mike Brown decided that success to him meant delivery of all software products on time and within budget. To this end he decreed that there would be absolutely no changes allowed on his project. (A succession of baselines was to be developed during the life cycle; however, Mike did not consider these evolutionary changes to be changes at all, but rather the normal progress of software development.) He informed all his software engineers of his decision to prohibit change and stated that each baseline would be a one-time delivery only, that is, would not be updated after issuance. He thus not only saved time and money by processing no changes, but he also conserved resources through elimination of document maintenance.

As the project went on, the software engineers found this rigid policy unworkable. In the processes of development and of testing, the programmers discovered discrepancies in the current or preceding baselines. Several engineers had ideas for changes that they believed would have a beneficial effect on the final product. Since no changes were allowed on this project, the engineers had recourse to only two alternatives: they could ignore the desirable or needed changes, or they could ignore the strictures against making changes. Since the engineers were generally conscientious, most of them chose the latter course and made the changes sub rosa. After all, they reasoned, it was so easy to effect the changes in both documentation and code, and unit testing should uncover any problems arising from making code changes.

The project proceeded blissfully for a number of months, with Mike supremely confident that he had discovered the road to project success. Then the axe fell—integration of the code modules began. Unaccountably (to Mike at least), integration testing yielded a seemingly unending stream of reports of problems with the software code. At the same time, Mike's users, witnessing the integration tests, complained that the system performed functions they had not asked for, and did not perform some functions they had requested. To his dismay, Mike watched helplessly while his project passed its delivery date and budget ceiling, with no certainty as to when a system satisfying his customers' needs could be obtained. □

In this story, Mike Brown tried to prevent change. The result was disaster. As the software engineers acquired experience on the project, they saw things not previously perceived or recognized. These insights gave rise to the need for changes, which Mike had prohibited—with disastrous results.

Since change on a software project is inevitable, it makes better sense to acknowledge its existence and to attempt to control it. We have illustrated this important principle in Figure 4.2. Figure 4.2a shows a project where an impenetrable barrier has been erected to prevent all change to a product. In the instance illustrated, an apparently needed change (to replace the lower-case "r" with an upper-case "R" for consistency within "PrODUCT") has been repelled and rejected without consideration. In Figure 4.2b, we illustrate an attempt to control changes to a product. The replacement of the lower-case "r" by an upper-case "R" has been considered and allowed to proceed, while the replacement of the "T" in one type font by a "T" in a type font different from that of the rest of the product has been prevented from proceeding (to avoid creating an inconsistent product).

Our use of the word "attempt" in this discussion of Figure 4.2 regarding controlling change is deliberate. Just as it is possible to run a red traffic light while driving, so it is possible to make an uncontrolled change to a product, particularly when that product is software. We believe that the risk resulting from uncontrolled software changes can be even greater than

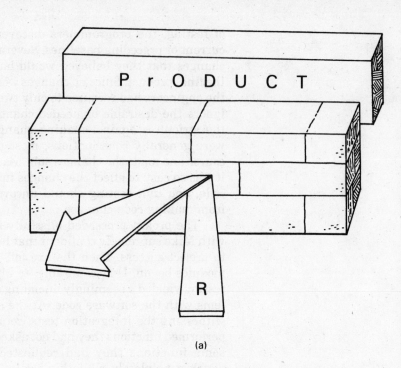

FIGURE 4.2. (a) Don't try
to prevent change—
(b) Attempt to control it.

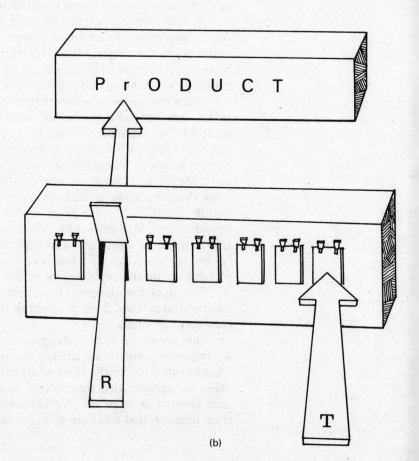

the risk in our traffic control analogue resulting from running a red traffic light at a busy intersection!

Preventing all changes has the appeal of apparently not perturbing schedules and budgets, but as the story above illustrates, there are substantial risks with this approach. The need for extensions of schedules and budgets is likely to become evident in the late stages of a project. Schedules and budgets may also change as a result of controlled changes, but in a controlled and visible manner.

To ensure that candidate software changes are processed in a visible and traceable manner, we need a controlling mechanism that channels these candidate changes to the appropriate project participants. This controlling mechanism is the organization that we call the configuration control board (CCB). In Figure 4.3, we portray the CCB as a control tower that controls the movement of software from stage to stage in the life cycle and in the area that we marked "Review" in the middle of the life cycle in Figure 2.7. As we proceed through this life cycle, the need arises to consider one or more candidate changes to the software product under development (or to previously developed products). To address this need (which may occur at any point within a life cycle stage), we symbolically close a gate, as indicated in Figure 4.3, that diverts us from the outer loop of the life cycle into the area marked "Review." In the review area, we assess these candidate changes, determine their impact on the software development effort, and make appropriate decisions. These decisions include specifying what to do with the candidate changes (e.g., implement them, reject them, or hold them in abeyance), which software products to modify (e.g., none, the one currently under development, products developed in previously visited life cycle stages), and what revisits, if any, to make to other life cycle stages.

Readers who have some background in configuration management will immediately recognize the CCB as the control organization historically used by the CM process to control modifications and enhancements to a system. On some projects, the CCB may also control changes to the computer code. In our context, the CCB performs the broader function of managing all change on a software project during all stages of the life cycle. This function includes both evolutionary and revolutionary change, and software in both textual (document) and coded forms. After we describe its relationship to the change control process, we examine the operation of the configuration control board in great detail in the next section.

Although Figure 4.3 shows a path from the outer loop to the inner area marked "Review" near the end of each stage, this diversion path may occur anywhere within a stage. For evolutionary changes, the diversion occurs whenever a software product is generated. If a product goes through several drafts, there will be a diversion path for each draft. The end

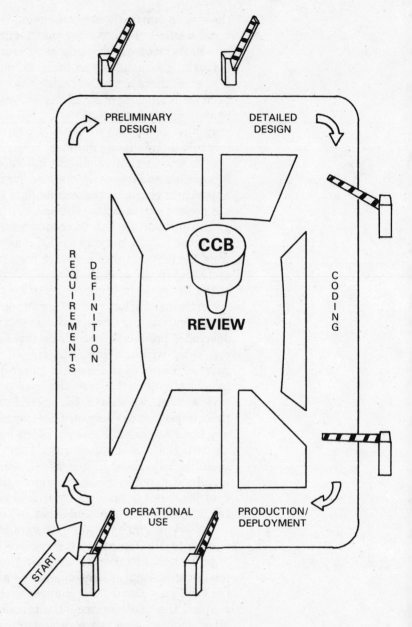

FIGURE 4.3. The CCB is the control activity for the change process conducted during the review of changes.

of each stage does not occur until the software product(s) comprising the baseline for the next stage has (have) been approved.

For revolutionary changes, the diversion path to the review area may connect to any point within the stage. For example, a developer at any point during the Coding Stage may detect a facet of the design omitted during the Detailed Design Stage. The designer submits a report of this omission, and the review process is initiated. Or during the Preliminary Design Stage a user may notice a requirement that has not surfaced before. He immediately initiates the review process by sub-

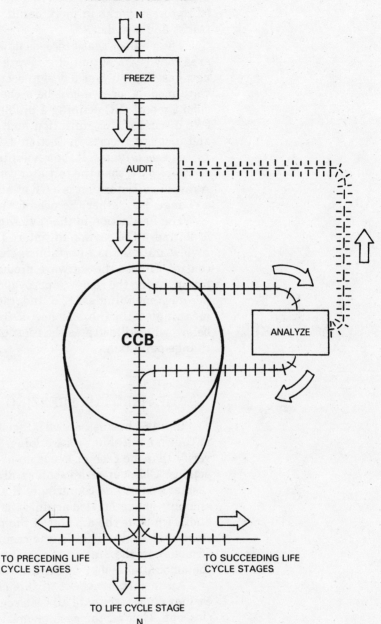

FROM LIFE CYCLE STAGE
N

FREEZE

AUDIT

CCB

ANALYZE

TO PRECEDING LIFE
CYCLE STAGES

TO SUCCEEDING LIFE
CYCLE STAGES

TO LIFE CYCLE STAGE
N

FIGURE 4.4. A detailed view of the review area of the life cycle shown in Figure 4.3—CCB control can be likened to the process of redirecting a train by switches.

mitting a request for change. So we see that there can be a multitude of paths connecting any life cycle stage in Figure 4.3 to the review area.

The diversion down the path to the review area occurs whenever a change arises. That is, every change—whether evolutionary or revolutionary, large or small, of major or minor impact—is reviewed and evaluated by the change control process. The paths that a change takes during the change control process are controlled by the CCB. In Figure 4.4, we have magnified the review area to show generically how the change control process works in more detail, using the analogy of train tracks and switches.

The product that proceeds down the path into the review area may be an output of software development proposed as a new baseline, such as a design document or the code for a software module, or it might be a change request (CR) or an incident report (IR) defining a problem observed on the system. (We discuss the organization and content of change requests and incident reports in Section 4.4.) We refer to this product as a *review initiator*. If the review initiator is a new or updated software part, then the initiator contains the proposed change. A review initiator that is a CR or an IR usually does not specify a change, but rather the need for a change.

The first action in the review process shown in Figure 4.4 is to freeze the review initiator. The purpose of freezing the review initiator is to establish the basis for the review and control. Unless the software product initiating the change is frozen during the review, approval or disapproval of the change becomes meaningless. To understand why change becomes meaningless in the absence of freezing, consider the story below, which illustrates the relationship between freezing and change definition.

THE NEED FOR FREEZING—A STORY

In retail businesses, cash register operations are reviewed at the end of a shift or a workday. This review is conducted to verify that the cashier keeps an accurate accounting of transactions. Closeout of a cashier's drawer involves totaling the cashier's sales and counting of the cash in the drawer. These amounts are reconciled against the preceding baseline for this audit, which is the amount of the money in the drawer at the start of the shift. That is, the cashier's sales plus the amount of money in the drawer at the start of the shift should equal the amount of money in the drawer at closeout.

An important aspect of this closeout process is that the cashier must terminate all cash register operations during the closeout. That is, the cashier must make no sales, receive no payments, and make no change. Effectively, the contents of the cash drawer and the sales for that cashier are frozen while the closeout (review) is conducted.

Consider the implications of trying to close out a cashier's drawer at a busy fast-food store while the cashier continues to make sales, receive payments, and make change. The checker determines and records the total sales at the beginning of the closeout. Of course, the cashier will add to these sales as the cash is being counted, but the checker will not have a record of their amount. As the checker is counting the amount of cash in the register, the cashier is adding to and subtracting from the various denominations in the drawer, both counted and uncounted. Modifications to the counted amounts are, of course, not recorded by the checker.

When the checker completes the cash count, he calculates the sum of the cash amount at the beginning of the shift plus the total sales. He expects this sum and cash count to be equal for successful closeout, but he will not find that to be true so long as the cashier continues to do business. Redetermining the total sales or recounting the current cash will change the amounts compared but will not change the end result—the inequality will persist as long as the cashier continues to do business, i.e., as long as he does not freeze the operation of his register and the contents of his cash drawer. ☐

Imagine the frustration and futility of trying to close out under the circumstances cited in the story above. Any count of the cash in the drawer would be meaningless—it would not represent the total cash in the drawer at *any* moment in time. Under these circumstances, conduct of a closeout would be a waste of time.

Similarly, as indicated in Figure 4.4, a software product must first be frozen if its review is to be meaningful. For example, the result of a review might be the establishment of the software product initiating a review as a baseline. If the product has meanwhile been modified substantially, then the baselined product does not represent the current product. And if the CCB directs the originator to make certain specific modifications to the product, the originator may be unable to respond fully and correctly if the product has already been changed in the specified portions that were to be modified.

The choice of the word *freezing* is deliberate. The action here is not to cast a software part in concrete, that is, to attempt to prevent forever any change to that software part. (Remember our discussion earlier in this section that change is inevitable.) Rather, our intent in freezing is to *control* change. When a change becomes necessary and is approved, the software item can be thawed, changed, and then refrozen. In this manner, we can accommodate change while still maintaining continuous visibility into the current state of the software and traceability of the software from one change to subsequent ones.

The identification function is part of the freezing process. If a software product has not been previously labeled by the product's developer, then the product assurance organization should identify the product and its contents at the time of freezing the product. (It is not significant what organization performs this identification, but because identification is largely a subjective exercise, one organization should perform all identification throughout the life cycle. In this manner, consistency is achieved in application of the identification standards prescribed for a project.) Recalling the first line of Figure 3.3, identification entails attaching a label to the review initiator itself and to each part of the item. These labels provide visibility into the evolutionary and revolutionary change being reviewed. Without these labels, we are reduced to referring to software as, for example, "the second paragraph of the latest version of the preliminary design" or "that piece of code that failed last Tuesday." Such references are often not specific enough to be useful in communicating among project members (recall Figure 2.10). In fact, they could be extremely misleading. Consider, for instance, the "latest" version of a preliminary design. Two people attempting to discuss the second paragraph of their latest version of a preliminary design may each be discussing a different entity. It is entirely possible that a person might not receive an issue of a document. It is even more likely that a person receiving an unidentified document would confuse it with other unidentified issues of the document. He might, as a result, ignore the new document (considering it to be the same as the old document) or subsequently consult the old document because he does not recognize that a newer edition exists. The subjects of freezing and identification are further discussed in Chapter 6.

The second action in the review process shown in Figure 4.4 is to audit the review initiator. Because Chapter 5 discusses auditing in depth, we only touch upon the subject here. Auditing entails comparing the review initiator with one or more other items (recall the product assurance balance shown in Figure 3.11). These items could be a set of standards, a preceding baseline, a preceding draft of the initiator, or the software requirements specification. Those items used in the comparison are a function of the nature of the review initiator, as we illustrate later in this section. The objective of auditing is to make visible the discrepancies between the review initiator and the items with which it is compared. These discrepancies are documented in an audit report, which along with the review initiator itself is submitted to the CCB for consideration.

We next consider the box in Figure 4.4 labeled "CCB." This box represents the decision-making body that determines the disposition of each change. Its function is analogous to the control tower in a railroad switching yard, determining the destination of the rolling stock using switches.

The first determination that the CCB makes is whether further analysis of the review initiator is needed prior to CCB determination of its disposition. Generally, the CCB would bypass this analysis only for small problems with evident solutions that can be quickly implemented. For example, presented with a preliminary design specification and an audit report listing discrepancies observed in the preliminary design specification, the CCB may decide that the discrepancies in the audit report make the changes required obvious enough that no further analysis is needed (e.g., a discrepancy might state that the preliminary design is incomplete in that it has not addressed one of the functions in the requirements specification). On the other hand, the CCB may consider that further analysis of a discrepancy should be conducted to define sufficiently the change needed (e.g., a section in the detailed design is ambiguous or cannot be understood, or a discrepancy indicates that the preliminary design specification and the requirements specification are inconsistent in that the design is based on achieving a substantially faster response time than was required).

Figure 4.4 shows that the analyze function supports the CCB but is not part of the CCB meeting. When the CCB decides that analysis of the review initiator is needed, it effectively turns the switch in Figure 4.4 to route the review initiator to the organization doing the analysis. Upon completion of the analysis, that organization generally returns the review initiator and the results of its analysis to the CCB.

The nature of the analysis differs according to the type of change proposed and the directions provided by the CCB. The analysis might consist of one of the following:

> A complete investigation into the impact of the change and the resources required to implement it (e.g., for a change request)

> A formulation of the precise change to be made (e.g., for an incident report that clearly requires a code change, or for a discrepancy in an audit report that points to ambiguous text)

> A determination of the scope of the problem and the exact changes required to implement a solution (e.g., for an incident report whose cause is not immediately obvious, or whose solution may require changes in a number of different software parts)

The CCB may, of course, direct that other analyses of a problem or a proposed change be performed.

When the CCB directs that a proposed change be analyzed, the analysis is often conducted by the seller's development organization, although on occasion other organizations may be involved in the analysis (e.g., the buyer's product assurance organization may analyze a proposed change to a product assurance plan). When the analysis is completed, the results are presented to the CCB for further consideration of the proposed change.

The review initiator, the audit report, and the analysis report are the *technical* inputs to the CCB for determination of the disposition of the change. The analysis report formulates the proposed change (if not done on the review initiator) and assesses its impact. For evolutionary changes, the audit report records discrepancies between the proposed change (a proposed new or updated baseline) and the requirements specification and between the proposed change and the predecessor baseline. Other considerations affecting the CCB's decisions may be political (e.g., assuagement of a user who may feel that he has been ignored), schedule (e.g., the effect of making changes on the date that the system becomes operational), or economic (e.g., the amount of money remaining to effect changes). Based on these considerations, the CCB decides on a disposition of each change. This decision is analogous to throwing a switch to determine the path in the software life cycle subsequently taken. For example, if the CCB accepts a software product developed during a given life cycle stage (an evolutionary change) and establishes it as a baseline, the path chosen is to the beginning of the next life cycle stage (i.e., the tollgate at the end of the current stage in Figure 4.3 is effectively opened). The CCB may decide that a software product requires reworking before it is acceptable; in this case the path selected returns to the current life cycle stage.

When the CCB approves a revolutionary change, revisits to one or more life cycle stages may be necessary. For example, a change request may cause a return to the Requirements Definition Stage to amend the requirements specification, with subsequent revisits to the other stages in succession as the change is implemented in a sequence of evolutionary changes. As another example, approval of an incident report arising during acceptance testing may cause a revisit to the Detailed Design Stage to modify the design, followed by coding of the change and its testing. In some circumstances, the CCB may direct a revisit to a succeeding stage. (For example, an incident report written on an operational system may result in a revisit to the Detailed Design Stage to correct the problem. While performing that correction, a coding error is discovered and the CCB, in approving its resulting code correction, may specify a revisit to the Coding Stage.)

The decisions that the CCB makes are documented in CCB meeting minutes. These minutes allow management and project participants to see what is happening on a project, and make software changes manifest and traceable from their origination to their archiving. In Chapter 6, we discuss and give examples of CCB meeting minutes.

The alternative path in Figure 4.4 from the analysis process to the audit process (indicated by dashed lines) might be considered for use in some circumstances. For example, suppose the audit of a draft preliminary design document reveals that a section of the design has been stated ambiguously. The development organization rewrites the section and normally presents its proposed resolution to the CCB. The CCB might approve the proposed resolution, and the approved change would be made to the preliminary design document. But suppose the revision to the section in the preliminary design document does not solve the problem (e.g., the section is still ambiguous) or introduces a new problem (e.g., the revised section is inconsistent with a later chapter in the document). These defects in the revision may not be evident to the CCB, particularly if the revision is substantial in scope or depth. If the CCB baselines the document as revised, false starts may occur as the project proceeds from its faulty baseline, thereby wasting considerable resources (recall Figure 1.3).

How does the CCB become aware of such defective revisions? Following the normal path shown in Figure 4.4, the CCB may not become aware of these defects until the design document is next updated or until the software produced in the next stage is audited. At this point, considerable time and money may have been wasted. To avoid such waste, the alternate path shown in dashed lines in Figure 4.4 could be used. In this case, the development organization, on completion of its analysis, provides its proposed resolution directly to the audit organization. The auditors would reaudit the revised section of the preliminary design document and send both the revised section and the audit results to the CCB for its consideration. Any remaining ambiguities, inconsistencies, or other discrepancies are made manifest to the CCB before it determines the disposition of the proposed change. Through the use of the alternative path rather than the normal path, discrepancies may surface earlier in the life cycle, thereby avoiding subsequent wastage. Of course, conducting the reaudit costs money and takes time, but it potentially saves much more money and time. Using the alternative path is a specific instance of the philosophy of "pay now versus pay much more later" illustrated in Figure 1.3. (A more detailed example of the use of the alternative path is presented later in this section.)

Now that we have described the change control process shown generically in Figure 4.4, we illustrate this process with three specific examples. The first example is an evolutionary change—presentation of a draft detailed design specification at the end of the Detailed Design Stage. The other two examples are of revolutionary change—first, submission at any point in the life cycle of a proposed amendment to the requirements, and second, submission by a user of an incident report while the system is in operational use.

EXAMPLE 1: CHANGE CONTROL FOR A DRAFT DETAILED DESIGN SPECIFICATION

For this example, we assume that a project has been in the Detailed Design Stage of the life cycle in Figure 4.3 and that the development organization has just produced a draft of the detailed design specification (DDS). Because of the tollgate in

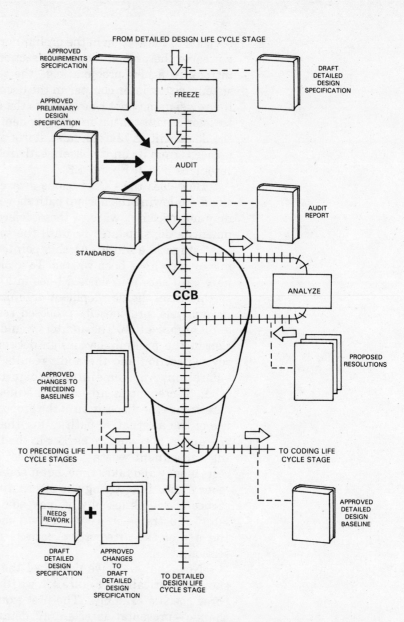

APPROVED
REQUIREMENTS
SPECIFICATION

DRAFT
DETAILED
DESIGN
SPECIFICATION

FREEZE

APPROVED
PRELIMINARY
DESIGN
SPECIFICATION

AUDIT

AUDIT
REPORT

STANDARDS

CCB

ANALYZE

PROPOSED
RESOLUTIONS

APPROVED
CHANGES TO
PRECEDING
BASELINES

TO PRECEDING LIFE
CYCLE STAGES

TO CODING LIFE
CYCLE STAGE

NEEDS
REWORK

APPROVED
DETAILED
DESIGN
BASELINE

DRAFT
DETAILED
DESIGN
SPECIFICATION

APPROVED
CHANGES
TO
DRAFT
DETAILED
DESIGN
SPECIFICATION

TO DETAILED
DESIGN LIFE
CYCLE STAGE

FIGURE 4.5. Change control of an evolutionary change—Submission of a draft detailed design specification.

the Detailed Design Stage, the draft detailed design specification has been diverted into the review area. The processing of this evolutionary change is shown in Figure 4.5.

The draft DDS is first frozen by placing a copy under the control of the product assurance organization; i.e., from this point on, the draft DDS cannot be changed without CCB action. If the draft DDS exists on an electronic medium, copies of both the electronic medium form and the hard-copy form are placed under control. At this time, the draft DDS is also identified by the product assurance organization if it was not identified by the development organization. Identification entails labeling both the document itself and its contents. (We present the details on how to identify a document in Section 6.1.)

The draft DDS is next presented to the auditors in the

product assurance organization,[1] who compare the draft DDS with the following three documents:

The CCB-approved requirements specification (on this project, this document has been established as the Requirements Baseline)

The approved preliminary design specification (on this project, this document is the predecessor baseline to the draft DDS)

The standards established for this project

As a result of this comparison process (which is discussed in the next chapter), the auditors produce an audit report describing their findings in terms of the discrepancies observed in the course of the comparisons.

The draft DDS and the audit report are presented to the CCB for its consideration. Each discrepancy in the audit report is considered individually. The first decision the CCB makes on a discrepancy is whether the discrepancy must be analyzed to provide further information on which the CCB can base its decision. If analysis is necessary, the discrepancy is sent to the organization designated by the CCB (typically the development organization), which determines the cause of the discrepancy, assesses its impact on the project, and proposes a resolution to the discrepancy (i.e., the precise change proposed). This information is provided by the analyzing organization to the CCB.

The CCB considers the resolution recommended for each discrepancy and either approves the resolution, rejects it, or returns it to the analyzing organization for further investigation.

When all the discrepancies have been considered and resolved, the CCB considers whether to baseline the draft DDS in light of the audit report on it, the CCB's own perusal of the document, and the approved resolutions to the audit report discrepancies. The CCB makes one (or, in some circumstances indicated below, more than one) of the following decisions relative to the DDS, resulting in an exit from the review area to the life cycle stages as shown in the exits from the three-way switch in Figure 4.5:

The CCB approves the draft DDS and establishes it as the Detailed Design Baseline (DDB). With this baseline established, the project can proceed into the Coding Stage, i.e., the Detailed Design Stage tollgate in Figure 4.3 has effectively been raised. It is not necessary for the audit report to show no discrepancies for this decision to be made. The CCB may decide to establish the Detailed Design

---

[1] It is not mandatory that a separate product assurance organization conduct this audit. We advocate an independent product assurance organization for performing this and other audits, but alternatives are possible. It is essential that the audits be conducted, regardless of what organization conducts them. However, the organization conducting the audits should be objective and unbiased. (Recall the discussion of this point in Section 3.1. See also Exercise 3.10.)

Baseline with discrepancies still outstanding, if the discrepancies were considered sufficiently small in number and impact. (Such discrepancies would subsequently be resolved by the CCB. These resolutions might, among other things, require that changes be made to the Detailed Design Baseline, i.e., that the baseline be updated. The review process for this proposed update to the DDB would be identical to that shown in Figure 4.5, except that the Detailed Design Baseline would be used for the audit instead of the approved Preliminary Design Baseline.)

The CCB sends the draft DDS back to the developers for reworking, along with a list of discrepancies and their resolutions. In this case, the Detailed Design Stage is reentered. The approved resolutions are implemented, and the draft DDS is updated. When the draft DDS has been updated in response to the discrepancy list, the updated draft DDS is again subjected to the review illustrated in Figure 4.5.

The CCB approves changes that require updates to preceding baselines. These baselines might be, for example, the Requirements Baseline or the Preliminary Design Baseline. The need for such changes might arise from discrepancies observed during the audit. The proposed resolution of a discrepancy may reveal that the cause of the discrepancy lies not in the draft DDS but in one of the preceding baselines. As a result of the CCB decision to change one or more of the preceding baselines, the path is taken to the stage where each baseline to be updated was originally developed. (A result of this revisit to a life cycle stage could be that it triggers more revisits. These subsequent revisits [recall Figure 4.1] might be forward in the life cycle, or backward, or might skip stages.) As each baseline is updated, it is reviewed in the same fashion as shown in Figure 4.5. Note that this CCB decision may be made in addition to one of the two above decisions. □

The preceding example is representative of the review process as it applies to evolutionary changes. The names of specific software products and life cycle stages may vary from those in Figure 4.5, but the basic process remains the same.

A question that arises after consideration of the preceding example is "What does the development organization do while this review process is in progress?" After all, the review process must take some time for the conduct of an audit, for analysis of discrepancies, and for the considerations of the CCB. Does the development organization simply mark time (at considerable expense) during this review period? The answer to the question is that the developers should not be idle during this review period following development of a draft software product. There are usually a number of productive things they can do. If there are incomplete portions of the draft software product currently under review, the developers can finish those portions and have them ready for the next issue of the software product. They can assist in the completion of other software products being developed in the current life cycle stage. They can start their planning and preliminary work for the subsequent life cycle stage. Through informal liaison and discussions with the auditors, the developers can find out about discrepancies uncovered by the auditors in the software product under review, investigate them, and be prepared with recommended resolutions when they are formally received. And usually the developers are involved in the analysis of discrepancies and in the deliberations of the CCB.

We now illustrate the Figure 4.4 review process for two revolutionary changes—first for a proposed amendment to requirements, and second for a user report of unexpected behavior in an operational system.

EXAMPLE 2: CHANGE CONTROL FOR AN AMENDMENT TO REQUIREMENTS

An amendment to the requirements on a project can be originated at any time during the life cycle. Whenever it is originated, the amendment is submitted for review as shown in Figure 4.6.

The proposed amendment to requirements is first frozen by the product assurance organization. This action entails assigning an identification label and placing a copy of the proposed amendment under control by putting it in a master file of proposed amendments to requirements.

The auditors next compare the proposed amendment with the following items:

The Requirements Specification (i.e., the Requirements Baseline), to determine whether the amendment is truly a change to the requirements and to ascertain which of these requirements the proposed amendment affects

Previously submitted amendments to requirements, to determine whether the proposed amendment has previously been proposed (i.e., whether the proposed amendment duplicates one previously considered or currently being processed)

The proposed amendment is then submitted to the CCB, whose first decision is to determine whether the proposed amendment should be analyzed. In general, the proposed amendment is assigned to an investigating organization (typically the development organization) for analysis in a specified time frame. However, the CCB might bypass this step if it were not considered necessary. For example, if the audit determines that a proposed amendment is a duplicate of one previously considered by the CCB, there is no need to analyze the proposed amendment a second time—the CCB has already made its decision relative to this proposed amendment. In such a case, the CCB might proceed directly to reject the more recent submis-

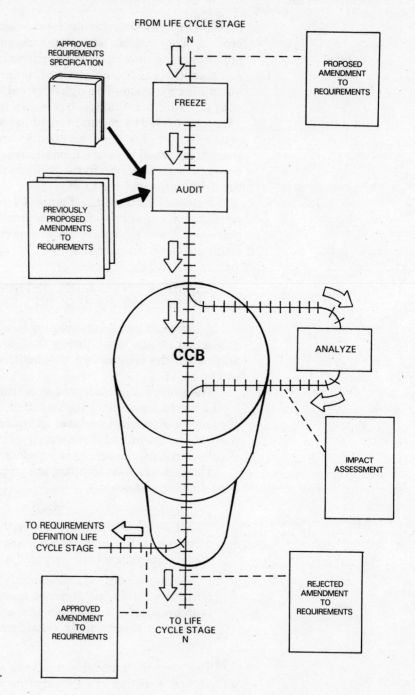

FIGURE 4.6. Change
control of a revolutionary
change—A proposed
amendment to requirements.

sion of the proposed amendment. This rejection is unrelated to
the CCB decision on the first submission of the proposed
amendment and merely reflects that the CCB will not consider
the later submission.

If the CCB decides that the proposed amendment to requirements needs to be analyzed, the investigating organization performs the analysis and prepares an impact assessment.

This impact assessment contains the following information:

An assessment of the impact of the proposed change on the project software products, i.e., what must be changed and how

An assessment of the impact of the proposed change on project resources such as time, manpower, and costs

A delineation of the benefits and liabilities of possible alternatives to the proposed change

With the impact statement in hand, the CCB determines the disposition of the proposed amendment to requirements. As shown in Figure 4.6, the CCB throws the switch in one of the two following directions:

The CCB may approve the amendment to requirements. When this decision is made, the path to the Requirements Definition Stage is taken. There the developers implement the approved change to the requirements by updating the Requirements Baseline. Note that all other established baselines will usually also have to be updated to maintain congruence among the baselines.

The CCB may reject the proposed amendment to requirements. In this case, the originator of the proposed amendment is informed of the decision, the proposed amendment is archived (for reference in case the same amendment is proposed again), and the project continues the life cycle in its current stage. □

Observe in the foregoing example that an amendment to requirements (a revolutionary change), when approved, gave rise to a set of updates to currently established baselines (evolutionary changes). Note also that the process shown in Figure 4.6 is independent of whatever life cycle stage the project is in when the proposed amendment to requirements is originated.

Our second example on revolutionary change deals with an incident report. We discuss the incident report in Section 4.4; for now, regard it as a report from a user of an operational system, describing an abnormal or unexpected behavior of the system.

EXAMPLE 3: CHANGE CONTROL FOR AN INCIDENT REPORT

The review process in this example is initiated by an incident report (IR) generated by a user actually using the system during the Operational Use Stage. As in our preceding two examples, the first step in the review process is to freeze the review initiator, i.e., the incident report (see Figure 4.7). The product assurance organization assigns a label to the IR and places a copy of the IR under control by putting it in a master file of incident reports.

The auditors conduct an audit at this point by checking

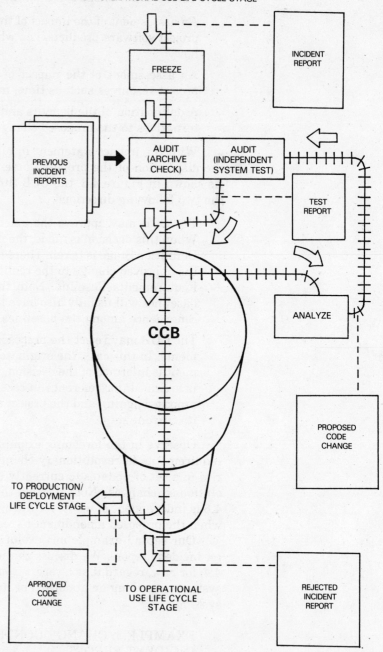

INCIDENT
REPORT

FREEZE

PREVIOUS
INCIDENT
REPORTS

AUDIT
(ARCHIVE
CHECK)

AUDIT
(INDEPENDENT
SYSTEM TEST)

TEST
REPORT

CCB

ANALYZE

PROPOSED
CODE
CHANGE

TO PRODUCTION/
DEPLOYMENT
LIFE CYCLE STAGE

APPROVED
CODE
CHANGE

TO OPERATIONAL
USE LIFE CYCLE
STAGE

REJECTED
INCIDENT
REPORT

FIGURE 4.7. Change control of a revolutionary change—A user-submitted incident report.

the archive to see if the incident reported in the IR has previously been reported and/or resolved. If the IR is a duplicate of a pending IR (one that has not yet been resolved), the CCB, at its first decision point, may decide to reject the IR (the project team is currently trying to resolve the incident under another IR), to dispense with further processing of the IR, and to return to the Operational Use Stage. If the IR is not a duplicate or is a duplicate that was thought to be previously resolved (it appears that the previous resolution did not resolve the incident), the CCB generally sends the IR to an investigating organization (typically, the development organization) for analysis.

In this example, as shown in Figure 4.7, the analysis determined that a correction to the code was necessary to resolve the incident. The development organization prepares a proposed code change, but rather than sending it to the CCB it uses the alternative route introduced in Figure 4.4 by sending the proposed code change to the system test team.

The test team, a group independent from the development organization, audits the proposed change by conducting system tests of the provisionally changed software code. That is, the test team takes the changed software code, integrates it with the existing code, and tests the resulting system in a live or nearly live environment. The purpose of these tests is to ascertain whether the reported incident is successfully resolved by the code change and whether any deterioration of other system capabilities results from the change. The test team reports its findings to the CCB.

The CCB, using its switch capabilities, can direct the IR along the following three paths, shown in Figure 4.7:

> If the test report indicates that the incident has not been satisfactorily resolved, the CCB may direct that the investigating organization reanalyze the IR and prepare a new proposed change.

> If the test report indicates that the proposed code change has satisfactorily resolved the incident without harmful side effects (i.e., without introducing problems in other system capabilities), the CCB may approve the proposed change and route it to the Production/Deployment Stage for production and dissemination of the modified software.

> The CCB may decide to reject the IR, in which case return is made to the Operational Use Stage and the originator is informed of the action. Such an action might be taken if the IR is a duplicate of a pending IR, or if the IR does not represent a problem with the software code (e.g., it may have resulted from an operator error or from a user's misperception of the system's capabilities). ☐

The foregoing example shows only one of several routes that an IR might take during the change control process. For example, the resolution of the IR might be to modify one or more baselines, to amend the software requirements, or to modify one of the other project products (say, a user's manual).

The preceding three examples are exemplifications of the generic change control process occurring in the review area of the software life cycle. Figure 4.4, which shows this generic change control process, is an enlargement of the review area shown in Figure 4.3. To close out this section, we now further explain the process of change control by focusing on the control tower labeled "CCB" in Figure 4.4 and by considering some of the issues that might be raised in that forum. For this purpose,

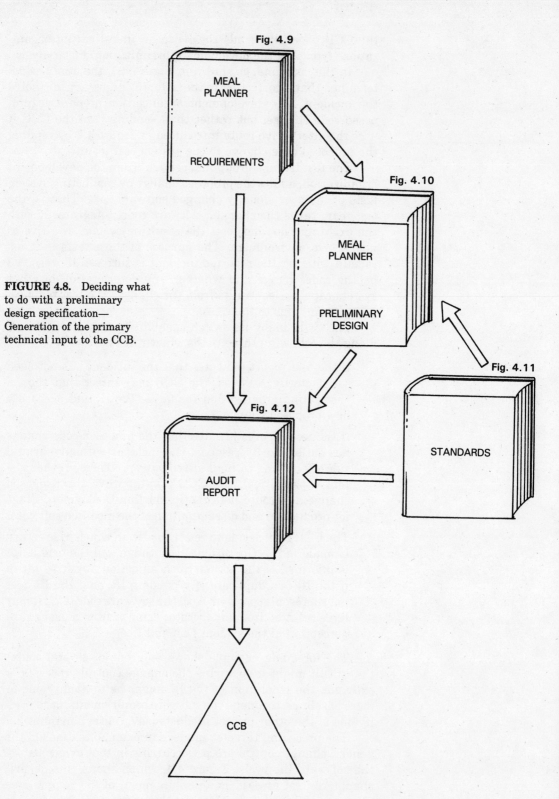

FIGURE 4.8. Deciding what to do with a preliminary design specification— Generation of the primary technical input to the CCB.

178

we use a sample problem highlighting issues that might face a CCB that is considering a preliminary design specification.

EVOLUTIONARY AND REVOLUTIONARY CHANGE CONTROL—A SAMPLE PROBLEM

Background and Question

Assume you are a member of a CCB supporting the development of a system called MEAL PLANNER, an automated tool to assist dietitians, nutritionists, and others in planning the specific contents of meals. Assume further that the development of this system is currently in the Preliminary Design Stage and that the following are some specifics pertaining to this development effort (see Figure 4.8, which establishes the context for this sample problem):

A. The software requirements specification shown in Figure 4.9 has been developed and approved by the CCB as the basis for preliminary design work.

B. A draft of the preliminary software design specification, shown in Figure 4.10, has been audited against the requirements specification in Figure 4.9 and against the documentation standard shown in Figure 4.11. The results of this audit are shown in Figure 4.12.

FIGURE 4.9. Requirements specification used in Section 4.2 sample problem.

MP-01
Version 1.2

Software Requirements Specification
for System MEAL PLANNER

1.0 <u>Introduction</u>

This document specifies the functions to be performed by the software component of System MEAL PLANNER. These functional requirements constitute the basis for subsequent System MEAL PLANNER software design and code.

2.0 <u>System Overview</u>

The purpose of System MEAL PLANNER is to assist dietitians, nutritionists, and other individuals needing to plan the specific content of meals. More specifically, this system shall determine the following:

- **Given the name of a food and its quantity, MEAL PLANNER shall return the following information:**
  - **The number of calories in that serving of food.**
  - **The number of grams of protein in the serving.**
  - **The number of grams of carbohydrates in the serving.**
  - **The number of grams of fat in the serving.**
  - **The percentages of calories in the serving deriving from protein, fat, and carbohydrate.**

Continued

- Given a meal consisting of two or more foods and the quantity of each, MEAL PLANNER shall return the analogues to the items listed in the first bullet above for the entire meal (i.e., the total number of calories in the meal, the total number of grams of protein in the meal, etc.).

For example, System MEAL PLANNER will, in response to the user-input information

STEAK, 4 ounces,

indicate the number of calories in this 4-ounce serving of steak, the number of grams of protein in the serving, and so forth. Similarly, System MEAL PLANNER will determine the corresponding information for a meal consisting of the following foods:

STEAK	4 oz.
FRENCH FRIES	6 oz.
BROCCOLI	$3\frac{1}{2}$ oz.
CHOCOLATE ICE CREAM	1 cup
ORANGE JUICE	8 oz.
FRENCH BREAD	3 oz.
BUTTER	1 tbsp.

It is assumed that the MEAL PLANNER software will be operated on computer hardware including a keyboard that will be used to enter the names of foods and their quantities, a video device that will be used to display the results of MEAL PLANNER software calculations, and a printer that will be used to generate hard copy of the information displayed on the video device. It is also assumed that the following nutritional information on the 2000 foods listed in Appendix A to the MEAL PLANNER System Specification will be available on a magnetic medium (i.e., tape or disk) accessible by the System MEAL PLANNER processing unit:

- The number of calories per unit weight or volume.*

- The number of grams of carbohydrate per unit weight or volume.
  (1 gram of carbohydrate contains 4 calories).

- The number of grams of protein per unit weight or volume.
  (1 gram of protein contains 4 calories).

- The number of grams of fat per unit weight or volume.
  (1 gram of fat contains 9 calories).

3.0 Software Functions

The System MEAL PLANNER software shall perform the following functions in response to the user-supplied input of a single food and its quantity or a list of foods and their quantities:

- Calculate the entities itemized under the two bullets in paragraph 2.0.

- Display the above results on the video device.

- Print the above results on the printer.

- Display an error message if the user enters a food not contained in the MEAL PLANNER database.

---

* For each food, nutritional information will be listed in the MEAL PLANNER database in terms of the unit generally used for that food. Thus, for example, nutritional information on foods such as meat, fish, cheese, and poultry is per the weight unit "ounce" (e.g., calories per ounce). Nutritional information on foods such as ice cream and cooking oil, on the other hand, is per the volume unit "cup," while nutritional information on foods such as butter and margarine is per the volume unit "tablespoon."

FIGURE 4.9. *(Continued)*

Preliminary Software Design Specification
for System MEAL PLANNER

1.0 Background and Introduction

Dietitians, nutritionists, and individuals concerned about the food they eat can benefit from an automated aid that helps them plan the specific content of meals. The purpose of System MEAL PLANNER is to provide such an automated aid.

This specification sets forth the preliminary software design for System MEAL PLANNER. More specifically, this document describes in broad terms how the software requirements delineated in the System MEAL PLANNER Software Requirements Specification are to be implemented. The specifics of this design will be prescribed in the System MEAL PLANNER Detailed Design Specification, which in turn will serve as the basis for computer code development.

2.0 System Capabilities

As prescribed in the System MEAL PLANNER Software Requirements Specification, the software shall perform the following functions:

- Given the name of a food and its amount, MEAL PLANNER shall return the following information:

    - The number of calories in that food serving.

    - The number of grams of protein, carbohydrate, and fat in the serving.

    - The percentage of calories in the serving deriving from protein, carbohydrate, and fat.

- Given a meal consisting of two or more foods, and the amount of each, MEAL PLANNER shall return the analogues to the items listed above for the entire meal (i.e., the total number of calories in the meal, the total number of grams of protein in the meal, etc.).

3.0 System Environment

The particular hardware that is to host the MEAL PLANNER software is to be determined (TBD). The MEAL PLANNER design assumes that the software will be operated on hardware consisting of a keyboard that will be used to enter the names of foods and their amounts, a video device that will be used to display the results of MEAL PLANNER software calculations, a printer that will be used to generate hard copy of the information displayed on the video device, and a central processing unit that will perform the operations dictated by the software code. A magnetic storage device (TBD) will host nutritional information on the 2500 foods that make up the MEAL PLANNER database.

4.0 Design Description

This section describes the preliminary design for the following four software functions

Continued

FIGURE 4.10. Preliminary
software design specification
based on requirements
specification in Figure 4.9.

(see Software Requirements Specification, paragraph 3.0):

- Calculate the entities listed in paragraph 2 above.
- Display the calculation results on the video device.
- Print the calculation results on the printer.
- Display on the video device an error message if the user enters a food not contained in the MEAL PLANNER database.

4.1 Calculation Function Design

The software shall determine the number of calories, grams of protein, fat, and carbohydrate, and the calorie percentage of each of these latter three entities, in a serving of food F_i of amount Q_i as follows:

Let:

Q_i = amount of F_i input by user in units consistent with the units for F_i in the MEAL PLANNER database (e.g., for a 3-ounce serving of steak, Q_i would be 3).

CAL_i = number of calories in Q_i units of F_i.

$CARB_i$ = number of grams of carbohydrate in Q_i units of F_i.

PRO_i = number of grams of protein in Q_i units of F_i.

FAT_i = number of grams of fat in Q_i units of F_i.

$UCAL_i$ = number of calories in one unit of F_i (from MEAL PLANNER database).

$UCARB_i$ = number of grams of carbohydrate in one unit of F_i (from MEAL PLANNER database).

$UPRO_i$ = number of grams of protein in one unit of F_i (from MEAL PLANNER database).

$UFAT_i$ = number of grams of fat in one unit of F_i (from MEAL PLANNER database).

$PCARB_i$ = percentage of calories in Q_i units of food F_i deriving from carbohydrate.

$PPRO_i$ = percentage of calories in Q_i units of food F_i deriving from protein.

$PFAT_i$ = percentage of calories in Q_i units of food F_i deriving from fat.

Then:

CAL_i = $Q_i \times UCAL_i$

$CARB_i$ = $Q_i \times UCARB_i$

PRO_i = $Q_i \times UPRO_i$

FAT_i = $Q_i \times UFAT_i$

$PCARB_i$ = $4 \times CARB_i/CAL_i = 4 \times (UCARB_i/UCAL_i)$

$PPRO_i$ = $4 \times PRO_i/CAL_i = 4 \times (UPRO_i/UCAL_i)$

$PFAT_i$ = $9 \times FAT_i/CAL_i = 9 \times (UFAT_i/UCAL_i)$

Continued

FIGURE 4.10. *(Continued)*

The software shall determine the number of calories, grams of protein, fat and carbohydrate, and the caloric percentage of each of these three entities, in a meal consisting of N foods F_i of amount Q_i as follows:

Let:

MCAL	=	number of calories in meal.
MCARB	=	number of grams of carbohydrate in meal.
MPRO	=	number of grams of protein in meal.
MFAT	=	number of grams of fat in meal.
PMCARB	=	percentage of calories in meal deriving from carbohydrate.
PMPRO	=	percentage of calories in meal deriving from protein.
PMFAT	=	percentage of calories in meal deriving from fat.

Then:

$$MCAL = \sum_{i=1}^{N} CAL_i = \sum_{i=1}^{N} Q_i \times UCAL_i$$

$$MCARB = \sum_{i=1}^{N} CARB_i = \sum_{i=1}^{N} Q_i \times UCARB_i$$

$$MPRO = \sum_{i=1}^{N} PRO_i = \sum_{i=1}^{N} Q_i \times UPRO_i$$

$$MFAT = \sum_{i=1}^{N} FAT_i = \sum_{i=1}^{N} Q_i \times UFAT_i$$

$$PMCARB = 4 \times (MCARB/MCAL) = 4(\sum_{i=1}^{N} Q_i \times UCARB_i)/(\sum_{i=1}^{N} Q_i \times UCAL_i)$$

$$PMPRO = 4 \times (MPRO/MCAL) = 4(\sum_{i=1}^{N} Q_i \times UPRO_i)/(\sum_{i=1}^{N} Q_i \times UCAL_i)$$

$$PMFAT = 4 \times (MFAT/MCAL) = 4(\sum_{i=1}^{N} Q_i \times UFAT_i)/(\sum_{i=1}^{N} Q_i \times UCAL_i)$$

4.2 Display Function Design

To be determined (TBD) pending choice of video hardware selection.

Continued

FIGURE 4.10. (*Continued*)

4.3 Print Function Design

TBD pending choice of printer hardware selection.

4.4 Error Message Function Design

TBD.

FIGURE 4.10. *(Continued)*

Preliminary Software Design Specification Standard

The Preliminary Software Design Specification (PSDS) contains an overview of the design for the software component of a system. It describes the design approach by functional area and the identification of the data required by the software. Once approved, the PSDS is expanded during the Detailed Design Stage of the life cycle with the details needed by programmers to produce software code during the Coding Stage. These details are packaged in a Detailed Software Design Specification (DSDS) subsequently described in this standard. The format and content of the PSDS are specified below.

1.0 Background and Introduction

State the purpose of the document. Briefly describe the overall objective of the system whose preliminary software design is to be presented in this document. State the scope of the document to include a description of its organization and contents. List all references applicable to the content of this document.

2.0 System Capabilities

Paraphrase or otherwise delineate the requirements stipulated in the software requirements specification to be addressed by the software design.

3.0 System Environment

Describe the hardware that is to host the software being designed. If applicable, also indicate external interfaces to this hardware.

4.0 Design Description

Describe the design approach for accomplishing the functional capabilities delineated in paragraph 2.0. Where applicable, indicate all mathematical formulas to be used in performing computations and other data manipulations. Indicate an approach for acceptance testing each functional capability -- that is, testing the software after it is integrated into the system to determine if the system is ready for delivery to the customer.

FIGURE 4.11. Extract from documentation standard governing the format and content of the preliminary design specification in Figure 4.10.

Report of Audit
of
System MEAL PLANNER Preliminary
Software Design Specification

Version 1.0 of the System **MEAL PLANNER** Preliminary Software Design Specification (MP-04) has been audited against the **MEAL PLANNER** Software Requirements Specification (MP-01 Version 1.2) and against the project documentation standard (STDS-MNL-02). The discrepancies listed below were uncovered during the audit.

Conformance with Documentation Standard (QA Findings)

1. The standard stipulates that paragraph 1.0 of the preliminary design specification should "include a description of ... [the design specification's] organization and contents" and should also include a list of "all references applicable to the content" of the specification. Paragraph 1.0 of the draft design specification does not appear to address these items. For completeness, these items should be addressed.

2. The standard stipulates that paragraph 3.0 of the preliminary design specification should "describe the hardware that is to host the software being designed." In the draft design specification, this hardware is indicated as TBD. For completeness, this hardware should be specified -- if not in the preliminary design specification, certainly in the detailed design specification. Otherwise, it is unlikely that coding can be accomplished.

3. The standard stipulates that paragraph 4.0 of the preliminary design specification is to "describe the design approach for accomplishing the functional capabilities delineated in paragraph 2.0." Four such capabilities are delineated, but the design of only one capability (calculation function) is described. For completeness, the design of the other three capabilities (display function, print function, and error message function) should be specified. The design specification notes that the design of the display and print functions is TBD pending hardware selection. Thus, as indicated in Finding 2 above, to avoid coding delays, it would seem that hardware selection needs to be accomplished -- certainly no later than detailed design. Regarding the error message function, paragraph 4.4 of the preliminary design specification lists the design of this function as TBD. It would seem that this design does not depend on hardware selection and therefore can be addressed at this time. At a minimum, it would seem that the specific error messages to be generated, and the conditions giving rise to their generation, can be specified at this time. For completeness, this design issue should be addressed, preferably in the preliminary design specification (as opposed to the detailed design specification).

4. The standard stipulates that paragraph 4.0 of the preliminary design specification also is to "indicate an approach for acceptance testing each functional capability." The draft design specification does not address acceptance testing. For completeness, this issue should be addressed so that acceptance test planning can proceed. Regarding this testing, has it been decided who is responsible for writing the testing approach to be incorporated into the preliminary design specification -- the development staff or

Continued

FIGURE 4.12. Partial report of an audit of the preliminary design specification in Figure 4.10.

the product assurance staff? This issue should be resolved so that the preliminary design specification can be completed.

Conformance with Requirements Specification (V&V Findings)

1. Paragraph 2.0 of the requirements specification indicates that the MEAL PLANNER database is to contain nutritional information on 2000 foods. Paragraph 3.0 of the preliminary design specification indicates that this database is to contain nutritional information on 2500 foods. For consistency, this apparent discrepancy should be resolved.

2. The last formula in paragraph 4.1 of the preliminary design specification, which prescribes how to calculate the percentage of calories in a meal deriving from fat, reads as follows:

$$PMFAT = 4 \times (MFAT/MCAL) = 4 \left(\sum_{i=1}^{N} Q_i \times UFAT_i \right) / \left(\sum_{i=1}^{N} Q_i \times UCAL_i \right)$$

Paragraph 2.0 of the requirements specification indicates that 1 gram of fat contains 9 calories. It would therefore appear that the number 4 appearing in the above formula should be replaced by the number 9 [by comparison, the formula for the quantity $PFAT_i$, the percentage of calories in a food serving deriving from fat, is given in paragraph 4.1 of the preliminary design specification as follows:

$$PFAT_i = 9 \times FAT_i/CAL_i = 9 \times (UFAT_i/UCAL_i)].$$

3. As noted in QA Finding 3 above, the preliminary design of the display function, print function, and error message function is specified as TBD. Therefore, the degree of conformance of the design of these functions to requirements cannot be determined at this time.

Other Findings

Paragraph 3.0 of the requirements specification stipulates that System MEAL PLANNER is to "display an error message if the user enters a food not contained in the MEAL PLANNER database." The scope of this requirement is not clear. For example, does this requirement mean that the user is expected to enter a food name exactly as it appears in the database or else the system will respond with an error message (i.e., synonyms such as "green beans" for "string beans" will not be treated as equivalent names). For completeness, the scope of this requirement should be clarified.

FIGURE 4.12 *(Continued)*

C. The System MEAL PLANNER CCB is now meeting to decide what to do with the preliminary design specification (whether to establish it as the baseline for subsequent detailed design work, thus approving the evolutionary change from requirements to preliminary design, or whether to return the preliminary design specification to the development staff for reworking; recall Figure 4.4). With the preceding as background, what are some evolutionary and revolutionary change issues that the CCB should consider regarding the preliminary software design specification (and possibly the requirements specification)?

As discussed earlier in this section, the audit report is the primary technical input to the CCB's decision-making process (other inputs include things such as unexpected budget cuts, personnel turnover, or political factors such as a CCB's conjecture about the current willingness of the customer to agree to unanticipated changes). In the subsequent discussion, it is assumed for simplicity that the audit report in Figure 4.12 is the sole basis for the System MEAL PLANNER CCB's software change actions (see Exercise 4.13 at the end of this chapter, which deals with some of the implications of sources other than an audit report pertaining to CCB software change action). Based on the audit findings recorded in Figure 4.12, we therefore have the following evolutionary and revolutionary change issues regarding System MEAL PLANNER development that the CCB should consider:

A. QA Finding 1 points out an omission primarily of form from the preliminary design specification. It is arguable whether the omitted information significantly detracts from the readability of the document. Describing the organization and contents of the document in its first paragraph probably makes the document easier to read, but particularly for a small document (where organization is presumably simple), such tell-them-what-you-are-going-to-tell-them descriptions may be superfluous. Regarding the auditor's comment pertaining to the missing reference list, it would probably be worthwhile to give a complete citation of the System MEAL PLANNER Requirements Specification (since it is referred to in paragraph 2.0) so that, for traceability, it is clear to which version of the requirements specification the preliminary design specification is linked. If the CCB decides to approve QA Finding 1 for implementation, the resultant changes to the preliminary design specification would be considered evolutionary because they are called for by the documentation standard and are thus planned.

B. QA Finding 2 indicates that the hardware that is to host the MEAL PLANNER software has not yet been specified. The auditor then goes on to indicate, both in this finding and in QA Finding 3, what impact this hardware issue has on software development. The auditor further indicates that it may not be necessary to resolve this issue during preliminary design (despite what the documentation standard calls for), but the issue needs to be resolved during the Detailed Design Stage of the life cycle. If the CCB decides to approve QA Finding 2 for implementation (either now or during the Detailed Design Stage), then the resultant hardware changes to the preliminary design specification would be considered evolutionary (for the same reason cited in A, above). These (hardware) changes would in turn precipitate (evolutionary) software changes to paragraphs 4.2, 4.3, and 4.4 in the preliminary design specification currently indicated as "to be determined (TBD)."

C. QA Finding 3, as indicated in B, above, deals with the TBD items in paragraphs 4.2, 4.3, and 4.4 of the preliminary design specification. Regarding paragraph 4.4, the auditor points out that some of the design of the MEAL PLANNER error message function can (and should) be addressed in the preliminary design. If the CCB decides to approve this part of QA Finding 3 for implementation, then (for the reasons stated in A, above) the resultant change to the preliminary design specification would be considered evolutionary.

D. QA Finding 4 deals with the omission of an approach for acceptance testing of the four System MEAL PLANNER software functions. This omission is a product assurance issue that, as the auditor suggests, derives from an apparently lingering management oversight—some organization should be assigned responsibility for writing the acceptance testing portions of the preliminary design specification. If the CCB decides to approve QA Finding 4 for implementation, the resultant changes to the preliminary design specification would be considered neither evolutionary nor revolutionary *software* changes, since they are not part of the MEAL PLANNER software design but rather a means for ultimately determining whether code resulting from this design does what it is supposed to do. Recalling the definition of product assurance given in Section 1.1, however, it can be argued that these changes are an integral part of the evolution of MEAL PLANNER software from requirements definition to operational code and are thus evolutionary.

E. V&V Finding 1 points out a numerical discrepancy between the requirements specification and the preliminary design specification. If the CCB decides to approve this finding for implementation, the resultant change (which might be to either document or to both) would probably be considered revolutionary. For example, suppose the CCB determined that the value of 2000 in the requirements specification was what the customer wanted. Then the value of 2500 in the preliminary design specification would have to be changed to 2000 to reflect the *planned* number of items in the MEAL PLANNER database (i.e., the evolution of the system calls for 2000 items; any number other than 2000 precipitates a change that was not planned).

F. V&V Finding 2 points out an apparent error in a mathematical formula specified in the preliminary design. If the CCB decides to approve this finding for implementation, the resultant change would be considered revolutionary (the presumption being that proper interpretation of the requirements specification would not have given rise to the change so that change can be considered unplanned—i.e., revolutionary).

G. V&V Finding 3 appears on the surface to be a repetition of QA Finding 3, but in reality each finding makes visible a different aspect of the same problem. The problem is that the design of three capabilities is specified as "to be determined." QA Finding 3 not only points out the failure of the cited paragraphs to conform to the project documentation standard, but also warns of the impact of these omissions on subsequent stages. V&V Finding 3, on the other hand, looks backward at the requirements specification and warns that the absence of a design for these three capabilities prevents assessment of design congruence to requirements. These issues are both pertinent and should be considered by the CCB when it decides how to resolve this problem of evolutionary change.

H. The finding specified under Other Findings in the audit report raises an issue pertaining to the requirements specification that apparently was not raised when this specification was audited and previously approved by the CCB (a frequent occurrence on many software projects, as was pointed out in Chapter 2—recall the king and the wizard in Figure 2.8). If the CCB decides to approve this finding for implementation, the resultant changes to the requirements specification would be considered revolutionary, because they were not planned when the requirements specification was originally formulated.

The preceding discussion has brought out a broad range of evolutionary and revolutionary change issues pertaining to a relatively simple software development project. Our experience indicates that many of the issues discussed above arise on actual software projects—small (and simple) and large (and complex).

In this section, we have looked at the change control process in some detail. Our discussion and illustrations show that the focal point of this processing is the configuration control board. It is now time to explore the CCB in more depth—to ascertain what it is and how it works.

As a final note for this section, we point out that the change control process discussed in this section—with the CCB as the focus of all change processing—is not the only way to process software changes. Readers interested in considering alternative ways to process changes should work Exercises 4.3 and 4.12.

4.3 Examination of the CCB

In the preceding section, we showed that the configuration control board was the central element in the change control process. We introduced the CCB as a decision-making body—establishing baselines, approving discrepancy resolutions, directing revisits to life cycle stages, and authorizing updates of baselines. In this section, we focus on this board and discuss who sits on it, what decisions it makes, and how it operates. The purpose of this in-depth examination is to bring to light the important considerations associated with planning for, establishing, and sustaining this central element in the change control process.

Who sits on the CCB? To answer this question, recall Figure 2.13, which showed the three disciplines that contribute to the achievement of software product integrity:

Management, including both senior and project management

Development, including analysis, design, engineering, coding, unit and subsystem testing, installation, and training

Product assurance, including quality assurance, test and evaluation, configuration management, and verification and validation

Because the synergistic efforts of these three disciplines are needed to achieve software products with integrity, and because the CCB is the forum that is central to the product assurance function of change control, it seems only reasonable that the CCB should include all three disciplines in its membership—that is, the CCB should have representatives on it from management, from the developers, and from the product assurance practitioners. Now, this does not mean that a CCB should be permanently staffed with a representative from each subfunction mentioned above, for example, with a coding representative and a training representative, among others. Many CCB meetings will be concerned with neither coding nor training. The CCB should be permanently staffed with at least one representative from management, from development, and from product assurance, with additional representation provided according to the subject matter under consideration at any particular meeting. Remember that the CCB is a forum for the exchange of information, whose purpose is to make change control decisions. It is essential to this purpose to have representation from and interaction among all concerned parties relative to whatever matter is under consideration.

In this discussion of representation on the CCB, we have not said which archetypical project participant provides the representatives. After all, each of the three archetypical project participants—the user, the buyer, and the seller—may have its own project management, as well as its own development and product assurance staffs. Which archetypical participant should provide representatives to the CCB? We believe they all should. Ideally, the CCB should include management, development, and product assurance representatives from the user, from the buyer, and from the seller. It may not always be practical to have all these representatives (for example, the user may be many thousands of miles away from the buyer and seller), but to the extent possible the CCB should be established as an integrated one. What better forum exists for interaction of the user, buyer, and seller in the control of change on a project? Such a CCB greatly increases the visibility of the changes under consideration and of the viewpoints of all project participants. The result should be better change control decisions.

Up to this point, we have discussed *the* CCB, as if it were a single board managing all change. In practice, many projects will have more than a single CCB to manage change within a project. Several factors are involved in the decision regarding how many CCBs to establish on a project, as discussed in the following paragraphs.

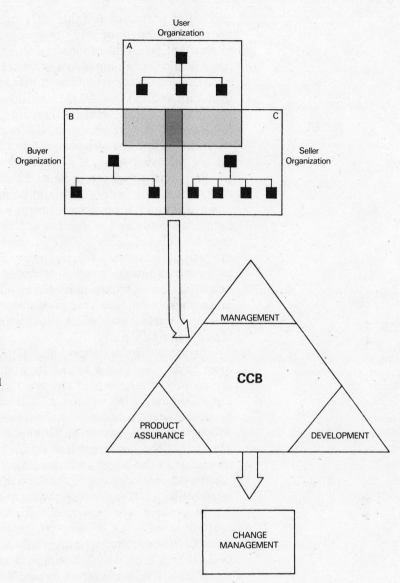

FIGURE 4.13. CCBs provide forums for units of each organization within the user/buyer/seller triumvirate—or for pairs of these organizations, or for all three organizations—to interact continually and effectively on a software project for the purpose of managing change.

One of these factors is the individual and collective needs and concerns of the user, the buyer, and the seller. Figure 4.13 shows the effect of this factor on the establishment of CCBs. The figure shows how organizational units of the user, the buyer, and the seller, encompassing the disciplines of management, development, and product assurance, can meet together to form an integrated CCB. The shadings in the figure indicate various combinations of the user, buyer, and seller joining in an integrated CCB. The lighter shading represents a user/buyer CCB (overlap of A and B), a user/seller CCB (overlap of A and C), and a buyer/seller CCB (overlap of B and C). The darker shading represents a user/buyer/seller CCB (overlap of A, B, and C).

It may be argued that creating a CCB consisting of buyer

and seller personnel is inherently unworkable. Project managers, either buyer or seller, would generally rather not have unpleasant or unfavorable news (such as the need to make a large number of changes to a software product that should be near the end of its development) divulged in a public forum. It is human nature to put off public disclosure of an organization's problems in the expectation that timely solutions to the problems can be developed within the organization. If such solutions can be found, there is no need to make the problems public. On the other hand, if such solutions are not forthcoming, the problems may have to be surfaced publicly at some later date, when they generally would be more difficult and costly to solve. The CCB provides a forum where such problems can be made visible and where the entire project team can focus on their solution. The earlier in the life cycle that problems are introduced to the CCB, the more likely it is that a software product with integrity can be achieved. The authors have seen numerous cases where joint buyer/seller CCBs have proven quite workable in resolving problems. Section 7.1 presents several real-world experiences illustrating the benefits of joint buyer/seller CCBs.

In some circumstances, one of these organizations (i.e., user, buyer, or seller) may validly wish to convene a CCB comprised only of members of its own organization. For example, the seller may wish to hold a CCB meeting with only seller personnel present to consider the first draft of a document that will eventually be baselined. This CCB would increase the likelihood that the document had product integrity before it was presented to the buyer and user. When this seller CCB is satisfied with the document, it would be presented to an integrated buyer/seller CCB for consideration as a baseline.

In general, the preferred integrated CCB would be the user/buyer/seller CCB indicated in Figure 4.13. The buyer/seller CCB shown in the figure might be convened, for example, to consider a draft detailed design document, in which the user would have a minor interest. A user/buyer CCB might meet to consider baselining the requirements specification, prior to its delivery to the seller for fulfillment. The user/seller CCB shown in Figure 4.13 might consider the resolution of incidents arising in operational software, provided the incidents had no impact on cost and schedule. (If these incidents did, the buyer would be most interested in participating in the discussion.)

A second factor in determining the number and kind of CCBs to establish is the system development issues that might be faced on a project. Figure 4.14 shows a hierarchy of system development issues, along with a sample of each issue and a CCB that might be established to handle the issue. The hierarchy shown is not unique; we use it here for expository purposes. In the figure, the level of hierarchy is indicated by appropriate indentation. Within every project, there are system issues and, in many projects, system external interface issues to be addressed. Within the system, there are subsystem issues

SYSTEM DEVELOPMENT ISSUE HIERARCHY	SAMPLE ISSUE	CCB HIERARCHY
System	Can I add this new function to my system in 3 months?	System CCB
Subsystem	Are the design specifications for functions F14 and F15 of Subsystem S1 mutually consistent?	Subsystem CCB
Hardware	Should I buy or build a black box to perform system function F1?	Hardware CCB
Software	Is the computer code in conformance with the design specification?	Software CCB
Internal Interfaces	Do the software database organization and hardware disk access times allow lookup of a Los Angeles telephone number within one second?	Hardware/Software CCB
Intersubsystem Interfaces	Should altitude transmitted from Subsystem S1 to Subsystem S2 be in units of feet or nautical miles?	Subsystem Interface CCB
System External Interfaces	What messages can I pass from my system to System Q via existing Communications Link L1?	Intersystem CCB

FIGURE 4.14. A CCB hierarchy generally derives from the hierarchy of issues associated with system development and their perceived significance.

and intersubsystem interface issues to be considered (for systems having major, identifiable subsystems). Within each subsystem, there are hardware, software, and internal (hardware/software) interface issues to be resolved.

Issues like those suggested in Figure 4.14 exist for almost every project, but all the CCBs shown in the figure would not necessarily be established on every project. Which ones should be established for a project vary from project to project. The key elements to consider when deciding whether an issue is significant enough to merit creation of a separate CCB include project size and complexity, and criticality and importance of the issue within a project. Those issues for which CCBs are not established are subsumed by the next highest issue in the hierarchy for which a CCB is established. For example, on a small project, only a System CCB might be established; all the issues shown in Figure 4.14 would be considered by this board. Consider, on the other hand, a very large project where each subsystem is an operational system in itself. In this case, the full spectrum of CCBs shown in Figure 4.14 might be constituted. (The authors are aware of several large Department of Defense systems that use a CCB hierarchy like that shown in Figure 4.14—see, for example, Project Venus in Section 7.1.)

Because the focus of this book is on software, we have highlighted the software issue in the hierarchy and the Software CCB in Figure 4.14. Most software issues are handled at this level. However, you should be aware that some software-related issues are handled at other levels in the issue hierarchy. For instance, see the sample issue for subsystem in Figure 4.14—the consideration of design specifications clearly has software-related aspects as well as hardware-related aspects. On some projects, the software issue is refined into subissues for which separate CCBs are established. The authors are familiar with a project, for example, in which a Software Incident Report CCB and a Software Change Request CCB were established (see Project Jupiter in Section 7.1).

A third factor to consider in planning for the establishment of CCBs is the level of expertise needed for each CCB. Consider a CCB whose members are managers of the various organizations represented at the CCB. Such a CCB would have difficulty making informed decisions on issues involving the technical details of the project. The management-oriented members of the CCB may not have the technical background to understand the problems or resolutions presented to them. A similar difficulty arises if the CCB consists of engineers and staff personnel and is faced with making decisions concerned with project policy. This latter CCB probably would not have the expertise or the authority in policy concerns to make proper decisions.

A solution to the above difficulties is to staff the CCB with both managers and technical personnel from the three disciplines shown in Figure 2.13. This solution carries the disadvantage that, for some period of time, every member of the CCB would be noncontributing (and probably bored). It is not an effective use of project personnel.

Another solution is to create several CCBs, each having a restricted area of decision-making and a membership with the appropriate level of expertise. One approach that we have seen function successfully using such levels is to constitute a CCB composed of managers from the three disciplines shown in Figure 2.13 and a CCB composed of technical personnel from those disciplines. The scope of the management-level CCB extends to resource allocation, budgets, schedules, and policies; technical details are not considered. On the other hand, the technical-level CCB concentrates on the detailed technical aspects of the project. Matters arising at a CCB meeting that do not fall within the appropriate level of expertise of that CCB are referred to the other CCB.

In planning for the CCBs to use on a project, there are thus three factors to consider—the involvement of the user, buyer, and seller; the system development issues to be handled; and the levels of expertise required. Applying these factors to their extreme could lead to the creation of a bewildering array of CCBs, whose prime effort would probably be deciding what the area of responsibility for each CCB should be! We certainly do not suggest that. We are suggesting that these three factors should be rationally considered in the context of each project when planning the establishment of a hierarchy of CCBs.

A real-world example of the results of considering these factors is shown in Figure 4.15. This figure shows the hierarchy

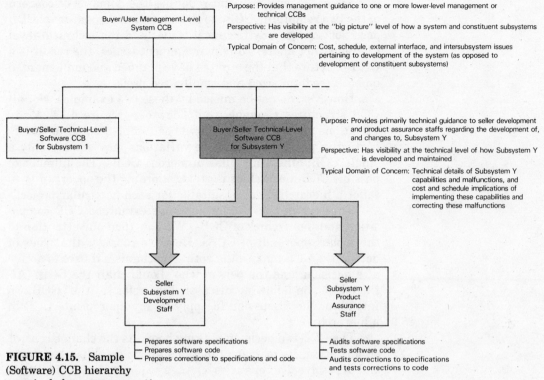

Purpose: Provides management guidance to one or more lower-level management or technical CCBs

Perspective: Has visibility at the "big picture" level of how a system and constituent subsystems are developed

Typical Domain of Concern: Cost, schedule, external interface, and intersubsystem issues pertaining to development of the system (as opposed to development of constituent subsystems)

Purpose: Provides primarily technical guidance to seller development and product assurance staffs regarding the development of, and changes to, Subsystem Y

Perspective: Has visibility at the technical level of how Subsystem Y is developed and maintained

Typical Domain of Concern: Technical details of Subsystem Y capabilities and malfunctions, and cost and schedule implications of implementing these capabilities and correcting these malfunctions

FIGURE 4.15. Sample (Software) CCB hierarchy organized along management/technical and user/buyer/seller lines illustrating how management and technical CCB guidance effects and affects software change.

of CCBs and their relationship to the seller's development and product assurance staffs on a large project concerned with military command and control. This project is a "system of systems"; that is, each subsystem is a large, independently operating system, interfacing with the other subsystems via high-speed data links. The CCB hierarchy consists of a buyer/user management-level system CCB and a buyer/seller technical-level software CCB for each subsystem. Note in Figure 4.15 that the relationship between the Software CCB for Subsystem Y and the seller's development and product assurance staffs for Subsystem Y is one of technical guidance and is not a line of authority. Note also that the domains of concern for the two levels of CCB overlap—the management-level CCB addresses some technical issues, and the technical-level CCB addresses some managerial issues. Finally, observe in the figure caption that the first time the word "software" appears it is placed in parentheses; this notation is intended to emphasize that the System CCB is not constrained to consider only software.

But not every product assurance manager is faced with large-sized projects. You might well ask for an example of a CCB hierarchy for a medium-sized or small-sized project. Figure 4.15 with a few modifications can also serve as an example of a CCB hierarchy for such projects. If one removes all subsystem CCBs from Figure 4.15, except for that for Subsystem Y; relabels the retained Subsystem Y CCB as the Software CCB (for the entire system); and redefines the domains of concern of the two remaining CCBs so that the management-level CCB does not address any technical issues and the technical-level CCB does not address any management issues, the result is a CCB structure that the authors have planned and implemented on both medium-sized and small-sized projects.

However, do not be misled by these two examples. Not all CCB structures resemble that shown in Figure 4.15. Many variations are possible and have been implemented to satisfy particular project needs. Some variations may employ only a single CCB; others may use numerous CCBs. The number of possible CCB hierarchies is great, affording the opportunity to tailor a hierarchy that is suitable for each particular project.

Thus far in this section we have examined CCB composition and hierarchies of CCBs. We now turn our attention to the modus operandi of CCBs. Here we consider the types of decisions a CCB makes, the voting mechanism it uses to arrive at a decision, and the person who should chair the CCB. (Although in the following discussion we refer to "the" CCB, we intend for the discussion to apply to any appropriate CCB in a hierarchy.)

The CCB is a decision-making body. As the change control organization, its primary functions are to establish baselines and to resolve discrepancies, change requests, and incident reports that come before it. When considering a draft baseline, the CCB may elect either to accept or to reject the draft baseline (see Figure 4.16). Acceptance is not necessarily predicated upon there being no outstanding discrepancies against the draft baseline. Although such a goal is desirable, practical considerations often dictate that the CCB establish a baseline and postpone resolution of any outstanding discrepancies to some later agreed-upon date. Rejection of a draft baseline could be based on its noncongruence with its predecessor baseline or its requirements, or on other discrepancies, such as its internal inconsistency or its failure to satisfy specified standards. When the CCB rejects a draft baseline, it provides a list of approved changes to the draft baseline. The development organization reworks the draft baseline to incorporate the changes and submits the revised draft baseline to the CCB for approval.

In light of the above decision alternatives, let us reconsider Figure 4.5, which shows the change control of an evolutionary change. Note from this figure that the CCB is considering establishing a baseline and resolving discrepancies uncovered during the audit. The acceptance of the baseline causes the path to be taken to the next stage (the Coding Stage in Figure 4.5). Rejection of a draft baseline leads to a return to the current life cycle stage. Any approved change to the draft baseline also causes a return to the current stage. Approved changes to preceding baselines cause the paths to the appropriate preceding life cycle stages to be taken.

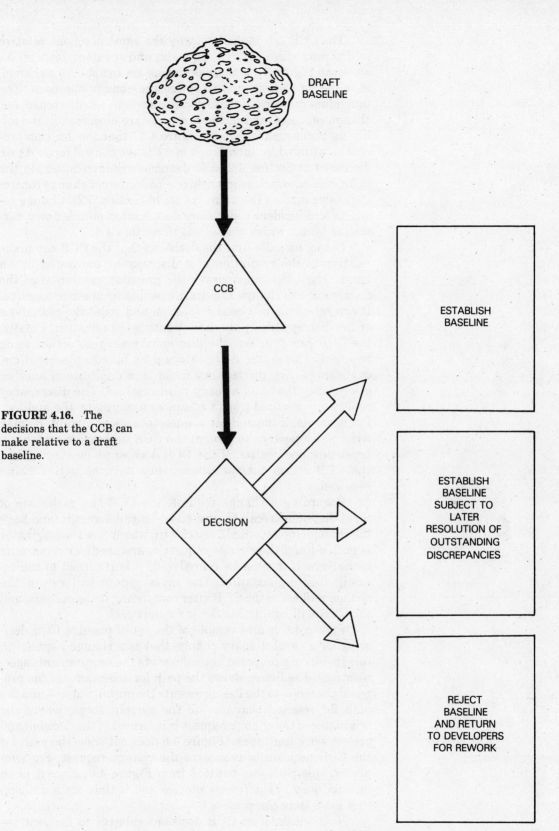

FIGURE 4.16. The decisions that the CCB can make relative to a draft baseline.

DRAFT BASELINE

CCB

DECISION

ESTABLISH BASELINE

ESTABLISH BASELINE SUBJECT TO LATER RESOLUTION OF OUTSTANDING DISCREPANCIES

REJECT BASELINE AND RETURN TO DEVELOPERS FOR REWORK

The CCB can make basically the same decisions relative to discrepancies, change requests, and incident reports. As shown in Figure 4.17, these decisions are to approve a change, to make no change, and to revise the change approach. The individual nuances of these decisions relative to discrepancies, change requests, and incident reports are discussed in the following paragraphs. Note in Figure 4.17 that the decision process is initiated by submission of a change control form. As we discussed in Section 4.2, discrepancies are introduced via the audit report, which is in essence a collection of change control forms (we discuss the audit report in Section 5.2). Change requests and incident reports are documented on their own particular forms, which we discuss in Section 4.4.

Let us consider first the decisions that the CCB can make relative to the resolution of a discrepancy uncovered by an audit. The CCB can approve the proposed resolution of the discrepancy to change the draft baseline or another baseline. It can reject the proposed resolution and order the reanalysis of the discrepancy by the investigating organization. Finally, the CCB can close out the discrepancy with no action being required. This latter decision could be based on several circumstances. The discrepancy could be a duplicate of another discrepancy that had already been resolved. The discrepancy could have resulted from a misunderstanding by the auditor. For example, if the auditor is uncertain about a point, he may write a discrepancy to prompt the CCB to consider whether a problem indeed exists. If the CCB decides no problem exists, the CCB closes out the discrepancy with no action being required.

Regarding a change request, the CCB can make one of three decisions (recall Figure 4.17)—it can accept it (and have the change implemented), reject it (in which case the originator is notified and the change request is archived), or require its reanalysis. If it must be reanalyzed, it is returned to the investigating organization. The investigators will return the change request to the CCB after completing its reanalysis, and the CCB will again consider it for approval.

Figure 4.6 is an example of the set of possible CCB decisions for a revolutionary change that is a change request (in this instance, a proposed amendment to the requirements specification). The figure shows the path for acceptance of the proposed change—to the Requirements Definition Stage—and the path for rejected changes—to the current stage, where the originator of the change request is informed of the decision and project work continues. (Figure 4.6 does not show the path for the CCB decision to reanalyze the change request. For simplicity, this path was omitted from Figure 4.6, since it is an internal loop in the review process and is thus not a decision that exits from the process.)

Next we consider CCB decisions relative to incident re-

FIGURE 4.17. The decisions that the CCB can make relative to a change control form.

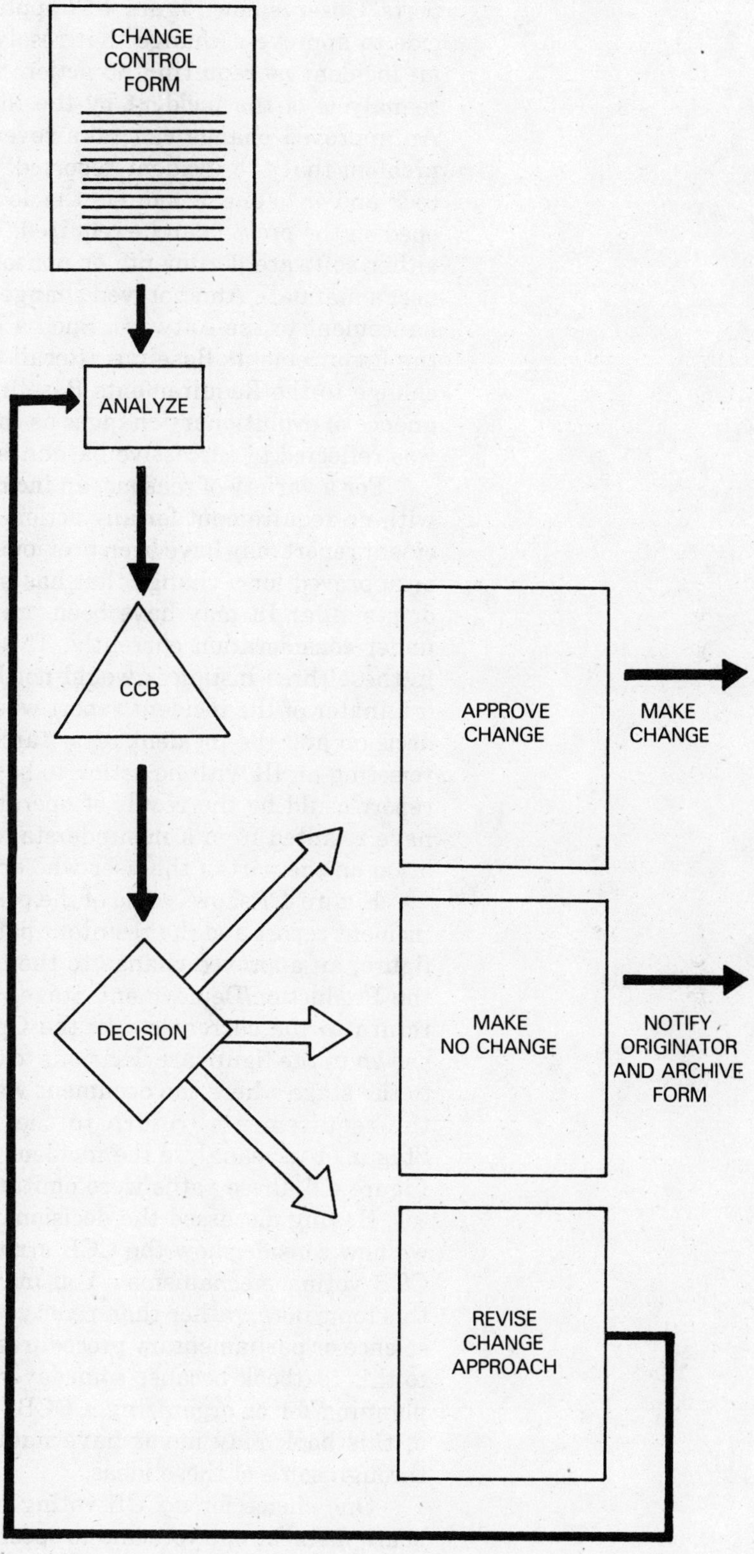

CHANGE CONTROL FORM

ANALYZE

CCB

DECISION

APPROVE CHANGE → MAKE CHANGE

MAKE NO CHANGE → NOTIFY ORIGINATOR AND ARCHIVE FORM

REVISE CHANGE APPROACH

ports. Observe how Figure 4.17 applies here. The CCB can decide to approve a change that resolves the incident, to reject an incident as requiring no action to be taken, or to require reanalysis of the incident by the investigating organization. An approved change can take several forms. To correct the problem that the incident reported, a change to the software code and/or to one or more of the documents previously developed on the project can be required. These documents could be either software documents or nonsoftware documents (e.g., a user's manual). An approved change could also require an enhancement to the software. Such a change would be made to the Requirements Baseline. (Recall from Section 4.2 that this change to the Requirements Baseline would precipitate a sequence of evolutionary changes as the change in requirements was reflected in successive baselines.)

For a variety of reasons, an incident report can be rejected with no requirement for any action to be taken. A similar incident report may have been previously considered and rejected or approved for a change that has not yet been implemented, or a similar IR may have been previously submitted and be under consideration currently. The duplicate incident report in these three instances would not be considered further; the originator of the incident report would be notified of the CCB decision and the incident report archived. Another reason for rejecting an IR with no action to be taken is that the incident report could be the result of operator or user error. It could have resulted from a misunderstanding of the software operation on the part of the user who originated it.

Figure 4.7 shows some of the possible CCB decisions on an incident report and the resultant paths taken. As shown in the figure, an approved change to the code results in a return to the Production/Deployment Stage. A rejection results in the return to the current stage, the Operational Use Stage. Not shown in the figure are decisions to correct a document (return to the stage where the document was developed), or to amend the requirements (return to the Requirements Definition Stage), or to reanalyze the incident report. As was the case in Figure 4.6, these paths were omitted for simplicity.

Having discussed the decisions that the CCB may make, we now consider how the CCB arrives at those decisions (i.e., CCB voting mechanisms). You may wonder why we address this topic here, rather than refer you to a textbook on political science or parliamentary procedures. We have added this topic to this textbook because someday you may be responsible for planning for or organizing a CCB, and because some readers of this book may never have had the opportunity to think through some of these ideas.

One choice for a CCB voting mechanism is to give each board member one vote and to specify that the majority effects a decision (what constitutes a majority must be specified in the directive establishing the CCB). To those of us raised in a democratic tradition, this voting mechanism has obvious appeal—all views are considered equally, and everyone is a part of the decision process (and therefore probably more interested in the proceedings). But watch out! This form of voting mechanism could lead to stacking the vote by one organization. For example, if the seller's entire development organization came to a CCB meeting, it might outvote the rest of the membership and make all the decisions conform to its organization's wishes. Another disadvantage of the one-person-one-vote voting mechanism is that politics could be introduced into the voting process ("If I vote to approve items A and B that you are interested in getting approved, will you vote to approve items C and D that I am interested in getting approved?"). The result is CCB decisions based on vote trading and not on the technical merits of each item considered.

A possible modification to the one-person-one-vote voting mechanism would be to give a vote to each organization represented on the CCB rather than to each individual. This method loses some of its democratic appeal—indeed, it is a republican process. (Note that both "democratic" and "republican" begin with a lower-case letter!) But it still keeps everyone involved in the decision process. The possibility of politicking still exists in this method, but the ability to stack the vote is prevented—the number of votes remains constant, regardless of how many members of one organization attend a meeting.

Another voting mechanism to consider is to achieve a consensus of all the board members on each item under consideration. By *consensus* we mean the informal agreement (no vote counting) of most of those present at a meeting. This method permits the expression of all viewpoints and retains the interest of all board members. It is more expeditious than voting by individuals or organizations, and it tends to inhibit politicking. But what if the CCB cannot achieve consensus? No decision can be made in such a case, unless a mechanism to break deadlocks has been included in the CCB's charter. Such an escape mechanism might be to give all the votes to a single person when it is necessary to break a deadlock.

Giving all the votes to a single person (say, for the moment, the chairman of the CCB) could be the voting mechanism used by a CCB under all circumstances. Such a dictatorial method certainly fosters decision-making, but it may quickly stifle the interest of the other board representatives. If the chairman never considers their views, listens to their comments, or consults with them prior to making a decision, they will have little interest in the CCB proceedings or even in attending the meetings. The chairman must recognize his potential for limiting participation and take positive measures to encourage input and discussion from all CCB members. He needs the visibility that their input provides if he is to make good change control decisions.

TABLE 4.1.   ADVANTAGES AND DISADVANTAGES OF CANDIDATES FOR CCB CHAIRMAN

CCB Chairman Candidate	Advantage(s)	Disadvantage(s)
Seller's project manager	Responsible for project development and maintenance Probably most technically competent of managerial personnel	May not have the buyer's interests at heart
Buyer's project manager	Bears the prime responsibility to the user for product integrity Puts up the money to fund the project	May not be technically competent to render reasonable decisions regarding software changes
Seller's product assurance representative	Change control is one of his prime responsibilities	May be biased toward seller's interests at the expense of the buyer May be too technically oriented, slighting management considerations
Buyer's product assurance representative	Change control is one of his prime responsibilities	May not be sensitive to certain project issues that may affect the feasibility of implementing changes approved
Seller's and buyer's project managers, serving jointly	Buyer and seller equally represented Each bears the prime responsibility for the project within his organization	Has potential for deadlock

We need to say a few words here about the chairman of the CCB. The selection of this person is especially important when he or she has all the votes. Under the other voting mechanisms, the selection of the chairman is less critical, the primary duties of the chairman in these cases being to keep the board on track with its agenda and to keep discussion focused on the issues. So let us consider possible choices for CCB chairman when all the votes for the board are given to that person. To enlarge the scope of the selection, let us further assume that the CCB is composed of buyer and seller representatives. Table 4.1 shows for several candidates some considerations pertinent to the selection of a CCB chairman. You can observe from that table that there are advantages and disadvantages to selecting any of the candidates listed there. On each project, you must weigh the considerations given in this and the preceding paragraphs and in Table 4.1 in selecting a CCB chairman and a CCB voting mechanism for making decisions.

This discussion completes our examination of the CCB. We have now discussed the types of changes on a project, the process of change control, and the organization at the focus of this process. To complete our study of software change control, we need only discuss the paperwork supporting the change control process. The next section addresses this topic. Strictly speaking, paperwork support of the CCB is a bookkeeping function, to which Chapter 6 is devoted. The software change control portion of the bookkeeping function is included in the current chapter because it is so closely involved in the change management process.

4.4 Paperwork Support of the CCB

Paperwork! The very mention of the word probably makes you grimace. Yet the paperwork support of the CCB is essential if the change control process is to be visible and traceable. In this section, we discuss why paperwork is necessary in change control and then show you how to develop and use a set of change control forms. We take this approach (rather than presenting "the" forms that you must use) because you will want to tailor your change control forms to your particular project and environment. To this end, we first derive a typical set of forms needed to support the CCB. We provide guidelines on forms design, and then lead you through the design of one of these forms, the incident report, in a sample problem. We show you examples of the other needed forms. We conclude the section with three general scenarios covering all the situations that could precipitate a software change and illustrate the use of the sample forms in these scenarios.

Is paperwork really necessary to support the change control process? The authors have not met anyone who would not agree that some paperwork is necessary to control change; it appears to be widely viewed as a "necessary evil." Perhaps it would seem less evil if one considered that the alternative (no paperwork) might well lead to statements by the project participants such as:

Exactly what change am I being asked to approve?

I've got an angry user on the telephone. Does anyone remember what problem she reported last month?

No, I haven't made that change—I didn't know it had been approved.

I'm ready to make the change now, but I forget the details of the elegant solution that our recently departed guru recommended. Does anyone know how I can reach him?

You were right—this problem is the same one we had last fall. I've found the report of the old problem, but I can't find out how we solved it. I guess I'll have to solve it all over again.

Statements like these indicate a lack of visibility and traceability in the change control process. Forms make manifest the visibility and traceability that the CCB provides to the change control process. The use of a form to record a problem, to recommend that a change be made, or to indicate a CCB decision immediately captures that event and makes it uniformly visible to all project participants. Instead of becoming the subject of guesswork, the event is made concrete. Capturing the event and using cross-references between forms provides traceability between events connected with the change control process.

Figure 4.18 illustrates this concept that forms (in conjunction with the CCB) give visibility and traceability to the change control process. In the figure, a change control event p (e.g., the occurrence of an incident at a user site) has been recorded on form type A. A subsequent event q (e.g., the promulgation of a notice announcing an approved change) causes form type B to be generated. The act of recording events p and q has made the change control process more visible. The increased visibility is shown symbolically in Figure 4.18 by the enlarged letters and arrow in the field of view of the binoculars. In Figure 4.18, event q is related to event p (e.g., event p could be an incident, while event q could be the promulgation of the resolution to the incident). Traceability between events p and q is symbolically shown in Figure 4.18 by the arrow connecting event p to event q. On the actual forms that we discuss later in this section, traceability between these events is attained by a pointer to form type B placed on form type A, and by a pointer to form type A placed on form type B. (Note that Figure 4.18 does not imply that every project event is recorded on a form. Indeed, the opposite is true—many events on a software project are not recorded on forms [e.g., a meeting of a CCB].)

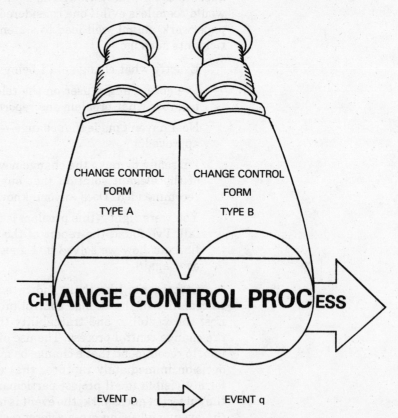

FIGURE 4.18. Forms (in conjunction with the CCB) give visibility and traceability to the change control process.

TABLE 4.2.   FOR EACH EVENT IN THE CHANGE CONTROL
PROCESS, INFORMATION MUST BE RECORDED TO PROVIDE
VISIBILITY AND TRACEABILITY TO THE PROCESS

Event	Information to Be Recorded
Initiation	Identification of the originator and of the environment, statement of the problem
Freezing	Identification of the problem
Audit	Discrepancies uncovered
Analysis	Cause, impact, and recommended resolution
Decision	CCB action
Implementation	Statement of what is to be changed

Now that we have shown you that paperwork is necessary
to the change control process, let us consider how we might
choose a set of forms to support that process. (Note that we do
not construct the process to match existing forms, but rather
the reverse.) The basic events in the change control process
(recall Figure 4.4) and some information to be recorded about
each event are shown in Table 4.2. All these events shown in
the table result in providing information relative to a pending
change. However, the information obtained from an audit is
generally recorded in an audit report (as discussed in Section
5.2), and no separate change control form is needed to support
this event. The information gathered from the other events
listed in Table 4.2 is captured on change control forms.

Before selecting a set of change control forms, let us consider a categorization of changes that includes one more level
of depth than evolutionary and revolutionary change. This
categorization we characterize by the following three
questions:

Revolutionary Change

Do we want something not already in the software or something that extends what is already there? (Briefly stated:
Do we want something new or different?)

Is something in the software at variance with the requirements specification? (Briefly stated: Is something wrong?)

Evolutionary Change

Should we establish this product as a new or updated baseline? (Briefly stated: Should we baseline this product?)

We contend that this categorization includes all possible
changes to the software in a system. It is instructive to recall
the king's question in the first frame of Figure 2.8 ("Can you
stop the rain?"). Where does this question fit into the above
categorization? We believe that the question could relate to
either category under revolutionary change. The king could

TABLE 4.3. A SET OF FORMS TO SUPPORT THE CHANGE CONTROL PROCESS

Category	Form	Process Events Recorded
Do we want something new or different?	Change Request (CR) Impact Assessment (IA)	Initiation, freezing, decision Analysis
Is something wrong?	Incident Report (IR)	Initiation, freezing, analysis, decision
	Software Change Notice (SCN)	Implementation
Should we baseline this product?	None	

want something different to happen (i.e., something other than rain), or he might think that his requirements (unstated, in the cartoon) have not been fulfilled (e.g., the requirements may have specified that it not rain on the day in question).

We next derive a set of forms to support the change control process by allocating to various forms the basic events occurring in the process of answering the three questions above. Note that each process event for a category must be recorded either on one of the forms postulated or in some other established place (e.g., the results of an audit of an IR may be reported in the minutes of a CCB meeting). Table 4.3 shows a set of forms resulting from one allocation of the change control process events.[2] Observe from the table that the implementation event is not recorded on any form for the first category of change. This omission is deliberate—when the CCB approves a change to add something new or different, the implementation almost always initially involves the updating of the requirements specification. The republication of the requirements specification is sufficient notice of the implementation of the change.

We create no form to provide visibility and traceability to the process of baselining an evolutionary change. A form is not needed simply because the information that would be recorded on such a form is recorded someplace else. The initiation event information is found within the change itself, that is, within the proposed new or updated software baseline. The identification of the change is generally added to the software baseline during the freezing event. The results of the audit are recorded in an audit report. As discussed in Section 5.2, the analysis of the audit findings is recorded and presented to the CCB in a report.[3] The decision of the CCB is recorded in the CCB minutes. Implementation of the change—when the change is approved—is indicated on the change itself. Therefore, no addi-

---

[2] In Chapter 5, we introduce a variation of the incident report called a test incident report (TIR). Although the TIR is a change control form, we postpone our discussion of it to Chapter 5 because of its intimate relationship to the acceptance testing process, described there.

[3] In Chapter 5, we point out that audit findings can be collectively documented in an audit report or individually documented in IRs. This latter approach for documenting audit findings uses IRs and SCNs. This use of change control forms for evolutionary change processing is discussed in Chapter 5.

tional forms are required to support baseline change processing.

The names given to these change control forms vary widely in the industry. For example, others may term what we call an incident report a software trouble report, a system problem report, or a discrepancy report. The names given the forms are not significant, but merely a matter of personal preference. The authors prefer, for example, the term "incident report" because of its less pejorative connotations.

Similarly, the set of forms in Table 4.3 is not unique—that is, it is not the only set of forms that could be specified to support the software change control process. For example, the Department of Defense uses a form called an engineering change proposal (ECP) that is a combination of our change request and impact assessment forms. You might want to designate for each of your projects your own set of forms based on a different allocation of process events to forms. The set we propose is provided primarily for exemplification purposes, although in our experience it has proven to be a workable and effective set.

We now turn to how to design your forms. For this purpose, we work through a sample problem to design the IR form. We then present you with examples of the other forms in the set we specified in Table 4.3 (which were designed using techniques similar to those used in the sample problem). You might want to design your own forms for your particular project and its environment, or you might tailor the sample forms we provide to suit your project and environment.

In designing forms, keep in mind the following considerations. Most important is that the form capture the data you need to record. Of almost as great importance is consideration for the people who will be filling out the forms. Each form should be simple to fill out. It should be easy to read, should clearly label each item as to what is wanted, and should indicate acceptable values if a range of values or a code is used. Make it easy for the person filling out the form, and you will be rewarded with complete and correct data entry. Make it difficult for the person filling out the form, and you will get inaccurate, incomplete, and invalid data entered.

Generally, every change control form should contain information in the categories listed in Table 4.4. If a form records data on more than one event, information in some categories must be recorded for each event (e.g., the originator category or the event description category). The originator category includes information not only on the initiator of the form but also on each person who fills out a part of the form in response to an event. The subject category is concerned with identifying what the form is addressing, whether it is documentation or software code. The subject is the same for all events recorded on a form. Therefore, subject information need be placed on a form only once, regardless of how many events are recorded on

TABLE 4.4. GENERIC CONTENT OF A CHANGE CONTROL FORM

Category	Content
Originator	Information in this category must identify the person filling out the form and his organization and telephone number, so that he can answer questions relative to the data he enters. If the form records several events, each person filling out a part of the form must be identified.
Subject	The subject of the form, be it document or code, must be precisely identified, including its environment if appropriate, so that a reader can locate it or reconstruct it, if necessary. Cross-references to other forms are another means of identification of subject.
Event description	This category contains the information that is to be recorded about each event. It might describe a problem, the impact of an incident, the recommended resolution of an incident, or the approved disposition of a proposed change.
Approval	Some events may require the approval of one or more authorities before further action can occur. For such events, the form must record these approvals.

the form. Event description is recorded for every event covered by a form. The specific data elements used to contain the event description vary widely, depending upon the event recorded and the desires of each project's management. Approvals may not be needed for all events and should be placed on the form only for events that do require them, as specified in project policy directives.

The specification of data elements and layout of a change control form depend upon the project and the software environment in which the form will be used. To show you how Table 4.4 can be applied to the design of a form, we next develop (in a sample problem) the design of an incident report.

DESIGNING AN
INCIDENT REPORT
FORM—A SAMPLE
PROBLEM
Background and Problem

As part of the seller's product assurance planning group at the beginning of a medium-sized project,[4] you have decided to implement a set of forms for supporting the change control process. One of these forms is an incident report (IR). This form is to be used to record data for the revolutionary change control events of initiation, freezing, analysis, and decision when something in the software is apparently wrong (see Table 4.3). Design this IR form, giving at least one reason for each item included on the form.

[4] By a *medium-sized* project, we mean a project having roughly ten to twenty persons working on it full-time. Exercise 4.14, which defines small-sized and large-sized projects, asks you to consider the implications of removing this assumption.

The IR form we are designing will record data for four events in the change control process. We first decide on each element for each event, using Table 4.4 as a guideline. Then we lay out these elements so that the format is understandable, easy to use, and well organized. Figure 4.19 is the result of this form-design process. We now explain in detail how we arrived at the figure.

A. *Initiation Event.* The name, organization, and telephone number of the incident originator are placed on the form so that the originator may be contacted should questions arise. Organization and full telephone number are important here,

FIGURE 4.19. Example of an incident report (IR) form and associated events that it documents.

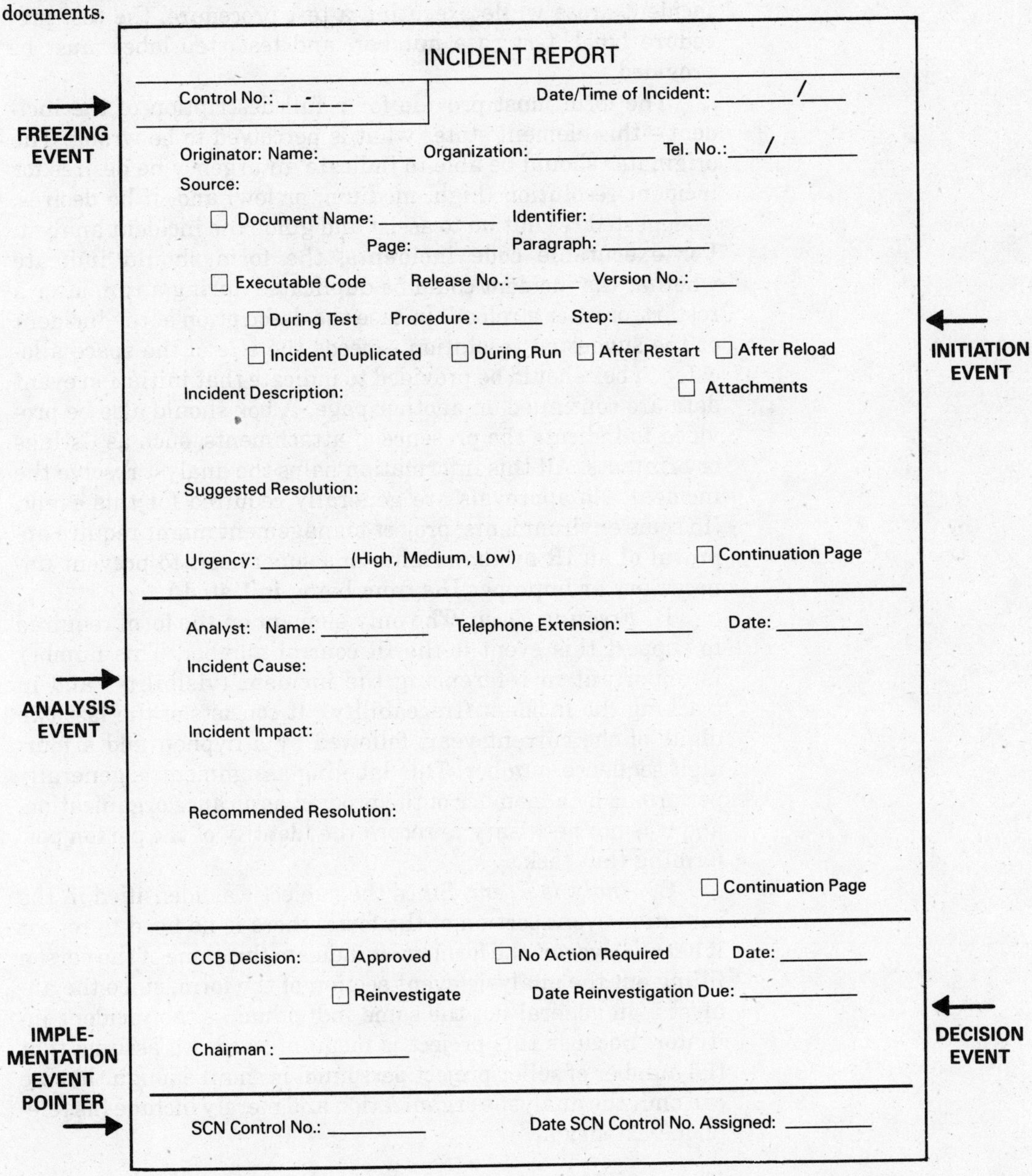

INCIDENT REPORT

Control No.: __ - ____   Date/Time of Incident: _____ / ____

Originator: Name: _____ Organization: _____ Tel. No.: __ / _____

Source:

☐ Document Name: _____ Identifier: _____

Page: _____ Paragraph: _____

☐ Executable Code   Release No.: _____ Version No.: ____

☐ During Test   Procedure : _____   Step: _____

☐ Incident Duplicated   ☐ During Run   ☐ After Restart   ☐ After Reload

Incident Description: ☐ Attachments

Suggested Resolution:

Urgency: _____ (High, Medium, Low)   ☐ Continuation Page

Analyst: Name: _____ Telephone Extension: _____ Date: _____

Incident Cause:

Incident Impact:

Recommended Resolution:

                                                        ☐ Continuation Page

CCB Decision: ☐ Approved   ☐ No Action Required   Date: _____

                 ☐ Reinvestigate   Date Reinvestigation Due: _____

Chairman : _____

SCN Control No.: _____   Date SCN Control No. Assigned: _____

FREEZING EVENT

INITIATION EVENT

ANALYSIS EVENT

IMPLE-MENTATION EVENT POINTER

DECISION EVENT

since the IR may be originated by anyone in the user's, buyer's, or seller's organization.

Next, the form should record the subject of the incident, that is, the document or computer code involved in the incident and its environment. This information allows a reader of the IR to locate its subject or to reconstruct it, as may be necessary to analyze or audit the IR. The form records the date and time of the incident for traceability. The incident could result from a problem in the documentation or in the executable code. For a document, the document name, label, page, and paragraph number are required to locate the subject of the incident. For the executable code, we want release number and version number to pinpoint which code is involved in the incident. If the incident arose while executing a test procedure, the test procedure label, test case number, and test step label must be provided.

The form must provide for a full description of the incident—this element states what is perceived to be wrong. The originator should be able to indicate an urgency he desires for incident resolution (high, medium, or low) and, if he desires, a suggested resolution to assist and guide the incident analyst. For executable code incidents, the form should indicate whether the incident could be duplicated during a run, after a restart, or after a reload. In case the description of the incident or the suggested resolution exceeds the size of the space allocated, a box should be provided to indicate that initiation event data are continued on another page. A box should also be provided to indicate the presence of attachments, such as listings or printouts. All this information helps the analyst resolve the incident. No approvals are generally required for this event. (In some environments, project management might require approval of an IR by the originator's supervisor, to prevent unnecessary or improper IRs from being initiated.)

B. *Freezing Event.* The only element on the form required to support this event is the IR control number. This number is important in referencing the incident (visibility) and in tracking the incident (traceability). It consists of the last two digits of the current year, followed by a hyphen and a four-digit sequence number. This labeling assignment is generally performed by a member of the product assurance organization, and it is not necessary to record the identity of the person performing that task.

C. *Analysis Event.* Since the subject was identified in the initiation event section of the form, there is no need to repeat it here. However, the form must indicate the name of the person filling out the analysis-event section of the form, since the analyst is in general not the same individual as the incident initiator. Because this project is medium-sized, we assume that the number of seller project personnel is small enough that we can omit the analyst's organization and merely include his telephone extension.

The analyst must indicate on the form his analysis of the incident cause and of the incident's impact on the project, and a recommended resolution of the incident. Recall from Section 4.3 that this resolution may recommend that a change be made or that no action be taken as a result of the IR. If a change is recommended, the precise change recommended should be included in the recommended resolution. Provision should be made for a continuation sheet for the event description, if necessary. No approvals are generally required for this event. (In some environments, approval of the analyst's work by his supervisor might be required.)

D. *Decision Event.* In our approach to change control processing, the CCB is always responsible for this event. (See Exercise 4.3 for consideration of alternative ways to process software changes without using a CCB.) Thus, no entry on the form is needed to indicate who fills out this section. The subject can also be omitted from this section, since it already appears on the form. The event description is the CCB decision. The allowable CCB decisions, as we discussed in Section 4.3 (recall Figure 4.17), are the following: change approved, no action required, or reinvestigate (with reinvestigation due date stipulated). The signature of the CCB chairman is needed on the form for approval of the decision.

In addition to using data elements for the four events served by the form, we add for traceability one data element— a possible cross-reference to an SCN—from the implementation event (recall Table 4.3). This information is generally recorded by a member of the product assurance organization. No originator, subject, or approval data are recorded for this event, because they are recorded on the SCN referenced.

Using the foregoing data elements and adding elements for the dates of change control events for traceability purposes, we developed the IR form shown in Figure 4.19. The figure also shows the change control events that the form documents. Since different people usually fill out the elements for each event, the form has been organized and ruled into a separate part for each event.

The sample problem shows how the generic content specified in Table 4.4 was applied as appropriate to each of the events covered by the form. The form was also specifically tailored to the project for which it was designed (for example, recall the discussion in C above about the analyst's organization and telephone extension). This latter feature is very important. Organizations usually redesign their change control forms from project to project, even when the project team remains relatively the same. Generally, such changes are made because each project is organized somewhat differently, or the software environment is changed, or the change control process is modified. Such changes may necessitate changing the change control forms too. That is why we do not give you the only forms

```
┌─────────────────────────────────────────────────────────────────┐
│                    SOFTWARE CHANGE NOTICE                         │
│  ┌──────────────────────────┐                                    │
│  │ Control No.: _ _ – _ _ _ _│                    Date:_____   │
│  └──────────────────────────┘                                    │
│                                                                    │
│  Originator: Name: _____     Telephone Extension: _____   │
│                                                                    │
│  Changes Implemented:                                             │
│    Software      Software     Version/    Type of Software    IR  │
│     Name         Identifier   Revision    (Doc. or Code)   Control No. │
│                                                                    │
│                                                                    │
│                                                                    │
│                                                                    │
│                                                                    │
│                                                                    │
│                                                     ☐ Continuation Page │
│                                                                    │
│  Approval:                                                         │
│                                                                    │
│  Software Development Manager: _____    Date: _____    │
│  Product Assurance Manager: _____     Date: _____    │
│  Project Manager: _____     Date: _____    │
└─────────────────────────────────────────────────────────────────┘
```

FIGURE 4.20. Example of a software change notice (SCN) form.

to use, but instead give you examples and guidelines on how to develop your own forms.

The sample problem developed a form for an incident report to record the process events specified in Table 4.3. Examples of the remaining three forms specified in Table 4.3 are shown in Figures 4.20, 4.21, and 4.22. Figure 4.20 presents an example of a software change notice (SCN). This form records information from the implementation event. When an IR requiring changes to document(s) and/or code is approved by the CCB, the changes are made by preparing change pages for the document(s) and by modifying a copy of the currently baselined source code. The change is then accomplished by placing the change pages and modified source code under control, accompanied by an SCN to notify all project participants that the changes have been made. One SCN can serve as the implementation notice for multiple IRs. Notice that, per Table 4.4, Figure 4.20 contains originator data, subject identification (IR reference), event description (changes implemented), and approvals. Changes implemented can be continued on another page.

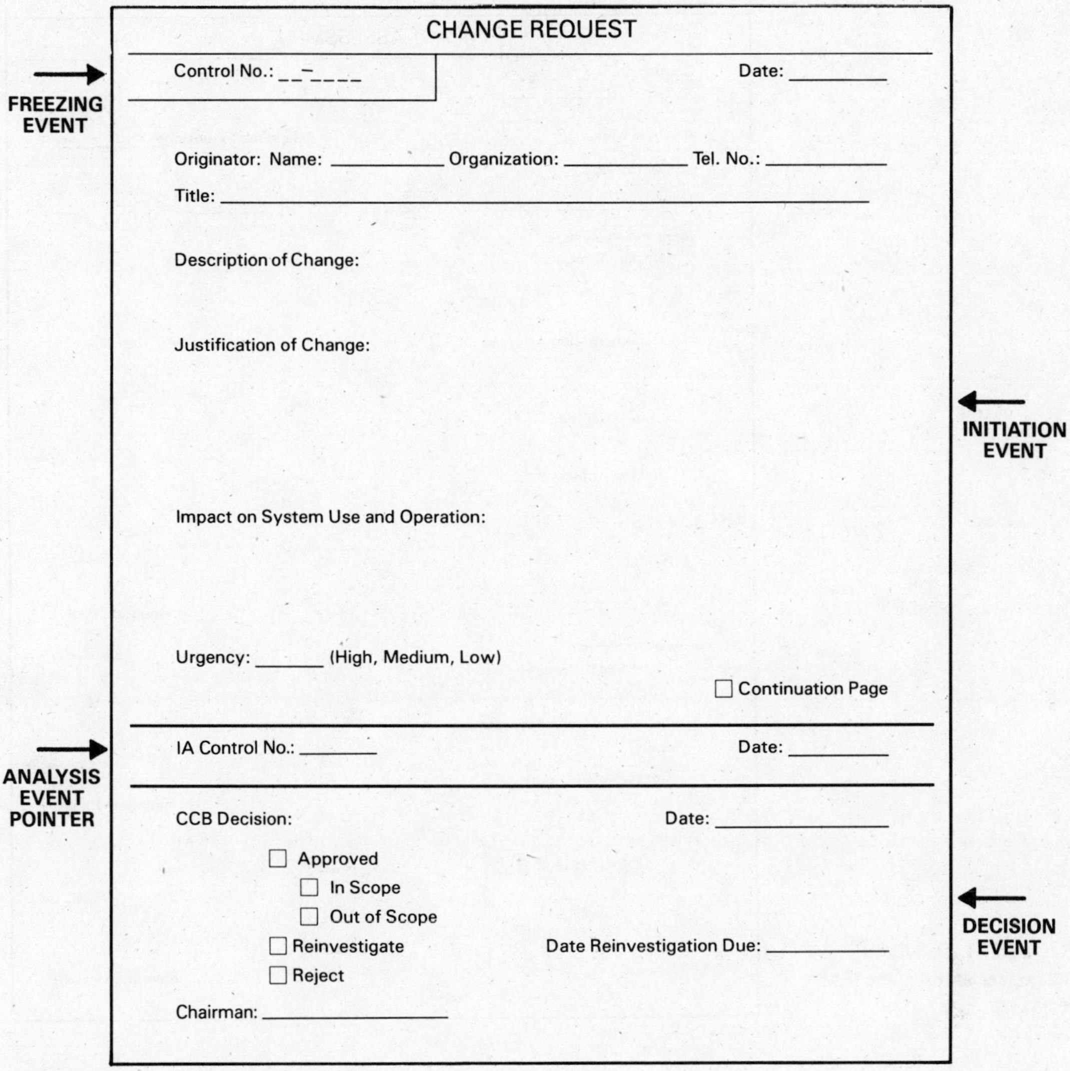

CHANGE REQUEST

Control No.: __–____   Date: _____

FREEZING EVENT

Originator: Name: _____ Organization: _____ Tel. No.: _____

Title: _____

Description of Change:

Justification of Change:

INITIATION EVENT

Impact on System Use and Operation:

Urgency: _____ (High, Medium, Low)

☐ Continuation Page

IA Control No.: _____   Date: _____

ANALYSIS EVENT POINTER

CCB Decision: Date: _____

☐ Approved
  ☐ In Scope
  ☐ Out of Scope
☐ Reinvestigate   Date Reinvestigation Due: _____
☐ Reject

DECISION EVENT

Chairman: _____

FIGURE 4.21. Example of a change request (CR) form and associated events that it documents.

Figure 4.21 is an example of a change request (CR) form. As Table 4.3 indicates, the CR records the initiation of a request for a change, as well as the freezing and decision events. A CR is initiated whenever something new or different is desired by any project participant. The CR describes the change desired, the justification for making the change, and the impact on the use and operation of the system of implementing the requested change. Notice from Figure 4.21 that a CCB-approval decision could be adjudged as either within the scope of existing contracts or out of scope of existing contracts (thus requiring modification of those contracts). In addition to incorporating into the CR data elements for the initiation, freezing, and decision events, we include for traceability a cross-reference to the impact assessment form for this CR from the analysis event. The

```
                        IMPACT ASSESSMENT
   Control No.: _ _ – _ _ _                        Date: _____

   Analyst: Name:_____        Telephone Extension:_____
   CR Control No.: _____
   Title: _____

   Technical Analysis:
       Design Approach:



       Documentation Affected:



       Code Affected:


       Testing Approach:




                                                  ☐ Continuation Page
   Impact Analysis:
       Schedule Considerations:


       Manpower Considerations:


       Cost Considerations:
                                                  ☐ Continuation Page
   Alternatives:



                                                  ☐ Continuation Page
```

FIGURE 4.22. Example of an impact assessment (IA) form.

form is organized and ruled into separate parts for each person filling out the form. Provision has been made to continue initiation event data on a separate page.

Figure 4.22 shows an example of an impact assessment (IA) form. This form records the results of the analysis event of the revolutionary change control process when something new or different is desired. The IA is filled in as a result of a CR.

The event description on the IA form is composed of three parts:

Technical analysis: The approach to be used in designing the proposed change, the software (documentation and code) affected by making the change, and the approach to be used in testing the system after the code has been changed

Impact analysis: Considerations of schedule, manpower, and costs to implement the proposed change

Alternatives: A brief discussion of alternatives to the proposed change, with benefits and liabilities provided for each alternative.

Each part may be continued on another page.

Now that we have a sample set of forms, let's take a look at how they might be used. In Figure 4.23, we present three scenarios showing the use of the change control forms and the interaction of the forms with the CCB. Each of these scenarios deals with one of the three categories of change proposed previously in this section (recall Table 4.3). To illustrate these scenarios, we provide examples of filled-out change control forms in Figures 4.24 through 4.27.

Consider the first scenario, the one initiated by a desire to build something new or different. This scenario is the change control process shown in Figure 4.6. To initiate this scenario, the originator fills out the upper part of a CR, as illustrated in Figure 4.24. (This CR and the other filled-out forms introduced later are based on System MEAL PLANNER, introduced and discussed in Section 4.2.) This CR is presented to the CCB, which assigns it to an analysis group. The results of this analysis are documented in an IA (see example in Figure 4.25), which is then submitted to the CCB. (The product assurance organization fills out the middle part of the CR for traceability.) With the IA in hand, the CCB makes a decision on disposition of the CR. The results of this decision are added to the bottom part of the CR (Figure 4.24). Since, in our example, the CCB decision was to approve the proposed change, the evolutionary change control process is initiated as the now-approved change is reflected in successive baseline updates, starting with the

FIGURE 4.23. Scenarios showing the use of change control forms.

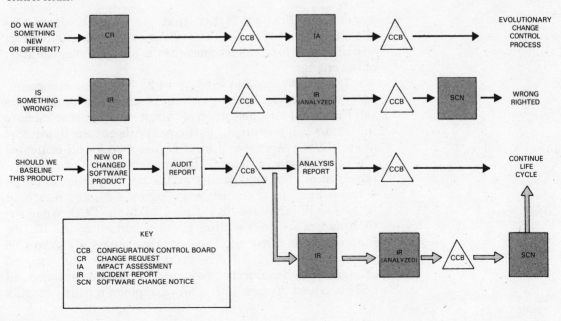

```
                    CHANGE REQUEST

Control No.: 88-0019                          Date: 15 Mar 88


Originator: Name: Tom Green   Organization: Natl. Meals  Tel. No.: 909/555-9567
Title:  MEAL PLANNER Database Update Capability

Description of Change:    Provide the capability to add foods (and their associated
data) to the database. A capacity of up to 500 additional foods should be provided.

Justification of Change: This capability is needed for two reasons:
a.  We need to be able to use local and regional names for foods currently in the data-
    base (e.g., "snap beans" for "string beans").
b.  We need to be able to use local and regional foods not currently in the database
    (e.g., she-crab soup).

Impact on System Use and Operation:
    Our nutritionists can use local names and foods, avoiding manual labor and need to
    remember unfamiliar names.


Urgency: High  (High, Medium, Low)
                                                       ☐ Continuation Page

IA Control No.: 88-0012                       Date: 20 Mar 88


CCB Decision:                      Date: March 24, 1988
    ☒ Approved
    ☐ In Scope
    ☒ Out of Scope
    ☐ Reinvestigate          Date Reinvestigation Due: _____
    ☐ Reject
Chairman: Mary White
```

FIGURE 4.24. Example of a completed change request (CR), showing use of the form in answering the question "Do we want something new or different?"

system specification. Notice that the CCB considers this change to be out of scope of the existing contract. The contract will thus have to be changed prior to the actual implementation of the change.

The second scenario in Figure 4.23 treats the change category characterized by the question "Is something wrong?" (Recall Figure 4.7 for illustration of this process.) This scenario is initiated when any project participant fills out the upper part of an IR. (See the upper part of Figure 4.26 for an example.) The IR is introduced to the CCB, which assigns it to an analysis organization. The analyst fills out the middle portion of the IR with his analysis of the IR, as in Figure 4.26, and returns it (shown as IR [analyzed] in Figure 4.23) to the CCB. When the CCB makes its decision, the decision portion of the IR (see Figure 4.26) is filled out. The example change in Figure 4.26 was approved by the CCB. The developers prepare the approved change, and when the change is ready for implementation, an SCN is issued. Figure 4.27 is an example of a filled-out SCN

```
                        IMPACT ASSESSMENT

    Control No.: 88-0012                          Date:  20 Mar 88


    Analyst:  Name:  Hugh Brown           Telephone Extension:   8197

    CR Control No.:  88-0019

    Title:   MEAL PLANNER Database Update Capability

    Technical Analysis:
        Design Approach:  Create an additional subsystem for database update. Include
    data entry, data validation, and database update functions. Modify current user
    interface.

            Documentation Affected:
    System Specification, Requirements Specification, Design Specification, User's
    Manual
            Code Affected:  Code for additional subsystem will all be new. MMI
    (Man-Machine Interface) Subsystem will need to be modified for this capability.

            Testing Approach:
    Updated product must be acceptance tested by our company T&E Group. Particular
    attention must be focused on user interface, storage capacity limits, and system perfor-
    mance.

                                                        ☐ Continuation Page


    Impact Analysis:
        Schedule Considerations:
            5 months, starting about 1 May 1988.

        Manpower Considerations:
            18 man-months

        Cost Considerations:
            $150,000                                    ☐ Continuation Page

    Alternatives:  Users could inform us of the database modifications needed. We
    could update the database and send them a new database. This alternative
    would cost less, but may not be satisfactory to users in terms of responsiveness and
    their dependence on our company for database updates.

                                                        ☐ Continuation Page
```

FIGURE 4.25. Example of a completed impact assessment (IA) for change request shown in Figure 4.24.

that might result from the IR shown in Figure 4.26. With the change made, the original wrong has been righted in a visible, traceable, and hence manageable manner.

The final scenario in Figure 4.23 deals with evolutionary change, as characterized by "Should we baseline this product?" This process is shown in Figure 4.5. The change process is initiated by presentation of the draft of a software product proposed as a new or updated baseline. This product is audited, and an audit report is provided to the CCB. The CCB assigns an analysis organization (usually the development organization) to analyze the discrepancies contained in the audit report. The results of this analysis are presented to the CCB in a report that provides a recommended resolution of each discrepancy. The CCB makes a decision on how to resolve each discrepancy and then decides whether to baseline the software product. Once the product is baselined, the project continues along the life cycle depicted in Figure 4.3.

INCIDENT REPORT

Control No.: _89-0012_   Date/Time of Incident: _890122/0900_

Originator: Name: _Jane Black_ Organization: _Nutrition, Ltd._ Tel. No.: _210/555-2467_
Source:

☐ Document Name: _____   Identifier: _____

Page: _____   Paragraph: _____

☒ Executable Code   Release No.: _88-2_ Version No.: _1.2_

☐ During Test   Procedure: _____   Step: _____

☒ Incident Duplicated   ☒ During Run ☐ After Restart ☐ After Reload

Incident Description: _Whenever a quantity in grams is entered in_   ☒ Attachments
MEAL PLANNER, all the output numbers are outlandishly high.
See attached listing for the results of entering "steak, 225 grams."

Suggested Resolution:

Correct gram-to-ounce converter.

Urgency: _Medium___ (High, Medium, Low)   ☐ Continuation Page

---

Analyst: Name: __John Blue__   Telephone Extension: __8226__   Date: __890130__

Incident Cause: The subroutine to convert grams to ounces (GRAMTOOZ)
is scaled incorrectly—100 times too high.

Incident Impact: For a single food entry, user must divide results by 100. For meals
entered in grams, the user must calculate results manually.

Recommended Resolution: In module GRAMTOOZ, change line 85 to
QUOZ = 0.03527 * QUGR

                                                              ☐ Continuation Page

---

CCB Decision: ☒ Approved   ☐ No Action Required   Date: _890214_

                 ☐ Reinvestigate   Date Reinvestigation Due: _____

Chairman: _Bob Redman_

SCN Control No.: _89-0030_   Date SCN Control No. Assigned: _890217_

FIGURE 4.26. Example of a completed incident report (IR), showing use of the form in answering the question "Is something wrong?"

As indicated earlier in this chapter and described further in Chapter 5, the last scenario in Figure 4.23 has a variation (shown by tinted arrows in the figure) that is used by some organizations. In this variation, when the CCB receives the audit report on a proposed new or updated baseline it does not have every discrepancy in the audit report analyzed and reported upon (with a recommended resolution) in an analysis report. A certain number of discrepancies can be easily and quickly resolved at the CCB meeting (for example, an inconsistency in the spelling of the software system name, or an ambiguous term that is readily clarified). For such discrepancies, there is no need to spend additional resources to analyze the problem and to document a recommended resolution—the CCB can make an immediate decision on each.

In this alternate scenario, when the CCB receives the audit

SOFTWARE CHANGE NOTICE

Control No.: *89-0030*   Date: _890217_

Originator: Name: _Nancy Greenfield_   Telephone Extension: _2194_

Changes Implemented:

Software Name	Software Identifier	Version/ Revision	Type of Software (Doc. or Code)	IR Control No.
GRAMTOOZ	4.2.1.14	3.4	Code	89-0012

☐ Continuation Page

Approval:

Software Development Manager: _Bill Blackburn_   Date: _17 Feb 89_

Product Assurance Manager: _Jim Brownlee_   Date: _890218_

Project Manager: Ann Whitemarsh *aw*   Date: Feb. 21, 1989

FIGURE 4.27. Example of a completed software change notice (SCN) for incident report shown in Figure 4.26.

report it considers each discrepancy in turn. If a discrepancy can be readily resolved, the CCB makes an immediate decision on it. If a discrepancy is not readily resolvable at the CCB meeting, the CCB directs that an IR be created describing the discrepancy. This IR is processed just as any other IR is processed. That is, the IR is analyzed (typically, by the development organization) and returned to the CCB with the results of the analysis (indicated as IR [analyzed] in Figure 4.23). If the CCB approves a change as a result of this IR, an SCN is issued when the change is implemented.

There is a variation to the second scenario shown in Figure 4.23 that arises occasionally at certain user installations. A number of such installations must operate around the clock. Most of these installations are operated by the government (particularly the Department of Defense), but increasingly some of them operate in the private sector (for example, some mail-order systems and some point-of-sale systems, such as all-night grocery stores). For these installations, a failure in their computer-based systems can have serious consequences. When something goes wrong with their software, these users have an emergency situation, for which the second scenario in Figure 4.23 is too lengthy to be responsive. Is the change control process bypassed for such emergencies? Not at all. A procedure that is responsive to the emergency situation and yet maintains control should be developed in the product assurance plan for systems at such installations.

One procedure to handle such situations that we have observed in successful operation is as follows:

When a site liaison representative of the seller (responsible for continued system maintenance) is notified by site personnel of an emergency situation, he contacts the appropriate software analyst. The analyst evaluates the problem to ensure that there is sufficient data to repair it, that the problem is not the result of improper system usage by the operator, and that the problem is not a duplicate of an incident report. He then proceeds to resolve the problem by the most expedient means available. When he has a solution, he contacts, by telephone, at least one member of the CCB (using teleconferencing facilities, if possible) to obtain approval prior to disseminating the solution. When approval is obtained, he sends the necessary corrections to the site having the problem. No attempt is made to obtain a solution that is elegant or efficient or that will last beyond the time required to develop a permanent correction— what is desired is a solution that quickly returns the site to operational status and that prevents further system degradation.

When the solution has been sent to the site, the analyst fills out an IR on the incident and on the next working day submits the IR (to obtain a permanent solution) and the temporary solution (other sites may need the same temporary fix) to the CCB.[5]   □

In this procedure, notice that the basic change control process is abbreviated but not omitted. Even in these emergency circumstances, a CCB meeting of sorts is convened. Visibility and traceability are maintained under all circumstances. (The interested reader should also consider Exercise 4.4, which probes issues associated with software emergencies and the need for change control.)

This discussion completes our examination of the forms that support the change control process. In this section, we have shown that paperwork is necessary to provide visibility and traceability in the change control process. We discussed how you could develop the forms that you might need on a project. We also provided a set of forms as examples and illustrated their use.

---

[5] Paraphrased from a configuration management directive governing the maintenance of a large military command and control system installed at multiple sites and required to be operational twenty-four hours a day (see Project Venus in Table 7.1).

4.5 Summary

In this chapter, we focused on the mechanics of the first of the three product assurance functions in the model we introduced in Figure 3.10—change control. After presenting the two broad classes of change that are continually occurring on a software project (evolutionary change and revolutionary change), we discussed in depth the process of change control, the organization and procedures to accomplish it, and the paperwork to support it. We pointed out and illustrated that the focal point of the change control process is the CCB. This most important organization is the control activity for the entire change process, both evolutionary and revolutionary.

The role we defined for the CCB in this chapter is broader in scope—as regards evolutionary change control and revolutionary document change control—than is generally granted to it by others (notably the Department of Defense). Perhaps some readers would be more comfortable in referring to this group as a committee—the title used is immaterial. What is important is that a group like the one we have here called a CCB be established to control the change process in a disciplined, visible, and traceable manner.

We have presented the CCB as a decision-making body controlling software changes. The CCB must consider each evolutionary or revolutionary change and figuratively cast a ballot like that shown in Figure 4.28. But how does the CCB know which choice to make on its ballot? To formulate an answer to this question, recall our discussion in Section 4.2 of the technical inputs to the CCB—the review initiator, the audit report, and the analysis report. Of these technical inputs, the audit report directly assesses whether a software change appropriately addresses a customer's need. We should look then at the audit report and at the audit that spawns it to determine what the CCB needs to make decisions on changes.

FIGURE 4.28. What does a CCB need to know to determine that a software change appropriately addresses a customer's need?

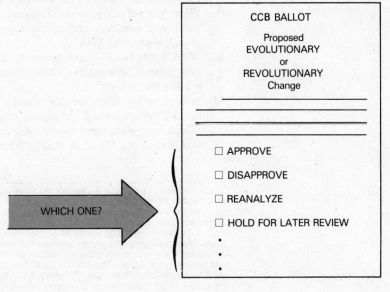

In discussing the change control process, we made frequent reference to the audit function. The next chapter goes into this second product assurance function in depth. The allusions to auditing in the context of change control in this chapter should make you better prepared to appreciate the importance of the audit function. Recall the balance that we illustrated in Figure 3.11. In this chapter, we have seen how the balance is brought to a position where we have product integrity. In the next chapter, we look at how to use the weights on the balance.[6]

EXERCISES   **4.1**   In his book *Quality Is Free: The Art of Making Quality Certain* (New York: McGraw-Hill Book Company, 1979), Philip Crosby includes a case study to demonstrate, using a real-life example, how to implement a quality improvement program. Part of the example is a running dialogue among some members of the staff of a (nonsoftware) company that is having problems and is attempting to institute a quality improvement program. In a meeting where they are trying to pinpoint the sources of their problems, one of the staff members makes the following observation:

> It is apparent to me that most managers, us included, are so concerned with today, and with getting our own real and imagined problems settled, that we are incapable of planning corrective or positive actions more than a week or so ahead (p. 207).

Barry Boehm, in his article "Verifying and Validating Software Requirements and Design Specifications" (*IEEE Software,* vol. 1, no. 1 [January 1984]), begins with the following dialogue among participants on a software project just getting started:

> Don't worry about that specification paperwork. We'd better hurry up and start coding, because we're going to have a whole lot of debugging to do (p. 75).

(a) In what sense is Boehm's dialogue excerpt echoing the attitude expressed in Crosby's dialogue excerpt?

(b) What type of change—evolutionary or revolutionary—do you think will dominate the software project alluded to in Boehm's dialogue excerpt? Why?

(c) What do the two dialogue excerpts suggest to you about a possible relationship between evolutionary and revolutionary changes on a software project?

(d) In Section 2.4, when we introduced the life cycle depicted in Figure 2.7, we discussed the notion of revisits to life cycle stages. Which type of change—evolutionary or revolutionary (or both)—is a revisit to a life cycle stage? Why?

---

[6] Senior managers may want to consider the following exercises before proceeding to the next chapter: Exercise 4.3, on alternative ways to process software changes; Exercise 4.11, on large software projects and the CCB concept; Exercise 4.12, on alternatives to the centralized change control approach. Most of the exercises in this chapter concern the CCB and therefore should be of interest to project managers and product assurance managers. These managers may particularly want to consider the following exercises before proceeding to the next chapter: Exercise 4.1, on specification paperwork and evolutionary and revolutionary change; Exercise 4.2, on CCB activities; Exercise 4.3, on alternative ways to process software changes; Exercise 4.8, on changing software in operational use; Exercise 4.12, on alternatives to the centralized change control approach.

(e) Consider the excerpt from Crosby's dialogue in the context of a software project. In light of your responses to (c) and (d), does it make sense to plan for revolutionary change on a software project? Why (not)? Is the idea of "planned revolutionary change" a contradiction in terms (recall the definition of revolutionary change given in Section 4.1), or is it something that a prudent software project manager may want to incorporate into his management approach? Why (not)?

(f) One way to reduce the cost of evolutionary change might be to do away with "that specification paperwork" referred to in Boehm's dialogue excerpt. Assume that such a cost reduction would result. Why might such a cost reduction seemingly paradoxically precipitate a cost escalation on a software project? (*Hint:* Consider what Crosby is referring to when he states in his book with a conviction clearly based on experience, "It is always cheaper to do the job right the first time" [p. 271].)

(g) Suppose you were involved in a software project whose goal was to produce software code that, once it was made operational, would never be augmented with new capabilities or with enhancements to existing capabilities. On such a project, would it be all right to not "worry about that specification paperwork"? Why (not)? (*Hint:* Recall (b), (c), and (f).)

(h) Unlike the supposition in (g), most software code, once it becomes operational, is continually being augmented with new capabilities or enhancements to existing capabilities. Given this state of affairs, and recalling your response to (g), what can you conclude about "that specification paperwork" and its impact on the cost of evolutionary and revolutionary change?

4.2 In this chapter, we emphasized that the fundamental responsibility of a software CCB is to approve, monitor, and control software (evolutionary and revolutionary) changes. Given this statement of responsibility, consider the following questions:

(a) Which of the activities listed in Table E4.1 should a CCB perform? (For each activity, give at least one reason why it should or should not be performed by a CCB.)

(b) Assume that the primary purpose of a software project staff meeting is to review the progress of the project with the principal project participants and to make decisions about how the project should proceed. With this assumption, which of the activities listed in Table E4.1 should be accomplished at a software project staff meeting and why?

(c) Based on your answers to (a) and (b), write down at least three ways that CCB meetings and project staff meetings can complement each other. Is it essential that these two types of meetings be mutually exclusive with respect to the activities they accomplish? Why (not)?

(d) What are at least two advantages and two disadvantages of merging CCB meetings with project staff meetings?

(e) Is it necessary to call the forum for software control a "CCB" (or some equivalent name that explicitly mentions or implies the notion of software change control)? Why (not)?

4.3 The discussion in Section 4.2 advocates that the CCB should be the center of change control for any software project. Succinctly stated,

TABLE E4.1. LIST OF CANDIDATE CCB ACTIVITIES FOR EXERCISE 4.2

a. Reviewing proposed changes to a software design document

b. Considering a proposal to change a contract between a software buyer and a software seller to include the development of additional software capabilities not delineated in the existing contract

c. Approving patch code (an emergency repair that permits continued use of operational software capabilities until a permanent change can be implemented)

d. Logging incident reports (IRs)

e. Analyzing an IR to determine whether computer code needs to be changed

f. Labeling a listing of computer language code for purposes of identifying software parts

g. Reviewing a software design document to determine whether previously approved changes have been incorporated

h. Approving a software product assurance plan

i. Approving a project manager to head a software development effort

j. Reviewing an audit report that documents inconsistencies between a software design specification and a software requirements specification

k. Reviewing the results of an acceptance test of software code showing discrepancies between output generated by this code and output specified in requirements and design documentation from which the code was presumably developed

l. Reviewing a proposed change to a software part

m. Approving a software documentation standard that is to govern the format and content of specification and test documentation to be produced on a software project

n. Recording CCB minutes

o. Archiving CCB minutes

p. Reviewing CCB minutes from the previous CCB meeting to confirm their accuracy

q. Reviewing a schedule of software product deliverables to determine whether these deliverables are being produced on time and within budget

r. Reviewing a plan to change a software project's organizational structure (e.g., to change the chain of command regarding which individual or organizational entities report to one another)

s. Reviewing a dry run of a presentation of project status that is eventually to be given to senior management (i.e., management not involved in the day-to-day affairs of the project)

t. Approving software code for delivery to a customer

this philosophy stipulates that the CCB should lie at the focus of evolutionary and revolutionary change processing. There are, of course, many alternative ways to process software changes. Listed in Figure E4.1 are four of these alternatives. (In addressing the following questions, you should keep in mind the concepts of visibility and traceability introduced in Chapter 2.)

(a) What are at least two advantages and two disadvantages of each alternative specified in Figure E4.1 in terms of the likelihood that—
1. Proposed changes will be properly evaluated before they are approved for incorporation into products?
2. Approved changes will be properly incorporated?

(b) For each advantage you specified in (a), indicate whether that is an advantage or disadvantage of the CCB change control philosophy discussed in Section 4.2. Do the same thing for each disadvantage you specified in (a).

(c) Assume that alternatives 2, 3, and 4 in Figure E4.1 are extremist change control approaches in the sense that they tie the hands of the customer, the developer, or both. With this assumption, and imagining how you might respond to (a) if it included alternatives "in between" these extremes, what do your responses to (b) indicate about the CCB change control approach discussed in Section 4.2 vis-à-vis alternative change control approaches in general?

FIGURE E4.1. Four alternative ways to process software changes without using a CCB (Exercise 4.3). Quote reprinted by permission of the publisher, *Datamation*® magazine, © copyright by Technical Publishing Company, A Dun & Bradstreet Company, 1984—all rights reserved.

ALTERNATIVE 1

The approach to developing software systems embodied in the life cycle in Figure 2.7 (or similar life cycles) is often termed "traditional" or "classical" to distinguish it from other or "innovative" approaches. One such innovative approach that was introduced in the late 1970s is "rapid prototyping" (for an overview of this approach, see, for example, J. Connell and L. Brice, "Rapid Prototyping," *Datamation*, vol. 30, no. 13 (August 15, 1984), pp. 93-100; recall also Exercise 2.7). In rapid prototyping, a user is presented with a working prototype "rapidly" (i.e., relatively early in the project). This prototype generally contains enough functional capability to allow the user to play with it and thereby determine what he really wants (recall the wizard and the king in Figure 2.8). Regarding this fact of life, Brice and Connell make the following observation in advocating the techniques of rapid prototyping:

> System developers are motivated to satisfy user requirements, but traditional development methods are often at odds with this desire. The techniques of rapid prototyping are based on the fact that the complete set of essential system requirements will not be discovered until the user has a chance to experiment with a working model of the system. The rapid prototype will accommodate new requirements easily, regardless of when they are discovered. In rapid prototyping, changes are made to successive versions of a prototype through user and developer utilization of these prototype versions. Requirements and design specifications are not frozen before coding is initiated. Instead, these specifications are finalized *after* the user obtains a prototype version that meets his approval. Thus, in rapid prototyping, change control is virtually indistinguishable from the development process (p. 94).

ALTERNATIVE 2

The developer unilaterally makes changes to software products (i.e., software code and predecessor specification documentation) but is obligated to inform management what these changes are after they have been made. These changes may or may not be in response to specific customer requests (i.e., some changes may be in response to modified or new requirements put forth by the customer while other changes may result simply from the developer's perception that a product needs to be modified).

Continued

ALTERNATIVE 3

The customer unilaterally decides what changes are to be made and dictates these changes to the developer. (Assume that the customer is willing to pay the developer whatever the developer says a change will cost; assume also that folded into this cost is that the dictated change must be incorporated on or before a date specified by the customer.)

ALTERNATIVE 4

The customer and developer mutually agree at the outset of a project that the following stipulations will govern changes to software products throughout the project:

(1) While a product is being developed (the first time), the customer and developer will hold periodic meetings at which technical interchanges between the customer and developer will take place to ensure that there is mutual agreement on the product's contents. The only record of these technical interchanges will be a modified product that will be the subject of a subsequent meeting.

(2) Once the customer and developer mutually agree that a product needs no further work, its contents cannot be changed except to correct an error (e.g., design flaw, conflicting requirements, computer code logic error) that the customer and developer both agree exists. The customer and developer will then come to an agreement as to the change needed to correct the identified error. The only record of this agreement will be a product (or products) incorporating the agreed-upon change.

FIGURE E4.1 ***(Continued)***

4.4 Section 4.2 described the steps in evolutionary and revolutionary change control emphasizing the central role of the CCB (recall Figures 4.4, 4.5, 4.6, and 4.7). These steps obviously take time. When a software system becomes operational and subsequently appears to malfunction, the time available to restore the system to operation often is in short supply. Under such "emergency" circumstances, it might seem that time simply does not permit the convening of a CCB meeting for purposes of considering what revolutionary changes may be needed to restore the system to operation. As a starting point for probing some of the issues associated with software emergencies and the need for change control, consider the following scenario (derived from actual experience), which we assert is representative of many software maintenance situations:

System ABC is operating at a user site. This software system is being maintained by the seller who developed the software. This maintenance activity consists of a seller software analyst stationed at the user site who is able to communicate, via telephone, user software problems to the seller plant and receive instructions for correcting these problems.

*One night the system crashes. Frantic, the user rouses the site analyst out of bed and demands immediate corrective action. Half asleep, the site analyst looks at the state of the system. After a number of attempts to fix the problem, the analyst creates and installs a patch that seems to fix the problem. (*Note: *By a* patch, *we mean that the coded* *form of software is modified prior to the modification of the documentation on which the code is based. Depending upon the particular project and its environment, the patch may be made to source code or to executable code.) When it appears that the user is satisfied that the system is working properly, the analyst goes home to go back to sleep. The next morning, the analyst returns to the user site and sees that the system seems to be working all right. Feeling no pressing need, the analyst does not report the incident of the night before to his home office, and it is soon "forgotten."*

Based on the information given in the preceding scenario and the discussion of software change control in this chapter, consider the following:

(a) Can the CCB concept be applied in the scenario described? (Indicate yes, no, maybe, or some combination of these possibilities, and give at least one reason to support your answer.) (*Hint:* Remember that some fires not only cannot be extinguished by water but will intensify when attacked by such a response.)

(b) If your answer to (a) was other than "no," describe in a paragraph how a CCB could have been convened and what it could have accomplished. (*Hint:* Do participants in a CCB meeting have to be situated at the same location?)

(c) Recalling the concept of visibility from Section 2.2 and the discussion of change control paperwork in Section 4.4, indicate at least one thing that the site analyst should have done—if not immediately after patching the code, at least after he got a good night's sleep.

(d) Suppose the site analyst in the scenario goes to work for another company. Give at least one reason why his patch may not be "forgotten." (*Hint:* What assumption are the site analyst's replacement and the analysts at the seller plant likely to make regarding the operational computer code? Are software patches generally like salve applied to a cut, or are they more akin to an antibiotic injection?)

(e) From your answers to (c) and (d), infer at least one thing about the need for some form of change control under *any* circumstances. (*Hint:* What do you need to determine under *any* circumstances before changing software code?) Regarding time-critical situations in particular, what advantages do two or more knowledgeable people have over an individual when it comes to making the determination to change software? Do these advantages generally outweigh the apparently obvious advantage of an individual acting on his own—quick reaction?

4.5 Using the definitions of *evolutionary change* and *revolutionary change* introduced in Section 4.1, indicate for each change listed in Table E4.2 whether it is evolutionary or revolutionary (or both) and give one reason to support your answer.

TABLE E4.2.   LIST OF POSSIBLE CHANGES TO A SOFTWARE
                       SYSTEM FOR EXERCISE 4.5

a. A change intended to correct a logic error in a portion of computer code

b. The first issue of a specification that is the developer's interpretation of customer requirements set forth in a contractual statement of work

Continued

c. The first issue of a baseline document that further details the information set forth in a previously approved baseline document

d. A revision to the document defined in c above that introduces something new or enhances what is already there

e. A revision to the document defined in c above that corrects something in c

f. A proposal to add a capability to an operational software system

g. A revision to a software design document incorporating the change in item f above when the change has been approved (by a CCB)

h. A patch (an emergency repair that permits continued use of operational software capabilities until a permanent change can be implemented) to computer code operating improperly at a user site

i. The proposed deletion of a function from a functional specification document

j. The addition of comment statements to properly operating computer code for the purpose of clarifying what the code does

k. Changing the name of a variable in properly operating computer code to make it consistent with a design specification from which the code was derived

l. Changing the name of a variable in improperly operating computer code to make it consistent with a design specification from which the code was derived, with the expectation that the changed code will properly operate

m. Converting computer code written in one language (e.g., FORTRAN) to its equivalent in another language (e.g., BASIC)

n. Combining the computer code making up two properly operating subroutines into a single functionally equivalent subroutine

o. Modifying properly operating computer code in response to a customer whim

---

4.6   Section 4.4 described the paperwork associated with establishing and maintaining control over software evolutionary and revolutionary change. A complaint often voiced about the efficacy of software product assurance is that such paperwork tends to impede rather than facilitate software product development. It is further argued that this paperwork has a tendency to feed on itself and grow until it mires project participants in a seemingly endless sea of bureaucratic tasks. With these observations as background, and recalling the discussion of software change processing in Sections 4.2 and 4.3, consider the following:

(a)   What effect do you think each of the factors listed in Table E4.3 has on determining the extent to which events at CCB meetings should be documented and the extent to which change control forms such as those discussed in Section 4.4 should be used to support these meetings? Indicate your response in terms of one of the following two possibilities:

As the factor increases, the need for such paperwork increases.

As the factor increases, the need for such paperwork decreases.

Give at least one reason to justify your response.

TABLE E4.3. FACTORS AFFECTING SUPPORT TO CCB MEETINGS TO CONSIDER IN EXERCISE 4.6

a. Number of project participants

b. Length of project

c. Criticality of the software to overall system operation (e.g., if the software fails, is there a manual backup that will permit system operation to continue?)

d. Frequency of CCB meetings

e. Length of CCB meetings

f. Complexity of software being developed

g. Likelihood that human lives will be lost if software operates improperly

h. Likelihood that a large financial loss will result if software operates improperly

i. Experience of software development staff

j. Experience of software project manager

k. Number of software products to be developed

l. Incentive award in a software contract (e.g., the earlier a product is satisfactorily delivered, the greater the award)

m. Sophistication of software customer

(b) Based on your responses to (a), what types of software projects should tend to have small or modest change control paperwork needs? What types of software projects should tend to have large change control paperwork needs?

(c) How might you use your responses to (a) to determine on a given software project how much software change control paperwork is enough, thereby minimizing the bureaucratic tangle alluded to in the introduction to this exercise?

4.7 The discussion in this chapter focused on issues pertaining to *software* CCBs—i.e., CCBs responsible for dealing with software matters. Software, of course, is but one component of a system (recall Figure 4.14). In many instances, it is essentially the only component that is undergoing development (the other components, such as computer hardware, communications gear, and people being "off-the-shelf" and ready to run). However, on many system development efforts other system components, in addition to software, are being developed. For such efforts, the issue of change control generally magnifies in complexity. Frequently, for example, software changes need to be considered in the context of a changing hardware environment, and in some instances it may be better to change hardware than to change software. With the preceding as background, consider the following questions (assume that the context for these questions is a system development effort involving the parallel development of software and computer hardware that is to host this software):

(a) What are at least two advantages and two disadvantages of holding *only* joint CCB meetings (meetings attended by representatives from both the hardware and software development organizations)?

(b) What are at least two advantages and two disadvantages of holding *only* separate hardware CCB meetings and software CCB meetings (CCB meetings where representatives are from the hardware development organization only or software development organization only)?

(c) What are at least two advantages and two disadvantages of holding (1) hardware CCB meetings where primarily hardware issues are dealt with but representatives from the software development organization may attend as deemed appropriate by the hardware CCB and (2) software CCB meetings where primarily software issues are dealt with but representatives from the hardware development organization may attend as deemed appropriate by the software CCB?

(d) What are at least two advantages and two disadvantages of holding the two sets of CCB meetings referred to in (c) and, in addition, holding system-level CCB meetings where representatives from both the hardware and software development organizations attend? (In these meetings, primarily issues that have an impact on the system as a whole [e.g., system performance such as system response time to user queries] are dealt with.)

(e) Based on your answers to the preceding parts of this exercise, what are some policies governing CCB meetings that may be desirable to establish on a system development effort involving both hardware and software development? *Hint:* An example of such a policy might be the following:

Every N *weeks a software CCB meeting shall be held whose scope is limited to software changes that do not appear to have an impact on hardware; every* N *weeks a hardware CCB meeting shall be held whose scope is correspondingly limited; every* 2N *weeks a system-level CCB meeting shall be held whose scope is limited to software changes that may impact hardware, hardware changes that may impact software, and issues that are neither hardware-specific nor software-specific.*

4.8 Typically, after software is coded and installed for operational use, code changes do not get reflected in predecessor representations (such as, e.g., design specifications). Consider the following questions pertaining to how this typical software maintenance (classically speaking) problem might be addressed:

(a) Should a CCB be convened to review and approve the changes to the documents before the documents are changed? (Indicate yes, no, maybe, or some combination of these three, and give at least one reason to support your answer.)

(b) Should an audit be performed to determine the effect of these changes on the contents of the documents before the documents are changed? (Indicate yes, no, maybe, or some combination of these three, and give at least one reason to support your answer.)

(c) If your answer to (b) was not "no," what should be done with the results of the audit and why?

(d) Should an audit be performed on the documents after they are changed? (Indicate yes, no, maybe, or some combination of these three, and give at least one reason to support your answer.)

(e) If your answer to (d) was not "no," what should be done with the results of the audit and why?

(f) If the cost of revising the documents and reissuing new ones would be excessive because of budget constraints, how might application of the concepts discussed in Section 4.4 help provide economical updates to these software representations? (Indicate your answer in a short paragraph.)

(g) Would you change your responses to the preceding parts of this exercise if the two lead-in sentences to this exercise were replaced with the lead-in below? If so, how and why? If not, why not? *Typically, while software is first being coded (i.e., subsequent to detailed design but prior to operational use), or even before coding begins, it becomes apparent that changes to predecessor (presumably reviewed and approved) design and requirements documentation may be needed. Consider the following questions pertaining to how this typical documentation updating problem might be addressed. . . .*

(h) Based on your responses to the preceding parts of this exercise, what might you conclude about the nature of CCB activities before and after coding begins?

(i) Based on your response to (h), and recalling the discussion of evolutionary and revolutionary change in Section 4.1, what might you conclude about the nature of software development (those activities that precede first operational use of software code) and (classical) software maintenance (those activities that follow first operational use of software code)? Are they inherently different? Why (not)?

4.9 An issue that often needs to be considered on a software project is how frequently a CCB should meet. The following questions focus on some trade-offs associated with resolving this issue:

(a) What relationship generally exists between CCB meeting frequency and the concept of visibility as defined in Chapter 2? Why?

(b) What relationship generally exists between CCB meeting frequency and the concept of traceability as defined in Chapter 2? Why?

(c) In general, to what extent might each of the factors listed below influence CCB meeting frequency and why?

1. Product delivery dates
2. Length of project
3. Average length of CCB meetings
4. Experience of software development staff
5. Likelihood that human lives will be lost and/or a large financial loss will result if software code to be developed operates improperly
6. Number of software products to be developed
7. Complexity of software products to be developed
8. Sophistication of software customer
9. Trend of the software problems being encountered. (For example, is the number of problems increasing or decreasing over the last few CCB meetings? Is the perceived seriousness of the problems increasing or decreasing over the last few CCB meetings?)

4.10 In his book *Software Defect Removal*, Robert Dunn has a chapter entitled "Requirements and Design Reviews." This chapter focuses on a number of topics pertaining to the review of software products developed during the life cycle stages that precede the Coding Stage.

One section describes the mechanics of conducting these reviews. Included in this description is a discussion of who should chair a review meeting. This discussion begins:

> . . . The review has been called, the documentation has been distributed and the participants have gathered to make common cause in a room with sufficient table space to spread out the material. Who presides? A likely candidate to chair the meeting is the software quality assurance representative. Chairpersons of business meetings are the ones who most often take on the job of distilling the proceedings into some sort of record, and software quality engineers are going to take their own minutes anyway, simply because they are software quality engineers. Also, they neither feed nor are fed by the work reviewed, with the consequence that of the technically cognizant persons who participate in reviews, they are likely to be the most objective. As an alternative, the person calling the review may also serve as chairperson. (R. H. Dunn, *Software Defect Removal* [New York: McGraw-Hill Book Company, 1984], p. 90.)

With the above excerpt as background, and assuming that Dunn's requirements and design reviews are akin to CCB meetings dealing with evolutionary changes as discussed in this chapter, consider the following:

(a) Given that Dunn's notion of software quality assurance is akin to our notion of software product assurance, what do you think Dunn means by "Software quality engineers are going to take their own minutes anyway, simply because they are software quality engineers"? Do you think that this characteristic is a good reason for making the software quality (product) assurance representative at the meeting the chairperson? Why (not)?

(b) What do you think Dunn means by "They neither feed nor are fed by the work reviewed"? Do you think that this characteristic really makes the software quality (product assurance) engineer the most objective of the technically cognizant persons who participate in the review (recall the triangle diagram in Figure 2.13)? Why (not)? Should objectivity be the main criterion used to select a person to chair a review? Why (not)?

(c) In the above excerpt, Dunn indicates that the person calling the review is an alternative choice to serve as the review chairperson. Refer to Figure 2.13. Assume that someone from the management or development (but not product assurance) disciplines calls for the review. Write down at least two advantages and two disadvantages of this alternative choice (over the software quality engineer choice), and give at least one reason for each advantage and disadvantage that you list. Consider the following specific choices:

1. The software project manager
2. The software project manager's boss
3. The member of the software development staff whose work is the subject of the review
4. A member of the software development staff whose work is not the subject of the review but who is working on the project
5. A member of the software development staff who is not part of the project

(d) Based on your answers to the preceding parts of this exercise, who would you select to chair a requirements or design review? Give at least two reasons to justify your choice.

4.11 The Association for Computing Machinery (ACM) sponsors a number of special-interest groups. The Special Interest Group on Software Engineering (SIGSOFT) publishes an informal newsletter called *Software Engineering Notes,* which is "concerned with the design and development of high-quality software." The October 1984 issue (vol. 9, no. 5) included an article by Dick Dunn entitled "Two Observations on Large Software Projects" (pp. 8–10). The author introduces his article with the following statements:

> The observations which follow come from observing and participating in several large software projects over the past few years. I present them as observations—hypotheses, if you will—without any attempt to prove them. The intent is to stimulate discussion (p. 8).

In the spirit of the author's expressed intent, we present below excerpts from the section of his article that deals with his second observation—namely, that "the main function of design reviews, structured walk-throughs, and like design techniques is to buy time" (p. 9). The author then proceeds to elaborate on this observation:

> We realize how serious it is to find a design error late in a project, after a lot of code has been written and tested. The later it is found, the more trouble it causes, so a considerable emphasis has been placed on developing techniques to find problems early. There are many different names for them, but they have common characteristics—circulated documents or meetings in which concerned parties review and discuss a (somewhat abstracted) specification of the project. Significantly, they produce some sort of report—issues resolved or needing resolution, status, plans—but always something "visible."
>
> In fact, any group of competent people working toward a common goal will get together one way or another to work out plans and problems! Even a single person working on a difficult problem has to come to agreements with himself on how to do things. Moreover, sometimes it just takes a while for all of the ramifications of a big problem to become apparent—it might take a week of "real time" to solve a problem even though it only takes four hours of work during that week.
>
> The actual mechanisms for achieving this planning and problem-resolution are not important as long as it happens. However, it can be disconcerting to management . . . to see the members of a project spending long coffee breaks talking, taking three-hour lunches together away from the office, or just plain sitting at a desk staring into space—especially when they have no tangible evidence of work being done! There is a temptation to accelerate the design/planning phases or to start some coding early, just to produce something visible. In this context the functions of the popular techniques (i.e., design reviews, etc.) become clear:

They provide visible "recognized" activities (meetings) to serve the functions that might otherwise be performed in a largely informal manner.

They produce tangible results—documents with a formal status, typically produced according to a predictable schedule.

They provide activities to fill the time while people ruminate on problems, thus allowing them to "look busy" as well as be busy.

So far, what I have said indicates that the various meetings and documents are benign, achieving their ends even if not in the way they purport to do so. This may not be quite true.

Software is hand-crafted, not mass-produced. Each software project has different needs, problems, and goals. If the design methodology is insufficiently general, the final product may be damaged by trying to bend it to an inappropriate design tool. For example, HIPO (hierarchic input-process-output) charts simply won't work for some projects because they presuppose a model which is not an abstraction of any reasonable solution to the problems.

The intermediate steps (meetings, documents) of design techniques can grow to be goals in themselves. If this happens, the project will tend to be more influenced by people who are good at "generating paper" or wielding influence in meetings than by the more technically qualified people.

Programmers (in a generic sense—anyone who produces software) are at best an eccentric and obstinate lot. A few meetings and documents may be OK, but if there are too many, they will rebel. If you overconstrain a skilled person, you are giving an indication of some distrust. Obviously, this won't be received kindly.

Can we demonstrate that formal design techniques are not only performing their intended function, but doing so as a *direct* consequence of the actions performed? If not, can we achieve the same goals without the excess motion? (pp. 9–10).

Based on Dunn's remarks above and the CCB concept set forth in this chapter, consider the following:

(a) In what sense are the remarks in Dunn's first paragraph ("We realize . . .") a restatement of the CCB concept set forth in this chapter?

(b) How might the arguments in Dunn's second through fourth paragraphs be used to justify a CCB concept like that set forth in this chapter on software projects of *any* size?

(c) How might the arguments in Dunn's fifth through seventh paragraphs be used to tone down or reject a CCB concept like that set forth in this chapter?

(d) Propose an answer to Dunn's first question in his final paragraph, based on the philosophy set forth in this chapter.

(e) Propose an answer to Dunn's second question in his final paragraph by attacking the philosophy set forth in this chapter.

(f) Based on your responses to the preceding parts of this exercise, derive at least three trade-offs that you think need to be considered in establishing a project product assurance program whose implementation will be *necessary* to project progress (and thus will do much more than just buy time in the sense used by Dunn).

4.12 This chapter sets out a software management philosophy that places the CCB at the center of project activities. That is, all candidate software changes—evolutionary or revolutionary—are to be brought before the CCB for review and either approval or rejection. (*Note:* See Exercise 4.3 for alternative approaches to change control not involving CCBs.)

Alternatives to this change management philosophy are certainly available. The items listed below are intended to stimulate your thinking regarding the relative merits of such alternatives vis-à-vis the centralized philosophy described in this chapter.

(a) Suppose you wanted to establish a CCB that would review only potential changes that exceeded certain predetermined thresholds (e.g., that would require more than x amount of money to code, and/or that would require more than y weeks to design and code, and/or that would require the addition of a new subsystem). All other changes to code and/or predecessor design and requirements specifications would be implemented unilaterally by the development organization (e.g., refinements to code to enhance existing capabilities, correction of spelling errors, clarification of design logic). With this supposition, consider the following:

1. List at least three advantages that this change control approach has over the centralized approach described in this chapter, and give at least one reason for each advantage that you list.

2. Compared to the centralized change control approach, does this alternative offer greater or lesser visibility and traceability? Give at least three reasons to justify your answer.

3. Based on your answers to 1 and 2, list at least three characteristics of a project (such as the number of software product developers) that you think would be the most significant in helping you to decide whether this alternative or the centralized approach would be beneficial to the project. Define what you mean by "beneficial," and give at least one reason to justify each characteristic that you list.

(b) Suppose you work in a company that develops and sells a variety of software products. Suppose also that these products are bought and used by customers who are widely dispersed geographically. In addition, suppose you have maintenance agreements with most of these customers that obligate you to implement their (evolutionary and revolutionary) change requests (the total number and magnitude of these requests being specified in each maintenance agreement). Finally, suppose the number of customers that you have is such that on any business day you must handle one hundred or more incident reports and change requests, each of which must be analyzed when it is received (usually by telephone). Most of these incident reports and change requests must be resolved within a day or two, with a small percentage (say, 10 percent) requiring software code modification and the remainder requiring either documentation changes or verbal instructions to customers regarding how to properly use the software they have. With these suppositions, consider the following:

1. List at least three disadvantages associated with trying to utilize the CCB approach described in this chapter in the highly dynamic environment just described. Give at least one reason for each disadvantage that you list.

2. Using the disadvantages you listed in 1 as a guide, modify

the CCB approach described in this chapter to accommodate the environment just described. Define your modified change processing approach in terms of modifications of the evolutionary and revolutionary change control flows depicted in Figures 4.5, 4.6, and 4.7.

3. In terms of the visibility and traceability it affords, how does the change processing approach you defined in 2 compare to the centralized change processing approach described in this chapter?

(c) Suppose you work in a company that has developed and installed a software system at a number of geographically dispersed locations. Suppose also that this system supports military applications at these locations and that it must be operational twenty-four hours a day, seven days a week. Finally, suppose your company has a software analyst at each of these sites who is responsible for correcting user-discovered bugs and implementing user-requested enhancements that do not exceed a prespecified number of new or modified lines of source code. Specifically, each of these analysts has the authority, in consultation with the user, to change code and associated documentation. In addition, each analyst is responsible for submitting in writing to your company's headquarters facility each code change or documentation change within one week of its implementation. With these suppositions, consider the following:

1. List at least three advantages of this change control approach over the centralized approach described in this chapter, and give at least one reason for each advantage that you list.

2. Compared to the centralized change control approach, does this alternative offer greater or less visibility and traceability? Give at least three reasons to justify your answer.

3. List at least three circumstances where it might be useful to couple the CCB apparatus described in this chapter to this alternative. For each circumstance you list, indicate at least one reason why this coupling is advantageous if not necessary for maintaining control over the software system.

(d) Based on your answers to the preceding parts of this exercise, do you think it is necessary on *any* software project to establish a CCB that makes decisions in the manner described in this chapter to handle at least some of the changes that are to be made to the software? If your answer is "yes," give at least three reasons to justify your answer. If your answer is "no," list at least three types of environments or software projects where you believe all software changes may be implemented by individuals without the intervention of a CCB to govern these activities.

4.13 Recall the sample problem on evolutionary and revolutionary change pertaining to System MEAL PLANNER in Section 4.2 and consider the following:

(a) Suppose the money allocated to documentation on the project is in short supply. Would this situation alter how you, as a CCB member, would consider accepting or rejecting the audit findings discussed in the sample problem? If so, which findings and why? If not, why not?

(b) Suppose that a MEAL PLANNER test plan has been produced that specifies the approach to be used in testing each of the four MEAL PLANNER software functions. Would this alter how you, as a CCB member, would consider accepting or rejecting the auditor's QA Finding 4 on testing (see Figure 4.12)? If so, why? If not, why not?

(c) Suppose that the hardware that is to host the MEAL PLANNER software will not be selected until the beginning of the Detailed Design Stage of System MEAL PLANNER development. With this supposition, reconsider the questions posed in (a).

(d) Suppose that the System MEAL PLANNER under development is a prototype that will undergo trial-use only by members of your company (which is also developing the system). Suppose further that the purpose of this trial use is to refine the prototype so that the refined version can be marketed by your company to the general public. With these suppositions, reconsider the questions posed in (a).

4.14 The sample problem in Section 4.4 on designing an incident report (IR) form stated that the form was needed on a medium-sized project. This stipulation had an influence on at least two data elements (analyst's organization and telephone extension) on the form. Consider the following:

(a) Redesign the IR form as specified in the sample problem in Section 4.4, based on its use on a large-sized project. By a *large-sized* project, we mean one having roughly fifty or more persons working on it full-time. Give at least one reason for each change you would make in Figure 4.19.

(b) What changes would you make to the IR form shown in Figure 4.19 if you wished to use the form on a small-sized (roughly four to eight full-time personnel) project. Give at least one reason for each change you would make.

(c) From the sample problem in Section 4.4 and (a) and (b) above, what can you infer about the relationship between the IR form and the size of a project? Why?

4.15 Recall the blank impact analysis (IA) form in Figure 4.22 and the filled-in IA form in Figure 4.25. Consider the following:

(a) The impact assessment form does not contain much detail (e.g., the design approach is given, but no details of the design are provided). Should the IA form contain data elements that ask for more detail (e.g., replace "Design Approach" with "Design Changes," or "Documentation Affected" with "Documentation Changes")? Why (not)?

(b) If you answered (a) that the IA form should not contain more details of the change, how and when should such details be presented to the CCB?

(c) The filled-in IA form in Figure 4.25 lists an alternative to providing System MEAL PLANNER with a database update capability. Assume that your company developed, installed, and maintains System MEAL PLANNER. What two potential configuration management problems did the analyst overlook in his discussion of the alternative (your company updates the database in response to a user's request and sends the updated database to the user)?

4.16 The software change notice (SCN) can be used both as a notice of the implementation of a software change (as in this chapter) and as a control form for placing changed software (both documents and code) in a development library. Discuss the advantages and disadvantages of this additional usage for this form. Should the SCN form be changed to reflect this usage? How?

4.17 Suppose you are proposing a set of forms to support change control. Rather than use or tailor the set of forms shown in Table 4.3, you decide to reduce the project paperwork by using only two forms. These forms are a change request (CR) to answer the question "Do we want something new or different?" and an incident report (IR) to answer the question "Is something wrong?" All events in the change control process will be recorded on each form. With the preceding as background, consider the following questions:

(a) How would you modify Figure 4.21 (CR form) to record all events involved in processing a proposed change for something new or different? Why?

(b) How would you modify Figure 4.19 (IR form) to record all events involved in processing an incident report? Why?

(c) From your responses to (a) and (b), what can you infer about the relationship between the number of forms used for change control support and the totality of information to be recorded on those forms? Justify your answer.

REFERENCES AND ADDITIONAL READINGS

1. Bazelmans, R. "Evolution of Configuration Management." *ACM SIG-SOFT Software Engineering Notes*, vol. 10, no. 5 (October 1985), pp. 37–46.

   This paper describes the origin and evolution of the term "configuration management." Most of it is devoted to the evolution of various automated aids that have been developed to facilitate the control and tracking of changes to software code. The discussion of these aids augments our discussion of the software change process in this chapter for the special case that the software product is computer code.

2. Bersoff, E. H., V. D. Henderson, and S. G. Siegel. *Software Configuration Management: An Investment in Product Integrity*. Englewood Cliffs, N.J.: Prentice-Hall, 1980.

   Chapter 4 of our book extends some of the ideas on configuration control discussed in chapter 5 of the above book.

3. Buckle, J. K. *Software Configuration Management*. London: Macmillan, 1982.

   This book is a more compact treatment of the subject of software configuration management than the Bersoff et al. book (Reference 2; see also references to this book in preceding chapters)—150 pages versus 350 pages. Chapter 5 of the Buckle book treats the topic of configuration control as it applies to software products that are not computer code; chapter 6 treats the same topic as it applies to computer code. These two chapters offer a point of view on software change control that is different from our treatment in Chapter 4. Our treatment emphasizes the role of the CCB, but Buckle's treatment focuses on the individual steps needed to transform a draft software product into a frozen, controlled entity. A CCB-like body is part of this transformation process. Although not called a CCB, Buckle refers to a class of people involved with document control called "the approval authorities" that functions in a manner similar to the CCB as we describe it in this chapter. On pages 86–87, Buckle discusses the control of operationally deployed software (i.e., what is classically referred to as "maintenance"). At the center of this control mechanism is a control committee responsible for assessing and approving requests for change to this operational software (i.e., a CCB-like body).

4. Dunn, R. H. *Software Defect Removal*. New York: McGraw-Hill Book Company, 1984.

This book could also be titled *Software Product Assurance*. It contains ideas that both complement and contrast with the ideas in our book (see Exercise 4.10). The following excerpt from the book's preface explains why the book was written:

> If we can improve our processes for removing defects (unless an explicit distinction is made, I use the term to refer to both detection and correction), we will have made concomitant progress in improving program quality. Stories relating the effects of software defects are legion. . . . What I think is worth mentioning is that we have no reasonable way to reckon the cost exacted by the effects of program defects. Intuitively, however, we know that low quality levels have resulted in too many hours spent at reconciling credit accounts, finding the several tons of frozen fish sent to the wrong warehouse, recovering the errant spacecraft, and placating the patrons waiting in line at the bank while someone tries to bring up the crashed teller network (p. xii).

Chapter 11 ("Configuration Control") offers some complementary and contrasting views on the ideas we present in our Chapter 4. For example, on page 298 the author discusses the functions of the CCB and includes the following comments:

> References to the board's functions in earlier discussions . . . suggest that the board is a decision-making body. This is an overstatement, except in theory. At a project level, one would expect that decisions to authorize work on an enhancement or the repair of nettlesome but not critical problems would be made elsewhere, although the people engaged in these deliberations might well include those who attend SCCB [software CCB] meetings.

Regarding implications of this quote, see Exercises 4.3, 4.11, and 4.12.

5. Evans, M. W. *Productive Software Test Management*. New York: John Wiley & Sons, 1984.

In several places, this 218-page book touches on the subject of software control in the context of testing. Of particular relevance to the discussion in this chapter and the discussion in Section 5.3 is the material found on pages 73–77 and 166–167 of Evans' book, which includes a brief discussion of the role of the CCB in support of testing. The discussion of configuration management during development testing on Evans' pages 121–122 offers a brief look at the notion of change control from the developer's perspective (as opposed to the product assurance perspective that we focus on).

6. Rosenau, M. D., Jr., and M. Lewin. *Software Project Management: Step by Step.* Belmont, Calif.: Lifetime Learning Publications/Wadsworth, 1984.

Chapter 17, "Handling Changes," addresses the subject of software change control. Although the treatment of the subject is cursory, the discussion on pages 242–247 complements the discussion in our Chapter 4 and touches upon the topics of software change review mechanics and the role of the CCB.

7. Uemura, K., and M. Ohori. "A Cooperative Approach to Software Development by Application Engineers and Software Engineers." *Proceedings of the 7th International Conference on Software Engineering,* Orlando, Florida, March 26–29, 1984. Washington, D.C.: IEEE Computer Society Press, 1984 (IEEE Catalog No. 84CH2011-5), pp. 86–96.

This article describes an innovative approach to software development that represents an alternative to the CCB-centered approach discussed in this chapter. Employed in a Japanese structural design and software engineering company, this approach is based on the use of an interpreter who serves to explain the functional design turned out by application engineers (e.g., civil engineers) to programmers responsible for code design, development, and debugging. The interpreter (who may or may not be a civil engineer) acts as a kind of intermediary between the wizard and the king portrayed in Figure 2.8 by helping the programmers achieve convergence with the application engineers (who are the customers, since the code being developed is to provide automated structural and civil engineering tools). The role of the interpreter thus serves a purpose similar to the role of the CCB described in this chapter. In addition to describing their software development approach, the authors report on results of applying the approach to two projects within their company. They compare their results with results based on company experience using the "traditional" approach to software development (i.e., no use of interpreters). This comparison indicates that the cooperative approach yielded greater productivity (expressed in units of man-days/kilolines of code produced) and better-quality products (expressed in terms of the average number of bugs uncovered after product release to the customer).

chapter 5

KNOWING ABOUT DISCREPANCIES IN SOFTWARE PRODUCTS

In the preceding chapter, we focused on the configuration control board and its role in establishing and maintaining control over evolutionary and revolutionary software changes. Left unanswered in that chapter was the following key issue:

How does the CCB know when a software change may be needed?

In this chapter, we turn our attention to this question. Our approach is, once again, from the perspective embodied in Figure 2.8. The king and the wizard in this figure are obviously separated by a discrepancy in understanding. Presumably, when the king responds to the wizard's question "What is it you really want?" the wizard will change the product he delivers to the king. So it is on a software project—a product is turned out and is then compared against what the customer asked for. If this comparison yields discrepancies, then the product (or, alternatively, what the customer asked for) will be changed until the discrepancies are resolved. Our purpose in this chapter is to describe the basic processes involved in comparing software products against one another to determine whether these products are being developed logically and are congruent with what the customer asked for. We term these basic processes *auditing*. We introduced the concept of auditing in Figure 3.10, where it was presented as one of the three fundamental product assurance functions. In Chapter 4, we showed the interrelationship of auditing with the change control process (recall particularly Figure 4.4). The description of auditing in the present chapter essentially completes the discussion begun in Chapter 4 of the mechanics involved in achieving convergence between the wizard (product developer) and the king (customer).

Figure 5.1 is an overview of the auditing process as it pertains to evolutionary changes. The process begins whenever a

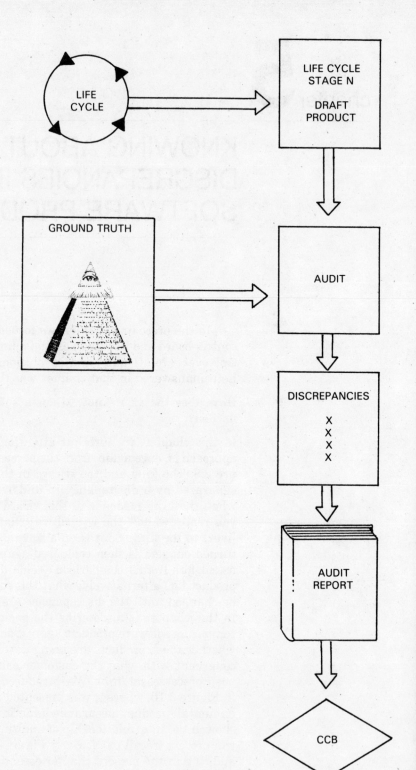

FIGURE 5.1. Auditing process overview.

draft software product is produced by the developers, and it ends with the delivery of an audit report to the CCB. The audit itself compares the draft software product against the ground truth.[1] (We discuss what constitutes ground truth for software audits in Section 5.1.) As a result of this comparison, discrepancies between the draft software product and the ground truth may be uncovered. These discrepancies are documented in an audit report, which is presented to the CCB for its disposition. (We discussed how the CCB handled audit reports and the discrepancies they contain in Section 4.2.) Observe that the auditing process depicted in Figure 5.1 is simply an expansion of the box labeled "Audit" in Figure 4.5.

The auditing process shown in Figure 5.1 applies to all software products, whether the software is documentation or code. However, there are differences in the details of the process, depending upon whether the software is documentation or code. We therefore discuss these two forms of software separately, in Sections 5.2 and 5.3, respectively.

In Chapter 4, we indicated (in Figures 4.6 and 4.7) that audits are also conducted when revolutionary changes are proposed. The auditing process for revolutionary change differs slightly from Figure 5.1—rather than a draft software product, the initiator of the audit is either a change request (CR) or an incident report (IR). Otherwise, the auditing process is the same for both evolutionary and revolutionary change. For revolutionary changes, the audit may consist of the following:

A comparison of a CR to a requirements specification (Figure 4.6) to ascertain which requirements are affected by the CR

An archive check to determine whether a CR (Figure 4.6) or an IR (Figure 4.7) has previously been proposed

An independent system test of changed code (Figure 4.7) to ascertain whether the changed code has successfully resolved the incident reported in an IR

The last audit is discussed in Section 5.3, along with audits of evolutionary code changes. Because of their simple, straightforward nature, the first two audits are not discussed further in the text, but are examined in Exercises 5.26 and 5.27.

This chapter is organized as follows:

In Section 5.1, we discuss the nature of discrepancies and the following general classes of discrepancies of which the

---

[1] By *ground truth*, we mean an established benchmark against which, by comparison, change is detected. If the ground truth is found to be faulty, it is corrected and then reestablished as the new ground truth. We have symbolized ground truth by the incomplete pyramid and eye from the reverse of the Great Seal of the United States. The pyramid represents permanence and strength, while its unfinished condition symbolizes the expectation of more work to be done to form a more perfect Union (*Facts About United States Money*, Department of the Treasury, Washington, D.C.).

CCB needs to be aware to effectively perform its decision-making function as described in Chapter 4:

Incongruities between a software product and project standards

Incongruities between a software product and predecessor products (including a customer's statement of need)

Incongruities between software code operating in a live or nearly live environment and a customer's statement of need and design documentation

Inconsistencies, ambiguities, grammatical weaknesses, and spelling errors within a software product

We illustrate each of these classes with examples to demonstrate how such discrepancies may precipitate evolutionary and revolutionary changes.

In Section 5.2, we go through the mechanics of cross-checking a document (a software product that is not computer code) against a predecessor software product, against a customer's statement of need, and against project-imposed standards. Thus, this section is a discussion of the mechanics of QA and V&V as defined in Section 3.1 (recall Figure 3.2). Then, we describe how to prepare an audit report documenting the results of this cross-checking. The section concludes with a sample problem illustrating the auditing of a highly simplified design document with a correspondingly simplified predecessor product and a simplified standard. This sample problem also includes an illustration and discussion of an audit report summarizing the results of cross-checking these simplified documents.

Section 5.3 parallels Section 5.2 in scope and content for the special case of a software product that is computer code. It is a discussion of the mechanics of T&E as defined in Section 3.1 (recall Figure 3.2). We address the topics of test planning, test procedure generation, and test reporting. We illustrate these three processes and their interplay with a sample problem.

In Section 5.4, we summarize the main ideas presented in the chapter and close by emphasizing the synergism of change control (presented in Chapter 4) and auditing (presented in Chapter 5).

5.1 The Nature of Discrepancies

In the introduction to this chapter, we stated that discrepancies may be uncovered when a software product is compared to the ground truth. In this section, we discuss the nature of these discrepancies which are the output of an audit (see Figure 5.1). We divide discrepancies into classes according to what the ground truth is for a given software product and illustrate each class with examples. We also discuss how discrepancies should be reported.

First, it must be noted that a discrepancy does not necessarily represent something that is wrong with a software product. This common misconception is only sometimes true. A *discrepancy*, quite simply, is an incongruity[2] observed as a result of comparing a software product with the ground truth. It is possible, of course, that a discrepancy represents something that is wrong in the software product. But a discrepancy could also represent something that is wrong with the ground truth (if the ground truth is incorrect, it must be corrected and then be reestablished as the ground truth). Furthermore, a discrepancy could result from a misunderstanding or an invalid assumption derived from the ground truth. (As a real-world example of such a discrepancy, consider a requirement "to calculate the point of intercept" of one ship by another. This means to those knowledgeable in the application—military command and control—that a maneuvering ship assumes a course and speed such that the maneuvering ship and a nonmaneuvering ship arrive at the same point—the point of intercept—at the same time. This requirement was misinterpreted by the nonseagoing software designer, who designed software to calculate the point of *intersection* of the tracks of two ships by extrapolating their current courses.) In this case, the ground truth should be clarified and the software product modified to reflect the clarification of the ground truth. Finally, it is possible that a discrepancy, upon analysis, does not really represent an incongruity between a software product and the ground truth. Consider the situation where an auditor is not sure whether an incongruity exists. If the auditor does not report this possible incongruity and it does indeed exist, an incongruity would not be made visible. Therefore, the auditor faced with this situation should report the possible incongruity. Other project personnel in the CCB forum should be able to resolve whether the discrepancy exists. If it does not exist, it is simply rejected by the CCB. This approach of "when in doubt, report" is designed to prevent discrepancies from slipping through the cracks. However, this approach should not be carried to extremes—the introduction of an excessive number of frivolous discrepancies wastes time and money.

Managers particularly should be aware that every discrepancy does not necessarily represent something wrong with the software product being audited. We have often seen busy managers base their evaluation of a new software product purely upon the number of discrepancies uncovered in a software product audit, as if every discrepancy represented an error in the new product. The preceding paragraph shows how unfair such an evaluation may be—the discrepancies might

---

[2] Recall the notion of congruence shown in Figure 3.4. An *incongruity* is an absence of congruence, that is, an incongruity is a part in a software product that cannot be associated with any part in another, related software product.

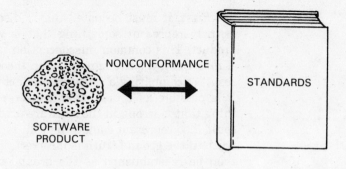

NONCONFORMANCE

SOFTWARE
PRODUCT

STANDARDS

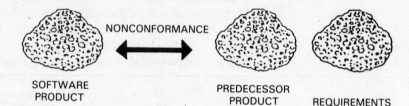

NONCONFORMANCE

SOFTWARE
PRODUCT

PREDECESSOR
PRODUCT

REQUIREMENTS

FIGURE 5.2. Top-level
taxonomy of software
discrepancies.

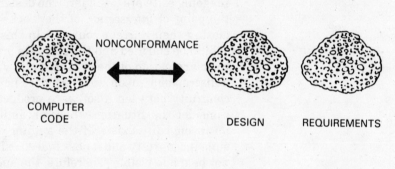

NONCONFORMANCE

COMPUTER
CODE

DESIGN

REQUIREMENTS

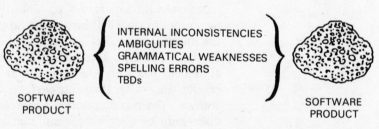

INTERNAL INCONSISTENCIES
AMBIGUITIES
GRAMMATICAL WEAKNESSES
SPELLING ERRORS
TBDs

SOFTWARE
PRODUCT

SOFTWARE
PRODUCT

represent problems with the new product, problems with the
ground truth, or no problems at all. A manager can make a
better evaluation if he bases it not on the number of discrepancies in the audit report but on the decisions the CCB makes
on the discrepancies uncovered by the audit. Analysis of such
decisions would reveal how many and how substantial are the
changes to be made to the software product and to the ground
truth. This information would provide a better evaluation of
the new software product than would a count of the discrepancies in the audit report. Discrepancies that result in no
changes being made to any product should not be considered
in evaluating either the software product or the ground truth.

A discrepancy should be reported in specific, objective, and neutral terms and should contain the rationale for addressing the discrepancy. A discrepancy should be specific in designating the software part(s)—in the software product being audited and/or in the ground truth—that are incongruous and in stating what the incongruity is. The report of a discrepancy should objectively state facts and should neither express opinions nor make assumptions. A discrepancy report should be neutral in that it does not assert that either the software product or ground truth is wrong, but only that they differ. A properly worded discrepancy would not include statements such as:

"Section 1 of the document is poorly worded and is therefore difficult to understand."

"The reliability requirement is nonsensical. Whoever wrote it obviously has no understanding of how software operates."

"Although the design meets all its requirements, the design of the database retrieval capability, in my opinion, is too cumbersome to function in an optimum manner."

In the balance of this section, we provide a number of sample discrepancies written using the above precepts, most of them modeled on actual discrepancies observed by the authors.

It is convenient to classify software discrepancies according to the specific comparison process (with a specific ground truth) that uncovers them (recall Figure 3.11). A top-level classification of discrepancies that may arise from software audits is shown in Figure 5.2. Four different comparison processes are shown in the figure. The software products involved in these comparisons are shown on the left-hand side of the figure, and the various ground truths are shown on the right-hand side.

The first row in Figure 5.2 represents the comparison of a software product to a set of standards established for a project, which is the ground truth for this comparison. The software product is assessed as to its conformance with each standard in this set. The discrepancies shown in Table 5.1 are examples

TABLE 5.1. EXAMPLES OF QUALITY ASSURANCE
DISCREPANCIES

Subsection 4.2 of the design document defines the five software modules that make up Subsystem S2. Four of these modules are specified as having error exits. No error exits, however, have been specified for module MS2(3) of this subsystem. Paragraph 7.3.4 of the programming standard stipulates that all modules should have error exits. This apparent discrepancy between the description of module MS2(3) and the programming standard should be resolved for compliance.

The System ABC Requirements Specification does not conform to paragraph 2.1.6 of the company's documentation standard. Paragraph 2.1.6 of the documentation standard stipulates that every requirements specification must state its database backup and restoration needs. The System ABC Requirements Specification is silent on this issue. For completeness, this apparent omission should be addressed.

---

of incongruities that might result from this type of comparison. Both examples shown in Table 5.1 illustrate that considerable savings in resources may be achieved through a timely audit (recall Figure 1.3). In the first example, an apparent design error is uncovered prior to commencement of coding, while in the second example the absence of an important (and potentially complex) function from the statement of need is revealed. We consider this issue further in Section 5.2 (see also Exercises 5.7 and 5.11).

In Chapter 3, we discussed the assessment of conformance of a software product to standards and labeled this process software quality assurance (SQA). We also indicated in Section 3.1 that the process of SQA was included in the discipline of software product assurance (recall Figure 3.2). The first row of Figure 5.2 illustrates how the process of SQA fits into the audit function of software product assurance.

The second row of Figure 5.2 shows a comparison of a software product to a ground truth composed of two items—the predecessor software product and the requirements specification. The comparison of a software product to a predecessor software product was labeled as verification in Section 3.1, and the comparison of a software product to the requirements specification was labeled as validation in that section. The second row of Figure 5.2 thus illustrates how the process of verification and validation (V&V) that we defined in Section 3.1 is included in the audit function of product assurance.

A special case of this comparison process exists when the predecessor product of a software product being audited is the requirements specification. The requirements specification is the only item in the ground truth in this case, and the comparison of the software product to the requirements specification is both a verification and validation.

For both verification and validation, the comparison determines whether the two products are congruent (recall Figure 3.4). Determining congruency is a two-step process. The auditor first must find software parts in both products that match as to subject, and then must determine whether those software parts match in content. For example, suppose an auditor is comparing a preliminary design specification (PDS) to a requirements specification (RS). Assume that he finds a paragraph in the requirements specification on the subject of drawing circles. He searches the preliminary design specification for material on that subject and finds an entire section devoted to drawing circles. Having found a match in subject between the two products, he next compares the paragraph in the RS to the section in the PDS to see whether they have the same content. If the only difference between these two software parts is the greater detail that is anticipated in the PDS, he has located a pair of congruent parts in the two products. That is, if a software part or parts in one product matches in subject and content a software part or parts in the other product, then the software parts are congruent. If a software part in one product does not match in subject any software part in the other product, then an incongruity exists. An incongruity also exists if a software part or parts in one product matches in subject a software part or parts in the other product, but does not match in content. These and all other incongruities are reported as discrepancies.

Finding software parts that match in subject is generally not a trivial task. Recall from Figure 3.4 that congruence between software products can be a one-to-one, a many-to-one, or a one-to-many relationship. Further, where incongruities exist, there may be parts in one product that have no match in subject in the other product.

There are several ways for an auditor to determine these subject matches. One way is to search the entire predecessor product for each software part in the software product to locate all subject matches. Since the predecessor product is searched from beginning to end for each software part in the software product, this method is thorough (it finds all subject matches), but it can be extremely time-consuming (and thus expensive). This high resource expenditure generally makes this method not feasible for software products of some size.

A practical alternate method of finding subject matches is shown in Figure 5.3. In this method, a two-way comparison is made. In the first comparison, each part in the software product is compared to the predecessor product to locate a part that

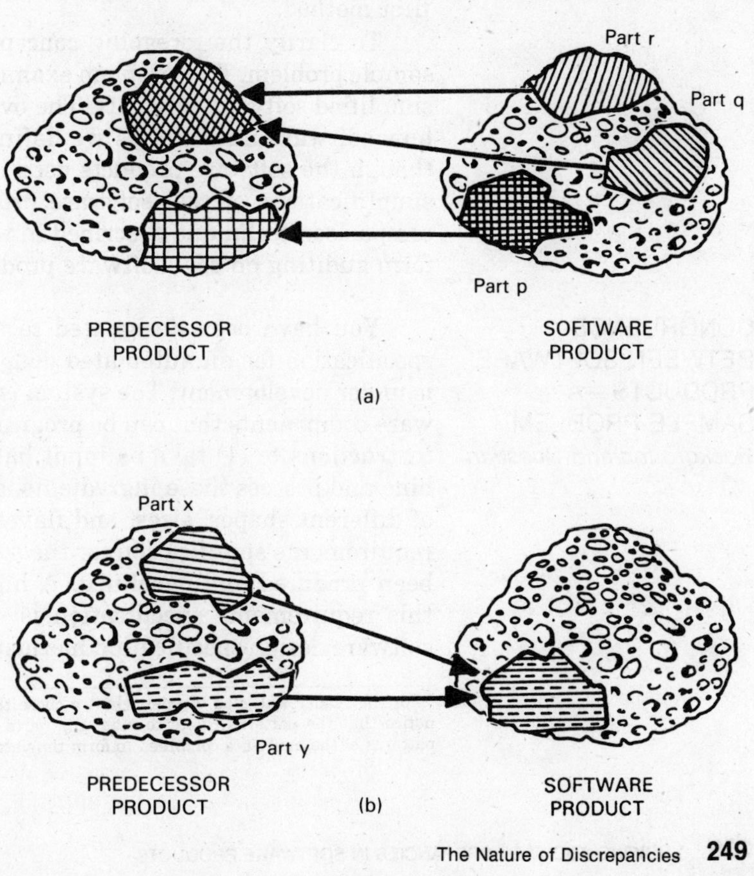

FIGURE 5.3. Auditing seeks to determine (a) whether each part in a software product has an antecedent in a predecessor product, and, conversely, (b) whether each part in this predecessor product has a corresponding part in the software product. Through this two-way comparison, auditing establishes the extent to which the two products are congruent.

matches in subject. (Notice that the search does not necessarily have to cover the entire predecessor product for each software product part—the search continues only until the first matching part is found.)

For example, in Figure 5.3(a), part p is compared to the predecessor product until a subject match is found. Then part q and part r are similarly matched. Notice that parts q and r both match to the same part in the predecessor product. This relationship is a one-to-many relationship in terms of the predecessor product to the software product.[3]

The second comparison for finding subject matches is the converse of the first: each part in the predecessor product is compared to the software product to locate a part that matches in subject. For example, in Figure 5.3(b), part x is compared to the software product until a subject match is found. Then part y is similarly matched. Notice in this case that parts x and y both match to the same part in the software product. This relationship is a many-to-one relationship in terms of the predecessor product to the software product.

This two-way comparison finds, in a nominal amount of time, all one-to-one, many-to-one, and one-to-many relationships, as well as predecessor product disconnects (parts in the predecessor product that have no subject matches in the software product) and software product disconnects (parts in the software product that have no subject matches in the predecessor product). It is considerably less time-consuming than the first method.

To clarify the foregoing concepts, consider the following sample problem. This problem examines the audit of two highly simplified software products. The overall purpose is to explain how software auditing as we define it is actually done. Although the software products used in the sample problem are simplifications of real software products, we stress that the comparison technique described in the problem is how we perform auditing on real software products.

CONGRUENCE BETWEEN SOFTWARE PRODUCTS—A SAMPLE PROBLEM
Background and Question

You have been designated to audit the software design specification for an automated doughnut-making system that is under development. The system is to consist of a set of hardware components that can be programmed via a set of software instructions to (1) take as input baking ingredients, (2) combine and process these ingredients, and (3) produce doughnuts of different shapes, sizes, and flavors as output. A functional requirements specification for the software for this system has been produced and baselined. A highly simplified version of this requirements specification is shown in Figure 5.4. The software design specification has just been produced and is now

---

[3] For the reader who may wonder why we chose the particular patterns in Figure 5.3, notice that the patterns relate to matching parts (on a many-to-one relationship, the patterns of the many are combined to form the pattern of the one).

**Functional Requirements Specification for
Programmable Subsystem of
Automated Doughnut-Making System**

1.0 Introduction

This document specifies the functions to be performed by the programmable subsystem of the Automated Doughnut-Making System (ADMS). This document is the basis for all software to be developed for ADMS.

2.0 System Overview

ADMS consists of the following two subsystems:

a. Hardware Subsystem (requirements separately documented)

b. Software (Programmable) Subsystem

3.0 Software Subsystem Functions

The Software Subsystem shall perform the functions listed in the subparagraphs below.

3.1 Input Processing Function

This function shall drive all hardware components that receive doughnut ingredients.

3.2 Recipe Processing Function

This function shall process ingredients to produce doughnuts in accordance with recipes keyed in from a keyboard. The following set of primitive keyboard instructions shall be accommodated:

3.2.1 Add. Add the ingredients specified to the bowl.

3.2.2 Mix. Mix the ingredients in the bowl at the speed and for the time specified.

3.2.3 Roll. Roll out the mixture on the cutting board.

3.2.4 Cut. Cut out the dough for either regular (with hole) or filled doughnuts.

3.2.5 Bake. Bake the doughnuts for the time and at the oven temperature specified.

3.2.6 Fill. Fill doughnuts with ingredient specified.

3.2.7 Dust. Dust doughnuts with ingredient specified.

3.3 Output Processing Function

This function shall drive all hardware components that package the baked doughnuts.

FIGURE 5.4. Simplified functional requirements specification for Programmable Subsystem of Automated Doughnut-Making System.

```
┌────────────────────────────────────────────────────────────────────┐
│                      Design Specification for                        │
│                    Programmable Subsystem of                         │
│                   Automated Doughnut-Making System                   │
│                                                                      │
│    • • •                                                             │
│                                                                      │
│  2.0   Software Subsystem Architecture                               │
│                                                                      │
│    • • •                                                             │
│                                                                      │
│  2.2   Ingredient Receipt Component                                  │
│                                                                      │
│    • • •                                                             │
│                                                                      │
│  2.3   Recipe Processing Component                                   │
│                                                                      │
│    • • •                                                             │
│                                                                      │
│        2.3.1   Mix Module                                            │
│                                                                      │
│                a.  Purpose. This module will alternately add         │
│                    specified ingredients to the mixing              │
│                    bowl  and mix the contents of the bowl for        │
│                    specified times.                                  │
│                                                                      │
│        • • •                                                         │
│                                                                      │
│        2.3.2   Roll Module                                          │
│                                                                      │
│        • • •                                                         │
│                                                                      │
│        2.3.3   Cut Component                                         │
│                                                                      │
│                a.  Purpose. This component will cut out doughnuts.   │
│                    It consists of the following                     │
│                    two modules:                                     │
│                                                                      │
│                    1.  Regular Cut Module:  this module cuts         │
│                        doughnuts with a hole in each one.           │
│                    2.  Fill Cut Module:  this module cuts            │
│                        doughnuts without holes.                     │
│        • • •                                                         │
│                                                                      │
│        2.3.4   Bake Module                                          │
│                                                                      │
│        • • •                                                         │
│                                                                      │
│        2.3.5   Fill Module                                          │
│                                                                      │
│        • • •                                                         │
│                                                                      │
│        2.3.6   Glaze Module                                         │
│                                                                      │
│        • • •                                                         │
│                                                                      │
│  2.4   Doughnut Packaging Component                                  │
│                                                                      │
│    • • •                                                             │
└────────────────────────────────────────────────────────────────────┘
```

FIGURE 5.5. Partial
design specification for
Programmable Subsystem of
Automated Doughnut-Making
System.

TABLE 5.2. MATCHING OF DESIGN SPECIFICATION TO REQUIREMENTS SPECIFICATION FOR PROGRAMMABLE SUBSYSTEM OF AUTOMATED DOUGHNUT-MAKING SYSTEM

Design Specification		Requirements Specification	
2.0	Software Subsystem Architecture	3.0	Software Subsystem Functions
2.2	Ingredient Receipt Component	3.1	Input Processing Function
2.3	Recipe Processing Component	3.2	Recipe Processing Function
2.3.1	Mix Module	3.2.2	Mix
2.3.2	Roll Module	3.2.3	Roll
2.3.3	Cut Component	3.2.4	Cut
2.3.3a1	Regular Cut Module	3.2.4	Cut
2.3.3a2	Fill Cut Module	3.2.4	Cut
2.3.4	Bake Module	3.2.5	Bake
2.3.5	Fill Module	3.2.6	Fill
2.3.6	Glaze Module	?	
2.4	Doughnut Packaging Component	3.3	Output Processing Function

ready for audit. This software design specification is partially shown in Figure 5.5. (Only a partial specification is shown in order to simplify the problem.) Based on the specifications provided, what discrepancies do you observe as you audit the design specification?

Solution Approach

A. We first determine the matches in subject between the requirements specification (predecessor product) and the design specification (software product). Even though these specifications are simplified products, we use the two-way comparison method described earlier (recall Figure 5.3) to locate subject matches.

For the first comparison, we compare the parts in the design specification to the parts in the requirements specification. This comparison yields the subject matches shown in Table 5.2.

For the second comparison, we compare the parts in the requirements specification to the parts in the design specification. This comparison yields the subject matches shown in Table 5.3.

This method locates all the subject matches that exist in this case, as can be verified by a quick scan of the two specifications (feasible only because the specifications are so simple). Notice that the first comparison (Table 5.2) picks up the one-to-many relationship (i.e., one in the predecessor product to many in the software product) connected with the Cut function. The many-to-one relationship (i.e., many in the predecessor product to one in the software product) connected with the Add and Mix functions is detected by the second comparison (Table 5.3).

Also notice that two disconnects are located. The first comparison reveals that the Glaze module in the design specifi-

TABLE 5.3. MATCHING OF REQUIREMENTS SPECIFICATION TO DESIGN SPECIFICATION FOR PROGRAMMABLE SUBSYSTEM OF AUTOMATED DOUGHNUT-MAKING SYSTEM

Requirements Specification		Design Specification	
*3.0	Software Subsystem Functions	2.0	Software Subsystem Architecture
*3.1	Input Processing Function	2.2	Ingredient Receipt Component
*3.2	Recipe Processing Function	2.3	Recipe Processing Component
3.2.1	Add	2.3.1	Mix Module
*3.2.2	Mix	2.3.1	Mix Module
*3.2.3	Roll	2.3.2	Roll Module
*3.2.4	Cut	2.3.3	Cut Component
*3.2.5	Bake	2.3.4	Bake Module
*3.2.6	Fill	2.3.5	Fill Module
3.2.7	Dust	?	
*3.3	Output Processing Function	2.4	Doughnut Packaging Component

* This matching was initially determined during the comparison shown in Table 5.2.

cation has no match in the requirements specification. Evidently a developer (probably expressing his personal taste) added a capability to the design to produce glazed doughnuts, a capability not contained in the requirements. This disconnect would be reported as a discrepancy—the CCB must decide whether this glaze capability is not desired and thus should be removed from the design specification, or whether this capability, initially overlooked, is indeed desired, in which case the requirements specification would be amended to incorporate this capability.

The other disconnect becomes evident on the second comparison—the design specification does not address the requirement to dust doughnuts. This omission is also a discrepancy to be reported to the CCB.

B. Our next step in the audit process is to determine whether the parts of the design specification and the requirements specification that match in subject also match in content. In this sample problem, we provide little content in the specifications. However, in the content that is provided, there is one incongruity. When requirements specification (Figure 5.4) paragraph 3.2.2 for mixing is compared to design specification (Figure 5.5) paragraph 2.3.1a, we observe that the requirement that mixing be done at specified speeds is omitted from the design specification. This omission would be reported as a discrepancy.

This sample problem illustrates the mechanics of determining the congruence of two software products in the sense depicted in Figure 5.3. Do not be misled by the ease with which our deliberately simple software products could be audited. In the real world, auditing of voluminous specifications is a labor-intensive task. While auditing can consume considerable resources, it potentially saves even more resources through early detection of problems. Auditing is another example of the concept of "pay now versus pay much more later" that we introduced in Section 1.2 (recall Figure 1.3).

This task of assessing congruence between software products can be simplified by the developer of the products. He might include in each software part of each product the labels identifying the matching software parts in the predecessor product and in the requirements specification. Alternatively, he might produce a traceability matrix, linking software product part labels to part labels in the predecessor product and in the requirements specification. For either method, the auditor should verify the accuracy and the completeness of the information provided.

To complete our discussion of the second row of Figure 5.2, we present in Table 5.4 examples of discrepancies that might be uncovered through verification and validation. Notice in that table in the first verification discrepancy that a feature is observed in the detailed design that is not specified in the preliminary design specification. This excursion from the requirements will consume additional resources to develop. (We discuss excursions from customer requirements further in Project Mars in Section 7.1.) The CCB may not be willing to spend these resources for something not needed by the customer, in which case it would direct that the feature be deleted from the design. On the other hand, the CCB may decide that the feature has sufficient benefit to be included in the system. If that is the decision, the CCB would direct that the requirements specification be modified to include the feature. Observe how the auditor, in reporting this and other discrepancies, helps answer the question we posed at the beginning of this chapter: "How does the CCB know when a software change may be needed?"

The third row of Figure 5.2 is actually a special case of the second row. When the software product is computer code, it is verified against the software design specification and validated against the requirements specification. However, a listing of source code is generally not used for these comparisons. Rather, the following process is typically used (Section 5.3 elaborates on this process). Detailed test plans and test procedures are prepared based on the design and requirements specifications. Then the computer code is transformed to an executable form. This code is executed in a live or nearly live environment using the written test procedures. Discrepancies are reported whenever the results expected from a test differ from the actual results observed during test execution.

In Section 3.1, we introduced this process of exercising computer code and assessing its functionality under the label of test and evaluation (T&E) (recall Figure 3.2). We indicated in Section 3.2 the close relationship of T&E and V&V and asserted that the process of T&E was included in the audit func-

TABLE 5.4. EXAMPLES OF VERIFICATION AND VALIDATION DISCREPANCIES

Verification Discrepancies

Subsection 1.3 of the detailed design document (System Architecture) provides a summary description of each of the system's subsystems. This description includes a reference to Subsystem S13. Section 2.2 of the preliminary design specification, which specifies the system's subsystems, makes no reference to a Subsystem S13. This apparent discrepancy should be resolved for consistency.

Subsection 3.6 of the detailed design document (System Displays) defines the format and content of each of the displays that can be generated at a user terminal. In describing the time that may elapse to generate displays, this section contains the following statement: "The amount of time required to generate the display shown in figure 3.6-3 depends in part upon the scale specified by the user for the map background. If this scale is greater than fifty (50) miles to the inch, the software will require at least five (5) seconds to generate and display the map following completion of the user input requesting generation of the display." This statement appears to be inconsistent with the response time performance requirement specified in subsection 3.1 of the preliminary design specification, viz., the response time between entry of a display request and the display of a response must be less than 4 seconds. (This performance requirement is derived from paragraph 6.7 in the requirements specification.) This apparent discrepancy should be resolved for consistency.

Validation Discrepancies

The detailed design specifies that the search algorithm in module S4.8 will sequentially search the tray table to determine which trays are currently lined up at their discharge chutes (and therefore must be tilted to discharge their contents). This design logically follows from the preliminary design specification, which stated in paragraph 3.4.2 that subsystem S4 would, for each increment of tray sorter travel, tilt all trays aligned with their discharge chutes. However, analysis indicates that a sequential search would be too slow to satisfy paragraph 5.2.2 of the requirements specification, which specified that the system must be capable of tilting all 980 trays of the tray sorter on any one increment of tray sorter travel. This apparent discrepancy should be resolved for conformance.

Paragraph 6.2 of the requirements specification states that the system must be available 24 hours per day, 7 days per week. The preliminary design specification does not address this requirement. This discrepancy should be resolved for completeness.

tion of software product assurance. We have now seen in the first three rows of Figure 5.2 how the processes of QA, V&V, and T&E respectively form part of the audit function and serve as a means to classify audit discrepancies. The CCB needs to be aware of these classes of discrepancies to perform its decision-making function effectively.

Examples of discrepancies that might be reported as part of this T&E class are shown in Table 5.5. Notice in these discrepancies that no references are made to the specific software parts in the design and requirements specifications to which the computer code is being compared. Such references should be contained in the written test procedures and need not be repeated in the reports of the discrepancies. Since the computer

TABLE 5.5. EXAMPLES OF TEST AND EVALUATION DISCREPANCIES

In step 16 of test procedure 4-2, the expected response to the terminal command "CIRCLE (8,10.4,5)" was that a circle would be drawn on the terminal display at coordinates (8,10.4) with a radius of 5 units. The actual result of the entry of this command was the display of an ellipse on the terminal, centered at coordinates (8, 10.4) with a minor axis of 10 units and a major axis of 14 units.

Upon entry of the command "GRAPH (BAR)" at step 98 of test procedure 6A (having previously entered the parameters for a bar graph in preceding test steps), a bar graph was displayed on the terminal with alternate bars going up and down and with bar magnitudes 200 times larger than the values previously entered. What was expected at this step was the display of an error message stating that negative values were not allowed in drawing bar graphs.

---

code being tested is a complete system, it is generally not known which parts of the computer code are being tested in any test step.

We now return to Figure 5.2. The fourth row of the figure represents self-comparison; that is, the ground truth (recall Figure 5.1) is the software product itself, so that the software product is being compared with itself. Since the first three rows of Figure 5.2 are manifestations of the processes of QA, V&V, and T&E, respectively, the reader might assume that the fourth row of this figure is a manifestation of the fourth product assurance process introduced in Section 3.1—configuration management (CM). But this assumption would not be correct; the fourth row of Figure 5.2 is not related to CM. It is, however, related to the process of verification and validation. Self-comparison is a form of V&V in the sense that one portion of the product may be compared not to a preceding product but to a preceding portion of the same product to determine internal consistency. The preceding portion of the product can be considered to be a predecessor product (verification) or the requirements for the latter portion of the product (validation).

A self-comparison may uncover a variety of internal discrepancies. These discrepancies could be categorized as a lack of consistency, of clarity, of completeness, and of testability. Defects in consistency and clarity may be found in any software product; defects in completeness and testability may be found in requirements specifications, as we subsequently explain.

Inconsistencies may arise between different portions of the software product. Frequently, a software part is introduced at one point in a product and subsequently is expanded upon at some other point in the product. If these two presentations of the software part are inconsistent, one (or both) of them may be incorrect, such as an incorrect figure or table reference in a specification. If an incorrect software part is used as the basis for subsequent development, errors in subsequent software products will result. An inconsistency may also exist when a pointer to another part of the product is inaccurate. This inconsistency could also confuse the developer and lead to errors in subsequent software products. As a third example, an inconsistency may also exist when the front part of, say, a design specification refers to three subsystems included in the design while the remainder of the specification only describes two of these subsystems (some might argue that this inconsistency is also an example of a defect in completeness).

A software product may lack clarity for several reasons. A statement in a specification may be ambiguous or may lead the reader to make unwarranted assumptions. A grammatical weakness may confuse a reader so that he either misinterprets a specification or makes (possibly invalid) assumptions as to its meaning. (Reference 5 in Chapter 2 provides an illustration of this problem involving the use of the word "too.") Spelling errors can also lead to confusion and to resources wasted developing something that is not desired. Now do not get the idea that we advocate that the auditor function as a technical editor. The auditor certainly can assist the technical editor by pointing out typographical errors observed in the process of his scrutiny of the software product. But the auditor should be alert for and report as a discrepancy any spelling error that has an impact on the development effort. For example, one of the authors once audited a voluminous design specification that contained five different spellings of the name of an error-checking routine. It was not clear whether a single routine was being specified or whether five different error-checking routines were desired.

Lack of clarity in a software product can lead to misinterpretations, unwarranted assumptions, or confusion, with the result that resources could be wasted in the development of subsequent software products. This waste results from the development of undesired capabilities and from a failure to develop desired capabilities. Each instance of a lack of clarity in a software product should be documented as a discrepancy.

When a self-comparison is performed on the requirements specification, the document is checked for two other attributes—completeness and testability. The requirements specification lacks completeness if the auditor, based on his experience and his knowledge of the customer's needs, detects that the specification overlooks whether the resultant software code will actually work and be useful (such as the omission of a performance requirement stipulating how rapidly the software is to respond to a user query). Completeness is also lacking if a requirement is marked TBD (To Be Determined) or something similar. (Missing parts and TBDs in other software products are considered verification discrepancies—they indicate that a software product does not logically follow from its predecessor product.)

The requirements in a requirements specification are also assessed as to their testability during self-comparison. Testability is the ability to write a test procedure, which when executed in a live or nearly live environment (i.e., during T&E) demonstrates that the capability under consideration has been incorporated into computer code as stipulated in the requirements specification. A frequently occurring testability discrepancy is the requirement that a software system be user friendly. Unless "user friendliness" is defined in functionally specific terms (e.g., "the syntax of all user-entered commands shall follow the rules of informal written English"), the requirement that a software system be user friendly is inherently untestable.

Examples of discrepancies resulting from self-comparison are shown in Table 5.6. The examples include discrepancies involving inconsistency, lack of clarity, and incompleteness. We included no examples of discrepancies arising from a lack of testability, preferring instead, in the following sample problem, to highlight the difficulty of defining requirements that are testable and to suggest an approach for auditors to assess testability.

TABLE 5.6. EXAMPLES OF SELF-COMPARISON
DISCREPANCIES

Paragraph 4.3.4.5 (Number of Terminals to be Supported) of the requirements specification indicates that the system is to be capable of supporting up to fifty (50) terminals. This paragraph appears to be inconsistent with the discussion in section 1 that suggests that a maximum of fifteen (15) users will be able to access the system simultaneously. This apparent discrepancy should be resolved for consistency.

Section 1 of the design document (System Overview) contains several different spellings of the same system name. These discrepancies should be corrected for consistency.

Subsection 3.1 of the requirements specification (Performance Requirements) contains the following statement: "The system response time to a user query input at a terminal device shall not exceed three (3) seconds." The definition of "system response time" does not appear to be specified anywhere in the document. Does it mean, for example, "the time that elapses between the instant the user presses the RETURN key on the terminal device at the end of his query until the instant the system's response to the query first appears on the terminal's display device"? This point should be clarified.

The second sentence of the fourth paragraph of section 1 of the design specification is not understood. This issue should be addressed for the sake of clarity.

Section 2 of the requirements specification (System Overview), which contains a discussion of the system capabilities to be automated (i.e., capabilities to be supported by software functions), does not contain a corresponding discussion of the capabilities to be supported by computer hardware and communications equipment. This issue should be addressed for the sake of completeness.

Section 5 of the requirements specification is entitled "Performance Requirements." Subsection 5.4 (Response Time Requirements) is listed as To Be Determined (TBD). For completeness, this discrepancy should be resolved.

REQUIREMENTS
DEFINITION AND
TESTABILITY—A
SAMPLE PROBLEM
*Background and
Questions*

Suppose a computer system is supporting the operations of a meteorological satellite. Among other things, this satellite is monitoring weather activity over various parts of the earth. In support of this monitoring, suppose the computer system includes the capability to allow its users to define rectangles on the earth's surface that serve as reference areas for weather observations (e.g., to observe what percentage of the time the area is cloudless). Suppose further that this capability is defined in paragraph 4.2.7 of the requirements specification for the computer system. Paragraph 4.2.7 of the requirements specification is shown in Figure 5.6.

Which of the six requirements listed in Figure 5.6 are testable? Recall that testability means that each requirement is sufficiently defined in the paragraph to permit the development of written test procedures that could then be used to demonstrate that the requirement is or is not satisfied in the coded form of the software. If a requirement is not sufficiently defined to permit the development of such procedures, how would you augment the requirement statement to make it testable? (*Note*: Some parts of this sample problem require knowledge of trigonometry in order to be completely understood. However, it is not necessary to understand the mathematical details of the exercise completely in order to understand the testability issues addressed. The mathematics has been incorporated into the problem to illustrate in specific terms the types of mathe-

FIGURE 5.6. Portion of requirements specification for Meteorological Satellite Monitoring System.

**Requirements Specification for
Meteorological Satellite Monitoring System**

4.2.7 Rectangles on the Surface of the Earth

To support quantitative analysis of weather observations made from the meteorological satellite, the system shall provide the capability to define rectangles on the surface of the earth. These rectangles shall conform to the following specifications and limitations:

a. The rectangles shall be oriented such that the north and south sides lie along (constant) lines of latitude, and the east and west sides lie along (constant) lines of longitude.

b. The maximum dimension of any side shall not exceed 80 nautical miles.

c. The maximum area of any rectangle shall not exceed 3,600 square nautical miles.

d. All rectangles shall lie between 75° North and 75° South latitude.

e. Each rectangle shall be defined by specifying the latitude and longitude of its northeast and southwest vertices.

f. No more than 200 rectangles shall be accommodated by the system at any one time.

---

matical issues that testers may face in the real world. The mathematical issues discussed in this sample problem are derived from the authors' actual software project experience.)

Solution Approach

In general, a software requirement is testable if we can describe an exercise of the requirement that can be performed on the computer hosting software code to be tested. Presumably such an exercise can then be broken down into a set of test steps that a tester can perform and a corresponding set of expected results that a tester can compare with the observed operation of software code. In the following discussion, we examine the six requirements in question from this perspective. That is, we describe an exercise that might be performed and what a tester might look for to determine whether computer code embodies each of these requirements.[4] It is assumed that data can be entered into the host computer system via a keyboard; it is also assumed that the system response to this input can be observed on a display device and, if desired, on a printout.

A. For requirements *a* and *e* (see Figure 5.6), the tester could define a rectangle by inputting the latitude and longitude of its northeast and southwest vertices. The tester could then observe on the display device the resultant figure to see whether its borders lie along the latitudes and longitudes defined by the vertices. (Presumably the figure will be displayed on a map background showing lines of constant latitude and longitude making visual comparison with the expected result possible. If no such map background is part of the system being tested, it may be necessary for the tester to instrument the code being tested so that it displays such a background or otherwise indicates where the figure lies on the surface of the earth.) The preceding discussion thus represents a test of the two requirements in question in that it describes an exercise that a tester can perform to confirm that a rectangle can be constructed that lies along lines of constant latitude and longitude as defined by the latitude and longitude of the rectangle's northeast and southwest vertices.

B. For requirements *b* and *c* (see Figure 5.6), it is necessary to perform mathematical computations in order to determine expected results. To do these computations, it is necessary to know what model is being used for the shape of the earth. This model is not indicated in paragraph 4.2.7 of the requirements specification. If this model is not indicated elsewhere in

---

[4] In Section 5.3, we examine the process of converting such exercises into test procedures, i.e., a set of test steps that a tester can perform. These test steps are accompanied by a set of expected results. When the tester executes the test steps, he compares the result of software code operation against these expected results. If the results of this code operation do not agree with the expected results, the tester writes a test incident report to document this discrepancy (see Section 5.3). In the current sample problem, we focus on conceptualizing such exercises. Of course, strictly speaking, until such exercises are converted to performable test steps, requirements testability has not been formally demonstrated.

the specification, then requirements *b* and *c* are untestable. To see the significance of the need to prescribe an earth model, assume that the requirements specification indicates elsewhere that the earth is a sphere of radius $R = 3440$ nautical miles. With this assumption, it is then possible to write down the following distance and area formulas that could be used to check requirements *b* and *c*:

$D1$ = great circle distance of the east or west side of the rectangle = $R(LAT2 - LAT1)$

where

$LAT1$ = latitude of the rectangle's southern border (in radians)[5]

$LAT2$ = latitude of the rectangle's northern border (in radians)

$D2$ = small circle distance of the north or south sides of the rectangle = $R(LON1 - LON2)\cos(LAT)$

where

$LON1$ = longitude of the rectangle's western border (in radians)

$LON2$ = longitude of the rectangle's eastern border (in radians)

LAT = latitude of the rectangle's northern or southern border as appropriate

cos = cosine function

A = area of rectangle = $R^2(LON1 - LON2)[\sin(LAT2) - \sin(LAT1)]$

where

sin = sine function[6]

If the earth is not assumed to be a sphere (but, say, an ellipsoid), the above distance and area formulas may have to be modified or replaced to account for deviation from sphericity. (The extent to which modification or replacement may be required depends in general on the accuracy required; that is, for completeness the requirements specification should probably indicate the accuracy required for distance and area computations.) Using the above formulas, the tester could then define various rectangles by specifying their northeast and southwest vertices such that (1) some of these rectangles have one or more sides that exceed 80 nautical miles, (2) some of these rectangles have no sides

---

[5] One radian is equal to 180°/pi or 57.2957795 . . . degrees. It is a unit of angular measure frequently used in engineering and scientific computations.

[6] In the above formulas for distance and area, the following sign conventions are assumed: (1) latitudes above the equator are positive, and latitudes below the equator are negative (e.g., 30°S = −0.52 radians); (2) longitudes to the west of the prime meridian are positive, and longitudes to the east of the prime meridian are negative (e.g., 30°E = −0.52 radians). The above sign conventions assure that the distance and area formulas given above yield positive values for any point on the earth's surface.

exceeding 80 nautical miles, (3) some of these rectangles have an area exceeding 3600 square nautical miles, and (4) some of these rectangles have an area less than 3600 square nautical miles. The tester could thus enter these vertex pairs and then observe on the display device the result of entering these pairs. In those cases where the vertex pairs yield rectangle side lengths no greater than 80 nautical miles and an area no greater than 3600 square nautical miles, the display would presumably show the rectangles corresponding to the vertex pairs input; otherwise, the display would presumably respond with some error diagnostic indicating the offending length and/ or area. As was indicated in A, above, the tester may have to instrument code being tested so that it displays the values of rectangle side lengths and areas if the code is otherwise not required to do so. The preceding discussion thus indicates that, in order to test requirements b and c, it is necessary to know the model being used for the shape of the earth. This discussion also indicates that the details of this shape depend on the accuracy required for distance and area computations (e.g., required computational accuracies may be such that it is sufficient to assume that the earth is a sphere, because changes to distance and areas that would result by assuming a nonspherical earth would be smaller than the required accuracies of the values of these quantities). Consequently, unless the requirements specification were augmented to address earth-model (and computational-accuracy) issues, requirements b and c would have to be considered untestable.

C. For requirement d, the tester could extend the scope of the tests used to exercise requirements a and e by including rectangles whose northern borders lie above 75° North latitude and other rectangles whose southern borders lie below 75° South latitude. Vertex pairs defining such rectangles would presumably cause the software to respond with some error diagnostic indicating the offending border(s). Thus, this requirement can be considered testable.

D. For requirement f, the tester could again extend the scope of the tests used to exercise requirements a and e by inputting up to 200 pairs of acceptable vertices (vertex pairs that do not violate requirements b, c, and d). It should be noted that, for repeatability, accomplishment of the testing of requirement f would probably benefit from automated support. For example, it may be useful to store the (up to) 200 vertex pairs on some mass storage device (say, a disk). Then, through a keyboard-entered command, these pairs could be read into the system, each pair (quickly) generating a figure on the display device and storing the figure on a mass storage device for subsequent reproduction on a printer, so that the resultant hard copy could be carefully analyzed subsequent to test execution to explicitly check that (at least selected) rectangles corresponding to the vertex pairs input were properly generated. Following this exercise, the tester would attempt to create additional rectangles in excess of 200 by entering additional vertex pairs. When the number of rectangles stored on the mass storage device exceeds 200, the system would presumably respond with some error diagnostic indicating that the system limit of 200 stored rectangles has been exceeded. Thus, the preceding discussion indicates that requirement f is testable. This discussion also indicates that testing this requirement would probably be greatly facilitated by at least automating the process of inputting test data.

The solution approach just presented illustrates in specific terms what is meant by "requirements testability." As this discussion demonstrates, it is important to specify requirements as precisely as possible. Otherwise, they may be untestable—and if they are untestable, the wizard's question posed in Figure 2.8 remains unanswered. Also, the discussion of the testability of requirements b and c brings to light a challenge that typically faces a tester. If a tester does not have specific expertise in an area to be tested, it may be necessary for him to do some detailed analysis of the implications of testing that area. Thus, in the case of requirements b and c, the tester, if not conversant with computations on the surface of a sphere, would need to dust off his mathematics books to locate formulas that would help him generate expected results. In general, a good tester need not be an expert on the technical details of what he is to test. He does, however, have to be able to invoke his analytical skills to seek answers to questions raised by the capabilities he is to test.

As a final point in our discussion of audit discrepancies, we suggest that you compare Figure 5.2 with Figure 3.11, which presented an analogue to software product assurance in the form of a balance and set of weights. The left-hand pan of the balance contains a software product, and one of the weights is placed on the right-hand pan to effect a comparison. The parallelism of this analogue to Figure 5.2 is evident—the weights in the analogue are the items in the ground truths shown to the right of the arrows in Figure 5.2. The balance and set of weights are a good analogue of the audit function and represent the QA, V&V, and T&E processes.

Now that we have looked at the nature of discrepancies and analyzed the classes of discrepancies, it is time to investigate the audit process itself.

5.2 The Auditing Process for Documents

Figure 5.1 presented an overview of the audit process from the creation of a draft software product to the arrival of an audit report at the CCB. In the last section, we focused on some of the specific elements in that generic audit process—on software products, on ground truth, and on discrepancies. Now we move from the generic process to a specific audit process—the process for auditing software products that are documents. (The audit process for software products that are computer code is described in Section 5.3.) In so doing, we take a larger view than we took in Section 5.1, not concentrating on the individual

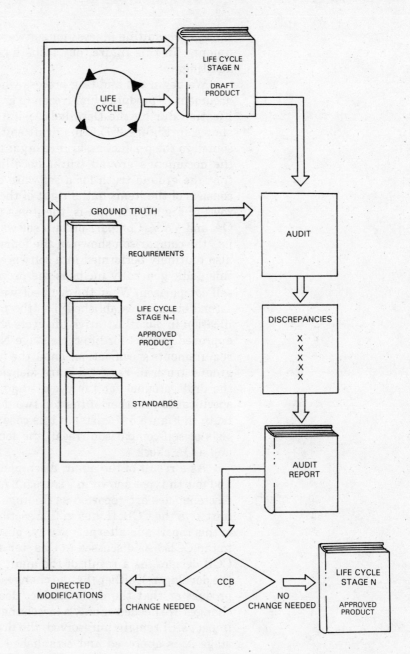

FIGURE 5.7. Overview of auditing process for software products that are documents.

The following labels appear within the figure:

LIFE CYCLE

LIFE CYCLE STAGE N DRAFT PRODUCT

GROUND TRUTH

REQUIREMENTS

LIFE CYCLE STAGE N-1 APPROVED PRODUCT

STANDARDS

AUDIT

DISCREPANCIES
X
X
X
X
X

AUDIT REPORT

DIRECTED MODIFICATIONS

CCB

CHANGE NEEDED

NO CHANGE NEEDED

LIFE CYCLE STAGE N APPROVED PRODUCT

elements of the process but focusing on the audit process as a whole and on its position within the change control process. We also discuss the format of the audit report and alternative ways to report discrepancies. We conclude the section with a sample problem that illustrates in specific terms how to report discrepancies resulting from an audit of a preliminary design against requirements.

We introduced the process of auditing a software product that is a document in Chapter 4. Recall Figure 4.5, which shows the change control process for a draft detailed design. The focus in that figure was the CCB. By slightly generalizing that figure and merging it into Figure 5.1, we obtain Figure 5.7, which shows the auditing process for software products that are documents. In this figure, our focus has now been changed to auditing.

We begin the auditing process whenever a draft software document is produced and frozen (e.g., a detailed design specification during the Detailed Design Stage of the life cycle shown in Figure 2.7). This draft software document is presented to the product assurance organization for audit against the document's ground truth. Recalling Figure 5.2, observe that the ground truth for a software document in Figure 5.7 consists of the items to the right of the arrows in the first two rows of Figure 5.2, that is, the items used in the processes of QA and V&V. Comparison of a software document to itself—i.e., the comparison shown in the fourth row of Figure 5.2—is also routinely performed in a software document audit. Thus, this audit generally includes the processes of QA, V&V, and self-comparison. When the draft software document is to be the second baseline established (i.e., the preliminary design specification in our illustrative life cycle shown in Figure 2.7), the approved product for life cycle stage $N-1$ in Figure 5.7 is the requirements specification. Thus, the top two documents in the ground truth in Figure 5.7 are identical. For the case where the draft product for life cycle stage N is the requirements specification, neither of the top two documents in the ground truth in Figure 5.7 exists; in this case an audit generally consists of self-comparison (recall the fourth line in Figure 5.2) and a QA check.

As a result of the audit, discrepancies of the first, second, and fourth types shown in Figure 5.2 may be uncovered. These discrepancies are reported as findings in an audit report submitted to the CCB. (Later in this section we discuss the format of this report and alternative ways of submitting discrepancies to the CCB.) As discussed in Chapter 4 (recall Figure 4.5), the CCB decides, as a result of the audit report (and analysis by the developers), either that no changes are needed for the draft product or that the draft product does need changing. If no changes are needed or only a few changes with relatively minor impact still remain unresolved, the draft product for life cycle stage N is approved and established as a baseline (e.g., the Detailed Design Baseline if stage N is the Detailed Design Stage). If changes are needed, the modifications directed by the CCB are made in the current stage to the draft product for life cycle stage N, or previous stages are revisited to change software documents in the ground truth, namely, either the requirements specification or the approved product for life cycle stage $N-1$. When changes are to be made to the draft product for stage N, the draft product, when changed, will be reintroduced to the auditing process. When a revisit to a previous stage is directed, the approved product for that stage is updated and the auditing process for the previous stage is initiated.

The preceding discussion completes a walk-through of the auditing process shown in Figure 5.7. Once a draft product is introduced to the process, it cycles through the audit and control process as many times as necessary until the CCB decides that no changes to the draft product are needed or that the remaining unresolved discrepancies are few enough in number and minor enough in impact to allow baselining of the product pending their resolution. Notice that the reference to stage N in Figure 5.7 applies to any life cycle stage producing a document. For example, source code listings (which are software documents) produced during the Coding Stage could be audited against the requirements specification and the detailed design specification using the process shown in Figure 5.7. (However, this particular audit is seldom conducted. Generally, the coded form of the software produced during the Coding and Production/Deployment Stages is audited by means of the T&E process described in Section 5.3. Our experience indicates that this latter process is generally more cost-effective and more effective in uncovering discrepancies than the process of auditing source code listings.)

Earlier we mentioned that the discrepancies uncovered in an audit were documented in an audit report that was presented to the CCB (recall Figures 5.1 and 5.7). A suggested format for this audit report—one that has been used by the authors on several projects—is shown in Table 5.7. All the subjects in the table have been addressed in previous chapters except for software identification (paragraph 4.2) and bookkeeping (paragraph 4.7). These two subjects are discussed in Chapter 6. Notice in the audit report that the auditor's objective findings are clearly separated from any of his subjective opinions. Also observe that, in addition to discrepancies uncovered by quality assurance, verification and validation, and self-comparison processes, various discrepancies may be uncovered as a result of software identification and through development of a traceability matrix.[7]

As we discussed in Chapter 4, the CCB considers the audit report in deciding what action to take regarding whether to baseline a software product. In addition, the CCB considers and takes action on each discrepancy contained in the audit report findings. The first action that the CCB takes upon receipt of the audit report is to have the development organization analyze those discrepancies whose cause and resolution are not clearly apparent (recall the Analyze box in Figure 4.4). The analyzers present to the CCB a recommended resolution for each such discrepancy. If the resolutions of all the discrepancies are obvious, the CCB can dispense with this analysis step. With

---

[7] A *traceability matrix* is a document that traces each software part in a requirements specification to its corresponding software part(s) in each subsequent software product and to the test documentation whose execution validates the requirements embodied in the software part. Recall Table 2.1 in Section 2.3.

TABLE 5.7. SUGGESTED FORMAT FOR A SOFTWARE AUDIT REPORT

| | Date |
| Software Audit Report Title | Document Number |

Section 1. Introduction

1.1 Purpose. This paragraph states the purpose of the audit report, which is to provide the results of an audit of a particular software product for a particular project.

1.2 Identification. This paragraph identifies the software that was audited, the date the software audit was completed, and the names of the auditors.

1.3 Project references. This paragraph provides a brief summary of the references applicable to the history and development of the project under which the audit was conducted.

1.4 Overview. This paragraph provides a brief overview of the contents of the report.

Section 2. References

This section lists all the documents applicable to the report.

Section 3. Procedure

This section describes the procedure used in the conduct of the audit with reference to the specific documents or other entities used in the process. Any assumptions made or constraints imposed relative to the audit are listed here.

Section 4. Findings

This section presents the objective findings uncovered as a result of the audit.

4.1 Conformance to standards. This paragraph reports the findings of the quality assurance check in terms of structure, format, content, or methodology. (The applicable standards may be externally imposed, such as governmental standards imposed on a contractor, and/or internally imposed, such as corporate or project management guidelines.)

4.2 Software identification. This paragraph presents the results of identifying the software parts. A representation of the configuration of the parts may be provided here or placed in an appendix. Any difficulties in labeling the parts will also be listed here.

4.3 Traceability matrix. This paragraph shows the traceability between the requirements specification and the software product. It also details disconnects between the requirements specification and the software product, and between the preceding baseline and the software product.

4.4 Results of verification. This paragraph presents the discrepancies observed as a result of verifying the software product.

4.5 Results of validation. This paragraph lists the discrepancies observed in the course of validating the software product.

4.6 Results of self-comparison. This paragraph presents the discrepancies uncovered as a result of product self-comparison, i.e., of comparing a software product with itself to assess the clarity, consistency, completeness, and testability of the product.

4.7 Bookkeeping. This paragraph lists the software parts that were changed as a result of an update to a software product. It also lists the approved changes, i.e., the change requests and incident reports, incorporated in the software product.

Section 5. Conclusions

This section presents the conclusions formulated by the auditors based upon the findings of the audit. It should be noted that the conclusions represent the judgment of the auditors and are thus primarily subjective, as contrasted to the objective findings of the audit given in Section 4.

Continued

TABLE 5.7. (Continued)

Software Audit Report Title	Date Document Number

Section 6. Recommendations
   This section provides the auditors' recommendations as a result of conducting the audit. This section also represents the judgment of the auditors and is thus primarily subjective.

Adapted from W. L. Bryan, S. G. Siegel, and G. L. Whiteleather, "Auditing Throughout the Software Life Cycle," *Computer,* vol. 15, no. 3 (March 1982), p. 64. Reprinted by permission of the publisher.

a recommended resolution available from the analysis report, the CCB proceeds to make its decision on each discrepancy in the audit report. Such decisions are recorded in the minutes of the CCB. (We discuss CCB minutes in Chapter 6.)

   Several alternatives to this method of handling audit reports might be used to record, report, and resolve the discrepancies uncovered by an audit. One such alternative was discussed in Section 4.4 and illustrated in the third scenario shown in Figure 4.23. In this scenario, the audit report is prepared as described above. When the CCB first considers the audit report, it again divides the discrepancies into those whose resolution is apparent and those whose resolution is not apparent (and therefore require some analytical work). For the former class, the CCB proceeds directly to make its decisions, which are recorded in the CCB minutes. For the latter class, an incident report (recall Figures 4.19 and 4.26) is prepared for each discrepancy in the class. These IRs are generally given to the development organization for analysis. From then on, the IRs are processed in the same manner as IRs generated in response to incidents—the developers complete the analysis portion of the IR, the CCB makes its decision, and if a change is approved, an SCN is used to promulgate the change.

   This method (selectively creating IRs) provides better visibility and traceability than the first method described (processing the audit report without creating IRs). However, there is a price to pay for this increased visibility and traceability: increased resources are required to handle and process the IRs.

   Another method that the authors have used for reporting and processing discrepancies provides even greater visibility and traceability for discrepancies. In this method, every discrepancy uncovered during an audit is reported as a separate incident report. These IRs are handled and processed just like those IRs created as a result of incidents (recall the second scenario in Figure 4.23). An audit report is still prepared in this method, but there is no need to report the discrepancies uncovered in the audit. Here, the audit report simply summarizes and categorizes the discrepancies reported as IRs. Again, for the increased visibility and traceability afforded by this method, there is an increased price to pay for handling and processing the IRs. Note that the processing of every IR requires time and money, even if the discrepancy documented by the IR has small impact and its resolution is immediately obvious.

The foregoing paragraphs have presented the following three methods for the CCB to process discrepancies uncovered in an audit report:

1. Assign entire audit report to development organization for analysis; resulting analysis report provides recommended resolution for every discrepancy.
2. Categorize discrepancies into those whose resolution is apparent and those whose resolution is not apparent; process former category immediately; create an IR for every discrepancy in the latter category; process IRs as for an incident (see Figure 4.7).
3. Create an IR for every discrepancy in audit report; process IRs as for an incident.

These three methods are listed in ascending order of visibility, traceability, cost, and time. The CCB should carefully weigh the benefits and liabilities of these three methods of recording and processing audit discrepancies when establishing its mode of operation at the beginning of a project.

To close out this section, we present a sample problem that illustrates the concepts of uncovering and reporting discrepancies. The problem is cast in the form of an audit of a system preliminary design specification to predict the point differential between the two teams involved in a football game. Even if you are not a football fan, work through this problem. No knowledge of defensive formations or blocking assignments is required to follow it. Do not bypass this problem just because it contains some mathematical formulas. The formulas are not germane to our discussion of the audit; they are used only to make the design complete and to give the problem an element of realism. Instead of presenting the entire audit report, only the findings of the audit have been included. This approach eliminates material not pertinent to our discussion (such as Sections 1, 2, and 3 shown in Table 5.7).

AUDITING A SOFTWARE PRODUCT THAT IS NOT COMPUTER CODE—A SAMPLE PROBLEM
Background and Question

Figure 5.8 shows a one-page requirements specification for a software system (called System PREDICT) that is to predict the point differential of a football game based on information pertaining to the two teams involved in this game. Assume that this specification constitutes the Requirements Baseline for this software development effort (i.e., it has been approved by a CCB in the manner shown in Figure 4.5). Figure 5.9 shows a draft of a preliminary design specification for this software system. Assume you are an auditor whose task is to audit this preliminary design specification draft against the System PREDICT Requirements Baseline shown in Figure 5.8, and that you are to submit your findings to a CCB whose function is to determine whether this draft should become the System PREDICT Preliminary Design Baseline. Assume that this baseline will be used to develop a detailed design from which computer code will be developed. Finally, assume that an auditor should

Requirements Specification for System PREDICT

PRED-S1
Version 1.1

This requirements specification delineates the capabilities for a system called PREDICT whose overall purpose is to predict the point differential of a football game based on certain information regarding the two teams involved in the game. This information shall include the following:

1. The won-lost record of each team in all regular season games played prior to the game whose outcome is to be predicted.
2. The total number of points scored and allowed by each team in all regular season games prior to the game whose outcome is to be predicted.
3. The scores of any previous regular season games involving the two teams.
4. Injuries to key players on each team.
5. The likely weather conditions at game time and the previous performance of each team under similar conditions.
6. Which team is playing at home.
7. The effect of the game on each team's post-season playoff chances.

System PREDICT shall, given the information listed above, predict the point differential between the two teams to within 25 percent of the actual point differential.

FIGURE 5.8. Requirements specification used in Section 5.2 sample problem.

Draft XXX
PRED-D1

Preliminary Design Specification for System PREDICT

This specification sets forth the preliminary design for System PREDICT, whose overall purpose is to predict the point differential of a football game based on certain information regarding the two teams playing the game. This specification thus delineates the algorithm for computing this point differential in terms of the seven factors specified in the System PREDICT Requirements Specification. Table PRED-D1-1 delineates this algorithm.

Using the values from Table PRED-D1-1, point differential, PD, is computed by subtracting the Team 2 value in the table from the corresponding Team 1 value, multiplying this difference by a weighting factor, and summing these results over all seven factors. That is, PD is computed from the following mathematical formula:

$$PD = \sum_{J=1}^{7} [(\text{FACTOR } j)_{\text{TEAM 1}} - (\text{FACTOR } j)_{\text{TEAM 2}}] W_j$$

Continued

FIGURE 5.9. Preliminary design specification used in Section 5.2 sample problem.

where

$W_j = 1$ for $j = 1, 2, 4, 5, 7$
$W_j = 2$ for $j = 3$
$W_j = 3$ for $j = 6$

If PD is greater than zero, Team 1 is predicted to beat Team 2 by PD points; otherwise, Team 2 is predicted to be the winner (unless PD = 0, in which case the game is rated a tossup).

Table PRED-D1-1			
FACTOR #	FACTOR DEFINITION	TEAM 1	TEAM 2
1.	If the team won-lost record is at least 0.500, give the team 1 point; otherwise, give the team 0.	(FACTOR 1) TEAM 1	(FACTOR 1) TEAM 2
2.	If total number of points scored by the team minus total number of points allowed by the team in all previous regular season games is greater than zero, give the team 1 point; otherwise, give the team 0.	(FACTOR 2) TEAM 1	(FACTOR 2) TEAM 2
3.	Let $\underline{X}$ be the average of the point differential in any previous regular season game involving the two teams (computed by subtracting Team 2's score from Team 1's score and dividing by the number of games played). If $\underline{X}$ is greater than zero, give Team 1, 1 point and Team 2, – 1 point; otherwise, give Team 2, 1 point and Team 1, – 1 point.	(FACTOR 3) TEAM 1	(FACTOR 3) TEAM 2
4.	If $\underline{N}$ is the number of key players on the team who will miss the game because of injury, give the team – N points.	(FACTOR 4) TEAM 1	(FACTOR 4) TEAM 2
5.	If the weather conditions at game time are $\underline{C}$ and the team has won more often than it has lost under these conditions during the regular season, give the team 1 point; otherwise, give the team – 1 point.	(FACTOR 5) TEAM 1	(FACTOR 5) TEAM 2
6.	If the team is playing at home, give the team 1 point; otherwise; give the team 0.	(FACTOR 6) TEAM 1	(FACTOR 6) TEAM 2
7.	If the team is in playoff contention, give the team 1 point; otherwise, give the team 0.	(FACTOR 7) TEAM 1	(FACTOR 7) TEAM 2

FIGURE 5.9. (*Continued*)

ideally be a neutral, objective reporter of discrepancies, that he should be as specific as possible in reporting discrepancies, and that he should offer rationale to justify why each discrepancy should be addressed. With these assumptions, and with the information contained in Figures 5.8 and 5.9, what discrepancies between the documents shown in these figures might you, as an auditor, report to the CCB?

Solution Approach

Figure 5.10 contains findings of the audit. In the following discussion, we comment on these findings to provide insight into how an audit might be conducted and into the specifics of what an audit might uncover.

A. In the auditor's finding 1 (Figure 5.10), he goes through each of the seven classes of information listed in Figure 5.8 and comments on what has been done in carrying them through to preliminary design. Here we see explicit examples of how an auditor addresses the question of whether a software product logically follows from a predecessor product and whether a software product embodies what the customer asked for. In performing these comparisons, we see how the auditor sheds light on potential ambiguities in the Requirements Baseline (e.g., finding 1c) and potential omissions in the preliminary design specification (e.g., findings 1e and 1f). While much of what the auditor has to say in finding 1 exemplifies the classical argument "Where do requirements end and where does design begin?" the auditor raises issues for the CCB that it may not have considered when it approved the Requirements Baseline and that the CCB may wish to address in the Requirements Baseline before design proceeds much further (and requirements ambiguities become more difficult to resolve). Thus the auditor provides the vital function of raising the visibility of the software development process to a level where apparently significant development issues can be dealt with at a time when their resolution may cause little or no schedule or resource impact (this example illustrates the "pay now versus pay much more later" message portrayed in Figure 1.3).

B. In the auditor's finding 2, he points out an apparent disconnect between requirements and design (i.e., something called for in the Requirements Baseline appears to have been omitted in the design). The auditor then points out that the requirement omitted from the design may need to be reconsidered because it is unclear how any design developed can be *proven* to satisfy the omitted requirement (recall the sample problem on the testability of requirements discussed in Section 5.1). To help the CCB deal with this issue, the auditor offers some suggestions as to how the requirement may be stated in terms that designers and coders can deal with. Again, it should be noted that in this finding the auditor raises the visibility of the software development process to a level where the CCB can deal with significant requirements issues long before they become deeply embedded in design (and code). In terms of the comic strip in Figure 2.8, the auditor is helping the wizard get an answer to his question (presumably before the king runs out of time, money, or both).

C. The auditor's findings are expressed in objective terms, using noninflammatory language. The findings are generally specific (in most cases supported by example) and supported by rationale. The overall result is that the auditor has probably provided the CCB with the information it will need to make intelligent, informed decisions about what should be done with draft XXX of the preliminary design specification and whether the Requirements Baseline should be updated.

FIGURE 5.10. Findings of an audit of the preliminary design specification in Figure 5.9 against the requirements specification in Figure 5.8.

Discrepancies Uncovered from an Audit of the System PREDICT Preliminary Design Specification

An audit of draft XXX of the System PREDICT Preliminary Design Specification (PDS) against the Requirements Baseline (RB) has been performed. The following discrepancies between the two items were uncovered during the audit:

1. The RB lists seven classes of information that are to be used to predict the point differential. For each of these classes, the PDS appears to make some assumptions regarding how the information in the class is to contribute to the point differential. These assumptions are listed below. Therefore, to ensure that the requirements set forth in the RB are being properly interpreted, it is suggested that these assumptions be reviewed, and if deemed appropriate, be reflected in the RB. Also listed below are some apparent discrepancies between the RB and PDS. It is suggested that these discrepancies be resolved.

   a. The PDS assumes that the intent of the RB regarding a team's won-lost record is that, if it has a non-losing record, then the team is given 1 point in computing the point differential. The RB is silent as to the quantitative relationship between a team's won-lost record and its contribution to the point differential (e.g., in contrast to the PDS, another possible interpretation of the RB requirement is that the larger the difference between a team's wins and its losses, the greater should be the contribution to the point differential [assuming the team's wins exceed its losses]).

   b. The PDS assumes that the intent of the RB regarding a team's point differential is that, if a team has scored more points than it has allowed, then the team is give 1 point in computing point differential. As was the case with the won-lost information class, the RB is silent as to the quantitative relationship between a team's point differential and its contribution to the predicted point differential of the game (e.g., in contrast to the PDS, another possible interpretation of the RB requirement is that the larger the difference between the number of points the team has scored and the number of points it has allowed, the greater should be the contribution to the predicted point differential of the game [assuming the points scored exceed the points allowed]).

Continued

c. The PDS assumes that the intent of the RB regarding the scores of any previous regular season games involving the two teams is that, if the average of the point differential of these scores is greater than zero, then Team 1 is given 1 point in computing the point differential of the game to be played and Team 2 is given -1 point. As was the case with the preceding two information classes, the RB is silent as to the quantitative relationship between the point differential in previous games played by the two teams and its contribution to the point differential of the game to be played (e.g., in contrast to the PDS, another possible interpretation of the RB requirement is that the most recent game played between the two teams should count more than previous encounters, which is not reflected in a simple average over previous scores [it should be noted that the RB is somewhat ambiguous in that it does not indicate whether previous regular season games are restricted to the current season or include previous seasons, and, if so, how many previous seasons; from the PDS, it would appear that the designer interpreted the RB to encompass games played in the current and previous seasons, because the two teams generally only meet at most twice during a regular season, so that, if the intent of the RB was to include only the current season, there would be no need to perform the average indicated in the PDS]). It should also be noted that the PDS is silent on what value is to be assigned to the predicted point differential if the average point differential in previous games is exactly zero. The PDS should cover this contingency so that programmers can specify this logical possibility in the code they will write for System PREDICT.

d. The PDS assumes that the intent of the RB regarding injuries to key players is that there is a linear relationship between the number of key players injured and the number of points to be subtracted from the point differential. The RB is silent as to this relationship, and other relationships are, of course, possible (e.g., ones that take into account who the injured player is -- for example, a quarterback may be worth twice as much to a team as a key defensive player).

e. The PDS assumes that the intent of the RB regarding (predicted) weather conditions at game time is that, if a team won more games than it lost under similar weather conditions in the past, then one point is given to that team in computing the point differential. The RB is silent as to the quantitative relationship between weather conditions and previous performance under such conditions. Many other interpretations of the RB are of course possible. Furthermore, the PDS does not appear to deal with the possibility that one or both teams may be playing under weather conditions that one or both have not played under previously (e.g., a team may be in its first season and may come from the South where snow never falls, and may be playing a team in blizzard-like conditions).

f. The PDS assumes that playing at home is worth 1 point in the predicted point differential. The RB is silent as to how much playing at home should be worth. Furthermore, the RB, and thus the PDS, do not address the possibility that some games may be played at a neutral location (i.e., where no team would be considered "home" in terms of fan support). For completeness, this possibility should be addressed in the RB and PDS.

g. The PDS assumes that if a team is in playoff contention, then it is given 1 point in computing the point differential. The RB is silent as to how much being in

Continued

FIGURE 5.10.   (*Continued*)

playoff contention is worth in terms of computing predicted point differential. Of course, many other quantitative relationships are possible (such as one that takes into account whether the game being played will determine if one or both teams will be eliminated from post-season play).

h. The PDS assumes that, to compute the predicted point differential, the results obtained from each of the seven information classes are to be summed and weighted with the weighting factors specified in the PDS. The RB offers no guidance as to how the information classes are to be weighted with respect to one another. For completeness, such guidance should probably be included in the RB.

2. The RB stipulates the following performance requirement for System PREDICT:

"System PREDICT shall . . . predict the point differential between the two teams to within 25 percent of the actual point differential."

This performance requirement does not appear to be addressed in the PDS. That is, the PDS is silent as to the estimated error associated with the mathematical formula given in the PDS for computing predicted point differential. More fundamentally, it is not clear how the performance requirement can be proven a priori to be satisfied (e.g., it is not clear how it can be proven that any mathematical relationship relating, say, injuries to key players and the effect of these injuries on the score of a game is accurate to within so many percentage points). It is therefore suggested that the RB performance requirement cited above be reviewed to determine if it can be verified with respect to any formula that may be proposed in the PDS. Is it the intent of the user to "verify" the formula by applying it to historical data (for example, the scores involving all teams in the league for the past ten years) and adjusting the formula parameters until agreement with these historical data is obtained with the desired degree of accuracy? If so, then perhaps the RB should be modified to reflect this intent to provide a more specific basis for design work.

FIGURE 5.10. (*Continued*)

This sample problem illustrates typical discrepancies uncovered during an audit and how to report them. The audit report makes explicit the assumptions used by the software developers in creating a design, so that the CCB can confirm whether the assumptions are valid. (See Exercise 5.2 for further exploration of the assumptions in the System PREDICT specifications. See also Exercises 5.21 and 5.25 for additional aspects regarding audits of the System PREDICT Preliminary Design Specification.)

5.3 The Auditing Process for Computer Code

In the preceding section, we described the auditing process for software in the form of documentation. We now turn to the complementary auditing process for software in its other form—when the software is computer code. The generic model of the auditing process that we showed in Figure 5.1 still applies when computer code is being audited—a life cycle product (i.e., code) is compared to its ground truth (recall from the third row of Figure 5.2 that the ground truth in this case is the design and requirements specifications), and discrepancies observed during the comparison are reported to the CCB. But the details of the process are substantially different from those of the process for auditing software documentation described in the preceding section.

We begin by looking at the preparations made prior to conduct of the audit. This is followed by a sample problem that illustrates how to construct a test procedure. We next look at the auditing process in detail and observe how the auditing (testing) cycle causes software code to converge to a product with no or few discrepancies. This product then can be delivered to the user.[8]

We indicated in Section 5.1 that when the life cycle software product to be audited is code we term the process test and evaluation (T&E), a process that was first formally introduced in Section 3.1 (recall Figure 3.2). T&E is an assessment of whether software code is congruent with requirements and design specifications. But in T&E we do not generally determine this congruency by comparing source code listings (a document form of code) directly with the requirements and design specifications. Rather, computer code is put in its executable form and, through execution in a live or nearly live environment, is indirectly compared with the two specifications through use of test plans and procedures (see Figure 5.11). These test plans and procedures[9] are derived from the requirements and design specifications (we discuss this later in this section). Each test procedure specifies the results expected from performing specific operations on computer code. When the specific operations are executed on code, the actual results observed are recorded and compared with the expected results contained in the test procedures. Any differences between the expected and observed results are reported as discrepancies. Thus, the requirements and design specifications are the ground truth for this audit, but are involved in the audit comparison only indirectly (i.e., through the test plans and procedures).

We stated above that T&E was conducted in a live or nearly live environment. By this we mean an environment that is identical to or closely approximates the environment in which the user operates. In the life cycle shown in Figure 2.7, the actual testing occurs just before the software system is delivered to the customer. This testing is referred to in the literature by several names; we arbitrarily refer to it as acceptance testing, because it usually occurs just before the customer accepts the system for operational use. The purpose of acceptance testing is to demonstrate that operating computer code satisfies the user's needs. Since the user's needs include op-

---

[8] We are using "converge" here in the mathematical sense of "approaching a limit," the limit in this case being code with no discrepancies. Because such discrepancy-free code is rarely realized in practice, we believe that "converge" is an appropriate way to characterize the objective of the testing cycle. See Exercise 5.6.

[9] Recall from our discussion in Section 3.1 that *test plans* specify a set of tests whose execution demonstrates that the final software product satisfies the requirements specification. A *test procedure* is a sequence of steps defining how to perform one of the tests specified in a test plan.

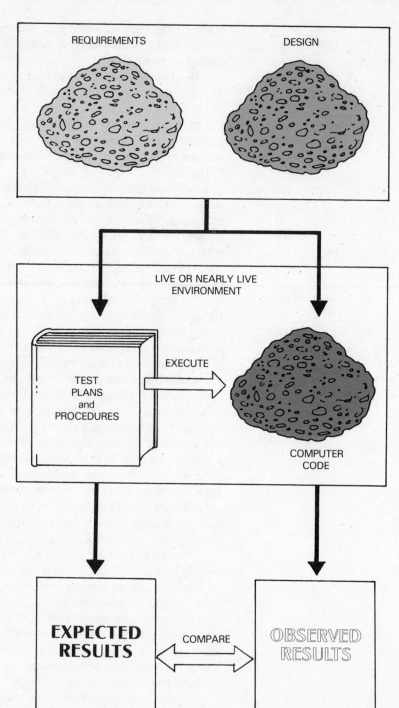

FIGURE 5.11. T&E assesses the extent to which computer code embodies the design and requirements. In T&E, the code is executed in a live or nearly live environment (i.e., in an environment that is identical to or approximates the user's environment) using written test plans and procedures derived from the design and requirements. The expected results specified in this test documentation are compared to observed results obtained from computer code execution. This comparison reveals the extent to which the code embodies the design and requirements.

erating the system in his own environment, we must conduct the acceptance tests in a live or nearly live environment. Performing the tests in some other environment (e.g., the development environment) would not demonstrate that the computer code satisfies the user's needs.

T&E activity is not confined to the Coding and subsequent

stages of the life cycle. In fact, T&E activity extends throughout the life cycle. It generally begins right after the requirements specification is baselined, with the initiation of efforts to develop a test plan. A test plan is concerned with such items as test organizations, test schedules, test resources, test personnel and their responsibilities, the approach to be used to test the system, and, most important for our current consideration, a list of tests to be executed during acceptance testing. This list is derived from the requirements, with one or more tests planned to be conducted to demonstrate the satisfaction of each requirement. (A single test could be used to demonstrate the satisfaction of more than one requirement.) Thus, the test plan links tests to specific requirements. As an aid to the reader, we provide in Table 5.8 a suggested format for a software test plan. Note especially the contents of that table's section 3.0, on testing approach. This section of our book discusses methods and procedures for developing the testing approach for a test plan.

TABLE 5.8. SUGGESTED FORMAT FOR A SOFTWARE TEST PLAN

	Date
Test Plan Title	Document Number

1.0 *INTRODUCTION*
This section gives introductory information regarding the project, the system to be tested, and the testing approach as indicated in the subsections below.

1.1 *Purpose.* This subsection identifies the project and stipulates the purpose of the test plan by indicating what the document contains (e.g., organizational responsibilities, test approach, test schedule). It is a "tell-them-what-you-are-going-to-tell-them" subsection.

1.2 *Scope.* This subsection specifies the project software releases encompassed by the plan. For example, a project may extend over several years with one or more software releases scheduled per year. In this case, Subsection 1.2 specifies which of these releases the plan addresses.

1.3 *System Overview.* This subsection describes the system that is to be exercised by the testing approach specified in the plan. This overview serves to identify aspects of the system operation that will be the focus of the plan's testing approach.

1.4 *Testing Approach Overview.* This subsection gives an overview of the approach specified in Section 3.0. This overview is often of particular interest to management, especially senior management, who may have neither the time nor the inclination to read Section 3.0. For example, if Section 3.0 spells out a multi-level approach to testing, Subsection 1.4 should briefly indicate the objective and scope of each of the test levels.

2.0 *APPLICABLE REFERENCES*
This section lists the references applicable to the test plan. In general, these references include project standards, a product assurance plan that establishes the context for project testing, and software specifi-

Continued

TABLE 5.8.   SUGGESTED FORMAT FOR A SOFTWARE
TEST PLAN (*Continued*)

	Date
Test Plan Title	Document Number

cation documents (such as requirements and design specifications) from which the code to be tested is developed.

3.0 *TESTING APPROACH*

This section describes the approach (but not the detailed test steps) to be used to test the system described in Subsection 1.3. This description includes specifying the types of tests to be performed (such as tests designed to exercise the system functions one by one without regard to how these functions may be used operationally, tests designed to exercise sequences of functions that approximate operational use of the system, tests designed to stress the system to its design limits and possibly beyond these limits), and a list of tests to be executed during acceptance testing. This section also describes how test procedures are to be specified. In addition, it describes how test incidents are to be reported and CCB activity in connection with test incidents.

4.0 *TEST MANAGEMENT REQUIREMENTS*

This section indicates how the testing described in Section 3.0 is to be managed including a delineation of the responsibilities of each project organization involved with testing.

5.0 *PERSONNEL REQUIREMENTS*

This section delineates the responsibilities of those individuals who are to perform the testing (such as the test director, test witnesses, and test operators).

6.0 *HARDWARE REQUIREMENTS*

This section describes the hardware needed to support testing. This description includes the configuration of hardware components on which the software to be tested is to operate. It also includes any hardware needed to support test procedure development and other hardware tools (such as simulators that model the operation of external systems interfacing with the system being tested).

7.0 *SOFTWARE REQUIREMENTS*

This section describes the software needed to support testing. This description includes the software code that is the object of the testing. It also includes software tools such as compilers and simulators that may be used to model the user's operational environment if the testing is not to be performed in the user's operational environment.

8.0 *SCHEDULE*

This section specifies the schedule for testing activities, generally spanning the period between test plan publication and the publication of a test report that gives the results of test procedure execution.

Subsequent to the baselining of the detailed design specification, each test listed in the test plan is developed into a step-by-step test procedure that demonstrates satisfaction of the requirements specified for the test in the test plan. The steps in the procedures are designed to assess whether the requirement(s) to be demonstrated by the procedures have been satisfied by computer code. Information on actions to be taken or commands to be used within a test step, and on the results to be expected from those actions or commands, is obtained from the design specification. We thus can see that the set of

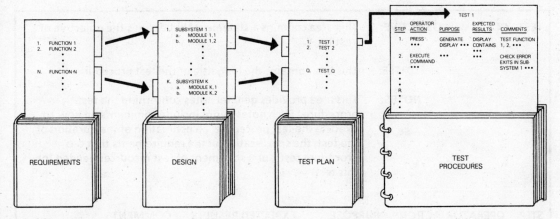

STEP	OPERATOR ACTION	PURPOSE	EXPECTED RESULTS	COMMENTS
1.	PRESS •••	GENERATE DISPLAY •••	DISPLAY CONTAINS •••	TEST FUNCTION 1, 2, •••
2.	EXECUTE COMMAND •••	•••	•••	CHECK ERROR EXITS IN SUB-SYSTEM 1 •••

TEST 1

REQUIREMENTS

1. FUNCTION 1
2. FUNCTION 2
 •
 •
N. FUNCTION N
 •
 •

DESIGN

1. SUBSYSTEM 1
    a. MODULE 1,1
    b. MODULE 1,2
 •
 •
K. SUBSYSTEM K
    a. MODULE K,1
    b. MODULE K,2
 •

TEST PLAN

1. TEST 1
2. TEST 2
 •
 •
Q. TEST Q
 •

TEST PROCEDURES

FIGURE 5.12. Acceptance testing documentation thread—From requirements to test procedures.

test procedures reflects both the requirements and the design of the software system. Each test procedure should contain within it a pointer to the requirement(s) that the procedure tests. We thus have traceability (see Figure 5.12) among the four documents concerned with T&E—the requirements and design specifications, which are the ground truth for the audit, and the test plan and procedures, which are the surrogates of the two specifications for the conduct of the acceptance tests. Observe in Figure 5.12 how this traceability is achieved. The requirements specification establishes a list of functions that the software is to perform. Software designers translate these requirements into a design specification that designates subsystems and modules needed to satisfy the requirements. The requirements specification and design specification are often traced to each other through use of a traceability matrix, as we noted in Section 5.2. The test plan, as described above, lists the tests to be performed during T&E and links each test to one or more requirements. This linkage is usually added to the traceability matrix, so that there is traceability from the requirements through the specification documentation to the tests that demonstrate that computer code satisfies the requirements. Finally, in Figure 5.12, each test procedure should contain pointers to the requirement(s) that the procedure tests and to the portions of the detailed design that were used in the creation of the test procedures. This traceability is important in determining that all requirements have been accounted for in the test procedures, and, when differences are observed between the expected and actual results, in determining which requirements are unsatisfied.

We recommend that the test procedures be written in the five-column format shown in Figure 5.13, which we have successfully used on a number of projects. The elements of the format are as follows:

Header. This section of the test procedure provides identification of the test, states the objective of the test, gives the long title of the test, and provides notes on how to

TEST XX.Y	OBJECTIVE:	This area contains a statement that defines the objective of Test XX.Y.
	TITLE:	This line contains the long title of the test procedure.
	NOTES:	This area provides general notes concerning the test procedure. Such notes might include comments on how to execute the test procedure, an estimation of the duration of the test, the specification of the requirements that the procedure tests, or a statement of test resources needed for this test.

STEP	OPERATOR ACTION	PURPOSE	EXPECTED RESULTS	COMMENTS
N	Describes the actions taken by the person who is executing the test procedures.	Describes the reason for the step.	Describes the expected response of the system to the action specified in the Operator Action column.	Contains additional information such as boundary data, dependencies among test steps, an estimate of elapsed time associated with executing the step, suggested excursions from the test step, a discussion of the rationale for the step or operator action, or the test underlying the step, and the overall objective of a set of test steps. May also contain pointers to requirements documentation and/or design documentation.

[Document No.]
[Release No.]   [Page No.]

FIGURE 5.13. Five-column test procedure format. Adapted from W. Bryan and S. Siegel, "Making Software Visible, Operational, and Maintainable in a Small Project Environment," *IEEE Transactions on Software Engineering*, vol. SE-10, no. 1 (January 1984), p. 65. Reprinted by permission of the publisher.

conduct the test, on the estimated duration of the test, on requirements tested, and on test resources (e.g., test data) needed for the test.

Column 1: *Step.* This column provides a (usually sequential) identifying number for each step.

Column 2: *Operator Action.* This column specifies the precise action taken by the tester (e.g., entry of a keyboard command or pressing a function key) in executing a particular step. The information in this column comes from the detailed design specification.

Column 3: *Purpose*. This column explains why the tester took the action specified in column 2—that is, what the tester expects to accomplish by his actions.

Column 4: *Expected Results*. This column describes the response of the system to the action taken by the tester in column 2. The information in this column comes from the requirements and the detailed design specifications. When the test is performed, the information in this column is compared to observed results as each test step is executed in order to uncover any discrepancies.

Column 5: *Comments*. This column contains a variety of information that may be useful to the tester. Figure 5.13 provides a number of suggestions for information to put in this column.

Note particularly the linkages of the test procedure to the requirements specification and the detailed design specification in the header (under Notes) and in the Comments column of Figure 5.13. These linkages provide the traceability shown in Figure 5.12.

Having introduced a test procedure format, we now illustrate in the following sample problem how to construct a test procedure using that format. Test procedures are a key element in performing T&E. If a test procedure is not properly constructed, the test procedure may not achieve its purpose of demonstrating that operational computer code satisfies some specified requirement(s). (*Note:* This sample problem, like the one presented at the end of the preceding section, contains some mathematics, in particular some elementary analytic geometry. As in that preceding problem, it is not necessary to understand the mathematics in the following sample problem to understand the T&E issues dealt with. The mathematics has been included to give the problem an element of realism.)

PREPARING TO AUDIT A SOFTWARE PRODUCT THAT IS COMPUTER CODE—A SAMPLE PROBLEM ON TEST PROCEDURE CONSTRUCTION
Background and Question

Figure 5.14 shows a one-page extract from a requirements specification for a software system called SHAPES. This system is to permit a user sitting at a computer terminal with a display device to construct various geometric shapes. Figure 5.15 shows a portion of the System SHAPES Design Specification that defines the design of the circle-drawing capability called for in the System SHAPES Requirements Specification shown in Figure 5.14. Assume that these two specifications constitute respectively the Requirements Baseline and the Detailed Design Baseline for System SHAPES (i.e., they have been approved by a CCB in the manner described in Section 4.2). Also assume that you are a tester whose task is to perform acceptance testing on System SHAPES. Assume further that you have already prepared a test plan for this purpose and that Figure 5.16 shows an extract from this test plan that defines tests for exercising the SHAPES circle-drawing capability whose design is specified in Figure 5.15. Using the five-column format shown in Figure 5.13, how would you construct a test

REQUIREMENTS SPECIFICATION
FOR SYSTEM SHAPES

The purpose of System SHAPES is to permit a user sitting at a computer terminal with a display device to construct various geometric shapes. To achieve this purpose, the system shall perform the following functions:

1. Draw complete geometric shapes on a display in response to user-supplied inputs. The shapes that shall be accommodated are those listed in table 1 below, which also shows the corresponding user-supplied input.

Table 1. Geometric Shapes to Be Constructed from User-Supplied Input

SHAPE	INPUT
1. Circle	Radius, center of circle
2. Square	Length of side, center of square
3. Equilateral triangle	Length of side, center of triangle
4. Circular arc	Radius, angular width of arc, center of arc
5. Ellipse	Semi-major axis, semi-minor axis, center of ellipse

2. The border of geometric shapes generated shall be one of the following as selected by the user:

   a. Solid line
   b. Dashed line
   c. Dotted line

FIGURE 5.14. Portion of requirements specification used in sample problem on test procedure construction.

DESIGN SPECIFICATION FOR SYSTEM SHAPES

2.2 Circle-Drawing Subsystem

2.2.1 Computational Procedure

This subsection describes the design of the Circle-Drawing Subsystem of System SHAPES. The purpose of this subsystem is to draw circles on a display device based on a user-supplied radius, a user-supplied circle center, and a user-supplied code specifying the type of border

Continued

FIGURE 5.15. Circle-drawing portion of design specification for System SHAPES used in sample problem on test procedure construction.

(solid line, dashed line, or dotted line). The following processing steps specify the operation of this subsystem:

1. Let the user-supplied border codes be defined as follows:

    A = solid line
    B = dashed line
    C = dotted line

2. If (x_o, y_o) are the coordinates of the circle center and R is the circle radius, then a point (x,y) on the circle is given by the following formula:

    $$(x - x_o)^2 + (y - y_o)^2 = R^2$$

3. The above formula shall be used to compute the coordinates of a point on the circle. There are three cases to consider -- one for each border desired. The processing steps for each case are specified below.

    Case 1: Solid Line (Border Code = A)

    a. For each value of y, compute a corresponding value of x using the above formula rewritten to cover the four quadrants of the circle as follows:

        $x = x_o \pm [R^2 - (y - y_o)^2]^{1/2}$ for y between y_o and $y_o + R$

        (" + " is for the first quadrant and " − " is for the second quadrant);

        x = same formula as above for y between y_o and $y_o - R$

        (" − " is for the third quadrant and " + " is for the fourth quadrant).

    b. For the first and second quadrants, start with y = y_o and then obtain new values of y by incrementing by 0.001 until y = $y_o + R$ is reached.

    c. For the third and fourth quadrants, start with y = y_o and then obtain new values of y by decrementing y_o by 0.001 until y = y_o - R is reached.

    d. Connect two successive points (x_n, y_n) and (x_{n+1}, y_{n+1}) by a solid line by invoking the line-drawing algorithm specified in appendix A and display the result using the display algorithm specified in appendix B.

    Case 2: Dashed Line (Border Code = B)

    a. Follow steps a, b, and c in case 1 except that y is to be incremented or decremented by 0.003 instead of 0.001.

    b. Connect every other pair of successive points (x_n, y_n) and (x_{n+1}, y_{n+1}) by a solid line by invoking the line-drawing algorithm specified in appendix A and display the result using the display algorithm specified in appendix B.

    Case 3: Dotted Line (Border Code = C)

    a. Follow steps a, b, and c in case 1 except that y is to be incremented or decremented by 0.002 instead of 0.001.

Continued

FIGURE 5.15. *(Continued)*

b. Display the points calculated in <u>a</u> above using the display algorithm specified in appendix B.

2.2.2 <u>User Interface</u>

To access the Circle-Drawing Subsystem of SHAPES, the user shall utilize the following command:

CIRCLE (RADIUS, X, Y), CODE

where

RADIUS = user-supplied radius in the format **NN.NN**, where **NN.NN** must lie in the range 0.50 to 10.00 inclusive. The first **N** is optional.

X = user-supplied abscissa of the circle center in the format ± **N.NN**, where **N.NN** must lie in the range of 0.00 to 5.00 inclusive.

Y = user-supplied ordinate of the circle center in the same format and having the same range as **X**.

[Note: The center of the display device is assumed to lie at (X,Y) = (0.00,0.00); the width of this device is assumed to be 25.00 units and its height is assumed to be 22.00 units.]

CODE = user-supplied border code whose allowable values are A, B, or C as defined in 2.2.1 above.

2.2.3 <u>Error Conditions</u>

Table 2.2-1 below defines the error diagnostics that shall be generated using the algorithms specified in appendix C whenever the command specified in 2.2.2 above is not used as indicated there.

Table 2.2-1. Circle-Drawing Subsystem Error Diagnostics and Their Causes		
<u>DIAGNOSTIC CODE</u>	<u>DIAGNOSTIC</u>	<u>CAUSE(S)</u>
CE1	COMMAND SYNTAX ERROR	Command name misspelled (e.g., CIRCEL) Command string parameter mistake or punctuation error [e.g., CIRCLE(3.50,0.50,),A]
CE2	RADIUS OUT OF RANGE	Value of parameters out of range [e.g., CIRCLE(11.09,0.50,0.00),B]
CE3	CENTER ORDINATE AND/ OR ABSCISSA OUT OF RANGE	Value of parameter X and/or parameter Y out of range [e.g., CIRCLE(5.67,0.50,7.05),C]
CE4	BORDER CODE NOT A, B or C	Value of parameter code out of range [e.g., CIRCLE(3.00,0.50,0.50),D]

FIGURE 5.15. (*Continued*)

TEST PLAN FOR SYSTEM SHAPES

3.3 Circle-Drawing Tests

This subsection defines the tests for exercising the circle-drawing capabilities of System SHAPES. All tests are intended to be performed at a computer terminal with a display device. The computer terminal will accept tester-supplied inputs, and the display device will show the SHAPES response to these inputs. Two tests are defined -- test 1, which exercises the command CIRCLE with in-range values as defined in subsection 2.2.2 of the design specification; and test 2, which exercises the error diagnostics defined in subsection 2.2.3 of the design specification.

3.3.1 Test CD.1

The objective of this test is to verify that command CIRCLE draws circles when proper command parameter values are input. Selected in-range values of the command parameters will be input, and the displayed circles will be viewed to determine whether they are constructed according to subsection 2.2.2 of the design specification.

3.3.2 Test CD.2

The objective of this test is to verify that the error diagnostics appearing in table 2.2-1 of subsection 2.2.3 of the design specification are produced when command CIRCLE is improperly used. Selected out-of-range values of the command parameters will be input, and the display will be viewed to determine whether the diagnostics specified in table 2.2-1 appear.

FIGURE 5.16. Portion of test plan for System SHAPES used in sample problem on test procedure construction showing circle-drawing tests based on the design specification in Figure 5.15.

procedure for Test CD.1, defined in Figure 5.16? In constructing this test procedure, keep in mind that it is to be part of a test procedures document such as the one shown in Figure 5.12 and that the execution of these test procedures will be used to test and retest the SHAPES software code until the CCB decides that this code is ready for operational use.

Solution Approach

Figure 5.17 shows the first three steps of a test procedure designed to implement Test CD.1 as defined in the SHAPES Test Plan extract given in Figure 5.16. In the following discussion, we comment on Figure 5.17 to provide insight into the specifics of how a test procedure is constructed from a test plan and from design and requirements specifications.

A. At the top of the procedure in Figure 5.17, the overall objective of the test is stated. This statement is essentially the same statement that appears in subsection 3.3.1 of the test plan shown in Figure 5.16. Thus, this statement provides explicit traceability between the test procedure and the test plan. It also provides quick insight into the intent of the test. This quick insight is particularly helpful when a test consists of hundreds of individual steps. Under such circumstances, it is

TEST CD.1	OBJECTIVE:	The objective of this test is to verify that command CIRCLE draws circles when proper command parameter values are input.		
	TITLE:	Command CIRCLE Parameter Check.		
	NOTES:	1. No improper parameter values are to be input (see test CD.2).		
		2. In addition to the parameter values used in the test steps below, other (proper) values should also be input to extend the breadth and depth of the test.		

STEP	OPERATOR ACTION	PURPOSE	EXPECTED RESULTS	COMMENTS
1.	Enter CIRCLE(1.00,0.00,0.00),A	To draw a circle of radius 1.00 centered at (0.00,0.00) with a solid-line border.	A circle of radius 1.00 appears in the center of the display with a solid-line border.	Steps 1 - 10 explicitly exercise subsection 2.2.2 of the SHAPES Design Specification, which implements the capabilities
2.	Enter CIRCLE(5.00,0.00,0.00),B	To draw a circle of radius 5.00 centered at (0.00,0.00) with a dashed-line border.	A circle of radius 5.00 appears in the center of the display with a dashed-line border.	specified in the first line of table 1 in the SHAPES Requirements Specification and in paragraph 2 of that specification.
3.	Enter CIRCLE(10.00,-0.50,-0.50),C	To draw a circle of radius 10.00 centered at (-0.50,-0.50) with a dotted-line border.	A circle of radius 10.00 centered at (-0.50,-0.50) (i.e., slightly below and to the left of the center of the display) appears on the display with a dotted-line border.	
4.	•••	•••	•••	

FIGURE 5.17. Portion of System SHAPES Test Procedures derived from the System SHAPES Test Plan extract shown in Figure 5.16.

difficult to perceive by looking at such a long list of steps what system design aspects or requirements the procedure is trying to test. The statement of test objective appearing at the top of the procedure helps alleviate this difficulty. In a test procedure document consisting of hundreds or thousands of tests (not uncommon for systems of even moderate complexity), the absence of an objective for each test can make the comprehension of the set of test procedures impossible. Particularly in these circumstances, a statement of the overall objective of each test is essential for proper interpretation and use of the document.

B. Below the statement of objective in the test procedure, the title of the test appears. This title is generally a mnemonic aid that augments the test identifier shown to the left of the statement of objective (i.e., Test CD.1 in Figure 5.17). It provides insight into the nature of the test (which in this case is a check of the parameters appearing in a user command). As such, the test title complements the statement of objective appearing above it.

C. Below the test title are two notes that provide amplifying comments on the test as a whole. Specifically, the notes in Figure 5.17 address the following points:

1. The first note essentially defines the scope of the test (namely, that only proper parameter values are to be input). This note also points to another test (using the test identifier CD.2) which will deal with improper (i.e., out-

of-range) parameter values. The former type of test is often termed *positive testing,* while the latter type of test is often termed *negative testing.*

2. The second note suggests some excursions from the written procedures that should be performed. The excursions are for the purpose of extending the breadth and depth of the test. The development of written test procedures is generally an extremely labor-intensive activity. Consequently, it is often simply not possible to write down all the test steps needed to exercise comprehensively all or even most aspects of a requirement or a design that is the object of a particular test. To strike some sort of compromise between this real-world constraint stemming from limited resources and the need to perform thorough testing, a test procedure write-up often includes suggestions (such as the one in the second note) for performing test steps that are not explicitly shown in the write-up but that are straightforward variations or extensions of test steps shown. In the context of the test procedure depicted in Figure 5.17, an example of such variations might be the following:

The purpose of the first test step shown in the figure is to draw a circle of radius 1.00 in the center of the display with a solid border. The purpose of the second step is to draw another circle with a different radius also in the center of the display but with a dashed-line border. The purpose of the third step is to draw another circle with a radius that differs from the radii used in steps 1 and 2. Also, this third circle is to be centered somewhere other than in the center of the display and, in contrast to the first two circles, it is to have a dotted-line border. It is thus clear from these steps that the strategy of test CD.1 is exactly that prescribed in subsection 3.3.1 in the test plan shown in Figure 5.16—namely, the use of *selected* in-range values of CIRCLE parameters to construct different circles. From the comments appearing in the Comments column in Figure 5.17, it appears that this strategy is also followed in steps 4 through 10 (which are not shown in the figure). Now, from subsection 2.2.2 of the SHAPES Design Specification, it is evident that there are many more in-range combinations of parameter values for the CIRCLE command than can be incorporated into ten steps in the manner indicated in Figure 5.17. On the other hand, these combinations are clearly variations of the steps shown. Thus, for example, one set of such variations of step 1 might be the following:

CIRCLE(R,0.00,0.00), A

where R is allowed to vary from 0.50 to 10.00—the minimum and maximum values respectively for this parameter (as indicated in the design specification)—in increments of, say, 0.1. Such an excursion from step 1 in the written procedure would represent a fairly thorough testing of the capability to draw solid-line circles centered at the center of the display whose radii completely cover the allowable range for this parameter. □

D. The information in each of the three test steps shown is based primarily on subsection 2.2.2 of the design specification (as noted in the Comments column in Figure 5.17). For example, the information in the Operator Action column (i.e., what the tester has to input to elicit a response from the code being tested) is a particular realization of the command format specified in that subsection; also, the information in the Expected Results column is derived directly from the design specified in that subsection. This heavy reliance on design documentation occurs frequently in test procedure development work. The primary reason is that test procedures are generally written at the "button-pushing" level of detail and such detail is often not found until the Detailed Design Stage of the life cycle.[10] The Comments column in Figure 5.17, in addition to linking test steps back to the design specification, also links the steps back to the requirements specification. Thus, through this linkage, it is possible after test step execution to determine in specific terms the extent to which customer requirements (in this case, the capability to draw circles on a display) are embodied in the computer code. This information is precisely what a CCB needs to determine whether computer code needs to be modified before it is delivered to the customer for operational use.

E. Regarding the information in the Expected Results column, note that this information needs to be expressed in terms that permit a tester to observe the response of the system so he can effect a meaningful comparison between this information and the actual system response. This comparison is the heart of the test execution activity, because from this comparison come discrepancies that the CCB uses to make its decision regarding release for operational use of the code being tested. (A question that should be considered here is whether the information in the Expected Results column in Figure 5.17 is sufficiently specific to permit this comparison; see Exercise 5.11 at the end of this chapter. Recall also the sample problem on requirements testability discussed in Section 5.1.)

The preceding discussion gives some idea how a test procedure can be constructed from a test plan and specification documentation. From this discussion, you should now be able to construct a test procedure for Test CD.2 defined in subsection

---

[10] User interface information such as that shown in Figure 5.15 is sometimes not included in design documentation but is instead incorporated into a user's manual (i.e., a document specifying how a user is to use a system). Under such circumstances, it is necessary to cite the user's manual as a reference in the test procedures. In addition, to establish traceability with design (and requirements), it is a good idea to link this user's manual reference to the portion of the design documentation from which the information in the user's manual is presumably derived.

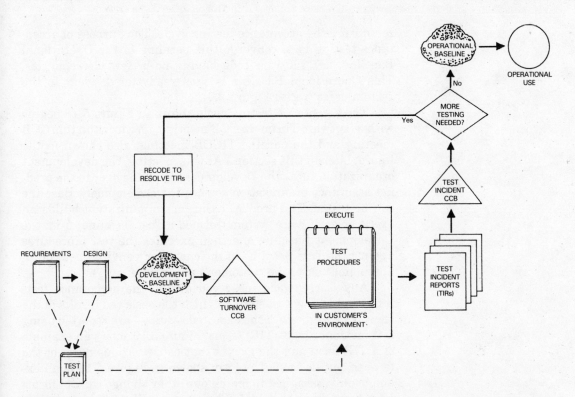

FIGURE 5.18. Acceptance testing cycle.

3.3.2 of the test plan shown in Figure 5.16. Construction of this test procedure is the subject of Exercise 5.23 at the end of this chapter.

The set of test documentation discussed—test plan and test procedures—is not the only set possible. For example, the federal government often adds an intermediate document. This document, the test specification, outlines each test procedure prior to formulation of the procedure steps. Other variations of test documentation include the use of different names for test entities (e.g., a test procedure may be known as a test case) or the use of a hierarchy of tests (e.g., test groups/test procedures/test cases). None of these variations modifies the primary concept we are discussing—specific written test documentation derived from appropriate sections of the requirements and design specifications must be developed prior to the beginning of acceptance tests.

Now that we have looked at the preparation of the test plan and test procedures—activities that must precede the actual audit of the code—we are in a position to discuss the auditing process itself. This process, which we term the *acceptance testing cycle* in the case of auditing computer code, is shown in Figure 5.18. We show the requirements specification and the design specification in the figure to reflect that not only is computer code derived from them, but so too are the test plan and test procedures. Code to be acceptance tested is placed in a Development Baseline upon the completion of coding and unit and integration testing (see footnote 4 in Chapter 3) and at the beginning of the acceptance testing cycle. This baseline is frozen during the acceptance testing cycle. The purpose of acceptance testing is to converge this baseline to the Operational Baseline, i.e., software code having no or few discrepancies. This Operational Baseline is then ready for delivery to the system users (recall Figure 2.7).

The acceptance testing cycle shown in Figure 5.18 begins with a Software Turnover CCB meeting. (We focus on this CCB meeting and the parallel TICCB meeting, also shown in the figure, later in this section.) At this meeting, the development organization turns the Development Baseline over to the product assurance organization so that the Development Baseline can be tested. The product assurance organization builds an executable software system (termed a Test Baseline) from the Development Baseline and then executes the test procedures against the Test Baseline in the customer's environment or an approximation to the customer's environment.

Any discrepancies observed during the acceptance testing—that is, any test step for which the observed results of the step do not agree with the expected results—are reported using test incident report (TIR) forms. Figure 5.19 shows an example of a TIR form and the events that cause various parts of the form to be filled out. The form shown in Figure 5.19 is an example only, designed to match our other change control forms introduced in Section 4.4. The reader will probably want to create his own form, using the form design principles discussed in Section 4.4. Our TIR form is a simplification and amalgamation of the IR and SCN forms introduced in Section 4.4 in Figures 4.19 and 4.20, respectively. (We chose this design for this form because the test incident report process is basically a simplified version of answering the question "Is something wrong?")

Upon completion of a period of testing, the TIRs are presented to the Test Incident CCB as shown in Figure 5.18. After reviewing the TIRs, the CCB makes a decision on whether to continue the acceptance testing cycle. If the CCB believes, from the number and type of TIRs presented to it, that the software is ready for operational use, it establishes the Development Baseline as the Operational Baseline. If the CCB decides that the software is not yet ready for operational use, it gives the TIRs to the developers, who attempt to resolve them. The developers update the Development Baseline with resolutions to the TIRs. Thus begins another acceptance testing cycle. These cycles continue until the CCB determines that the software code is ready for operational use. With each pass through the cycle, the number of discrepancies observed from execution of the test procedures should be reduced, until no or few TIRs are outstanding. If the CCB believes that the outstanding TIRs are noncritical in nature, the CCB establishes the Operational Baseline. (Remember that the test procedures embody the requirements and design specifications, the ground truth for computer code.)

Let us now take a closer look at how the TIR form in Figure

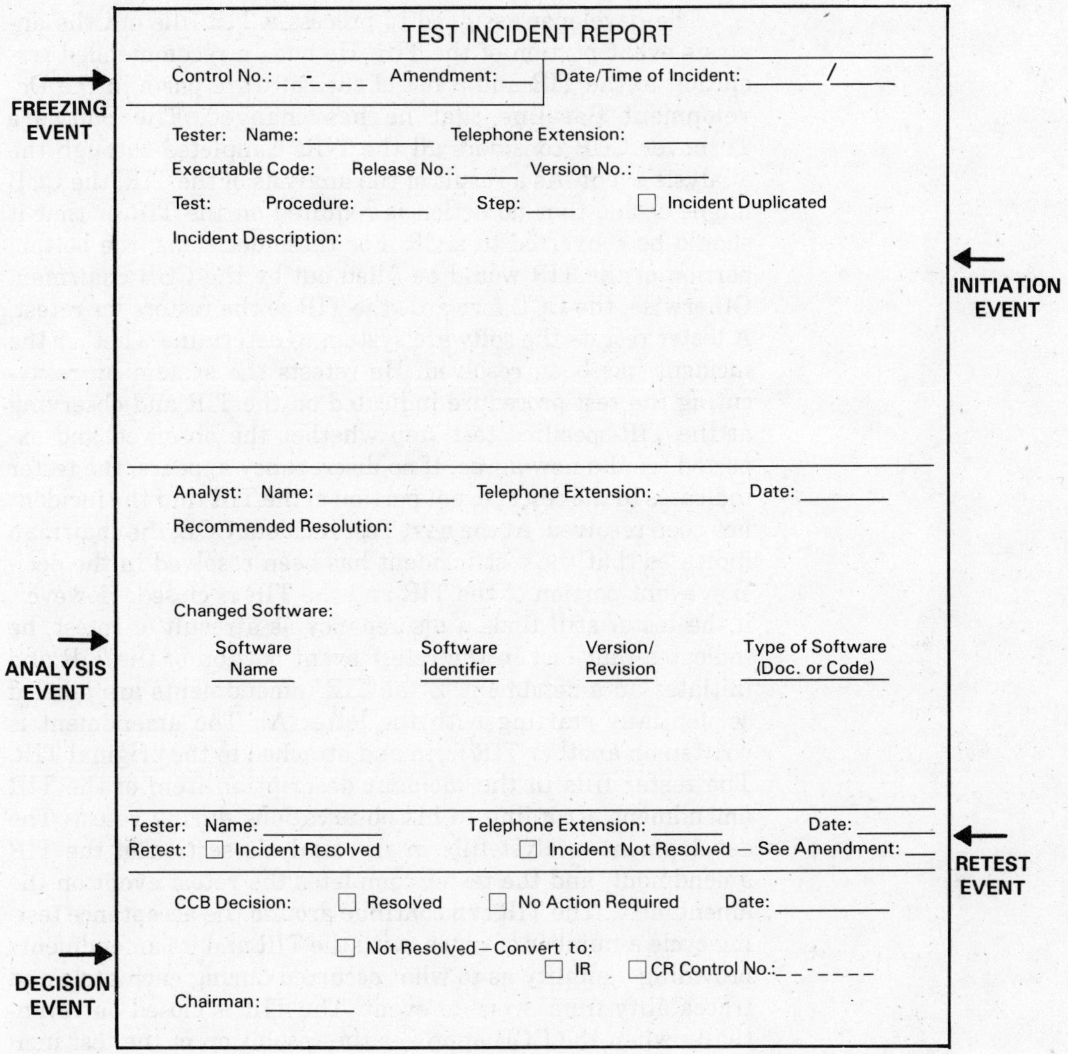

TEST INCIDENT REPORT

FREEZING EVENT → Control No.: __-_____ Amendment: ___ Date/Time of Incident: ______/_____

Tester: Name: Telephone Extension: ____

Executable Code: Release No.: _____ Version No.: _____

Test: Procedure: _____ Step: _____ ☐ Incident Duplicated

Incident Description:

← INITIATION EVENT

Analyst: Name: ______ Telephone Extension: _____ Date: ______

Recommended Resolution:

Changed Software:

ANALYSIS EVENT →

Software Name	Software Identifier	Version/ Revision	Type of Software (Doc. or Code)

Tester: Name: ______ Telephone Extension: _____ Date: _____

Retest: ☐ Incident Resolved ☐ Incident Not Resolved — See Amendment: ___

← RETEST EVENT

CCB Decision: ☐ Resolved ☐ No Action Required Date: ______

DECISION EVENT →

☐ Not Resolved—Convert to:

☐ IR ☐ CR Control No.:__-____

Chairman: ______

FIGURE 5.19. Example of a test incident report (TIR) form and associated events that it documents.

5.19 is processed in relation to the acceptance testing cycle in Figure 5.18. When a tester executing test procedures observes a discrepancy, he fills out the initiation event portion of the TIR and gives it to the bookkeeper in the product assurance organization. The bookkeeper assigns a control number to the TIR in the freezing event portion of the TIR and presents all accumulated TIRs to the CCB at the Test Incident CCB meeting. At that meeting, the CCB might decide that no action is required on the TIR or might decide to convert the TIR either to an incident report (IR) or a change request (CR). Conversion to an IR might occur if the CCB establishes the Operational Baseline at the Test Incident CCB—any residual TIRs are converted to IRs at that time. For any one of these three decisions, the CCB chairman fills out the decision event portion of the TIR. If the CCB decides to send the TIR to the developers for resolution, no entry is made in the decision event portion of the TIR.

The developer assigned to process a TIR fills out the analysis event portion of the TIR. He adds a recommended resolution to the TIR and a list of the software parts in the Development Baseline that he has changed. The Software Turnover CCB considers all the TIRs completed through the analysis event. As a result of the analysis of the TIR, the CCB might decide that no action is required on the TIR or that it should be converted to a CR. For these decisions, the bottom portion of the TIR would be filled out by the CCB chairman. Otherwise, the CCB forwards the TIR to the testers for retest. A tester retests the software system to determine whether the incident has been resolved. He retests the system by reexecuting the test procedure indicated on the TIR and observing at the TIR-specified test step whether the observed and expected results now agree. If no discrepancy appears, the tester indicates in the retest event portion of the TIR that the incident has been resolved. At the next Test Incident CCB, the chairman indicates that the test incident has been resolved in the decision event portion of the TIR and the TIR is closed. However, if the tester still finds a discrepancy as a result of retest, he indicates that fact in the retest event portion of the TIR and initiates an amendment to the TIR (amendments are labeled sequentially starting with the letter A). The amendment is written on another TIR form and attached to the original TIR. The tester fills in the incident description item of the TIR amendment according to his observations during retest. The development analyst fills in the analysis section of the TIR amendment, and the tester completes the retest event on the amendment. The TIR can continue around the acceptance testing cycle a number of times, with the TIR and its amendments providing visibility as to what occurred during each cycle and traceability from event to event. The TIR is closed out eventually when the CCB approves the resolution of the test incident, converts it to an IR or CR, or requires no code or document changes to be made.

We now take one more excursion through the acceptance testing cycle, this time with emphasis on the CCB meetings and their interaction (see Figure 5.20). As we proceed through the testing cycle, observe how visibility is provided at every step in the cycle through minutes of CCB meetings, through use of TIRs, through written test procedures, and through documented baselines. With this visibility provided at every event in every cycle, we attain traceability. We have a trace of baseline changes and test incident report processing from CCB minutes and other bookkeeping reports (see Chapter 6, especially Figure 6.15) and from test procedures linked to the requirements and design specifications. Visibility and traceability are particularly important during the acceptance testing cycle. Generally, the scheduled software code delivery date is rapidly approaching. The software code is being changed frequently and rapidly. Without good visibility and traceability, it is easy to lose control over the software. Test incidents may be over-

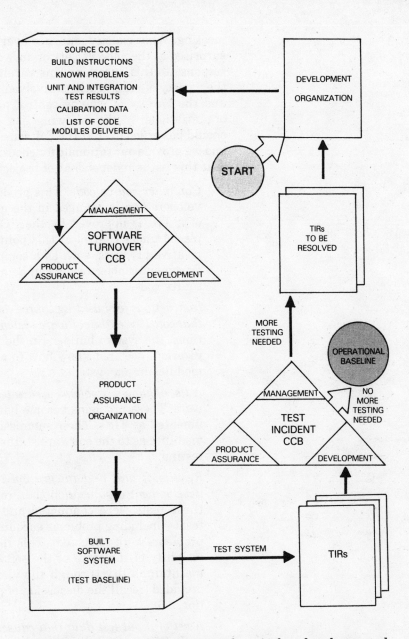

FIGURE 5.20. The interaction of the Software Turnover CCB and Test Incident CCB during the acceptance testing cycle.

looked or go unreported; they may be misplaced and never addressed. Resolutions to TIRs may be found, but code may not be corrected. Corrected code may never be retested, and harmful side effects from code changes or improper corrections may never be uncovered. The Development Baseline may not converge to an Operational Baseline, but may actually diverge with an increasing number of test incidents from testing cycle to testing cycle. Visibility and traceability are essential if we are to achieve convergence.

The starting point in our tour through the testing cycle shown in Figure 5.20 occurs when the development organization turns over, let us assume, a new software system (that is, one that has not yet had any acceptance testing) to the product assurance organization at the Software Turnover CCB meeting. What exactly is turned over? The authors have been surprised at the wide variety of answers they have received in response to this question. This variety may be a reflection of the variety of organizations involved in software development and the variety of change control procedures used by those organizations. In the following list, we state the items that should be turned over at the Software Turnover CCB meeting, and we provide our rationale for choosing each item (we believe that this list is independent of project organization):

Computer source code. This product is created by the developers and is changed in the event that the resolution of a TIR is approved by the CCB. It must therefore be placed under control at this point. Other source code derivative products, such as a computer source code listing or computer object code, can be generated from computer source code.

Instructions for building source code modules into an entity that constitutes the software system. Without these instructions, the system builder (in the product assurance organization) does not know how to assemble the source code modules into a system.

A list of known problems associated with the delivered software. These problems become baseline discrepancies documented as TIRs. Their submission to the CCB provides visibility as to the software status and averts unnecessary testing.

Results of unit and integration testing conducted by the development organization (i.e., reports that indicate how these tests were conducted and the outcomes of these tests—including problems encountered and whether these problems were corrected). This information increases the visibility of the state of the software code and promotes maintainability through the visibility and traceability provided (recall the discussion of product integrity in Section 2.6).

A set of input test data that causes the software to operate and the corresponding output data. This information is used not to test the software (the test procedures provide an independent set of data for testing) but to calibrate the software system.[11]

A list of the computer source code modules delivered. This list identifies the software parts delivered.

The minutes of the CCB meeting should specify what was turned over at the meeting, list the known software problems,

---

[11] When we wish to check the state of the software quickly, we can feed the input test data into the system and observe the output data. If the output data do not match the output test data, we know that some software part is missing (e.g., it may not have been turned over at a Software Turnover CCB) or has been changed. Basically, something that worked before no longer works. Notice that if the output data match the output test data we have not learned anything about the state of the software. Software could be missing parts or be changed and not be detected by this calibration test.

TEST INCIDENT REPORT

Control No.: _90-1066_   Amendment: ___ | Date/Time of Incident: _901110/2130_

Tester: Name: _Amy Blue_   Telephone Extension: _2174_

Executable Code: Release No.: _90-3_ Version No.: _2.1_

Test: Procedure: _EL2_   Step: _49_   [x] Incident Duplicated

Incident Description:

Expected ellipses to be drawn with semi-major axis oriented north-south. When ellipse with semi-major axis = 5000 miles was drawn, semi-major axis was oriented northeast-southwest.

Analyst: Name: _Jack Lemon_   Telephone Extension: _1492_   Date: _901115_

Recommended Resolution:

Register overflow. Use double precision arithmetic whenever semi-major axis greater than 2000 miles.

Changed Software:

Software Name	Software Identifier	Version/ Revision	Type of Software (Doc. or Code)
ELIPCALC	5.2.1	1.6	Code
ELIPDRAW	5.2.4	2.1	Code

Tester: Name: _Peter Rose_   Telephone Extension: _8214_   Date: _901118_

Retest: [x] Incident Resolved   [ ] Incident Not Resolved — See Amendment: ___

CCB Decision: [x] Resolved   [ ] No Action Required   Date: _19 Nov 90_

[ ] Not Resolved — Convert to:
    [ ] IR   [ ] CR Control No.: __-_____

Chairman: _Sally Plum_

FIGURE 5.21. Example of a completed test incident report (TIR) showing an incident resolved on its first retest.

establish priorities for testing the software, and set a date when the testers will end the test period and submit any TIRs to the CCB.

Following the Software Turnover CCB meeting, the software configuration management personnel of the product assurance organization place the delivered source code modules under control[12] in the Development Baseline and then, using the build instructions provided at the turnover meeting, build an executable software system that is termed the *Test Baseline*. The product assurance testers, using the previously written test procedures, exercise this baseline in a live or nearly live environment. As a result of this testing, they may generate TIRs. For exemplification purposes, assume that the TIR shown in Figure 5.21 was generated (the software system being tested is the subsystem of previously discussed System SHAPES that draws ellipses; assume for the present discussion that these ellipses are drawn on a map of the earth's surface). The tester fills out the initiation event portion of the form and submits it to the product assurance bookkeeper, who assigns it the con-

---

[12] This control is established through a software development library, discussed in Section 6.3.

trol number 90-1066. TIR 90-1066 and all other TIRs written during this test period are submitted to the next meeting of the Test Incident CCB. At this meeting, the software system is returned to the development organization for correction of TIRs. Each TIR is discussed in turn; if the CCB can resolve a TIR at the meeting, it does so and closes the TIR. For example, if the TIR is a duplicate, or results either from a misunderstanding by the tester or from an error in the test procedures, the CCB usually decides to take no action on a TIR, and the TIR is closed (in the case of an error in a test procedure, the testers correct the errant test procedure and rerun the test). The CCB might also decide that a TIR represents a capability not currently required by the requirements specification. Such a TIR may be converted by the CCB to a change request, i.e., the CCB will consider amending the requirements after an impact assessment has been made. The TIR is closed, and the CR is processed as described in Section 4.2. The CCB may also decide that it will not change the requirements to respond to the TIR, in which case the TIR is closed and the originator notified. At this particular Test Incident CCB meeting, TIR 90-1066 (Figure 5.21) is recognized as a problem and is sent to the development organization for resolution. The minutes of this Test Incident CCB should include a list of all TIRs submitted, a list of those TIRs resolved, the designation of any software capabilities that should be given particular attention because of the number or impact of TIRs pertinent to those capabilities, and the date of the next Software Turnover CCB meeting, at which the development organization will turn the software back over to the product assurance organization for further testing (see Section 6.2 for a discussion and an example of these CCB minutes).

The development organization analyzes and attempts to resolve as many TIRs as possible in the time period allotted. The analysis event portion of each TIR resolved is filled out at this time. In the case of TIR 90-1066, shown in Figure 5.21, two modules were adjudged to be faulty by the analyst (from the development organization), ELIPCALC and ELIPDRAW. The developers obtain a copy of each of these two modules from the software development library and correct them to resolve the test incident.

At the subsequent Software Turnover CCB meeting, all resolved TIRs are presented to the CCB. For TIRs requiring changes to code modules (such as TIR 90-1066), the corrected source code modules (including ELIPCALC and ELIPDRAW) are also turned over to the product assurance organization. In the process of resolving TIRs, the development organization often uncovers additional discrepancies (these might even include areas of uncertainty in the various specifications for the project). These discrepancies are reported as TIRs and introduced at this Software Turnover CCB meeting. The minutes of this CCB meeting should document all TIRs returned to the CCB and their resolutions, all new TIRs introduced at the meeting, and the date when the Test Incident CCB would be held (see Section 6.2 for a discussion and an example of these CCB minutes).

After this meeting, the product assurance organization substitutes the corrected source code modules in the Development Baseline. The software system (Test Baseline) is rebuilt to include the corrected code modules. Then the testers exercise the Test Baseline again, using their test procedures.

During this testing period, particular attention is paid to the procedure test steps where resolved TIRs were first observed. If a discrepancy still exists at a particular test step, an amendment to the TIR is prepared and attached to the TIR. With regard to TIR 90-1066, the tester found no discrepancies at step 49 of procedure EL2, and so indicated that the incident was resolved in the retest section of the TIR. At the next meeting of the Test Incident CCB, the CCB, noting that TIR 90-1066 had been resolved on retest, marked the decision event section to indicate that the incident had been resolved and then closed the TIR.

The Test Incident CCB also decides when the testing cycle terminates. Ideally, the cycle terminates when no TIRs result from the execution of the test procedures and no residual unresolved TIRs exist. However, we live in a far from ideal world and must have other mechanisms to allow us to exit the testing cycle. Even if TIRs are outstanding at the end of a cycle, the CCB may elect to terminate the cycle if the number of outstanding TIRs is relatively few and the impact of the TIRs on system operation is relatively minor. Another consideration is whether the software has tended toward stability in the last few cycles. If the number of TIRs outstanding at the end of each cycle is steadily decreasing, the system appears to be stable and is converging to the Operational Baseline. Other considerations regarding when to terminate the testing cycle include the arrival of the required delivery date of the system to the customer and the exhaustion of funds available to conduct testing. These last two considerations often override any other considerations on when to terminate the testing cycle. However, it is often more cost-effective to let slip a delivery date in favor of doing more testing to reduce the number of discrepancies—even at added expense to the developer. (For further consideration of this subject, see Exercises 5.6 and 7.2.)

Regardless of the reason for terminating the testing cycle, all outstanding TIRs should be converted to incident reports. These IRs are processed in the manner described in Section 4.2.

It should be noted that when the testing cycle is terminated the system often has outstanding discrepancies. Although this situation is less than ideal, observe that product assurance has made these discrepancies visible, has provided a mechanism for resolving them in a visible, traceable manner, and has increased the likelihood that the delivered product is readily maintainable. These observations should provide some peace of mind to the user receiving this software. At least he knows what problems he might face and that someone is working on their solution.

Contrast the foregoing situation to a situation where no testing cycle (with its audit and control functions) is provided. On most projects, a testing period is planned between the completion of coding/unit testing/integration testing and the date of delivery of the software code to the customer. The delivery date is usually fixed; it is generally very difficult to change a delivery date. On the other hand, the date of completion of coding/unit testing/integration testing frequently tends to slip toward the delivery date. The net result of such slippage is a reduction of the testing period. Usually there are no plans to pass through the testing period more than once. The testing period is often viewed as a "kick-the-tires" final inspection just before delivery, from which at most only a few discrepancies are expected. With this concept, no recycling through a testing period is necessary. If there are only a few discrepancies in the computer code, this approach works satisfactorily. But if there are any substantial number of discrepancies, the testing period could become chaos without any product assurance to audit and control during the testing. The testing period could become a time of frenzied activity—testing, correcting code in response to test incidents, and retesting all going on in parallel in a period of time that usually has been abbreviated due to slippage of the completion date of the computer code. Reports of test incidents could be misplaced, corrected code could be overlooked, code changes could counteract other code changes. When the delivery date arrives (and delivery *will* occur on the specified delivery date), the state of the software is unknown. What discrepancies still exist? What discrepancies have been overlooked? In the period of frenzied testing activity, there is no time to document the changes made to the code or even to record which modules were changed. Under these circumstances, maintenance of the software becomes very difficult.

In this section, we looked in detail at the auditing process as it applies to computer code. We showed how this audit of code against requirements and design specifications is accomplished by executing code operating in a live or nearly live environment using written test procedures, the process we call T&E. We pointed out how product assurance gives visibility during the acceptance testing cycle to the state of the Development and Operational Baselines through CCB minutes, TIRs, and written test procedures, and provides traceability during the transition from the Development Baseline to the Operational Baseline. In Section 3.2 we stated that T&E and auditing were equivalent processes. We believe that the discussion in this section demonstrates this equivalence.

5.4 Summary

In this chapter we concentrated on the mechanics of uncovering discrepancies in software products. Before the CCB can approve changes to attain and maintain software products with integrity, it must first know the state of software products as they evolve and incidents arising from the exercise of the software product that may indicate a need for changes. This knowledge is acquired through the performance of audits that uncover discrepancies in software products.

A discrepancy is not a statement of something wrong with a software product but rather an incongruity observed as a result of comparing a software product with the ground truth. We can categorize discrepancies by looking at the types of comparisons from which they arise. These types of comparisons turn out to be the processes of quality assurance (QA), verification and validation (V&V), test and evaluation (T&E), and self-comparison.

We looked at the auditing process in detail, first for software products that were documentation and then for software products that were code. The former, shown in Figure 5.7, includes the processes of QA, V&V, and self-comparison. The latter, depicted in Figure 5.18, includes the process of T&E. In many organizations, these processes are performed by different groups of people and treated as if they had nothing in common. Yet careful inspection of Figures 5.7 and 5.18 reveals that these two forms of audit are equivalent. They are indeed specific instances of the generic model of an audit shown in Figure 5.1.

In Chapters 4 and 5 we concentrated on the review area first introduced in Figure 2.7. This review area is the arena in which product assurance is performed. In Figure 4.4 we showed this area in detail, including the functions of audit and control. In the balance of Chapter 4, we focused on the control function, particularly the CCB, while this chapter focused on the audit function. Figure 5.1, which is essentially a repetition of Figure 4.4, reflects this different focus.

Although Figures 4.4 and 5.1 focus on different functions, we should keep in mind that the figures represent the same process. The functions of control and audit are interdependent and related. These functions complement each other and jointly contribute toward attaining software products with integrity. Their relationship is illustrated in the model of product assurance in Figure 3.10.

We have not yet addressed the third function of product assurance shown in Figure 3.10—bookkeeping. That is the subject of the next chapter.[13]

---

[13] Senior managers may want to consider the following exercises before proceeding to the next chapter: Exercise 5.3, on the value of auditing software products; Exercise 5.9, on the scope and depth of auditing; Exercise 5.16, on the scope of acceptance testing; Exercise 5.17, on independent product assurance. Project managers and product assurance managers may want to consider the following exercises before proceeding to the next chapter: Exercise 5.2, on specification ambiguity and incompleteness; Exercise 5.3, on the value of auditing software products; Exercise 5.4, on a software product assurance charter; Exercise 5.5, on assigning priorities to discrepancies; Exercise 5.6, on discrepancy reporting and its relationship to CCB operation; Exercise 5.8, on the role of and need for independent acceptance testing; Exercise 5.14, on management imposition of constraints on discrepancy reporting; Exercise 5.16, on the scope of acceptance testing; Exercise 5.22, on an alternative acceptance testing cycle.

Many of the following exercises are based on the authors' actual software project experiences.

5.1   In Section 5.2, we went through the mechanics of checking a software product that is not computer code by self-comparison; we also discussed the mechanics of cross-checking this type of software product against a predecessor product and other points of reference such as project-imposed standards. The purpose of this exercise is to help you to think through these mechanics by performing such self-comparison and cross-checking on small extracts from software products. For this purpose, Figure E5.1 sets out a paragraph assumed to be extracted from a requirements document for a software system under development called System ABC. Figure E5.2 sets out a paragraph assumed to be extracted from a preliminary design document for System ABC (presumably this design document was published some time after the requirements document and is based on the requirements document). Assume that you are auditing these two documents and that you have determined that the extract in Figure E5.2 corresponds, at least in part, to the extract in Figure E5.1. With these assumptions, consider the following:

(a) Write down at least two discrepancies you might submit against the requirements document extract in Figure E5.1.

(b) Give at least one reason why discrepancies such as those you noted in (a) might initially go undetected (i.e., when the requirements document was initially issued).

(c) What concept introduced in Chapter 2 can be used to justify including the first sentence in paragraph 8.5.4.2 of the preliminary design document? To an auditor, what is the value of such a sentence? Answer this question also from the perspective of the software customer and the software developer.

(d) Write down at least two discrepancies that you might submit against the preliminary design document extract in Figure E5.2 *without referring to the requirements document extract.*

(e) Write down at least two discrepancies that you might submit regarding the mutual consistency of paragraph 3.2.3 in the requirements document and paragraph 8.5.4.2 in the preliminary design document.

FIGURE E5.1. System ABC Requirements Document extract used in Exercise 5.1.

3.2.3 Mathematical Support Function Requirements

Subsystem MATH shall provide a capability to construct polygons on a map background. Specifically, this capability shall include the following:

a.   The ability to specify a polygon with a minimum of 2 vertices and a maximum of 36 vertices.

b.   The ability to specify a polygon with an area up to 25,000 square nautical miles.

c.   Vertices shall be specified as latitude in degrees, minutes, and seconds (North or South) and longitude in degrees, minutes, and seconds.

d.   When an error is detected, the calculations shall be aborted and the user notified.

8.5.4.2 Polygon Construction Design Overview

Paragraph 3.2.3 in the System ABC Requirements Document stipulates that Subsystem MATH shall provide a capability to construct polygons on a map background. This capability shall be implemented using the following design approach:

a. Subroutine **POLY** will be the name of the module that will perform all polygon calculations in System ABC.

b. **POLY** will be called by subroutines TBD.*

c. **POLY** calls subroutines SIN, COS, TAN, and ERROR.

d. **POLY** uses algorithm WELL-KNOWN to construct polygons from vertices input. This algorithm comprises the main portion of the code in POLY.

e. **POLY** first checks to see if the number of vertices input is less than 3 or greater than 36. If so, then subroutine ERROR is called and the calculation is aborted. If not, WELL-KNOWN is entered.

f. Upon completion of the calculation, control is returned to TBD.*

*Note: TBD is an acronym standing for "TO BE DETERMINED."

FIGURE E5.2. System ABC Preliminary Design Document extract used in Exercise 5.1.

(f) Where would you submit the discrepancies referred to in (a), (d), and (e)? For what purpose?

5.2 Recall the sample problem on System PREDICT in Section 5.2. In that problem, we presented an audit report (Figure 5.10) on the preliminary design specification (PDS) (Figure 5.9) which pointed out that the PDS appeared to contain a number of assumptions relative to the Requirements Baseline (RB) (Figure 5.8) and recommended that the assumptions (if deemed appropriate by the CCB) be reflected in the RB. Some would argue with the audit report on the basis that the specifications in the PDS were not derived from assumptions but resulted from (undocumented) discussions between the designers and the customer (i.e., the specifications reflect user needs). With the preceding as background, consider the following:

(a) Even if the specifications were developed as a result of considerable discussion between the designers and the customer, do you think that the results of these discussions (the so-called "assumptions") should be reflected in the RB? Why (not)? (*Hint:* Consider the needs of the maintenance programmer.)

(b) Give three engineers in your organization a copy of the System PREDICT Requirements Specification in Figure 5.8 and ask them to draw up a design for the system. Compare the resulting designs to each other and to the design shown in Figure 5.9. What does this comparison tell you about the ambiguity of the System PREDICT Requirements Specification (RS)?

(c) Give three programmers in your organization a copy of the System PREDICT Preliminary Design Specification (PDS), but do not give them access to the RS. (This constraint is not atypical. Programmers are frequently handed a design and told to code it without any access to the requirements specification.) Have the programmers code System PREDICT from the PDS. Compare the resulting code to the requirements specification by testing the code. Then compare the test results obtained from the three sets of code. What does this latter comparison tell you about the ambiguity of the System PREDICT PDS?

5.3 Suppose you are a manager of a software product assurance organization. Suppose further that your organizational charter includes auditing in the sense described in this chapter. With these suppositions, and recalling what we said in this chapter about auditing generally being a labor-intensive activity (and therefore expensive), consider the following:

(a) Write down at least two arguments (use one or two sentences for each argument) that you would use to convince your management that expenditures for auditing will pay for themselves. (*Hint:* Recall Figure 1.3.)

(b) Suppose your management asks you the following question:

Can we ever be sure in advance that the "pay now" approach of performing audits early in the life cycle will save time and/or money later in the life cycle?

How would you answer? (Indicate either "We can be sure" or "We cannot be sure," and then write down at least one reason to support your answer.) (*Hint:* What is the message underlying that well-known sales pitch for automobile oil filters that uses the slogan "You can pay me [the purveyor of oil filters] now, or pay him [an auto mechanic] later!")

(c) Are there times you should try to convince your management that expenditures for auditing will *not* save time and/or money but are still necessary? (Indicate yes or no, and then write down at least one reason to support your answer.) (*Hint:* Consider the implications of software failure in certain types of systems.)

(d) If your answer to (c) was "yes," does this imply that there are times that auditing may reduce the integrity of a software product (recall from Chapter 2 that two of the attributes of a product with integrity are that it meet cost expectations and that it meet delivery expectations)? Why (not)?

(e) Recalling (b), does the value of auditing (its benefit versus its cost) diminish as it is applied later in the life cycle? Indicate yes, no, or maybe, and give at least one reason to support your answer. (*Hint:* Recall the game board portrayal of the life cycle in Figure 2.7 and consider what "later in the life cycle" really means.)

(f) From your answers to the preceding parts of this exercise, write down at least one conclusion about the value of auditing software products.

5.4 Suppose you have just been appointed to manage a newly formed software product assurance organization. As one of your first tasks, you set about defining a charter for this organization. Assume that the product assurance concept to be set forth in this charter is the concept propounded in this book (in particular, as explained in Chapter 3 and detailed in Chapters 4 and 5). Assume further that you are now about to write the section of the charter that itemizes the specific QA, V&V, and T&E activities that you want your organization to perform. Listed in Table E5.1 are activities pertaining to software products. From this list, select the activities you would incorporate into the QA/V&V/T&E

section of the charter, and give at least one reason to justify each activity you select. Also, for each activity you do not select, give at least one reason why you believe (based on the product assurance philosophy described in this book) such an activity does not belong in a software product assurance charter.

TABLE E5.1. SOFTWARE PRODUCT ACTIVITIES FOR EXERCISE 5.4

1. Comparing a listing of computer code against a predecessor detailed design document to see if the code logically follows from the design

2. Comparing a listing of computer code against a contractual statement of work to see if the code satisfies contractual requirements

3. Comparing a software design document against a documentation standard to check for conformance with the standard

4. Examining the derivation of a mathematical formula appearing in a design document to check that the formula is correct

5. Checking a software specification for internal consistency

6. Examining a listing of computer code for spelling errors

7. Checking a software specification document for grammatical and spelling errors

8. Executing software code on hardware according to a test procedure and comparing the results of executing this test procedure with the results predicted by the test procedure

9. Executing a simulation of a software system and comparing the simulation results with a document specifying the functions that the actual software code will perform when it is built to see if these functions are being performed

10. Comparing a specification of software functions against a contract from which the specification was directly developed to determine whether the specification and contract are consistent

11. Checking a design document to determine whether alternative design approaches could have more efficiently and/or compactly (e.g., in terms of hardware needed to load and execute the software code that might result from the design) satisfied customer needs as stipulated in a requirements specification

12. Checking a standard (such as a documentation standard) that is to be imposed on a software project to see if it is internally consistent and appropriately addresses project needs (e.g., does a documentation standard stipulate more, or fewer, document types than those called for in the project's statement of work?)

13. Monitoring a software project's product delivery schedule to determine whether software products are being delivered on time

14. Monitoring a software project's labor expenditures (e.g., the number of management, development, and product assurance hours expended to produce a particular software product) to determine whether software products are being developed within budget

15. Recording the minutes of software CCB meetings

16. Reviewing a revised software product to determine whether CCB-approved changes to the product have been properly incorporated into the product

Continued

17. Checking the internal consistency of a contractual statement of work specifying requirements for a software system

18. Reviewing reports of discrepancies written by your organization against software products to determine if the reports are relevant and appropriately worded

19. Reviewing test procedures written by your organization to determine if they adequately exercise software requirements specified in a requirements document

20. Logging and archiving CRs and IRs

5.5 In Sections 5.2 and 5.3, we described how the primary results of QA, V&V, and T&E activities (i.e., reports of discrepancies) provide the CCB membership with visibility into the state of software products. In Chapter 4, we described how this visibility enables the CCB membership to make intelligent, informed decisions regarding changes to these products. Within the frame of reference established in Chapter 4 regarding the role of the CCB (or CCBs) on a software project, and within the frame of reference established in Sections 5.2 and 5.3 regarding the relationship of QA/V&V/T&E discrepancy reporting to CCB operation, consider the following:

(a) Under what circumstances might it be desirable to assign priorities to discrepancies (by "priority" we mean an indicator that suggests the level of a discrepancy's perceived importance or its perceived impact on software development and/or maintenance cost and/or schedule and/or performance with respect to other discrepancies)? Why?

(b) List at least three disadvantages associated with assigning priorities to discrepancies, and give at least one reason to justify each disadvantage you list.

(c) Recall the three groups of disciplines shown in the triangle in Figure 2.13—management, development, and product assurance. For each group, list at least one advantage and one disadvantage of assigning it the responsibility of prioritizing discrepancies.

(d) Based on your answers to the preceding parts of this exercise, derive at least three ground rules for assigning priorities to discrepancies that you as a software project manager might find useful to establish on your software project. For each rule you derive, give at least one reason that this rule might help you better manage your project.

5.6 Recall the discussion in Sections 5.2 and 5.3 regarding discrepancy reporting and its relationship to CCB operation, and consider the following:

(a) Hypothesize at least three situations that would compel you as manager of a software development effort to constrain the project's CCB to declare a software product acceptable *only* if the CCB receives an audit report citing *no* discrepancies. (*Hint:* Under what circumstances might it be desirable, if not compulsory, to establish a policy of "zero-defect software" on a project? What implications might such a policy have on the guidance that you as the software project manager might give to the product assurance organization regarding the types of discrepancies they should report?)

(b) Hypothesize at least three considerations that might compel you as a software project manager to ignore (or postpone resolution of) discrepancies submitted to the CCB (or directly to you).

(c) Based on your answers to (a) and (b), derive at least three ground rules for invoking a "zero-defect software" policy that you as a software project manager might find useful to establish on a software project headed by you. For each rule you derive, give at least one reason why this rule might help you better manage your project.

5.7 Consider a software package that is in the midst of the Coding Stage (recall Figure 2.7). Assume that this coding activity is based upon, and proceeds from, an approved detailed design specification. Assume also that this design specification is derived from an approved requirements specification. Finally, assume that you are a part of a team of independent testers in the process of writing step-by-step test procedures intended to exercise the software code in an operational environment against the requirements and detailed design specifications. With these assumptions as background, consider the following:

(a) Suppose the detailed design specification is silent on a detail that you need regarding how to specify one or more steps in a test that you are attempting to write. Which of the actions listed below should you take so that you can get on with your job? Why?
1. Talk to the coders to find out how they are handling the design ambiguity
2. Write a discrepancy against the detailed design specification
3. Make up test steps based on your interpretation of the detailed design specification
4. Some combination of 1, 2, and 3
5. Some combination of 1, 2, and 3 and something else (What is this "something else"?)
6. None of the above (If you select this "action," specify what action[s] you would take and why.)

(b) Suppose you discover an ambiguity in a paragraph in the requirements specification as a result of attempting to construct a test to exercise the paragraph. Which of the actions listed below should you take so you can get on with your job? Why?
1. Talk to the customer to find out what he really wants
2. Write a discrepancy against the requirements specification
3. Make up a test based on your interpretation of the requirements specification
4. Go to the corresponding portions of the detailed design specification for clarification
5. Write a note to the software project manager indicating that the requirement in question is ambiguously stated and therefore untestable
6. Some combination of 1–5
7. Some combination of 1–5 and something else (What is this "something else"?)
8. None of the above (If you select this "action," specify what action[s] you would take and why.)

(c) If the software control mechanisms described in Chapters 4 and 5 are in place on a software project, are the situations posited in

(a) and (b) of only academic interest because they are unlikely to occur? Why (not)?

(d) What does your response to (c) suggest to you about the need to change software? What does it mean that a requirements specification or some other specification has just been approved so that it is now "frozen"? What is the purpose of freezing such entities if they are (soon) going to change anyway? Would it be more desirable to generate only generally worded requirements and design specifications, and then let the developers and testers thrash out the details among themselves? Why (not)?

5.8 Suppose you are a manager of a product assurance organization within a company that provides QA, T&E, V&V, and SCM services. Suppose further that you have been providing independent product assurance services to a customer who has been using another company to develop a software system. Part of your responsibility has been to audit unit and integration testing (see footnote 4 in Chapter 3) performed by the developer; you are also responsible for preparing and executing acceptance tests for purposes of helping the customer decide whether to accept the various major releases of the software system being turned out by the developer approximately every six months. Finally, suppose your customer has been rethinking whether he really needs your independent testing services and asks you to write a memorandum explaining the role of and need for an independent acceptance tester. Figure E5.3 is a partially completed version of this memorandum. Based on concepts set forth in this and preceding chapters, complete this memorandum by supplying arguments in the places indicated in brackets in the figure. If you find the structure in the figure too confining, compose a memorandum from scratch using the ideas in the figure as a starting point.

5.9 In this chapter, we described processes by which the CCB can be kept abreast of the extent to which software products are being developed logically and are congruent with what the customer asked for. These processes we variously described as audits, tests, quality assurance checks, or reviews. As with many concepts pertaining to software product assurance, no uniform definitions exist regarding:

What such processes should be called

The scope and depth of such processes

For example, consider the following excerpt from Dunn, *Software Defect Removal* (Reference 4 in Chapter 4 of our book), regarding the distinction between *inspection* and *review*:

"Inspection" is an often used synonym for "review." I prefer not to use it. Once a year the state of New Jersey inspects my car and declares it safe (or, with equal likelihood, unsafe pending adjustments). Once a year a mechanic approved by the Federal Aviation Agency and about to enrich himself at my expense inspects my airplane and confirms that it is still airworthy. My new tennis racket was inspected by No. 17. I rather think of inspections as wheel pulling, cable stretching, lamination counting operations attended by dark scowls and followed by red tags. By contrast, we *review* books, concerts, and plans for urban rehabilitation, each, like our software products, the result of laborious cognitive processes. And in the process of these reviews, we are forced to make decisions

TO:	The Customer	15 May 1994
FROM:	Product Assurance Manager	Memo ID: J52
SUBJECT:	Why Independent System-Level Testing	

An "independent" tester is an organization separate from the development organization whose role on a software project is the following:

> To assess whether or not software code, executing in a live or nearly live environment, meets its objectives.

Generally, the objectives of system-level testing (independent or otherwise) are to ensure the following:

(1) The software code units (or modules) operating as a system satisfy the user's requirements and performance criteria (i.e., it is assumed that the developer has performed unit and integration testing to squeeze out aberrations such as coding syntax errors and unit interface mismatches).

(2) The system operates in accordance with its user's manual and operator's manual.

(3) The system operates for some prespecified period of time without failure in the environment for which it was designed.

(4) When the system fails, it can be returned to operation after only a brief delay.

(5) The system does not lack required parts.

As we subsequently explain, the above objectives are more likely to be achieved by an independent tester.

The software developer is generally too close to his work to frequently see what is not there. Combined with the natural human tendency to be partial toward one's own handicraft, this closeness often inhibits the scope and depth of the developer's testing activities. An independent tester,

> [Complete this paragraph by explaining how an independent tester is better able than the developer to meet each of the five objectives listed above.]

The software development process is inherently difficult to visualize. Independent testing raises the visibility of this process as follows:

> [Complete this paragraph by listing at least three ways independent testing raises the visibility of the software development process.]

For many years, other industries have relied on independent testers to establish credibility of their products in the eyes of client communities they wish to reach. These communities have come to accept as a given that a product's innate quality is perhaps best demonstrated through analysis by an independent (and thus presumably impartial) agent.

> [Complete this paragraph by explaining why the sentiment expressed in the first two sentences of this paragraph may apply even more forcefully to the software industry.]

> [If you feel it is appropriate, add a concluding paragraph or paragraphs here.]

FIGURE E5.3. A partially completed justification for independent system-level testing (Exercise 5.8).

supported not by gauges that read "pass" or "fail," but by judgment (p. 89n).

Based upon Dunn's remarks above and the discussion of auditing/testing presented in this chapter, consider the following:

(a) What are software analogues to Dunn's inspection activities of "wheel pulling" and "cable stretching"?

(b) Based on your responses to (a), how do the software analogues to wheel pulling and cable stretching (which ostensibly are designed to detect such things as weak points and other potential problems) raise the visibility of the software development process? How do they inject traceability into this process?

(c) Describe at least two ways that the software analogues to wheel pulling and cable stretching are similar to the auditing/testing processes discussed in this chapter. Describe at least two ways that the software analogues to these two inspection activities differ from the auditing/testing discussed in this chapter.

(d) Based on the discussion in this chapter, what are software analogues to the "dark scowls" and "red tags" to which Dunn refers?

(e) Recall the balance shown in Figure 3.11, which portrays our concept of software product assurance. With this picture in mind, indicate whether you agree or disagree with Dunn's final sentence regarding the distinction between *inspection* and *review*. That is, is software product assurance as we define it strictly an exercise in judgment, or can it be an exercise supported by gauges that read "pass" or "fail" (or something in between)? Why (not)?

(f) Assuming that most software developers are professionals whose primary interest is to produce first-rate products (and who can be relied upon to conduct internal audits/reviews and tests of these products), should software product assurance be restricted to the analogues of wheel pulling and cable stretching (so that, for example, project resources can be conserved)? Why (not)?

(g) By insisting that an entity other than the development organization perform software product assurance on a project (wheel pulling or otherwise), are we in effect saying that the development organization cannot be relied upon or trusted to produce first-rate products? Continuing this reasoning, are we therefore saying that the software product assurance organization and the software development organization must be adversaries on a project and must interact primarily through confrontation? Why (not)?

5.10 (*Note:* This exercise assumes some background in mathematics. It is intended to probe some of the nuances pertaining to the auditing of software design documentation that specifies mathematical formulas that are to be transformed into computer code. Its purpose is to highlight issues that the auditor should be particularly sensitive to when examining software products containing mathematical expressions. Although mathematical formulas are generally a precise method for specifying something, the auditor must remain aware that such formulas often are interpreted by nonmathematicians during the process of converting these formulas to computer code. As a result, specifications containing mathematical formulas frequently need amplifying or clarifying information that would be considered superfluous in some other context, such as a mathematics or science textbook.) Figure E5.4 shows an extract from a software design specification giving a mathematical formula to be coded into a subroutine that is to support various computations as indicated in the paragraph. This paragraph

5.3.8 Equation for a Geodesic on the Earth's Surface. A geodesic is a line that represents the shortest path between two points lying on some surface. On the earth's surface, a geodesic is the shorter of the two great circle arcs linking the two points. This paragraph specifies the functional relationship between a latitude v on a geodesic and its corresponding longitude w where the geodesic is assumed to link the point at the latitude and longitude (v1, w1) to the point at the latitude and longitude (v2, w2) as shown in the figure below.

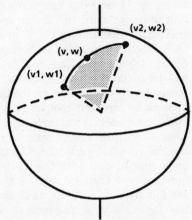

In terms of the quantities depicted in the above figure, the functional relationship linking v and w is the following:

$$v = \tan^{-1}[A\sin(w-B)]$$

where

$$A = \frac{[\tan^2(v1) + \tan^2(v2) - 2\tan(v1)\tan(v2)\cos(w1-w2)]^{1/2}}{\sin(w1 + w2)}$$

$$B = \tan^{-1}\left[\frac{\tan(v1)\sin(w2) - \tan(v2)\sin(w1)}{\tan(v1)\cos(w2) - \tan(v2)\cos(w1)}\right]$$

The derivation of this formula is given in appendix F. This formula shall be coded in a separate subroutine. This subroutine shall return a value for v when supplied values for w, v1, w1, v2, and w2. This subroutine shall support the following computations:

a. Determination of the intercept of a low-flying cruise missile with a ship platform moving along the course described by the formula specified in paragraph 5.3.3 above.

b. Determination of the shortest possible travel time for an aircraft departing from (v1, w1) and landing at (v2, w2) in support of the troop deployment algorithm specified in paragraph 4.6.1 above.

c. Determination of the additional time required to travel between (v1, w1) and (v2, w2) when other than a geodesic is traversed as specified by the nongeodesic formulas given in paragraphs 5.3.6 and 5.3.7 above.

FIGURE E5.4. Design specification extract pertaining to Exercise 5.10.

also specifies the geometrical interpretation of the mathematical formula and indicates that the derivation of the formula is to be found in an appendix to the design specification. Assume that, outside of this paragraph and this appendix, the design specification contains no other information regarding the formula. Also, assume that this design specification will be the sole basis for the coding activity. With these assumptions, and using Figure E5.4, consider the following:

(a) Using your knowledge as a mathematician, and keeping in mind that the coder using this design specification may not be a mathematician, what amplifying information would you suggest to the CCB should be included in paragraph 5.3.8 of the design specification to reduce the likelihood that the formula in the paragraph will be coded improperly? (*Hint:* Consider what "improperly" means here. For example, mathematicians know how to deal with division by zero, but computers do not, unless they are told explicitly. As another example, mathematicians know how to distinguish between radians and degrees, but computers do not, unless they are told explicitly. As a third example, mathematicians know how to deal with the multiple branches of trigonometric functions and their inverses, but computers do not, unless they are told explicitly. As a fourth example, mathematicians know how to deal with square roots of negative numbers and when to expect them, but computers do not, unless they are told explicitly.)

(b) List at least two ways that you as an auditor might use the information you would presumably find in appendix F of the design specification to audit paragraph 5.3.8.

(c) Give at least two reasons why it may be a good idea to audit the information you would presumably find in appendix F of the design specification. List at least three things that you would look for in this appendix F audit.

(d) In your opinion, should the coder be expected to look at appendix F? (Indicate yes, no, or maybe, and give at least two reasons to justify your answer.) Should your answer to this question influence your audit findings? Why (not)?

(e) Subparagraphs 5.3.8a, 5.3.8b, and 5.3.8c cross-reference paragraphs 5.3.3, 4.6.1, 5.3.6, and 5.3.7. For each of these paragraphs, indicate at least one thing you might look for in these paragraphs while auditing paragraph 5.3.8, and give at least one reason for looking at each thing that you indicate.

(f) In light of your answers to the preceding parts of this exercise, is it reasonable to assume that a CCB will be able to deal with your audit findings of paragraph 5.3.8 and appendix F since many of the audit findings will be of a highly mathematical nature? (Indicate yes, no, or maybe, and give at least three reasons to justify your answer.) (*Hint:* Recall from Section 4.3 that on some projects it may be necessary to have a tier of CCBs. Why? If a CCB will not be the beneficiary of your audit findings, who should be? Why?)

5.11 Suppose you work for an independent product assurance organization. Among other things, this organization is monitoring the integration testing efforts of a company that is building a software system for the customer for whom your organization is working. Suppose also that you are constantly lobbying with your customer for greater visibility into integration testing through more thorough documentation of integration test procedures. Your customer, on the other hand, is frequently at the mercy of deadlines imposed by the system user that he serves. As a result, your customer has a tendency to relax some of his testing documentation "needs." With these suppositions about the customer environment and your job, imagine you have just completed the review of an integration test procedure and have submitted the following findings:

1. Portions of the expected results depend on knowing the formulas used to compute certain quantities. For example, table 1 in the test procedure folder lists the expected values of areas for polygons on the surface of the earth. In order to determine whether these values are correct, the folder should include the mathematical formulas used to determine these area values. Without these formulas, it is not possible to compare these values with the values appearing in the computer output included in the test procedure folder. These formulas are also needed to determine whether the polygon areas are being calculated as surfaces in three dimensions or as planar approximations to these three-dimensional surfaces.

2. The test procedures do not indicate how information in incoming messages is used to determine the areas referred to in the paragraph above. Without this information, it is not possible to determine whether the data elements in these messages are being correctly processed. Without this determination, it is not possible to validate explicitly whether the test is exercising the requirements allocated to it as specified in paragraph 2.3 of the test procedure folder. For clarity and completeness, the test procedure folder should explicitly indicate how data element values in the incoming messages are transformed into the area values shown in table 1 of the folder.

Suppose that after you submit the above comments your customer informs you (not unexpectedly) that your comments are merely concerned with test procedure documentation and do not bear on the test itself—particularly since the area values shown in table 1 of the test folder match those appearing in the computer output included in the folder. Your customer therefore informs you that he does not intend to direct the developer to revise the test procedure folder. Finally, suppose that this test procedure folder (as well as other integration testing folders) will be used repeatedly in testing of future upgrades to the software system as part of regression testing activities (by *regression testing* we mean the testing of existing capabilities in a system in which new capabilities have been added). With the preceding information as background, consider the following:

(a) List at least two reasons why you should attempt to convince your customer that it is in *his* best interests to direct the developer to address your comments in his testing documentation.

(b) Suppose your customer tells you, after you give him the reasons you list in (a), that the developer has no time now to address your comments because code has to be debugged and delivered to the customer. List at least three reasons that you might give your customer at this point as to why the developer has no time now *not* to address your comments.

(c) Suppose, after giving your customer the reasons you list in (b), your customer rejects your rationale and stands his ground. List at least two constructive suggestions you might make to your customer regarding what could be done to ameliorate the situation so that the next time the test is run resources will not have to be wasted trying to determine whether the test has explicitly demonstrated what it was supposed to demonstrate. Should you volunteer to address your own comments and upgrade the developer's test procedure folder for him? Why (not)?

(d) In your opinion, should a product assurance organization be forceful in the manner indicated in preceding parts of this exercise, or should this organization merely submit its comments and do no further lobbying for their acceptance? (Whichever position you choose, give at least three reasons to support your choice. You may also choose to support both positions. If so, indicate the circumstances under which you would support each position and why.)

5.12 Assume that Table E5.2 is part of a requirements specification for a software system under development. This table is intended to define how records in certain files are to be created and updated in response to receipt of two different message types (M1 and M2). It is also intended to specify the conditions under which error diagnostics are sent to a system user in response to receipt of these two types of messages. Suppose you are a member of an independent product assurance organization responsible for testing the software under development to ensure that it conforms to the requirements specification. Suppose also that your specific responsibilities include developing and executing a written test procedure for exercising the rules shown in Table E5.2. With this information as background, consider the following:

(a) Write a step-by-step test procedure that explicitly exercises all the rules specified in Table E5.2. Use the five-column format shown in Figure 5.13 to document your procedure.

(b) Suppose that, instead of just two message types, Table E5.2 were expanded to include 200 message types; suppose also that instead of two if-then relations the table were expanded to include ten if-then relations. Would the test specification approach implied by Figure 5.13 have been a practical way to exercise this augmented set of message processing rules? Why (not)?

(c) How does the test specification format shown in Figure 5.13 facilitate the tester's job in helping the CCB do its job of making decisions about software changes?

(d) Considering your responses to the preceding parts of this exercise, what are some real-world considerations that need to be addressed when preparing test procedures whose overall objective is to demonstrate explicitly that software code is doing what the customer asked it to do?

TABLE E5.2. MESSAGE PROCESSING RULES FOR EXERCISE 5.12

	Rules			
	1	2	3	4
If message type received is	M1	M1	M2	M2
If record exists in File A	Yes	No	Yes	No
Then				
Create new record in File B		X		X
Update existing record in File B	X		X	
Send error diagnostic to user		X	X	

5.13 We have repeatedly emphasized the advantages of an independent auditor. In particular, we have asserted that an independent auditor is better able than the developer to see what is not there as well as what is there. Furthermore, we have emphasized that, in addition to performing verification and validation checks, a good auditor performs internal consistency checks and is sensitive to language ambiguities, spelling errors, and other information defects. This exercise is intended to probe some of the nuances of these aspects of auditing by considering an extract from a software product. Figure E5.5 depicts a paragraph from a software design specification. This software part describes the display to be produced in a military system. The display is to be used by a weapons officer for the purpose of determining (1) whether weapons are to be employed (presumably in a rapidly unfolding conflict) and, if they are to be employed, (2) the types of weapon (conventional and/or nuclear) and (3) their number(s). With this information and Figure E5.5 as background, consider the following:

(a) While reviewing the paragraph in Figure E5.5, what other parts of the specification would it be useful to examine? Why?

(b) Is there a possible (nontrivial) spelling error in the paragraph? If so, what is it and how would you report it to the CCB?

(c) Are there ambiguities in the paragraph? If so, how would you report them to the CCB?

(d) Considering what may be at stake if the code resulting from this part of the design fails to work properly, what suggestions would it be worthwhile to forward to the CCB (in addition to the items alluded to in (b) and (c))? Remembering that you should clearly distinguish between your objective and subjective findings, how should you report these suggestions to the CCB?

FIGURE E5.5. Design specification extract pertaining to Exercise 5.13.

3.5.2 <u>Weapons Employment Display</u>.   The purpose of this display is to provide the weapons officer with weapons employment options. The contents of this display shall be governed by the value of **DCODE** set in the manner described in paragraph 3.3.2 above. The following table specifies the display contents in terms of this value:

<u>DCODE</u>	<u>DISPLAY</u>
0	CONVENTIONAL WEAPONS ARE NOW TO BE EMPLOYED; PRESS FUNCTION KEY F1 FOR TYPE AND NUMBER
1	NUCLEAR WEAPONS ARE NOW TO BE EMPLOYED
2	PRESS FUNCTION KEY F2 FOR OPTIONS
3	NO WEAPONS ARE TO BE EMPLOYED

For other values of DCODE, refer to the error code defined in paragraph 7.2.

5.14 A criticism sometimes leveled against product assurance is that it tends to focus on relatively minor problems (from the perspective of overall software project objectives). One result of this focus is that inordinate amounts of project resources may be devoted to addressing these minor problems at the expense of addressing what in hindsight turns out to be major problems. On the one hand, it may be desirable for project management not to impose constraints on the kinds of discrepancies an auditor is to report because such constraints might unduly complicate the auditor's task and result in distorted audit reports. (For example, suppose an auditor is directed not to report any spelling errors or poorly phrased wording. Some spelling errors or poor wording may be obvious and may not obscure the intended meaning of a software product. Other spelling errors or poor wording may be subtle and obscure or invert the intended meaning of a software product. See, for instance, Figure E5.5 in the preceding exercise.) On the other hand, it may be desirable for project management to impose constraints on the kinds of discrepancies an auditor is to report because such constraints will help project management better obtain the type of information that it (project management) needs to do its job (i.e., to make intelligent, informed decisions as to how the project is to proceed). With the preceding as background, consider the following (in responding to the items below, assume you are a member of a product assurance organization):

(a) List at least three things you might do before starting an auditing task to raise the likelihood that your audit report will not overwhelm your customer with minutiae, and give at least one reason for each thing that you list.

(b) Suppose your customer directs you not to report on spelling errors or poor wording in a software product. Suppose further that while auditing a software product you come across what you believe may be spelling errors or poor wording that do require visibility. For example, suppose you encounter the following sentences in a detailed design document that, once approved, will be turned into computer code:

The area A of a rectangle on the surface of the earth shall be calculated using the formula

$$A = R^2W[sin(X2) - sin(X1)]$$

where

R = *3440 nautical miles = mean radius of earth*
W = *angular width of rectangle in radians = longitude spanned by rectangle*
X1 = *southernmost latitude of rectangle*
X2 = *northernmost latitude of rectangle.*

The value of W *shall be determined from a table by relating an angular width code to an angular width value that can be found in the table. The value of* X1 *cannot exceed 90° and must be such that* X1 *is less than* X2*; the resulting sign may be positive or negative.*

In your opinion, are there instances of poor wording or possible spelling errors in the above example? If so, what are they? Would you report them to your customer despite his direction to you? Why (not)? If you would not report these instances to your customer, is there anything in the above example that you would report to your customer? If so, what and why? If you would report the poor wording or possible spelling errors to your customer, how would you report these instances together with other things that you might report regarding the above example so that wheat and chaff are not intermingled? (*Hint:* Consider what constitutes a nitpick versus what constitutes a potentially substantive finding in the context of the above example.)

(c) (This part of the exercise is for readers who have been, or are currently, involved in a software project.) Take a software specification document (e.g., a requirements specification or a design specification)—it can be a draft or a product that was delivered to a customer—and audit it (or a small portion of it if the document is more than 10 to 20 pages). Restrict yourself to locating the following types of discrepancies:

1. Poor wording
2. Possible spelling errors
3. Internal inconsistencies

If you were auditing this specification for the actual customer for whom it was intended, which of the above types of discrepancies that you found would you report to him? Why?

(d) Based on your responses to the preceding parts of this exercise (and your own software project experience in addition to that called upon in (c)), list at least three criteria that you might use on an actual software project to help you as an auditor to decide when to report poor wording or spelling errors and when not to. For each criterion you list, give at least one reason why the criterion can help reduce the likelihood that your audit report will overwhelm your customer with minutiae.

5.15 Suppose you are a software auditor in an independent product assurance organization. Suppose further that your responsibilities on a particular software project include verifying that mathematical computations being performed by software code are correct. Finally, suppose in a particular test the following situation exists:

A formula, currently unknown to you, is being used in software code to compute a quantity X *whose correctness you want to check. Call this (unknown) formula* F_{code} *so that*

$$X_{code} = F_{code} \ (input \ parameters)$$

where

X_{code} *is the value of* X *computed by the software code for a given set of input parameters.*

Now, suppose you have determined (e.g., from requirements documentation) that X *can be computed from two formulas,* F_{exact} *and* F_{approx}. F_{exact} *calculates exact values of* X, *but it may degrade overall system performance because of the computational burden it places on computer hardware.* F_{approx} *yields approximate values of* X *(*F_{approx} *is known to be a good approximation from, say, statements made in the requirements specification) and, in contrast to* F_{exact}, *does not degrade overall system performance.*

The following is a specific example of F_{exact} *and* F_{approx} *based on an actual application involving the calculation of the area* X *of a rectangle on the surface of the earth oriented between two parallels at latitudes LAT1 and LAT2 and stretching longitudinally WG radians:*

$$F_{exact} = R^2(WG)[sin(LAT2) - sin(LAT1)]$$
$$F_{approx} = R^2(WG)(WT)cos[(LAT2 + LAT1)/2]$$

where

R = *radius of the earth*
WT = LAT2 − LAT1 *(in radians)*

F_{approx}, *which assumes that the spherical rectangle can be replaced by a planar trapezoid, approximates* F_{exact} *very well if* LAT1 *and* LAT2 *are within a few degrees of one another.*

With the preceding as background, consider the following:
(a) To perform your verification task, which of the entities listed below are *necessary* for you to know? For each entity that you select, give at least one reason to justify your selection.
  1. X_{code}
  2. F_{code}
  3. X_{exact} (i.e., the [exact] value of X obtained from F_{exact})
  4. X_{approx} (i.e., the [approximate] value of X obtained from F_{approx})
  (*Hint:* Consider the pros and cons of the following argument: "My job is to determine that the quantity X_{code} agrees with the expected value of X. To simplify my job, I will ask the developer what formula F_{code} he is coding. With this formula, I will simply do a manual calculation to determine X which I will consider as my expected result that I will compare with X_{code} during testing.")
(b) Why consider using F_{approx} at all if F_{exact}, which yields an exact value for the quantity being tested, is available? (*Hint:* What is the meaning of "exact" in this case?)
(c) Suppose that F_{code} is not a coded version of F_{exact}. Is it legitimate for test verification purposes to compare X_{code} to X_{exact}? Is this comparison tantamount to comparing apples with oranges? Why (not)? (*Hint:* What is the acceptance tester's responsibility with regard to testing this code?)
(d) Suppose the requirements specification stipulated that the software system must calculate values of X to within a specified accuracy. Suppose further that the tester observes that actual values of X_{code} he obtains during a test differ from the expected values by more than the specified accuracy. Must the tester know (or ascertain) and report which value (actual or expected) is inaccurate? If your answer is "yes," explain how he determines which value is inaccurate. If your answer is "no," who do you feel should know or ascertain this information?
(e) Even if you indicated in (a) that it was not *necessary* to know F_{code} for test verification purposes, is there value for these purposes to know what F_{code} is? Why (not)? (*Hint:* Consider the case that $F_{code} = F_{approx}$.)

5.16 Suppose you are a manager of a software product assurance organization in a company that develops and maintains customer software systems that support military applications. Because of the nature of these applications, the software systems must operate continuously (twenty-four hours a day, seven days a week); when the software fails, the system must be restored as soon as possible. Suppose further that your boss, somewhat unhappy with previous performances of your testing staff, has made you responsible for preparing and executing tests for an upcoming new release of a currently operational message-processing system. More specifically, he has instructed you to devise a battery of tests that, in his own words, will "wring out" the new release. The overall objective of these tests, he informs you, is to feel reasonably confident that, at the successful completion of the tests, the software system can be released to the customer for installation at his site for operational use. After pondering your boss's guidance, you return to him with the list of categories of tests shown in Table E5.3 and the criteria shown below that define your interpretation of what "wringing out" the release means.

The system will operate in accordance with the operator's manual.

The system will operate continuously for at least several days before going down.

The system can, after going down, be returned to operation with delays of no more than several minutes.

The system will perform at least as responsively as it did during the release being replaced.

The system will not operate with a capability less than that provided in the release being replaced.

The system will not be missing parts.

After reviewing the above criteria and Table E5.3, your boss is impressed. He then informs you that you have a limited budget for testing. As a first step toward bringing your testing program in line with the budget, the boss asks you to prioritize the seventeen categories listed in Table E5.3 (the ultimate objective being to decide which categories can be shoehorned into the budget and which categories will have to be dropped). The basic guidance that your boss gives is that you are to perform this prioritization so that the categories at the top of the list (i.e., with highest priorities) are the most likely to satisfy the six confidence criteria given above. Perform this prioritization, and give at least one reason to justify each of the seventeen rankings you assign. (*Hint:* To get your thinking started, you may wish to read the article cited in Reference 9 of this chapter.)

5.17   A criticism sometimes leveled at the concept of independent product assurance is that it is good at raising questions but not good at supplying answers (to these and other questions). Consequently, it is frequently argued that product assurance offers no added value to a project. The questions product assurance raises may indeed be legitimate. However, if product assurance cannot provide answers to at least some of these questions, maybe it would be more cost-effective if there were no product assurance. Such questions, if they were significant, would, it is argued, be raised (and presumably answered) by the developers and/or management. With the preceding as background, consider the following:

(a) Would developers and management necessarily raise the same questions regarding software products that an independent product assurance organization would? Why (not)? In responding to this question, give examples of at least ten questions that you think might be asked about a software product. Indicate who (i.e., developers, managers, product assurance practitioners, or some

TABLE E5.3. TEST CATEGORIES FOR ACCEPTANCE TESTING
(EXERCISE 5.16)

1. Tests to demonstrate that the new capabilities resident in the new release work.

2. Tests to determine that selected old capabilities (i.e., capabilities that were part of previous releases) work.

3. "Operational tests" to determine the system's ability to operate in a representative operational environment. These tests are divided into the following two subcategories:

   a. Composite testing, whose purpose it is to show that the system correctly passes information between subsystems. In contrast to the capability demonstration tests in 1 and 2 above, which exercise the operator/system interface on a command-by-command basis, the composite tests follow various messages (which are not operator-initiated as opposed to commands, which are) through the entire system and show that they are processed correctly, that the appropriate subsystems are notified of their existence, and that the correct output is generated.

   b. Stress testing, whose purpose it is to show that the system is capable of handling large amounts of data in concert with considerable operator activity. In contrast to the capability demonstration tests discussed in 1 and 2 above (which, as indicated in *a* above, exercise the operator/system interface), the stress tests exercise the system with levels of input and activity beyond those expected to occur on site. If run for a period of several days, these tests can address the testing criterion of "feeling confident that the system will operate continuously for at least several days before going down."

4. Tests to determine the correct operation of the communications interface linking the system with the outside world.

5. Tests to determine the correct operation of system initialization procedures (for example, an assessment of the ability to generate an operational system of the correct configuration from dead start) and system utilities. These tests can address the testing criterion of "feeling confident that the system can, after going down, be returned to operation with delays of no more than several minutes."

6. Tests to determine system performance. These tests can address the testing criterion of "feeling confident that the system will perform at least as responsively as it did during the release being replaced" and the testing criterion of "feeling confident that the system will not operate with a capability less than that provided in the release being replaced."

7. Tests to determine the number of the software modules exercised during other categories of tests (which, among other things, indicate the presence of dead code).

8. Tests that examine the integrity of individual software subroutines and function subprograms including checks such as the following:

   a. Boundary value checks of subroutine and function subprogram arguments (e.g., checks to see what happens when values of the wrong type or magnitude are passed to a subroutine).

   b. Logic checks (e.g., checks to see if conditional statements execute

---

Continued

correctly and checks to see if error conditions are properly returned in the case of incorrect inputs).

(NOTE: It could be argued that tests such as those indicated above should be performed as a matter of course by the software developers. While this argument may hold in an ideal world, in the real world it should be recognized that most software developers generally do not prepare comprehensive so-called unit tests of their work. The product assurance organization should recognize this fact of life and at least spot-check the integrity of individual software modules.)

9. Tests that examine the integrity of two or more software subroutines and/or function subprograms working in concert with one another. Such integration tests check that subprograms are properly communicating with one another (e.g., passing values of arguments correctly). These tests represent a logical progression from the tests identified in 8 above. The idea would be to combine subprograms into progressively larger entities and perform tests at each point in the progression. (NOTE: It could be argued that such tests should be performed as a matter of course by the software developers. However, the product assurance organization should assume responsibility for at least some highly selective integration testing [particularly involving subroutines and function subprograms appearing for the first time in the release being tested]. It should also be noted that integration tests and tests identified in 8 above will require that the product assurance organization develop software code [i.e., driver programs and associated data that exercise the subprograms to be tested].)

10. Tests that check the system build process (i.e., the process by which the individual software subroutines are compiled and link edited into a system ready for operational use).

11. Tests that check the operating system supplied by the vendor of the hardware that hosts our software.

12. Tests that check the structure and content of the (relatively static) database against the database specification.

13. Tests that explicitly verify new (and old) capabilities with respect to detailed design documentation (from which software code is presumably produced).

14. Tests that verify whether incident reports (IRs) supposedly fixed in the new release and previous releases have indeed been fixed.

15. Tests that verify whether test incident reports (TIRs) supposedly fixed in the new release and previous releases have, indeed, been fixed (including verifying that TIRs acknowledged as unresolved in previous releases have indeed been resolved).

16. Tests that make the system fail and prescribe ways for returning the system to operation. These tests can address the testing criterion of "feeling confident that the system can, after going down, be returned to operation with delays of no more than several minutes."

17. Tests that indicate how long the system can stay up—so-called "reliability" tests (e.g., by installing the system at the customer site a week or so before scheduled delivery so that its operation can be monitored during this predelivery period).

combination of these three) is most likely to raise these questions, and give at least one reason to substantiate your selection of each question. An example of a question and its context might be the following (which is adapted from an actual software project):

On page 3 of the detailed requirements document, the following statements appear:

> *It is required to compute the area of a rectangular region anywhere on the surface of the earth to an accuracy of 0.1 square nautical mile. A "rectangle" is here defined to consist of an east side and a west side each oriented along a meridian and a north side and a south side each at a constant latitude.*
>
> *What model of the earth is the basis for the formula or computational scheme that is to be used to calculate the area of a rectangle to the accuracy specified? This model does not appear to be specified elsewhere in the requirements document. To provide explicit direction to the designers, and for subsequent maintainability purposes, this model should be specified.*

(b) List at least two reasons why it may not be desirable for an independent product assurance organization to answer questions that it asks regarding software products it audits.

(c) Listed below are situations similar to ones we encountered on software projects as members of independent product assurance organizations. Keeping in mind the preamble to this exercise and your responses to (a) and (b), indicate in a paragraph or two how you, as a member of an independent product assurance organization, might handle each situation.

1. You have reviewed the initial draft of a software product and found definitions of certain key terms either missing or ambiguously stated. Your technical background is such that you could easily supply the missing definitions and reword the ambiguous ones so that they are clear. (Does your response to this situation change if "initial draft" is replaced by "second draft," "third draft," . . . "draft *N*"?)

2. You have reviewed the third draft of a software product and found that it does not address key issues you raised in your review of the preceding two drafts. Furthermore, the third draft is more obscure than its predecessors. Sensing that development of this software product is not moving forward, you decide that extreme (but constructive) action is called for. You therefore decide to show the developer by a specific example how you think the product should be developed. How do you proceed? The following are types of actions you might consider:

   • Write a detailed annotated outline of your view of what the product should look like

   • Write one section or chapter with a cover memorandum that caveats this write-up with remarks such as "the enclosed write-up may not be technically accurate but is intended to present a detailed *model* of what Section X should look like."

3. You have examined a computational subroutine and deduced the formula that is coded in the subroutine. Other than the

subroutine listing, the justification and limitations of this formula are not documented. You proceed to determine the model and the approximations underlying this formula and in the process deduce its limitations. As a result, a number of trade-off issues occur to you, such as "Should this formula with its inaccuracies be replaced by a formula that performs an exact computation but at a cost of increased computation time?" How do you proceed? The following are types of actions that you might consider:

- Submit your derivation of the formula to the developer for incorporation into his documentation of the subroutine
- Submit your list of trade-off issues to the customer and/ or developer for analysis and resolution
- Both of the above

5.18 Suppose you have a software subroutine written in language X that you need to convert to language Y as part of an upgrade to a system that you are supporting. Assume the following regarding this subroutine:

1. Other than the listing of the subroutine and a few handwritten, obscure notes about what the subroutine does, no other documentation exists.
2. The programmer who developed the subroutine has long since departed, and no one else is available to explain to you the inner workings of the subroutine.
3. You are fluent in language Y but somewhat rusty in language X, which, however, is similar to language Y (such as FORTRAN and PL/1).
4. The subroutine takes in certain numerical values and through a formula and a table lookup consisting of several thousand entries returns a numerical value.
5. The formula that the subroutine uses is not documented, but with some effort on your part you could deduce it by reading the language X code.
6. The subroutine, although not used often, appears to have worked correctly for several years on the system that is in the process of being upgraded (you have gathered this information through some casual conversations with present and past users of the system—as best they can recall). You have been able to obtain a table of values that the language X version of the subroutine generated for a selected set of input values.
7. A specification document exists that defines the quantity that the language Y version of the subroutine is to determine.

Now, suppose you have succeeded in rewriting the subroutine in language Y and you are ready to test the rewritten code. Because you have many other things to do, you really cannot afford to spend too much time on this testing activity. Furthermore, as a result of this time constraint, you have been unable to decipher what formula the subroutine uses (your conversion effort from language X to language Y consisted primarily of replacing language X constructs with their counterparts in language Y and transcribing the table lookup values). You thus decide to test the converted subroutine by inputting the values mentioned in 6, above, and comparing them with the output values mentioned in 6. You perform this test, and the values generated by the language Y version agree with the values generated by the language X version. With the preceding as background, consider the following:

(a) What has the test you performed demonstrated regarding the language Y version of the subroutine and why?

(b) What should a test of the language Y version of the subroutine demonstrate and why?

(c) Even though you have neither the time nor the mathematical background to conduct additional tests, your professionalism compels you to turn for additional testing to an independent test organization supporting the system upgrade. List at least three things you would suggest that this organization do to test that the subroutine as converted satisfies its requirements as specified in the document referred to in 7 above and give at least one reason to justify each.

(d) In your opinion, is it really necessary to perform the additional tests alluded to in (c)? Why (not)? (*Hint:* In responding to these questions, do not think in theoretical or altruistic terms. Consider the real world of software development, where there is generally more work than can be accomplished by available resources, and where testing is often viewed as "something to be done if time permits" and as a questioning of a developer's competence.)

5.19 Suppose you are a member of an independent product assurance organization supporting a multiyear, multimillion-dollar software project with the following characteristics:

1. The software drives a system that must be operational around the clock.

2. If the software fails, military operations may be disrupted.

3. Every three to six months, enhancements and new capabilities are incorporated via software releases that replace the currently operational software.

4. Part of the software is a set of mathematical routines left over from a forerunner of the current system that was in operation over five years ago. Except for source code listings of these routines no documentation exists, and the developers of these routines have long since departed the scene. Consequently, there is no record of the formulas, assumptions, and limitations embodied in these routines. Furthermore, the developer of the current software has no maintenance responsibility regarding these routines and has been directed by the customer to use the routines as furnished (i.e., these routines constitute customer-furnished software). Finally, these routines supply numerical results to a broad range of capabilities in each new software release.

In conjunction with your auditing and testing activities over several software releases, your concern is rising that the software may be performing inconsistent and incorrect computations. You wish to take some action regarding this concern. You consider the following courses of action:

Talk with the developer to see whether he would be willing (if the customer will foot the bill) to analyze and document the mathematical routines described in 4 above.

Write a memorandum to your customer documenting your concern which includes your analysis of one of the mathematical routines, a description of how this routine is probably being improperly used in the current software release, and your conjecture that such improper use extends to other routines.

Document one or two of the routines and write a memorandum to your customer with this documentation attached. In the memorandum, you explain that the customer-furnished software routines need to be documented (either by the developer or by a customer organization) along the lines of the attached routines and give your reasons.

Meet with the customer, explain your concern, and recommend that he take immediate steps to have the customer-furnished routines documented.

Do nothing now, and wait until users of the system start complaining to your customer that the system does not appear to be generating correct numerical results.

With the preceding as background, consider the following:

(a) Which course of action listed above would you pursue (you may choose more than one) and why?

(b) Suppose characteristic 2, listed above, were replaced by the following:

If the software fails, nobody will be killed, injured, or suffer large financial loss.

Would you change your response to (a)? Why (not)?

(c) Would you change your response to (a) if characteristic 3 were replaced by the following?:

Every 9 to 18 months, enhancements and new capabilities are incorporated via software releases that replace the currently operational software.

(d) Would you change your response to (a) if characteristic 1 were replaced by the following?:

The software drives a system that must be operational eight hours a day, five days a week.

(e) Would you change your response to (a) if the substitutions of (b), (c), and (d) were all made?

5.20 A task often performed by an independent product assurance organization is the monitoring of the testing activities of the development organization. On many software projects, the development organization is responsible for performing unit and integration testing of the software code under development as a prelude to acceptance testing (typically performed by the product assurance organization). Given this testing scenario, and given the concept of software product assurance portrayed by the balance in Figure 3.11, how do you think an independent product assurance organization should perform "monitoring of the testing activities of the development organization"? In particular, consider the alternatives listed below and indicate the strengths and weaknesses of each. Discuss these strengths and weaknesses from the perspectives of the customer, the development organization, and the product assurance organization.

Test Monitoring Alternatives

1. Observing the development organization execute tests and documenting the observations

2. Reviewing the development organization's test plans, procedures, and results, and documenting the findings of this review
3. Doing both 1 and 2
4. None of the above (For this alternative, describe and analyze a process that differs from 1, 2, and 3.)

5.21 Assume that you comprise the entire product assurance organization assigned to System PREDICT (discussed in Section 5.2).
(a) Using the format given in Table 5.7, write a complete audit report on the System PREDICT Preliminary Design Specification (shown in Figure 5.9). Assume that the System PREDICT Requirements Specification (see Figure 5.8) has been baselined as the Requirements Baseline. Assume further that an appropriate documentation standard has been specified for the project.
(b) Write a test procedure for conducting T&E of the code for System PREDICT. Postulate actual test results that might be obtained if the test procedure were executed. Report the hypothetical test results.

5.22 In Figure 5.18, we described an acceptance testing cycle based on an alternating sequence of development/resolution periods and testing periods. Consider the alternative scheme described in the next paragraph, which the authors have seen work successfully. This alternative is characterized by having the development/resolution periods and test periods run concurrently.

In this scheme, the development group uses the computer system on one shift, and the test group uses the computer system on a second shift. A brief CCB meeting is generally held every day between the two shifts. Incident reports arising from testing are presented at the CCB meeting daily (each of these meetings is the equivalent of the Test Incident CCB meeting shown in Figure 5.18). Changed software code is released only periodically, however, say, weekly or biweekly (each of these meetings is the equivalent of the Software Turnover CCB meeting shown in Figure 5.18). Otherwise, the testing cycle remains the same as that shown in Figure 5.18.

With the preceding as background, consider the following questions:
(a) What would be two advantages and two disadvantages of this concurrent testing/resolution cycle?
(b) What is the greatest risk to the project of using this concurrent testing/resolution cycle? Why?
(c) What product assurance process can reduce this risk? How? (*Hint*: Consider what needs to be done to ensure test repeatability both from the perspective of the development organization and of the product assurance organization.)

5.23 The test plan for System SHAPES lists two tests (CD.1 and CD.2) to be executed to test the circle-drawing capability of the system (see Figure 5.16). A portion of a test procedure for Test CD.1 is given in Figure 5.17. Using Figure 5.17 as a guide, write the companion to test procedure CD.1, namely test procedure CD.2, to verify error diagnostics. Use the five-column format introduced in Figure 5.13.

5.24 An automobile with a manual transmission owned by one of the authors is equipped with an on-board microcomputer that helps the driver achieve, in the words of the automobile's owner's manual, "the best fuel economy at any acceleration." Ten times a second the computer samples the following four variables: engine speed, car speed, accelerator position, and "how hard [the engine] is working." At the point when better fuel economy could be obtained by upshifting, the microcomputer switches on a lamp on the instrument panel. This computer is part of the standard package provided by the manufacturer (i.e., it did not cost additional money). After driving the car awhile, when the lamp suggested shifting at unexpected points the owner began to wonder if there were any bugs in the software and if the (unknown) fuel economization algorithm really worked.

With the preceding as background, consider the following questions:

(a) Is this function of economical upshifting testable by the seller? By the user? If your answer to either question is "yes," write an appropriate test procedure(s) to show that the microcomputer function satisfies the stated capability. If your answer is "no," state why it is not testable. (*Hint:* Recall the sample problem on requirements testability in Section 5.1.)

(b) Suppose the manufacturer wished to charge for this feature— after all, it could considerably reduce the car owner's fuel expenditures. If you considered the feature to be untestable by the user, how might the seller use product assurance to help convince the user to buy this feature?

5.25 Conduct your own audit of the System PREDICT Preliminary Design Specification (shown in Figure 5.9) against the System PREDICT Requirements Specification (Figure 5.8). Document your findings. Then consider the following questions:

(a) Did you find any discrepancies beyond those documented in our audit findings shown in Figure 5.10? If so, describe the discrepancies.

(b) Do you take exception to any discrepancies that we reported in Figure 5.10? If so, why?

(c) Do your answers to (a) and (b) suggest that, despite our arguments to the contrary, auditing is not primarily an objective exercise in comparison? Why (not)?

(d) Do your answers to (a) and (b) suggest that more than one auditor should audit a given software product under certain circumstances? If so, list at least three circumstances where multiple audits of a software product may be not only useful but also necessary. If you believe there are no circumstances that might justify multiple audits of a software product, give at least three reasons to support your position.

5.26 In the introduction to this chapter, we mentioned that an audit of revolutionary changes may consist of a comparison of a CR to a requirements specification to ascertain which requirements are affected by the CR. Because of its straightforward nature, we indicated there that we would not discuss this aspect of auditing in the text. The intent of this exercise is to pursue this aspect of auditing. For this purpose, recall Figure 4.9, which contains the System MEAL PLANNER Requirements Specification discussed in connection with the sample problem in Section 4.2; recall also the completed CR in Figure 4.24, which calls for an enhancement to System MEAL PLANNER. Compare this CR to the requirements specification in Figure 4.9. Which requirements in this document might be affected by this CR? How would you report to a CCB your findings resulting from this comparison? Should you also compare this CR to the System MEAL PLANNER Preliminary Software Design Specification shown in Figure 4.10? If so, how would you report to a CCB your findings resulting from this comparison? If not, why not?

5.27 In the introduction to this chapter, we mentioned that an audit of revolutionary changes may consist of an archive check to determine whether a CR or an IR that is submitted to a CCB duplicates a previously submitted CR or IR. Because of its straightforward nature, we indicated there that we would not discuss this aspect of auditing in the text. The intent of this exercise is to pursue this aspect of auditing. For this purpose, consider the following:

(a) Suppose a CR is submitted that calls for a new capability for a currently operational system called System ABC. Suppose further that all System ABC CRs and IRs are stored on a word-processing system that has the capability to do a search through its database of CRs and IRs to locate key words and phrases defined by the searcher. Recalling the CR and IR forms shown in Figure 4.21 and 4.19 respectively, describe how you would use this word-processing system to determine whether the CR submitted is already being addressed by previously submitted CRs and/or IRs. Describe generally how you would report the results of such an archive search to a System ABC CCB.

(b) Repeat (a) for an IR that is submitted.

REFERENCES AND ADDITIONAL READINGS

1. Beizer, B. *Software System Testing and Quality Assurance*. New York: Van Nostrand Reinhold Company, 1984.

    We cited this book in Chapter 3 (Reference 1) because chapters 1, 2, and 10 are pertinent to the ideas presented in our Chapter 3. We include it in this chapter because its chapters 3–9 are pertinent to the ideas presented in Section 5.3, which deals with the mechanics of testing.

2. Bryan, W. L., S. G. Siegel, and G. L. Whiteleather. "Auditing Throughout the Software Life Cycle." *Computer*, vol. 15, no. 3 (March 1982), pp. 57–67.

    This article contains forerunners of many concepts and ideas appearing in this chapter.

3. Deutsch, M. S. *Software Verification and Validation: Realistic Project Approaches*. Englewood Cliffs, N.J.: Prentice-Hall, 1982.

    This book complements and extends many of the concepts discussed in this chapter. It encompasses the auditing of software products that are not computer code and the auditing of software products that are computer code. The book also addresses the subject of independence of the auditing organization from the development organization. In particular, chapter 11 deals with the topic of an independent test organization, while chapter 13 deals with the topic of an independent V&V contractor (a contractor who is not part of either the customer organization or the software development organization).

4. Evans, M. W. *Productive Software Test Management*. New York: John Wiley & Sons, 1984.

This book (a companion to Evans et al., *Principles of Productive Software Management*, Reference 4, Chapter 2) examines the subject of software testing from the management perspective rather than from the technical, "how-to-do-it" perspective of most books on the subject. The book's preface states its purpose and scope:

> This book guides the software manager through the software testing morass. The book will identify the individual components and test levels that must be integrated into a cohesive structure, and outline how the testing program is to be planned and managed. It will identify tools, techniques, and methodologies that must be incorporated if testing is to succeed (p. v).

Evans' book thus complements our discussion of testing and management of the testing cycle in Section 5.3. His rationale for writing the book is that there is a testing crisis in the software industry—namely, that many software project managers do not adequately plan for testing because testing is typically done toward the end of the project, and thus, in their concern for dealing with short-term milestones, they often forget the milestones farther down the road that also must be reached if success is to be achieved (we return to this point in Section 7.2). The author sets the stage for his discussion of the testing crisis (and his subsequent discussion of how to deal with the crisis) by telling the following story:

> The software manager glumly walks into the conference room to face the assembled staff of supervisors and senior technical personnel. The state of the group is universal fatigue and clearly evident general depression—brought about by overwork and frustration. As the manager faces the group, their eyes turn to him for guidance. What has happened? Despite all the work and staff commitment, the system that has been so laboriously developed through the sacrifices of so many has failed because of an inability on the part of the project team to integrate the various software components into an operational configuration and to demonstrate its functional integrity. The money has been spent, the schedule has been exhausted, and the project is far from complete. People working on the project are at the breaking point. Everyone in the room asks the same questions: What happened? What could we have done differently? Where do we go from here? (p. 1).

Our experience confirms the depressing tale related above—software projects in which software testing was poorly planned or in which testing was introduced as an afterthought were not successful.

5. Hetzel, W. *The Complete Guide to Software Testing*. Wellesley, Mass.: QED® Information Sciences, 1984.

Explaining the purpose and orientation of his book, the author states:

> The quality of systems developed and maintained in most organizations is poorly understood and below standard. This

book explains how software can be tested effectively and how to manage that effort within a project or organization. It demonstrates that good testing practices are the key to controlling and improving software quality and explains how to develop and implement a balanced testing program to achieve significant quality improvements (p. vii).

The scope of this book extends beyond the exercising of computer code. For example, it includes chapters on testing requirements and on testing design (which address "testing" techniques that can be used before code is developed as well as after code is developed), and thus supplements the ideas in our Chapter 5. The quotation above shows that the author stresses the relationship between software testing and achieving software quality. He defines quality software as software that meets requirements (p. 7). Consequently, the author's approach to testing is consistent with our approach to auditing—namely, the use of visible and traceable means to obtain an answer to the wizard's question posed in Figure 2.8. In addition to chapters devoted to the mechanics of testing, the author concludes the book with four chapters devoted to the management of the testing function.

6. Joyce, K. J. "The Art of Space Software." *Datamation*, vol. 31, no. 22 (November 15, 1985), pp. 30–34.

This article recounts in nontechnical terms some of the software problems that NASA's space shuttle program encountered and some of the product assurance practices that were used to reduce the likelihood of bugs finding their way into software code. The article provides interesting insight into product assurance issues on large software projects where software failure could mean the loss of human life in view of literally a worldwide audience. Of particular relevance to this chapter is the discussion of the eight levels of testing of flight software used by NASA so that the software can be labeled as "man-rated," that is, the operation of the software code is reliable to the extent that a person's life can depend on it. (Although the January 1986 space shuttle disaster which killed seven astronauts was not the result of a software failure, one of the recommendations in the report issued by the Presidential Commission formed to reduce the risks of future space shuttle flights was that NASA should establish an Office of Safety, Reliability, and Quality Assurance; see the excerpt from this report given in Exercise 3.10.)

7. Juris, R. "EDP Auditing Lessens Risk Exposure." *Computer Decisions*, vol. 18, no. 15 (July 15, 1986), pp. 36–42.

This article discusses how EDP auditing applied during software development can help protect against disaster when the computer code becomes operational. The concept of EDP auditing described in this article is allied with, but distinct in certain ways from, the concept of software auditing discussed in this chapter and elsewhere in this book. It is allied with this concept in the sense that, in the words of the article, "because . . . [EDP] auditors don't design system specifications or write code, they have enough distance to be able to ask questions that perhaps no one else on the development team would ask" (p. 38). The concept of EDP auditing is distinct from our concept of software auditing with respect to what is used for the ground truth and with respect to focus. In our concept of software auditing as set forth in this chapter, the ground truth is dynamic, beginning with the requirements specification and standards and evolving to successor software products (recall Figure 5.7). Any element of this ground truth (e.g., the requirements specification) can be changed by the CCB during any stage in the life cycle as we discussed in Chapter 4 (recall Figure 4.6). In EDP auditing, on the other hand, the ground truth is essentially static, being derived from industry standards for operational control (e.g., controls for maintaining database integrity such as limiting database updating to authorized users), security (e.g., limiting access to certain kinds of information such as company personnel salaries), and accountability (e.g., maintaining a trace of transactions processed). Requirements specifications and other software products are compared to these standards by the EDP auditors, and where a product (including the requirements specification) differs from industry standards, the product is considered discrepant. With respect to focus, our concept of software auditing is concerned with the satisfaction of the software requirements set forth in the requirements specification. EDP auditing, on the other hand, focuses on reducing or eliminating the risks to which an application can expose an organization rather than focusing on the functional requirements that the application presumably embodies. Of course, if such risks are not incorporated into the requirements specification, our concept of software auditing does not consider such risks as part of the auditor's ground truth. However, the software auditor should consider such risk issues in his audit of the requirements specification and document them in Section 5 and/or Section 6 of his audit report—recall Table 5.7. Such risk issues may then be addressed by the CCB, and changes to reduce the risks may subsequently be incorporated into the requirements specification through a CCB-approved amendment to this specification as indicated in Figure 4.6.

To illustrate the potential value of EDP auditing, the article discusses an incident involving a major bank where industry standards for control, security, and accountability were apparently inadequate or lacking in the bank's operational software. As a result, during one business day when the number of bank transactions significantly exceeded the number that had ever been previously encountered during one day, the software (through a design flaw) failed and caused the bank to lose about $5 million in interest in one night! In Section 7.1, we discuss this particular bank incident from the point of view of the product assurance concepts set forth in this book.

8. Parnas, D. L., and D. M. Weiss. "Active Design Reviews: Principles and Practices." *Proceedings of the 8th International Conference on Software Engineering*, Imperial College, London, August 28–30, 1985. Washington, D.C.: IEEE Computer Society Press, 1985 (IEEE Catalog No. 85CH2139-4), pp. 132–135.

This article presents some ideas on the subject of auditing software designs that complement some of the ideas presented in this chapter and in our Chapter 4. The following words from the article's abstract (p. 132) describe its purpose and content:

This paper describes an improved technique, based on the following ideas, for reviewing [software] designs.
1. The efforts of each reviewer should be focused on those aspects of the design that suit his experience and expertise.

2. The characteristics of the reviewers needed should be explicitly specified before reviewers are selected.
3. Reviewers should be asked to make positive assertions about the design rather than simply allowed to point out defects.
4. The designers pose questions to the reviewer, rather than vice versa. These questions are posed on a set of questionnaires that requires careful study of some aspect of the design.
5. Interactions between designers and reviewers occur in small meetings involving 2–4 people rather than meetings of large groups.

The above list shows that the article deals with some alternative mechanisms to our audit/CCB approach for reviewing and changing software products.

9. Petschenik, N. H. "Practical Priorities in System Testing." *IEEE Software*, vol. 2, no. 5 (September 1985), pp. 18–23.

This article addresses the frequent question "How much testing is needed to have a reasonable degree of confidence that a software system is ready for operational use?" Noting that, for large software systems in particular, "'thorough testing' can pass the limits of practicality" (p. 18), the article describes a test case selection methodology successfully used to maintain an actual system (a large database application). In particular, the article (p. 21) presents the following three priority rules that provide criteria for selecting some test cases over others so that the selected test cases answer the question posed above:

Rule A: Testing the system's capabilities is more important than testing its components.

Rule B: Testing old capabilities is more important than testing new capabilities.

Rule C: Testing typical situations is more important than testing boundary value cases.

The article discusses the rationale for these rules and provides insight into the practical aspects of software system testing. As such, it complements our discussion of software acceptance testing in this chapter.

10. Suydam, W. E., Jr. "Need for Software Testing Moves into Spotlight." *Computer Design*, vol. 24, no. 15 (November 1, 1985), PennWell Publishing Company, Advanced Technology Group, pp. 54–62.

This article gives a nontechnical overview of software testing techniques, their purpose, and their advantages and disadvantages, complementing our discussion in Section 5.3. It also contains some interesting observations on the way testing is viewed in the software industry, the cost-benefits of testing, and the extent to which software testing can be automated. On the way testing is viewed in the software industry, the article states:

Many software developers still treat software testing more as a black art than as a science. For such firms, software testing is an impromptu affair that's often viewed as an obstacle to shipping the software rather than an intrinsic part of software development (p. 54).

Reinforcing a point we make several times in this book, the article continues: "But for software testing to be most efficient and effective, it should be planned from the beginning of a project" (p. 54). On the cost-benefits of testing, the article quotes E. F. Miller, an authority on software testing, and states the following, which reflects some of the ideas presented in this chapter:

"Programmers do a pretty good job of debugging, but they do a lousy job of testing," says Dr. Edward F. Miller, . . . a vendor of software-testing tools and services. The distinction between testing and debugging is important for understanding why so many software bugs exist.

Testing detects and defines defects in a program, usually by a comparison of actual input and output of the program with the expected results for a given set of inputs. Debugging simply removes the detected defects. . . .

[Miller] does provide statistics to back up his claim [about programmers doing a lousy job of testing]. According to Miller, typical software contains an average of 50 defects per 1000 lines of code. He claims that proper testing and debugging can reduce that defect rate to about 0.5 defects per 1000 lines—a hundredfold reduction. "The cost of that testing," he says, "is about 30 to 40 percent above normal production costs, in exchange for which the software developer knows that thoroughly tested software is going out the door." In contrast, Miller places the cost of shipping inadequately tested software at 200 times the cost of preventive testing and repair, not including the attendant bad publicity when defective software goes awry (p. 62).

Miller then offers some quantitative support for our "pay-now-versus-pay-much-more-later" assertion regarding the efficacy of product assurance. On the extent to which testing can be automated, the article, quoting the author of a commercial automated testing tool, concludes with the following analogy:

[The automated test tool author] compares programs for automated testing to recipes. Imagine a cooking school where cakes are tested automatically. "The machines could tell you whether you included proper amounts of the various ingredients in a cake. That tells you whether you've properly followed the recipe." But the recipe itself is under test.

"You can surely automate analysis in that form, . . . but you can never have anything automated tell you whether the result tastes good to people. So, I don't think you can ultimately automate testing." In software testing, as in cooking, the proof of the pudding is still in the taste (p. 63).

In terms of the ideas presented in Section 5.3, we observe that an effective way to determine objectively the taste of a software product is through independent test of software code using written procedures based on stated customer requirements, followed by CCB evaluation of the test incidents resulting from test execution.

chapter **6**

BOOKKEEPING

In Chapter 4, we took the life cycle game board that we introduced in Chapter 2 (recall Figure 2.7) and described the basic elements needed to visibly and traceably process evolutionary and revolutionary software changes throughout a project's march around this game board. We have seen how the configuration control board (CCB) acts as the project lens that focuses the activities of three sets of disciplines—management, development, and product assurance (recall Figure 2.13)—in the search for an answer to the wizard's question to the king in Figure 2.8, "What is it you really want?" In Chapter 5, we delved deeper into the technical aspects involved with answering this question. There we described the basic auditing processes used to compare software products against one another. The purpose of these comparisons, we emphasized, is to determine whether the products are being developed logically and whether they embody what the king (customer) asked for. Figure 6.1 summarizes these fundamental notions from Chapters 4 and 5.

In Section 4.4, we discussed the forms needed to give visibility to and establish a trace of events pertaining to software changes. In Sections 5.2 and 5.3, we discussed techniques for documenting audit findings. In this chapter, we take an in-depth look at these and other bookkeeping issues. Our purpose is to describe the bookkeeping required to support the CCB and auditing activities discussed in Chapters 4 and 5. (Recall Figure 3.10, which shows how the change control and auditing processes feed data into the bookkeeping function.) Without this bookkeeping, the software life cycle game depicted in Figure 6.1 cannot be played with a reasonable expectation of winning (i.e., of developing software products with integrity). As we illustrate in Figure 6.2, this bookkeeping effects synergism between the change control process and the auditing process. This synergism serves to link and coordinate the activities of the management, development, and product assurance organizations throughout the march around the life cycle game board in pursuit of an answer to the wizard's question.

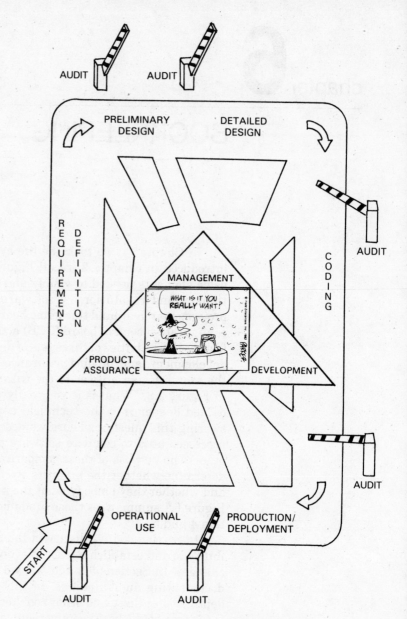

FIGURE 6.1. Marching around the software development game board—the pursuit of an answer to the wizard's question. Cartoon by B. Parker and J. Hart, *The Wizard of ID*, September 30, 1983. Reprinted by permission of Johnny Hart and North America Syndicate, Inc.

In Figure 6.2, when a software product is created or updated it is audited and an audit report is produced (recall Figure 5.1). This audit report is archived by the bookkeeping function and then submitted to the CCB. Following the CCB meeting, a set of meeting minutes is produced (we discuss the subject of CCB meeting minutes in Section 6.2). These minutes may contain actions that could require changing the software product. Thus, we can see from the figure that bookkeeping is a bridge between these change control and audit processes, providing them with visibility and traceability. (Note in the figure that the box labeled "Bookkeeping" shows only two important events out of all the events recorded by the bookkeep-

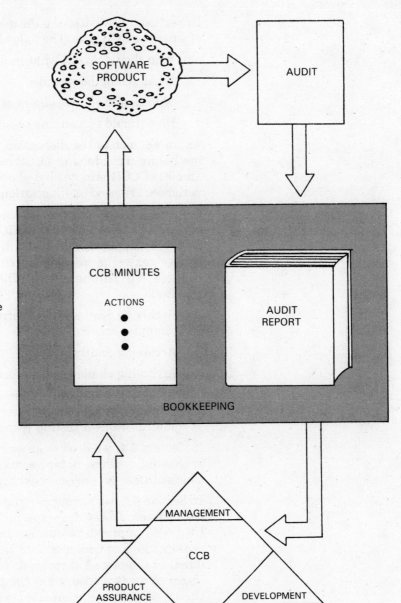

FIGURE 6.2. Bookkeeping effects synergism between the change control process and the auditing process.

ing function. This chapter is concerned with bookkeeping for all recorded events.)

Our approach in this chapter is as follows:

In Section 6.1, we discuss how to identify software parts. The following topics are addressed:

How identification raises the visibility of the development process and enhances its traceability

How to label software parts

How to record and disseminate software labels

Principles of software part identification

In Section 6.2, we describe the mechanics of keeping track of what the CCB does. The following topics are addressed:

Who should record what goes on?

What should be recorded?

Who should receive copies of what is recorded?

How should corrections be made to what is recorded?

As an adjunct to the discussion of the above topics, the mechanics of conducting a CCB meeting are described. Examples of CCB minutes based on the authors' project experiences are used as illustrations.

In Section 6.3, we describe the mechanics of keeping track of project activities other than CCB meetings. The models for this description are the evolutionary and revolutionary change control processes discussed in Section 4.2 (recall Figures 4.5 through 4.7). The following topics are addressed:

Archiving draft and final software products (including computer code)

Archiving audit reports

Archiving change control forms

Archiving project plans, procedures (e.g., test documents), and memoranda (e.g., a charter delineating joint user/buyer testing responsibilities)

In Section 6.4, we discuss automated aids (such as word-processing systems, database management systems) that can facilitate the project bookkeeping task.

In Section 6.5, we summarize the main ideas presented in the chapter. To set the stage for the discussion given in Chapter 7 of product assurance in the real world, we also recount the key concepts (and their relationships) introduced in Chapters 1 through 6. These concepts define the *theory* of product assurance. Chapter 7 portrays how this theory needs to be modulated when applied in the real world of limited resources, tight schedules, and customers who change their minds.

6.1 Identifying Software Parts

The identification of software parts is an essential task within the bookkeeping function of product assurance. To understand why identification is so essential, recall Figure 2.10. That figure shows two views of a software product—a monolithic view and a view of the product divided into identified parts. Perhaps you recall (from Section 2.5) the difficulty of describing the change that occurred in part (a) of Figure 2.10. Suppose the members of a CCB were discussing that change and that as a result of that discussion several modifications to the change were proposed and approved. It is highly unlikely that the members of the CCB would have a consistent view of the change under discussion or of the modifications made to it.

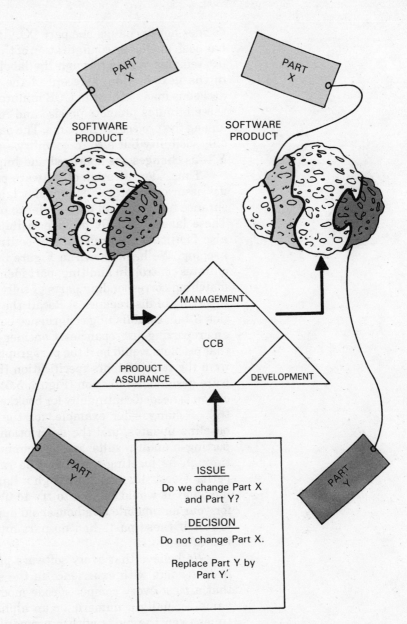

FIGURE 6.3. Identification
is needed to achieve
consistent communication
among software project
participants.

Within the figure:

PART X

PART X

SOFTWARE PRODUCT

SOFTWARE PRODUCT

MANAGEMENT

CCB

PRODUCT ASSURANCE

DEVELOPMENT

PART Y

PART Y

ISSUE
Do we change Part X
and Part Y?

DECISION
Do not change Part X.

Replace Part Y by
Part Y′.

Without having a software product with identified parts, communication about that product or changes to it is severely hampered.

Contrast the foregoing situation to that shown in Figure 6.3. In this figure, the CCB is considering whether to change two parts of a software product. The two parts at issue are clearly delineated and identified with attached labels.[1] The CCB has visibility into those parts of the software product for which a change has been proposed. In this case, the CCB approves the replacement of one part (Y) by another (Y′) and

[1] Recall from Section 2.5 our definition of software configuration—a relative arrangement of software parts. To be meaningful, a specific configuration must have its parts identified (recall Figure 2.11). Thus, in Figure 6.3 we have only partially shown the configuration of both software products.

decides not to change one part (X). After the approved change has been made, the configuration of the modified software product remains visible through the labels on its parts. As shown in the next section, a record of the issue discussed and the decisions made is kept in CCB minutes. The part identifiers in these minutes promote precise and consistent communication among the project participants. The part identifiers provide not only visibility but also traceability—e.g., from Part Y to Part Y'—as changes are approved and implemented.

Thus, identification of software parts is essential to product assurance because it provides labels that the product assurance functions can use to refer to particular software parts. These labels not only provide visibility and traceability but also facilitate the functions of control, auditing, and bookkeeping. We have shown in Figure 6.3 how identification facilitates control. In auditing, part identification is essential for matching corresponding parts of software products and in the reporting of discrepancies. Recall the sample problem in Section 5.1 on establishing congruence between software products and reporting discrepancies. Consider how much more difficult that problem would be if the paragraph numbers were removed from the requirements specification (Figure 5.4) and the software design specification (Figure 5.5). Software part identification is needed continually for bookkeeping related to the control of change—for example, for the recording of baselines, baseline updates, and the description of changes; for the reporting of audit results; and for communicating CCB decisions through its meeting minutes. The rationale for this need is perhaps best illustrated through a hardware analogue. Imagine what it would be like to try to obtain replacement parts for your automobile or a household appliance such as a refrigerator if these parts had no part numbers or other unique identifiers.

We believe that every software product should be identified. Readers with experience in the software industry know that almost every computer code module is identified with a name—usually a numeric or an alphanumeric label. (Sometimes even the parts within a module are identified—with statement numbers, paragraph names, or code labels.) But other software products, i.e., software documents, are generally only assigned an identifier for the document as a whole. The parts within a document are not usually identified as software. For the reasons given at the beginning of this section, identification should be extended to the software parts comprising the document. When the software parts within a document are not identified, the result is similar to the situation shown in Figure 2.10(a).

We already discussed in Section 4.2 the point at which a software product is identified. Recall from Figure 4.4 that the first step in the review process of a software product is to freeze the product, i.e., put it under control. To do this properly, it is necessary to identify the product—that is, assign labels to the product and all the software parts within it. Thus, identification is the first task of the freezing function in the review of a software product.

In this section we have mentioned the concept of *identification* without defining or exemplifying it. The act of identifying a software product consists of assigning a unique label to the product as a whole and to each software part[2] within the product, and then recording and disseminating those label assignments, so that the label/software part relationship is communicated to all project participants.

There are a number of ways to assign a label to a software part. One simple method is to assign sequential numbers to software parts—when each software part in a product is first recognized, it is assigned the next sequential number in some project- or organization-specified series. The same number should be used for a given software part throughout the life cycle. A software part that is described (in increasing detail) in a number of documents should be assigned the same number in each document. For this reason, the auditor of a document may also perform the task of identifying it. When the auditor establishes congruence between a software product and a predecessor product (recall Figure 5.3), he can give the software parts in the new product the same labels that their corresponding parts have in the predecessor product. This sequential method of labeling parts is commonly used for labeling hardware parts (recall Figure 2.11). The sequential method is also generally used to label change control forms, such as IRs and CRs. Note that this method provides no information about the configuration of the software product, that is, the relative arrangement of its parts.

A method that, in addition to providing a label for each software part, also provides information on the configuration of the software product is described in detail and well illustrated in chapter 4 of Reference 2 listed at the end of this chapter. In this method, each software part is assigned an acronym "SCI" (meaning "software configuration item") followed by a multilevel index. Each level of index represents a parent-child relationship. For example, a software part labeled $SCI_{1,2,3}$ is the third child of the second child of a parent (generally, SCI_1 represents the software system as a whole). This method is well suited for software developed in a top-down fashion, i.e., software that is tree-structured. However, it does need some modification for software that is not tree-structured.

---

[2] Recall from the discussion in Section 2.5 that determining what constitutes a software part is a subjective exercise. Sometimes, the CCB may stipulate how a software product is to be subdivided into software parts. In other instances, particularly on Department of Defense projects, software parts (at least at a gross level) are specified in a contract before the project begins (such a contract may specify, for example, that the seller is to deliver ten computer software configuration items [CSCIs]).

Yet another method, intermediate between the sequential numbering and the hierarchical numbering methods described above, uses paragraph numbers to label software parts. This method makes use of the fact that many specification documents (particularly those produced for the federal government) are subdivided into hierarchically numbered paragraphs. The number of each paragraph containing software can be used as a label for that software. Even though paragraphs in these documents are numbered hierarchically, the software labels do not necessarily indicate a relative arrangement of parts. For example, part 4.6.2 is not necessarily the second child of part 4.6 (paragraph 4.6.1 may not discuss software), nor is part 4.5 necessarily the fifth child of part 4 (paragraphs 4.1, 4.3, and 4.4 may not discuss software).

Although we stated earlier in this section that the software parts within a document are not usually identified, software documentation is commonly subdivided into numbered paragraphs, and such subdivision incidentally labels the software parts. Because not every paragraph contains a software part, the identification function here need only designate which paragraphs contain software parts—the labels have already been assigned. A disadvantage of this method is that the same software part appearing in several documents cannot be assigned the same part number.

The second part of the act of identifying a software product, after each software part has been assigned a label, is to record and disseminate the label assignments. The label assignments can be recorded in three ways, as shown in Figure 6.4—on the software product itself, in a list, or in a tree diagram. Recording the labels directly on the software product as shown in part (a) of Figure 6.4 solves the dissemination problem—whoever views the product views the identified software parts for that specific product. For documents, the labels may be handwritten in a margin of a master copy or, preferably, typed in the document text. Of course, if the paragraph number is used as a label, the software product is already labeled. In this case, the only identification task is to mark which paragraphs represent software parts, say, by inserting an asterisk in front of the paragraph number.

Computer code is more difficult to label than documents. Identification labels are often inserted into source code. Since the source code is readable by humans through terminals and listings, the identification of a software part can be readily determined. However, other forms of computer code, such as object code, executable code, and code executing on hardware, are not readable by humans. Although labels can be placed in such code, it is generally not possible to read them. One technique for making labels readable in code is to insert source code in each software part that generates a message on a display terminal (e.g., "SOFTWARE PART 1,2,3,5 IS NOW EX-

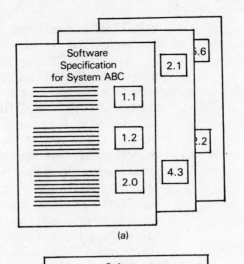

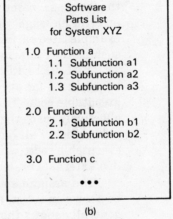

FIGURE 6.4. Three techniques for identifying software parts: (a) placing labels in the software product next to the parts, (b) creating a separate list of software parts, (c) creating a treelike diagram showing the parts and their hierarchical relationships.

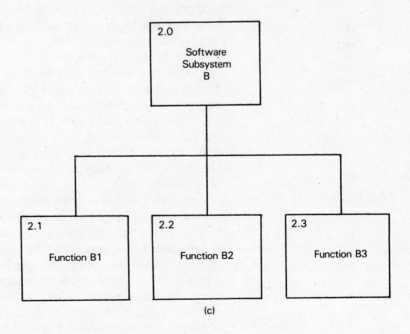

ECUTING") whenever the software part is executed. This technique effectively labels executing code.

Another technique for labeling code not readable by humans is to place in each module of the source code a label disguised as the name of a nonexistent module (for example, a statement such as EXTERNAL REFERENCE SCI123 might be inserted in the source code of one module; here the name SCI123 takes on the appearance of another module called SCI123 which does not exist). This disguised label will be included in the object code (which is unreadable by humans) created from the source code. Utility software, often referred to as a "linking loader," creates executable code from object code for a number of software parts. For each object code module, this linking loader attempts to locate a software part having the disguised label as a name. Since a software part having the label as a name does not exist, the linking loader produces an error message which includes the identification label (in the example cited earlier using the name SCI123, an error message such as the following might be produced: UNSATISFIED EXTERNAL REFERENCE SCI123). Such an error message will be produced for every object code module being placed in the executable code. This technique accomplishes two purposes: it effectively reads the label in an object code module, and it provides a list of all modules (i.e., software parts) included in the executable code (which is indeed executable since the unsatisfied externals are never called).

The assignment of labels to a software product may also be shown in a list, such as in part (b) of Figure 6.4. This list generally shows the label and the name of each software part in the product. The list is often indented to indicate hierarchy. When the parts list is thus indented, a relationship of the parts is implied. Consequently, such a parts list documents the configuration of the software.

The third technique for recording label assignments is in a tree diagram—see part (c) of Figure 6.4. The nodes in the tree (each node is represented as a box in the figure) represent the software parts. Each node is marked with the label and the name of a software part. The branches of the tree (the lines connecting the nodes) represent relationships between software parts. Thus, this method also records the software configuration.

To illustrate these three methods of recording label assignments, the following sample problem is provided. The problem is based upon the functional requirements specification for the Automated Doughnut-Making System introduced in Section 5.1 and uses the paragraph numbering method of assigning labels. (The sample problem focuses on methods of recording label assignments and is not concerned with how something is determined to be a software part. The reader interested in this subject should consider Exercise 6.16.)

IDENTIFICATION OF
AUTOMATED
DOUGHNUT-MAKING
SYSTEM—A SAMPLE
PROBLEM
Background and Problem

Figure 5.4 depicted the functional requirements specification for the programmable subsystem of the Automated Doughnut-Making System (ADMS). Using paragraph numbers as labels, identify the software parts in the functional requirements specification, recording the labels (1) in the software product, (2) in a list, and (3) in a tree, as shown in Figure 6.4.

Because we are using paragraph numbers as labels, the functional requirements specification is already labeled. However, we must determine what subdivisions of the specification represent software. By looking at the subdivisions in Figure 5.4 and comparing their contents to the definition of software given in Figure 2.1, it is determined that paragraphs 2.0b, 3.0, 3.1, 3.2 (and all its subparagraphs), and 3.3 all represent some part of the software subsystem of ADMS.

To record the labels in the functional requirements specification (see Figure 6.4(a)), we mark each such paragraph and subparagraph with an asterisk to indicate that it is a software part. The resultant identified specification is shown in Figure 6.5.

The software parts list corresponding to Figure 6.4(b) for the ADMS Programmable Subsystem is shown in Figure 6.6. The list is created by arranging the software parts in hierarchical order and assigning their paragraph numbers as labels. The names of the software parts are included with the labels for the parts. The software names are indented to indicate the relative arrangement of the software parts, i.e., the software configuration. Observe that this method of reporting label assignments is easily maintained using a word processor.

Figure 6.7 shows how the configuration of the ADMS Software Subsystem might be depicted in the form of a tree (see Figure 6.4(c)). Each box contains the part label and a brief name for the part. The lines connecting the boxes show the relationship between the boxes. In Figure 6.7 this relationship is one of inclusion, i.e., part 3.0 includes parts 3.1, 3.2, and 3.3. Because of its freedom and flexibility in graphic layout, the tree form of recording label assignments shows the software configuration (i.e., the relative arrangement of software parts) better than either of the other two methods. However, the tree must be redrawn every time any part of the tree is changed. This task is relatively simple if a graphics terminal is available; otherwise, performed manually, the task can be extremely time-consuming for diagrams of even moderate complexity (e.g., for trees containing four or five levels of hierarchy). (Note from Figure 6.5 that the same software part is described in paragraphs 2.0b and 3.0—thus, the redundant reference to paragraph 2.0b is omitted in Figures 6.6 and 6.7.)

This sample problem shows that each technique for recording label assignments has advantages and disadvantages. Which to use on a specific project depends on factors such as

---

Version 1.2
August 14, 1990

Functional Requirements Specification for
Programmable Subsystem of
Automated Doughnut-Making System

1.0 Introduction

This document specifies the functions to be performed by the programmable subsystem of the Automated Doughnut-Making System (ADMS). This document is the basis for all software to be developed for ADMS.

2.0 System Overview

ADMS consists of the following two subsystems:

a.   Hardware Subsystem (requirements separately documented)

*b.   Software (Programmable) Subsystem

*3.0 Software Subsystem Functions

The Software Subsystem shall perform the functions listed in the subparagraphs below.

*3.1 Input Processing Function

This function shall drive all hardware components that receive doughnut ingredients.

*3.2 Recipe Processing Function

This function shall process ingredients to produce doughnuts in accordance with recipes keyed in from a keyboard. The following set of primitive keyboard instructions shall be accommodated:

*3.2.1   Add. Add the ingredients specified to the bowl.

*3.2.2   Mix. Mix the ingredients in the bowl at the speed and for the time specified.

*3.2.3   Roll. Roll out the mixture on the cutting board.

*3.2.4   Cut. Cut out the dough for either regular (with hole) or filled doughnuts.

*3.2.5   Bake. Bake the doughnuts for the time and at the oven temperature specified.

*3.2.6 Fill. Fill doughnuts with ingredient specified.

*3.2.7 Dust. Dust doughnuts with ingredient specified.

*3.3 Output Processing Function

This function shall drive all hardware components that package the baked doughnuts.

* = software part

FIGURE 6.5. Identified functional requirements specification for Programmable Subsystem of Automated Doughnut-Making System.

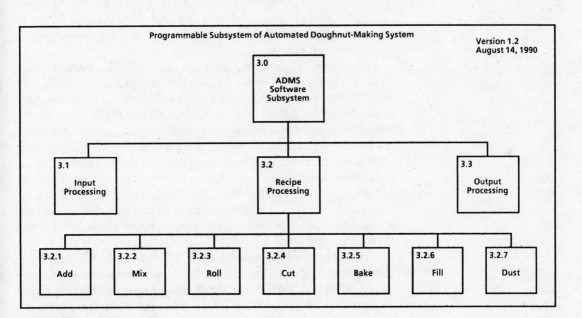

Version 1.2
August 14, 1990

Software Parts List for
Programmable Subsystem of
Automated Doughnut-Making System

3.0	ADMS Software Subsystem
3.1	Input Processing
3.2	Recipe Processing
3.2.1	Add
3.2.2	Mix
3.2.3	Roll
3.2.4	Cut
3.2.5	Bake
3.2.6	Fill
3.2.7	Dust
3.3	Output Processing

FIGURE 6.6. Example of identification in the form of a parts list for Automated Doughnut-Making System Software Subsystem.

FIGURE 6.7. Example of identification in the form of a tree for Automated Doughnut-Making System Software Subsystem.

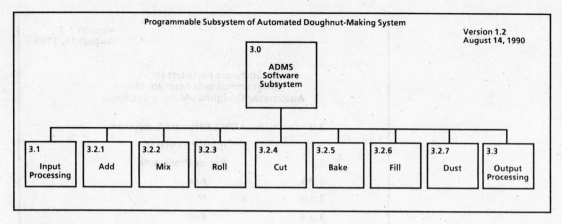

FIGURE 6.8. An alternative identification of Automated Doughnut-Making System Software Subsystem.

the software tools available, the project participants, the magnitude of the project, and frequently the personal preferences of the project manager.

We want to stress that configuration identification[3] is a subjective activity. The identification shown in Figures 6.5, 6.6, and 6.7 is not the only one possible. The programmable subsystem of the Automated Doughnut-Making System (ADMS) could also be identified as shown in Figure 6.8. Figures 6.7 and 6.8 represent two different but equivalent ways of viewing the same software entity.

How were Figures 6.7 and 6.8 derived? The person who created Figure 6.7 decided to identify the parts in ADMS by using functional decomposition. The relationship that he used to partition the software was "is included in." He first determined that input processing, recipe processing, and output processing are the three functions included in ADMS. (He might have stopped identifying at this point, if the resultant four-node tree were sufficient for his purposes in identifying ADMS.) Then he decided that the functions of add, mix, roll, cut, bake, fill, and dust are included in the function of recipe processing. He thus created the eleven-node, three-level tree shown in Figure 6.7.

The person who created Figure 6.8 approached his task of identifying ADMS by listing the functional requirements contained in the ADMS Functional Requirements Specification (Figure 6.5). The relationship he used to partition the software was "is a function of." After analyzing Figure 6.5, he decided that input processing, add, mix, roll, cut, bake, fill, dust, and output processing are functions of ADMS. He thus created the ten-node, two-level tree shown in Figure 6.8.

[3] *Configuration identification* is a more inclusive term than *software identification*. The latter term refers to the assignment of labels to software parts. The former term is concerned not only with the assignment of labels to software parts, but also with the relative arrangement of those parts. (Recall the definition of software configuration in Section 2.5.)

It is thus clear that partitioning a software product into parts is primarily a subjective exercise. A software product does not have a unique configuration or set of software parts. (The subjectivity of software identification is further explored in Exercise 6.9 at the end of this chapter.) The important principle here is to create *some* partition of every software product, to disseminate it to all project participants, and to keep it current as the software product changes throughout the project life cycle. This identification provides a vocabulary for communication among project personnel and for facilitating the functions of control, audit, and bookkeeping. (For example, in CCB discussions the CCB members can use software part labels rather than lengthier and possibly ambiguous titles or descriptions, and in audit reports the source of a discrepancy can be clearly related to a software part by using its label.)

Because identification is a subjective exercise, one organization should perform all labeling on a product throughout the project life cycle. Having a single organization perform identification provides greater consistency in labeling from product to product. Also, with this approach, labeling of a product can be more easily related to the labeling of predecessor products, which in turn improves traceability from product to product (see Exercise 6.10). Generally, the product assurance organization should identify software products as they are frozen at the beginning of the review process. Note, however, that if paragraph numbers are used for labeling on a project, the development organization actually assigns labels as it creates a software product. In this instance, the product assurance organization still performs identification by determining which paragraphs contain software and are included in the identified configuration (for example, as in Figure 6.5, by adding asterisks in front of paragraphs identified as software parts). (See Exercise 6.16 for issues pertaining to how something is determined to be a software part and how to determine the number of part identifiers to associate with information in the document that is software.)

In this section, we looked at the need for and purpose of identifying software parts. We explored who should do the identification and what, how, and when to identify. In the next section, we show the application of identification as we discuss another important bookkeeping function—creating and maintaining minutes of CCB meetings.

6.2 Keeping Track of CCB Meeting Results

We introduced the configuration control board (CCB) in Chapter 4 and described how it injected visibility and traceability into the process of controlling evolutionary and revolutionary change. In Chapter 5, we elaborated on the role played by the CCB in evolutionary change as it considered the results of audits and tests. Thus far, we have only briefly mentioned one other important facet of CCB operation—the production

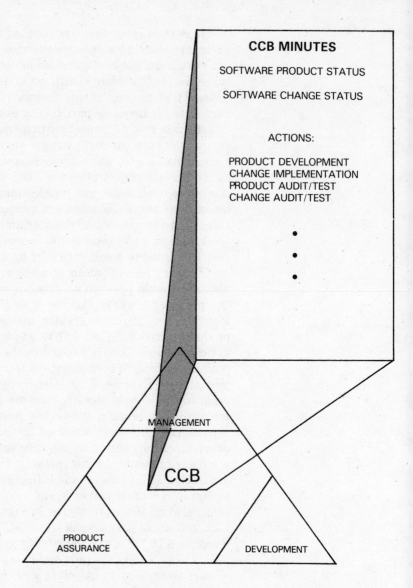

CCB MINUTES

SOFTWARE PRODUCT STATUS

SOFTWARE CHANGE STATUS

ACTIONS:

PRODUCT DEVELOPMENT
CHANGE IMPLEMENTATION
PRODUCT AUDIT/TEST
CHANGE AUDIT/TEST

•
•
•

MANAGEMENT

CCB

PRODUCT
ASSURANCE

DEVELOPMENT

FIGURE 6.9. CCB minutes give visibility into CCB proceedings.

and maintenance of formal minutes for every CCB meeting. In this section, we discuss and illustrate this important bookkeeping task in detail.

To some, the recording and publication of minutes for a meeting is an unnecessary formalism instituted by a pretentious manager. But this is to miss the point completely. The minutes of a CCB meeting are essential to provide an accurate, precise, and thus visible account of the proceedings of the CCB, both for the CCB members and for other project participants. Figure 6.9 illustrates this point—the minutes provide a recorded view into what was said and decided at a CCB meeting. The minutes record the status of software products and changes and each action decided upon. For each action, responsibility is assigned and a schedule for its accomplishment is established. The series of CCB meeting minutes forms a trace of the functioning of the CCB over the project life cycle.

Have you ever left a meeting feeling that you understood what had been decided at the meeting, only to discover in a later discussion with a colleague that his understanding differed from yours? Have you ever known a meeting decision to be overlooked and forgotten because it was not written down? If you are a senior manager, have you ever wondered whether a project under your cognizance was progressing satisfactorily? These situations can all be corrected by publication of meeting minutes. To convince you further of the benefit of publishing CCB meeting minutes, we provide you with the following story, which is an adaptation from an actual project.

LACK OF VISIBILITY OF PROJECT MEETINGS—A STORY

Paul Little, the seller's project manager on Project PQR, was familiar with CCBs but did not believe in their value. He authorized the leader of his development group, Peter Anderson, to make changes in computer code (deviating from the design specifications) as Peter saw fit. Paul met frequently with the user/buyer; usually he was the only person from the seller's company present. No record of any of the meetings with the customer was ever made.

Near the beginning of Project PQR, a lengthy meeting between the user/buyer and seller was held (at the user/buyer's request) to ensure that the requirements for the project were clearly understood. The requirements review meeting was attended by most of the seller's project staff and by a number of users. During the meeting, a question was raised about the laconically stated requirement that "all data entries shall be fully validated."[4] A user stated that the Project PQR system was to perform all the data entry validation checks performed by the existing system (which Project PQR was replacing), plus several new and more complex data validation checks that were urgently needed. Unfortunately, the current system was not well documented and no list of the current data validation checks existed. The user agreed to "dig out" from current com-

---

[4] Validation of data entries entails checking every data entry to ensure that the values entered for a data element are allowable. For example, for the entry of all-numeric calendar dates, the following data validation checks might be performed:

For month, the value must be greater than or equal to 01 and less than or equal to 12. For day of month,

   For month = 01, 03, 05, 07, 08, 10, or 12, the value must be greater than or equal to 01 and less than or equal to 31.

   For month = 04, 06, 09, or 11, the value must be greater than or equal to 01 and less than or equal to 30.

   For month = 02,

      For year divisible evenly by 4, value must be greater than or equal to 01 and less than or equal to 29.

      For year not divisible evenly by 4, value must be greater than or equal to 01 and less than or equal to 28.

puter source code all the current data validation checks and to inform the seller what these checks were. No minutes were kept of this meeting on user needs.

A week later, the user orally presented to Peter (the seller's development group leader) a number of data entry validation checks for the current system. Peter noted these items, but did not see fit to publish the list or to keep any written record of his meeting with the user. He followed up the meeting by assigning data validation checks to appropriate development group members. A month later, he suddenly resigned from the company to accept an opportunity with another company.

Mary Rose, head of the seller's test team (who was not present at the requirements review meeting), was unable to obtain a list of the data validation checks to be performed by the Project PQR system. In frustration, she designed tests to ascertain that the system performed data validation checks that seemed reasonable to her. (Unfortunately, what her tests ascertained fell far short of the user's needs in this area.)

On the day before the Project PQR system was to be demonstrated to the user prior to delivery, Paul told his (new) development group leader, Sally Vines, that at his meeting with the user that morning the user said he was anxiously awaiting demonstration tomorrow of one of the new, complex data validation checks (first introduced at the requirements review meeting). Sally was surprised. She told Paul that she had never heard of the requirement and certainly had not programmed it. Paul was aghast. He told Sally that two months before, at one of his meetings with the user, the user had asked if that specific capability would be in the delivered system. Paul had confidently told the user that the desired capability would be in the first delivery of software code.

Frantically, Sally and her group set about to add the missing capability in the few hours still left. Regrettably, they did not succeed in getting the new capability to work properly at the next morning's demonstration. In fact, at the demonstration it soon became evident that their frantic efforts had caused several other previously checked-out data validation checks to work improperly. Concerned by the improper performance of the system, the user requested additional demonstration of all the data entry validation checks he needed. This demonstration revealed that none of the new capabilities had been coded and that a number of capabilities used by the current system had been omitted. The user was greatly upset and refused to accept the software. With much chagrin, the seller's project team went back to work and a few months later delivered to the user a software system that the user found acceptable. Paul, the project manager, had departed one month earlier to seek employment elsewhere. □

In our story, it turned out that no one remembered the data entry validation checks introduced at the requirements review meeting. Everyone assumed that the list of validation checks the user gave Peter contained *all* the checks that the user desired. Since the list of validation checks that the user gave to Peter was never written down, but rather was passed along orally, some checks got lost in the oral transfers. The abrupt departure of Peter caused loss of the only information the seller had about data entry validation checks to be incorporated in the new system. All the above problems could have been avoided if minutes of each meeting[5] had been recorded and published. The developers would have had visibility into what to develop. The testers would have had visibility into what to test. The user would have had visibility into what he would be receiving in his completed system. The departure of the development group leader would not have had an impact on this visibility. The production of minutes here would have saved considerable time and money for the project.

We now turn our attention to the mechanics of keeping track of what the CCB does. Let us consider first who should record the minutes of a CCB meeting. Some people consider taking minutes to be a purely clerical job and would use a person trained in secretarial skills (e.g., shorthand) for this task. Such a person would generally not be involved in the discussion within the CCB and therefore could devote full attention to keeping the minutes. A CCB secretary with shorthand skills could produce a verbatim transcript of a CCB meeting if required. On the negative side, a person with secretarial skills generally is not technically cognizant of the CCB discussion and therefore might not know when CCB decisions had been reached.

Another possible CCB secretary would be a member of the development staff responsible for implementing CCB-approved changes. Such a person would be most knowledgeable on the software and possible changes to it, i.e., in understanding what the CCB discusses and decides. However, that very understanding would probably involve him in the subjects under discussion and distract him from his secretarial duties. Further, his organizational allegiance may bias his recording (for example, a CCB agreement that a change would be implemented by a certain date might be recorded as an agreement that the developers would *attempt* to implement the change by that date).

A member of the product assurance organization could serve as CCB secretary. He certainly would be technically cognizant of the CCB discussions and decisions. He may well get involved in the CCB discussion, but his involvement is usually focused on the CCB reaching a decision rather than on the decision itself. Since the product assurance practitioner is not

---

[5] We consider these meetings to be meetings of a CCB even though they were not so labeled. The rationale for this viewpoint is that each of these meetings dealt primarily with evolutionary and revolutionary changes to the Project PQR system.

involved in implementing software changes, he is likely to have a dispassionate viewpoint of the proceedings. This neutral viewpoint should be reflected in his recording of the minutes. Indeed, in our experience, the secretary of the CCB has most often been someone from the product assurance organization.

What should be recorded in the CCB minutes? The most fundamental items to record are the results of discussions of agenda items, action assignments, and decisions of the CCB. These items could be quite wide-ranging (depending upon the CCB charter for a project). However, the most important subjects relative to its change control responsibilities are software products and software changes. The status of each item discussed and the action taken on each must be recorded in the minutes. Other subjects that should be recorded include the results of audits and of tests, the establishment of baselines, and the implementation of software products and changes. At the end of the minutes, a summary of actions to be taken is included, with responsibility for action and due date explicitly stated. A suggested format for CCB minutes is presented in Table 6.1. Rationale for including some of the items shown in Table 6.1 follows:

An identifier and date—to give visibility to the minutes and to make them traceable

A list of attendees and their organizational affiliation—to record who participated in the decision-making

A list of organizations not represented at the meeting—to record whose viewpoints were *not* considered in the decision-making

The status of the minutes of the preceding meeting, including any necessary corrections—to assure that the trace of CCB minutes is correct and accurate

The time and place of the next meeting—to give visibility to the schedule for the next meeting

A list of people receiving copies of the minutes—to inform each recipient who else has received the information contained in the minutes (and to expand project visibility outside the CCB meeting participants, if desired)

Recording the status of the minutes of the preceding meeting (the fourth item above) is particularly important for traceability purposes. The minutes should show that the preceding meeting minutes were correct as recorded or that they needed specific corrections and were approved as corrected.

A copy of the minutes should be distributed to every person who attends the meeting. Copies should also be sent to each member of the CCB who was not present at the meeting and to appropriate senior managers. These minutes let them know exactly what happened at the meeting. The presence of the

TABLE 6.1. FORMAT FOR CCB MINUTES

Memorandum	Date Identification Number

To: Distribution [see bottom]

From: [Typically, the memo is from the CCB secretary]

Subj: Minutes of System XYZ Configuration Control Board (CCB) Meeting

Ref: [Typically, the minutes from the preceding CCB meeting are cited here]

1.0 *[Date of Meeting]*

2.0 *[List of meeting attendees and their organizational affiliation]*

     2.1 [List of organizations not represented at the meeting who typically participate]

3.0 *CCB Actions*

The subparagraphs under this paragraph contain a record of what happened at the meeting to include things such as the following:

Approval of and changes, if any, to the minutes of the preceding CCB meeting (or meetings)

Presentation and/or disposition of IRs, SCNs, CRs, IAs, TIRs

Discussion of audit (including test) findings and decisions regarding how discrepancies are to be resolved

Presentation (or overview) of a candidate software baseline (i.e., a draft product such as a draft design specification in conjunction with a design review)

Turnover of computer code from the development organization to the product assurance organization for (acceptance) testing

Discussion of new issues (such as a new capability for which a CR has not yet been formulated).

4.0 *Action Items*

This paragraph lists the who/what/when resulting from the items addressed in paragraph 3.0 as assigned during the meeting, typically by the CCB chairman. This list becomes part of the agenda for subsequent CCB meetings. A typical format for this list is the following:

No.	Action Item	Action Agent	Due Date	Paragraph Reference
[Action item identifier]	[Brief description of action]	[Organization or individual responsible for the action]	[Date action is to be completed]	[Pointer to subparagraph in paragraph 3.0 that gives the context for the action]

5.0 *[Time and place of next CCB meeting]*

Distribution:

Listed here are the individuals or organizations that are to receive copies of the minutes. This list typically includes all individuals listed in paragraph 2.0 and management personnel who desire visibility into the status of System XYZ.

names of senior managers in the distribution list of the minutes contributes to the third aspect of visibility we presented in Section 2.2—making management visible to project participants.

Next, let us briefly consider the mechanics of a CCB meeting relative to the keeping of minutes. The first item of business at every CCB meeting is to consider the minutes of the preceding meeting. Any corrections desired are introduced, considered, and either approved or disapproved. If there are no corrections, the minutes are approved without correction. Otherwise, the minutes are approved as corrected.

As each item on the agenda is discussed and a decision is made, the CCB secretary records that decision. When the secretary is not sure what decision has been reached by the CCB, the secretary should stop the proceedings and ascertain precisely what was decided. At the end of the CCB meeting, the secretary should summarize the decisions made by the CCB and the actions to be taken.

To close out this section, we present and discuss minutes of four different types of CCBs. These minutes are based on the authors' project experiences, but they are adapted to relate to the projects used as examples earlier in the book. The minutes follow the format shown in Table 6.1. The four types of meetings are (1) a software CCB considering an evolutionary change (e.g., a proposed draft of a new baseline; see Figure 6.10); (2) a software CCB considering revolutionary changes (see Figure 6.11); (3) a Test Incident CCB (considering the results of an acceptance test; see Figure 6.12); and (4) a Software Turnover CCB (considering the results of resolving TIRs; see Figure 6.13).

Note from Figures 6.10 through 6.13 that all the CCBs have representatives from the user, the buyer, and the seller (recall Figure 4.13). For clarity, instead of using fictitious organizations in these figures, we indicate each person's organization by his affiliation (user, buyer, or seller) and group (management, development, or product assurance). We also indicate in brackets information as to position (e.g., manager, secretary, chairman) for some of the CCB members in order to show how these positions relate to the CCB. The bracketed information would not normally appear in CCB minutes.

Figure 6.10 shows the minutes of a CCB considering an evolutionary change, namely, CR 88-0019 to System MEAL PLANNER (see Figure 4.24). This change request had previously been approved by the CCB and, as indicated in the impact assessment (Figure 4.25) as one of the steps in implementing the change, the development organization has produced a draft of the revised version of the MEAL PLANNER Software Requirements Specification. One of the seller's developers presents an overview of this software product, followed by delivery of an audit report on the draft software product by a person from the buyer's product assurance group. The CCB considered

June 1, 1988
MPCCB - 88/8

To: Distribution

Thru: Mary White, MEAL PLANNER CCB Chairman

From: Jim Limerick, MEAL PLANNER CCB Secretary

Subj: Minutes of MEAL PLANNER Configuration Control Board (CCB) Meeting

Ref: (a) MEAL PLANNER CCB minutes MPCCB-88/7 dated May 25, 1988

1.0 Date of Meeting: May 31, 1988

2.0 Attendees:

Bill Blackburn	Seller/Development [manager]
Hugh Brown	Seller/Development
Jim Brownlee	Seller/Product Assurance [manager]
Tom Green	User/Management
Polly Lemonsky	Buyer/Development
Jim Limerick	Buyer/Product Assurance [secretary]
Ned Rosebud	Buyer/Development
Walt Silverstone	Seller/Product Assurance
Mary White	Buyer/Management [chairman]
Ann Whitemarsh	Seller/Management [project manager]
Stan Tanbrook	Buyer/Product Assurance

2.1 Organizations Not Represented: none.

3.0 CCB Actions:

3.1 Reference (a) was approved as published.

3.2 Action items from previous meetings resolved: none.

3.3 Hugh Brown presented an overview of Version 1.4 of MP-01, Software Requirements Specification for System MEAL PLANNER. This version is the result of applying CR 88-0019 to the previous version. CR 88-0019 added the capability to update the MEAL PLANNER database.

3.4 Stan Tanbrook presented an audit report documenting the results of auditing Version 1.4 of MP-01. After considering the audit report, the board made the following disposition of the audit report findings:

3.4.1 Findings 1, 3, 4, 5, 8, 10, 11, 14, 17, 19, and 20 had recommended resolutions proposed by the auditor or by a board member. These resolutions were approved by the board for implementation (i.e., revision of Version 1.4 of MP-01). These approved changes are identified as IR 88-0097.

3.4.2 Findings 6, 7, 9, 12, 15, and 16 require further analysis. IRs 88-0098, 88-0099, 88-0100, 88-0101, 88-0102, 88-0103, respectively, will be originated by the Seller/Product Assurance Group for these findings. The IRs are assigned to the Seller/Development Group for investigation and analysis.

Continued

FIGURE 6.10. Minutes of a software CCB meeting considering an evolutionary change.

3.4.3   Findings 2, 13, and 18 require no action be taken. After discussion, the board decided that these findings represented misunderstandings by the auditor and that no problems existed.

3.5   Ned Rosebud raised the issue as to whether the user had a need to delete foods from the database. (CR 88-0019 asked only for the capability to add foods to the database.) Tom Green, the originator of CR 88-0019, stated that, while he only asked specifically to add foods, he implied in the title of the CR ("...database update capability") that he also had a need for the capability to delete foods. The board moved to add this capability to Version 1.4 of MP-01, identifying this change as approved IR 88-0104.

3.6   The board took no action on baselining Version 1.4 of MP-01, pending the resolution of IRs 88-0098 through 88-0103, and the implementation of approved IRs 88-0097 and 88-0104.

4.0   Action Items:

No.	Action Item	Action Agent	Due Date	Paragraph Reference
88-212	Implement IR 88-0097	Seller/Development	July 1, 1988	3.4.1
88-213	Analyze IRs 88-0098 through 88-0103	Seller/Development	July 8, 1988	3.4.2
88-214	Implement IR 88-0104	Seller/Development	July 15, 1988	3.5
88-215	Baseline MEAL PLANNER Requirements Specification Version 1.4	MPCCB	July 16, 1988	3.6

5.0   Next Meeting: Tuesday, June 7, 1988, at 2:00 p.m. in the Main Conference Room.

Distribution:
All attendees
Tim Graystone [Buyer/General Manager]
Al Plumtree [Seller/President]

FIGURE 6.10. *(Continued)*

all the findings in the audit report. For eleven of these findings, the CCB felt no need for further analysis and approved them for implementation. These findings resulted in changes to be made to the software requirements specification. An incident report (IR 88-0097) was written to cover this set of approved changes, in order to give them visibility and accountability (i.e., to enable them to be tracked until implemented). The CCB decided that six of the audit report findings required further analysis before the CCB made a decision. Incident reports were originated for each of these findings (recall the alternative scenario in the bottom line of Figure 4.23 and the discussion of this alternative scenario in Section 4.4). The CCB decided that no action was required on three of the audit report findings. The auditor may have been unsure about whether discrepancies existed, and so gave the issues visibility by reporting them as findings. The broad representation on the CCB, with its range of viewpoints, was able to resolve these issues as not being discrepancies.

One of the buyers raised the issue of an apparent inconsistency, not previously observed, in change request CR 88-0019. The CCB decided that a capability desired by the user was missing from the software requirements specification and directed that it be added (identifying the change as IR 88-0104 for visibility and traceability). When reading paragraph 3.5 in Figure 6.10, you should recall the conversation between the wizard and the king in Figure 2.8.

In all the minutes shown in Figures 6.10 through 6.13, note that senior management of both the buyer and the seller is included in the distribution of the minutes. From these minutes, senior management gains visibility into the progress of the project.

CCB meetings generally are not held solely to discuss one type of change. For purposes of instruction, we prepared separate sample minutes for evolutionary and revolutionary changes; in general, however, a CCB would consider both types of change at the same meeting. The CCB minutes shown in Figure 6.11 are for a meeting considering only revolutionary changes.

In Figure 6.11, notice that a correction has been made to the minutes of the previous meeting (paragraph 3.1.1). Whether corrected or not, minutes of the previous meeting should always be approved by the CCB. Figure 6.11 shows (under paragraph 3.0) the handling of an action item from a previous meeting, the consideration of an emergency incident that occurred two days before, and the processing of four incident reports. Notice that all these items resulted in the generation of additional action items, which are summarized in paragraph 4.0. One of the IRs (IR 89-0012) is illustrated in Figure 4.26. This IR was approved, as shown in paragraph 3.4 of the minutes (Figure 6.11) and in the next-to-lowest section of the incident report (Figure 4.26). Since the action directed in Section 3.4 of the minutes (Figure 6.11) is to submit a software change notice, an SCN, such as in Figure 4.27, would be prepared and submitted by one of the seller development staff. Observe in paragraph 2.1 of Figure 6.11 that representatives of two groups normally present at the CCB meeting did not attend this one. In the distribution list at the end of the minutes, the names of the missing representatives are included so that they can be apprised of the meeting results.

The minutes shown in Figures 6.12 and 6.13 relate to consecutive CCB meetings that might occur during an acceptance testing cycle. Recall Figure 5.20, which shows the interaction of these two types of CCB meetings during the acceptance testing cycle. Section 5.3 discussed these CCB meetings and the contents of their minutes. Figure 6.12 is the minutes for a Test Incident CCB, and Figure 6.13 is the minutes for the subsequent Software Turnover CCB.

Recall that Figure 5.21 presented a completed test incident

To: Distribution

Thru: Bob Redman, MEAL PLANNER CCB Chairman

From: Jim Limerick, MEAL PLANNER CCB Secretary

Subj: Minutes of MEAL PLANNER Configuration Control Board (CCB) Meeting

Ref: (a)   MEAL PLANNER CCB minutes MPCCB - 89/5 dated February 7, 1989

1.0   Date of Meeting: February 13, 1989

2.0   Attendees:

Bill Blackburn	Seller/Development [manager]
John Blue	Seller/Development
Jim Brownlee	Seller/Product Assurance [manager]
Nancy Greenfield	Seller/Development
Jim Limerick	Buyer/Product Assurance [secretary]
Bob Redman	Buyer/Management [chairman]
Harriet Rose	Buyer/Product Assurance
Walt Silverstone	Seller/Product Assurance
Ann Whitemarsh	Seller/Management [project manager]

     2.1   Organizations Not Represented: Buyer/Development Group
                                                        User/Management

3.0   CCB Actions:

     3.1   Reference (a) was approved with the following modification:

           3.1.1   Paragraph 3.3: Add Nutrition, Ltd., to the list of sites to which Release 89-3 will be delivered.

     3.2   Action item from previous meeting was resolved as follows:

           3.2.1   Action item #89-0032, second installation of Release 89-3: Bill Blackburn stated that the installation of Release 89-3 at National Meals was completed with only a few minor problems. The installation notes remain the only item to be completed for the installation. Delivery of the installation notes will be carried as an action item for the Seller/Development Group; action due by March 15, 1989.

     3.3   Harriet Rose stated that an emergency incident had been reported by Diet Plus, Inc., two days ago. It was assigned control number IR 89-0015. The incident involved the calculation of the total calories in a meal. John Blue, with the concurrence of Ann Whitemarsh and Bob Redman, had sent a patch to Diet Plus, Inc., by wire, but did not test the patch. The board moved that the Seller/Product Assurance Group test the patch immediately, and that the Seller/Development Group determine a permanent fix by February 17.

Continued

FIGURE 6.11. Minutes of a
software CCB meeting
considering revolutionary
changes.

3.4 Recommended resolutions to the following IRs were presented to the board and the following decisions were made:

IR No.	Presenter	Disposition	Action	Action Agent	Due Date
89-0010	Nancy Greenfield	No action required	Notify originator	Seller/Product Assurance	890217
89-0012	John Blue	Approved	Submit SCN	Seller/Development	890218
89-0013	John Blue	Reinvestigate	Reanalyze IR	Seller/Development	890220
89-0014	Nancy Greenfield	Approved	Submit SCN	Seller/Development	890218

4.0 Action Items:

No.	Action Item	Action Agent	Due Date	Paragraph Reference
89-0046	Deliver installation notes to National Meals.	Seller/Development	890315	3.2.1
89-0047	Test patch for IR 89-0015	Seller/Product Assurance	890214	3.3
89-0048	Analyze IR 89-0015	Seller/Development	890217	3.3
89-0049	Notify originator of IR 89-0010 no action required.	Seller/Product Assurance	890217	3.4
89-0050	Submit SCNs for IRs 89-0012 and 89-0014	Seller/Development	890218	3.4
89-0051	Reanalyze IR 89-0013	Seller/Development	890220	3.4

5.0 Next Meeting: Tuesday, February 21, 1989, at 10:00 in the Main Conference Room.

Distribution:
All attendees
Tim Graystone [Buyer/General Manager]
Tom Green [User/Management]
Polly Lemonsky [Buyer/Development]
Al Plumtree [Seller/President]

FIGURE 6.11. (*Continued*)

report (TIR 90-1066). Figure 6.12 shows that the TIR 90-1066 was written in the testing period just prior to the Test Incident CCB, and Figure 6.13 shows that a code change was developed in response to TIR 90-1066 just prior to the Software Turnover CCB. This code change evidently resolved the test incident, since Figure 5.21 shows that the incident was resolved on the next retest of the software system. Against the background of the incident report processing flow shown in Figure 4.7, a traceability thread can be seen linking the minutes in Figure 6.12 (paragraph 3.4), the minutes in Figure 6.13 (paragraph 3.4), and the TIR in Figure 5.21 (from the dates on this form and on the two sets of minutes).

These sample minutes complete our discussion of the important bookkeeping task of keeping and publishing CCB minutes. In the next section, we discuss other project events that should be recorded.

```
                            MEMORANDUM                          November 13, 1990
                                                                SCCB - 90/40

To:     Distribution

Thru:   Sally Plum, SHAPES CCB Chairman

From:   Helen Gray, SHAPES CCB Secretary

Subj:   Minutes of SHAPES Configuration Control Board (CCB) Meeting

Ref:    (a) SHAPES CCB minutes SCCB - 90/39 dated November 5, 1990


1.0  Date of Meeting: November 12, 1990

2.0  Attendees:

        Jane Black           User/Management
        Bill Blackburn       Seller/Development [manager]
        Amy Blue             Buyer/Product Assurance
        Hugh Brown           Seller/Development
        Jim Brownlee         Buyer/Product Assurance [manager]
        Helen Gray           Seller/Product Assurance
        Nancy Greenfield     Seller/Development
        Jack Lemon           Seller/Development
        Sally Plum           Buyer/Management [CCB chairman]
        Peter Rose           Buyer/Product Assurance
        Ann Whitemarsh       Seller/Management [project manager]

     2.1   Organizations Not Represented: Buyer/Development Group

3.0  CCB Actions:

     3.1   Reference (a) was approved as published.

     3.2   Action items from previous meetings resolved: none.

     3.3   Release 90-3, Version 2.1 was turned over to the Seller/Development Group.

     3.4   Amy Blue [Buyer/Product Assurance test leader] presented to the board 105 TIRs (numbered 90-
           1006 through 90-1110). There was extensive discussion of TIRs 90-1024 through 90-1032, which
           describe problems related to the new menus defined in the SHAPES Detailed Design Specification.
           Bill Blackburn [Seller/Development manager] indicated that he would have his staff give particular
           attention to this set of problems.

     3.5   It was agreed that the Seller/Development Group would return the Release 90-3 software code to
           the Buyer/Product Assurance Group on November 19, 1990 for additional testing.

4.0      Action Items: none.

5.0      Next Meeting: Monday, November 19, 1990 at 3:00 p.m. in the Auxiliary Conference Room.

Distribution:
 All attendees
 Tim Graystone [Buyer/General Manager]
 Sue Pinkerton [Buyer/Development]
 Al Plumtree [Seller/President]
```

FIGURE 6.12. Minutes of a
Test Incident CCB meeting.

MEMORANDUM   November 20, 1990
                                                        SCCB - 90/41

To: Distribution

Thru: Sally Plum, SHAPES CCB Chairman

From: Helen Gray, SHAPES CCB Secretary

Subj: Minutes of SHAPES Configuration Control Board (CCB) Meeting

Ref: (a) SHAPES CCB minutes SCCB - 90/40 dated November 13, 1990

1.0 **Date of Meeting:** November 19, 1990

2.0 **Attendees:**

Jane Black	User/Management
Bill Blackburn	Seller/Development [manager]
Amy Blue	Buyer/Product Assurance
Hugh Brown	Seller/Development
Jim Brownlee	Buyer/Product Assurance [manager]
Helen Gray	Seller/Product Assurance
Nancy Greenfield	Seller/Development
Jack Lemon	Seller/Development
Sally Plum	Buyer/Management [CCB chairman]
Peter Rose	Buyer/Product Assurance
Ann Whitemarsh	Seller/Management [project manager]

2.1 **Organizations Not Represented:** Buyer/Development Group

3.0 **CCB Actions:**

3.1 Reference (a) was approved as published.

3.2 Action items from previous meetings resolved: none.

3.3 Release 90-3, Version 2.2 was turned over to the Buyer/Product Assurance Group.

3.4 Of the 105 TIRs turned over at the CCB meeting on November 12, 1990, 100 TIRs have been corrected via code changes (TIRs 90-1006 through 90-1085 and 90-1091 through 90-1110).

3.5 Bill Blackburn [Seller/Development manager] stated that TIR 90-1086 was the result of the improper operation of the system by the Buyer/Product Assurance Group and therefore no corrective action was required. Jim Brownlee [Buyer/Product Assurance manager] said that he would correct the pertinent test procedure to provide appropriate clarification to the testers.

Continued

FIGURE 6.13. Minutes of a
Software Turnover CCB
meeting.

3.6 Bill Blackburn submitted TIRs 90-1111 through 90-1130. He indicated that solutions and associated code had been developed for TIRs 90-1111, 90-1123, and 90-1127 through 90-1130. He also indicated that resolutions for the remaining new TIRs have not yet been developed. There was some discussion about TIR 90-1124, which Bill Blackburn felt may not really be a problem because the SHAPES Requirements Specification was vague in the area of concern. Bill Blackburn stated that he wrote TIR 90-1124 to obtain clarification on the matter. The board decided that the issue raised in TIR 90-1124 was indeed a problem.

3.7 It was agreed that the Buyer/Product Assurance Group would return Release 90-3, Version 2.2 to the Seller/Development Group on November 26, 1990.

4.0 Action Items: none.

5.0 Next Meeting: Monday, November 26, 1990, at 3:00 p.m. in the Auxiliary Conference Room.

Distribution:
  All attendees
  Tim Graystone [Buyer/General Manager]
  Sue Pinkerton [Buyer/Development]
  Al Plumtree [Seller/President]

FIGURE 6.13. (*Continued*)

6.3 Project Event Recording

Recall our definition of traceability from Section 2.3—"the thread that links one event to another." Traceability is one of the fundamental concepts of this book. The recording of project events is basic to establishing traceability. If project events are not recorded, a trace linking those events cannot be shown. Recall Figure 2.6, which defines traceability by illustrating some of the events involved in the change control process and the links between them. If one or more of the rectangles or the links between them were omitted, traceability would be destroyed (e.g., if Events n, o, and p were not recorded, it would not be evident how the missing piece in Event m had been added as shown in Event q).

Recording project events is therefore necessary to realize traceability. Which events to record (of the many occurring on a project) is a function of how much and what traceability is desired. A decision on how much traceability is needed on a project should be made early in project planning, keeping in mind that it costs money to record events. There must be a balance between the amount of data collected and the cost of collecting the data. If some events are unnecessarily recorded, money will be wasted. If too few events are recorded, traceability is reduced with the result that money will also be wasted (recall Figure 1.3).

Event recording is comprised of three parts—recording what happened (i.e., what is the event?), recording when it happened, and archiving the event product. By *event product*, we mean an entity produced during an event (such as CCB

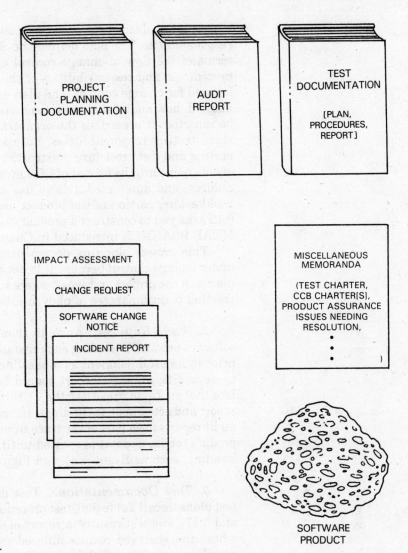

PROJECT
PLANNING
DOCUMENTATION

AUDIT
REPORT

TEST
DOCUMENTATION

[PLAN,
PROCEDURES,
REPORT]

IMPACT ASSESSMENT

CHANGE REQUEST

SOFTWARE CHANGE
NOTICE

INCIDENT REPORT

MISCELLANEOUS
MEMORANDA

(TEST CHARTER,
CCB CHARTER[S],
PRODUCT ASSURANCE
ISSUES NEEDING
RESOLUTION,
•
•
•
)

SOFTWARE
PRODUCT

FIGURE 6.14. In addition to CCB minutes, what by-products of evolutionary and revolutionary change should be archived? Some examples.

minutes as discussed in the preceding section). Figure 6.14 presents some other event products, which we describe in the following paragraphs.

EXAMPLES OF EVENT PRODUCTS

1. Project Planning Documentation. Project planning documentation includes project plans, system development plans, software development plans, and product assurance plans (or sometimes configuration management plans and quality assurance plans). Schedules for the project should also be included. We briefly discuss here the product assurance plan. The other project planning documentation is treated at length in Reference 3 listed at the end of this chapter and in other books on software project management.

A project product assurance plan serves as the basis for all product assurance within a project. It specifies the organizations involved in product assurance and delineates their responsibilities. The plan defines the change control process in terms of the flow of change control events, the composition, procedures, and responsibilities of the CCB, and the forms to be used for change control. The plan describes what should be audited, how audits should be conducted, and how they should be reported. It prescribes the organization for testing and assigns testing responsibilities. Formats for test incident reporting and test procedure construction are prescribed. Project events to record, the format of CCB minutes, identification procedures, and automated aids to use are all described in the bookkeeping portion of the product assurance plan. (Exercise 6.19 asks you to construct a product assurance plan for System MEAL PLANNER introduced in Chapter 4.)

This project planning documentation is not usually put under change control because it is not software. However, it is placed in the project archives,[6] where it generally serves as the starting point for traces of plan fulfillment.

2. Audit Reports. An audit should be conducted on each software product (including each update to a software product) prior to its establishment as a baseline. As a result of each of these audits, an audit report should be produced in a format like that in Table 5.7. After the CCB has considered the audit report and acted upon its findings, the report is archived. These audit reports form part of the trace from the time each software product (or its update) is created until its establishment as a baseline, such as Event n does in Figure 2.6.

3. Test Documentation. Test documentation includes test plans (recall Table 5.8), test procedures (recall Figures 5.13 and 5.17), and test results (a report of steps in test procedures where the observed results differed from expected results—recall the completed TIR form in Figure 5.21). These test documents link to each other, and to the requirements specification, to the design specification, to CCB meetings, and to TIRs (recall Figures 5.18, 5.20, and 5.21). Thus, it is possible to trace from any requirement to the test procedure that validates the requirement to the TIRs resulting from executing the test procedure, or to the test report that states that no TIRs were written in testing that requirement.

4. Change Control Forms. Change control forms—IRs (and TIRs), SCNs, CRs, and IAs, as we have chosen to exemplify

---

[6] By *archiving*, we mean the collecting and filing of project data into a repository for safekeeping and reporting of status. Data archived can be changed as specified by the approving authority for the particular product under consideration. By *controlling*, we mean the filing of project data into a repository for safekeeping, reporting of status, accountability, and maintenance of integrity. Data controlled can be changed only as specified by the CCB after successful completion of the change control process. By these definitions, archiving is a subset of controlling.

them—are an important part of the tracing of the change control process. The forms link with each other (e.g., an IR points to the corresponding SCN, and the SCN points to the IR[s] to which it relates; recall Figures 4.26 and 4.27), to software products from which they arise, and to CCB meetings at which they are considered. Some of these forms (e.g., IRs) contain a trace within them as the various parts of the form are filled out by people in different organizations (recall Figure 4.26). In addition to being archived, these multiple-entry forms are tracked as they pass from person to person. This tracking is usually performed by the product assurance organization, which periodically issues reports on the status of the change control process. If available, an automated tool (see discussion in Section 6.4) can easily track the change control forms and report on their status.

5. Software Products. The software products (whether code or documentation) and all updates to them are placed under formal change control. As we indicated in footnote 6, this form of recording event data is more stringent than archiving. Formal change control must be invoked for software because software is malleable and easily changed. If formal change control is not established, visibility of the software among all project participants is lost and the software development traceability thread is broken. Software products are traced from one stage to the next in the software life cycle, as the software evolves and matures in its journey from a requirements specification to operational software. They are also linked to CCB minutes, audit reports, project plans, test documentation, and change control forms.

6. Miscellaneous Memoranda. A miscellaneous category includes such items as test charters, CCB charters, and memoranda on product assurance issues.

A test charter might be drafted if the user and buyer jointly agreed to plan and conduct the acceptance tests for a software project (this joint testing is a worthwhile albeit rarely used procedure; see Exercise 6.11). For this joint endeavor, the functions, responsibilities, authority, and lines of communication of both parties must be clearly established. These items would be specified in a test charter, an example of which is outlined in Table 6.2.

The charter for a CCB comprised of only one organization (e.g., a seller CCB) would usually be promulgated in the project product assurance plan. However, for CCBs comprised of seller/buyer, seller/user, buyer/user, or seller/buyer/user personnel, it is preferable to draft a separate CCB charter delineating the responsibilities and authority of all parties, the membership, chairmanship, voting rules, and procedures to be followed by the board.

TABLE 6.2.   OUTLINE OF A JOINT USER/BUYER TEST CHARTER

	Date
Charter Title	Document Number

References.
The test charter is headed by a list of references pertinent to the software project. In general, these references include governing test plans and/or product assurance plans, project standards, and software specification documents (such as requirements and design specifications) from which code to be tested is developed.

1.0   *Purpose.*
Section 1 of the test charter indicates the user and buyer organizational elements whose testing responsibilities are to be delineated in subsequent sections of the charter. This section also gives background on the project, typically by pointing to one or more of the references listed above (e.g., a project product assurance or test plan). This background information provides the project context for the testing activity that the charter addresses.

2.0   *Scope.*
Section 2 of the test charter identifies the specific software releases encompassed by the charter. For example, a project may extend over several years with one or more software releases scheduled for each year. In this case, Section 2 specifies which of these releases are to be included within the scope of this charter, and which testing activities (e.g., integration testing, acceptance testing) are included.

3.0   *Organizational Element Testing Responsibilities.*
Section 3 defines the testing responsibilities for the organizational elements that are to be involved in the project testing activities. Each organizational element mentioned in Section 1 is addressed in a separate subsection. For example, if Organizational Element X is a user organization, then responsibilities delineated in Subsection 3.X might include items such as the following:

> Provide expertise in the user systems that are to be supported by the software to be tested
>
> Assist the buyer (which would be an organizational element whose responsibilities are delineated in another part of this section of the charter) in preparing test plans and test plan updates
>
> Define test procedures down to the individual steps to be performed to exercise system functions specified in the requirements specification (one of the references presumably listed in the charter's reference section)
>
> Perform testing using the procedures resulting from the preceding responsibility
>
> Assist the buyer in preparing reports documenting the results of tests performed.

If Organizational Element Y is a buyer product assurance organization, then responsibilities delineated in Subsection 3.Y might include items such as the following:

> Train user personnel in how to do software testing
>
> Write test plans with the assistance of user organizational elements
>
> Establish and maintain the technical test environment by creating and controlling test databases, test programs, and test program job streams, and by constructing procedures explaining how these items are to be created and maintained

Continued

TABLE 6.2. *(Continued)*

Charter Title	Date Document Number
Perform testing of the technical test environment	
Perform testing of selected software functions as a double-check on user-performed functional testing	
Prepare reports, with the assistance of user organizational elements, documenting the results of tests performed.	

The responsibilities delineated in this section for each organizational element may range from simple lists of one-line statements such as those shown above to multiple-paragraph elaborations for each of these one-line statements.

4.0 *Organization Chart.*
Section 4 depicts the relationship of the organizational elements whose responsibilities are delineated in Section 3 and the relationship of these elements to the overall project organization. This section indicates the testing chain of command and clarifies, for example, how test discrepancies included in test reports are to be resolved (i.e., where the buck is to stop so that computer code that does what it is supposed to do ultimately results).

The memoranda on product assurance issues that might be archived can be quite diverse. For example, such issues might include a discussion of what types of testing are required, are desired, and are feasible on a project (see Exercises 5.8 and 5.16); or a discussion of the validation of a model used in the project and the test data to validate it. These events trace forward to development events and backward to events that spawned them (e.g., an incident report or an audit report). □

Notice how the recording of the events and data shown in Figure 6.14 and of CCB minutes effects synergism between the change control and auditing functions (recall Figure 6.2). A visible trace is maintained from software products to audit reports to CCB minutes to IRs to more CCB minutes to SCNs. Bookkeeping, change control, and auditing are truly integrated into the software development process.

When are events recorded? The items in Figure 6.14 make it evident that this event recording occurs throughout the life cycle (including the review area) shown in Figure 2.7. Software products are developed in every stage of the life cycle (except for the Operational Use Stage). CCB meetings occur and minutes are taken in the review area, which is entered at least once in each stage of the life cycle. Incident reports and change requests may be originated at any point in the life cycle. Bookkeeping, particularly event recording, continues throughout the life cycle.

Within subprocesses of the life cycle (e.g., the change control process or the acceptance testing cycle in the review area), a number of events are recorded. Recall Figure 4.5, which shows the change control process for an evolutionary change, namely, the submission of a draft preliminary design specifi-

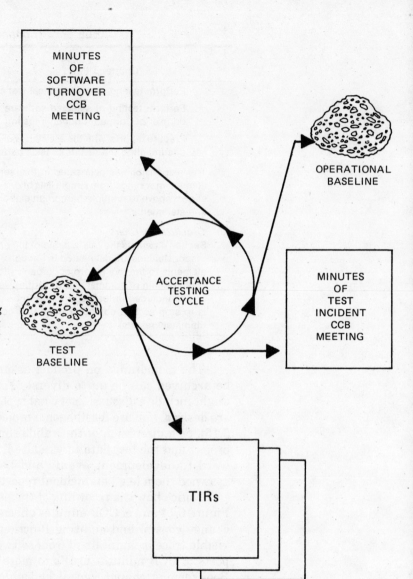

FIGURE 6.15. Bookkeeping during the acceptance testing cycle.

cation. Some of the events that should be recorded in the archive for this project are shown in that figure. The reader should be able to identify other events that should be recorded during this particular change control process (see Exercise 6.12).

Let us consider the events to be recorded during an acceptance testing cycle, such as shown in Figure 5.20. The events generally recorded during such a cycle are shown in Figure 6.15. Entry into this cycle is at the Software Turnover CCB meeting. As a result of this meeting, a set of minutes is produced (see Figure 6.13 for an example of Software Turnover CCB minutes). Subsequent to the meeting, the product assurance organization builds and freezes a version of the software termed the Test Baseline. The Test Baseline is executed in a live or nearly live environment using detailed step-by-step test procedures. As a result of this and subsequent testing, a number of TIRs are generated—each another event to be recorded. Next, the Test Incident CCB meets to consider the TIRs. The minutes issued for the Test Incident CCB meeting are also placed in the archive (see Figure 6.12 for an example of Test Incident CCB minutes). When the TIRs have been resolved by the developers, another Software Turnover CCB meeting is held, and the cycle begins to repeat. As the cycle continues, these same events occur until, at a Test Incident CCB meeting, a decision is made to terminate the cycle. At this point, the Operational Baseline is created—another event that is recorded in the archive. Thus ends the testing cycle, leaving in its wake a succession of CCB minutes, TIRs, and Test Baselines, and finally an Operational Baseline.

Thus far in this section, we considered putting software and other products (in the form of documentation and code) into an archive, without discussing the nature of the archive. As we stated earlier in this section, an archive is a repository for software and other products. It need not be a single entity— generally, the archive for a project has a hard copy component and an electronic medium component. Documentation that exists only in hard copy is archived in the hard copy component. However, documentation created on some electronic medium is archived on that medium, usually with hard copy produced and archived for convenience of reference. The version on the electronic medium is the master copy of such documentation.

Computer code, since it is almost always created as source code on a magnetic medium, is archived on that magnetic medium. Often a listing of software source code is produced and archived. Sometimes, archived source code is compiled and the resulting object code is also retained on the electronic medium of the archive. Source code on the electronic medium always remains the master copy of the software code.

Access to view items placed in the archive is freely granted to all authorized persons (for example, an audit report may be made available to all project personnel, but not to nonproject personnel). Changes to archived items may be made only by an authorized change-approving authority (e.g., only an auditor should be able to change his audit report, say, to correct errors of fact—such corrections should, of course, be brought up at CCB meetings and thereby be made visible).

The portion of the archive containing software products is often termed a software library or a software development library.[7] A library is distinguished from the rest of the archive by the degree of control exercised over it. This control is exercised to ensure that only CCB-approved changes are made to the library. In some libraries, this control is extended to prevent access to software items by project personnel without

---

[7] On some projects, the library is constrained to hold only code. Documentation tends not to be controlled on such projects. The authors do not advocate this approach. In Exercise 6.17 we ask you to consider the advantages and disadvantages of this approach.

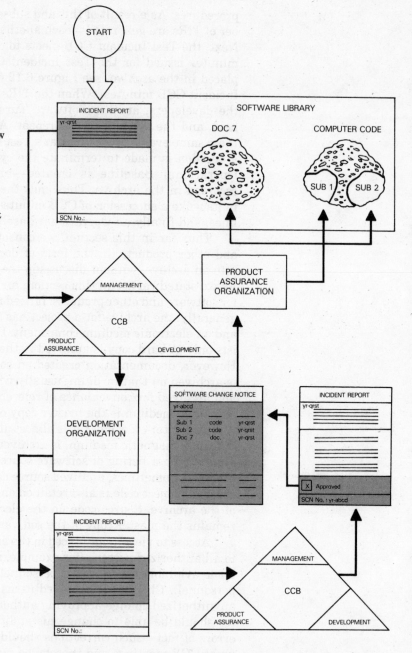

FIGURE 6.16. An overview of the mechanics of maintaining a software library showing the central role of the software change notice (SCN) as the authorization for the product assurance organization to change the library.

authorization (e.g., a developer may not be allowed to obtain a copy of a program for correction unless he is making a CCB-approved change).

In the schema of change control forms that we developed as an example in Chapter 4, we use the SCN not only to notify project personnel of the implementation of a change but also to serve as the authorization to change software in the library. Figure 6.16 shows the use of the SCN as a change authorization in the context of processing an incident report. This figure parallels Figure 4.7, which shows the steps in processing an incident report. In Figure 6.16, the bookkeeping accomplished during the processing of an IR is emphasized. Notice at the starting point in the figure that the IR has been through the freezing activity and has been identified as *IR yr-qrst* by the product assurance organization. The top part of the IR was filled in by the initiator (recall Figure 4.19 for an IR form). The IR then goes to the CCB, which in this particular case assigns it to an investigator in the development organization (however, the IR might be assigned to other organizations). The investigator fills in the middle portion of the IR with his analysis and recommended resolution. The IR is again presented to the CCB, which approves the recommended resolution. The approval is added to the decision-event section of the IR. The SCN control number (*yr-abcd*) may be assigned by the product assurance organization when the recommended resolution is approved by the CCB, or when the SCN is approved by the project manager (see Figure 4.20 for an SCN form). When the CCB approves the IR, the development organization acquires copies of the software to be changed (in Figure 6.16, these are code units Sub1 and Sub2 and document Doc7), makes the approved changes, and fills out the SCN (recall Figure 4.27, which is an example of a filled-out SCN). The SCN is approved by the software development manager, product assurance manager, and the project manager, and delivered, along with the changed software, to the product assurance organization. If the SCN was not assigned a control number upon approval by the CCB, the control number is now assigned. The product assurance organization updates the software (namely, Doc7, Sub1, and Sub2) on the library as authorized by the approved SCN. Observe that, during this process, the status of the IR is visible at all times, the process is completely traceable from its start to finish (the CCB minutes—which are not shown in Figure 6.16—further promote this traceability), and a trace of the contents of the software library is maintained. (In Figure 6.16, we use shading on the IR and the SCN forms to highlight how the sequence of filling out these forms helps establish traceability.)

In this section, we explored project event recording from the viewpoint of what is recorded, when events are recorded, how events are recorded—and most important, why events are recorded—to provide the traceability to make the evolution of a software product manifest so that its subsequent evolution can be more effectively managed. In the next section, we explore the role of automated aids in supporting software product assurance.

6.4 Automated Aids to Software Product Assurance

This section describes software product assurance automated aids and explains their potential use on a software project. Such aids can increase productivity on a project. They usually support the function of bookkeeping. In change control, no automated replacement for the interchange of ideas and of information that occurs in the forum of a CCB has been developed. In auditing, no substitute for the human ability to compare two software products is yet available. Automated

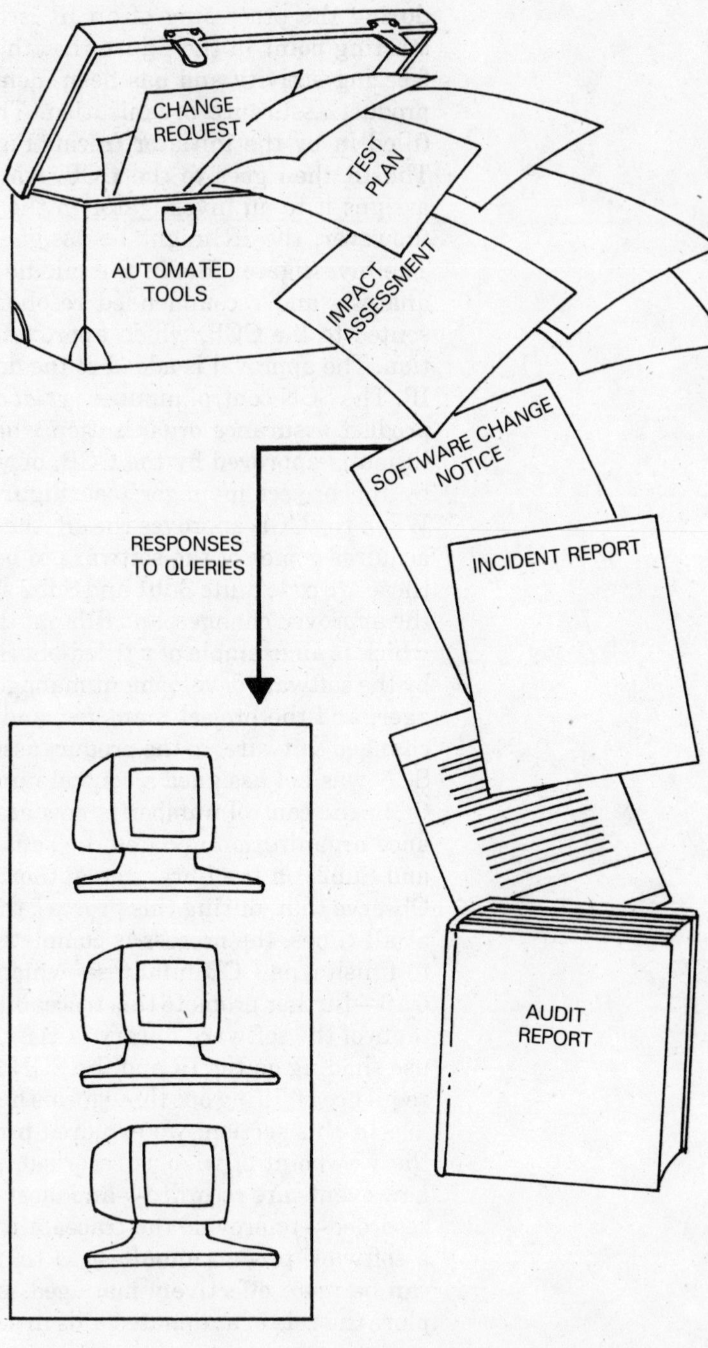

FIGURE 6.17. Automated tools improve visibility by making greater amounts of information available to more people and making it easier for more people to query the project information archive. These factors, in turn, increase project productivity.

Labels in figure: CHANGE REQUEST, TEST PLAN, IMPACT ASSESSMENT, AUTOMATED TOOLS, SOFTWARE CHANGE NOTICE, INCIDENT REPORT, RESPONSES TO QUERIES, AUDIT REPORT

aids can be and have been developed to help with the bookkeeping tasks of identification and project event recording, storing, and reporting. As shown in Figure 6.17, these automated tools contribute to an increase in project productivity by improving visibility: (1) by making greater amounts of information available to people and (2) by making it simpler for people to obtain responses to queries. Key to the first way of improving visibility is the ability to enter bookkeeping data into a computer in such fashion that it can be easily retrieved.

If event products are recorded in a database, the products can be later retrieved by project personnel. For example, a developer might retrieve an approved, but not yet implemented, change request to assess its impact on an incident report that he is investigating. Such a retrieval may allow better coordination between project participants and prevent wasted resources.

The second way that an automated bookkeeping tool improves project visibility is to provide responses to queries levied against the project archive and to provide reports, which are basically responses to prespecified queries. Depending upon the database, and the system's ability to formulate queries and to retrieve data, these extracted data could be far-ranging and complex in nature. For example, the project manager may want to see a list of all IRs that are approved but not yet implemented. Or an auditor may want to know about all uses of a key phrase in a software product that he is auditing. Notice in the preceding examples that the retrieval of bookkeeping data can be helpful to change controllers and auditors. Even if their basic functions cannot be automated, change controllers and auditors can obtain meaningful and useful data in response to database queries. For example, a CCB member may want to know how many IRs have been written on a specific software part, or an auditor may want to know the CCB resolutions of all discrepancies that he originated when he audited a certain software product.

Having established the benefit of automated tools for bookkeeping, let us look at the tools available. Regrettably, the authors have not found any general-purpose tools that could be applied to perform bookkeeping on every project. Nor do we feel that such tools can be developed. Every project is unique—whether it be the management style of the project manager, the particular needs of the customer, the design approach selected by the developers, or the acceptance testing approach used by the product assurance organization. Even though the generic change control process shown in Figure 4.4 may apply from project to project, the details of the processes generally do not allow the use of a general-purpose automated bookkeeping tool. Recall our development of a set of change control forms in Section 4.4. We said there and reiterate here that the set of forms and the content of each form vary among projects. Developing an automated tool to track the status and processing of the change control forms is a basic and relatively easy task. Yet no general-purpose tool can be used for this task if every set of change control forms is different.

If no general-purpose automated tool is available for bookkeeping, what can be done to obtain automated aids for software product assurance? A number of tools sold commercially do at least some automated bookkeeping. The National Bureau of Standards Institute for Computer Sciences and Technology collects information about the very dynamic field of software tools and publishes reports on software tool availability, usefulness, and usage. A search of these reports may locate a commercially available tool that is readily applicable to your project. Such a search may also locate a tool that helps support your product assurance process, even if the tool is not compatible with the way you perform the process. Having a mutually incompatible tool and process that the tool is supposed to aid, you can proceed in one of two directions—you can tailor the tool to support the process, or you can tailor the process to match the tool. The former choice can be quite difficult and expensive; it is often less expensive to develop your own tool. The latter course can be inexpensive to implement, if project personnel can adjust to doing things the software tool's way. Often project personnel refuse to invest the time or effort to change their way of doing business. In such cases, the automated tool goes unused or is circumvented. For example, the authors once observed an automated software library with comprehensive capabilities that went completely unused on a project. When the developers discovered that they could not compile any programs that they put in the library or use programs in the library as files to be included in source program compilations, they ceased putting programs in the library until just before the software was turned over for acceptance testing.

Another way to acquire a software tool to help with bookkeeping is to develop it. The time and cost of developing a tool specifically designed for a project must be considered, but the benefits of getting a tool that serves your particular needs are considerable. Not only would the tool be useful—but it would be used, making it possible to achieve the increased productivity suggested in Figure 6.17. A word of caution, though, on developing your own product assurance tools: *Do not* follow the procedure described in the story below.

THE TOOL THAT FAILED—A STORY

The product assurance manager on a large-scale project decided he wanted an automated product assurance tool for his project. He assembled key members of his staff and announced his plan to build an interactive software configuration status accounting system called System ICARUS. He waived any specification of requirements because he knew exactly what he wanted. He rattled off six general functions that were to be implemented, and spent the remainder of the brief meeting eliciting a "design" for System ICARUS. This design consisted of about twenty data element names scribbled on a blackboard. The design was not written down except in the personal notes of some of the staff members present.

Because the project product assurance organization was not available to develop the software, the product assurance manager acquired the services of two programmers assigned to a different project. They were given two weeks to code the "design." It actually took three months until a portion of System ICARUS was declared operational, even though only limited testing had occurred.

When the data-entry clerks used the system, they found that the entry of data was laborious, slow, error prone, and very difficult to correct. The product assurance manager found that the system could not respond to several queries he wanted to make. Other product assurance personnel complained that the system could not produce one of their most important reports and that, despite its stated purpose (configuration status accounting), System ICARUS maintained neither configuration nor status! Other project personnel found that they had to learn a new, complicated query language and a large number of programmer-oriented names of variables, many of which had no relation to the data they contained. As a result, these personnel never levied a query against System ICARUS.

The system was modified so that the product assurance manager could get a response to his queries. All other recommended changes to the system were arbitrarily rejected by the product assurance manager.

When his changes had been made, the product assurance manager publicly announced within his company with great fanfare that System ICARUS was operational. This announcement, accompanied by a number of demonstrations of the new system, was made even though a number of significant bugs existed, the system had not been fully tested, and no documentation for the system existed other than a rudimentary user's manual.

Following the announcement, the system was laboriously fed by the data-entry clerks for over a year. During this period, few reports were generated and fewer queries were made. Then, like its namesake,[8] the system disappeared one day (as quietly as the product assurance organization could make it disappear). (See Exercises 7.4 and 7.10 for other issues related to this story.) □

In this story (which is modeled on an actual project), the product assurance organization was guilty of not practicing what it preached. Neither a requirements specification nor a design specification was produced. The initial effort was on database design, followed thirty minutes later by the beginning of coding. Without documentation, no auditing was possible, and the system was not maintainable. Testing was inadequate and incomplete—the developers apparently only tested the software with proper values for proper fields on a menu. Changes were processed not by a user/buyer/seller CCB but by

---

[8] In Greek mythology, Icarus and his father Daedalus wanted to leave Crete to escape the wrath of King Minos. Daedalus made wings of feathers and wax for both of them, and they flew away from Crete. Unfortunately, Icarus flew too close to the sun. The wax melted and Icarus fell into the sea. Since the user (Icarus) specified no thermal tolerance, the developer (Daedalus) probably ignored thermal considerations in his design. There is no record of a user's manual alerting users to this system limitation. The only testing of the system appears to have been after installation. It should also be noted that the developer/user (Daedalus) made it safely to Sicily.

arbitrary buyer decision. In short, none of the product assurance practices recommended in this book was followed.

Since general-purpose tools to aid software product assurance are usually not available, we recommend that the product assurance organization start off a project by getting acclimated to the project environment. During this acclimation period, it should determine the most labor-intensive tasks that are candidates for automated support. Then, using technology existing in the project environment, automated aids should be developed. This approach was used on a project on which both authors participated. Faced with a substantial regression testing task, the product assurance organization methodically constructed a tool that facilitated construction of test procedures (allowing flexibility in changing test scope and parameters) and that automatically executed the resultant test procedures. This tool proved extremely useful because it increased the productivity of the product assurance organization and facilitated the development of more comprehensive test procedures.

6.5 Summary

In this chapter, we explored the product assurance function of bookkeeping to observe how it effects synergism between the other two product assurance functions—change control and auditing. We began by observing that software part identification provides visibility and traceability to the software development process by supplying the language of reference for the product assurance functions. We next explored the who, how, why, and what of taking CCB minutes and observed that, by making manifest the proceedings of the CCB, the minutes gave to senior management and project participants visibility into the change control process. We then discussed the archiving of a wide variety of software products and other project products during the change control process and the acceptance testing cycle. This recording of project events is needed to provide the traceability required to manage the evolution of a software product. Finally, we looked at how automated tools for the bookkeeping function could increase visibility on a project, yielding increased productivity.[9]

This discussion completes Chapter 6. Before proceeding to the final chapter of the book, we summarize in Figure 6.18 the key concepts included in the first six chapters of the book. Notice in the figure that the relationship between the key concepts in the various chapters is indicated by repeated use of symbols. For Chapters 3–6 in the figure, we shaded the symbol

---

[9] Senior managers may want to consider the following exercises before proceeding to the next chapter: Exercise 6.3, on items to include in a project status accounting summary for management's benefit; Exercise 6.4, on information that should be kept in a project archive and its intended use. Project managers and product assurance managers may want to consider the following exercises before proceeding to the next chapter: Exercise 6.3, on items to include in a project status accounting summary for management's benefit; Exercise 6.4, on information that should be kept in a project archive and its intended use; Exercise 6.11, on a user/buyer test charter; Exercise 6.19, on writing a software product assurance plan.

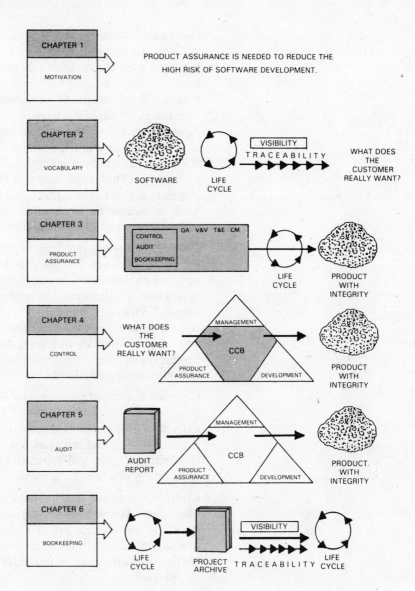

FIGURE 6.18. Key concepts from Chapters 1–6 and their relationships.

on which each chapter focused. An overview of each chapter is as follows:

Chapter 1 provided motivation for reading the book by citing the high risk of software development and the ability of software product assurance to reduce that risk.

Chapter 2 provided a working vocabulary for use throughout the book. We defined software and indicated that it encompassed both documentation and computer code. We introduced the notion that the software life cycle is a series of recyclings through a sequence of life cycle stages. We illustrated the two prime contributions of software product assurance—visibility and traceability. Finally, using a comic-strip dialogue between a wizard and a king, we posed the basic software project management challenge—to achieve convergence between a customer's perception of his need and the software developer's perception of that need.

Chapter 3 introduced the elements of software product assurance in terms of the four processes of quality assurance (QA), verification and validation (V&V), test and evaluation (T&E), and configuration management (CM), and of the three functions of control, audit, and bookkeeping. We emphasized that application of these elements of product assurance throughout the life cycle increases the likelihood of achieving our goal in software development—a software product with integrity.

Chapter 4 investigated in depth the control function of product assurance. We discussed the control of revolutionary and evolutionary changes, which arise from attempts to answer the question the wizard in Figure 2.8 asks the king—"What is it you really want?" We emphasized how the configuration control board (CCB) focuses the activities of the disciplines of management, development, and product assurance to resolve these changes so that a product with integrity results.

Chapter 5 concentrated on the second product assurance function, auditing. We pointed out that auditing is basically the comparison of a software product with its ground truth. We emphasized that the resulting audit report is the primary technical input to the CCB in the process of controlling changes to achieve a product with integrity.

Chapter 6 focused on the bookkeeping function of product assurance. We showed how, throughout the software life cycle, project events are recorded in the project archive. We described how these data provide visibility and traceability that allow better management and development on the project.

Now that we have investigated the three product assurance functions individually in detail, we shift our focus and look at product assurance as a whole. In our final chapter, we examine real-world applications of product assurance to ascertain whether product assurance really works—that is, whether product assurance assures the development of software products with integrity.

EXERCISES   **6.1**   Figure E6.1 depicts a memorandum that represents minutes of a CCB meeting for a project in which the software has achieved its operational state. Thus, these minutes deal with issues pertaining to revolutionary change (e.g., the fixing of latent defects) and evolutionary change (e.g., consideration of expanded capabilities or new requirements). Based on the information in the memorandum shown in Figure E6.1, consider the following:

```
┌──────────────────────────────────────────────────────────────────────────┐
│                           MEMORANDUM                                        │
│                                                                            │
│ TO:          Distribution                                                  │
│ FROM:        CCB Secretary                                                 │
│ SUBJECT:     CCB Minutes for Project Q                                     │
│ REFERENCE:   (a) CCB Minutes dated July 7, 1990                            │
│                                                                            │
│ 1.0    Date of Meeting: July 14, 1990                                      │
│                                                                            │
│ 2.0    Attendees: Sam, Harry, Joe, Mary, Sandra, Foster                    │
│                                                                            │
│ 3.0    CCB Actions:                                                        │
│                                                                            │
│ 3.1    Reference (a) was approved with the following change:               │
│                                                                            │
│ 3.1.1  In paragraph 3.2.5, change "Incident Report (IR) 18" to "IR 81."    │
│                                                                            │
│ 3.2    Items contained in the Action Items paragraph of reference (a) (paragraph 4.0) were │
│        resolved as follows:                                                │
│                                                                            │
│ 3.2.1  IR 39 status -- Sam indicated that the reported problem was, in fact, not a problem.  The │
│        "incident" resulted from improper use of the system by the operator. │
│                                                                            │
│ 3.2.2  The patch in response to IR 42, which was sent to User X, did not work. │
│                                                                            │
│ 3.3    Change Request (CR) 105 was introduced.  An impact assessment (IA) will be prepared │
│        and presented for CCB review and approval.                          │
│                                                                            │
│ 3.4    IR 51 was presented.  The board agreed that the reported incident resulted from an │
│        error in the User's Manual.  Mary was assigned the action for correcting the User's │
│        Manual.                                                             │
│                                                                            │
│ 4.0    Action Items:                                                       │
│                                                                            │
│                  Due           Action        Paragraph/                    │
│        No.  Item  Date         Agent         Reference                     │
│                                                                            │
│        1    IR 51   July 28    Mary          3.4                           │
│                                                                            │
│ 5.0    Next Meeting: July 21, 1990                                         │
│                                                                            │
│ Distribution:   President                                                  │
│                 Division Manager for Project Q                             │
│                 CCB attendees                                              │
│                                                                            │
└──────────────────────────────────────────────────────────────────────────┘
```

FIGURE E6.1.
"Maintenance" CCB minutes pertaining to Exercise 6.1.

(a) Write down at least one item missing from the upper right-hand corner of the memorandum.

(b) Write down at least one piece of information that might be useful to include in paragraph 2.0 after each attendee's name.

(c) Recalling the concept of traceability, write down at least one reason for including information in the minutes such as that given in paragraphs 3.1 and 3.1.1.

(d) Suppose reference (a), cited in the memorandum, did not need to be changed. Would it be useful to include a statement to that effect in place of the statement given in paragraph 3.1? (Indicate yes or no and write down at least one reason to support your answer.)

(e) Recalling the concept of visibility, write down at least one action that the CCB should take regarding IR 39 (paragraph 3.2.1).

(f) Recalling the concepts of visibility and traceability, write down at least two additional items that you would indicate in paragraph 3.2.2 regarding the patch in response to IR 42.

(g) Write down at least one piece of information regarding the IA (recall Figure 4.22) in paragraph 3.3 that might have been useful to include in the paragraph.

(h) Write down the term introduced in Chapter 2 that might be used to characterize the linkage between the CR and IA in paragraph 3.3.

(i) Write down the name of the form introduced in Chapter 4 that might be used to document the result of Mary's action in paragraph 3.4.

(j) Write down the term introduced in Chapter 2 that might be used to characterize the inclusion of paragraphs 3.4 and 4.0 in the minutes.

(k) Write down at least one item missing from paragraph 5.0.

(l) Recalling the concept of visibility, write down at least one reason for including the president and the division manager for Project Q in the distribution list of those individuals who are to receive the CCB minutes (assume that these two individuals do not generally attend CCB meetings).

6.2 Figure E6.2 depicts a memorandum that represents minutes of a CCB meeting convened for the purpose of accomplishing a design review of a document. The document is a detailed design for a software system called System ABC. Assume that this document, once the CCB approves it, becomes the System ABC Detailed Design Baseline from which computer code is to be produced. Assume also that an auditor has reviewed the document prior to the meeting and has submitted his report to the CCB. This report is referenced in the memorandum. With this information as background, and based on the information in the memorandum shown in Figure E6.2, consider the following:

(a) Write down at least one reason for putting a date and/or number on the memorandum (as shown in the upper right-hand corner of the memorandum).

(b) Write down at least one piece of information that might be useful to include in each of the references cited at the beginning of the memorandum.

(c) Write down at least one piece of information that might be useful to include in paragraph 2.0 after each attendee's name.

(d) Regarding paragraph 3.1, write down at least one reason why it is useful for Bob to give a presentation on his document rather than just opening the CCB meeting with the other members of the CCB asking Bob questions.

(e) Regarding paragraph 3.2a, indicate at least one reason why the statement in this paragraph may be preferable to the statement "Page 34 would be revised to read 'X = A + B'."

(f) Regarding paragraph 3.2b, indicate the term that might be used

September 12, 1989
CCB/89-21

MEMORANDUM

TO: Distribution
FROM: CCB Secretary
SUBJECT: CCB Minutes for System ABC Detailed Design Review
REFERENCE: (a) System ABC Detailed Design Document
(b) Auditor's Report of System ABC Detailed Design Document
(c) System ABC Preliminary Design Document

1.0 Date of Meeting: September 10, 1989

2.0 Attendees: Bob, Alex, Nancy , Maxine, Astrid

3.0 CCB Actions:

3.1 Bob, the author of reference (a), presented a 30-minute talk on the contents of reference (a).

3.2 Following Bob's presentation, questions were asked by the other attendees regarding specific points in reference (a). As a result of these questions, the following changes to reference (a) were agreed to:

a. Software part 2.2 on page 34 would be revised to read "X = A + B."

b. The wording of software part 3.7 on pages 86 and 87 would be changed to be consistent with the wording of software part 3.0 in reference (c), the System ABC Preliminary Design Document.

c. The three misspellings in the Table of Contents would be corrected.

3.3 The CCB Secretary presented for approval the changes to reference (a) recommended in reference (b).

3.4 The CCB approved reference (a) as the System ABC Design Baseline (DB) with the changes noted in paragraphs 3.2 and 3.3.

3.5 The CCB decided not to reissue reference (a).

Distribution: President
CCB attendees

FIGURE E6.2. Design Review CCB minutes pertaining to Exercise 6.2.

to characterize the linkage implied by the references to software part 3.7 and software part 3.0.

(g) In light of what is indicated in paragraphs 3.4 and 3.5, what kind of information is missing from paragraphs 3.2b, 3.2c, and 3.3?

(h) In light of what is indicated in paragraph 3.5, what purpose, other than recording what happened and when, does the memorandum serve?

(i) Assume that the president indicated in the distribution list at the end of the memorandum does not generally attend CCB meetings. What term introduced in Chapter 2 can be used to characterize

TABLE E6.1. POSSIBLE STATUS ACCOUNTING SUMMARY ITEMS FOR EXERCISE 6.3

a. Baseline status (e.g., which baselines have been approved, which are being audited)

b. The number of change requests (CRs) awaiting resolution

c. The number of CRs resolved since the last status accounting summary

d. The number of incident reports (IRs) awaiting resolution

e. The number of IRs resolved since the last status accounting summary

f. The number of approved IRs for which the approved changes have yet to be implemented

g. The number of software change notices (SCNs) which have been approved since the last status accounting summary

h. Oldest/newest CRs awaiting approval

i. Oldest/newest IRs awaiting resolution

j. Oldest/newest approved IRs awaiting implementation

k. Estimated cost of, and schedule for, implementing each approved CR

---

the value of including the president on the memorandum's distribution list?

6.3 Suppose you are a project manager responsible for ensuring proper implementation of revolutionary software changes to a system called System XX which has already been turned over to the user. Suppose also that you work for the company that developed System XX. As a result, you are also responsible for selling enhancements to this system and ensuring proper implementation of the resulting evolutionary changes. Table E6.1 lists items that might be included in a project status accounting summary provided to you by your company's product assurance organization (which is supporting your project with services such as those described in Chapters 4, 5, and 6). For each of the items in this table, indicate whether you would or would not want it included in a (one- or two-page) status accounting summary, and give at least one reason to support your answer. Assume that the project status accounting summary would be produced with a frequency specified by you (for example, in conjunction with each project CCB meeting as a supplement to the CCB minutes). (*Hint:* In considering these items, it may be helpful to recall the concepts of visibility and traceability introduced in Chapter 2.)

6.4 Recall the discussion in Section 6.2 regarding keeping a record of what the CCB does, and recall the discussion in Section 6.3 regarding keeping a project archive. With these discussions in mind, consider the following:

(a) From each of the perspectives listed below, write down at least one reason why project historical records (e.g., a collection of minutes of CCB meetings, an archive of all pending and resolved/approved CRs and/or IRs) may be important while the project is ongoing.

(1) Seller perspective

(2) Buyer perspective

(3) User perspective

(b) Write down at least one way each of the individuals listed below might use project historical records after a project is successfully (or unsuccessfully) completed.

(1) Seller

(2) Buyer

(3) User

(c) Write down at least two reasons why a software project manager, or some other individual vested with project responsibility, would *not* want project records compiled and archived.

(d) Considering your responses to (c), list at least two circumstances where it might be desirable to purposely omit items from the project record. Give at least three examples of such items.

(e) Considering your responses to (c) and (d), suggest at least two ways that a software project might be too visible. Does such an overabundance of visibility mean that the project has too much product assurance? Why (not)?

(f) Suppose you are software product assurance manager on a software project that is politically and technically sensitive (e.g., the success of the project implies the rise of your organization and the fall of a sister organization, or the success of the project implies a technological breakthrough and concomitant marketing advantage over your business competition). Because of the sensitivities, the software project manager has given you the following guidance regarding your project responsibilities:

(1) No minutes are to be recorded at project CCB meetings.

(2) All results of software product audits are only to be communicated orally to the product developers.

(3) Detailed, written step-by-step procedures to test the software code prior to customer delivery can be produced but, per (2) above, the results of executing these procedures are only to be communicated orally (at CCB meetings).

Recalling your responses to (c), (d), and (e), would you choose to negotiate a compromise with the project manager regarding your responsibilities? If so, how (in terms of the three items listed above)? If not, for each of the three items listed above, describe in a paragraph or two how you would carry out your responsibilities (e.g., describe how you would respond to a request from the project manager for the results of an audit that were reported at a CCB meeting held one month ago).

6.5 A typical software development and maintenance problem is that associated with ensuring that object code appropriately reflects the source code from which it was (supposedly) generated. Suppose on a particular project that the source code developers and the audit team consistently agree during code reviews that source code used to solve a particular problem should, in fact, provide a solution. Suppose also that when this code is subjected to acceptance testing it periodically (and apparently randomly) fails to operate properly (i.e., the executing code does not produce results predicted by the written test procedures). With these suppositions as background, consider the following:

(a) Write down at least two ways that bookkeeping information might provide insight into why the code failures occur.

(b) Write down at least two kinds of status information that might provide insight into why code failures occur, and explain how each kind that you identify might provide this insight. (*Hint:* Consider some of the forms discussed in Section 4.4.)

(c) In your opinion, which of the individuals listed below should have some responsibility for making inferences from the kinds of information you listed in (b)? (For each individual you select, give at least one reason to justify your choice.)
  (1) Bookkeeper
  (2) Auditor
  (3) Developer (i.e., the coder and/or his boss)
  (4) Project manager
  (5) Other (indicate the individual or individuals you have in mind)

(d) Suppose that, after much head-scratching, the code developers and the audit team finally determine why the code failures occur. Suppose also that they make this determination primarily from information *not* available in the project bookkeeping archive. How might this experience be exploited with regard to subsequent project bookkeeping activities in support of resolving future code failures?

6.6 Suppose you are a CCB secretary responsible for taking minutes at CCB meetings. Imagine that at one particular meeting the following events take place regarding revolutionary and evolutionary changes to an operational system called WONDER:

Three IRs are discussed. One results in approval of a change to two code modules, one results in approval of a change to the Design Baseline, and one requires further analysis.

The results of an audit of a detailed design specification are presented, and the members of the CCB approve two changes to this specification based upon this audit.

A report is received from a board member of a previously approved patch that did not work when installed.

A CR calling for a new WONDER capability is initially presented.

Using the examples for CCB minutes given in Figures 6.10 and 6.11 as guides, and using your imagination to fill in the details pertaining to the events listed above, prepare a set of minutes for the CCB meeting in question. Assume that this CCB meets every two weeks and is attended by representatives from the organization that developed WONDER and representatives from the WONDER user community. Assume also that the developer and the user representatives each include members from the management, product development, and product assurance disciplines (recall the triangle diagram in Figure 2.13).

6.7 On certain software projects, it may be necessary to convene frequent CCB meetings (say, every week), but it may be impractical to gather the involved parties in one location with the required frequency (e.g., because the project is supported by a number of geographically dispersed development and/or user organizations). Under such circumstances, the only practical means for conducting CCB meetings may be through teleconferences. Using the discussion of CCB minutes in Section 6.2 as a starting point, list at least three ways that keeping a record of CCB teleconferences might differ from keeping a record of CCB meetings involving participants gathered in the same room. How might the outline for CCB minutes given in Table 6.1 need to be modified to accommodate these differences? Address these issues for each of the following levels of teleconferencing capability:

(a) The CCB participants can communicate with one another during a meeting only via telephone.

(b) The CCB participants can communicate with one another during a meeting via telephone and video.

(c) The CCB participants can communicate with one another during a meeting via telephone, video, and electronic mail.

6.8 Throughout this book we have discussed the idea of revisits to life cycle stages. The purpose of this exercise is to probe some of the nuances of what "when something happened on a software project" means. For this purpose, suppose that you are participating in a project that has produced computer code that is in operational use. Suppose further that you are part of a CCB that meets regularly to process the three general types of changes shown in Figure 4.23. With the preceding as background, consider the following:

(a) When you participate in a CCB meeting to consider the first class of changes indicated in the figure (do we want something new or different?), which of the life cycle stages shown in Figure 2.7 do you think you are in? Why?

(b) Reconsider (a) for the second class of changes in the figure (is something wrong?).

(c) Reconsider (a) for the third class of changes in the figure (should we baseline this product?).

(d) What do your answers to the preceding parts of this exercise suggest to you about the relationship between the concept of life cycle stage and the concept of time? For example, can you be in two different stages at the same time? Can you be in one stage at two different times?

(e) Do your responses to (d) suggest to you that, despite what we said in Section 2.4, the concept of life cycle stage is not helpful in managing software development? Why (not)?

(f) What do your responses to (d) and (e) suggest to you about the way product assurance bookkeeping should be performed on a software project? For example, is it helpful to label and track items such as those shown in Figures 6.10, 6.11, 6.12, 6.13, 6.14, and 6.15 by life cycle stage? Is it useful for tracking purposes to distinguish a design document, for example, that is produced the first time the Detailed Design Stage is entered from a design document that is produced after the Operational Use Stage is entered? Is it useful to distinguish evolutionary changes from revolutionary changes that a CCB considers? Is it useful to call a CCB meeting a "design review" when it considers whether to baseline a design document in order to distinguish it from a CCB meeting that considers only IRs written against an operational system?

6.9 (*Note:* This exercise should be done with a group of at least ten people, such as might be found in a university or seminar class.) Have ten people identify the software parts in the System PREDICT Requirements Specification shown in Figure 5.8, using the three techniques for identifying software parts depicted in Figure 6.4. Compare the ten sets of results. What do these results suggest to you about software part identification?

6.10 Apply all three software part identification techniques depicted in Figure 6.4 to the System PREDICT Requirements Specification in Figure 5.8 and the System PREDICT Preliminary Design Specification in Figure 5.9. Use these identification labels to rewrite the audit findings in Figure 5.10 involving these two documents. What does this rewrite suggest to you about the utility of the software part identification techniques in Figure 6.4? For example, do they contribute to visibility and traceability? Why (not)?

6.11 Refer to the user/buyer test charter outline in Table 6.2. List three advantages and three disadvantages of using an approach implied by such a charter to conduct acceptance testing on a software project. What project characteristics (such as size, duration, or complexity of the application) do you think are most important for determining whether such a test charter should be instituted on the project? Using Table 6.2 as a starting point, devise a test charter for an actual software project with which you were or currently are associated. Do you think such a charter would facilitate or complicate the testing activity on this project? Why?

6.12 Refer to the evolutionary change control flow depicted in Figure 4.5. Name the events in that flow that you think should be recorded by the product assurance bookkeeping function. Give at least one reason for recording each event you select. (*Hint:* Recall Figures 2.4 and 2.6.)

6.13 Figure 6.16 gives an overview of the mechanics of maintaining a software library in connection with revolutionary change. How would you modify that figure so that it applies to evolutionary change?

6.14 Recall Figure 5.20, which depicts the interaction of the Software Turnover CCB and the Test Incident CCB during the acceptance testing cycle. On some projects a document called a "release note" is prepared in conjunction with this testing cycle. Assume that the basic purpose of a release note is to inform the user of the new capabilities and known problems in the software that is being tested for release to the user. At what point(s) in the Figure 5.20 cycle do you think a release note should be prepared? What specific information derived from the testing cycle do you think the release note should contain? Why?

6.15 Compare the requirements specification in Figure 6.5, which has been identified using the technique depicted in Figure 6.4(a), to the same requirements specification as it appears in Figure 5.4. What key piece of identification information appearing in Figure 6.5 is missing in Figure 5.4?

6.16 Suppose you are a member of a software development organization and are handed a draft software document (e.g., a detailed design specification) that is being readied by your organization for the CCB process such as that depicted in Figure 4.5. Suppose further that, except for paragraph numbers, this document contains no information that could be used to identify software parts. Recalling the three techniques for identifying software parts shown in Figure 6.4, describe how you would perform software identification on this document using each of these techniques. In particular, address the following issues:

How do you determine which information in the document is software?

How do you determine how many part identifiers to associate with information that you have determined to be software? (For example, how do you determine whether a chapter in the document describing software functions is to be given one identifier, or whether individual sections, subsections, or paragraphs are to be given identifiers?)

In doing this exercise, take an actual specification document and address the questions listed above in the context of this document (or take a part of the document, if the document is large—say, 100 pages or more). If you do not have an actual specification document, use one of the specification documents appearing in this book, such as the System PREDICT Requirements Specification (Figure 5.8), the System PREDICT Preliminary Design Specification (Figure 5.9), the System MEAL PLANNER Requirements Specification (Figure 4.9), or the System MEAL PLANNER Preliminary Design Specification (Figure 4.10). In what ways might a CCB or a contract defining the software development work to be done facilitate the software identification task? Show how these ways would influence how you would identify the document you are using in the exercise. Would you change your responses to the exercise if, instead of being a member of the software development organization, you were a member of a product assurance organization? If so, how? If not, why not? Would you change your response to the exercise if instead of a document you were handed computer code to identify? If so, how? If not, why not?

6.17   In footnote 7 in Section 6.3, we asserted that we do not advocate a software library that is constrained to hold only computer code (i.e., excludes documentation). List at least three advantages and three disadvantages of this approach. On what types of projects do you think such advantages might outweigh the disadvantages?

6.18   At the beginning of Section 6.3, we offered some broad guidance regarding which events to record on a software project. Using Figure 6.14 and Table 6.1 as a starting point, and keeping Figures 2.4 (visibility concept) and 2.6 (traceability concept) in mind, describe how you would decide which events to record on a software project. In this description, explicitly indicate how project characteristics such as the following govern project event recording:

Project size (as characterized by the number of people working on the project)

Complexity of the software to be developed (e.g., is the development effort a state-of-the-art adventure into the unknown, or is it an enhanced replication of something done previously many times?)

Project duration (e.g., is the project a three-month one-shot development effort, or a ten-year multiple-release development and maintenance effort?)

Consequences of software malfunction or failure (e.g., if the software malfunctions or fails, will people die, be injured, and/or suffer large financial loss?)

Project manager's management style (e.g., does the project manager depend on detailed project records?)

Senior management's interest in the project (e.g., if the project succeeds/fails, will senior management earn a big bonus/get fired?)

Project budget (e.g., is the budget so tightly constrained that barely enough money will be available to pay for the development organization's labor?)

Those of you who have software project experience may wish to work the exercise in the context of an actual project in which you were involved. In this case, indicate (1) what kinds of events were recorded, (2) what kinds of events should have been recorded and were not, and (3) what kinds of events that were recorded should not have been.

6.19 Using the guidance given in Section 6.3, write a product assurance plan for System MEAL PLANNER software development. Refer to Figures 4.9–4.12 and 4.24–4.27 for System MEAL PLANNER details. Use your imagination and software project experience to supply other details.

REFERENCES AND ADDITIONAL READINGS

1. Babich, W. A. *Software Configuration Management: Coordination for Team Productivity*. Reading, Mass.: Addison-Wesley Publishing Company, 1986.

   This 162-page book is intended for software project managers, senior programmers, and others responsible for coordinating the activities of programmers. It focuses on the code control aspects of configuration management (and is thus smaller in scope than Reference 2, below). According to the author, the goal of configuration management is "to maximize productivity by minimizing mistakes" (p. 8). To maintain reader interest in what some would consider a dry subject, the author illustrates a number of software-related issues with cartoon-like drawings. The book deals with a number of software bookkeeping issues pertaining primarily to computer code and therefore complements some of the discussion in this chapter. The final chapter of the book goes step-by-step through each phase of a life cycle (beginning with computer program design and ending with what the author terms "QA, Delivery, and Maintenance," where "QA" is used in a sense akin to our concept of acceptance testing). For each phase, the book describes the configuration manager's goals, the strategy for achieving these goals, and tools and procedures for implementing the strategy. Included in this description are some detailed bookkeeping suggestions, for example, bookkeeping in conjunction with code delivery to the customer (p. 149):

   > When it comes time to deliver the software [code], the configuration manager prepares a load image [i.e., executable form of the software system] using the most recent object code in the baseline. The load image is thoroughly tested by QA, and if it passes, is delivered to customers. The configuration manager carefully prepares a special derivation history, called a *version description document*, for the load image. The version description document shows:

   > The revision numbers of all package source codes and specifications that are represented in the configuration. This information, together with the lists of tools and parameters used to compile and link, allows the load image to be reproduced if necessary;

The list of all bug reports [i.e., TIRs] outstanding (unfixed) in the load image; and

A comprehensive list of differences between this customer delivery and the last one, including bugs that have been fixed and features that have been added.

This book is also intended as supplemental reading in a university software engineering course.

2. Bersoff, E. H., V. D. Henderson, and S. G. Siegel. *Software Configuration Management: An Investment in Product Integrity.* Englewood Cliffs, N.J.: Prentice-Hall, 1980.

    The principles and mechanics of software configuration status accounting are addressed in chapter 7 of Bersoff et al. Some of the ideas in our Chapter 6 are extensions of these principles and mechanics. Chapter 4 of the Bersoff book describes and illustrates thoroughly the principles and mechanics of software configuration identification that we touched upon in our Chapter 6.

3. Biggs, C. L., E. G. Birks, and W. Atkins. *Managing the Systems Development Process.* Englewood Cliffs, N.J.: Prentice-Hall, 1980.

    This 400-page book, part of the Touche Ross Management Series, offers an in-depth treatment of managing the development of systems with software content. Consistent with the spirit of the Touche Ross Management Series, this book is a how-to-do-it text on software system development management. Section 3 of this three-part text is entitled "Systems Development Standard Forms" and consists of 100 forms that help to structure documentation and to visualize the end-products of the system development process. This material provides detailed insight into the mechanics of bookkeeping of software system development and greatly extends many of the concepts introduced in this chapter.

4. Daniels, M. A. *Principles of Configuration Management.* Rockville, Md.: Advanced Applications Consultants, 1985.

    This 136-page book is intended for readers with no previous acquaintance with configuration management (hardware as well as software). Because it addresses configuration management principles (as opposed to the details of how to do configuration management), it is appropriate for senior managers and project managers looking to acquire quickly some insight into the subject, as well as for novice configuration management practitioners looking for an introduction to the discipline. Daniels' chapter 4 discussion of status accounting complements some of the discussion in our Chapter 6.

5. Perry, W. E. *Managing Systems Maintenance.* Wellesley, Mass.: QED® Information Sciences, 1981.

    This book, which is listed as Reference 9 at the end of Chapter 2 and is summarized there, emphasizes the mechanics of filling out forms pertaining to software change control and therefore complements and extends some of the ideas we present in this chapter. For example, chapter 6 in Perry's book presents forms and checklists to help in the recording of software problems and new requirements. The chapter also details how such forms are to be filled out.

6. *Third Software Engineering Standards Application Workshop*, sponsored by the IEEE Computer Society, San Francisco, October 2–4, 1984. Silver Spring, Md.: IEEE Computer Society Press, 1984 (IEEE Catalog No. 84CH2071-9).

This work consists of a set of papers and paper summaries presented at a 1984 workshop (attended by government, industry, and academia) that focused on software engineering standards. The following excerpt from the preface provides insight into its scope:

> The theme of this Third Software Engineering Standards Application Workshop . . . is "Standards in a competitive world." During the course of the workshop, we will listen to and discuss what is happening in the IEEE Software Engineering Standards Subcommittee and working groups, the standards activities within the federal government, software standards in the nuclear industry, and implementation and support of software standards within the private sector. Most, if not all, of the software standards that we will be discussing have a strong component or flavor of guidance. These software standards focus upon achieving higher quality software and a more productive work force. Software engineering standards do not yet encompass issues that affect interchange and interoperability, but that day is coming. Increasingly we will find that software standards are essential to maintain effective and competitive operations in today's world (p. v).

The brief articles from the workshop listed below address software bookkeeping issues. Because they deal for the most part with bookkeeping from a management perspective (the "why" of status accounting as opposed to the "how"), they should be of particular interest to senior managers and software project managers.

J. Vosburgh, "Position Paper on Data Collection Standards for Software Engineering," p. 17. This paper opens with the following statement: "We collect software engineering data to answer questions, so the standardization of data collection must begin with an understanding of why we are collecting data and what we plan to do with it." It concludes with a five-step recommendation for developing a software engineering data collection standard: (1) establish the questions, (2) determine data needed to answer the questions, (3) identify data collection tools, (4) describe the analysis to be performed, (5) derive example reports that will enable management to answer the stated questions. Much of the body of the paper gives the rationale for these five steps.

W. J. Ellis, "Data Collection: A Perspective," p. 18. This one-page paper gives a brief perspective of the history of software engineering data collection while pointing out that "data collection has become in itself a discipline, with lessons learned from experience."

F. E. McGarry, "Data Collection Standards," pp. 30–31. This paper begins with the following statement: "Over the past several years an increasing emphasis has been placed on the need for accurate and detailed software development data so that researchers may better understand and measure the software development process" (p. 30). It then makes the following observation regarding the basic incompatibility of many software engineering data collection activities:

Although there has been an increasing awareness of the measurement/data collection importance . . . and there has been noticeable growth in the data collection activities within major software development environments, the problem of inconsistency of data definitions across disciplines and the lack of commonality of terminology have continued to impose barriers to the general usage and effective interpretation of the available information (p. 30).

The paper concludes with a list of data collection questions for consideration (presumably by the workshop participants), including the following:

Should there be a set of data collection standards? If so, who should develop and maintain them?

What impact would data collection standards and the data collection process have on the software development process? (Cost, methodology, team structure . . .)

7. Zucker, S. "Automating the Configuration Management Process." *Proceedings of SOFTFAIR, a Conference on Software Development Tools, Techniques, and Alternatives*, cosponsored by the IEEE Computer Society, National Bureau of Standards, and Association for Computing Machinery (ACM) SIGSOFT, Arlington, Virginia, July 25–28, 1983. Silver Spring, Md.: IEEE Computer Society Press, 1983 (IEEE Catalog No. 83CH1919-0), pp. 164–172.

This paper describes a tool that automates in part the control and status accounting configuration management functions. It complements and extends some of the ideas presented in Chapters 4, 5, and 6 (recall Figure 6.17). In particular, it describes how much of the configuration management paperwork typically generated on large software projects can be virtually eliminated through the use of computer terminal display devices linked to a project configuration management database and linked to each other so that project participants (such as CCB members) can communicate with one another via electronic mail. The article offers some detailed insight into how automation can facilitate the status accounting associated with the tracking of change control forms such as those discussed in Section 4.4. It concludes with the following interesting observations regarding the potential job threat that automation poses for a configuration manager:

Initially the Configuration Manager viewed CMS [the name of the automated configuration management system] as a job threat. However, as he began to use and understand the system he came to appreciate that CMS was performing the drudge work as well as the security checks. When the computer refused to accept undocumented or unapproved changes the programmer could not blame it on a picky configuration manager. The configuration manager had time to do more interesting higher level tasks. He created information reports, and had a complete handle on the whole system. Currently, the configuration manager is a vocal advocate of CM automation. He is happy to demonstrate the system and is constantly suggesting new methods of system usage (p. 172).

In its penultimate paragraph, the article offers the following observation regarding a likely trend in the data processing field pertaining to the role of software and how automation may be able to help keep pace with this trend:

> As the field of data processing grows and the scope of projects becomes more and more software oriented, the need for strict discipline becomes extremely apparent. Maintenance of a large software system continuously requires the incorporation of new features, the correction of old features and continued performance improvement. Because software is more pliant than hardware, it is constantly used to absorb system changes. Configuration Management procedures must be applied throughout the life cycle of a product. Automation of these CM procedures will ensure the integrity of the product and the reliability of the entire system (p. 172).

If we substitute "product assurance" for "configuration management" in the fourth sentence quoted above, it should be evident that the thoughts expressed in the first four sentences echo ideas that we have reiterated throughout our book. Whether "automation of . . . CM [or other product assurance] procedures will insure the integrity of the product and the reliability of the entire system" will, of course, become apparent only as more software projects utilize such automated procedures. It should be kept in mind that "automation" in this context also implies "software." Thus, the use of automation to support product assurance of software projects poses a Catch-22 dilemma of sorts— namely, if software development is to be supported by something that itself results from software development, then we must ensure that such software does what it is supposed to do before it is used to help determine whether other software is doing what it is supposed to do (recall our story in Section 6.4 about the product assurance tool that failed).

chapter 7

CAN PRODUCT ASSURANCE REALLY WORK?

Philip Crosby was Vice-President and Director of Quality at International Telephone and Telegraph Corporation for fourteen years. During this period, he instituted a quality management program in this multibillion-dollar corporation that employs hundreds of thousands of people. Crosby's business environment had little to do with software, but he unquestionably plied his quality trade in the real world. In 1979, he wrote a book entitled *Quality Is Free: The Art of Making Quality Certain*. As we emphasized in the three sample problems in Chapter 1, managing software development and maintenance is perhaps a riskier venture than managing the development and maintenance of nonsoftware products. We believe that Crosby's message about quality is particularly apt for the software industry. The following is the essence of that message, which appears as the first two paragraphs in Crosby's book:

> Quality is free. It's not a gift, but it is free. What costs money are the unquality things—all the actions that involve not doing jobs right the first time.
> Quality is not only free, it is an honest-to-everything profit maker. Every penny you don't spend on doing things wrong, over, or instead becomes half a penny right on the bottom line. . . . If you concentrate on making quality certain, you can probably increase your profit by an amount equal to 5 to 10 percent of your sales. That is a lot of money for free.[1]

Translating Crosby's chain of reasoning to the business of making software, we contend that software product assurance is free. The preceding chapters have demonstrated why this must be so. We talked about "pay now versus pay much more later" (recall Figure 1.3). We talked about raising the likeli-

---

[1] P. Crosby, *Quality Is Free: The Art of Making Quality Certain* (New York: McGraw-Hill Book Company, 1979), p. 1.

hood of achieving software product integrity through the application of product assurance. We showed how the application of product assurance raises the visibility of the software development and maintenance process and injects traceability into this process, thereby transforming the process from an exercise in artistic expression to an engineering discipline.

Crosby asserts: "We must define quality as 'conformance to requirements' if we are to manage it."[2] Our concept of product integrity reflects this key observation (recall our concept of "good" software in Figure 2.14). How many times have we returned to the wizard's question in the comic strip in Figure 2.8? We purposely focused on this question because our experience in the software industry has been that, more often than not, this question is shunted aside in the rush to "get on with the coding."

But Crosby's nonsoftware experience aside, you, the reader, certainly have the right to ask:

Can product assurance really work?

This chapter offers a response to this question in terms of the concepts and techniques set out in the preceding chapters. By describing some of our real-world software experiences here, we demonstrate that applying these concepts and techniques can make a difference under certain circumstances, but does not *guarantee* software project success. We earnestly believe that, paraphrasing Crosby, product assurance "is not only free, it is an honest-to-everything profit maker." We also know that many in the software industry do not yet really *believe* that "what costs money (on software projects) are the unquality things—all the actions that involve not doing jobs right the first time." Like motherhood and apple pie, many will say that they are all for "doing jobs right the first time"—until it comes to putting a price tag on bids to win those jobs. Then, somehow, the "cost" of doing software product assurance is simply too great to include in bids that have any chance of winning in a competition.

Yet, recall Figures 1.4 and E1.1, where we portrayed the risks associated with any software development effort. Software success, i.e., achievement of a product with integrity, is never certain at the beginning or during the course of a software project. Winning in a competition for a software development job can result (and often has resulted) in losing by the time the project ends or is terminated. We have represented this element of uncertainty in Figure 7.1 by a pair of dice that might be cast periodically to determine an outcome during the march around the software development game board such as that depicted in Figure 2.7. Just as weighting dice increases the likelihood that certain faces will come up after a throw, putting visibility and traceability into a project through the application of software product assurance increases the like-

---

[2] Ibid., p. 17.

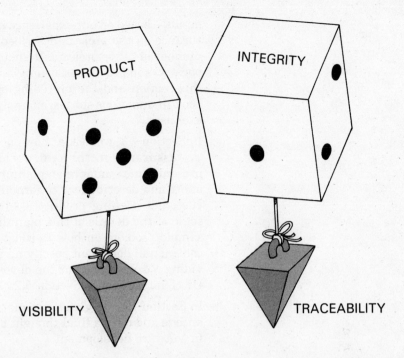

FIGURE 7.1. Nothing is certain in the game of software development. In playing this game, however, the roll of the project software development dice is more likely to come up PRODUCT INTEGRITY when, through the application of product assurance, the dice are weighted with visibility and traceability.

PRODUCT

INTEGRITY

VISIBILITY

TRACEABILITY

lihood that product integrity will be achieved on the project. We want our conceptual dice to read "Product Integrity" after each roll. To increase the probability of this outcome, we load the dice with weights marked "visibility" and "traceability." We have demonstrated throughout this book that we obtain these weights—visibility and traceability—through the practice of product assurance.[3]

This chapter is organized as follows:

In Section 7.1, we describe an experiment for scientifically determining product assurance effectiveness. However, because this experiment (or one equivalent to it) cannot rigorously be performed, we must fall back upon real-world experiences to demonstrate the effect of product assurance on projects. We therefore describe several projects from the viewpoint of the application of product assurance and of the project outcomes. These stories are intended to demonstrate that the ideas described in the preceding chapters have a legitimate place in the world of real software projects. The application of these ideas does not guarantee success, but their absence may guarantee disaster.

In Section 7.2, we show how software product assurance works in the real world of limited resources, time constraints, and software customers who change their

---

[3] Note that in Figure 7.1 we are specifically *not* depicting software development as a gambling process. Nor are we depicting the use of weights as a means of obtaining an unfair advantage over someone else. We use dice as a means of making probability manifest, as in mathematics texts on probability. Weights are used in Figure 7.1 to symbolize modification of these probabilities.

minds—based on our experience in performing product assurance on the projects described in Section 7.1 and on a number of other projects. It should be noted that our experiences in product assurance are reflected not simply in this section and the preceding one, but throughout this book in numerous stories, examples, sample problems, and exercises.

In Section 7.3, we look at how one gets started doing product assurance in the real world. For this purpose, we present some guidance on planning the product assurance effort and describe how to formalize this planning with a customer seeking product assurance support. To show some of the details of this planning process, we include a sample problem on how to construct a task order (i.e., a contractual document specifying work to be done) for providing V&V support for the development of System PREDICT introduced in Section 5.2.

In Section 7.4, we give a summary of what product assurance is and offer a final thought on the need for discipline in software development.

7.1 Real-World Application of Product Assurance

How effective is product assurance in achieving a software product with integrity? An experiment for scientifically demonstrating product assurance effectiveness is shown in Figure 7.2. This experiment involves the development of the same software system X by two different development groups. That is, the two groups are given the same requirements, and these requirements are assumed to remain unchanged throughout the development effort; from these requirements, the two groups are to produce software code embodying the same capabilities. To isolate the effect of product assurance, both development groups must be equally experienced, skilled, and talented. For the same reason, both groups would be constrained to develop the software using the same methods and tools. However, Development Group 2 would be supported by a product assurance group. The experiment as thus prescribed would evaluate the efficacy of the product assurance group, since there is no difference in merit between the two development groups. Upon completion of developing software system X by both development groups, the software code that each group produces (labeled X1 and X2 in Figure 7.2) would be compared relative to the five product integrity attributes defined in Chapter 2 (and any other measurable attributes agreed upon prior to the experiment) to determine which development group produced the "better" software (a criterion that also must be defined and agreed to prior to the experiment). If Group 2 produced the better software, then the product assurance group was effective in producing that better product. If Group 1 produced the better software, then the product assurance group was not effective in producing a better product.

Although we can postulate such an experiment, we assert

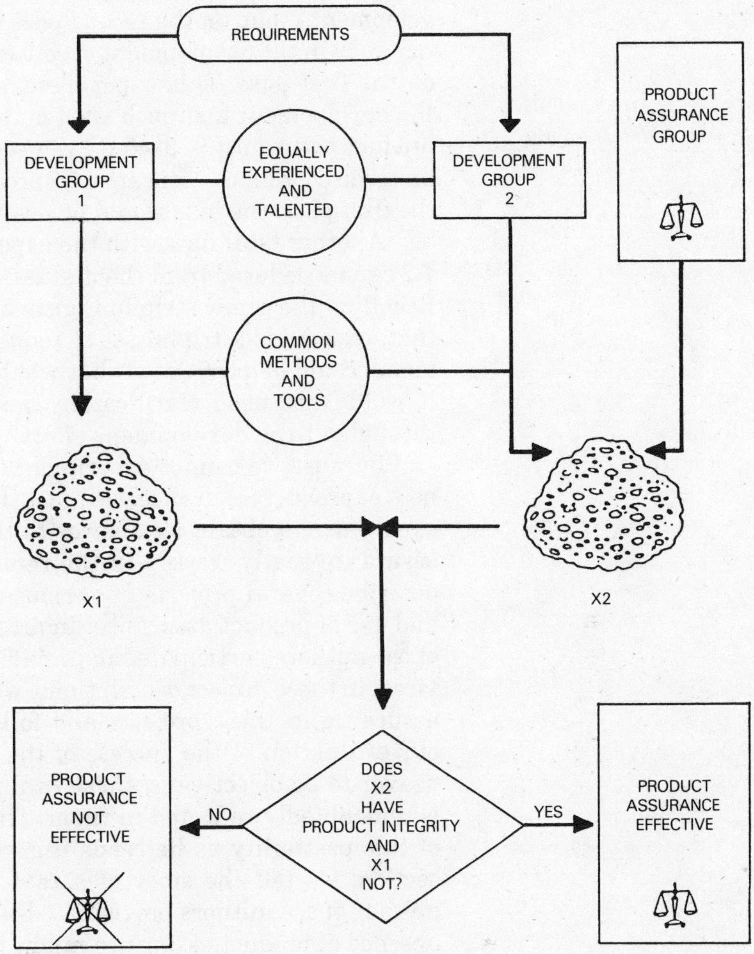

FIGURE 7.2. An experiment for scientifically demonstrating product assurance effectiveness. Two equally experienced and equally talented development groups, using common methods and tools, set out to produce software code embodying the same capabilities (i.e., both groups are given the same requirements, and these requirements are assumed to remain unchanged throughout the development effort). Group 1 turns out product X1 while group 2, supported by an independent product assurance group, turns out product X2. If X2 has integrity and X1 does not, then the effectiveness of (independent) product assurance has been demonstrated.

that an actual experiment based on this model is fatally flawed and that we cannot validly conduct the experiment. One flaw is in the requirement that both development groups be equally experienced, skilled, and talented. In the real world, this equality is not achievable, and we would find in our experiment that the difference between developing software system X with and without product assurance would be masked by the differences between individuals in the development groups.

An attempt could be made to overcome these individual differences by using the same personnel in both development groups and by developing software system X twice in sequence. That is, a group of developers could develop the system without support from the product assurance group. Then the same group of developers could develop the same system a second time, this time with the support of the product assurance group. The rest of the experiment remains the same in this alternative approach. Of course, the sequence of these two developments could be reversed, that is, product assurance support could be provided on the first development and not on the second.

This alternative experiment is also flawed, in that the development group on the second pass is more experienced—particularly in the development of software system X—than it was on the first pass. This experiment is therefore biased toward the development approach used on the second pass. That is, if product assurance is used on the second pass, the bias would be toward product assurance; if product assurance is used on the first pass, the bias would be away from product assurance.

Another fatal flaw with the experiment depicted in Figure 7.2 can be deduced from the discussions in preceding chapters. Recalling the comic strip in Figure 2.8, it is highly improbable that, except for a trivial set of requirements, a set of requirements could be postulated that would be so unambiguous that it would not need clarification (and therefore modification) throughout the development effort.

Because we cannot experimentally evaluate the effectiveness of product assurance, we must therefore turn to real-world experience to obtain an answer to the question "Can product assurance really work?" In the remainder of this section, we describe several projects of various magnitudes, applications, and use of product assurance. In all these projects, one or both of the authors participated in providing product assurance services. In these project descriptions, we stress the role of product assurance in these projects and follow each description with our evaluation of the success of the project. Although we endeavor to be objective in these evaluations, our personal bias is undoubtedly reflected in them. The reader should be aware of this possibility as he reads this section. At the end of this section, we tell the story of a real-life catastrophe in which neither of the authors participated—as an example of how the absence of product assurance might lead to a catastrophe. The lessons we can learn from these real-world experiences are presented in Section 7.2.

We begin our study of real-world experience in software product assurance by referring to Table 7.1, which gives a synopsis of the projects we describe. Inspection of the table reveals the wide variety among these projects in terms of their applications, their size, and their use of product assurance. (Fictitious names have been used for all the project names to avoid offending anyone with our evaluations.)

The first project described is a small one in the field of data communications.

PROJECT MERCURY

Project Mercury was a short-duration, fixed-price contract to provide data communications support to a large bank. A functional description and a design specification were developed and reviewed internally and then provided to the customer. These documents lacked sufficient detail and thus left open to question what the customer was getting. As a result, the customer submitted a steady stream of additional require-

PROJECT ID: MERCURY   *APPLICATION*: banking communications support
BUDGET ORDER OF MAGNITUDE: $100,000   *DURATION*: <1 year
PRIMARY PRODUCT ASSURANCE PROCESSES: T&E
PROJECT OUTCOME—PRODUCT ASSURANCE IMPACT: System not successful, due to lack of change control and auditing; testing helped bring system on-line; detailed written test procedures developed for this testing; although someone other than the developers wrote these procedures, they were executed by the developers as part of system acceptance.

PROJECT ID: VENUS   *APPLICATION*: intelligence support
BUDGET ORDER OF MAGNITUDE: $1 million/year   *DURATION*: 5–10 years
PRIMARY PRODUCT ASSURANCE PROCESSES: T&E, CM
PROJECT OUTCOME—PRODUCT ASSURANCE IMPACT: Each year, 1–2 major software releases deployed to users; project success correlated with degree of product assurance used; all software changes processed through a CCB that typically met every week or two; CCB *modus operandi* documented in a configuration management instruction.

PROJECT ID: MARS   *APPLICATION*: intelligence support
BUDGET ORDER OF MAGNITUDE: <$1 million   *DURATION*: 1 year
PRIMARY PRODUCT ASSURANCE PROCESSES: T&E, V&V, QA
PROJECT OUTCOME—PRODUCT ASSURANCE IMPACT: Requirements not pinned down; success was what was delivered; software development governed by customer-imposed standard (MIL-STD-483), which was open to a broad range of interpretation; to meet delivery schedules, product assurance resources sacrificed for additional programming.

PROJECT ID: JUPITER   *APPLICATION*: database management system
BUDGET ORDER OF MAGNITUDE: $50 million/year   *DURATION*: >10 years
PRIMARY PRODUCT ASSURANCE PROCESSES: T&E, V&V, CM
PROJECT OUTCOME—PRODUCT ASSURANCE IMPACT: Extensive product assurance by both buyer and seller; six configuration control boards in a two-level hierarchy; seller governed by a product assurance plan; high visibility and extensive analysis given to new requirements; requirements traced through all levels of testing.

PROJECT ID: SATURN   *APPLICATION*: logistics support
BUDGET ORDER OF MAGNITUDE: $3 million/year   *DURATION*: 5–8 years (planned)
PRIMARY PRODUCT ASSURANCE PROCESSES: QA, T&E, V&V, CM
PROJECT OUTCOME—PRODUCT ASSURANCE IMPACT: Buyer performed extensive product assurance, seller none; seller destroyed all traceability and visibility during coding stage; management showed lack of concern for product assurance warnings; project terminated near end of coding stage for first release (after approximately three years).

PROJECT ID: URANUS   *APPLICATION*: automated postal operations
BUDGET ORDER OF MAGNITUDE: $3 million/year   *DURATION*: 4 years
PRIMARY PRODUCT ASSURANCE PROCESSES: T&E, CM
PROJECT OUTCOME—PRODUCT ASSURANCE IMPACT: After a bad start, system successful; after one year, cost growth and schedule slippages led to top and middle management turnover within development organization; these problems resulted in part from a lack of visibility into software development.

PROJECT ID: NEPTUNE   *APPLICATION*: mail automation
BUDGET ORDER OF MAGNITUDE: $10 million (total)   *DURATION*: >10 years
PRIMARY PRODUCT ASSURANCE PROCESSES: T&E, V&V
PROJECT OUTCOME—PRODUCT ASSURANCE IMPACT: In its initial stages, project almost completely lacked product assurance; as a result, development work was halted; after several years, development work was resumed with a new team where emphasis was given to making development visible and traceable; as a result of this visibility and traceability, the software system was made operational and maintainable within three years of resumption of work (and more than nine years after the system was originally supposed to be operational).

ments (at no increase in price!) up until near the end of the project. These added requirements were not reflected in the documents and necessitated some recoding. Toward the end of the project, the customer became quite nervous about the state of his software and insisted that the final stages of coding be done at his site. Also, testing of the communications interface had to be conducted at the customer's site, since the seller could not test it in his plant.

Product assurance was invoked on this project only for T&E. Test procedures were written to assess the functional capability of the completed system. The continually changing requirements made it necessary to update the test procedures frequently. The developers executed the test procedures at the customer's site with the customer as witness. The few discrepancies observed during test execution were worked off within several days. □

Project Mercury was not a success. Even though a working system was delivered, it was delivered late and the seller lost money. The lack of visibility created by the absence of sufficient detail in the project documentation hurt the seller. The problem was exacerbated by the lack of a change control mechanism to evaluate additional requirements before they were approved. Product assurance played a minor role in this project, yet that role appeared to help get the system accepted. This limited product assurance role was unfortunate—installation of an auditing function and a change control function on this project could have reduced the magnitude of the problems and turned the project into a success.

The second project described is substantially larger, is long-term in duration, and involves more product assurance than Project Mercury.

PROJECT VENUS[4]

Project Venus produced software to support a military intelligence operation. This software support system was installed at approximately a half-dozen sites around the world. Because of the nature of the application, this system was to operate at these sites twenty-four hours a day, seven days a week. The system was maintained through a change control process that we refer to as the *major release* approach. This approach consisted of periodically (approximately every six months to a year) incorporating a group of enhancements into an existing operational baseline to create the subsequent operational baseline. When incorporated into an existing operational baseline (and installed at the sites), this group of enhancements (plus patches to resolve program "bugs"; see note in Exercise 4.4) constituted a major release. A major release

---

[4] This description is adapted from W. Bryan and S. Siegel, "Product Assurance: Insurance Against a Software Disaster," *Computer*, vol. 17, no. 4 (April 1984), pp. 75–83.

was thus a controlled way of upgrading an installed system in roughly uniform increments (in contrast to an approach that upgraded an installed system each time a change was approved—regardless of the magnitude of the change). The primary advantage of the major release approach was that it permitted changes to be more effectively integrated with one another and with capabilities in the current operational baseline. The primary disadvantage of the major release approach was that the customer generally had to tolerate system weaknesses and problems for a longer period of time.

The approach on Project Venus was to translate customer requirements (as articulated in a contract) into computer code by way of a sequence of progressively more detailed specifications. Each specification in the sequence was given visibility through a design review attended by the seller and customer. This design review was part of a change control process similar to that portrayed in Figure 4.5.

A CCB was established to focus project activities during the major release cycle. The CCB consisted of customer representatives and seller representatives. Jointly chaired by the seller's project manager and the customer's project manager, it met regularly (typically weekly) to process operational incidents submitted by users of the currently installed operational baseline. It also reviewed and approved change requests for enhancements to this baseline. Approved change requests precipitated the design review cycle just described. To raise the visibility of the chain of events linking one major release to the next, detailed minutes of CCB meetings were compiled, promulgated, and archived. The entire change control process was documented in a detailed configuration management instruction (see footnote 5 in Chapter 4).

Once a major release had been coded, unit tested, and integrated, the seller performed acceptance testing just as described in Section 5.3 (recall Figure 5.18). The CCB functioned as a Software Turnover CCB and as a Test Incident CCB during this period (recall Figure 5.20). The acceptance testing was followed by a demonstration to the customer. This demonstration typically consisted of customers executing the test procedures at the seller's facility (which approximated the customer's operational environment through simulated interfaces), augmented by customer excursions from these procedures. As a result of this demonstration, additional test incidents—that the customer would want fixed before the development baseline was installed for on-site testing—might have been generated. When this demonstration had been completed to the satisfaction of the customer, the development baseline was then installed at the user sites. Testing by the seller and/or customer agents (i.e., a test organization retained by the customer to perform independent T&E of the seller's code) was then performed on the development baseline operating in the customer's environment. Additional test incidents that the customer may have wanted corrected may have resulted from this T&E activity. When the customer felt that the development baseline was operating satisfactorily in accordance with the seller's and/or the customer agents' test procedures (except for any mutually acceptable discrepancies), the user stated in writing that the development baseline had been accepted. At that point, the development baseline became the new operational baseline.

For years, the seller had installed a number of major releases using this process or variations of this process. There appeared to be a direct correlation between effort spent on CM and T&E and the ease with which a major release was installed in a timely fashion at user sites. It was true that this process cost time and money and sometimes even delayed software installation. It was also true that it did not produce completely error-free releases. However, because of the visibility and traceability the process afforded, the errors that did remain were for the most part known (documented as test incidents) and were relatively easy to correct in subsequent releases.

This process was not always applied as a matter of course. Because the process took time and money and placed a burden on both the customer and the seller—particularly the design reviews and the frequent CCB meetings—the process was sometimes reduced in scope, and some elements were eliminated. On one occasion, because of a budget squeeze and political reasons, an attempt was made to install a major release without the CCB apparatus. The result? The release was almost a year late and experienced numerous difficulties in the field. ☐

On this project, the value of product assurance has been demonstrated, and the application of CM and T&E has been institutionalized. The project has been successful, except for the one release where product assurance was essentially eliminated. Seller management endeavored to avoid repeating this unhappy experience by insisting upon some form of CCB support even in the face of tightly constrained budgets. Here we have a situation where, on different releases of the same project (with essentially the same development staff), the releases on which product assurance was performed were successes, and the release on which product assurance was not performed was a failure. Compare this situation with the experiment shown in Figure 7.2. Project Venus approximated the alternative experiment discussed above where the same system was developed twice, once with and once without product assurance.

The next project described is one that also provided intelligence support, but the nature of this project is quite different from that of Project Venus. It was a one-time development, with the seller providing limited maintenance services for up to one year.

PROJECT MARS

Project Mars developed an intelligence support system to replace an existing one. The seller was obligated to maintain the system to a limited extent (i.e., to correct bugs) for a period of one year after acceptance. The customer's requirements were broadly stated in the contract and never specified in detail during the project life cycle. A functional description (a description of the functions the system is to perform) and a design specification were produced by the seller. An audit of both documents was conducted. Since there were no requirements delineated by the customer in writing, the only checks of the functional description were a self-comparison and a comparison with the prescribed documentation standard (recall rows 1 and 4 of Figure 5.2). The design specification was compared with the documentation standard and the functional description, but it could not be validated without a requirements specification. The audits uncovered differences in the interpretation of the standard and other discrepancies. Project Mars had no change control mechanism, and none of the discrepancies was ever resolved. In fact, the project manager ignored the audit reports, and as soon as the coding fell behind schedule he removed all funding for V&V and QA and used it to cover his programmers for an additional period of time.

The customer told the seller's project manager and development team manager orally about some of the customer's specific requirements. Some of these requirements were communicated to the development team and some were not. Further, the developers considered the design specification to be a guideline only, and they freely departed from it when they thought they had a "better" way to design the system. None of the customer's requirements or the developer's design changes was ever reflected in the documentation. At the end of the development period, the seller made a few cosmetic changes to the two documents and delivered them to the customer, even though they were badly out of date and did not fully meet documentation standards.

The seller established an acceptance test effort within his product assurance organization. In the absence of a requirements specification, this T&E group had to use the functional description as part of its ground truth (recall Figures 5.1 and 5.18). Since the documentation from which they had to write their test procedures was badly out of date, the testers became quite frustrated. None of the test procedures worked as the documentation said they should. This problem made the testers rewrite their test cases based on what they could find out from the developers. Some capabilities that had never been documented were never communicated to the T&E group, and therefore were never acceptance tested.

When the seller's T&E group ran through the acceptance tests with the customer observing, the tests ran smoothly, with only a few discrepancies uncovered. However, the customer was not satisfied. He had not seen a number of capabilities demonstrated. Some ad hoc tests were conducted. The discrepancies they uncovered were recorded but not well documented. Because the procedures for these tests were not written down, it was sometimes difficult to remember the sequence of keyboard entries leading up to a discrepancy. Often this situation meant that a discrepancy could not be duplicated. Such discrepancies were usually ignored.

These ad hoc tests also revealed some missing capabilities that the customer had expected to see. As a result, the customer would not accept the system. The seller began an effort to correct known discrepancies and to install missing capabilities. This effort dragged on for about three months and resulted in a substantial overrun for the project. □

Several factors contributed to the failure of Project Mars. As illustrated in Figure 7.3, one of the most important factors was the failure to obtain an agreed-upon, detailed requirements specification (which created dissension between the customer and the seller and within the seller's organization). The "wizard" on this project evidently never sought an answer to the question "What is it that you [the customer] really want?" The absence of focus on the requirements specification may have been a deliberate effort to guarantee "success" on the project. When there are no specific requirements defined for a project, there is nothing against which to measure the final software product. Thus, whatever works on the scheduled delivery date is delivered, and whatever gets delivered is assumed to be that which was required. Based on this assumption, product integrity is guaranteed no matter what the software contains or how it functions.

The other major problem on this project was the elimination of all product assurance effort except for T&E support. Changes occurred on the project, but they were often not visible and were never under control. The audits of the two documents were ignored, and the audit of the code (i.e., acceptance testing) was ineffective because the preceding documents were badly out of date. In fact, this project was one without visibility and traceability. The effective use of product assurance would have provided this visibility and traceability and would have increased the likelihood of achieving a true software success.

We turn next to a very large project with considerable product assurance—scaled to the size of the project.

PROJECT JUPITER

Project Jupiter was a large message-processing and database management system. The software in Project Jupiter was updated on a major release basis, in the same fashion as described in Project Venus. During the development of this updated software, both the buyer and the seller practiced product assurance comprehensively. The seller's product assurance ef-

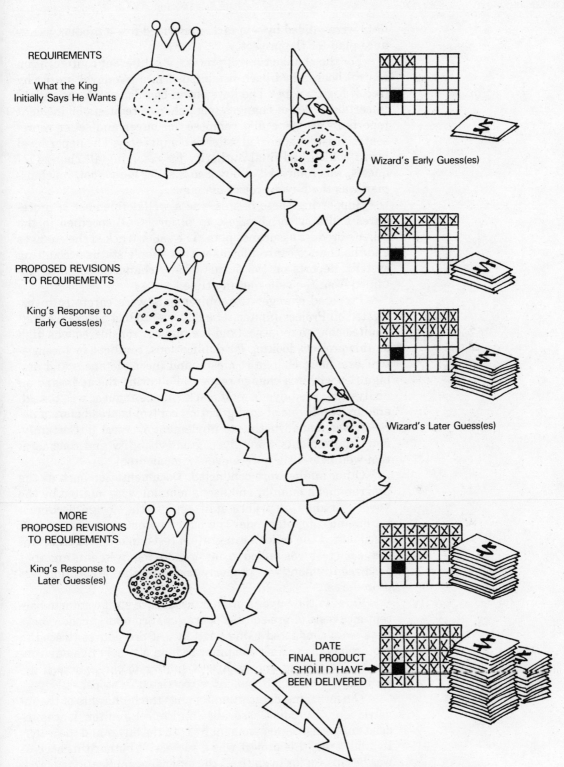

REQUIREMENTS

What the King
Initially Says He Wants

Wizard's Early Guess(es)

PROPOSED REVISIONS
TO REQUIREMENTS

King's Response to
Early Guess(es)

Wizard's Later Guess(es)

MORE
PROPOSED REVISIONS
TO REQUIREMENTS

King's Response to
Later Guess(es)

DATE
FINAL PRODUCT
SHOULD HAVE
BEEN DELIVERED

FIGURE 7.3. If requirements are not clearly delineated (i.e., if the king is not definitive regarding what he wants, and the wizard does not press for an answer), software development degenerates into a continuing guessing game. The wizard guesses what the king will accept, and the king guesses what he can get the wizard to produce. When there is no CCB to help the wizard and king resolve uncertainties, the result is often escalating costs and schedule slippages. Furthermore, this guessing game often breeds dissension between the wizard and the king.

407

forts were guided by—in fact, conformed to—a product assurance plan for the project.

For the change control process, six different configuration control boards had been established in a two-level hierarchy (recall Figure 4.14). The lower-level boards, which specialized in certain types of changes (e.g., change requests or incident reports), were generally composed of buyer and seller representatives—just one had seller personnel only. The upper-level board, which had final authority for resolving all change requests, was composed of buyer and seller personnel. Its chairman was the buyer project manager.

Supporting these boards was a well-defined set of procedures and a set of change control forms, all specified in the seller's product assurance plan. The seller tracked the changes and the change control forms with a simple status accounting system. Reports on the status of any change(s) could be obtained from the seller at any time.

Proposed changes to requirements were carefully investigated on Project Jupiter. The buyer's product assurance staff audited change requests (and the number considered was high on this project), looking for duplications, conflicts, or inconsistencies among change requests, and incompleteness and ambiguities within a change request. Following the audit and an analysis by the buyer's staff, each change request was considered by two levels of configuration control boards before a decision was made whether to implement or reject it. Certainly, new requirements were given great visibility and consideration well before they were ever implemented.

Other audits were conducted. Documentation such as the programmer's manual and user's manual were audited by the buyer's product assurance staff against the design documentation and computer code. The buyer's product assurance staff also audited the seller's integration tests, in order to ascertain that each test was linked to one or more requirements and that each requirement was properly tested by the integration test procedures.

Finally, the buyer's product assurance staff conducted acceptance tests of pre-release operational computer code. These tests were conducted using written test procedures (traced to requirements) against computer code in a nearly live environment. The testing approach was similar to the approach described in Section 5.3, but more restricted in scope. □

The foregoing description touches the highlights of the involvement of product assurance on Project Jupiter. It was indeed an extensive involvement by both the buyer and the seller. By and large, this project was a success. Whether this success was because of (or in spite of) the extensive application of product assurance on the project is a matter for speculation.

One additional point regarding this project needs to be made. The amount of product assurance to use on a project is truly dependent upon the amount of visibility and traceability desired. Project Jupiter management desired a high degree of visibility and traceability. As a result, the scale of product assurance activities was extensive. On smaller projects, product assurance still has much to offer, but it must be correspondingly scaled down in magnitude and scope. (Recall Figure 1.4 in our discussion in Section 1.3 and Figure E1.1 in Exercise 1.6; Project Jupiter is akin to the project portrayed in Figure 1.4.)

We next look at a project somewhat smaller than Project Jupiter that also practiced extensive product assurance. Yet, unlike Project Jupiter, this project ended in failure.

PROJECT SATURN

Project Saturn was a logistics support system to be developed over a period of years in multiple releases. The buyer formed an independent product assurance organization (that is, independent of the project manager) long before he selected a seller, and he charged it with performing all the product assurance services we advocate in this book. (Later in this project, the buyer placed the product assurance organization directly under the project manager.) The product assurance organization produced a comprehensive product assurance plan that specified all the methods and procedures to be used on the project to attain products with integrity.

For change control, the product assurance plan established two configuration control boards in a two-level hierarchy, specified the procedures to be used for change control, and provided the forms to support this process. Both CCBs had buyer and seller representatives and included buyer product assurance representatives.

Every document (whether a software product or not) was audited by the buyer's product assurance organization. Any discrepancies found during these audits were documented as incident reports (this is the alternative scenario depicted in the third row of Figure 4.23).

The buyer's product assurance organization also performed all the bookkeeping for the project. An automated status accounting system was developed for the project by the buyer's product assurance organization. It tracked incident reports and change requests, maintained a directory of baselines established, and traced the software configuration as it proceeded from requirements through design to code. The product assurance organization interfaced with the buyer's central library in control of computer code and provided its own control and library functions for documents.

For acceptance testing, the buyer established a joint user/buyer test team. The user personnel handled the functional aspects of the testing, and the buyer product assurance personnel addressed the technical side of the testing. (This team operated under a charter similar to that shown in Table 6.2.)

Notice that the product assurance provided on Project Saturn was instituted by the buyer. The seller on this project participated on the CCBs and responded to incident reports, but otherwise performed little product assurance. The seller had no product assurance organization of his own.

The seller generally proceeded quite independently of the buyer and user on this project. He determined the schedule by which he worked, and he determined the contents of each release. Unfortunately, he did not see the need to publish either the schedule or the release contents for other project participants. He would not let the buyer monitor his unit tests or his integration tests.

The project proceeded through the Requirements Definition, Preliminary Design, and first-release Detailed Design Stages and into the Coding Stage. As illustrated in Figure 7.4, the seller did not believe in documentation maintenance, so no baselines were ever updated (one baseline was actually discarded to avoid expending effort on correcting it). Further, the seller did not believe that the design specification, even though baselined, constrained him in coding in any way. As a result, and with the concurrence of the buyer's management, the seller, as he saw fit, modified the design as he coded. His departures from the Design Baseline were not documented and were not approved by the CCB. By this point, all traceability of the software had been lost and there was no visibility into the software design or code. Further, no control was being exercised over the software development. Despite warnings about these circumstances and their consequences by the product assurance group, the project continued on this path for some months until the seller turned the first-release software over to be acceptance tested. When the initial tests uncovered many problems, the user (who allocated the money to the buyer to acquire this system for him) decided to cut his losses and abruptly terminated the project (which not only put the seller out of work but also put the buyer's product assurance group out of work). □

Unlike Project Jupiter, which also had extensive product assurance effort, Project Saturn failed. Why did one project succeed while the other failed? In our opinion, there were a number of reasons that Project Saturn failed. We restrict ourselves to those pertaining to product assurance.

One prime reason Project Saturn failed was, in our view, the lack of a product assurance organization or product assurance effort within the seller organization (except for some perfunctory unit and integration testing). The large number of corrections required in every product the seller developed and the seller's reluctance to making the corrections created the impression that the seller had no interest in developing a product with integrity. This suggests that, if software success is to be achieved, both buyer and seller must *practice* product assurance (which means more than passive CCB involvement).

Another major cause of Project Saturn's downfall was the

FIGURE 7.4. On some software projects, the only software product that matters is computer code. On such projects, even if predecessor software products—such as requirements and design documents—are developed, they are viewed as historical (i.e., once produced, they are not updated to reflect subsequent changes). Each baselined product is abandoned once the successor product is baselined. This approach to software development results in computer code that is difficult and expensive to maintain because traceability is destroyed and, consequently, the context for change no longer exists. Furthermore, it is unlikely that the computer code embodies customer requirements.

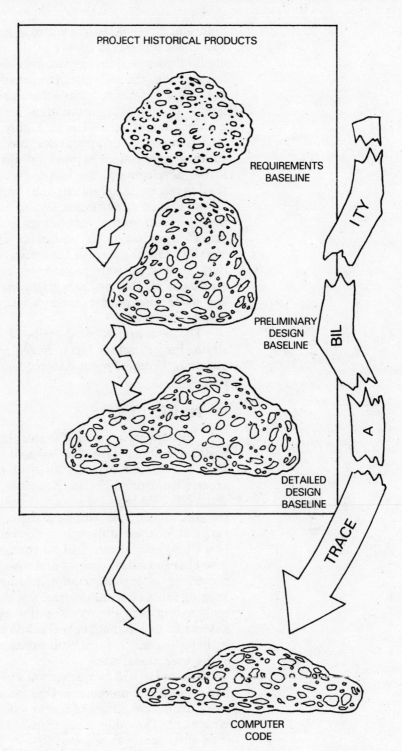

PROJECT HISTORICAL PRODUCTS

REQUIREMENTS BASELINE

PRELIMINARY DESIGN BASELINE

DETAILED DESIGN BASELINE

TRACEABILITY

COMPUTER CODE

411

failure of buyer management to demand that the seller (who was under contract to the buyer) maintain visibility and traceability throughout the project. Because buyer direction was not forthcoming, the seller set the schedule and release content, but would not communicate them to the other project participants. The buyer project management sided with the seller in not updating baselines (recall Figure 7.4) and in making unilateral (non-CCB-approved) changes. The more the product assurance organization pointed out discrepancies and problems in the development, the less the buyer project management tried to resolve the problems and the more it muzzled the product assurance organization (which worked for buyer project management), so that its findings got no visibility outside the project organization (in particular, user management got no visibility into the state of the software until, as indicated earlier, the first software release was acceptance tested). So our conclusion in the last paragraph applies again—both buyer and seller must practice product assurance if software success is to be achieved.

The next project we describe is approximately the same size as Project Saturn but involved a completely different application. Unlike Project Saturn, however, this project was a success.

PROJECT URANUS

The application area of Project Uranus was in automated postal operations—the development of a process control system. The system was installed at more than twenty sites around the United States. Each site had different hardware and a different physical layout. Consequently, the software for the system had to be parameterized and to be built in different versions for these different configurations. The seller had his own CCB, which controlled all changes to software code. The code change control process and associated bookkeeping were prescribed in a configuration management plan. The bookkeeping function included tracking of incident reports and operation of a code library. The library was operated with an automated tool that not only checked program modules out and in, but also compiled and built executable software for any one of the operational sites.

The seller had two acceptance test teams, each of which had its own test procedures. One team tested the software in-plant, using simulators to create a nearly live operational environment. The other team installed the software and tested it on-site (clearly they tested in a live environment).

The design of the software was never formally documented, so in the early months of the project there was little visibility into the software, and management had no visibility into what was happening on the project. Management was unable to perform its function, and the project fell behind schedule and went over budget. At this point, the buyer forced the seller to replace his top and middle managers and to augment his programming staff. Most of the product assurance functions used on the project were initiated at this time. With the visibility gained through the change control process and through closer relationships and exchanges within the programming group, the managers were able to gain visibility into what was happening on the project. Software development proceeded on schedule and within budget for the rest of the project. □

Here was a case in which a project headed for disaster was turned around at the midpoint of its development path. The replacement managers introduced product assurance to the project, and product integrity was subsequently achieved. It is not reasonable to postulate that this project success is wholly attributable to the instituting of product assurance midway through the project. However, we can assert that product assurance did contribute to the achievement of software success.

The final project we are going to describe involves the development of another process control system, again for automated postal operations. As in Project Uranus, adding product assurance to an ailing project contributed in no small measure to turning the project around.

PROJECT NEPTUNE

Project Neptune was actually performed twice, the first time without significant product assurance and the second time with it. The customer's original statement of requirements was exceedingly weak relative to system-level performance criteria. A key performance requirement—in-plant mail flow rate—was ill-defined and vague. There was little visibility provided on the project—little documentation, no change control or audits, not even a designated project manager. As a result, none of the problems within the requirements was brought to light or resolved. Two and a half years after development started (and one year after scheduled project completion), the software was subjected to system tests to determine its operational readiness. The system was adjudged not ready. This judgment was the beginning of a three-year period of test/fix/ retest which degenerated into a guessing game like that depicted in Figure 7.3—without success in developing a system that was acceptable to the customer. A particular problem during this entire period was whether the specified flow rate had been achieved. (It appears that neither the buyer nor the seller attempted to obtain joint concurrence on what flow rate meant in measurable terms.) At the end of this abortive test period, the seller walked off the job (seeking adequate payment for work performed), and the buyer placed the seller in default (for nonperformance of contract). At this point the system was four years late and 20 percent over budget. No documentation or code had been delivered. (No functional or design specification was required by contract, only as-built documentation—a variation from the situation depicted in Figure 7.4.) A year later, the buyer and seller settled their differences and terminated their contract.

One year later, another seller was given a contract to rectify the existing system's problems. This seller used an approach emphasizing visibility and traceability. His project team, although small in numbers (ten to twelve people), included system, hardware, and software engineers, a product assurance practitioner, and user personnel who would actually be operating the system in-plant. The first step in this rectification was to produce a requirements specification, to document what the system was supposed to do in specific and quantitative terms. When the customer agreed to this specification, it was established as the baseline against which the system was to be rectified. As a noteworthy sidelight, this requirements baseline was established approximately ten years after the buyer first solicited bids for the system he wanted developed. (The moral here, of course, is that it is never too late to prompt the king to stipulate what he wants so that the wizard can proceed [the converse of what is portrayed in Figure 7.3].)

After the Requirements Baseline was established, the rectification proceeded through the stages corresponding to those following the Requirements Definition Stage in Figure 2.7. New products were prepared during each stage, and products prepared during preceding stages were updated at the end of each stage to maintain traceability back to the requirements specification. These products were audited as they were produced. Written procedures to specify how to handle audit findings and changes to requirements were prepared. A form of configuration control board was established and met weekly. A test plan specifying a five-level testing approach was produced. Test procedures implementing this plan were written.

The software code on this rectification project was produced on time and, when tested, showed very few problems. The flow rate that had been the cause of so much controversy fully met its requirements (specified in the baselined requirements specification). As the software was formally accepted, all project documentation was updated to represent the as-built condition of the system and to provide a basis for incorporating enhancements and new requirements in future versions of the system. □

Project Neptune began with ill-defined requirements and in its early period provided little visibility or traceability with no product assurance performed. The disastrous results were turned around by a rectification effort which practiced extensive product assurance (on a scale consistent with the project). As a result of the visibility and traceability thus provided, the project ended successfully.

Project Neptune ends our description of the product assurance provided on a sampling of projects on which the au-

THE REAL WORLD

SOMETIMES WHEN WE APPLIED PRODUCT ASSURANCE,
PROJECTS SUCCEEDED.

SOMETIMES WHEN WE APPLIED PRODUCT ASSURANCE,
PROJECTS TERMINATED PREMATURELY OR FAILED.

OFTEN WHEN PRODUCT ASSURANCE WAS OMITTED, CUT
BACK, OR CUT OUT, PROJECTS FAILED OR LED TO DISASTER.

FIGURE 7.5. A summary of our experience regarding the "correlation" between the application of software product assurance and software project outcome.

thors have performed some product assurance tasks. Figure 7.5 summarizes our experience as embodied in these and other projects that we have been associated with. This figure correlates the application of software product assurance with software project outcome. Later in this chapter, we return to this figure and restate it in the form of a so-called product assurance guarantee.

We end this section with one more description of a real-world application, although neither author participated in this project. We include a description of this project because it illustrates the theme we have stated a number of times: "Pay now versus pay much more later" (recall Figure 1.3). Also, this project offers a dramatic example of the third item listed in Figure 7.5. We preface this description with the remark that, since neither of us participated in this project, we had to rely on public documents to obtain technical and other pertinent details. (The institution involved, perhaps understandably, chose not to give us any technical details on the incident and referred us to the public record.)

THE OVERFLOWED COUNTER—A REAL-WORLD INCIDENT[5]

In the fall of 1985, a large New York bank acting as a clearing agent for government securities had a computer system failure that prevented the bank from delivering securities to buyers and making payments to sellers. The symptom of this

---

[5] Sources for this incident include: "A Computer Snafu Snarls the Handling of Treasury Issues," *Wall Street Journal*, November 25, 1985, p. 58; "DP Nightmare Hits N.Y. Bank," *Computerworld*, December 2, 1985, pp. 1, 7; "The Federal Reserve Bank of New York Discount Window Advance of $22.6 Billion Extended to the Bank of New York," Hearing before the Subcommittee on Domestic Monetary Policy of the Committee on Banking, Finance, and Urban Affairs, U.S. House of Representatives, Serial No. 99-65, December 12, 1985; "Computer Snarled N.Y. Bank," *The Washington Post*, December 13, 1985, pp. D7–D8; "Bank Blames Nightmare on Software Flop," *Computerworld*, December 16, 1985, pp. 1, 12; "Gentlemen Prefer Platinum to Bonds—$32 Billion Overdraft," *ACM SIGSOFT Software Engineering Notes*, vol. 11, no. 1 (January 1986), pp. 3–7.

failure was that the computer was storing transaction data in the wrong locations, thereby corrupting the database. A backup copy of the database existed, but in their haste to correct the problem quickly the bank's programmers and operators evidently copied the corrupted database onto the backup database, leaving the bank with two copies of a corrupted database. Before bank employees could develop and test an emergency patch, the bank had accumulated a $32 billion overdraft on its cash account at the New York Federal Reserve Bank. (Incidentally, computer programmers, supervisory officials, senior management of the bank, outside computer consultants, and personnel from the original software system developer all took part in patching the software and in developing a permanent fix for the problem—a form of emergency CCB as we discussed it in Section 4.4.) The patch failed shortly before the transfer system was shut down for the night, but not before the patch had allowed the overdraft to be reduced to $24 billion. The bank was forced to borrow that amount overnight, mostly from the Federal Reserve Bank of New York, to balance its accounts. The interest on that borrowing amounted to about $5 million.

Meanwhile, during the patching operation, a separate group at the bank was implementing a permanent fix for the problem. This effort involved reviewing and possibly modifying 700 separate computer code modules, and took twelve hours to accomplish. When this effort was completed, the computer system functioned properly and cleared up the backlog of transactions before the close of the day.

The computer system involved had been in operation for eight years. Eight months before the incident, the software code had been modified to recognize and store information for up to 36,000 securities issues to be cleared daily. However, the day the incident occurred was the first time the number of issues being cleared exceeded 32,000. The incident was ascribed by the bank to a flaw in program design. More specifically, the problem appears to have been caused by the overflow of a 16-bit counter on a message input/output buffer. (The system probably began to misstore data when the number of issues exceeded 32,767, or $2^{15} - 1$.) □

The description of the incident given above (except for the parenthetical statements, which are our commentary) is extracted from sources set forth in footnote 5. The following comments represent our assumptions, evaluation, and opinions. The bank in question declined to discuss the incident with us, and so we were left with our own hypothesis.

We think that the bank apparently responded to the incident using good product assurance techniques. Evidently some forum or group was convened to approve the actions taken on installing a patch and in implementing a more permanent fix to the software. This forum is akin to our concept of a CCB. Further, we note that the patch was tested prior to its installation, another activity we strongly espouse. We do not know from the record whether the permanent fix was tested before it was installed (which was desirable), although we do know that a live capacity test was immediately applied to it upon start-up, in the form of processing a two-day backlog of securities issues. The alleged overwriting of the backup database by the corrupt database may indicate defects in control procedures or could reflect operator error in a period of stress—we have too little information on this aspect to make a reasonable evaluation. This corruption of the backup database would most likely have occurred in any event, however. The backup system probably contained the same (flawed) software as the on-line system. The application of the same high volume of transactions to the backup system should produce the same results (namely, a corrupted database) as were produced in the on-line database.

We also think that, when the capacity of the system was enlarged eight months prior to the incident, capacity performance testing was not adequately performed. At the congressional hearing on this incident, one bank official stated that the bank went live with newly developed software after everything had been tested under normal conditions with normal data, presuming that all instances that could make the programs fail had been tested. The bank evidently has some form of tests of a software system against benchmarks established as to volume of transactions and storage capacity requirements. The record does not state whether the bank or its software developer actually conducted any testing of the modified system to ascertain whether the system could handle a capacity of daily transactions approaching 36,000 (and most particularly, greater than 32,767). The number of issues trading through the system at the time of the software modification to expand capacity to 36,000 securities issues was roughly 3,000. With the modified system having a capacity ten to twelve times the then-current need, bank management may not have envisioned a need for testing the modified system for processing capability and storage capacity. To conduct such a test would not be simple or inexpensive. It might require the development of simulators and data generators, which would consume sizable resources. The planning, conduct, and evaluation of such a test might entail considerable investment in time and money. Yet conduct of this test is fundamental to ascertaining that the purpose of the modifications—to expand capacity to 36,000 issues daily—was achieved. Conduct of a capacity test would have been costly in resources (but certainly well below $5 million); however, it would probably have uncovered the counter problem and led to its solution without causing operational difficulties. Failure to conduct the test would save resources in the short term, but this failure, if we are correct in our assumptions, would seem to have ended up causing a $5 million loss. "Pay now versus pay much more later."

Incidentally, the chairman of the bank said that the flaw in the software was unforeseen and probably unforeseeable. We disagree with that latter viewpoint—we have already stated our opinion that a capacity test would have revealed the problem. It is also possible that an audit of the design specification (if one existed) might have uncovered this problem. On the other hand, an audit might not have discovered this problem. Auditors, after all, are not infallible. (It is possible that an audit of the design modification actually was performed. If it was conducted, clearly the problem was not discovered.) But even given the possibility that a design audit might not uncover this counter overflow problem, it becomes worthwhile to conduct the audit, considering the penalty resulting from this incident. For projects as critical as this one, the performance of product assurance is certainly cost-effective. (See Exercise 7.14, which considers product assurance applied to software whose malfunction could be life threatening. Also, recall Section 1.2, which has a pertinent sample problem.) However, we contend that the performance of product assurance is cost-effective for any project. The scope and depth of product assurance must be scaled to the magnitude of the project, but when this scaling is done, product assurance works and is cost-effective.

We are concerned that the bank's response to this incident is to seek ways to prevent its reoccurrence by concentrating on the *operational* stage of the software. Steps mentioned in the public record include installation of an improved diagnostic system, consideration of more effective backup systems, review of equipment and personnel in the bank's operations division, intensive consultation among clearing banks over system operation, and possible actions by the Federal Reserve Board in the event the incident or a similar incident recurs. These measures are all concerned with the operation of the fully developed software. We feel that these measures are worthwhile, but that the focus on software operation is misplaced. To prevent recurrences of software failure such as this one, emphasis should be placed on enhancing the likelihood of correct operation of future releases through application of product assurance, such as testing, *during development of the release software*. As we have argued throughout this book, such an approach contributes to achieving software product integrity, thus obviating stopgap operational measures. The costs of product assurance and of stopgap operational measures are comparable, but the application of product assurance has the greater likelihood of producing a product with integrity—and of preventing incidents such as this one from occurring. During the congressional hearing on this incident, the chairman of the bank involved was asked, as the second part of a two-part question, if he was confident that this kind of problem would not happen again at his facility. He overlooked answering this part of the question.

In this section, we described an experiment for scientifically demonstrating the effectiveness of product assurance on a project (recall Figure 7.2). Our inability to conduct this experiment forced us to present real-world data in the form of a number of project descriptions focused on product assurance.

These projects encompassed a variety of applications—they ranged from small to very large in terms of dollars and duration, they possessed a varied scope of product assurance application, and they included successes as well as failures. We believe that these descriptions show that product assurance can work, keeping in mind Figure 7.5. We leave you to draw your own conclusions.

In the next section, we present some perceptions resulting from our analysis of the foregoing descriptions and from our other product assurance experiences.

7.2 Perceptions of Software Product Assurance in the Real World

In the previous section, we described some of the real-world projects on which we have product assurance experience. In previous chapters, we presented product-assurance-related stories, examples, sample problems, and exercises based on the projects described in Section 7.1 and on other projects in which we participated. We now present some perceptions of how software product assurance works in the real world. These perceptions are based on our observations of, and induction from, our product assurance experiences.

One perception we have applies almost universally. We have observed certain behavior on almost every project with which we have come in contact. This behavior is that software managers tend to focus on short-range project goals, such as those goals shown in the foreground of Figure 7.6, and to overlook long-range project goals, such as those shown in the back-

FIGURE 7.6. Managers tend to focus on short-range goals. In the process, long(er)-range goals are forgotten or ignored.

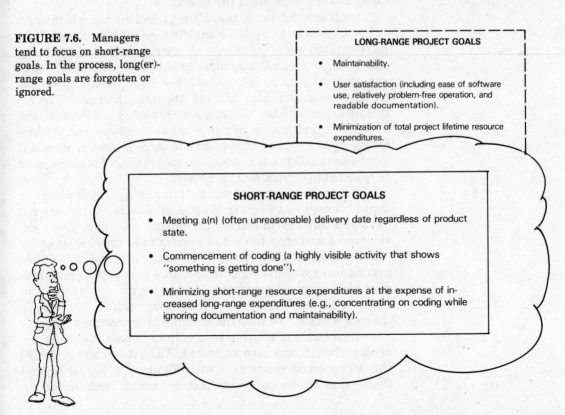

LONG-RANGE PROJECT GOALS

- Maintainability.

- User satisfaction (including ease of software use, relatively problem-free operation, and readable documentation).

- Minimization of total project lifetime resource expenditures.

SHORT-RANGE PROJECT GOALS

- Meeting a(n) (often unreasonable) delivery date regardless of product state.

- Commencement of coding (a highly visible activity that shows "something is getting done").

- Minimizing short-range resource expenditures at the expense of increased long-range expenditures (e.g., concentrating on coding while ignoring documentation and maintainability).

ground of that figure. This focus is understandable, even though it is undesirable. The project manager developing a software product probably thinks he will be evaluated by senior management solely on whether he gets some software system into the hands of the user on time and within budget. We now explore some of the implications of this management attitude in terms of the specific items listed in Figure 7.6.

Being generally conscientious, the project manager is interested in producing a system that satisfies the user's requirements, but in the real world this issue often becomes a secondary concern. Delivery date and budget are highly visible entities; if he fails to meet either one, the project manager will get a black mark on his record. Satisfaction of user requirements is not as readily visible as success in meeting delivery dates and in staying within budget. Besides, the customer may be very happy to have most of his requirements satisfied and may not complain or notice that some are not satisfied. The delivery date may have been arbitrarily set before the seller became involved in the project and may be quite unreasonable, yet it is almost sacrosanct on most projects. Thus, one of the project manager's goals is to deliver the software system—regardless of its state—on the appointed day. Any known unsatisfied requirements or problems uncovered by the customer can be resolved during a postdelivery cleanup or trial-use period. Of course, per Crosby's words that we quoted at the outset of the chapter, such cleanup does not come free (because something was not done right the first time).

Another short-range goal of the project manager is to begin coding as soon as possible—completeness, consistency, and logical compliance of the design with the requirements are of secondary importance. Commencement of coding is highly visible and gives an impression that the project is making progress, an impression that may be more apparent than real. The rationale appears to be that, since code is what is delivered, the sooner we start producing code, the more code we can produce by the delivery date. This rationale is, of course, true, but it overlooks the fact that much of the code produced often consists of rewrites to correct design defects.

The project manager wants to minimize his short-range expenditures to stay within his budget constraint. He may not have had any say in setting the budget for the software development and may think the constraint is unrealistic or insufficient, but nevertheless he seems to be bound to keep his expenditures within this limit. An area in which he might reduce his resource expenditures is updating documentation. For example, defects discovered in the design can be corrected in the code without updating the design. This action does conserve resources, but it effectively results in each baseline being discarded when its successor is created. We have already discussed this situation in connection with Figure 7.4. Recall in that figure that failure to update documentation leads to the destruction of traceability and to difficulty in maintaining the software.

But maintainability is a long-range goal for a project. Little maintenance is performed on the software during the short term (i.e., the period prior to first delivery), and when it is done it is less difficult because the original programmers are still present. Further, a project manager who is successful in the short term is generally rewarded by being made project manager on a comparable or more prestigious project. He seldom remains on the project after initial delivery, performing mundane maintenance. Thus, maintainability is of limited concern to the initial project manager.

Another area in which a project manager can reduce his short-term expenditures is product assurance. Note that the objective of product assurance—development of a software product with integrity (recall our definition of product integrity in Section 2.6)—differs slightly but significantly from the objective of a project manager. Both are concerned with staying within budget and schedule. But while product assurance endeavors to help the project manager satisfy *all* the user's requirements (and when they are not clear, to make them visible for the manager), the project manager is forced to attempt to satisfy as many user requirements as he can within the constraints of budget and delivery date. He generally cannot accommodate requirements that do not become manifest until after the project has started. After all, neither the budget nor the schedule takes these additional requirements into account.

The visibility and traceability afforded by product assurance may not always be welcomed by the project manager. In the previous chapters of this book, we discussed how these two attributes benefited a project manager, so let us consider here why visibility and traceability may be disadvantageous to a project manager. Product assurance attempts to make the user's requirements clearly visible and in the process may bring additional requirements to light. As we saw in the preceding paragraph, this visibility may make it even more difficult for the project manager to achieve his objective of delivering something on time and within budget. Product assurance also gives visibility to known user requirements that are not being satisfied as development proceeds. Because the project manager may believe that he must sacrifice some requirements in order to meet his budget and schedule, he may not welcome these shortfalls being made visible to others. Product assurance makes visible disconnects and the lack of traceability between successive software products. These problems generally require updating of documentation as part of their resolution. Since the project manager may be trying to conserve resources by not updating documentation, this visibility may also be unwelcome. Nor does the project manager generally welcome his senior management or the user gaining visibility into his problems.

For the reasons above, the project manager may not want to employ product assurance on his project. Weighing its benefits against the cost and liabilities (as he perceives them), he may choose to curtail or eliminate product assurance. He may also choose to limit the visibility provided by product assurance to not extend beyond himself. We have observed both these actions being taken and have seen the projects subsequently fail (for example, recall Projects Mars and Saturn in Section 7.1). See Exercises 3.10(f) and 6.4 for further consideration of these issues.

Consider some of the facets of user satisfaction, another long-range goal of a project. These facets include the ease with which the user can operate and apply the software, the number of latent software defects, and the readability and utility of operational, instructional, and maintenance documentation. None of these facets becomes evident during the short term. Thus, they are not the concern of the initial project manager, who will probably leave the project before they do become evident.

As a final consideration, notice that the focus of the project manager on minimizing short-range resource expenditures is counterproductive to the long-range goal of minimizing total expenditures over the project lifetime. The defects remaining in design documentation when design is curtailed and coding begins, coupled with the failure to update the documentation and the resultant loss of traceability, make the software more difficult and more costly to maintain, as indicated in Figure 7.4. Because software is in this "maintenance" stage much longer than it is under development, the total cost of the software over the project's lifetime is increased when short-term expenditures are minimized.

Members of the development organization often are in complete agreement with their project manager on short-range goals. Early commencement of coding and curtailment of project documentation are generally popular decisions among programmers. Further, note that, like the project manager, the programmers who initially develop software usually will not remain on the project subsequent to the postdelivery cleanup, i.e., during the "maintenance" stage. Maintainability is not of concern to them, but achievement of the planned delivery is.

We do not mean to blame the project manager for focusing on short-range goals. Given his circumstances and objective of on-time product delivery within budget, his focus on short-range goals is understandable. His objective may not even be of his own choosing. Senior management generally establishes budgets and delivery dates and assigns personnel. Having proposed to deliver software on a certain day for a certain cost, senior management is anxious that contract terms be met—to enhance the company's reputation, to satisfy a customer who may provide additional work for the company, and to make a profit on the contract. Notice also that there are generally separate budgets for development and maintenance. Such an arrangement does not foster the achievement of the long-range goal of minimizing costs over the lifetime of the project.

The customer often also causes the project manager and other project participants to focus on short-range goals. The customer asks for software by a certain date at a certain price. He seldom expresses any concern for long-range project goals, or if he does, he buries his concerns in vague, untestable performance requirements (e.g., "the system must be user friendly" or "the system must be easily maintainable"). As we often state in this book, what the customer wants (i.e., his requirements) is not always clear. But there is usually no doubt as to *when* he wants a software system and *how much* he will pay for it. This situation forces the project manager to set as his objective the delivery of software that meets as many of the customer's requirements as possible.

In our perception, the application of product assurance can help the customer and developer handle this real-world situation more effectively, as shown in Figure 7.7. The application of product assurance provides the visibility and traceability on a project that inform all project participants as to what the customer really wants, where the project has been, and what is currently happening on the project. If this visibility reveals that all the customer's requirements cannot be satisfied in the scheduled time or within the established budget, compromises can be satisfactorily made that tend to satisfy long-range goals (such as those shown in Figure 7.6). For example, we have had experience with customers who have been quite willing to extend the delivery date a reasonable period in order to obtain a software product that met all their requirements. We have also experienced the compromise shown in Figure 7.7. Here the customer has a need for some capability in the near term and has established those requirements he needs immediately and those he can defer until time or money becomes available to develop them. With the traceability provided by product assurance, the project team can determine what portions of the design and code and test procedures to include in the near-term delivery. Thus, when the customer receives computer code in the near-term delivery, that code should satisfy the customer's immediate needs. The remaining needs of the customer are subsequently satisfied by developing the rest of the design, code, and test procedures as necessary. Using this approach, documentation can be kept updated, issues of user satisfaction can be addressed, and software can be developed with features that allow it to be easily maintained.

In Figure 7.7, the customer has made a choice, tempered by the available time and money, as to what needs he must have satisfied in the near term, with the prospect of having the remaining requirements satisfied in the long term. Our perception of a different approach to resolving the problem of being unable to give the customer what he wants when he

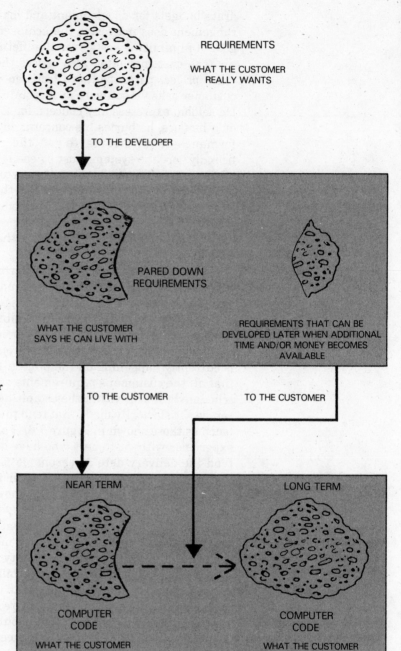

REQUIREMENTS

WHAT THE CUSTOMER
REALLY WANTS

TO THE DEVELOPER

PARED DOWN
REQUIREMENTS

WHAT THE CUSTOMER
SAYS HE CAN LIVE WITH

REQUIREMENTS THAT CAN BE
DEVELOPED LATER WHEN ADDITIONAL
TIME AND/OR MONEY BECOMES
AVAILABLE

TO THE CUSTOMER   TO THE CUSTOMER

NEAR TERM   LONG TERM

COMPUTER
CODE

WHAT THE CUSTOMER
RECEIVED

COMPUTER
CODE

WHAT THE CUSTOMER
MAY EVENTUALLY RECEIVE

FIGURE 7.7. In the real world, the customer cannot always get what he really wants when he wants it and at the price he wants to pay for it. Compromises may therefore be necessary. For example, after he submits his requirements to the developer, the customer may be told that not all these requirements can be incorporated into computer code by the time the customer says he needs the code and/or for the money the customer has available. Pressed for some capability in the near term, a customer is often willing to pare down or otherwise modify his requirements with the expectation that in the long term all his requirements can be incorporated into computer code. The application of product assurance helps the customer and developer deal effectively with such situations. This application provides the visibility and traceability needed to ascertain what can be done now and what must be deferred.

wants it and at the price he wants is shown in Figure 7.8. We have seen the Procrustean[6] approach illustrated in the figure used on a number of projects (for example, Projects Mars and Saturn among those shown in Table 7.1). In this approach, the developer, faced with the need to make some compromise, ar-

---

[6] In Greek mythology, Procrustes was an outlaw who invited travelers to stay at his house. He insisted that each traveler fit his iron bed precisely. If a traveler was too short, Procrustes would stretch the traveler's legs on a rack until he fit the bed. If a traveler was too tall, Procrustes would lop off the traveler's legs until he just fit the available bed.

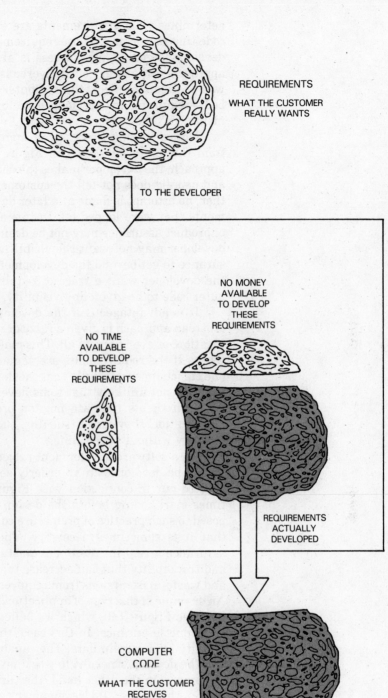

REQUIREMENTS

WHAT THE CUSTOMER
REALLY WANTS

TO THE DEVELOPER

NO TIME
AVAILABLE
TO DEVELOP
THESE
REQUIREMENTS

NO MONEY
AVAILABLE
TO DEVELOP
THESE
REQUIREMENTS

REQUIREMENTS
ACTUALLY
DEVELOPED

COMPUTER
CODE

WHAT THE CUSTOMER
RECEIVES

FIGURE 7.8. The Procrustean approach to software development—fitting customer requirements to computer code. On many software projects, it is often difficult to give the customer computer code embodying what he really wants because of, for example, budget or schedule constraints. In such instances, the developer, like Procrustes in Greek mythology, dismembers some of the customer requirements so that what remains is congruent with the computer code delivered to the customer. On these projects, success, by definition, is whatever is delivered.

bitrarily lops off requirements. These are requirements that the developer has neither time nor money to satisfy. This curtailment does not usually occur at the beginning of a project, and it is generally not given visibility when it does occur. Rather the curtailment typically occurs near the code delivery date and is given as little publicity as possible. The developer determines what requirements are satisfied by the computer code that is working. Those requirements are defined to be the developer's goal. Thus, success is always guaranteed in this approach—whatever gets delivered is defined to be that which was desired. In effect, the computer code is the Procrustean bed—requirements are lopped off until finally the requirements "fit" the code.

Notice in this Procrustean approach several differences from the approach shown in Figure 7.7. In the Procrustean approach, the developer makes the decision about what to omit and usually does not tell the customer what he has done. Further, no attempt is made at a later date to provide the requirements that were lopped off. In this approach, the application of product assurance may not be desired by the developer. The developer may not want the visibility provided by product assurance to get beyond the development organization. Nor does the developer want a trace of requirements through to computer code to be given any visibility.

It is advantageous if the developer who follows the Procrustean approach is given a fuzzy or vague requirements specification, or even none at all. This makes his success even more likely. If the requirements are vague or nonexistent, then no one can claim successfully that the developer has left anything out. It is not unlikely that some developers would prefer a set of requirements that are not too precise. Without a precise specification, they can pursue this "success is what you deliver" strategy without constraints.

On a software development project, the life cycle products should be developed in an orderly sequence. However, as we pointed out in connection with Figure 7.6, developers sometimes start coding before the design is complete. We are opposed to such practice of premature coding, but we do recognize that it is sometimes necessary. The application of product assurance even in these circumstances provides visibility and traceability that can decrease the likelihood of false starts and wasteful excursions from requirements (recall Figure 1.3). An example of this type of application happened on Project Jupiter (see Figure 7.9), which we believe illustrates the benefit of product assurance. In this case, the customer needed a capability by a certain date. The capability was broadly stated, and the developer needed to work out the particulars with the customer. On the other hand, the time period allotted did not permit the sequential development of requirements, design, and code. To solve this problem, a special group was formed, including analysts, programmers, and product assurance practitioners. This group developed the requirements and computer code satisfying those requirements in parallel. (Note that no design specification was produced in this effort, an omission that may ultimately precipitate maintenance problems.) A parallel development of requirements and code will almost certainly face troubles in the form of code that does not support

FIGURE 7.9. In the real world, some projects cannot follow a life cycle in which progressively more detailed products are developed in sequence. Even in such circumstances, the application of product assurance can increase the likelihood that products with integrity are developed. For example, as illustrated, in one particular project, a requirements specification was developed in parallel with computer code (without an intermediate design specification). The reason for this parallel and abbreviated development approach was a customer-imposed schedule constraint. The application of product assurance, primarily through auditing of the requirements drafts and code versions, injected a high degree of visibility into this development process. Through early recognition of potential discrepancies between the two products, wasted resources resulting from the false starts inherent in parallel development efforts were limited. The requirements and code were completed by the scheduled delivery date and were demonstrated to be congruent. To meet this date, project personnel worked extra hours. Thus, one product integrity attribute—schedule—was traded off against another—resource expenditures. Therefore, on this particular effort, the application of product assurance helped to achieve computer code that possessed the integrity attributes of congruence with customer requirements and delivery on time.

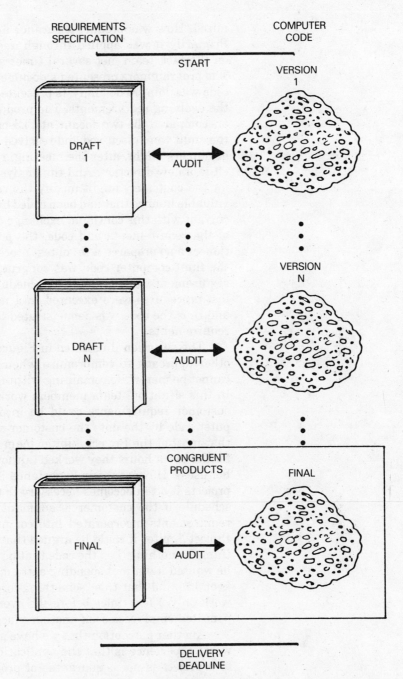

requirements and of requirements unsupported by code. Yet on this task such troubles did not occur; the task was completed by the scheduled delivery date, and the requirements and code were demonstrated by audit (test) to be congruent with each other. (Incidentally, test procedures were also developed in parallel with the requirements and code.) To be sure, there were some false starts and excursions from requirements during the task effort. But these difficulties were quickly uncovered by the product assurance function, and wasted effort was minimized. How was product assurance applied during this task? Primarily it was applied through auditing. Key participants on the task team met several times a week—a kind of CCB. The programmers presented a document describing what their code was doing. The analysts presented a document describing the evolving requirements. The product assurance practitioners compared the two documents. Discrepancies resulting from the audit were discussed and resolved at the meeting. The programmers might, after the meeting, revise some code or start off in a new direction. And the analysts (who were surrogates for the customer) might modify the requirements to reflect a valuable nuance that had been coded by the programmers. Concurrent with this continual exchange of information and audit of the requirements and code, the product assurance practitioners also prepared a set of test procedures to assess whether the final computer code was congruent with the final set of requirements. Just before the scheduled delivery date, these test procedures were executed in a nearly live environment, and thus the code was demonstrated to be congruent with the requirements.

The situation illustrated in Figure 7.9 also represents another approach to compromise when customer requirements cannot be met while remaining within budget and/or schedule. In this situation, team members worked overtime so that all customer requirements could be incorporated into the computer code by the date the customer stipulated. It turned out that most of the Project Jupiter team members were not paid for the extra hours they worked (although some were awarded bonuses). However, our experience indicates that on many projects it often becomes necessary to trade off budget against schedule if the customer is adamant about wanting certain requirements incorporated into computer code. Although on Project Jupiter it could be argued that the customer got something for nothing (i.e., the code that he wanted at the time that he wanted it without spending extra money), managers should keep in mind that this "something-for-nothing" approach will work only a few times before the overworked and undercompensated employees seek another place to work.

Another perception that we have gained through our real-world experience is that the application of product assurance to a project is not a guarantee of project success. In fact, as shown in Figure 7.10, sometimes the application of product assurance can contribute toward causing the curtailment or termination of a software product. In the project illustrated in Figure 7.10 (Project Saturn), a change control mechanism is in place, supported by an auditing process for all software products. In the first column, the Nth iteration of a software product has been audited and a certain number of discrepancies has been observed. These discrepancies have been considered by the CCB and solutions to them have been proposed and approved. The minutes reflect that the CCB is worried about the

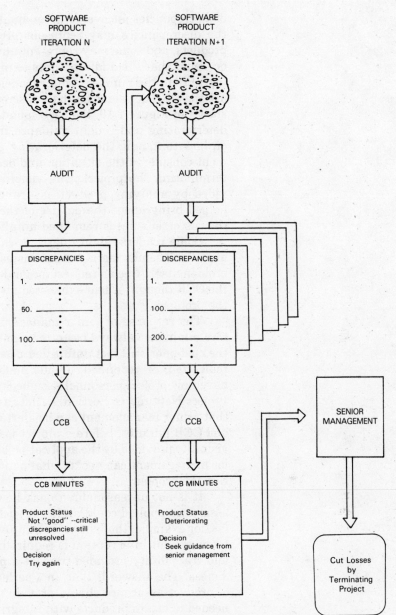

SOFTWARE PRODUCT ITERATION N

SOFTWARE PRODUCT ITERATION N+1

AUDIT

AUDIT

DISCREPANCIES

1. ⋮
50. ⋮
100. ⋮

DISCREPANCIES

1. ⋮
100. ⋮
200. ⋮

CCB

CCB

CCB MINUTES

Product Status
Not "good" --critical
discrepancies still
unresolved

Decision
Try again

CCB MINUTES

Product Status
Deteriorating

Decision
Seek guidance from
senior management

SENIOR MANAGEMENT

Cut Losses
by
Terminating
Project

FIGURE 7.10. Sometimes the visibility and traceability resulting from the application of product assurance may bring about the demise of a project.

state of the product. Certain critical discrepancies, supposedly resolved in previous iterations, have reappeared, i.e., they still have not been resolved.

The second column of Figure 7.10 represents the handling of the next (Nth + 1) iteration of the product. The audit results for this iteration of the product reveal that the number of discrepancies has greatly increased. The absolute number of discrepancies uncovered in an audit is not a meaningful measure of the state of the product audited. Not every discrepancy reported from the audit of a product represents a problem within that product (recall the discussion on evaluating the number of discrepancies uncovered in an audit in Section 5.1). Some of the discrepancies may represent problems with predecessor products, and some may represent auditor misunderstandings or issues that the auditor wants to make visible. More meaningful than the number of discrepancies uncovered in an audit are the CCB decisions on these discrepancies. In the situation shown in Figure 7.10, the CCB found the product status to be deteriorating and sought guidance from senior management on how to handle the deteriorating product. Senior management considered the situation and decided to cut its losses by terminating the project. The visibility and traceability provided by applying product assurance in this case actually helped bring about the demise of the project. Unfortunately, the customer's needs remained unfulfilled.

Some readers might question why the CCB sought guidance from senior management instead of trying to solve the problem itself. Such a request for guidance probably came after the CCB thought it had exhausted all possible ways to resolve the problem.

The response of senior management to situations of this sort might not always be to terminate the project. After all, the customer still has unfulfilled needs. The project might be redirected, or redefined, or put under new management, or have new project personnel assigned. (Recall the discussion of Project Neptune in Section 7.1.) The important point here is that senior management can be alerted, through audit reports and CCB minutes, before a project is out of control. With this visibility provided by the application of product assurance, senior management can decide what actions it should take to correct the problem.

It is not unreasonable to ask how a project with product assurance applied could arrive at such a sorry state of affairs (as, for example, that shown in Figure 7.10) that drastic senior management intervention is required. Shouldn't the visibility and traceability provided prevent a project from getting into a mess? The answer is that, in a perfect world, the application of product assurance should provide the checks and balances needed to attain products with integrity. But the real world is far from perfect, and as we subsequently explain, we can make no such guarantee for product assurance.

What we can guarantee for product assurance in this real world is shown in Figure 7.11. In this book, we do not give you a software development cookbook that will invariably lead you to success if faithfully followed. We do not believe that such a book exists or can be written. The purpose of the guarantee shown in Figure 7.11 is not to provide us with some sort of legal protection[7] regarding the ideas put forth in this book; rather it is an honest statement of what we believe product

---

[7] For comparison, the reader is referred to the guarantee accompanying almost any software package provided on a diskette. These guarantees generally provide legal protection to the seller of the package. The only thing they appear to actually guarantee the buyer is that the diskette can be read by a computer. See Exercise 7.16.

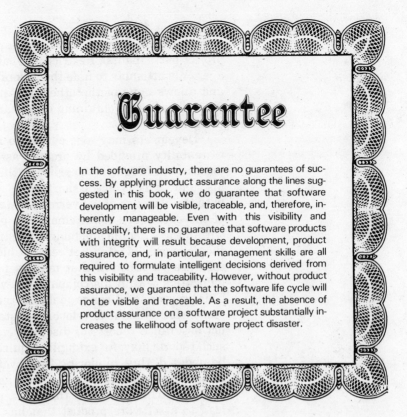

In the software industry, there are no guarantees of success. By applying product assurance along the lines suggested in this book, we do guarantee that software development will be visible, traceable, and, therefore, inherently manageable. Even with this visibility and traceability, there is no guarantee that software products with integrity will result because development, product assurance, and, in particular, management skills are all required to formulate intelligent decisions derived from this visibility and traceability. However, without product assurance, we guarantee that the software life cycle will not be visible and traceable. As a result, the absence of product assurance on a software project substantially increases the likelihood of software project disaster.

FIGURE 7.11. Product assurance does not guarantee software project success, but its absence may guarantee disaster.

assurance can and cannot provide to you. We are certain that, when product assurance is applied as we advocate in this book, visibility and traceability of the software on a project will be obtained. When the software on a project becomes visible and traceable, it becomes possible to manage that software as it evolves. We also guarantee the opposite—that when no product assurance is applied on a project, the software on the project will not be visible and traceable. Without this visibility and traceability, management is not likely to be informed, and thus the likelihood of failure or disaster on a software project becomes much greater.

However, we cannot go any further and guarantee that a product with integrity will result on a project where the software is visible and traceable (i.e., on a project where product assurance is performed). We cannot make this guarantee because even when product assurance is performed, lack of skills or ability in managers, developers, or product assurance practitioners may prevent attainment of a product with integrity.

Management (both project and senior) may choose to ignore the visibility and traceability (or a report of the lack thereof) provided to them (we have seen this happen more than once). As we said above, the likelihood of project failure or disaster is increased in this circumstance. In our experience, failure has inevitably occurred.

Sometimes project management may choose to muzzle its product assurance organization, or restrict its dissemination of information (for example, a project manager may not provide project status information to either senior management or project participants). Restricting visibility to the project manager only attempts to hide the lack of integrity in the software and allows none of the other project participants the opportunity to assist in obtaining a software product that does have integrity.

Developers may also choose to ignore the visibility and traceability provided by product assurance. Recall from our discussion of Figure 7.6 earlier in this section that developers also tend to focus on the short-range goals shown in the figure, with the objective of delivering software that satisfies as many of the customer's requirements as possible while remaining within the schedule and budget constraints. Consider also that the developer is often not responsible for maintenance of the software—a function that may be performed by another organization within his company or even by another company. This focus on short-range goals and the absence of maintenance responsibility make developers resistant to responding to product assurance reports of discrepancies or incidents. Because such reports may, for example, require that the documentation be updated, thus hindering the developer from achieving his short-range objective, the product assurance reports may be ignored. Achievement of this short-range objective does not lead to a software product that has integrity—customer requirements may not be satisfied, and traceability does not exist.

Product assurance practitioners may also contribute toward a project's not achieving a software product with integrity. The auditors might miss something critical during an audit—they are just as human as all the other project participants. This omission—or lack of visibility—may propagate from baseline to baseline. If the discrepancy overlooked is especially critical, the project could end up as a failure or even as a disaster. (Consider the possibilities if the spelling error for the DCODE = 1 display in Figure E5.5 is not detected, or if the substitution of nautical miles for feet in the space shuttle example in Reference 7 of this chapter were instead for a military defense system.) This risk is one reason that validation should be performed on every audit—a comparison is made between every software product and the requirements specification to assess their congruence and to reduce the risk of discrepancies being overlooked in any single audit. The use of more than one auditor to conduct an audit is another hedge against this risk, but cannot eliminate it.

For the foregoing reasons, we cannot guarantee that a project applying product assurance will achieve software products with integrity. Should product assurance be performed—should resources be spent on product assurance—if there is no guarantee that products with integrity will be achieved? The answer is yes—because product assurance is a hedge against disaster. Without product assurance, the likelihood is high that a project failure or disaster will occur. With product assurance, visibility and traceability are guaranteed and the likelihood of project software success is increased (but not guaranteed). Even Reference 8 listed at the end of this chapter—which experimentally concluded that independent verification and validation (IV&V) on small (4 to 12 man-years) flight dynamics projects was not cost-effective—stated that IV&V (substitute "product assurance") should be regarded as an insurance policy whose premiums should be paid when the consequences of failure were great. (For further consideration of this viewpoint, recall Section 1.2 and Exercise 1.4.)

In this section and the preceding one, we explored product assurance in the real world. In the preceding section, we looked at the application of product assurance on a variety of projects and evaluated the project outcomes. In this section, we took a different view of the real world in presenting some of our perceptions of how product assurance really works. Our presentation of these real-world experiences and perceptions demonstrates that product assurance does work (i.e., increases the likelihood of achieving software product integrity)—under certain circumstances.

In the next section, we turn from looking at technical issues relative to product assurance to some planning issues that must be addressed in preparing to perform product assurance.

7.3 Getting Started on a Product Assurance Task

In preceding chapters, we described the mechanics of doing product assurance. Understanding these mechanics is certainly necessary if product assurance is to be performed competently. However, it is also necessary to plan product assurance work intelligently before it is performed. In the following paragraphs we discuss the real-world problem of how to specify the product assurance task that is to be performed on a project. Our purpose in this discussion is not to give a comprehensive treatment of product assurance task planning. Rather our purpose is to bring to light some planning issues that typically need to be faced in preparing to do product assurance. These issues are in general no different from those planning issues faced by other software development tasks, but in their particulars they are unique to product assurance. Settling these issues is particularly necessary for an independent company performing product assurance, and usually they are settled as part of the contractual process. But settlement of these issues is also important when the product assurance organization is in the same company as the project manager and the development organization. Unfortunately, the issues are usually not even addressed in this circumstance, with resultant difficulties in the course of the project. The suggestions provided in this section are offered for the purpose of getting the reader started on planning a product assurance task.

When you contract with a painter to paint the outside of

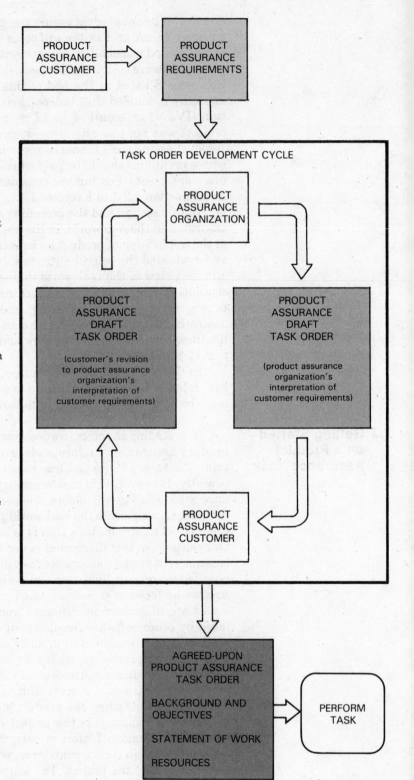

FIGURE 7.12. Application of product assurance disciplines the software life cycle. The work of the product assurance organization must itself be disciplined. To instill this discipline, this organization and its customer should agree in writing on the work to be performed before the work is begun. Hammering out such an agreement typically involves an iterative approach wherein customer product assurance requirements are first interpreted by the product assurance organization and then revised by the customer. Once it is agreed to by these two parties, the task order becomes the standard by which the customer can determine whether he is getting the product assurance he asked for. The task order may be changed during the course of product assurance work to reflect changing customer product assurance needs.

PRODUCT ASSURANCE CUSTOMER

PRODUCT ASSURANCE REQUIREMENTS

TASK ORDER DEVELOPMENT CYCLE

PRODUCT ASSURANCE ORGANIZATION

PRODUCT ASSURANCE DRAFT TASK ORDER

(customer's revision to product assurance organization's interpretation of customer requirements)

PRODUCT ASSURANCE DRAFT TASK ORDER

(product assurance organization's interpretation of customer requirements)

PRODUCT ASSURANCE CUSTOMER

AGREED-UPON PRODUCT ASSURANCE TASK ORDER

BACKGROUND AND OBJECTIVES

STATEMENT OF WORK

RESOURCES

PERFORM TASK

your house, you expect him to submit a proposal specifying what he is going to do and how much his work is going to cost. This proposal then becomes the basis for you and the painter to negotiate a contract for his services at a price you will pay for the work you want done. A similar scenario exists for product assurance services (see Figure 7.12). The customer (for product assurance services) issues a statement of his requirements. In response, the product assurance vendor submits a proposal to the customer (presumably a software development project manager or someone in authority overseeing a software development effort) specifying what the vendor is going to do to satisfy the requirements and what resources are required to do the work. The customer and the vendor iterate on this proposal until they agree on the work to be done and its cost. This written agreement becomes the standard against which task performance can be assessed. In the software world, this proposal can take many forms. For example, it can be a thick document containing hundreds of pages written in response to an often equally imposing request for proposal (RFP) document prepared by the customer. At the other extreme, this proposal can be a several-page task order. Because it is relatively simple in format yet serves to focus on important product assurance planning issues, we show this proposal as a task order and exemplify a task order in the sample problem below. However, we stress at the outset that such issues also usually need to be addressed in larger, more elaborate proposals or in proposals that fall somewhere between this extreme and the several-page task order extreme. What differentiates the proposals in this spectrum from one another is not the issues themselves but the complexity of the issues; in larger proposals, these issues are generally more complex, while in smaller proposals the issues are usually correspondingly reduced in complexity. Thus, the discussion that follows has broad applicability to the subject of product assurance planning.

Table 7.2 shows a format for a task order. This format, which is derived from task orders used on actual software projects, indicates the contents of each paragraph in the task order. To illustrate the meaning of some of the planning implications underlying Table 7.2, we consider the sample problem below.

PRODUCT ASSURANCE PLANNING—A SAMPLE PROBLEM
Background and Question

Recall the System PREDICT auditing sample problem discussed in Section 5.2. You will recall that the problem illustrated an audit of a preliminary design specification against a requirements specification. Assume that you are the product assurance manager for System PREDICT development. Assume further that the project is about to begin and that you need to draft a task order for V&V support for System PREDICT development. This V&V support is to include audits of the following documents to be produced by the software development organization:
1. Requirements Specification (RS)

TABLE 7.2. TASK ORDER FORMAT

Task Number	Date
Task Title	

Reference: The task order is headed by a list of references pertinent to the software project encompassing the task order, including the contract governing the task, project standards, products developed or to be developed by other tasks in the project, and related or companion task orders or documentation.

1.0 *Background and Objectives.*
Paragraph 1.0 of the task order gives background on the project that the work prescribed in the task order is to support. With this background established, it is then possible to meaningfully stipulate the objectives of the task, which are also included in paragraph 1.0 of the task order.

2.0 *Statement of Work.*
Paragraph 2.0 of the task order sets forth the statement of work. This statement includes the scope of the task, the task description, deliverables for the task, and customer-furnished equipment.

2.1 *Scope.* Paragraph 2.1 identifies the general work content and the system life cycle stages encompassed by the task order.

2.2 *Task Description.* Paragraph 2.2 specifies the items of work to be done. Presentations and formal reviews are indicated.

2.3 *Deliverables.* Paragraph 2.3 specifies what products are to be delivered under the task order and when they are to be delivered. Specified are the format of each product, the number of copies of each to be delivered, and when each is to be delivered to the customer.

2.4 *Customer-Furnished Equipment.* Paragraph 2.4 specifies the items of equipment and information that the customer must provide to the contractor to permit accomplishment of the work specified. This paragraph also provides an indication of where the task work is to be performed.

3.0 *Resources.*
Paragraph 3.0 of the task order specifies the estimated amount of all resources that are needed to perform the work specified in paragraph 2.2. To provide the customer with insight into the basis for the resource estimates, this section breaks out the resource requirements by contractor- or customer-specified labor category and by subtask.

2. Preliminary Design Specification (PDS)
3. Detailed Design Specification (DDS)

Assume that your organization is to audit each of the above documents and computer code resulting from the DDS. Assume further that the scope of the task does not include acceptance testing of this code, but that you will write a companion task order that picks up where this task order leaves off and covers acceptance testing. Also, assume that your contract with your customer (Company Q, which oversees both your work and the work of the software development organization, and is therefore to be the recipient of your draft task order) is called System PREDICT Independent Product Assurance Contract C-PA39 and contains a section specifying audit report formats. Finally, assume that your customer has prepared (1) a document called Product Assurance Plan for System PREDICT that prescribes the product assurance practices to be followed during System PREDICT development, (2) a documentation standards manual that prescribes the format and content of Company Q software specifications, and (3) a programming standards manual that prescribes guidelines for developing Company Q software code. With the preceding as background, how would you use the format in Table 7.2 to write a task order for V&V support for System PREDICT development?

Solution Approach

Figure 7.13 shows a task order based on the format given in Table 7.2 designed to provide V&V support for System PREDICT development up to, but not including, system acceptance testing. This task order highlights a number of product assurance task planning issues that usually need to be addressed if V&V work is to be accomplished without having an adverse impact on ongoing development efforts. These issues and how they are addressed in the task order are discussed below.

A. The task order is headed by an extensive list of references, all of which are cited at least once in the body of the task order. Examination of this list shows that it includes specific examples of the types of documents indicated in Table 7.2. By pointing to the items in this list, the task order can be

FIGURE 7.13. Task order for V&V support of System PREDICT development.

September 22, 1990

Company Q Task Order PRED-1
Verification and Validation (V&V) Support for
System PREDICT Development

Reference: (a) System PREDICT Independent Product Assurance Contract C-PA39
(b) Company Q document PAP-P1, Product Assurance Plan for System PREDICT, latest baselined version
(c) Company Q document Documentation Standards Manual (DSM), latest version
(d) Company Q document Programming Standards Manual (PSM), latest version
(e) Company Q document PRED-S1, System PREDICT Requirements Specification (RS)
(f) Company Q document PRED-D1, System PREDICT Preliminary Design Specification (PDS)
(g) Company Q document PRED-D2, System PREDICT Detailed Design Specification (DDS)
(h) Company Q Task Order PRED-2, Acceptance Testing Support for System PREDICT Development

1.0 Background and Objective. System PREDICT is an R&D software development project currently being undertaken by Company Q for the purpose of benchmarking various Company Q software development methodologies. Ostensibly, the System PREDICT

Continued

development effort is to produce a methodology for predicting the point differential of a football game based on information regarding the two teams playing in the game. It is anticipated that the result of this effort will lead to reliable methodologies for developing computational algorithms, relational databases, and man/machine interfaces.

Reference (b) describes the product assurance procedures for establishing and maintaining uniform configuration management (CM), verification and validation (V&V), quality assurance (QA), and testing practices during System PREDICT development and subsequent operational use. This document adapts the Company Q standards specified in references (c) and (d) to the special needs of the System PREDICT project.

The objective of this task is to provide V&V support for System PREDICT development according to the V&V procedures set forth in Section 7 of reference (b). Specifically, this task will produce audits of references (e), (f), and (g), and computer code to be produced from reference (g). Current System PREDICT project plans call for the development of the baselined version of references (e), (f), and (g) prior to code development. Thus, the intent of the audits of these items is to provide Company Q management visibility into System PREDICT evolution so that deviations from Company Q intentions come to light quickly and can therefore be dealt with cost effectively.

2.0 Statement of Work

2.1 Scope. The scope of this task is limited to audits of up to three drafts each of references (e), (f), and (g), and up to four versions of the code developed from reference (g). The scope of this task does not encompass acceptance testing of this code prior to its release for operational use. This acceptance testing support will be provided under a companion task order, reference (h).

2.2 Task Description. To meet the objective specified in paragraph 1.0 above, the contractor shall perform the following:

a. For each audit of reference (e), the contractor shall determine that the document is internally consistent and that requirements are unambiguously stated. The contractor shall document any inconsistencies or ambiguities in a report to be submitted to the System PREDICT Configuration Control Board (CCB) which, in turn, will be responsible for determining how these inconsistencies and ambiguities are to be resolved (according to the format specified in paragraph A.9 of reference (a) as modified by the procedures set forth in Subsection 7.6 of reference (b)).

b. For each audit of reference (f), the contractor shall determine that each requirement specified in reference (e) has been carried through to reference (f) and that each design element in reference (f) has a logical antecedent in reference (e) (i.e., that the design has not incorporated a capability not called for in reference (e)). The contractor shall document any such incongruities between references (e) and (f) in a report to be submitted to the System PREDICT CCB which, in turn, will be responsible for determining how the incongruities are to be resolved.

c. For each audit of reference (g), the contractor shall determine that each design element in reference (f) has been logically expanded to sufficient detail to permit coding of that element, that each requirement specified in reference (e) has been carried through to reference (g), and that there are no capabilities in reference (g) not called for in reference (e). The contractor shall document any such incongruities among references (e), (f), and (g) in a report to be submitted to the System PREDICT CCB which, in turn, will be responsible for determining how these incongruities are to be resolved.

Continued

FIGURE 7.13. (*Continued*)

d.   For each System PREDICT computer code audit, the contractor shall determine that each design element in reference (g) appears in the code, that each requirement specified in reference (e) has been carried through to the code, and that there are no capabilities in the code not called for in reference (e). The contractor shall document any such incongruities among System PREDICT code and references (e) and (g) in a report to be submitted to the System PREDICT CCB which, in turn, will be responsible for determining how these incongruities are to be resolved.

For each of the four types of audits specified above, the contractor shall also participate in the System PREDICT CCB meetings at which an audit report produced by the contractor is to be considered.

2.3 <u>Deliverables</u>. The deliverables specified below will be provided in the quantities and according to the schedule specified below.

a.   System PREDICT RS Audit Report (up to 3)

    (1) Five (5) copies according to the format specified in paragraph A.9 of reference (a) as modified by Subsection 7.6 of reference (b).

    (2) Within one (1) working day of receipt of the draft of reference (e).

b.   System PREDICT PDS Audit Report (up to 3)

    (1) Five (5) copies according to the format specified in paragraph A.9 of reference (a) as modified by Subsection 7.6 of reference (b).

    (2) Within two (2) working days of receipt of the draft of reference (f).

c.   System PREDICT DDS Audit Report (up to 3)

    (1) Five (5) copies according to the format specified in paragraph A.9 of reference (a) as modified by Subsection 7.6 of reference (b).

    (2) Within four (4) working days of receipt of the draft of reference (g).

d.   System PREDICT Computer Code Audit (up to 4)

    (1) Ten (10) copies according to the format specified in paragraph A.9 of reference (a) as modified by Subsection 7.6 of reference (b).

    (2) Within five (5) working days of receipt of the program listing of the computer code version.

e.   Weekly Task Progress Report

    (1) Two (2) copies according to the format specified in paragraph A.4 of reference (a).

    (2) On the first working day of each week following the week reported on.

2.4 <u>Company Q-Furnished Equipment</u>. To perform the audits specified in paragraph 2.2 above, Company Q shall furnish to the contractor one (1) master copy of each draft of references (d), (e), and (f) to be audited. Company Q shall also furnish five (5) copies of a complete listing of each version of System PREDICT computer code to be audited. All

Continued

FIGURE 7.13. (*Continued*)

work under this task order shall be performed at the contractor's facility except for participation in System PREDICT CCB meetings which will be conducted at Company Q facilities.

3.0 Resources. It is estimated that this task order will require 284 person-hours of effort allocated to the production of the deliverables specified in subparagraphs 2.3a through 2.3e above according to the labor categories specified in the table below. These labor categories are those defined in paragraph 9.9g of reference (a). For greater visibility, the resource estimates are broken out by each of the four types of audit specified in paragraph 2.2 above. Within each type, the resources shown are the totals for performing all audits of that type (e.g., for RS audits, the resources shown are for performing three audits).

Labor Categories, Audit Types, and Associated Levels of Effort
for Company Q Task Order PRED-1

LABOR CATEGORY	PERSON-HOURS			
	RS	PDS	DDS	Computer Code
Senior Computer Systems Analyst/Consultant*	16**	8**	8**	4***
Computer Systems Analyst	-	4	16	24
System Integrator	-	4	8	8
Programmer/Analyst	-	-	24	72
Project Secretary	8	16	24	40
TOTALS	24	32	80	148

* Task manager.

** Includes time for preparing weekly task progress reports.

***Time for preparing weekly task progress reports during the code audit period of this task; it is not anticipated that the task manager will participate in the code audits.

The table above accounts for the different emphasis in skills needed to perform auditing as System PREDICT proceeds from requirements definition (i.e., high-level system analysis) to coding (i.e., detailed data processing analysis). The above table also takes into account that one or more members of the audit team will participate in System PREDICT CCB meetings when the team's audit report is being acted upon by the PREDICT project staff.

FIGURE 7.13. (*Continued*)

specific without being long-winded. For example, paragraph 2.3 of the task order specifies the deliverables to be produced under the task order. By pointing to specific parts of references (a) and (b), the task order compactly delineates the format (and thus the expected content) of each task order deliverable. What the contractor is expected to produce and what the customer expects to receive are clearly identified at task outset, thus avoiding possible later misunderstandings between the contractor and the customer. For this reason, on projects lacking documents such as references (a) and (b) that specify deliverable formats, it is usually a good idea to include such format specifications in the task order (such as one-line statements of what each section or paragraph in a deliverable is to contain).

B. Paragraph 1.0 of the task order indicates that the System PREDICT development effort is essentially to be a testbed for other Company Q software development efforts. This background information serves to clarify the task objective subsequently stated in the paragraph. The audits to be performed under the task are intended to provide Company Q management with visibility into System PREDICT evolution. This visibility will thus afford management the opportunity to see what can go wrong—and what can go right—on software development, experience which presumably can be transferred to other Company Q software development efforts.

C. Paragraph 2.1 of the task order delineates the scope of the task by exploiting the list of references heading the task order. Included in this list are the documents to be audited under the task (namely, references (e), (f), and (g)). Also included in this list is the task order that prescribes product assurance work to be performed subsequent to the work prescribed in the V&V task—namely, acceptance testing (reference (h)). It should also be noted that paragraph 2.1 specifies the number of audits of each System PREDICT product encompassed by the task order. As we stressed in Chapter 5, an audit of a software product typically precipitates a revision to the product, which in turn generally precipitates another audit of the product (recall Figure 5.7). In planning product auditing work, it is therefore generally necessary to explicitly delineate the number of iterations in the audit/product revision cycle.

D. Paragraph 2.2 of the task order delineates the specifics of each of the four types of audits to be performed under the task. This delineation provides insight into what types of findings each audit will yield. It should be noted that the type of audit described in paragraph 2.2b of the task order is that which was presented as a sample problem in Section 5.2. It should also be noted that paragraph 2.2 indicates who is to receive each audit report (the System PREDICT CCB) and for what the report is to be used (resolving incongruities among software products). Thus, paragraph 2.2 describes the plan of activities that will achieve the objective set forth in paragraph 1.0.

E. A V&V task cannot be accomplished without the products to be audited. Thus, of necessity, the schedule of a V&V task is tied to the development schedule for these products. Paragraph 2.3 of the task order reflects this planning factor by tying the delivery date of an audit report to the date when the customer provides the product to be audited to the audit team.

F. Because the primary purpose of an audit is to assess

where a product under development is with respect to where it is supposed to be, the development of that product must, in general, be suspended while it is being audited. Thus, it is necessary to ensure that a reasonably comprehensive audit of a product be accomplished in a time frame that does not inordinately suspend product development. Paragraph 2.3 of the task order reflects this planning factor by calling for audit reports to be delivered within several days of receipt of the product to be audited. The delivery date estimates for the RS and PDS audits are based on the size and complexity of the RS and PDS sample specifications shown in the sample problem in Section 5.2 and include the time to review these specifications, write a draft of the audit report, and submit the report for management review, approval, and rewrite (if necessary), before delivery to the customer. The times for accomplishing the remaining audits shown in the task order are greater than the times planned for the RS and PDS audits. These greater times reflect the reasonable planning assumption that, as the development life cycle proceeds, products grow in size and complexity, which thus implies that the time to conduct audits of these products must correspondingly grow. This approach for estimating resources can be simplified if one or more products to be audited is already available during task order preparation.

G. The types of skills required for V&V work usually change as the development cycle proceeds. At project outset, high-level system analysis skills are generally needed to address issues such as requirements ambiguities and consistency. As development proceeds, the need increases for data processing skills. Paragraph 3.0 of the task order reflects this planning factor by including four different labor categories to support the various audits incorporated into the task order. In addition, the table in the task order explicitly shows the shift in skills required as development proceeds; greater computer systems analyst resources are to be applied to audits of products developed early in the life cycle, while greater programmer/analyst resources are to be applied to audits of products developed later in the life cycle.

H. Paragraph 3.0 of the task order also provides visibility into how task resources are to be allocated to support accomplishment of each of the four types of audits covered by the task order. The table included in this paragraph is essentially a resource allocation plan for accomplishing the work specified in paragraph 2.2 of the task order. This table can also help the task manager during task accomplishment to avoid cost overruns on the task by reminding him how much of which types of skills are needed for the audit at hand.

The solution approach just presented has highlighted a number of product assurance planning issues. Although the specific product assurance activity considered was V&V, many of the issues addressed apply to other product assurance activities. Thus, for example, had we considered the T&E product assurance activity, it would have been necessary to address resource allocation in a manner similar to that discussed in connection with the table in paragraph 3.0 of the task order in Figure 7.13. For the T&E task order, it would be useful to construct a table showing how resources are to be allocated, by labor category, to the activities of test plan development, test procedure development, test execution, and test reporting. In fact, Exercise 7.15 at the end of this chapter asks you to construct the analogue to the task order in Figure 7.13 for System PREDICT acceptance testing (i.e., reference (h) in Figure 7.13). As the preceding discussion attempts to demonstrate, planning for product assurance itself demands careful attention to detail.

7.4 A Disciplined Approach to Software Development

Throughout this book, we focused on the basic question that must be answered on any software project if a software product with integrity is to be developed. Turning to his customer, the software developer asks, "What is it you really want?" We went through a set of techniques that we call software product assurance to indicate how software development can be made visible and traceable, thereby raising the likelihood that the developer's response to the answer to this question will be to the mutual satisfaction of the developer and his customer. As recalled in Figure 7.14, we have described product assurance in terms of three fundamental functions—control, auditing, and bookkeeping. These functions must be performed on any software project to yield software products that do what they are supposed to do, are delivered on time, and are delivered within budget. In general, they should be performed by an organization independent from the development organiza-

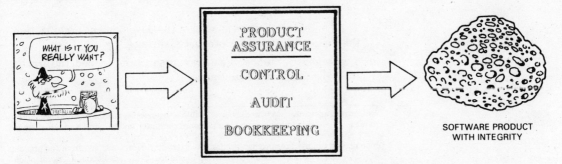

FIGURE 7.14. Product assurance—Techniques for reducing the risk embodied in the fundamental software development issue (the wizard's question) and achieving a software product with integrity. Cartoon by B. Parker and J. Hart, *The Wizard of ID*, September 30, 1983. Reprinted by permission of Johnny Hart and North America Syndicate, Inc.

tion. However, they can be performed by project management, the development organization, or any other organization supporting a software development project.

Whether we like it or not, we must now rely on software for things we do daily. In some cases, our very lives depend on the proper operation of software. Blaming mishaps in our lives on computer malfunctions is no longer something to chuckle about. A software malfunction can cause an automobile to swerve head-on into the path of another vehicle, a life-support system in a hospital to go haywire, a financial database in a bank to be destroyed. These possible events are no laughing matter.

It is time that software development is approached with the same degree of discipline as is done in other endeavors, such as aircraft manufacture and bridge construction. Professionals simply cannot continue to approach software development as a mind-expanding exercise in artistic expression. If this book at least caused you to think about doing software development in a more disciplined way than you did in the past, then we communicated our message. If, in addition, this book persuaded you to try some of its ideas, then we achieved our goal—helping you reduce the ever-present software risks of unsatisfied requirements, cost overruns, and schedule slippages.[8]

EXERCISES   **7.1**   The objective of this exercise is to compel you to think about how you would estimate the cost and type of product assurance activities for software projects with different characteristics. For this purpose, assume the following qualitative correlation between the general project characteristics listed below and the amount of product assurance needed (which is based on our real-world experience):

The more critical the software is to overall system operation, the greater the need for product assurance. (An example of software with high criticality would be software for a system that cannot operate at all if the software does not operate—that is, there is no manual backup.)

The lower the experience level of the development organization, the greater the need for product assurance.

The larger the number of software products developed, the greater the need for product assurance.

---

[8] Senior managers may want to consider the following exercises at the end of this chapter: Exercise 7.3, on the purchase price of a personal computer and a "parts and labor" guarantee; Exercise 7.8, on the production of software compared to the production of other products and the need for product assurance; Exercise 7.9, on soliciting from the product assurance organization its opinion of the competence of the development organization; Exercise 7.16, on software guarantees and software product liability. Project managers and product assurance managers may want to consider the following exercises at the end of this chapter: Exercise 7.2, on the application of product assurance and the resetting of product delivery dates; Exercise 7.4, on developing a product assurance tool in an undisciplined manner (a Catch-22 product assurance predicament); Exercise 7.5, on how much product assurance is (just) enough to achieve product integrity; Exercise 7.6, on the need for comments in computer code; Exercise 7.9, on soliciting from the product assurance organization its opinion of the competence of the development organization; Exercise 7.11, on recruiting for product assurance; Exercise 7.15, on preparing a T&E task order; Exercise 7.16, on software guarantees and software product liability.

TABLE E7.1. SOFTWARE PROJECT CHARACTERISTICS FOR EXERCISE 7.1

	Project 1	Project 2	Project 3
Total Project Budget	$12,000,000	$1,500,000	$20,000
Lines of Source Code (Estimated)	150,000	20,000	1,000
Development Schedule	25 Mo.	10 Mo.	3 Mo.
Veterans on Software Development Staff	80%	50%	0%
Software Products:			
Requirements Specification	Yes	No	No
Preliminary Design Specification	Yes	No	No
Detailed Design Specification	Yes	Yes	No
Source Code	Yes	Yes	Yes
Project Description	Note A	Note B	Note C

Note A: Project 1 is a large software project to which your entire organization (not just the product assurance element of this organization) has decided to devote the most appropriate resources. The software product is an integral part of a sophisticated state-of-the-art system. If the software fails to operate properly, there will be a significant financial loss (on the order of millions of dollars) to the organization as well as a major setback to the reputation of the entire organization. Figure E7.1 provides details regarding product delivery dates and other pertinent project events.

Note B: Project 2 is a medium-sized project, an in-house production of a software development tool to be used on most future software projects over the next seven years. The tool will be based upon a commercial product that has been used on numerous other applications. The description of this commercial product is well documented in the available literature.

Note C: Project 3 is a small project to model one aspect of the environment of a major software system under development. The model will be a small software program that will be discarded once the software system under development is delivered to the buyer. The project has been given to a new programmer who, though inexperienced, has demonstrated design and coding competency.

The larger the size of the software products, the greater the need for product assurance.

The greater the complexity of software products, the greater the need for product assurance.

The more tightly constrained the development schedule, the greater the need for product assurance.

In addition to the above, assume for this exercise that (1) you are a product assurance practitioner working in a company and (2) your boss has asked you to help plan the product assurance activities for three different software projects. Table E7.1 lists the salient characteristics of these three projects. Assume that both you and your boss are staunch advocates of the product assurance concepts discussed in this book.

(a) Weighing the parameters for Project 1 provided in Table E7.1 (including Note A), answer the following questions (justify each answer you give in terms of these parameters and the concepts of visibility and traceability):

   1. How often would you hold CCB meetings, and who should attend?

   2. Which of the software products listed in Figure E7.1 would you audit? (You may wish to consider this question in conjunction with question 3.)

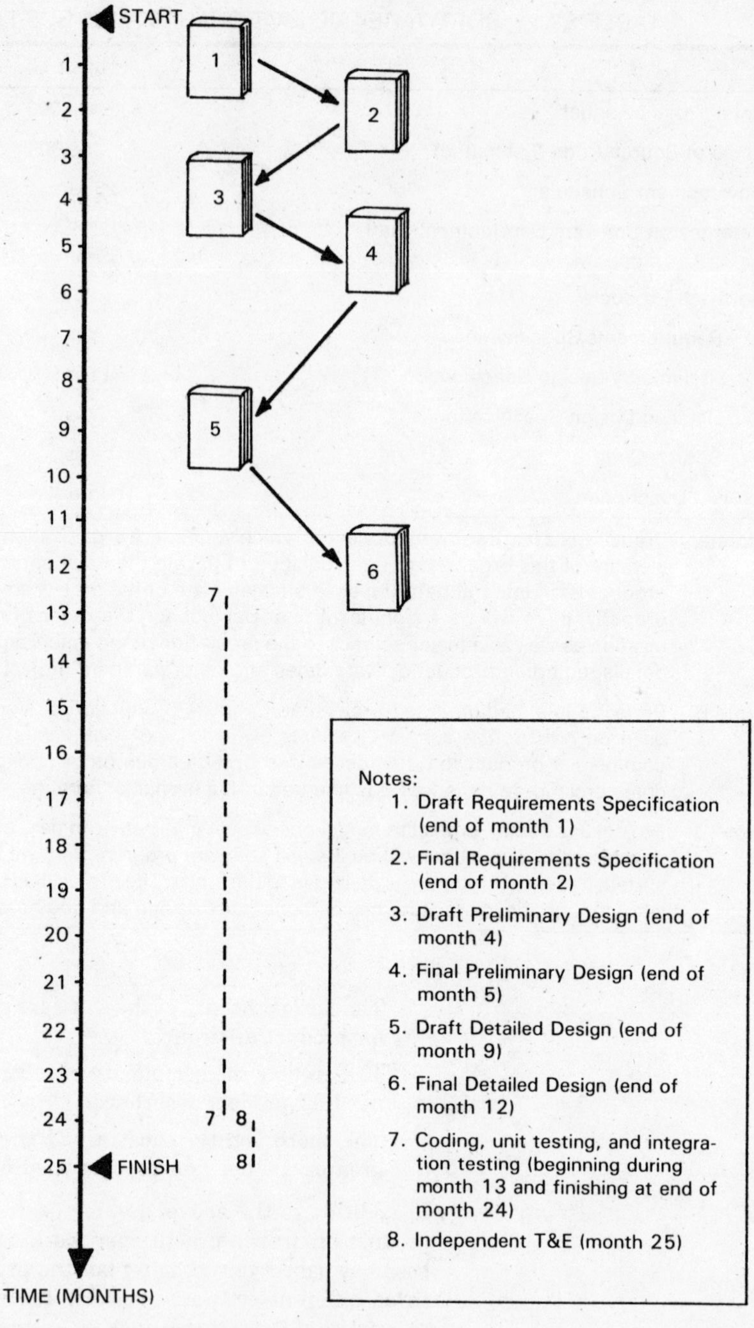

FIGURE E7.1. Project 1 schedule details for Exercise 7.1.

START

1
2
3
4
5
6
7
8
9
10
11
12
13
14
15
16
17
18
19
20
21
22
23
24
25 ◄ FINISH

TIME (MONTHS)

Notes:

1. Draft Requirements Specification (end of month 1)

2. Final Requirements Specification (end of month 2)

3. Draft Preliminary Design (end of month 4)

4. Final Preliminary Design (end of month 5)

5. Draft Detailed Design (end of month 9)

6. Final Detailed Design (end of month 12)

7. Coding, unit testing, and integration testing (beginning during month 13 and finishing at end of month 24)

8. Independent T&E (month 25)

3. Given that the software developers are planning to do unit and integration testing of the software code (see Figure E7.1, Note 7), how do you intend to exercise the software code in order to determine its acceptability for delivery to the user? (*Hint:* Consider such factors as test environment [e.g., live operational environment or simulated operational environment] and types of tests [e.g., *functional*, where individual functions are exercised without regard to how they might be used together in practice; *scenario*, where functions are ex-

ercised with regard to how they might be used together in practice; and *stress*, where the software is subjected to greater-than-anticipated loads].)

4. In addition to the activities specified in parts 1, 2, and 3, what other product assurance activities would you include in the planning?

5. How much of the total project budget (of $12 million) would you allocate to the product assurance activities listed in 1–4? Indicate how you arrived at this figure. Assume the schedule shown in Figure E7.1. Assume further that each document will consist of at least 100 pages and will be delivered in both draft and final form. In answering this question, you may wish to make reasonable assumptions as to product assurance parameters and factors (such as how many days or weeks are available for an audit, how many months are available for test planning, how many months are available for generation of step-by-step test procedures, how many tests will be needed to reasonably assure that a system malfunction will not result in a large financial loss, how many tests one tester can develop in a time frame that might be available for test preparation on a 25-month project, how many auditors will be needed to reasonably assure that no more than one draft of a document will be produced [because the project must be completed in 25 months], how many weeks during month 25 will be needed for test execution [taking into account code turnover between coders and testers to permit code changes in response to discrepancies uncovered during testing; recall Figure 5.20], how many weeks during month 25 will be needed to prepare a report documenting the results of test execution, how much a man-month of product assurance labor costs [possibly averaged over two or more labor grades], how many people will be required to support product assurance activities such as attending CCB meetings, compiling and archiving CCB minutes, and performing bookkeeping functions).

(b) Now consider Project 2. Construct an analogue to Figure E7.1 by making some reasonable assumptions based on the information in Table E7.1. Then, using Table E7.1 and this analogue to Figure E7.1, how would you change the answers you gave in (a), and why?

(c) Repeat (b) for Project 3.

7.2 In Section 2.6, we defined one of the product integrity attributes as "meeting delivery expectations." In Chapter 4, we portrayed how the CCB permitted visible and traceable processing of software changes (recall Figure 4.3), thereby increasing the likelihood of achieving software product integrity. In Chapter 5, we described how the CCB is informed of discrepancies in software products (recall Figure 5.1), thereby increasing the likelihood of achieving integrity in these products. With these three ideas in mind, consider the following:

(a) Suppose as a result of the visibility and traceability afforded by the CCB and auditing, it becomes evident that a software product whose development you are managing will not be completed in time to meet customer delivery expectations (e.g., V&V activities have uncovered discrepancies that cannot be resolved prior to a previously agreed-upon customer delivery date). You discuss this situation with your customer, and the two of you agree upon a new delivery date which represents your estimate of when the extant product discrepancies will be resolved. The new delivery date arrives, and you deliver the product to the customer as promised (with the discrepancies resolved). Since you succeeded in delivering the product "on time" (and presumably the product meets customer needs, because the discrepancies have been resolved), this product has integrity according to the definition given in Section 2.6. Does the scenario just described imply that injecting visibility and traceability into software development (via the techniques described in Chapters 4, 5, and 6) make "meeting delivery expectations" simply a trivial (and probably not very cost-effective) exercise in redefining delivery dates. Why (not)?

(b) Given the scenario in (a), does it follow that the product integrity attribute of "meeting delivery expectations" is devoid of meaning? Why (not)?

(c) The scenario portrayed in (a) could be interpreted as follows:

Time and money are expended (to support CCB operation and auditing) to make software development visible and traceable, which may cause the resetting of delivery dates, with the result that more time and money are expended meeting the new delivery dates.

Does it therefore follow that the product assurance philosophy advocated in this book is self-contradictory? Why (not)? Is the application of this philosophy nothing more than a self-fulfilling prophecy? If it is, is that necessarily undesirable, particularly from the perspective of a software project manager? If it is not a self-fulfilling prophecy, why is it not, and what does that imply as far as its value to a software project manager (and other project participants)?

7.3 Suppose you are about to purchase a personal computer. Suppose further that you have narrowed your choice down to two systems—Brand X and Brand Y—both of which satisfy your technical requirements. Brand X costs 25 percent more than Brand Y, but the Brand X software comes with a one-year "parts and labor" guarantee with the following stipulations:

For a period of one year after purchase, the vendor will correct at no additional charge to you any discrepancies between the operation of the software code and the documentation that is included with the original purchase of the Brand X system. These corrections may be either documentation changes, code changes, or both as mutually determined by you and the vendor.

For a period of one year after purchase, the vendor will correct at no additional charge to you any malfunction of the software code that stems from an obvious coding error (e.g., a menu display on a screen contains misspellings in column headings, an error message contains extraneous characters or misleading information, a display or printed output shows obviously and inappropriately truncated alphabetic or numeric data).

With the preceding as background, consider the following questions:

(a) Do you think it likely that the ultimate cost to you of buying and using the Brand X system will be greater than the ultimate cost of buying and using the Brand Y system? Indicate yes, no, or maybe, and give at least two reasons to support your answer.

(b) Listed below are three possible reasons why the Brand X purchase price is higher than the Brand Y purchase price. Which one would you select, and why?

1. The cost of developing Brand X software is greater than the cost of developing Brand Y software.
2. The vendor profit per Brand X sale is greater than the vendor profit per Brand Y sale.
3. The vendor profit per Brand X sale is about the same as the vendor profit per Brand Y sale, so that the extra Brand X cost is in effect the cost of a service contract.

(c) Assume that you *know* that the reason for the difference in the sale price between Brand X and Brand Y was reason 3 in (b). Would that encourage or dissuade you from Brand X? Why?

(d) Assume that the Brand X vendor sets his price based on the assumption that you and other potential customers will believe that reason 3 in (b) is primarily the reason for the higher Brand X purchase price. With this assumption, and assuming that Brand X's only competition is Brand Y, do you think that the Brand X vendor will make more sales than the Brand Y vendor? Why (not)? Do you think that the Brand X vendor will make more money than the Brand Y vendor? Why (not)?

(e) What do the preceding parts of this exercise have to do with software product assurance? (If your answer to this question is other than "nothing" or its equivalent, justify your answer in terms of specific principles and concepts presented in various chapters of this book.) (See also Exercise 7.16, which deals with software warranties and software product liability.)

7.4 Throughout this book we have stressed the need for disciplined software development and maintenance. In doing so, we have repeatedly indicated what can go wrong on a software project in the absence of discipline (recall, for example, our descriptions of Projects Saturn and Neptune in Section 7.1). However, we live in an imperfect world. Consequently, there are times when we may be confronted with situations that force us to make decisions that make us uncomfortable, to say the least. Consider, for example, the following situation based on the authors' actual experience:

Suppose you are the manager of a software product assurance unit that has been hired by a customer that has also hired some other company to develop, over a period of years, a large and complex software system. You are responsible for providing this customer with independent audits of the software products turned out by the developer, writing and executing test plans and procedures to determine for the customer whether software code is doing what it is supposed to do, and performing configuration management to keep track of the software products being developed. During your first year, you are reasonably successful in instituting many of the practices described in this book. Because of the magnitude of the development effort, however, your customer wants to leverage your product assurance efforts by having you develop some automated product assurance tools. Naturally, your customer wants these tools developed quickly so that you can get on with doing your job. So, in a one-hour meeting with you, your customer writes down on a piece of paper his "requirements" for an automatic auditing aid. He has instructed you to use his hardware and his data management system to get this auditing tool up and running within the next few weeks. Your customer instructs you that you can worry about documenting the tool after it is "up and running."

With the above situation in mind, consider the following:

(a) If you do not get the tool up and running as your customer asked, you run the risk, on the one hand, of not having your multiyear contract renewed because you may alienate your customer. On the other hand, if you proceed to develop the tool in the manner dictated by your customer, you run the risk of compromising your effectiveness as a product assurance agent because of damaged credibility (i.e., because you do not practice what you preach). Faced with this Catch-22 predicament, how would you try to satisfy your customer while at the same time assuaging your credibility fears?

(b) Is the situation described just another "real-world" proof that software product assurance is not really necessary, but only a "nice-to-have" function if time, resources, and/or project politics permit? (Indicate yes, no, or maybe, and give at least two reasons to support your answer.) (*Hint:* recall our story on the tool that failed in Section 6.4.)

(c) Would you fly in an airplane controlled in part by software whose development was audited in part by a tool produced under circumstances similar to those described in the situation above? Why (not)?

(d) Would you buy any software whose development was audited in part by a tool produced under circumstances similar to those described in the situation above? Why (not)?

(e) In light of your responses to (c) and (d), would you reconsider your response to (b)? If so, how? If not, why not?

7.5 In our experience we have observed that, on many software projects, there is reluctance, if not downright objection, to allocating resources to product assurance. Thus, an issue that needs to be addressed on every software project is the following:

How much product assurance is (just) enough to achieve product integrity?

To probe some of the specific nuances of this issue, consider the following situation:

Suppose you are a seller software project manager and you have just been assigned to head a software development effort that is about to start. Suppose further that the software to be developed is to be incorporated into a system whose operation is critically tied to the operation of the software. In addition, suppose that if the system fails to operate properly people may be killed or seriously injured and/or your company may suffer large financial loss. Finally, suppose you believe in the need for software product assurance but your budget is so tightly constrained that you have to make every dollar spent on product assurance count.

With the preceding as background, consider the following:

(a) You want to hold periodic CCB meetings to give visibility to and inject traceability into the process of evaluating and implementing software changes (in the manner described in Chapter 4). Write down at least two factors that you think are important for determining how frequently the CCB should meet, and give at least one reason to justify each.

(b) You want to audit software products in the manner described in Chapter 5 to gain visibility into the degree to which these products conform to customer requirements. Assume that the following software products are to be developed:

Requirements Specification (RS)

Detailed Design Specification (DDS)

Computer Code (CC)

With this information as background, consider the following questions:

1. Would you audit the RS? If so, when and why? If not, why not?

2. If you choose to audit the RS, how would you determine that the RS can serve as an adequate basis for authorizing initiation of DDS development? (In addressing this question, pay particular attention to the issue of how many RS audits should be performed and to what breadth and depth.)

3. How would you determine how many DDS audits should be performed to establish that the DDS is an adequate basis for authorizing initiation of coding?

4. Would you audit the CC against the DDS and RS through static analysis (i.e., visual comparison of the CC against the DDS and RS), or would you forgo this type of audit in favor of a more dynamic type of audit—namely, testing, whereby you execute the CC in an environment at least approximating the customer's operational environment using test procedures derived from the RS and DDS (as described in Section 5.3)? (In responding to these questions, justify each response with at least one reason.)

(c) Would you change your response to any of the preceding parts of this exercise if the failure of the software would *not* result in people being killed or seriously injured or your company suffering large financial loss?

(d) If you answered "yes" to (c), for which of the situations listed below would you have answered "no" to (c)? (Provide at least one reason to justify each "no" answer that you give.)

1. Failure of the software may result in people being killed and/or seriously injured.

2. Failure of the software may result in people being killed and/or your company suffering large financial loss.

3. Failure of the software may result in people being seriously injured and/or your company suffering large financial loss.

(e) If you answered "no" to (c) above, give at least two reasons to justify this answer.

(f) Based on your responses to the preceding parts of this exercise, construct a list of at least six criteria (expressed in terms of typical software project characteristics such as experience level of product developers, size of products, and schedule constraints) for estimating CCB meeting frequency and deciding what and how many times to audit on a software project. *Hint:* See Exercise 7.1. A sample criterion might be the following:

If the product developers, are, for the most part, inexperienced (say, 90 percent of the development staff has less than two years' design and coding experience), then CCB meetings should be scheduled with a frequency such that a number of meetings take place before the scheduled delivery of a product to the customer.

(g) Based on your responses to the preceding parts of this exercise, construct a list of at least six criteria that could be used to indicate when more product assurance than necessary is being applied on a software project. *Hint:* A sample criterion might be the following:

Audits of products corrected in response to previously performed audits typically uncover few significant discrepancies.

(*Note:* Regarding the sample criterion above, at issue is the trade-off between *explicitly checking* that corrections have been made versus *assuming* that they have been made. When is it practical to accept things on faith?)

(h) In the situational description at the beginning of this exercise, it was postulated that you were a *seller* software project manager. Now suppose you were the *buyer* software project manager on the same project. Would you change any of your answers to (a) through (g) in this new situation? Which ones and why?

7.6 *Computer* magazine, a monthly publication of the IEEE Computer Society, covers all aspects of computer science, technology, and applications. It is aimed at a broad audience whose interests are not limited to narrow specialties. A regular feature of *Computer* is "The Open Channel," which provides "a forum for the exchange of technical ideas." In the November 1984 issue (vol. 17, no. 11), D. A. Feinberg submitted a piece entitled "One Day in the Programming Department . . . ," reproduced below (from p. 94 of the issue). It is a dialogue between a programmer and his manager that presumably takes place just after the programmer has completed an apparently major programming task. Although the dialogue is somewhat exaggerated for effect, the scenario depicted is representative of some of our experiences in the software industry regarding trade-offs (recall Figure 7.6) between productivity (i.e., the need to get something done *now*) and maintainability (i.e., the need to keep and improve upon that something subsequent to its delivery to the customer). After reading this dialogue, you are asked to consider some questions and issues pertaining to these trade-offs.

"George Programmer reporting as ordered, Mr. Manager."

"Thank you, George. Please be seated."

"Yes, sir. What did you wish to discuss with me, sir?"

"George, you've just submitted that new process control system in the fastest time we've ever seen around here. I wanted to congratulate you on your fine effort."

"Why thank you sir."

"Unfortunately, your programming leader informs me that there is a critical flaw in your code."

"No way, sir. The system runs beautifully and meets or beats every requirement. Even the folks in Quality Control have certified the software for production usage. There is no flaw!"

"Yes, George, I've been fully briefed on those points. However, your leader tells me that there are no comments in any of your code. Is that really so?"

"Of course, sir."

"But, why not?"

"Well, sir, you know the new Programming and Operations Measures of Productivity Accounting System you instituted last year?"

"Yes, I'm quite familiar with POMPAS. For the first time in history, this company can objectively determine who is the most productive. It will allow us to award raises and promotions based on what a person really accomplishes; not just on personalities and clothing as we have done far too often in the past."

"Yes, sir. A great idea, sir. However, are you aware that the primary measure of programming productivity is the number of lines of code I produce per week?"

"Of course."

"Are you also aware that the program Quality Control uses to measure the number of lines of code I write excludes comments?"

"No, but what does that have to do with it?"

"Well, you see, sir, I get credit for the same number of lines of code whether they have comments or not. Since POMPAS now determines my raises and promotions, it is to my advantage to write as many real lines of code as possible each working day. Comments don't count; so I don't write any anymore."

"What!?"

"Sir?"

"You mean to tell me, George, that POMPAS doesn't take into account the effort required to write comments?"

"No, sir."

"But what will happen when new requirements force maintenance changes to your system?"

"I don't know, sir. I'm not in Maintenance, so that's really somebody else's problem. I'm going to be working on the new pipeline flow model as soon as I get back from vacation."

"But what if problems occur while you're gone? I don't mean to be insulting, but you know how things go when new software is first put into on-line production."

"Indeed I do, sir, but once Quality Control has certified software, it becomes a Maintenance responsibility."

"Oh yeah. Well I guess they can just work with your Internals Manual if they need to. Right?"

"Uh, well, sir, there isn't any Internals Manual this time."

"Huh?"

"Well, sir, you see, POMPAS doesn't give me any credit for lines of documentation, either. So I didn't do any. I never much liked writing in English, anyway, and, until the Quality Control group finishes its document-counting program, nobody gets any credit."

"But, but, but . . ."

"Can I go now, sir?"

(a) In the beginning of the dialogue, the manager says to the programmer that "there is a critical flaw in your code" because "there are no comments in any of your code." With these statements as a starting point, consider the following:

1. In what sense is the manager justified in asserting that the programmer's code is flawed, considering that the code apparently "runs beautifully" and even has Quality Control's blessing?

2. In what sense is the programmer justified in asserting that his code is not flawed?

3. Assume that the "Quality Control" referred to is similar to product assurance as discussed in this book. Indicate at least three ways that Quality Control could have been justified in blessing the programmer's code.

(b) Do your responses to (a) suggest that the manager, programmer, and Quality Control each did his job properly? If so, why is there a disagreement between the manager and the programmer? If not, who did not do his job properly and why? (Indicate "manager," "programmer," "Quality Control," or some combination of these three, and give at least three reasons to justify your answer.)

(c) In defending his position as to why he did not insert comments in his code, the programmer argues that he has no incentive to do so. The manager, in pleading his case, argues that the programmer's incentive should be to produce code that not only works *now* but can be made to work *later* after enhancements. Considering the programmer's response to this plea, do you think the manager is living in the real world by arguing the way he does? (Recall Figure E1.2.) How do you think the manager may have avoided this confrontation with his programmer? What does your response to this question suggest to you about the philosophy pursued on many software projects of (recall Figure 7.4) "let's code first and worry about documentation later"? Does the pursuit of such a philosophy really get the job done because it produces code sooner? Why (not)? Recalling Figure 7.6, do you think this manager is atypical of software managers? Or do you think the dialogue with his programmer awakened a realization that he needs to worry about long-range goals?

(d) Suppose you believe in the maintainability arguments put forth by the manager to justify including comments in code (and to justify the development of requirements and design documentation before coding is initiated). Given that at least some programmers are like the programmer in Feinberg's story, given that in the real world there is a tendency to "code first and document later—if time permits," and given that many people (particularly profit-sensitive senior managers) view such documentation and the product assurance activities needed to cross-check this documentation with computer code as diminishing software project productivity (recall Figure 7.6), write down at least three actions you, as a software project manager, would take at the outset of a project that you are to manage that might *realistically* head off the situation depicted in Feinberg's story. Give at least one reason for each action you write down. *Hint:* An example of an action to be insisted upon might be the following:

Action: Institute a set of documentation and coding standards that you and the development staff agree is acceptable (such standards might be mutually developed by the development and product assurance staffs). Obtain agreement from the development staff's management that each staff member will get credit in his performance appraisal for the degree to which his work adheres to these standards.

Reason: These standards will define in part the type of visibility and traceability management is expecting. By selecting standards that the development staff can live with—as opposed to dictating standards—and by tying developer performance to the degree of adherence to such standards, a carrot-and-stick mechanism is established on the project that raises the likelihood that software products will indeed conform to the standards (presumably without adverse impact on productivity). From the point of view of the product assurance staff, these standards become part of the official set of rules that all project participants recognize as defining the way the software development game is to be played. With this recognition, the likelihood is decreased that the contentious situation depicted in Feinberg's story will occur.

7.7 The U.S. National Bureau of Standards, through its Institute for Computer Sciences and Technology, publishes standards to improve the utilization and management of computers and automatic data processing in the federal government. One such series of standards is known as FIPS PUBs (Federal Information Processing Standards Publications). FIPS PUB 106, entitled "Guideline on Software Maintenance," explains its purpose as follows:

> Software maintenance accounts for approximately 60% to 70% of the application software resources expended within the federal government. In addition, the rapidly growing inventory of software systems is increasing the demand for software maintenance. Improved productivity in maintaining software, however, can offset these increases. Thus, the issue which must be addressed is not reducing the absolute cost, but rather improving the quality and effectiveness of software maintenance.
>
> This Guideline provides general guidance for managing software maintenance. It presents an overview of techniques and procedures designed to assist management in controlling and improving the software maintenance process. It addresses the need for a software maintenance policy with enforceable controls for use throughout the software life cycle, the management of software maintainers, and management methods which can improve software maintenance. It concludes that improvements in the area of software maintenance will come primarily as a result of the software maintenance policies, standards, procedures, and techniques instituted and enforced by management.
>
> This Guideline is intended for use by both managers and maintainers. It addresses the need for a strong, disciplined, clearly defined approach to software maintenance. It emphasizes that the maintainability of the software must be taken into consideration throughout the life cycle of a software system. Software must be planned, developed, used, and maintained with future software maintenance in mind. The techniques and procedures which are discussed in this Guideline are recommended for use in all federal ADP organizations (p. 4).

The guideline defines "software maintenance" as follows:

> Software maintenance is the performance of those activities required to keep a software system operational and responsive after it is accepted and placed into production (p. 4).

Section 5 of the guideline examines the issue of system maintenance versus system redesign—i.e., how to determine when the software component in the system has been so frequently and extensively modified that it would be more cost-effective to replace it rather than continue to recode and/or patch parts of what is already there. In examining this issue, the guideline lists eleven factors that may be useful to consider in determining whether to redesign rather than maintain what is already there. The guideline introduces these eleven factors as follows:

> Although maintenance is an ongoing process, there comes a time when serious consideration should be given to redesigning a software system. A major concern of managers and

software engineers is how to determine whether a system is hopelessly flawed or whether it can be successfully maintained. The costs and benefits of the continued maintenance of software which has become error-prone, ineffective, and costly must be weighed against that of redesigning the system.

When a decision has been reached to redesign or to stop supporting a system, the decision can be implemented in a number of ways. Support can simply be removed and the system can die through neglect; the minimum support needed to keep it functioning may be provided while a new system is built; or the system may be rejuvenated section by section and given an extended life. How the redesign is affected depends on the individual circumstances of the system, its operating environment, and the needs of the organization it supports.

While there are no absolute rules on when to rebuild rather than maintain the existing system, some of the factors to consider in weighing a decision to redesign or maintain are listed [below]. . . . These characteristics are meant to be general "rules of thumb" which can assist a manager in understanding the problems in maintaining an existing system and in deciding whether or not it has outlived its usefulness to the organization. The greater the number of characteristics present, the greater the potential for redesign (pp. 14–15).

Characteristics of systems which are candidates for redesign are as follows (p. 15):

1. Frequent system failures
2. Code over 7 years old
3. Overly complex program structure and logic flow
4. Code written for previous generation hardware
5. Running in emulation mode
6. Very large modules or unit subroutines
7. Excessive resource requirements
8. Hard-coded parameters which are subject to change
9. Difficulty in keeping maintainers
10. Seriously deficient documentation
11. Missing or incomplete design specifications

With the preceding as background, consider the following:

(a) For each of the eleven characteristics listed above, indicate at least one way they exacerbate software maintenance as defined on page 4 of the guideline. (*Hint:* Consider the hardware analogues to some of these characteristics as they apply, for example, to the problem of determining when to rid yourself of the car you currently operate and replace it with another car.)

(b) Based on your answers to (a), indicate at least one way that the product assurance techniques described in this book could avoid or lessen the likelihood of each of these eleven characteristics surfacing in connection with an operational software system.

(c) Eventually most software will have to be replaced no matter how carefully it may have been planned to meet evolving user needs. Given this fact of software life, and considering your responses to (b), list at least seven ways that the application of the product assurance techniques described in this book may help to provide early warning of the need to replace currently operational software with redesigned (i.e., essentially totally new) software.

(d) Based on your responses to (c), indicate at least three ways that software product assurance can aid in the planning of new software systems. What does this planning role suggest to you about a potential cost-benefit of software product assurance other than those day-to-day cost-benefits arising from visibility and traceability that we have frequently alluded to? (*Hint:* Consider what "spending time and money to save time and money" means in a global, as opposed to day-to-day, context of months or years of operational life of a software system.)

7.8 In February 1984, the United Nations Industrial Development Organization (UNIDO) published a report (number UNIDO/IS.440) entitled "Guidelines for Software Production in Developing Countries." Written by Herman Kopetz (a professor at Technische Universitaat in Vienna, Austria), this report has as its aim "to introduce some of the basic concepts of the information industry, particularly the software side, and to provide some guidelines for software production in the developing countries" (p. 2) (indicative of its tutorial flavor, the report contains a glossary of software terms). The 100-page report is divided into the following four sections:

1. Introduction, which addresses the question "What is software?" and discusses the role of software and hardware in the handling and processing of information
2. The need for a software policy in developing countries, which addresses why a (nonindustrialized) country should establish an organization, training facilities, and standards to exploit positive aspects of the information industry (such as using computers to support vocational training) and to reduce some of its negative consequences (such as inability to realize many beneficial applications of computers because understanding of the capabilities and potential of computers is lacking)
3. Organizing a software project, which touches on the topics of life cycle stages, software effort estimating, organizing a software project plan, and controlling a project
4. The software development process, which steps through software life cycle processes

(It should be noted that the report contains the following caveat on its cover: "The views expressed in this paper are those of the author and do not necessarily reflect the views of the secretariat of UNIDO.") At the beginning of section 3, the report makes the following observation about the production of software compared to the production of other products:

> If a comparison is made between the production of software and a more conventional product, then the first great difference is the visibility of the result. The software end-product consists solely of a set of carefully documented instructions for the computer—there is no tangible software product. The supervision effort required in determining development progress can be comparable with the development effort. . . . The development of conventional products is constrained by the laws of nature between relatively narrow limits (for example, the properties of materials), whereas the limits for software are set by complexity and the ability of human in-

tellect to cope with it. The constraints due to complexity are very difficult to explain and quantify for people who are not experienced in the field of software development. It is therefore necessary that each computer specialist be highly self-critical and be aware of his own limitations in any situation. The lack of physical constraints is also responsible for the often incorrect view that software is easy to change, does not require a long development time and can easily be made to fulfill new conditions (pp. 39–40).

With the preceding as background, consider the following:

(a) Citing inherent reduced visibility of the result of the software production process, the above excerpt asserts that "the supervision effort required in determining development progress can be comparable with the development effort." Explaining the nature of the constraints on the software production process, the above excerpt then asserts that "it is . . . necessary that each computer specialist be highly self-critical and be aware of his own limitations in any situation." In your opinion, are these two assertions the basis for an argument favoring the need for product assurance on a software project? (Indicate yes, no, maybe, or some combination of these three, and give at least three reasons to justify your answer.) (*Hint:* Consider this question in the context of the triangle diagram in Figure 2.13.)

(b) Regarding the last sentence in the above excerpt, is it incorrect to say "that software is easy to change . . . and can easily be made to fulfill new conditions"? (Indicate yes, no, maybe, or some combination of these three and give at least two reasons to justify your answer.)

(c) What does your response to (b) suggest about the need for product assurance on a software project?

(d) Suppose you were trying to sell the concept of software product assurance (along the lines discussed in this book) in your organization (which heretofore has had little exposure to the concept). Would you use the above excerpt (or selections from it) to help you with your selling campaign? If so, how? If not, why not?

7.9 Sometimes there is a tendency on the part of senior buyer/user management (and others having a vested interest in a software project) to solicit from the software product assurance organization its opinion of the competence of the development organization. The purpose of this exercise is to probe some of the issues associated with this tendency. With the preceding as background, consider the following:

(a) Conventional meanings of the word "competence" include "ability" and "fitness." Given these meanings, how would one go about determining the competence of a software development organization? Recalling the balance in Figure 3.11 that illustrates the concept of product assurance propounded in this book, list at least three reasons why a product assurance organization may not be in a position to make such a determination. Do these reasons make it unlikely that a product assurance organization can be considered competent to make such a determination? Why (not)?

(b) Suppose you are the manager of a product assurance organization. Suppose further that your customer has asked you to give him your opinion of the competence of the development organization. Finally, suppose that, for reasons such as those you listed in (a), you believe that your organization cannot really judge the competence of the development organization. With these suppositions, and keeping in mind that if you appear nonresponsive to your customer's needs you may lose your job, compose a paragraph or two indicating how you might respond to your customer.

(c) List at least three reasons why a customer may call upon the product assurance organization to render a judgment regarding the competence of the development organization.

(d) List at least three reasons why a product assurance organization may want to avoid being placed in a position to render a judgment regarding the competence of the development organization. (*Hint:* Consider what might happen if a project were in trouble but your judgment would indicate that the development organization is competent. Can the customer be incompetent?) Do these reasons suggest that a product assurance organization should refuse to render such a judgment? Why (not)?

(e) Based on your responses to the preceding parts of this exercise, do you think that a product assurance organization should be called upon to render a judgment on the competence of the development organization? Why (not)?

7.10 Product assurance organizations frequently develop tools to facilitate their tasks. For example, to support T&E activities that cannot be carried out in the customer's environment, it becomes necessary to develop tools that simulate this environment (such as message generators that simulate incoming message traffic which, in the customer's environment, would flow into the software system being tested via external communications links). However, such product assurance tools typically are not documented (e.g., design specifications, maintenance manuals, and/or user manuals either do not exist or, in instances where a tool has been in use a long time, are outdated); furthermore, as a result of this lack of documentation, use of the tools is often restricted to a small circle of people who were involved in their development (and eventually such tools tend to fall into disuse as these people move on to other activities). With the preceding as background, and recalling the software management principles espoused throughout this book, consider the following:

(a) Should the development and maintenance of product assurance tools (which themselves consist in whole or in part of software) be subjected to the same life cycle management processes that we have advocated in this book for the software whose development and maintenance is to be supported by such tools? Why (not)? In addressing these questions, consider the pros and cons associated with each of the following assertions:

1. Generally, product assurance schedules and budgets on a software project are so tight that there simply is not enough time and money to both formally develop product assurance tools and actually do product assurance. Just let the product assurance people develop these aids on their own time; the pressures of their product assurance tasks will naturally define for them the types of tools needed to make their already tightly constrained lives easier.

2. Tools that have direct applicability to more than one software project are rare; it simply is not cost-effective to formally develop product assurance tools for a given project when it

is more than likely that such tools will not work without at least some modification on some other project.

3. Even though a general-purpose product assurance tool is rare, it is worthwhile to allocate time and money to formally develop tools for a given project because there is always the chance such tools can be used more than once—either on possible extensions to this project or on some other project. Even if the tools require modification before they can be used on such extensions or other projects, by allocating the time and money to develop them "right," such modification to prolong the tools' use will be facilitated (i.e., will cost less time and money to effect than if their development were accomplished informally).

4. Software is software. Whether a piece of software is being developed as part of a contractually binding commitment between a customer and a software seller, or whether a piece of software is being developed in the absence of such a commitment with a possibility that the software will only be used once, software should be developed "right" (i.e., documented, tested, and so forth).

5. Product assurance should practice what it expects others to practice; if it develops software tools, it should subject this development to the same processes that it advocates for software development efforts outside its organization; otherwise, its credibility is suspect.

(b) If, as a result of responding to (a), you think there are at least some circumstances where product assurance tools should be formally developed, who should collect and document (and test) such tools for subsequent use (and possible marketing as a software product for use by other organizations)? Give at least three reasons to justify the individual and/or organization you designate for these tasks.

7.11 Suppose you are the manager of a product assurance department in a company whose main business is to develop and market custom software systems for a broad range of clients. Your department provides centralized product assurance support to other departments within the company responsible for developing and maintaining these software systems. Recently, your department has come under fire for not providing sufficiently experienced personnel to perform product assurance on several projects. You recognize that your department is indeed short on expertise. In addition to attempting to acquire this expertise through new hires from outside the company, you recognize that a source of needed expertise is right in your own company—members of other departments who have worked or are now working on projects that your department is responsible for supporting. With the preceding as background, construct a recruiting pitch that you might use on your company's senior management (and other department heads) to bolster your department's expertise (without alienating your fellow department managers). In constructing this recruiting pitch, consider working in one or more of the following ideas:

(a) A natural career progression for some of the company's junior staff members would be from the development departments (such as engineering, analysis, and coding), where they have acquired firsthand experience designing and/or building software products, to the product assurance department. From the corporate point of view, this approach would seem to make sense both in terms of capitalizing on an individual's experience and offering career advancement. The company should take the position that once an individual has acquired a certain level of expertise (and self-discipline), that individual can advance to a position that offers to broaden his grasp of system design and operation, thereby increasing the challenge to his skills. Be prepared in your recruiting pitch to deal with arguments from your fellow department heads such as the following:

The systems we build are so complex that my staff members—senior as well as junior—will never run out of challenges.

Good help is hard to find these days. I have enough trouble finding—and keeping—good people. Grow your own!

(b) It is often claimed that product assurance is a dead-end job. The argument typically used to support this claim is that product assurance does not do—it just looks at what others do. The implication is that looking at what others create is less creative and thus requires less ingenuity. Be prepared in your recruiting pitch to counter this argument that may be in the minds of some of the people whom you are trying to recruit.

7.12 In Section 7.1 and Figure 7.2, we described an experiment for scientifically demonstrating product assurance effectiveness. In that description, we pointed out why the experiment could not actually be performed. Recalling the discussion in Section 7.1 of the experiment's fatal flaws, construct an experiment that reduces the impact of these fatal flaws so that performing such an experiment at least gives an indication of the effectiveness of product assurance. (*Hint:* Devise a set of requirements that are reasonably unambiguous. Then devise a way for assembling two software development groups that have comparable experience and talent.) (*Note:* It may be worthwhile to run such an experiment in a university as part of a software engineering course. Conducting such an experiment would give the participating students firsthand appreciation of management and product assurance issues that typically arise on real-world software projects.)

7.13 Word-processing software is an application that is frequently available for use on personal computers. This software is also available for use with a variety of languages. Some interesting problems arise when it is desired to produce word-processing software that is supposed to accommodate two different languages with markedly different characteristics. In particular, consider word-processing software that is supposed to accommodate an Indo-European language such as English or French and a Semitic language such as Hebrew or Arabic. Indo-European languages are written from left to right, while Semitic languages are written from right to left. Suppose you were responsible for testing a word-processing system that was designed to satisfy the following general requirements:

Produce English text in a variety of fonts and styles (e.g., bold, italics, outline)

Produce Hebrew text (including vowel signs which can appear above, below, or inside consonants) in a variety of fonts and styles

Freely intermix Hebrew and English text in a single document

Make all editing capabilities available for use with either language (e.g., if right justification is available for English text, its counterpart [left justification] must be available for Hebrew text; if single spacing is available for English text, it must be available for Hebrew text; and for multicolumn printing single spacing in one language should be intermixable with double spacing in the other language)

Make whatever text appears on the computer system display device be identical to the text appearing on the computer system printer when editing is completed and a printout is desired

Devise a set of tests for exercising the requirements listed above by writing one or more paragraphs describing how you would test each requirement. For a subset of these test descriptions, develop step-by-step test procedures using the five-column format prescribed in Figure 5.13. Assume that you would execute these test procedures by using a keyboard attached to a display device to create and view text to be tested. Assume also that a printer is available to obtain a hard copy of any text generated. In your tests, you should be particularly sensitive to the seemingly innocuous last requirement listed above (in other words, as a tester, you should not make the assumption that what you see on the display device is what you will necessarily obtain on the printer). Also, because of this potential divergence between what you may see on the display and the corresponding printer hard copy, make sure that you think through how you will record the results of executing your test procedures.

7.14 Diabetes is a chronic disease that afflicts millions of people. It is essentially a disease of the pancreas which either inhibits or prevents this organ from secreting insulin. Insulin, a protein hormone, is needed to metabolize food by removing glucose from the blood and permitting it to enter body cells. There is no cure for this disease, but it can be controlled by a combination of exercise, diet, and medication. The medication that some diabetics require consists of insulin derived from animals (or so-called human insulin chemically produced from *E. coli* bacteria normally present in the intestines of humans) that must be injected under the skin to perform its function in humans. Advances in insulin therapy have seen the development of so-called insulin infusion pumps. These devices (about the size of a deck of cards) are worn by diabetics continuously. Their purpose is to mimic the function of a pancreas by continuously infusing a small amount of insulin into the body between meals and larger amounts to cover meals. These devices are essentially a mechanical device attached to an insulin-filled syringe which is driven by user-programmable software. The syringe is connected to a tube which in turn is connected to a needle that is typically placed in the stomach of the diabetic. By pressing buttons on the face of the infusion pump, the wearer can program the rate at which insulin is infused into the body between meals as well as the rate at which insulin is infused into the body at mealtime. Some of these devices allow the wearer to program different between-meal infusion rates to occur at different times of the day. This latter capability is particularly helpful to some diabetics because during the early morning hours (typically between 3 a.m. and 7 a.m.) these diabetics generally need more insulin than at other times during the day. Now, if through a software error, for example, an infusion pump malfunctioned so that it infused insulin at other than the programmed rates, the consequences could be life-threatening and possibly lethal. For example, an insulin overdose could place the diabetic in an irreversible coma while an underdose may put the diabetic in the hospital with too much glucose in the blood.

With the preceding as background, suppose you work for a company that produces programmable insulin infusion pumps and are responsible for testing the devices before delivery to the marketplace. Keeping in mind the potential legal consequences for your company should these devices fail to operate as programmed by the user, devise a set of tests for testing the following requirements:

The device shall permit the user to program up to four different between-meal infusion rates during a 24-hour period.

The device shall permit the user to infuse up to X_{max} units of insulin at mealtime in 0.25-unit increments.

The device shall issue an audible alarm to the user should infusion be interrupted because of a clogged needle or tubing.

First, develop narrative descriptions on the testing approach you intend to use to exercise each of the above requirements. Then, develop step-by-step procedures from each of these descriptions using the five-column format prescribed in Figure 5.13. (For useful background reading on some consequences of malfunctions in software-driven medical devices including insulin infusion pumps, refer to H. Bassen et al., "Computerized Medical Devices: Usage Trends, Problems, and Safety Technology," *IEEE Proceedings of the 7th Annual Conference of the Engineering in Medicine and Biology Society,* Chicago, September 27–30, 1985, pp. 180–185. This article is briefly summarized along with some other software failure stories [including the bank failure story we recount in Section 7.1] in "Letter from the Editor: Risks to the Public in Computer Systems," *ACM SIGSOFT Software Engineering Notes,* vol. 11, no. 1 [January 1986], pp. 2–12.)

7.15 Recall the sample problem in Section 7.3 pertaining to the preparation of the V&V task order shown in Figure 7.13. Construct the analogue to this task order for the acceptance testing task order cited as reference (h) in Figure 7.13.

7.16 An automobile, cruising at 60 mph, suddenly jumps the highway median strip and crashes head-on into another automobile traveling in the opposite direction. The occupants of the other automobile are all killed, but amazingly the driver of the automobile that jumped the median survives. Subsequent police investigation establishes that, at the time of the crash, this automobile was operating properly but that its driver had been drinking. The courts determine that this driver was liable for the deaths that occurred in the accident. As a result, the driver is fined and given a prison term.

Figure E7.2 shows a typical computer hardware warranty and a typical software "warranty" (although a specific vendor is cited in the two warranties for reasons of clarity, the wording shown is relatively independent of who the vendor may be). Of particular significance is that the software "warranty" is really not a warranty at all. As the "warranty" emphatically and unambiguously stipulates, if the software malfunctions or fails *for whatever reason* (e.g., vendor programming errors), the software buyer/user assumes full responsibility for the consequences of the malfunction or failure. To illustrate in specific terms the implications of such a "warranty," consider software that

APPLE COMPUTER, INC. ("Apple") warrants the Macintosh Main Unit, Keyboard, Mouse, and cabling against defects in materials and workmanship for a period of NINETY (90) DAYS from the date of original retail purchase.

If you discover a defect, Apple will, at its option, repair, replace, or refund the purchase price of the product at no charge to you, provided you return it during the warranty period, transportation charges prepaid, to the authorized Apple dealer from whom you purchased it or to any other authorized Apple dealer within the country of original retail purchase....

This warranty applies only to hardware products; Apple software media and manuals are warranted pursuant to a separate written statement.

(a)

FIGURE E7.2. A typical (a) computer hardware warranty, and (b) software "warranty." The above wording is taken from the Macintosh owner's manual, Apple Computer, Inc., Cupertino, CA, Apple Product #M1500, copyright 1984. Reprinted by permission.

Even though Apple has tested the software and reviewed the documentation, APPLE MAKES NO WARRANTY OR REPRESENTATION, EITHER EXPRESS OR IMPLIED, WITH RESPECT TO THIS SOFTWARE, ITS QUALITY, PERFORMANCE, MERCHANTABILITY, OR FITNESS FOR A PARTICULAR PURPOSE. AS A RESULT, THIS SOFTWARE IS SOLD "AS IS," AND YOU, THE PURCHASER, ARE ASSUMING THE ENTIRE RISK AS TO ITS QUALITY AND PERFORMANCE.

IN NO EVENT WILL APPLE BE LIABLE FOR DIRECT, INDIRECT, SPECIAL, INCIDENTAL, OR CONSEQUENTIAL DAMAGES RESULTING FROM ANY DEFECT IN THE SOFTWARE OR ITS DOCUMENTATION, even if advised of the possibility of such damages.

(b)

drives air traffic control display devices. Suppose this software mal-functions, with the result that two airplanes crash into one another, thus killing hundreds of people. A warranty similar to the one shown in Figure E7.2b issued by the air traffic control system vendor implies that the vendor is not liable for these deaths. (For legal background and details regarding software warranties and software product liability, see the references extracted from law journals listed at the end of this exercise.)

With the preceding as background, consider the following:

(a) Think of the automobile and its driver referred to at the outset of this exercise as a transportation system analogous to a computer system consisting of hardware and software. Viewed in this light, the driver in this transportation system is in a way similar to the software in a computer system, since the driver provides the instructions that make the transportation system hardware (i.e., the automobile) perform its basic function of controlled motion. There is general agreement that the automobile driver is responsible for his actions. From this point of view, do you think that the software "warranty" shown in Figure E7.2b seems at odds with common sense and, therefore, could be termed unreasonable, if not outrageous? Why (not)?

(b) Do you think the primary reason that "warranties" such as the one shown in Figure E7.2b are typical of the software industry is because the industry is unwilling to make the necessary commitment to provide a reasonable degree of assurance that software does what it is supposed to do? Our observation of the highly competitive software marketplace is that the first rule of survival is to win the software job and then, once the job is won, muddle through as best as possible in order to meet what is often an unrealistic delivery date (within budget, of course!). The conventional wisdom asserts that, for these reasons, there simply is not time to do the job right the first time. Do you think that these reasons underlie the "warranty" shown in Figure E7.2b? That is, do you think that, because few people expect software to be built right the first time (i.e., it is expected as a matter of course that software will contain bugs), it is simply not realistic to warrant software?

(c) Do you think that application of some of the product assurance techniques that we have discussed in this book can make the warranting of software realistic? More specifically, do you think that application of these techniques can make it realistic for a software vendor to warrant his software products with wording such as the following (adapted from Figure E7.2a and b):

> The vendor has tested the software code and reviewed the associated documentation. As a result, the vendor warrants, for a period of ONE (1) YEAR from the date of original retail purchase, this code and documentation against defects in workmanship. If you discover a defect, the vendor will, at its option, repair, replace, or refund the purchase price of the software code and its associated documentation at no charge to you, provided you return it during the warranty period, transportation charges prepaid, to an authorized vendor dealer. However, IN NO EVENT WILL THE VENDOR BE LIABLE FOR DI-

RECT, INDIRECT, SPECIAL, INCIDENTAL, OR CON-
SEQUENTIAL DAMAGES RESULTING FROM ANY
DEFECT IN THE SOFTWARE CODE OR ITS ASSO-
CIATED DOCUMENTATION, even if advised of the pos-
sibility of such damages.

(d) If you could purchase a software product with a warranty such
as that shown in (c) above, would you be willing to pay extra for
the software (much as you would pay for a service contract on a
hardware item)? Why (not)?

(e) Do you think that the restriction cited in the last sentence of the
warranty in (c) above is reasonable? That is, do you think that
if, for example, you suffer large financial loss as the result of
correctly using the vendor's software (although this software has
a bug in it), the vendor should not be legally responsible for the
loss you suffered? Why (not)? Do you think that application of
some of the product assurance techniques that we have discussed
in this book can make it feasible to warrant software without such
restrictions? Why (not)?

(f) Compare Figure E7.2b, a typical software warranty, to Figure
7.11, a software product assurance guarantee. What similarities
do you perceive in these two items? What differences?

The following references probe in considerable legal detail issues
pertaining to software warranties and software product liability:

Prince, J. "Negligence: Liability for Defective Software." *Okla-
homa Law Review*, vol. 33 (fall 1980), pp. 848–855.

Gemignani, M. C. "Product Liability and Software." *Rutgers
Computer and Technology Law Journal*, vol. 8 (spring 1981), pp.
173–204 (reprinted in *Defense Law Journal*, vol. 31 [July–August
1982], pp. 334–369).

Lanoque, S. "Computer Software and Strict Products Liability."
San Diego Law Review, vol. 20, no. 2 (March 1983), pp. 439–456.

Steinberg, S. R. "Disputes over Computer Software Warranties."
National Law Journal, vol. 5 (April 18, 1983), pp. 15–16.

Hall, D. A. "Strict Products Liability and Computer Software:
Caveat Vendor." *Computer Law Journal*, vol. 4 (fall 1983), pp.
373–400.

Durney, E. G. "The Warranty of Merchantability and Computer
Software Contracts: A Square Peg Won't Fit into a Round Hole."
Washington Law Review, vol. 59 (July 1984), pp. 511–531.

Raysman, R., and P. Brown. "Computer Law: Potential Liabilities
in Mass-market Software." *New York Law Journal*, vol. 192 (November 13, 1984), pp. 1, 3.

Davis, G. G., III. *Software Protection: Practical and Legal Steps
to Protect and Market Computer Programs*. New York: Van Nostrand Reinhold Company, 1985.

This last book, written by a computer attorney, is an in-depth treatment of computer law. Its contents are current to December 1, 1984.
Chapter 2 deals with the concept of software and should be compared
with our concept introduced in Section 2.1. Chapter 12 deals with the
subject of software warranties and thus provides useful background
for this exercise.

1. Baker, E. R., and M. J. Fisher. "A Software Quality Framework." *Concepts: The Journal of Defense System Acquisition Management*, vol. 5, no. 4 (autumn 1982), pp. 95–107.

   This article is from a special issue of the cited journal devoted to the subject of managing software. This journal is published quarterly by the Defense Systems Management College, Fort Belvoir, Virginia. As stated on its inside cover, the journal "is intended to be a vehicle for the transmission of information on policies, trends, events, and current thinking affecting program management and defense system acquisition." Most of the articles in the issue cited deal with the subject of managing software in this context—that is, with heavy Department of Defense orientation. However, this article does not have that orientation. It is a general expository treatment of the following concepts:

   Software

   Software quality

   Software quality program

   Software quality assessment and measurement (SQAM)

   Independent SQAM

   Software quality assurance

   As such, the article complements a number of the concepts appearing throughout our book (such as *software, product assurance*, and *independent software product assurance*). The following abstract of the article appears in the journal's table of contents and provides insight into the article's orientation:

   > It is the authors' contention that the ability of programmers and software designers to produce correct software lies at the heart of the difficulties in software management. Because it is a "human endeavor," software development is an "art" that, according to the authors, lacks discipline. They outline a quality program designed to instill such a discipline in software development and therefore improve the process and the product.

   Our discussion throughout this book shows we agree with the article's authors regarding the need to discipline software development.

2. Brooks, F. P., Jr. *The Mythical Man-Month: Essays on Software Engineering*. Reading, Mass.: Addison-Wesley Publishing Company, 1975.

   The preface of this classic and oft-quoted software engineering text begins:

   > In many ways, managing a large computer programming project is like managing any other large undertaking—in more ways than most programmers believe. But in many other ways it is different—in more ways than most professional managers expect (p. vii).

   The author was the project manager for the development of IBM's Operating System/360 project from 1964 to 1965. The book is a highly readable and often amusing case study of this project and includes related stories drawn from other sources. As the author indicates in the preface, it was written to answer "Tom Watson's [IBM president] probing questions as to why programming is hard to manage" (p. viii). The book is filled with stories that highlight the idiosyncrasies of software development and maintenance (as distinct from development and maintenance of nonsoftware entities). For example, in discussing software maintenance, the author describes how a software defect will often manifest itself as a local failure when in fact it is indicative of a far more global ill. This nonlocality characteristic of many software bugs, the author points out, presents a significant maintenance challenge. Any purported fix to such a bug must be tested not only "in the vicinity" of the code change precipitated by the fix, but ideally far away from this change to the outer reaches of the rest of the code. Citing a 1971 study of the history of successive releases in a large operating system, the author makes the following observations about the headache that software maintenance can become:

> [The authors of the 1971 study] find that the total number of modules increases linearly with release number, but that the number of modules affected increases exponentially with release number. All repairs tend to destroy the structure, to increase the entropy and disorder of the system. Less and less effort is spent on finding original design flaws; more and more is spent on fixing flaws introduced by earlier fixes. As time passes, the system becomes less and less well-ordered. Sooner or later the fixing ceases to gain any ground. A brand-new, from-the-ground-up redesign is necessary (p. 122).

The author concludes the above discussion with the observation that "[system] program maintenance is an entropy-increasing process and even its most skillful execution only delays the subsidence of the system into unfixable obsolescence" (p. 123). Our experience in the software industry is that Brooks' thermodynamic analogy of maintenance as an entropy-increasing process is applicable not only to the maintenance of operating systems but also to almost any software system. The Second Law of Thermodynamics stipulates that it is impossible for heat energy to flow spontaneously from a cold body to a hot body in contact with it because there is a tendency for natural processes to proceed toward a state of greater disorder (i.e., toward a state of greater entropy). Nobody has yet found a way to produce a system that violates the Second Law of Thermodynamics (the fabled perpetual motion machine). Yet many in the software industry seem to approach software development and maintenance with the attitude that the corresponding law in the software world (if we can extrapolate from Brooks' observation) can indeed be violated—that attitude being "code as quickly as we can and then test the code until all the bugs have been eliminated." We are thus led once again to the notion of "pay now versus pay much more later" (recall Figure 1.3).

3. Cort G., J. A. Goldstone, R. O. Nelson, R. V. Poore, L. Miller, and D. M. Barrus. "A Development Methodology for Scientific Software." Los Alamos National Laboratory Report LA-UR-85-1708, submitted to the Fourth Biennial Conference on Real-Time Computer Applications in Nuclear and Particle Physics, Chicago, Illinois, May 20–24, 1985. Also published in *IEEE Transactions on Nuclear Science*, vol. NS-32, no. 4 (August 1985).

Throughout our book, we emphasized the applicability of the software management techniques discussed to projects both large and small (recall Figures 1.4 and E1.1). Many people who have been exposed to these techniques in seminars that we teach believe that they are practical only for large projects, particularly because of the large amounts of documentation that our approach to software development calls for and the prominence that the CCB (with its attendant "overhead") plays in this approach. The article cited above relates the real-world experience of the Los Alamos Weapons Neutron Research (WNR) facility on small software projects using a methodology that (1) emphasizes the development and maintenance of comprehensive documentation and (2) uses a CCB for peer review of software products to determine compliance with standards and user requirements. The WNR software development approach is perhaps best summarized by the following excerpt from page 2 of the above article (which also gives some quantitative insight into what constitutes a "small project" in the WNR environment):

The software systems that are developed and maintained by the WNR staff can be characterized as mission-critical. . . . The operational lifetime of most of these systems is expected to be rather long—approximately ten years. The WNR methodology must, therefore, promote the development of highly reliable software that can be maintained by a small staff. We base this [software development and maintenance] strategy upon three assumptions.

1. *Large-scale methodologies are not suitable for use by projects of small or intermediate size.* Very effective methodologies already exist for managing software development projects. Historically, these strategies have been pioneered by, and perfected for, large-scale software development projects which can devote considerable resources to applying them. These methodologies usually require a dedicated staff to perform time intensive activities within a highly stratified management structure. A commitment such as this usually represents only a small fraction of the total resources available to a large project. The WNR staff, however, consists of approximately four full-time programmers and a single manager. As would most small or intermediate size projects, the WNR effort would be overwhelmed by the institution of a large-scale development methodology.

2. *Coding is the least important activity associated with any development or maintenance operation.* Coding should correspond to merely the translation of a sound design into an implementation. The most critical development activities are performed either before (specification and design) or after (testing) the coding phase. Most small projects (especially those of a scientific nature) emphasize the coding activity—often to the complete exclusion of the other phases. Reliability, consistency and maintainability are very difficult to introduce into an application during the coding phase, so many scientific applications are characterized by very low quality.

3. *Documentation is fundamentally more important than code.* Every software professional has been exposed to in-

adequately documented code, usually during a maintenance operation. The precedence of documentation over code, however, has far wider implications: over the entire software life cycle, complete documentation is crucial to the successful operation of any software system or component. In addition to adequate maintenance documentation, requirements must be fully documented (for comparison with validation test results). A carefully documented design is invaluable when the software requires enhancement or repair. Exhaustive documentation of test coverage, specific test cases and all test results is essential for validation and verification of subsequent versions. For these reasons, the WNR methodology emphasizes the development of complete, consistent and uniform documentation for every phase of the life cycle.

The above assumptions clearly echo many of the ideas regarding the need to discipline software development included in our book (recall, for example, what we say in connection with Figure 7.4 in Section 7.1). What we believe is particularly significant about the second and third assumptions is that they are applied, according to the first assumption, to projects in which the development staff presumably consists of *at most* five people. The role of product assurance in the form of testing, emphasized at the end of the third assumption, is also noteworthy. Of course, the disciplining of software development that results from these assumptions does not, as we have reiterated throughout this book, come free. Reflecting the "pay now versus pay much more later" attitude that we have discussed (recall Figure 1.3), the above article has the following to say on its next-to-last page about how much this disciplining may cost and what it yields in return:

Although the WNR methodology is designed to minimize the overheads imposed upon programmers and software managers, application of the methodology undoubtedly increases the development time for a software product. Estimates of the additional time required for software development are necessarily subjective, but a conservative estimate for this methodology indicates a programmer overhead of approximately 200%. Utilization of the configuration management strategy described is expected to place a burden of an additional 15% upon one participant.

The predicted overheads are based upon the increased effort that must be expended by each participant during the specification, design and testing phases (the time required for coding should actually decrease significantly). Peer reviews also consume a significant amount of time, both in preparation and execution. In order to maintain a proper perspective, however, it must be noted that the resulting software product is of significantly higher quality than a comparable system developed with traditional methods. Documentation is complete and accurate. Formal testing introduces a level of reliability that cannot be attained through the *ad hoc* exercising that might otherwise be performed. In summary, although the development time is tripled, the resulting software is exceedingly more reliable, maintainable and robust. This enhanced quality is expected to manifest itself in much longer mean times between failures as well as simplification of enhancement/repair activities.

The above words illustrate in semi-quantitative, real-world terms that it takes time and money to save time and money on software projects. The article concludes with the following observation regarding the trade-off associated with cutting back on the WNR methodology, thereby reducing the considerable overhead costs referred to above:

> The WNR methodology may also be tailored to the requirements of individual projects, particularly in terms of the degree of implementation and accompanying overhead. The simplest subset to implement retains the policy of evolutionary documentation and combines the specification and design phases. No peer reviews or formal testing are performed. This implementation significantly reduces the overheads associated with the methodology, although the quality of resulting software can also be expected to be much lower. The addition of peer reviews provides a very powerful means for improving software quality at the expense of increased overhead. A formal testing program and configuration management procedures then provide the full benefit (at maximum cost).
>
> Whatever the degree of implementation, the WNR methodology promotes enhanced software quality by shifting a major portion of the development effort to the early stages' of the life cycle. Regardless of project size, increased attention to specification and design issues will always produce a better result.

In our book, we have taken the position that "the increased attention to specification and design issues" cited in the last sentence quoted above can be effectively accomplished through a CCB apparatus supported by a technical auditing activity, and this apparatus, we assert, "will always produce a better result" (with the caveats discussed in Section 7.2).

4. Costello, S. H. "Software Engineering Under Deadline Pressure." *ACM SIGSOFT Software Engineering Notes,* vol. 9, no. 5 (October 1984), pp. 15–19.

This article presents a simple (mathematical) model to explain how to respond to the real-world problem of deadline pressure. The model is also used to explain the often-observed tendency to divert resources away from product assurance practices in the face of such pressure (recall the discussion of Project Mars in our Section 7.1). The article is not laden with mathematical symbology (the mathematical model described is simply a ratio involving a sum and product of readily understood quantities), so a background in mathematics is not necessary to assimilate the ideas the paper presents. The introductory paragraph, which captures the paper's orientation and style, reads:

> Software engineering is a disciplined approach to software development that ensures the quality and maintainability of software. Software engineering is composed of a great variety of practices, but for the purposes of this paper the realm of software engineering will be divided into two broad categories. The first category consists of structured *ways* of performing traditional software development activities. Structured coding and top-down design are examples of practices in this category. The second category, which is the main concern of this paper, consists of structured *activities* that are not part

of the traditional software development process. These "software engineering activities" include design review, code review, methodical documentation, and rigorous testing of modules and systems. Because these activities are not strictly necessary for producing minimally functional software, they increase the amount of time spent developing software. The time spent on software engineering activities is, of course, well spent. But its effects are not felt immediately—its benefits are most apparent *later* in the development phase and *after* the software is released. Software engineering must therefore be considered *an investment* (p. 15).

The second category of software engineering mentioned in the above excerpt—activities—contains elements akin to our product assurance functions. The final three sentences in the excerpt clearly echo the "pay (a little) now (for product assurance) to reduce the likelihood of paying (a lot more) later (for software lacking integrity)" philosophy espoused in this book. Commenting on the benefits of software engineering, the author uses the following pointed analogy:

> Just as a smoker finds the daily dose of nicotine more important than the risk of heart disease and cancer in the distant future, the software professional can find the allure of meeting the next deadline to be stronger than the future benefits of software engineering (p. 17).

Our experience is that (pursuing the author's analogy) undisciplined software professionals live out their lives much as an inveterate smoker responds to his nicotine needs. Furthermore, this experience reveals an overwhelming tendency for these software projects to contract the cancers of cost overruns, schedule slippages, and unsatisfied requirements. We never cease to be amazed how many software project managers harbor the feeling that these cancers cannot invade their projects and, despite the presence of danger signals, take no action to arrest the cancers (recall the discussion of Project Saturn in Section 7.1).

5. Hansen, H. D. *A Case Study of Successful Systems Development—Up and Running.* New York: Yourdon Press, 1984.

A book devoted entirely to the subject of a successful software project is rare (probably because people associated with software successes are in such high demand that they simply do not have time to write about their experiences). Hansen's book begins:

> This book presents a case study of an EDP system development project to computerize the $80 billion bond market of Denmark. Like the bumblebee, the project should not have been able to fly, but it was up and running on schedule without missing a day and without reducing the original expectations (p. 1).

The project was large (750 man-years of effort). Surveys were conducted in 1976 to consider how the tens of millions of paper bonds traded on the Copenhagen Stock Exchange could be reduced or eliminated. The actual start of the system development effort (in terms of design and development of software) began in March 1981 and continued into March 1983. On April 1, 1983, all Danish bonds (with a value of almost $80 billion) became paperless overnight. The structured analysis and design techniques pioneered by Yourdon and Constantine were used as the principal development aids. The role of product assurance is discussed in a number of places throughout the book (see the book's index under the entries "quality assurance," "testing system," and "walk-through"). A key element of the design effort was devoted to the development of data flow diagrams (DFDs; see T. DeMarco, *Structured Analysis and System Specification* [New York: Yourdon Press, 1979]), which described data flow in the bond system to be automated. Regarding a subset of these DFDs, the author makes the following point, which is worthwhile considering in the context of the wizard-king dialogue in Figure 2.8:

> You may ask, how can you spend two man-years on developing only 49 low-level DFDs? My answer is simply that you don't get them right on the first try. To the staff members of VP-Centralen [the nonprofit data center responsible for the development of the system], the number of DFDs produced must have seemed endless, since it is not a trivial job to draw correct DFDs. But, as they discovered later, the payoff is considerable in terms of quality if the time and energy are devoted initially to make them as accurate as possible (p. 69).

As the author subsequently points out, this accuracy was achieved through reviews (called walk-throughs) and the product assurance activity of checking DFDs for consistency (i.e., auditing). It should be noted how this admittedly laborious process of iterating on DFDs until they were "correct" (i.e., reflected user requirements) is just another example of the notion of "pay now versus pay much more later"— recall Figure 1.3 (see the discussion in Reference 2, above).

6. Johnson, D. G., and J. W. Snapper, eds. *Ethical Issues in the Use of Computers*. Belmont, Calif.: Wadsworth Publishing Company, 1985.

The preface to this book, which is a collection of thirty-three articles by different authors, explains its purpose as follows:

> While much has been written about computers and their future role in our lives, little attention has been paid to the ethical issues posed by increasing use of computers. What sort of code of conduct should bind computer professionals? Who, if anyone, should be liable for errors in computer programs? How much privacy are individuals entitled to when it comes to data stored in a computer? Do computers cause centralization of power? What sort of property rights should software designers have? This anthology pulls together articles that specifically address these questions together with more general philosophical pieces that broaden understanding of the issues (p. ix).

Particularly pertinent to the discussion in this chapter are the following articles which deal with issues of responsibility:

"Liability for Personal Injury Caused by Defective Medical Computer Programs" (p. 58)

"Liability for Malfunction of a Computer Program" (p. 67)

"Negligence: Liability for Defective Software" (p. 89)

"Punishment and Responsibility" (p. 95)

The second article cited above probes some of the difficulties facing the judicial system regarding negligence and computer programming. The author postulates that courts might classify computer programs as dangerous instrumentalities requiring the highest degree of care, because, for example, they might cause airplanes to collide under the wrong circumstances. The author considers this reasoning to be weak, since a computer program can be dangerous only if improperly constructed or used. A more likely standard for assessing liability is that computer programmers are professionals, who should be held to the level of care exercised by a reasonable member of the profession under similar circumstances. (One programmer has even been found guilty of committing malpractice!) However, the programmer may not qualify as a professional—no states have thus far enacted legislation licensing or regulating the conduct of computer personnel. If the programmer cannot be classified as a professional, he would be judged relative to liability as are other expert lay people, according to his skill and experience. It is entirely possible that the absence or presence of product assurance on a software development effort could be a factor in determining the outcome of litigation involving that effort (because of the presence or absence of visibility and traceability).

See also Exercise 7.16 that relates to software guarantees and software product liability.

7. Lin, H. "The Development of Computer Software for Ballistic-Missile Defense." *Scientific American*, vol. 253, no. 6 (December 1985), pp. 46–53.

This article discusses the problems that might face developers of software intended to guide battle management of the so-called "Star Wars" defense system. The ultimate goal of this system as stipulated in the interim charter of the Strategic Defense Initiative Organization "is to eliminate the threat posed by nuclear ballistic missiles." The article describes some of the major issues that were hotly debated within the software community regarding the feasibility of building software that would drive a system whose operation is intended to achieve this goal. The article gives a number of good examples of what can go wrong during software development, what has gone wrong during actual software projects (primarily ones involving weapon systems software), and why such problems would likely magnify on a project the size and complexity of the "Star Wars" effort (a team chartered by the Department of Defense estimated that the "Star Wars" software would require a minimum of 10 million lines of programming code; the author of the article contends that if the "estimate is low by a factor of only two, even a very optimistic software-development project will entail more than 30,000 man-years of work, or at least 3,000 programmers and analysts working for about 10 years" [p. 52]). The article discusses some of the product assurance issues facing such a large-scale effort—particularly the use of testing to locate and correct bugs. Regarding the problem of debugging real-time software (of which the "Star Wars" system is an example, since it must operate in response to events actually happening), the author offers the following quantitative insight into the difficulty facing developers of millions of lines of code:

> There is a final complication to debugging real-time software: even if an error can be located, attempts to eliminate it may not be successful. The probability of introducing an error (or more than one) while eliminating a known error ranges from 15 to 50 percent. Moreover, the majority of software-design

errors that appear after software is put into service do so only following extensive operational use. Experience with large control programs (one consisting of between 100,000 and two million lines of code) suggests that the chance of introducing a serious error in the course of correcting original errors is so large that only a small fraction of the original errors should be remedied (p. 52).

The author then translates the above comments into a "Star Wars" software development context:

In the context of comprehensive ballistic-missile defense, one should therefore ask about the consequences of an error that would manifest itself infrequently and unpredictably. The details of the first operational launch attempt of the space shuttle (in 1981) provide an example. The shuttle, whose real-time operating software is about 500,000 lines of code, failed to take off because of a synchronization problem among its flight-control computers. The software error responsible for the failure, which was itself introduced when another error was fixed two years earlier, would have revealed itself, on the average, once in 67 times (p. 52).

The ballistic-missile defense system and the space shuttle offer examples in the extreme of the need for visibility and traceability during software development that we have stressed throughout this book. While nearly all software development efforts are nowhere near the size of these examples, the space shuttle in particular is an actual project involving software that embodies the types of software problems typically encountered on software projects that span a broad range of size and complexity. For instance, the article tells of the following software-related problem during a June 1985 space shuttle mission that, we believe, exemplifies the types of problems frequently encountered on many small-sized and medium-sized software projects:

The crew of the space shuttle was to position the shuttle so that a mirror mounted on its side could reflect a laser beamed from the top of a mountain 10,023 feet above sea level. The experiment failed because the computer program controlling the shuttle's movements interpreted the information it received on the laser's location as indicating the elevation in nautical miles instead of feet. As a result, the program positioned the shuttle to receive a beam from a nonexistent mountain 10,023 nautical miles above sea level. This small procedural error was of little significance to the test itself, however; a second attempt a few days later was successful. Nevertheless, the event shows that even simple errors can lead to mission failure (p. 51).

We cannot overemphasize the significance of the author's observation in the last sentence in the above quote. As we have repeated many times in this book, a goal of product assurance is (recalling Figure 1.3) to spend time and money to uncover things like incorrect units being assumed in program code (nautical miles instead of feet) before the code becomes operational, thereby reducing the likelihood that more time and money will be spent later because an incorrect operation of the code required something to be done over again (or worse, such as a code misoperation or malfunction precipitating the loss of life, injury, and/or extensive material loss—see Exercise 7.14).

8. Page, G., F. E. McGarry, and D. N. Card. "A Practical Experience with Independent Verification and Validation." *Proceedings of the IEEE Computer Society's Eighth International Computer Software Applications Conference (COMPSAC 84),* Chicago, November 7–9, 1984, pp. 453–457. Silver Spring, Md.: IEEE Computer Science Press, 1984 (IEEE Catalog No. 84CH2096-6).

We have asserted throughout our book that the application of software product assurance raises the likelihood of achieving a software product with integrity. We have offered examples from the real world that we feel substantiate this assertion. A legitimate question to ask is this:

Are there documented instances where the application of software product assurance does *not* contribute to the achievement of product integrity?

This article appears to offer such an instance. It documents an independent verification and validation (IV&V) experiment performed at NASA Goddard Space Flight Center (NASA/GSFC) on software developed for spacecraft flight dynamic applications (e.g., maneuver control and attitude determination). Within this environment, software development was studied under a research project known as the Software Engineering Laboratory (SEL). The following excerpt from the article explains the role of this laboratory and the purpose of the IV&V experiment reported in the article:

> During the past 7 years, the SEL has studied more than 45 software development projects totaling more than 2 million lines of source code. Most flight dynamics projects are developed on a group of IBM mainframe computers using FORTRAN and assembler programming languages. The applications projects monitored by the SEL are largely scientific and mathematical in nature with moderate reliability requirements but with severe development time constraints that are imposed by a fixed spacecraft launch date. The development process typically takes between 18 and 24 months from the beginning of preliminary design to the end of software acceptance testing. Depending on mission characteristics, the size of a system ranges from 30,000 to 120,000 lines of source code, with an average of 30 percent reused from previous similar projects. An IV&V methodology was applied to two typical flight dynamics development projects in an attempt to determine the benefits of the approach. Each project was in development for 2 years and was approximately 65,000 lines of source code in size (p. 453).

The article reports the following conclusions resulting from the application of IV&V to the "two typical flight dynamics development projects":

> . . . The performance measures [of operational reliability, maintenance cost, requirements specification quality, system design quality, software implementation quality, testing effort, and development cost] indicate that the first application of an IV&V methodology in the flight dynamics environment
>
> Did not produce a more reliable product
>
> Did not detect errors earlier
>
> Did not improve maintainability

The overall conclusion is that IV&V is not cost-effective for NASA/GSFC's flight dynamics projects . . . (p. 456).

The seven performance measures listed in brackets above are each formally defined in the article. Following the above discouraging conclusion, the article offers the following more optimistic outlook:

Despite these results, it may be possible to better integrate the IV&V methodology into the software development process to make IV&V more cost-effective in the flight dynamics environment for

The right size effort

The right reliability requirement

Most ground-based flight dynamics projects require 8 ± 4 staff-years of effort. An IV&V methodology may be cost-effective for larger projects. For onboard (flight) systems with a more stringent reliability requirement, an IV&V methodology may be cost-effective for 5- to 6-staff-year efforts. In both these cases, an IV&V effort of approximately 15 percent of the development effort should be sufficient in the flight dynamics environment (p. 456).

Despite the foregoing conclusions, the article finishes with the following message, which echoes sentiments expressed in our book:

Software developers should keep in mind, however, that no software engineering methodology can replace technical and managerial expertise. It may be best to regard IV&V as an insurance policy: an additional premium that should be paid when the consequences of failure are great (p. 456).

9. Parikh, G. "Software Maintenance: Penny Wise, Program Foolish." *ACM Software Engineering Notes,* vol. 10, no. 5 (October 1985), pp. 89–98.

This article is a provocative account of the "maintenance mess" that faces the U.S. software industry (here, "maintenance" is used in the classical sense of "modification of software subsequent to its operational deployment"). The author cites the following as a primary cause of this "mess":

In most companies, development programmers also handle maintenance. Instead of using systematic maintenance processes and updating documentation, they rush through the work by patching the programs so they can get back to development work quickly. Over time, the programs become almost impossible to modify, and documentation deteriorates (p. 90).

These words reflect the "pay now versus pay much more later" syndrome that we have repeatedly mentioned in our arguments to justify the time and money spent on product assurance (recall Figure 1.3). Regarding what is needed to clean up the maintenance mess, the author makes the following observation:

Cleaning up the maintenance mess will be much more difficult and expensive than preventing it in the first place. By instilling "positive maintenance attitude," by encouraging the use of software maintenance techniques and tools and by providing maintenance training, many problems can be avoided (p. 90).

The thesis in our book is, of course, that the maintenance mess can be avoided if the product assurance principles we discuss are applied with commitment from the beginning of and throughout a software project.

Immediately preceding this article (on pp. 79–88) is an annotated bibliography on the subject of software maintenance prepared by the author. To guide a reader in selecting items to read, the entries in this bibliography (there are almost fifty) are partitioned into three overlapping categories—entries for all involved with software and software engineering, entries for more serious readers, and entries for postgraduate readers.

10. Perry, W. E. *Cleaning Up a Computer Mess*. New York: Van Nostrand Reinhold Company, 1986.

> The purpose of this book is stated in its preface:

> The only real solution to computer problems is to build application systems right the first time. The short-term solution is to adopt a process for identifying problems, diagnosing the cause, and then having a shopping basket full of solutions to use. The purpose of this book is to provide that corrective process (p. vii).

> The first chapter of the author's book is entitled "How Does a Computer Mess Originate?" He lists five "real causes of a computer mess," one of which is:

> Inability to implement user requirements correctly— The development of requirements does not appear to be a productive function to technicians. System design, programming, and testing are work for which you can see the results. Too many systems are built before the architect of the system has finished the blueprint. Too many users agree to a system before they know exactly what they are getting. Implementing what others say they want or agree is what they want is worthless if it doesn't do the needed job (p. 18).

> The above cause clearly recalls the wizard-king scenario that we have repeatedly discussed. The author restates this cause and the other four causes as "golden rules" of computer processing. The golden rule corresponding to the above-cited cause is the following, which echoes a message that we reiterate throughout our book:

> Golden Rule 4—Don't acquire or implement a computerized business application until the requirements have been thoroughly defined and agreed to by all parties (p. 18).

> Chapter 7 of Perry's book focuses on software issues and complements the discussion in our Chapter 7.

11. Spector, A., and D. Gifford, eds. "Case Study: The Space Shuttle Software System." *Communications of the ACM,* vol. 27, no. 9 (September 1984), pp. 872–900.

> This article is an interview conducted in May 1983 (several years before the January 1986 space shuttle catastrophe that killed seven astronauts) between the journal's Case Studies editors (Spector and

Gifford) and six people from IBM who were responsible for developing and maintaining the onboard software for NASA's space shuttle. The interview covers the following topics:

Project Overview (which focuses on the role of the onboard software)

The Shuttle Computers (which describes the onboard computer hardware)

Project Organization (which, despite the topic title, discusses software V&V, T&E, and CM)

Testing Facilities (which gives some details of the simulation techniques used to support shuttle software development)

Detailed System Operation—No Redundancy (which probes, without considering redundancy, some of the details of how the onboard software controls shuttle operation)

Redundant Set Operation (which focuses on how four of the five onboard computers frequently operate as a synchronized redundant set for reliability purposes)

System Problems (which discusses some of the problems, software and nonsoftware, encountered with the onboard system and how they were resolved)

The Interprocess Variable Problem (which examines a fundamental design decision that resulted in subsequent significant maintenance costs)

Concluding Remarks (which includes responses to the following questions: [1] What could the computer science research and development communities do to make efforts like the onboard space shuttle software simpler in the future? and [2] What kinds of onboard system are likely in more advanced space shuttles and space stations?)

One question asked in the area of software product assurance performed during the development of the onboard software had to do with the types of tests performed. The following is the response to this question given in the article:

For STS-1 [i.e., the first shuttle flight], when virtually all the code was new, we built a set of test cases that explicitly verified all the requirements just as we received them [from NASA and other contractors]. The independent verification group is expected to deliver error-free code, which is a goal we are asymptotically approaching. "Error-free" means 100 percent conformity to requirements, which is a massive verification job. For STS-1 we had about 50 people just testing guidance, navigation, and control (which excludes payload operations and the operating system). Those people worked about two years and built about 1000 test cases (pp. 882–883).

The above response shows that testing of the onboard shuttle software was an extremely large task by almost any scale of comparison. Given the magnitude of this task, it might be thought that traceability of test results back to specific requirements might be beyond the realm of practicality. In fact, the interviewer posed the following question addressing this traceability issue:

Could I point to any requirement on any page in those bookshelves [which evidently contained space shuttle requirements specifications] and ask you to say how you determined that your code met the requirement? (p. 883)

The following is the response:

Yes, I could show you (1) a test specification that tells you generically how am I going to test the requirement; (2) maybe four or five test procedures written up and reviewed in advance, detailing how that requirement is to be tested; (3) a set of test cases; and (4) a set of test case reports (p. 883).

Throughout this book we have emphasized the "pay now versus pay much more later" benefit of software product assurance (which is essentially equivalent to Crosby's "quality is free" investment policy quoted at the beginning of this chapter). In the interview with the space shuttle software development contractor, the question was asked, "On the whole, are you satisfied with your software engineering?" (p. 883). The following response to this question reveals how the "pay now versus pay much more later" and "quality is free" attitude apparently gained acceptance during the relatively long period of the onboard shuttle software development program:

The state of the art in software engineering has advanced significantly in the decade since we started this program [IBM started working on the software in 1974; as stated earlier, the interview with IBM in this article took place in 1983]. A more thorough approach to design reviews, code walk-throughs, and unit test inspections has been formulated. We've been able to start applying these techniques rigorously only in the last several years. We always did design and coding inspections, but not as meticulously as we do now. *Though these inspections are painful and expensive, we would apply that kind of rigor from the beginning if we had it to do all over again.* It's easier for people to get used to this kind of rigor if it's in place from the beginning, and *quite frankly, it's more cost-effective to discover our errors early in the process* (pp. 883–884; emphasis added).

It is true that the space shuttle has had its software problems (which received notoriety in the press), and some of these problems are discussed in the article (see pp. 896–900). As we have asserted many times in this book, the application of product assurance does not guarantee success (recall Figures 7.5 and 7.11). Some would argue that even with all the testing, etc., that was performed on the space shuttle software, there were instances where software failure literally prevented the shuttle from getting off the ground—so what was the benefit of all this product assurance activity? To this question, we would reiterate the response quoted earlier: "Quite frankly, it's more cost-effective to discover our errors early in the process." These words were spoken by someone who first managed the shuttle software independent verification organization and then subsequently took over both the development and verification organization (see p. 884 of this article for a discussion of how *independent* V&V worked with this organizational arrangement where one individual headed both development and verification; see also Exercise 3.10). Was this individual being self-serving because part of his responsibility was software verification? Or was this individual speaking as a software development manager who had learned through hard experience that "it's more cost-effective to discover our errors early in the [software development] process?" It is at least something to think about.

12. Waters, C. R. "Quality Begins at Home." *Inc.*, vol. 7, no. 8 (August 1985), pp. 68–71.

Throughout our book, we have stressed the "pay now versus pay much more later" benefit of practicing software product assurance (recall Figure 1.3). We have also stressed the need for commitment at all echelons of a software project to the practice of product assurance if this benefit is to be realized (recall from the discussion of Project Saturn in Section 7.1 what can happen if this commitment is absent). It does little good to institute a pro forma approach to product assurance or to circumvent for the sake of "expediency" product assurance checks that have been instituted. The article cited above recounts the trials and tribulations of a company that manufactures electronic components in its attempts to produce these components with integrity (in the sense that we use the word in this book). The article graphically portrays the hard lessons the company learned about "pay now versus pay much more later" and the need for commitment throughout all echelons of a company to a product assurance program. Achieving such commitment in the business world with its competitive pressures is a difficult and painful process. The article describes the pain associated with instituting a quality initiative within the company, and the difficulty of changing the habits and attitudes of the company's workers. Further, the article relates the problems involved in instilling a thoroughgoing approach to quality among the company's vendors and customers.

We have asserted many times in our book that, because software development is an exercise in manufacturing information and is thus inherently difficult to visualize (as opposed to hardware development, which involves the manufacture of objects with attributes that generally are easier to visualize), software development demands extra attention to those practices that raise the visibility of the development process. In this book, we have associated many of these practices with the concept of software product assurance. For this reason, even though the article cited above deals with a company that produces hardware and not software, we believe that the real-world lessons portrayed in the article carry over even more forcefully to the software industry.

13. Zimmerman, J. S. "The Right Stuff." *Datamation*, vol. 32, no. 2 (January 15, 1986), pp. 75–80.

This article tells the story of a large (i.e., hundreds of thousands of lines of computer source code), successful software project and discusses the reasons for its success. The project was in support of NASA's Earth Radiation Budget Experiment (ERBE) conducted in the mid-1980s to monitor the flow of energy into and out of the atmosphere. The article discusses how a number of the software management issues that we examine in our book were successfully addressed on this project. For example, the article discusses how answers to the wizard's question, "What is it that you (the user) really want?" were obtained. Also discussed are the "pay now versus pay much more later" issue and the issue of change control (recall Figures 1.3 and 4.13). Because the article is essentially free of technical jargon, it can be easily assimilated by senior management as well as by software specialists.

Page 78 of the article contains an inset labeled "16 Steps to Successful Systems Development." The inset essentially summarizes the lessons learned from the project. Some of these steps will be recognized as things that are discussed at length in this book (such as Step 9, which calls for the scheduling of regular reviews and is allied with our CCB concept, and Step 15, which calls for change management and which is the focus of our discussion in Chapters 4 and 5).

AUTHOR INDEX

SUBJECT INDEX

Note: f = figure, n = footnote, t = table

Preliminary design specification. *See* Design specification

Preliminary Requirements Definition Stage. *See* Life cycle stage

Preliminary requirements specification. *See* Requirements specification

Problem
defined, 99
example of, for software, 100–101
and wizard and king, 99

Procrustean approach to software development, 424–426

Procrustes, 424n, 425f

Product assurance. *See* Software product assurance

Product assurance guarantee, 431f

Product assurance organization
and acceptance testing cycle, 292, 293, 294, 295–298, 299
alternatives for, 137, 142–145
and answering questions it raises, 322
charter for, 304–306
as devil's advocate, 81
and freezing process, 170
functions of, 8, 304–306
and identification function, 349
independence of, 8, 12, 13, 123–124, 171n, 328, 443
and monitoring testing performed by development organization, 325–326
muzzling of, 431–432
and preparation of product assurance task order, 434f, 435
recruiting pitch to obtain staff for, 460–461
structuring of, 137, 142
use of, to assess development organization competence, 458–459

Product assurance plan. *See* Software product assurance plan

Product assurance planning. *See* Software product assurance planning

Product assurance practitioner
auditing techniques for, 241–276
bookkeeping techniques for, 338–378
labeling techniques for, 338–349, 388–389
and logical progression checking, 120
testing techniques for, 276–300

Product assurance processes. *See* Software product assurance processes

Product assurance task order. *See* Task order, product assurance

Product integrity, 73–74
and aim of software development, 76f, 78

attributes of, 73–76
and balance analogue for product assurance, 133, 134f
and bookkeeping function, 131, 335
and configuration control board, 192, 447–448
and configuration management, 113, 114
defined, 73–74
and difference between customer needs and performance criteria, 75
disciplines for attainment and maintenance of, 78–84
examples of, 77–78
and "good" software, 396
lack of, and product assurance, 432
and life cycle, 76–77
as a management evaluation aid, 88–89
and product assurance processes, 123, 124, 133, 450–452
and project management, 78f
and quality assurance, 111, 120
and reaudit, 130
and senior management, 78f
and software configuration validation, 114
and software maintenance, 74–75
and software project goals, 421, 432
and software success, 396
and standards, 138
and throw of project dice, 396–397
trade-offs of attributes of, 427f, 428
and triangle diagram, 78f
and user/buyer/seller organizations, 84–85
and verification and validation, 115
versus quality, 396
and visibility and traceability, 397

Product liability and software failure, 466, 473–474

Production/Deployment Stage. *See* Life cycle stage

Project
large-sized, defined, 237
medium-sized, defined, 208n
small-sized, defined, 237

Project A and rationale for establishing software baselines, 67–68

Project event products
defined, 364–365
examples of, 365–369

Project event recording, 364–373
defined, 364
during evolutionary change control, 388

project characteristics governing, 389–390
selecting events for, 389–390
and traceability, 364

Project failure and visibility and traceability, 431

Project goals, software, 419–423, 432
examples of
long-range, 130, 419f
short-range, 130, 419f
and management focus on, 419–423
and product integrity, 130, 421, 432

Project Jupiter, 194, 401t, 406, 408–409, 426–428

Project management. *See also* Software project management
plan for, 21, 22–23
product assurance as support discipline for, 81–82
and product integrity, 78f
and systems development, 29–30

Project manager, 84
as captain of software project ship, 10–14
and panoramic software concept, 38–39
and product assurance, 39
and product integrity, 78f
and visibility, 98

Project Mars, 255, 401t, 405–406, 422, 424, 471

Project Mercury, 400, 401t, 402

Project Neptune, 79n, 401t, 413–414, 430, 449

Project planning documentation, 365–366

Project PQR and lack of visibility of project meetings, 351–352

Project PRECIP. *See* Precipitation-day counting system

Project Q configuration control board minutes, 380–382

Project Saturn, 29, 401t, 409–410, 412, 422, 424, 449, 472

Project Uranus, 401t, 412–413

Project Venus, 193, 220n, 401t, 402–404

Prototype, rapid. *See* Rapid prototyping

Q

QA. *See* Software quality assurance

Quality, 396

Quality assurance. *See* Software quality assurance

Quality is free, 395, 480
and management concern for today (as opposed to future), 222

R

Radio tower as an analogue for product assurance, 12–13
Rapid prototyping, 89–90, 225f
Real-world software projects, 401t, 415–418
  computerization of Danish bond market, 472–473
  Earth Radiation Budget Experiment (ERBE), 481–482
  overflowed counter (bank software disaster), 331, 415–418
  Project A, 67–68
  Project Jupiter, 194, 401t, 406, 408–409, 426–428
  Project Mars, 255, 401t, 405–406, 422, 424, 471
  Project Mercury, 400, 401t, 402
  Project Neptune, 79n, 401t, 413–414, 430, 449
  Project PQR, 351–352
  Project Saturn, 29, 401t, 409–410, 412, 422, 424, 449, 472
  Project Uranus, 401t, 412–413
  Project Venus, 193, 220n, 401t, 402–404
  Space shuttle, 144–145, 330, 432, 475, 478–481
  Strategic Defense Initiative, 474–475
  System ATLANTIS, 155–156
  System ICARUS, 376–377
Reaudit, 130, 169
Redesign, characteristics of systems that are candidates for, 456
Regression testing
  defined, 313
  and tool construction, 378
Release note, 388
Request for proposal (RFP) and product assurance planning, 435
Requirement, 2
  ambiguity of, 92f, 407f
    and Project Neptune, 413
  and compromise with customer, 423, 424f, 428
  deferring of, 423
  defined, 2
  development of, in parallel with code, 426–428
  dismembering of, 425f
  examples of, 3
  excursions from, 9f
    defined, 10n
    and premature coding, 426, 427f
  and near term versus far term, 423, 424f
  and Procrustean approach to software development, 424–426
  misunderstanding of, example, 245
  reformulation of, and wizard and king, 158

  testability of, 258–259, 260–264, 273, 327
  as a weight for product assurance balance, 134
  and "user friendliness," 259
Requirements amendment, 173–175
Requirements Baseline. *See* Baseline
Requirements definition, 90–91
  and golden rule for avoiding computer mess, 478
Requirements Definition Baseline. *See* Baseline
Requirements Definition Stage. *See* Life cycle stage
Requirements review, chairing of, 232–233
Requirements specification, 38, 97
  for Automated Doughnut-Making System, 251f
  defined, 38, 97
  for Meteorological Satellite Monitoring System, 260f
  and testability of requirements, 260–264
  for precipitation-day counting system, 41, 46–48, 117f
  testing of, 49–50, 121–122
  relationship to design specification, 40, 47–48
  for Subsystem MATH of System ABC, 302f
  as a synonym for functional specification, 39, 40
  for System MEAL PLANNER, 179–180f
  for System PREDICT, 271f, 303, 326, 327
  labeling of, 387–388
  planning for audit of, 438f, 439f, 442
  types of, 40
Requirements testability. *See* Testability of requirements
Review
  versus audit, 308
  versus inspection, 310
Review initiator (as part of change control function)
  configuration control board processing of, 166–167
  defined, 164
  as technical input to configuration control board, 167
Review process. *See* Change control function
Revisit of life cycle stage. *See* Life cycle stage revisit
Revolutionary change, 152f
  and baseline update, 158
  candidate examples of, 227–228t
  defined, 151, 152f
  examples of, 152–153, 154, 188, 189
  and human fallibilities, 158
  inevitability of, on software projects, 157–158

  issues pertaining to, 380–382
  and need for paperwork, 222–223
  planning for, 223
  as precipitating evolutionary change, 158, 175
  rationale for distinguishing from evolutionary change, 156, 227–228
  reasons for, 158
  sample problem on (System MEAL PLANNER), 179–189
  and wizard and king, 158, 205–206, 380
RFP. *See* Request for proposal
Risk
  reduction of, through product assurance, 13, 23, 25, 136–137, 330–331, 379, 432, 444, 463
  and software development, 10–14, 22, 395

S

Sailboat-class software projects and product assurance, 22
Sample problem
  on auditing software that is not computer code, 270–276
  on congruence between software products, 250–254
  on designing an incident report form, 208–211
  on evolutionary and revolutionary change control, 179–189
  on identifying software, 345–347
  on preparing to audit computer code, 283–290
  on preparing a product assurance task order, 435–442
  on product assurance applied to a change request, 131–133
  for the product assurance practitioner, 14–17
  for the project manager, 10–14
  on requirements definition and testability, 260–264
  for the senior manager, 4–10
  on software concept, 38–39
  on visibility, 44–53
Scenario testing, defined, 446–447
Schedule slippage
  and acceptance testing, 300
  analogy with cancer, 472
  analogy with iceberg, 11, 22f
  and product assurance, 11
SCI. *See* Software configuration item
SCM. *See* Software configuration management
SCN. *See* Software change notice
Self-comparison (of a software product), 257–259
  examples of discrepancies uncovered by, 259t
  mechanics of, 302–303

and internal reference to
acceptance testing support,
437f, 438f, 441
and visibility, 442
TBD (To Be Determined), 187,
188, 246f, 258, 259t, 303f
Technical-level configuration
control board, 194–195
Technical review, 148
Tenacity (quality of a good quality
assurance worker), 147
Testability of requirements, 260–
264
assessment of, during self-
comparison of a
requirements specification,
258–259
example of, in System
PREDICT, 273
and independent verification and
validation, 99
sample problem on, 260–264
and user friendliness, 259
and wizard and king, 264
Test and evaluation (T&E), 115–
117, 276–300. See also
Acceptance testing; Testing
balance analogue for, 135
and configuration control board,
291f, 292–299
defined, 115, 277, 278f
ground truth for, 276, 277, 278f,
281
and peace of mind, 299
planning for, 116, 121
and precipitation-day counting
system, 121–122
and Project Mars, 405–406
and Project Mercury, 401t, 402
and Project Venus, 403–404
relationship to auditing function,
255–256
relationship to quality
assurance, 125
relationship to verification and
validation, 125
and System PREDICT, 443, 463
and traceability, 116, 281, 283
versus auditing source code
listings, 267
Test Baseline. See Baseline
Test charter
issues pertaining to, 388
need for, 367
outline for, 368–369t
Test Incident Configuration
Control Board (TICCB),
293, 294, 295f, 298, 299
example minutes for meeting of,
362f
and Project Venus, 403
Test incident report (TIR), 292–
294, 295–299
conversion of, to change
request, 298
conversion of, to incident
report, 299
example of completed form for,
297f

form for, 293f
processing of, 292–294
purpose of, 292
relationship to incident report
and software change notice,
292
as variation of incident report,
206n
and visibility and traceability,
294, 299
Testing, 16–17, 276–300. See also
Acceptance testing; Test
and evaluation
and achieving convergence
between computer code and
requirements, 17, 277
automating of, 263, 264, 333,
378
of automobile fuel
economization algorithm,
327
and bank software disaster,
416–417
and Coding Stage, 63, 278
cost of, 333
and defect reduction, 333
ground truth for, 255, 277, 281,
292
how much is needed, 332
importance of documentation of,
470
and incident report, 177
and instrumenting computer
code, 261, 263
and life cycle, 277, 278–279
of mathematical formulas, 318,
323–324
outline of user/buyer charter
for, 368–369t
and "pay now versus pay much
more later," 333
and peace of mind, 299
planning for, 121, 185–186f, 329,
333
and precipitation-day counting
system, 121–122
priorities in, 332
and Production/Deployment
Stage, 63
and Project Jupiter, 427–428
and Project Neptune, 414
and Project Saturn, 409, 410
and Project Venus, 403–404
of proposed code change, 177
relationship to auditing function,
255–256
relationship to change control
function, 177
and space shuttle, 479–480
and taste of software product,
333
and traceability, 17, 479–480
versus debugging, 333
versus inspection, 310
and visibility, 16, 48–50
and "wringing out" software,
319
writing procedures for, 283–290,
307

Testing, acceptance. See
Acceptance testing
Testing, composite, defined, 320t
Testing, functional, defined, 446
Testing, integration. See
Integration testing
Testing, negative, defined, 289
Testing, positive, defined, 289
Testing, regression
defined, 313
and tool construction, 378
Testing, scenario, defined, 446–
447
Testing, stress, defined, 320t, 447
Testing, unit. See Unit testing
Testing crisis, 329
Testing cycle. See Acceptance
testing cycle
Test plan, 16n, 279–280t
defined, 16n, 277n
outline for, 279–280t
relationship to software
specification
documentation, 116, 121–
122, 124, 255, 277, 279, 291
relationship to test procedures,
121, 280, 281f, 291f
for System SHAPES, portion
of, 287f
and traceability matrix, 281
Test procedure, 16n, 282f
as amalgamation of
requirements and design
specifications, 122
construction of, 283–290
actions involved with, 307–
308
as a labor-intensive activity,
289
defined, 16n, 129, 277n
example of, 288f
excursions from, 282f, 289
and expected results, 278f, 282f,
283, 290, 313
five-column format for, 281–
283, 282f
and integration testing, 312–314
purpose of, 283
relationship to software
specification
documentation, 116, 121–
122, 124–125, 255, 277,
280–281, 283, 291
relationship to test plan, 121,
280, 283–290, 291f
for System SHAPES, portion
of, 288f
tool for construction and
execution of, 378
and traceability, 281
Test specification, 291
Test team
as group independent from
development organization,
177
and Project Saturn, 409
skills needed for, 264
TICCB. See Test Incident
Configuration Control
Board

Time, concept of, and relationship
    to life cycle concept, 387
TIR. *See* Test incident report
Tollgate (for product assurance),
    169, 171
    and life cycle stage, 64
Tools for product assurance, 373–
    378. *See also* Automated
    aids
Traceability, 54, 55f, 56–57
    and acceptance testing cycle,
        294–295, 299, 300
    and alternatives to centralized
        configuration control board
        philosophy, 235, 236
    and audit report, 269, 270
    and bookkeeping function, 131,
        336, 380
    and change control forms, 203–
        204, 335
    defined, 54, 55f, 364
    and documentation produced
        out of sequence, 80
    and emergency change
        procedures, 220
    and freezing, 165
    and frequency of configuration
        control board meetings,
        231, 450–451
    and incident report form, 210,
        211
    and minutes for configuration
        control board, 351, 354,
        361, 381, 429f
    and paperwork, 203
    and product assurance, 56–57,
        58, 86, 88, 310, 379, 396,
        397, 406, 423, 426, 429f,
        430, 431, 432, 433, 448
    and product integrity, 397
    and project event recording, 364
    and project goals, 421, 432
    and project planning, 87
    and rapid prototyping, 90
    relationship to visibility, 56, 88
    and software product assurance
        guarantee, 431, 433
    and testing, 17, 281, 283, 479–
        480
    and wizard and king, 73
Traceability matrix
    defined, 57, 267n
    example of, 57t
    and testing, 281
    use of, for assessing congruence
        between software products,
        255
Trash cans and product assurance,
    9f, 28–29
Tree diagram (software
    identification technique),
    343f, 344
    example of, for Automated
        Doughnut-Making System,
        345, 347f, 348f
Triangle diagram, 78f
    and allocation of software
        project activities, 145–146

analogue to federal government,
    79–80
and checking and balancing, 79
and configuration control board,
    189–190, 191f
and prioritizing discrepancies,
    306
rationale for, 79
and user/buyer/seller, 84–85,
    191f
and wizard and king, 86, 336f

U

Uncontrolled change
    result of, 159
    risk of, and running a red light,
        159, 161
Unit testing, 116n
    and code changes, 159
    defined, 116n
    as distinguished from
        acceptance testing, 16
    and Project Saturn, 410
    relationship to acceptance
        testing, 291, 321t, 325
    relationship to test and
        evaluation, 116
Unreasonable expectations and
    software project failure, 137
Unsatisfied requirements
    analogy with cancer, 472
    analogy with iceberg, 11f, 22f,
        42–43, 51
Update (to a baseline), 158
    defined, 69n
    and revisits to life cycle stages,
        68–69, 172
User, defined, 84
User/buyer/seller
    and configuration control board,
        190–192
    relationship among, 84–86
User friendliness (and
    requirements testability),
    259, 423
User's manual
    defined, 116, 290n
    and incident report resolution,
        177, 200
    and test and evaluation, 116
    and test procedure, 290n

V

Validation, 115
    balance analogue for, 134
    of data entries, defined, 351n
    defined, 115
    example discrepancies of, 121f,
        256t
    potential redundancy of, 139
    and product integrity, 114
    rationale for performing on
        every audit, 432
V&V. *See* Verification and
    validation
Verification, 115
    balance analogue for, 134
    defined, 115

and error-free code, 479
example discrepancies of, 121f,
    256t
ground truth for, 248
as validation, 479
Verification and validation (V&V),
    115
    and auditing function, 244
    balance analogue for, 134
    defined, 115
    example discrepancies of, 121f
    ground truth for, 248
    and precipitation-day counting
        system, 120
    and product integrity, 115
    and Project Mars, 405
    relationship to quality
        assurance, 125
    relationship to self-comparison,
        257
    resources estimated for, 440f,
        442
    and System MEAL PLANNER,
        186f, 188–189
Visibility, 43f, 44–53
    and acceptance testing cycle,
        294–295, 299–300
    and alternatives to centralized
        configuration control board
        philosophy, 235, 236
    and audit report, 269, 270, 273
    and automated aids to software
        product assurance, 374, 375
    and baseline, 69–70
    and bookkeeping function, 131,
        336, 380
    and change control forms, 203–
        204, 335
    and checks and balances, 14
    and configuration control board,
        190, 192, 349
    defined, 43f
    and emergency change
        procedures, 220
    first aspect of, 44–50
    and freezing, 165
    and frequency of configuration
        control board meetings,
        231, 450–451
    and incident report form, 210
    and internal consistency
        checking, 45–46
    and life cycle stage, 60, 88, 95–
        96
    and logical progression
        checking, 46–48
    and minutes for configuration
        control board, 350f, 351–
        352, 354, 382, 429f
    and near-term versus long-term
        requirements, 423, 424f
    and product assurance, 15, 16,
        17, 44–53, 59, 86, 101, 310,
        379, 396, 397, 406, 423, 426,
        429f, 430, 431, 432, 433,
        448, 481
    and product assurance task
        order, 442

and product integrity, 397
and project goals, 421, 422
and rapid prototyping, 89
relationship to traceability, 56, 88
restricting of, 432
results of lack of, 44
and risk reduction, 13
sample problem on, 44–53
second aspect of, 50–52
and software product assurance guarantee, 431, 433
and standards checking, 45–46, 111
and systematically produced software, 80
and testing, 16, 48–50
third aspect of, 52–53, 105
and wizard and king, 73
Voting mechanism. *See* Configuration control board

W

Warranty
    hardware, 464f
    software, 463–466
Wizard and buyer/user
    cartoon for, 92f
    and requirements definition, 92
Wizard and king, 65f, 336f, 407f, 443f

and absence of requirements baseline, 68
achieving agreement between, 73, 151
and auditing, 241, 473
and auditing of System PREDICT, 274
and auditor, 274
and basic software management challenge, 90–91, 151, 379–380
and bookkeeping, 335
cartoon for, 65f
and change control function, 380
and change request, 131, 359
and configuration control board, 335
and Earth Radiation Budget Experiment (ERBE), 481
and evolutionary change, 380
and inflated and unreasonable expectations, 137
and king as archetypical customer, 151
and problem definition, 99
and product assurance, 73, 81, 443f
and Project Mars, 406, 407f
and Project Neptune, 414
and rapid prototyping, 89–90, 225f

relationship to computer mess, 478
and requirements definition, 65–66, 89–90, 90–91, 97–98, 189, 407f, 414
and requirements testability, 264
and revolutionary change, 158, 205–206, 380
and rush to "get on with coding," 396
and software development, 131
and software development game board, 336f
and software industry, 396
and software life cycle, 65–66, 90–91, 335, 336f
and System MEAL PLANNER, 189
and System PREDICT, 274
and triangle diagram, 86, 336f
use of interpreter as intermediary between, 240
and visibility and traceability, 73
WONDER, System. *See* System WONDER
"Wringing out" software, 318–319, 320–321t

Z

"Zero-defect software," 306–307